the computer book

WINDOWS® VISTA™ EDITION

the computer book

WINDOWS® VISTA™ EDITION

Rob Beattie

LONDON, NEW YORK,
MUNICH, MELBOURNE, DELHI

EDITOR Laura Nickoll
ART EDITOR Vicky Read
PRODUCTION CONTROLLER Wendy Penn
DTP DESIGNER Traci Salter

MANAGING EDITOR Adèle Hayward
CATEGORY PUBLISHER Stephanie Jackson
ART DIRECTOR Peter Luff

Produced for Dorling Kindersley Limited by
crosstees.eyes, The Lazy J Ranch,
Vancouver Island, Canada
EDITORIAL MANAGER Ian Whitelaw
EDITORIAL CONSULTANT Rob Beattie
SENIOR DESIGNER Andrew Easton
EDITOR Julie Whitaker

First published in Great Britain in 2007
by Dorling Kindersley Limited,
80 Strand, London WC2R 0RL

A Penguin Company

2 4 6 8 10 9 7 5 3

A CIP catalogue record for this book is available
from the British Library.

ISBN 978 1 4053 2547 9
Printed and bound in Slovakia by TBB

See our complete catalogue at
www.dk.com

About This Book

The Computer Book is an easy-to-follow guide to Windows® Vista™, exploring the Internet, creating documents and spreadsheets, using e-mail, managing digital images, and making a home movie.

THIS BOOK WILL HELP YOU TO GET the most out of your computer, whether you are a complete novice or an experienced user who is approaching Windows Vista for the first time or looking at programs you have never investigated. In a series of ten chapters, *The Computer Book* shows you how to make the most of a computer running Windows Vista, as well as introducing Microsoft's Internet Explorer, Notepad, WordPad, Word, Excel, Windows Photo Gallery, and Windows Movie Maker, plus Family Tree Maker.

Each chapter is divided into sections that deal with specific topics, and within each section you will find subsections that cover self-contained procedures. Each of these procedures builds on the knowledge that you will have accumulated by working through the previous chapters.

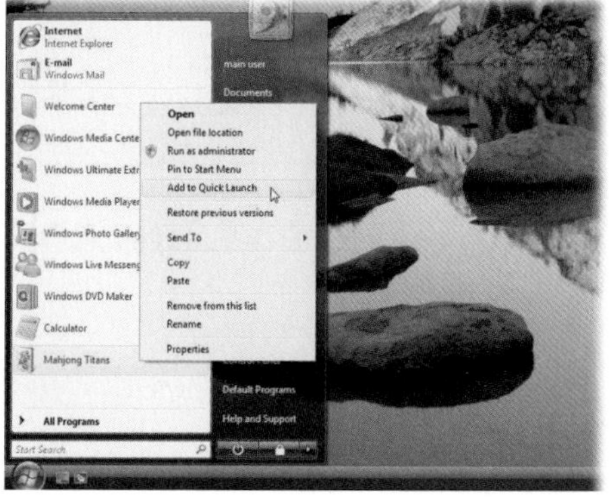

The sections and subsections use a step-by-step approach, and almost every step is accompanied by an illustration showing how your screen should look at that stage. The book contains several other features that make it easier to absorb the quantity of information that is provided. Cross-references are shown within the text as left- or right-hand page icons: and . The page number within the icon and the reference are shown at the foot of the page.

As well as the step-by-step sections, there are boxes that give additional information to take your knowledge beyond that provided on the rest of the page. Finally, at the back, you will find a glossary explaining new terms, and a comprehensive index.

For further information on computer software and digital technology, see the wide range of titles available in the *DK Essential Computers* series.

Contents

Introducing Windows

Welcome to Windows 10 • Exploring Vista 14
Using Windows 28 • A Typical Program 42
Personalizing Windows 54

Files and Folders

Exploring the System 64 • Getting Organized 72
Shortcuts and Links 96 • Searching for Items 100

Using the Internet

Introducing the Internet 108 • Exploring the Internet 114
Security Features 132 • Browser Plug-ins 140
10 Great Sites 146

Using E-mail

Introducing Mail 170 • Creating E-mail 176
Incoming E-mail 184 • Personalized E-mail 194

Staying Safe

What to Expect 200 • Windows Update 206 • Windows Firewall 212 • Malware Protection 216 • Sharing Your PC Safely 230

242

Using Programs

Basic Word Processing 244 • Introducing Word 260
Introducing Excel 278 • Genealogy Software 298

310

Enjoying Your Photos

Meet Photo Gallery 312 • Organizing Your Photos 322
Improving Your Photos 330 • Sharing Your Images 334

340

Playing Music and DVDs

Playing and Ripping CDs 342 • Managing Your Music 350
Buying Music Online 370 • Burning a Music CD 378
Playing DVDs 382 • Windows Media Center 386

394

Making Movies

Digital Movie Making 396 • Editing Your Movie 406
Adding Titles 418 • Adding Music 424
Your Finished Movie 430

436

Maintaining Your PC

Meet Your PC 438 • Keeping a Tidy House 448
System Protection 456 • Managing Programs 478
Windows Scheduler 486 • Keeping Your Data Secure 496

Glossary 506 • Index 509 • Acknowledgments 512

INTRODUCING WINDOWS

THE VAST MAJORITY OF HOME PCs use Microsoft Windows, an operating system designed to put a friendly face on top of the complex arrangements of ones and zeroes that computers use to get anything done. All new PCs come with the latest edition of Windows called Vista, which is the most advanced, most secure version so far and is the one we're using in this book. We'll start by taking you through the Windows desktop–where you'll spend much of your time–and then show you how to start and use a program, how to find your way around Vista's Start menu and Quick Launch toolbar, before exploring the Sidebar and its gadgets. We'll look at the programs that come free with Windows Vista and then use Calendar to show you how a typical program works. Finally, we'll take you into the Control Panel and explain how to personalize many aspects of the desktop, including background colors and images.

10 Welcome to Windows

14 Exploring Vista

28 Using Windows

42 A Typical Program

54 Personalizing Windows

Welcome to Windows

Vista has been designed from the ground up to be the friendliest, most powerful, and most secure version of Windows that author Microsoft has ever released.

What Is Windows Vista?

Windows Vista is an operating system, which means that it's an interface between the inner workings of the computer and the people who use it. Vista also comprises a suite of programs and accessories, and includes many improvements over the previous versions of Windows, in terms of both the way it looks and the way it works.

WHAT DOES IT DO?

- Instead of having to communicate with a home PC using complex code commands, Windows provides a set of attractive graphical objects that you control with a mouse.
- Moving the mouse across the desktop moves a small arrow called the cursor across the screen.
- Clicking the buttons on the mouse allows you to open menus, make selections, and interact with Windows and Windows programs to write letters, plan budgets, edit home movies, listen to music, enhance photos, browse the Internet, send and receive e-mails, and much more.

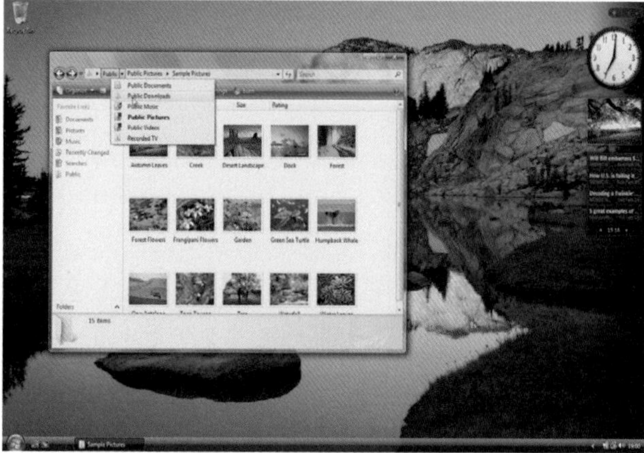

Technically Speaking...

Windows Vista works both on desktop PCs and on smaller battery-powered notebook computers. However, Vista also has notebook-specific features that make it easier to start and stop what you're doing and also extend the battery life of the portable PC.

KEY NEW FEATURES FOR THE EXPERIENCED USER

• BETTER SECURITY

Windows Firewall can now monitor both incoming and outgoing Internet traffic, making it better at stopping malevolent programs from interfering with your PC and preventing any that do get through from "phoning home" with personal information stored on your PC. It also includes Windows Defender, which scans your PC regularly for spyware, removing any it finds. (Vista does not include anti-virus software.)

• IMPROVED INTERFACE

Vista looks better than ever before, thanks to photo-realistic icons, redesigned menus and windows, a pleasing new typeface, and clever transparency effects. These come courtesy of the Aero interface, but it requires a fast PC, plenty of memory, and good graphics.

USER ACCOUNT CONTROL

This love-it-or-hate-it feature is designed to stop you accidentally doing something that may cause damage to your PC. It displays an "are-you-sure?" dialog box when you try to run programs or tasks that may affect the way the computer works at a basic level. Unfortunately, you still have to decide for yourself whether or not to complete the action.

• WINDOWS CALENDAR

At last, a decent built-in organizer for keeping appointments and "to do" lists. You can display different calendars, distinguishing them by color, and also publish or subscribe to Internet-based calendars.

• COMPREHENSIVE SEARCHING

When you're not busy, Vista quietly indexes all the files and folders you use most often, so when you want to search for something, you get results much more quickly. You can search from the Start menu and from within individual folders. Vista also looks inside your files, so it can find, for example, a particular word in a particular document.

• DVD BURNING

Vista is the first version of Windows to incorporate a DVD creation program as standard, so you can turn your home movies into DVDs that friends can enjoy on their own players.

• WINDOWS RE-ORGANIZED

Web-browser-style back and forward buttons improve the way windows are displayed, and a new Favorite Links pane allows faster access to the folders on your PC you use most often. Navigable drop down menus at the top of each window make finding your way round densely nested folders much easier, and a Preview pane displays files in miniature so you can look at their contents without opening them.

• BACKUP AND RESTORE

Instead of being hidden away as an afterthought, Vista includes a proper program to back up and restore your files. Users of the Ultimate Edition can also back up their entire PC, rather than just groups of files and folders.

THE WINDOWS VISTA DESKTOP

When you switch on your PC, the Windows Vista Desktop appears. It's the electronic equivalent of a real desktop and the jumping off point for everything you do with your PC. From here you can start and stop programs, search for files, connect to the Internet, play games, listen to music, and watch DVDs. As we'll see later in this chapter, you can also change the way the desktop looks, altering the way that icons are displayed, the color scheme, and the background screen image.

FEATURES KEY

❶ Recycle Bin
The Recycle Bin is where you put items you want to delete; they can still be retrieved until you actually empty it.

❷ Start Button
Click here to launch programs, open files and folders, or find items on your PC or the Internet.

❸ Quick Launch Toolbar
Frequently used programs are stored here 26.

❹ Taskbar
The Taskbar offers easy access to programs and documents that are open on the desktop, allowing you to switch between them quickly.

❺ Show/Hide Icons
Click this arrow to reveal or hide any additional icons in the Notification Area.

❻ Notification Area
This is for those programs that load automatically, such the Volume Control 27.

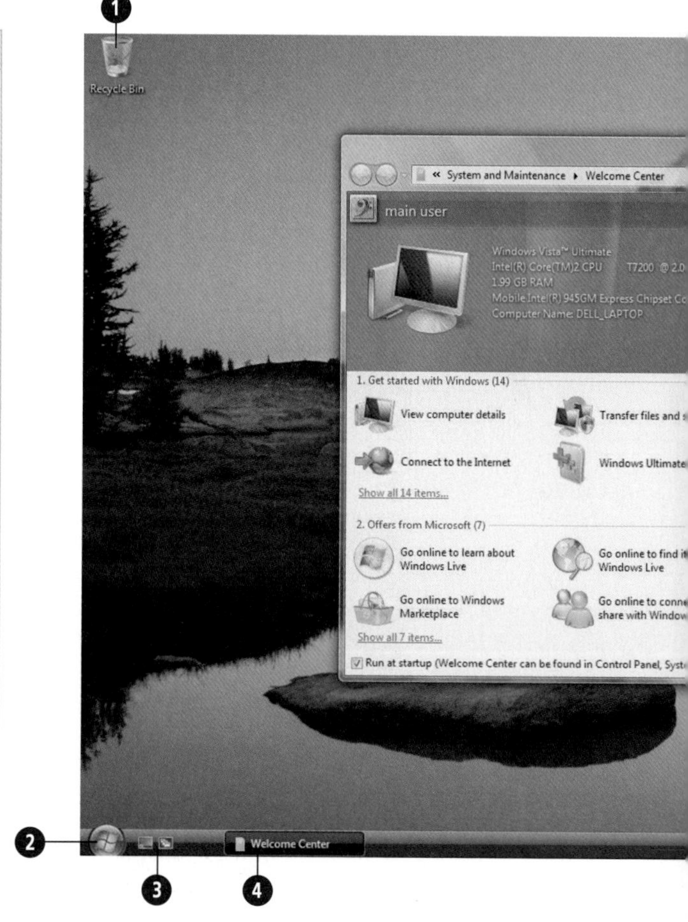

26 The Quick Launch Toolbar

27 The Notification Area

VISTA VERSIONS

The four main versions of Vista are Home Basic, Home Premium, Business, and Ultimate. Of these, Home Basic is for older or slower PCs, and Premium is the best choice for home users who want the fancy new interface and all the good entertainment features. Business lacks these but offers better backup and stronger networking, while Ultimate (used in this book) has the lot. Vista upgrades are cheaper than full versions because they require that you already have a copy of Windows XP running on your PC.

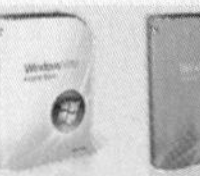

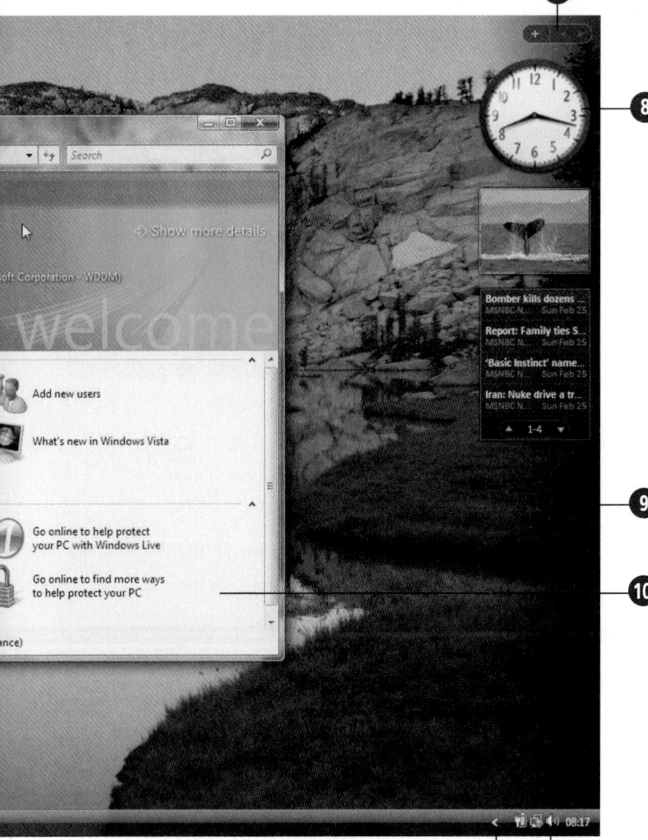

FEATURES KEY

❼ The Sidebar
The Sidebar is a part of the desktop that is reserved for storing Gadgets.

❽ The Clock Gadget
The Clock Gadget is one of many small but useful single-function programs included with Windows Vista; more are available on the Internet.

❾ Desktop Background
The Desktop Background can be any large single image or a number of smaller images repeated (or "tiled") to create an attractive pattern. Vista includes a number of both. You can also use one of your own photos or download a new image.

❿ Welcome Center
When you first start Windows Vista, the Welcome Center appears, offering a mix of information, tutorials, and special offers.

28 **The Sidebar**

30 **Adding a New Gadget**

Exploring Vista

Now we've been introduced to the Windows desktop, let's have a look at some of the things it can do, including launching and closing programs.

Selecting and Launching a Program

Although there are other ways to do it, most of the time we'll be using the **Start** button to open programs. This is a powerful feature that opens an electronic window onto the programs, files, and folders stored on your PC.

1 Opening the Start Menu

- Use the mouse to move the cursor over the **Start** button at the bottom left of the desktop.
- As you do, it "lights up" to indicate that the button is now ready to use.
- Click once on the **Start** button with the left mouse button and watch what happens next.
- After a moment the Start menu appears, listing the various folders on your PC, along with those programs Windows thinks you're most likely to want to use.

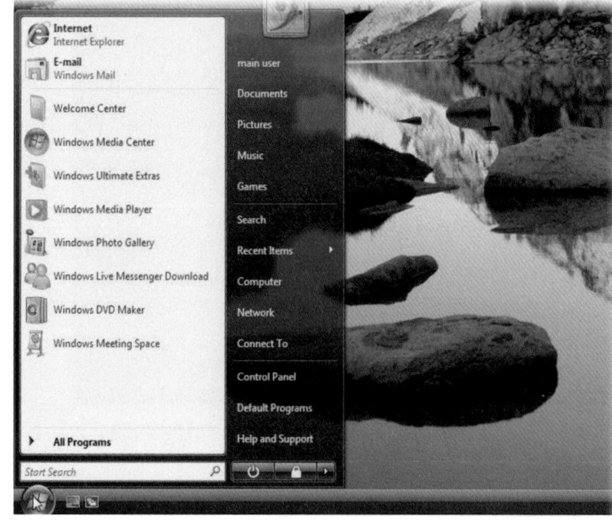

2 OPENING ALL PROGRAMS

● At the bottom of the left-hand side of the Start menu you will see an item called **All Programs**. Move the cursor over this and then click once with the left mouse button.

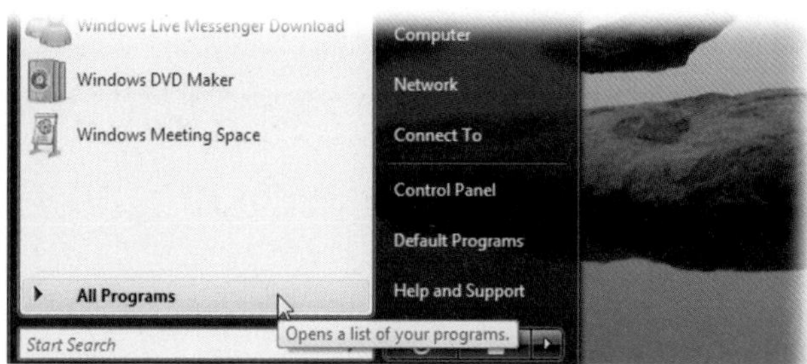

● Vista now shows not just the most commonly used programs but also all the folders (indicated by small yellow folder icons) that contain other programs stored on your PC.

● We're going to start by having some fun, so move the cursor up to the **Games** folder and click on it once with the left mouse button.

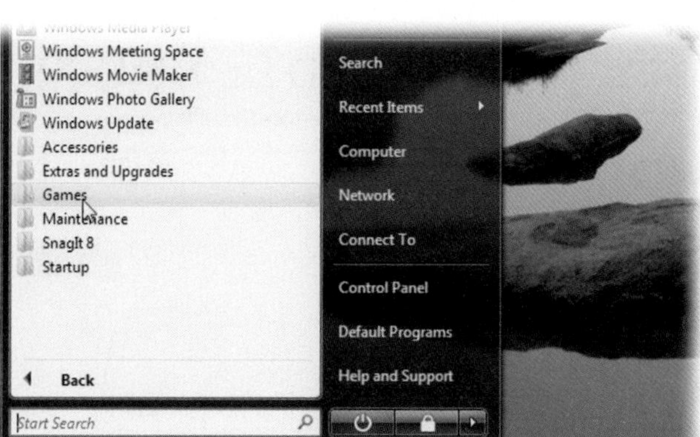

3 VIEWING FOLDER CONTENTS

● Notice that the Games folder stays where it is and that the contents (i.e. all the games inside the folder) are now displayed below it.

● Move the cursor so that it's hovering over **Mahjong Titans** and watch what happens to it.

● The cursor arrow changes into a pointing hand, indicating that this is a program that will launch when you click it.

● Click the **Mahjong Titans** icon to start playing the game.

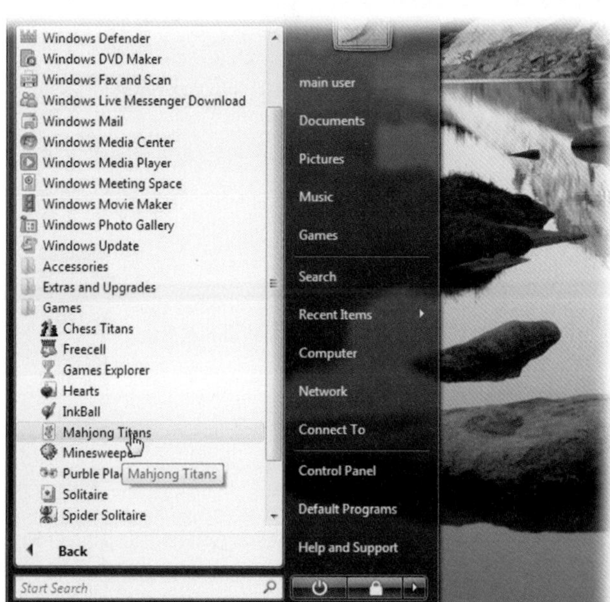

4 LAUNCHING THE PROGRAM

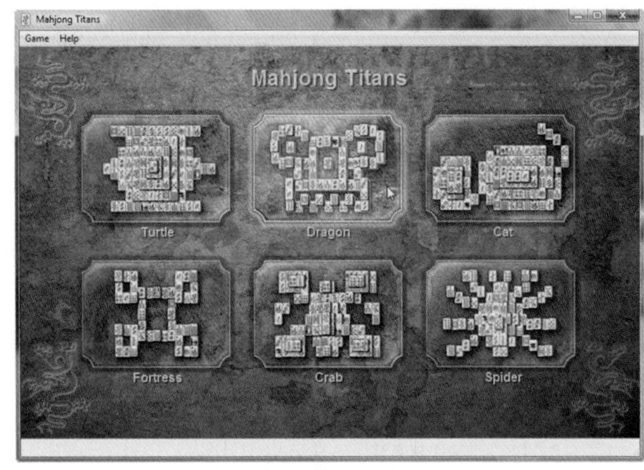

• After a moment, the game appears on the screen. Pick whichever layout you'd like to play–in this example it's the **Dragon** layout–and then click on it.

• You will notice that the Start menu automatically closes when the program is launched.

• And here's Mahjong Titans ready to be played. Notice how detailed the tiles look–this realistic appearance is one of the many impressive features of the new Vista.

5 LAUNCHING A SECOND PROGRAM

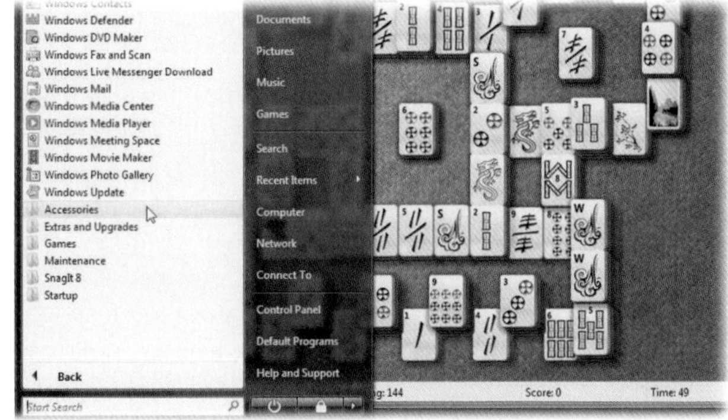

• Windows lets you run more than one program at once and allows you to quickly switch between them whenever you like.

• Click on the **Start** button, choose **All Programs** again, but this time click on **Accessories** to open that folder.

- As with **Games**, the Start menu opens the folder and displays the programs stored inside it as a list.
- Click on **Calculator** to launch the free calculator program that's included with Windows Vista.

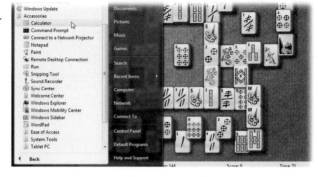

- The Calculator program opens, and here you see it running on top of the Mahjong Titans game.
- You can run any number of programs together at the same time by launching them one after the other like this. The only limiting factor is the amount of memory you have installed in your computer.

6 SWITCHING PROGRAMS

- We've already seen the Taskbar 12. It's a quick way to switch between different programs running on the desktop. As each new program is launched, it is represented on the Taskbar by a rectangle, like the two you can see at the bottom of the screen here. These rectangles represent Mahjong Titans and the Calculator program.

12 **Taskbar**

- In this case, neither program takes up the full screen, but some do, and one can be completely hidden behind another.
- To help you switch between them, Vista reveals a small thumbnail version of each program when you hover the cursor over the rectangle on the Taskbar.

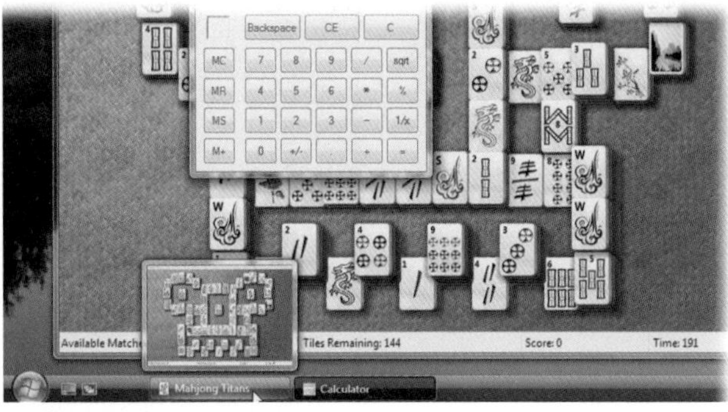

- Now try clicking the **Mahjong Titans** rectangle on the Taskbar with the left mouse button. As you do so, you'll see that the Mahjong Titans game moves to the front and the Calculator program disappears behind it. The Calculator is still there–you can still see it in the Taskbar–but it's now hidden behind the Mahjong Titans window.

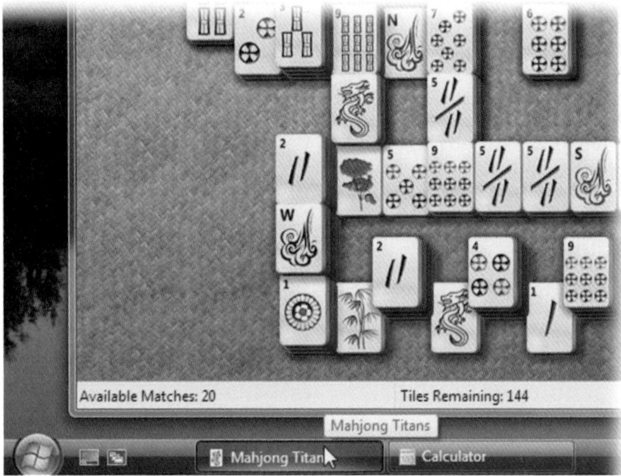

- Now, let's swap them around. Hover the cursor over the rectangle on the Taskbar and watch as the thumbnail is displayed to indicate that the program is still running, even though you can't see it.

● Click the **Calculator** rectangle and you'll see the program itself appear on top of the Mahjong Titans game. This feature is extremely useful when you're running several programs at the same time and you need to switch between them quickly.

7 CLOSING PROGRAMS

● Finally, let's close the programs. Move your cursor onto the small "X" at the top right-hand corner of the Calculator and then click it once with the left mouse button.

● Go to the top right of the Mahjong Titans window and do exactly the same to close this program.

● Congratulations. You've just opened, run, and closed your first Microsoft Windows Vista programs.

Exploring the Start Menu

We've already seen how the Start menu can be used to launch one or more programs, but there's much more to it than that. As Windows' main gateway, this is the starting point for much of what you will do on your PC. The Start menu also offers easy access to the main folders on your computer, including those in which Windows stores settings that you may need to change from time to time.

FEATURES KEY

❶ On/Off/Sleep
The buttons here provide various ways to switch off or shut down your PC safely.

❷ Start Search Box
To find something on your PC, just type its name (or part of its name) in here.

❸ Recent Programs
Windows Vista puts your most recently used programs on the Start menu so you can return to them quickly.

❹ Recent Items
Clicking here displays those files you've used recently.

❺ Popular Programs
Windows displays some of its more popular programs here.

❻ Internet/E-mail
Windows automatically adds these programs to the top of the Start menu.

❼ Easy Access
A list to the right of the Start menu displays the computer's main folders and programs such as Search and Help.

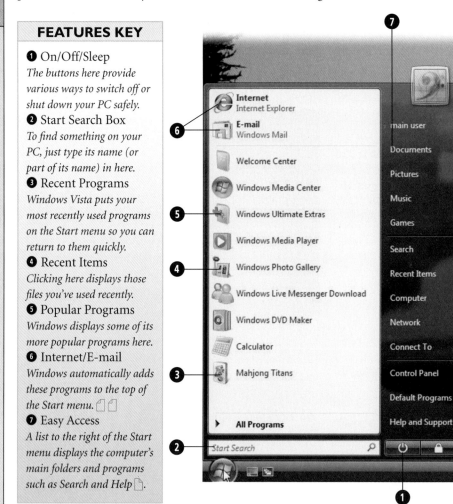

106 **Using the Internet**

168 **Using E-mail**

36 **Windows Help**

LOOKING INSIDE A FOLDER

- When we launched the Majong Titans program by going to **All Programs**, we saw a listing of all the programs in the Games folder, but we didn't actually open the folder.
- This time we're going to launch from within the folder, so click the **Start** button to open the menu.
- Now move the cursor across to the right-hand column and click once on the **Games** menu.

- After a moment, the Games folder opens on the desktop, displaying detailed icons representing each of the games currently installed on this computer.

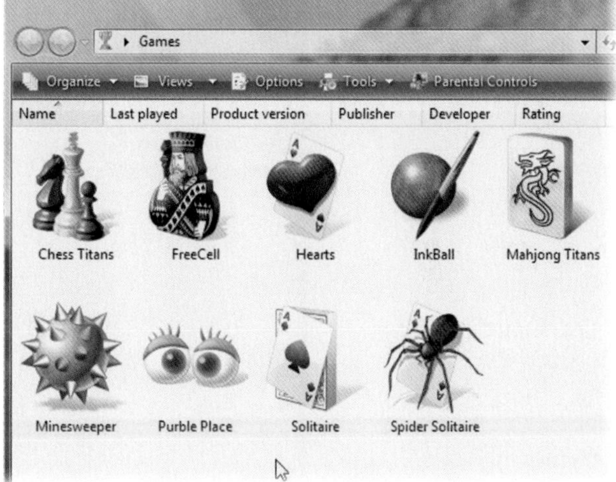

- By moving the cursor over any of these icons and then double clicking with the left-hand mouse button, you will open that game.

CUSTOMIZING THE START MENU

We've seen how the Start menu tries to help out by listing those programs it thinks you're going to use most frequently, but with a few mouse clicks you can make that decision for yourself; as well as changing other important aspects of how it works.

PINNING A PROGRAM TO THE START MENU

- We've seen that Windows puts programs for browsing the web and e-mailing right at the top of the Start menu because it thinks that's what we wants to do. We're now going to add our own program to this list, so that we can locate it easily.
- Click on the **Start** button and, when the menu opens, click on **Calculator** with the right mouse button. A pop-up menu appears.

- This menu offers a range of actions that we can apply to the chosen program. These include opening the program, copying it, and removing it completely from the list.
- Move your cursor to **Pin to Start Menu** and left click on it with the mouse.

● When you release the left mouse button, watch what happens. Windows Vista adds the Calculator to the programs at the top of the list. If you look closely, you can see a thin horizontal line separating this section from the rest of the menu.

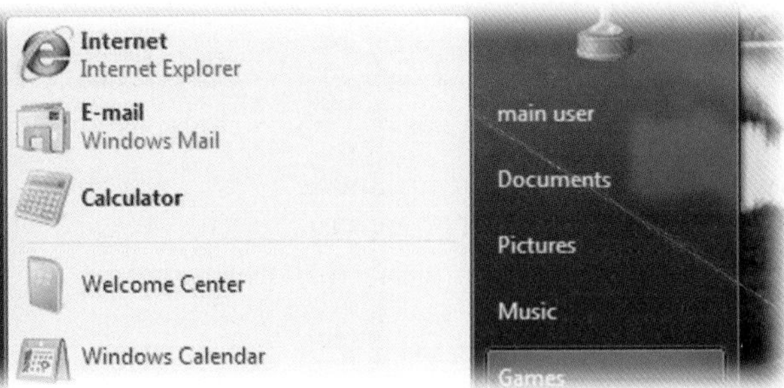

UNPINNING A PROGRAM

● You can also remove any programs that have been pinned to the top section of the Start menu.

● Just right click on the program you want to demote (here we're going to unpin the newly promoted Calculator), and choose **Unpin from Start Menu** from the pop-up menu by clicking it with the left mouse button.

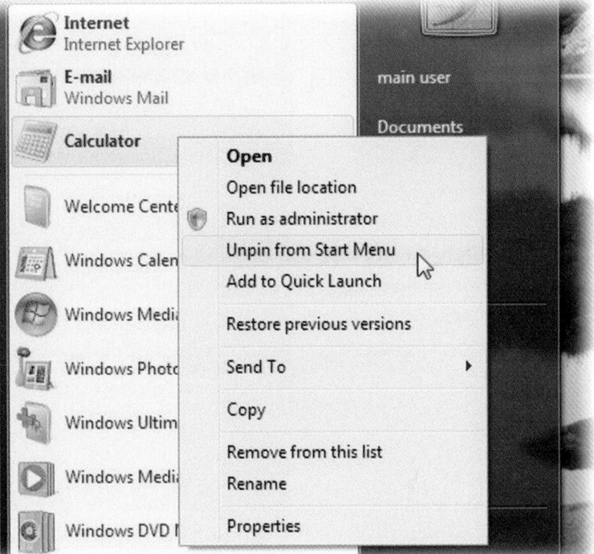

● And here's the result–the Calculator has moved back to its original position in the bottom half of the list. This kind of flexibility makes the Start menu a very powerful way to gain easy access to the programs you use all the time.

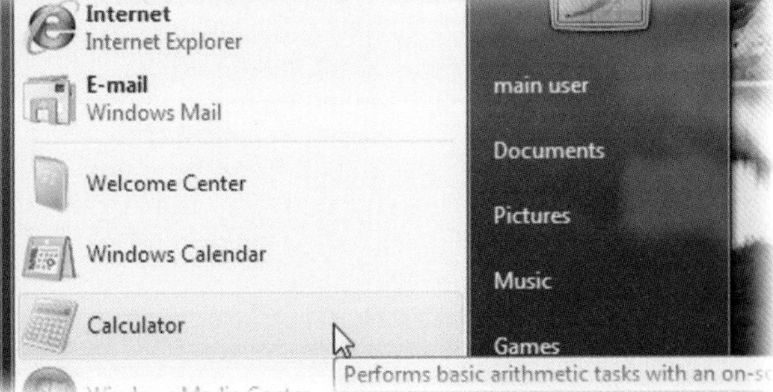

MODIFYING FOLDERS ON THE START MENU

- By default, folders on the Start menu are set to display the contents of the entire folder on the desktop when you click on them–just as the Games folder did .
- To change the way this works, click on the **Start** button and position the cursor in the menu without highlighting any programs.
- Click the right mouse button, and then click on the little **Properties** box that pops up to select it.

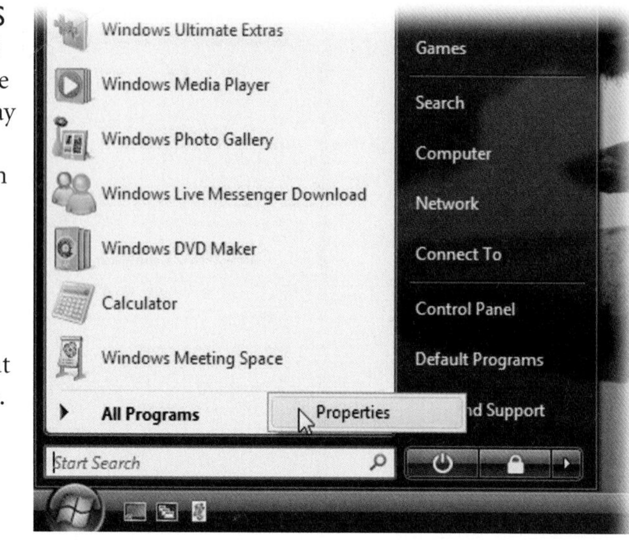

- When the **Taskbar and Start Menu Properties** dialog box opens, select the **Start Menu** tab and then left click on the **Customize** button at the top left.

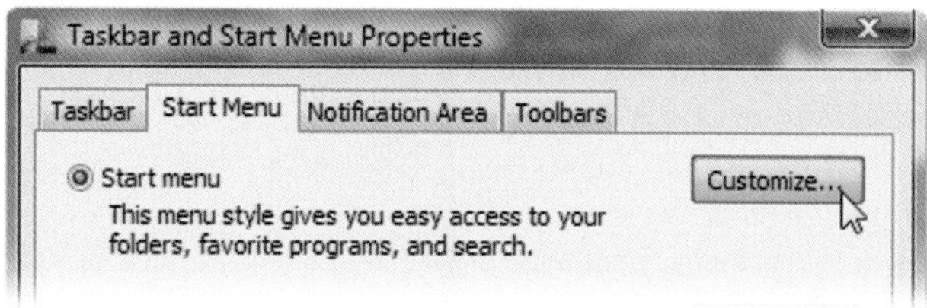

- In the middle of the dialog box you can see a long list of options waiting to be turned on or off with the mouse. They don't all fit within the window, so Windows thoughtfully provides a scroll bar on the right of the dialog box. Click on this with the left mouse button and, still holding the button down, drag it downward. You'll see the list in the middle of the window start to scroll up, like film credits.

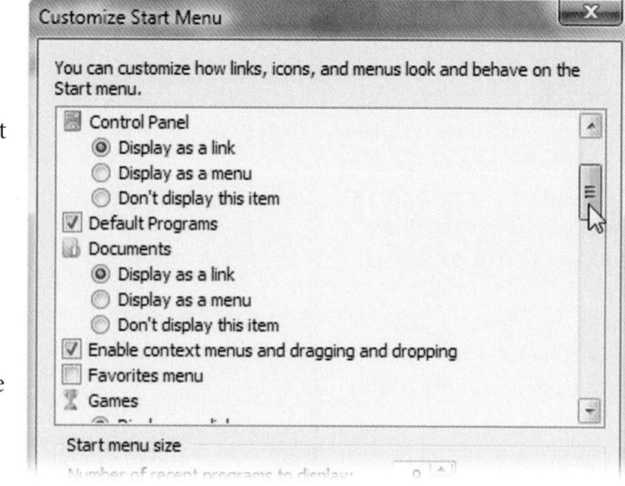

21 **Looking Inside a Folder**

● Scroll down until you come to the **Games** section. You will see that it is set to **Display as a link**, meaning that it opens the full window on the screen when you click on it.
● To save space, we'll choose the **Display as a menu** option underneath. Just click once on the radio button next to the option.

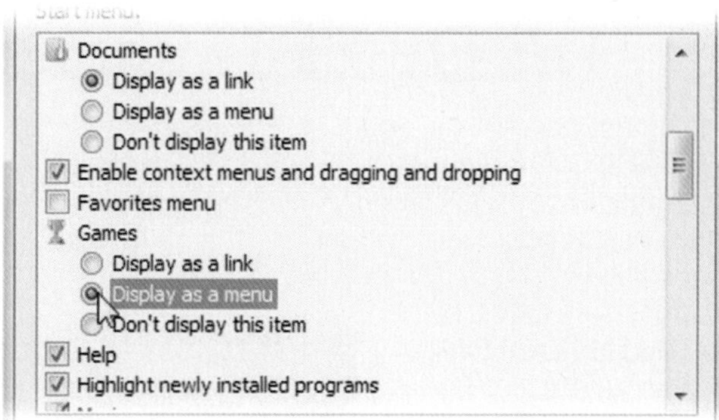

● Windows checks that you really want to make this change. Click **OK** to confirm your changes. (You can always go back to this dialog box and revert to the original settings if you change your mind later on).

● You now return to the **Taskbar and Start Menu Properties** dialog box, and are again asked to confirm the Start menu changes. Click on **OK**.

● And here's the result. When you open the Start menu now you'll see that there's an arrow next to the Games folder entry. Move the mouse to this arrow and the same games we saw earlier displayed in their own window now appear as a menu. Click on **Mahjong Titans** and the game will launch so you can play it.

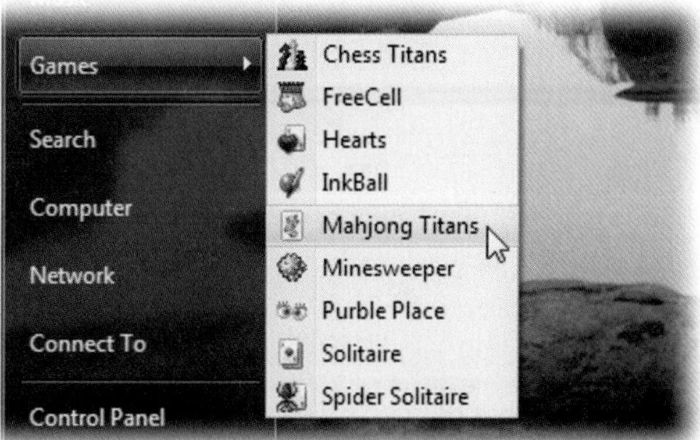

The Quick Launch Toolbar

Windows Vista just loves to launch programs, and the Quick Launch toolbar is yet another place to store those programs you use most frequently. It's particularly useful on smaller screens, where real estate is at a premium.

USING THE QUICK LAUNCH TOOLBAR

- The Quick Launch toolbar sits next to the Start menu at the left-hand end of the Taskbar. There are two programs there by default. The left one sends all open programs to the Taskbar to clear the desktop, and the other opens Vista's 3-D view, which is useful for flipping between open programs.

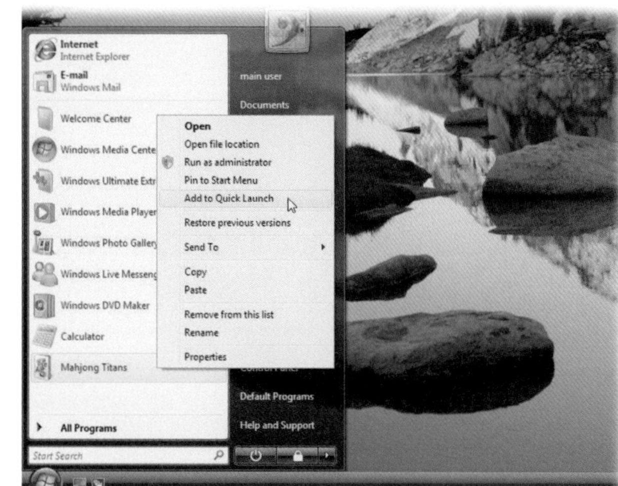

- As an example, let's add Mahjong Titans to the toolbar. Click on the **Start** button and then right mouse click on **Mahjong Titans**. Choose **Add to Quick Launch** from the pop-up menu by clicking it with the left mouse button.

- Vista instantly adds the Mahjong Titans icon to the Quick Launch toolbar, making it even easier to waste time than ever before! Other programs can be added to the Quick Launch toolbar in the same way.

THE NOTIFICATION AREA

At the right-hand end of the Taskbar, Vista keeps small programs that are loaded with the operating system itself. Typically they do such things as help to manage battery life in a notebook PC, tell you the time and date, or let you change the speaker volume.

VIEWING THE NOTIFICATION AREA

- These helper programs are represented by icons in the Notification Area. To save space, some are hidden "behind" the little arrow button. To reveal hidden programs, click the arrow.

- Let's have a look at the time and date program. Just hover the cursor over the time at the far end of the Notification Area and the date pops up, together with a calendar icon.

- You can usually open a program in the Notification Area by clicking on it once with either the left or right mouse button (there's no hard and fast rule about which one to use). In this case, clicking the left mouse button on the time opens a calendar and a clock, and allows you to change the date and time settings.

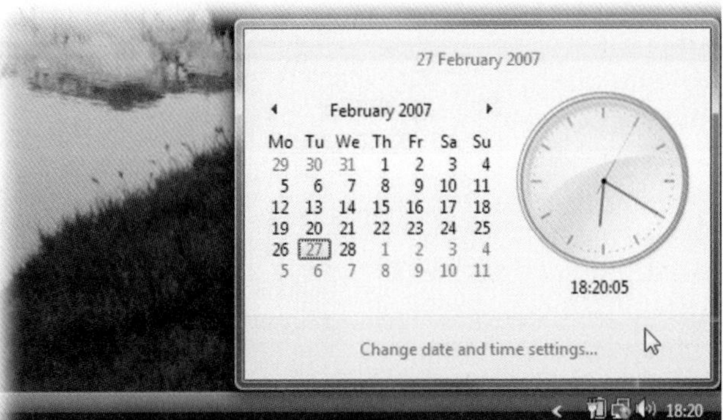

USING WINDOWS

Windows Vista offers a variety of features and programs to make your life easier, as well as plenty of hand holding so that you can quickly find answers to any questions that are puzzling you.

THE SIDEBAR

The Sidebar is a new Windows feature. It sits at the edge of the screen and acts as a "dock" for a range of Gadgets–small, useful programs that provide you with information and help you to stay organized. Vista automatically shows you a clock, a picture slide show, and–if you're connected to the Internet–rolling, up-to-date news headlines. Many of the Gadgets can be modified to suit your taste.

MODIFYING A GADGET

- Taking advantage of Vista's new transparency features, the Sidebar is see through until you hover the cursor on top of it. Then a solid vertical bar "swims" into view like this.

- Let's start by modifying one of the existing gadgets. Move the cursor until it's hovering over the clock at the top of the Sidebar.
- Now click on it once with the right mouse button.
- When the pop-up menu appears, click **Options** once with the left mouse button.

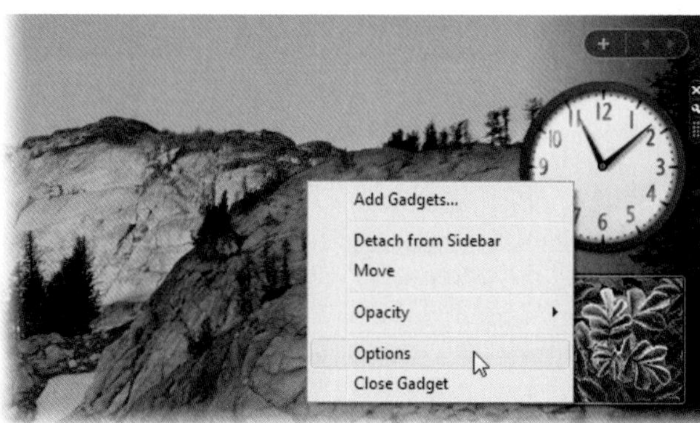

● This brings up the **Clock** options dialog. Here you can give the clock a name, change the time zone, and re-set the date and time for the whole PC.
● Below the clock you will see the words **1 of 8** with an arrow on each side. This indicates that there are different visual "looks" for the clock that you can choose from if you don't care for the one that is displayed by default.
● Click the right arrow once and you'll see a sharper and more modern look for the clock.

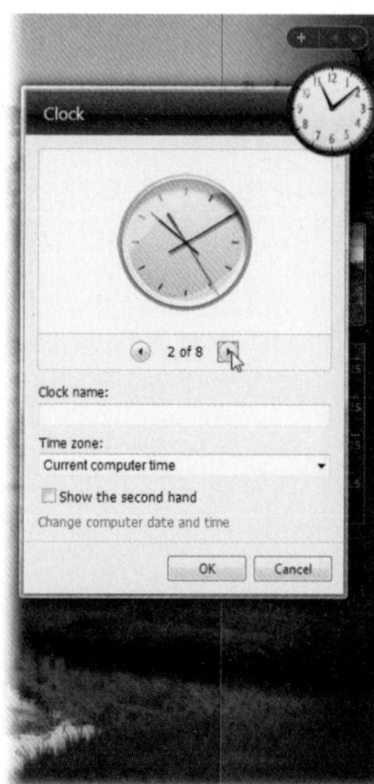

● As we've seen before, to confirm any changes, it's necessary to tell Windows that's what you want to do.
● Clicking **Cancel** will leave the clock unchanged, but if you like the look of this clock, click the **OK** button.
● Alternatively, use the arrow keys to scroll through the different clocks until you find one you do like and then click **OK**.
● The new look clock is in position. As it changes, you will see the hands sweep slowly round until they're telling the correct time. Visual tricks like this are among the things that make Vista a pleasure to use.

ADDING A NEW GADGET

● To add a gadget to the Windows Sidebar, move the cursor over the "+" sign at the top. After a moment it will highlight and you'll see the word **Gadgets** appear next to it. Click on this once with the left mouse button.

● Windows displays the gadgets that are included free with the operating system. As you can see, these include a weather gadget, a calendar, one for currency conversion, and an address book.

● To add, for example, the notes gadget, double click on the **Notes** icon with the left mouse button.

Clicking on this link takes you to a Microsoft website where you can find literally hundreds of additional gadgets that can be added to your Sidebar.

● Windows automatically pops the new gadget into position above those already on the Sidebar.

● Unless you want to add further items, close the gadgets window in the middle of the desktop by clicking the "X" in the top right-hand corner.

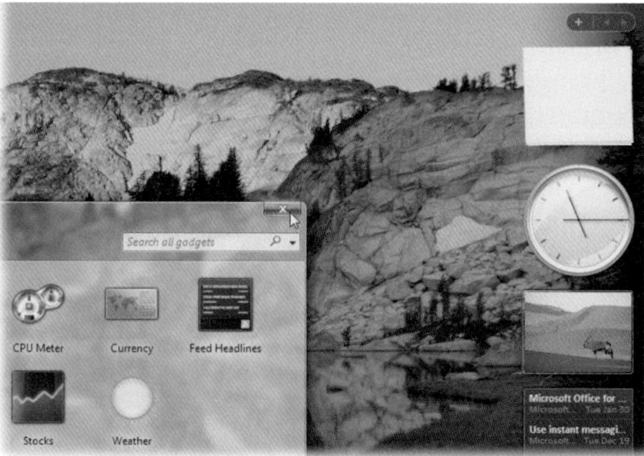

• The Notes gadget is ready to use. Simply click on it once with the left mouse button to select it and then start typing your reminder.

• As with the clock, it's possible to change various options associated with the Notes gadget. The writing on the note is a bit small, so let's make the text bigger.

• Right click on the bottom panel of the Notes gadget (where the cursor becomes an arrow) and then choose **Options** from the pop-up menu that appears.

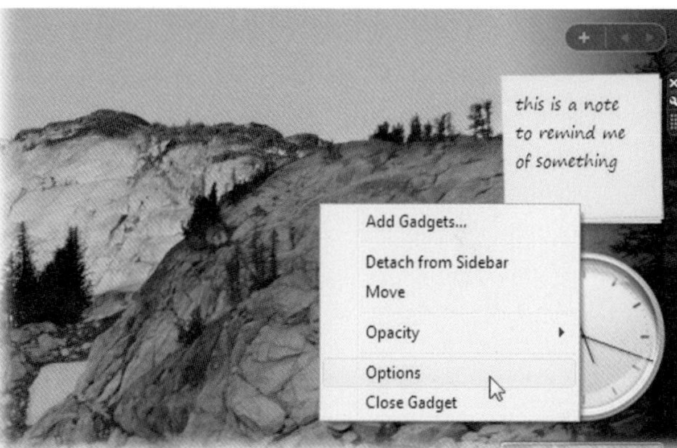

• The **Notes** dialog box appears onscreen. In the same way as the clock, it's possible to change the look of this gadget, in this case by scrolling through a range of six different colors.

• There are also options to change the font and the size of the text you type into your notes. The **Font Size** is currently **9** point.

• The downward pointing arrow in the **Font Size** box– a standard feature in Windows Vista–indicates the presence of a drop-down list of choices.

● Click on the arrow with the left mouse button, and a list of options drops down the screen.

● Here we're going to increase the size of any text we type into our Notes from 9 point to 12 point, so click once on **12** in the drop-down list.

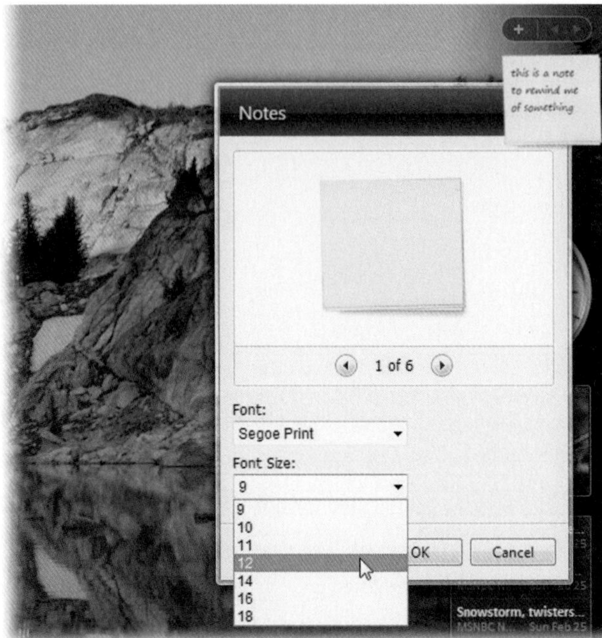

● You can see here that the **Font Size** box now shows **12** instead of **9**. However, as before, in order to confirm your changes you have to click the **OK** button.

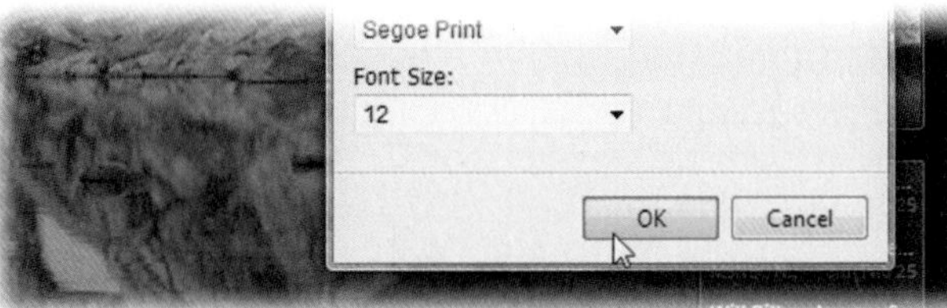

● The Notes menu closes, and the Notes gadget is back in position on the Sidebar with its new larger and more legible type.

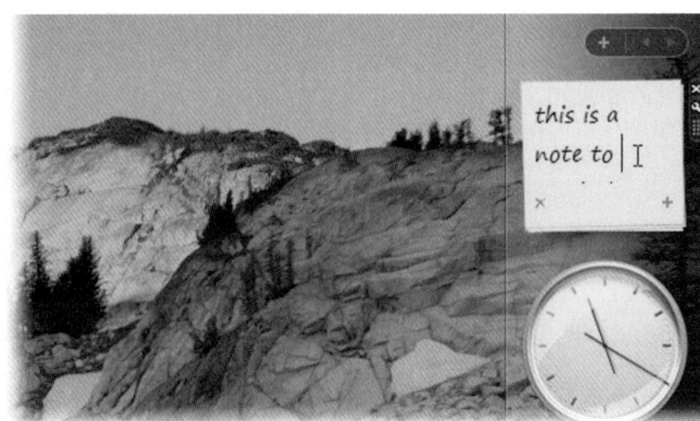

MOVING GADGETS TO NEW POSITIONS

- You can move Gadgets within the Sidebar or anywhere on the desktop.
- Hover your cursor over the Notes gadget and you'll see three small icons next to it–an "x", a wrench, and a tiny rectangular grip.
- Click on the grip with the left mouse button and drag the Notes gadget out onto the desktop.

- The Notes gadget increases in size, and the clock moves up the Sidebar to take the Notes' position.
- To create a new note, click the little green "+" sign at the bottom right-hand corner.
- Clicking the "x" at the bottom left corner deletes the current note.

- Your new note appears immediately and you can begin to type afresh. Note that the gadget tells you at the foot of the page that you're currently working on the second note. You can move between notes by clicking on the left- and right-pointing arrows.
- To return Notes to the Sidebar, grab the grip again with the cursor and drag it back to its earlier position.

KEY ACCESSORIES

As with previous versions of Windows, Vista includes a number of programs called Accessories that are useful for carrying out simple tasks, such as word processing, manipulating images, and drawing. They can't necessarily replace full-blown commercial alternatives, but they do a decent job and are well worth exploring. You will find the Accessories by clicking on the Start button to open the Start menu 15, clicking on **All Programs** to open the full list, and then clicking on **Accessories**. A selection of these helpful programs is shown here open on screen.

FEATURES KEY

❶ Paint
This is a good program for creating basic shapes with colored fills, text, and simple effects. Think of it as the electronic equivalent of a child's paint box.

❷ Sound Recorder
This is a fun accessory for recording sounds. You'll need a microphone but, after that, anything you record can be stored on your PC and used like any other Windows sound–for example to play when your PC starts up or to sound an alarm when an appointment occurs in Windows Calendar 44.

❸ Notepad
This is a simple program for writing and saving notes. For anything more complicated you're better off using Notepad's big brother, Wordpad (see ❹ opposite).

15 Opening All Programs

44 Recurrences and Alarms

OTHER PROGRAMS INCLUDED WITH WINDOWS VISTA

- **Windows Photo Gallery** for editing and organizing images (such as digital photos) stored on your PC.
- **Windows Media Player** for organizing video and music (such as songs bought from an online music service) on your PC, as well as creating your own CDs and playing back commercial DVDs.
- **Windows Movie Maker** for editing video shot with a digital video camera, adding credits, visual effects, and a sound track, and then copying the result to a DVD.
- A selection of housekeeping programs that help maintain your computer's performance, including Backup and Restore for keeping your data safe.

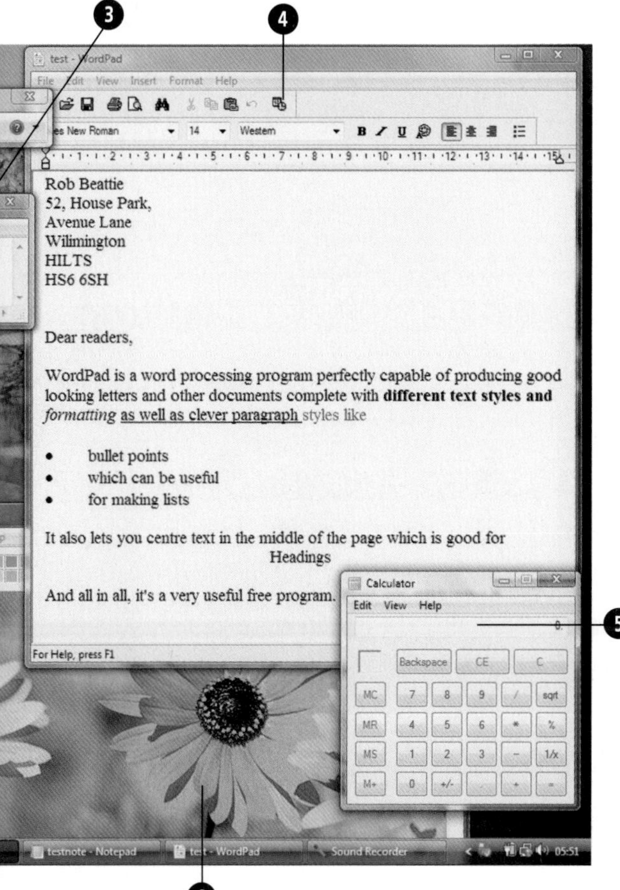

FEATURES KEY

❹ Wordpad
This is almost a proper word processing program, and it is certainly good enough for writing letters and other similar documents. It lets you change the way your text appears on the screen and the way it looks when you print it out. Wordpad includes simple paragraph formatting, such as bullet points and centered text.

❺ Calculator
An ultra useful, easy to use electronic calculator.

❻ Paint (again)
Windows lets you run some accessories more than once at the same time. Here the Paint program is being used to view one of the photos that's included with Vista.

❼ Games
Windows Vista has a range of games, including a powerful version of chess.

310 Enjoying Your Photos

340 Playing Music and DVDs

394 Making Movies

Windows Help

Whether you're an experienced Windows user coming to Vista for the first time or you've never used a PC before, it's likely that you'll need a helping hand at some point. Vista includes excellent help features that will aid you no matter what you're trying to do. Here we'll look at various ways to find answers to your questions.

FINDING GENERAL HELP AND SUPPORT

● To begin exploring Vista's help features, click the **Start** button and choose **Help and Support** on the right-hand side of the menu.

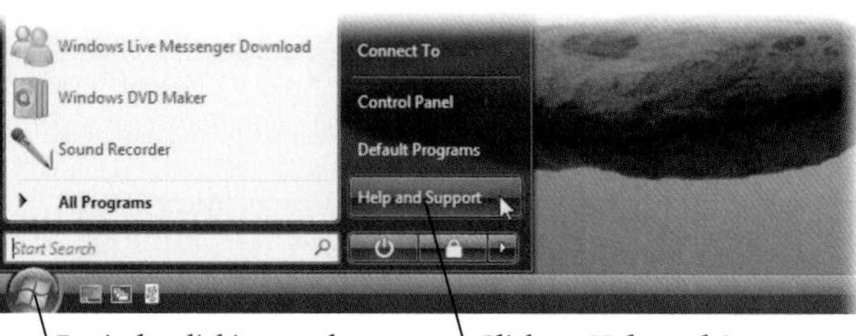

*Begin by clicking on the **Start** button*

*Click on **Help and Support** to open Vista's help features*

● This is the **Windows Help and Support** center, which offers various ways to help you out. You can click on any of the six icons at the top, seek help with specific common problems by clicking the links under the **Information from Microsoft** heading, or even get help from a friend.

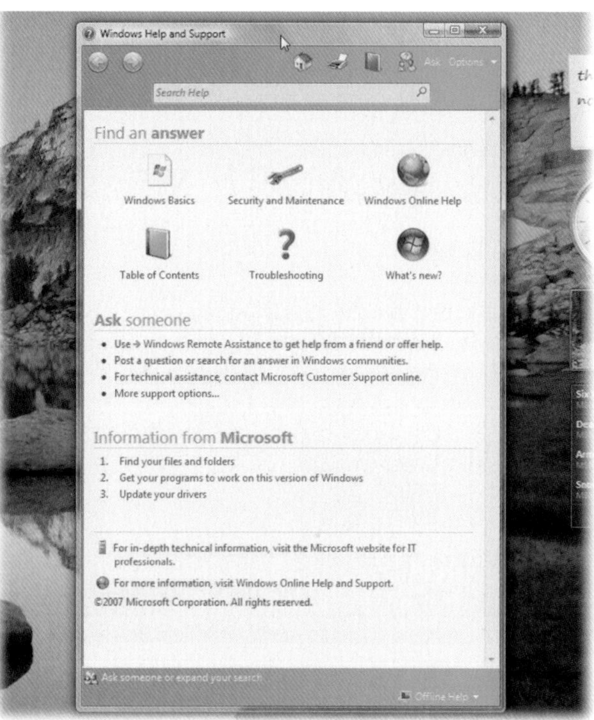

USING OPTIONS

If you can't find what you want on a help page, click the **Options** button and choose **Find (on this page)**. Then type in the word you're looking for and click **Next**.

● Let's suppose you're new to computers, and you just want to find out a bit more about how it all works.
● Move the cursor over the **Windows Basics** icon. It turns into a pointing hand to indicate a link to another part of the system.
● Click it once with the left mouse button.

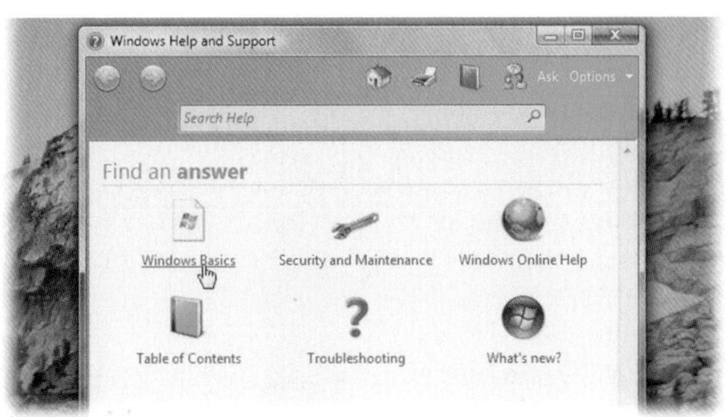

● Windows displays a page like the contents of a book. In effect, that's what it is, but each blue "chapter title" is a live link that will take you directly to that chapter.
● Move the cursor over **Parts of a computer**, and left click on it.

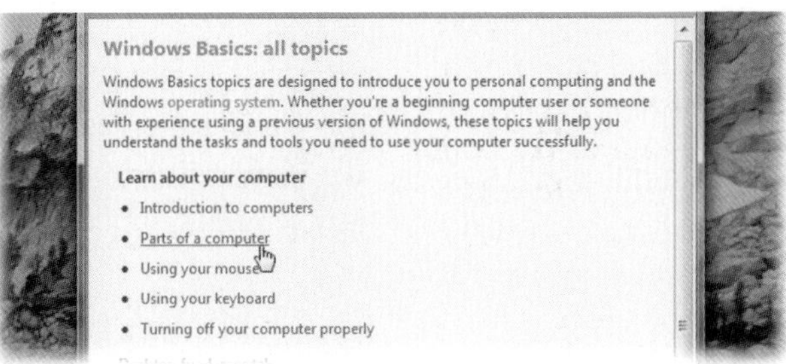

● And here's the **Parts of a computer** chapter, complete with an annotated illustration of a typical home PC set up.
● The descriptive text is black, but there is also blue bullet text on the right. As before, blue text indicates that each of these headings is a live link that will lead to a further sub-section within the help system.
● Follow one of these links by left clicking once on the **Monitor** heading.

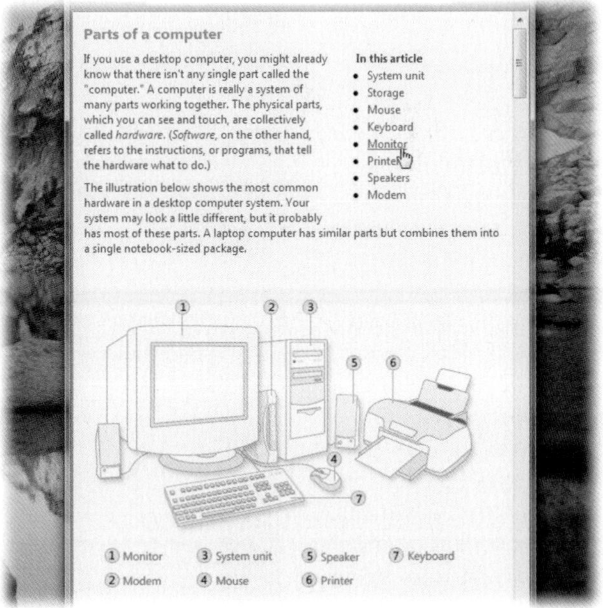

● Vista explains what a monitor is, how it works, and shows you what the two kinds look like–the older-style TV sets and the new flat panel type.
● Below the monitors, you can see that **Printer** is the section that follows. This was the next heading in the last screen, which tells us that all the topics are in a single page. The live link just took us further down the same page.
● We can also tell this from the scroll bar on the right-hand side of the window, which is three-quarters of the way down the window.
● To visit the other topics, you can scroll up or down by using the scroll bar.

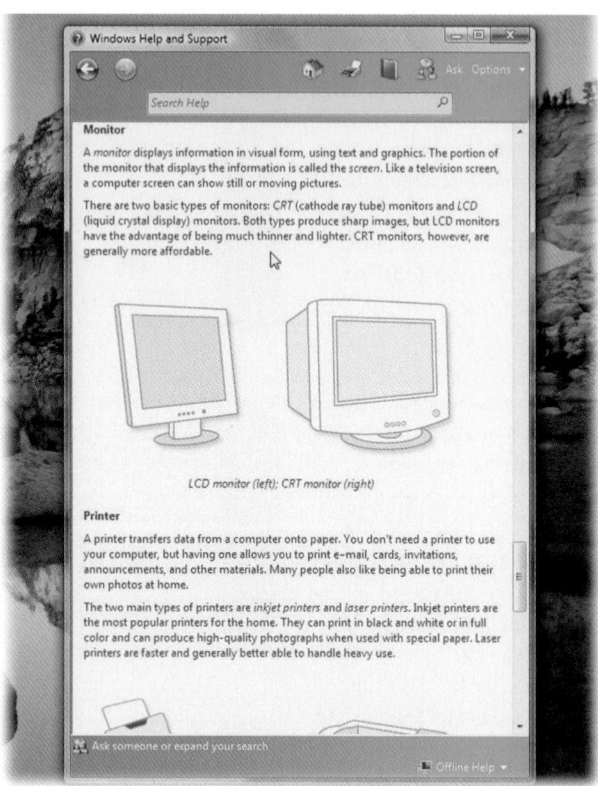

● To return to the last page you were on (**Windows Basics**) just click once on the **Back** button at the top left of the window.

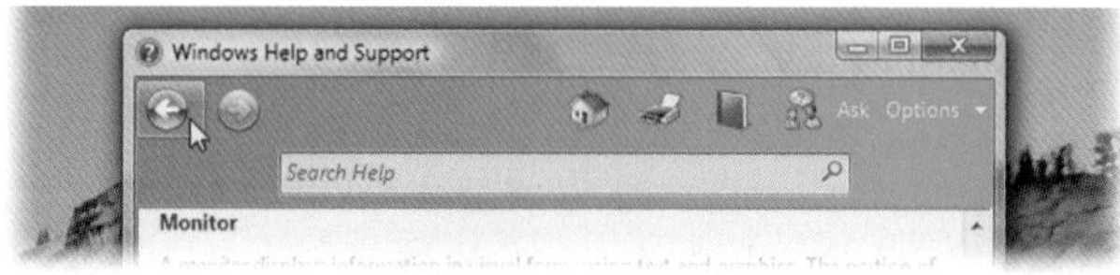

● Back on the **Windows Basics** page, you can see that when you've visited a link Windows helpfully changes the color of the text from blue to purple.
● To return to the opening help screen, click on the small house icon at the top, which represents "home".

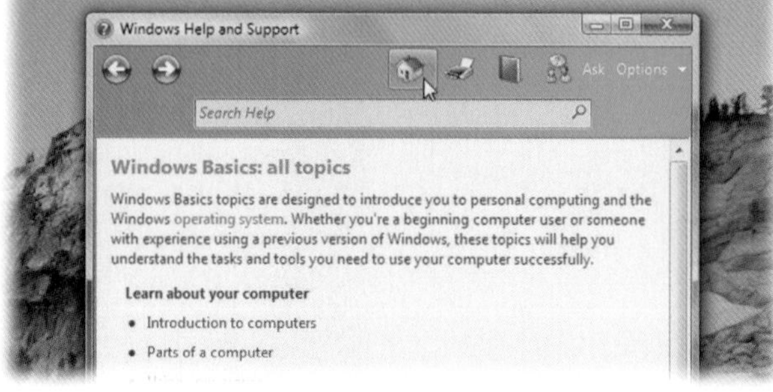

LOOKING FOR HELP ON A SPECIFIC TOPIC

● As we have seen, the Vista contents are arranged rather like a book.
● In order to find help on a particular topic, start from the opening help page and click on the **Table of Contents** icon.

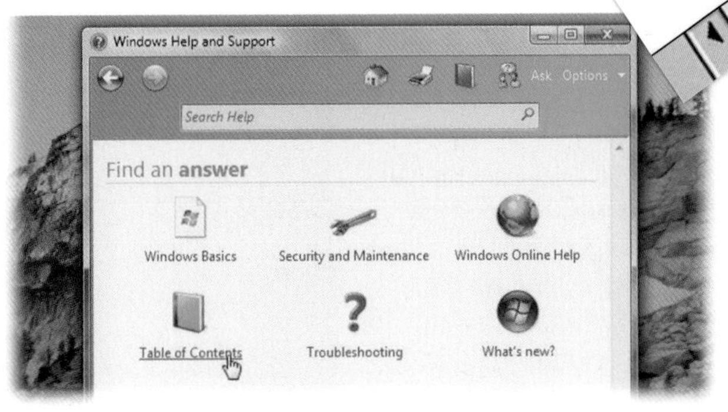

● The list of chapter headings that appears covers all of the major functions in Windows Vista.
● Clicking on any of these will take you to the relevant section. We want to find out how to play a music CD, so we'll click on the **Music and sounds** chapter heading.
● In the next screen, **Using Windows Media Player** looks like the right choice, so we'll click on that.
● We can retrace our steps using the **Back** button if this is the wrong choice.

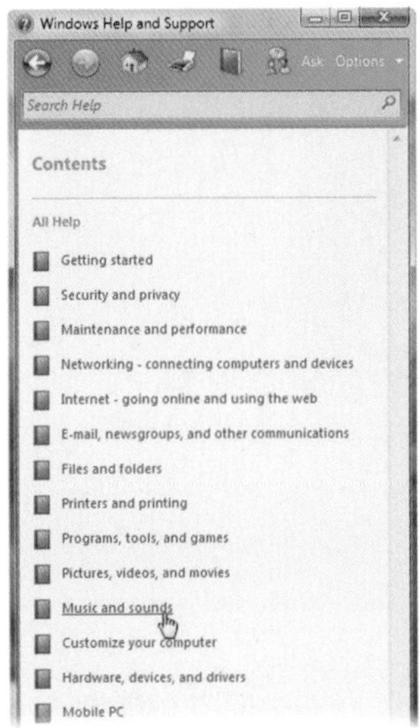

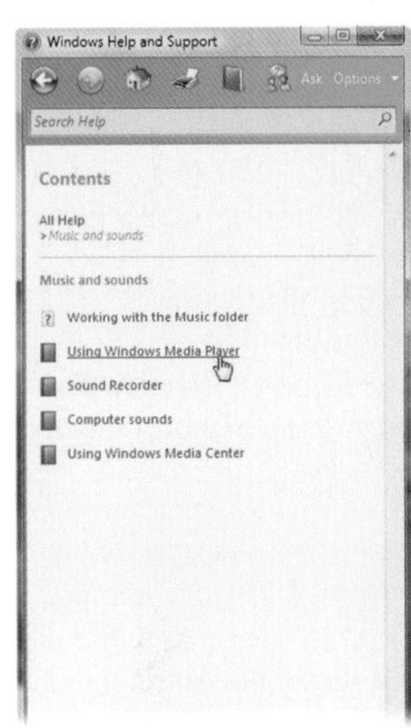

● The window that opens reveals another set of sub-headings, so we'll click **Playing music and video** and see where that takes us.

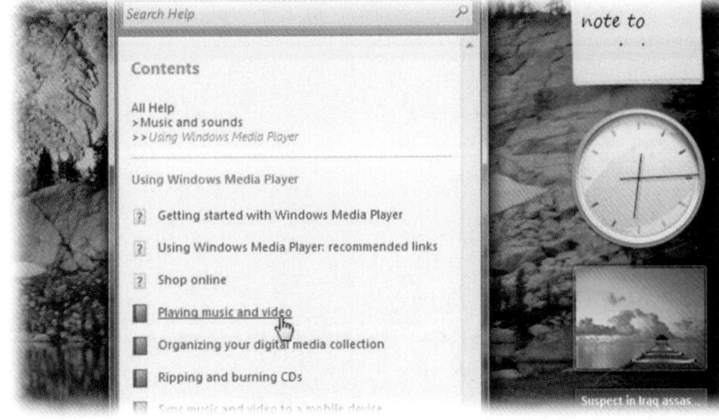

- In the next window, the first section looks the best bet here, so we'll click that.
- Note that in the top half of the box Windows lists all the chapters and sections we've visited. Each of them is a clickable link, so it's possible to jump straight back to the one you want, rather than having to keep clicking the **Back** button.

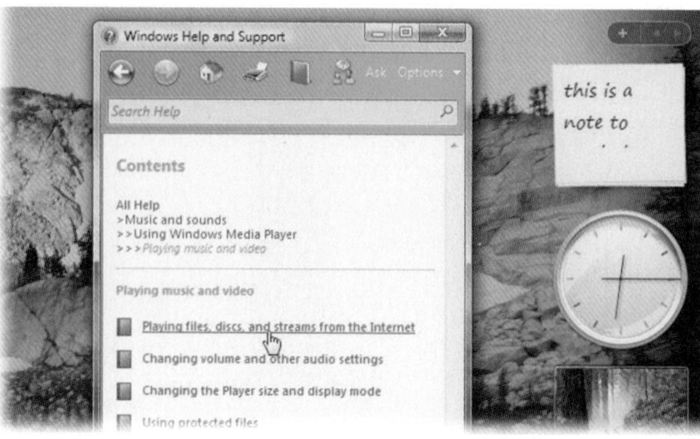

- In the window that opens, the headings have a question mark in a box next to them, rather than a blue book icon. This indicates that this is where the trail ends–hopefully with the answer. Click the **Play a CD or DVD** link to find out.

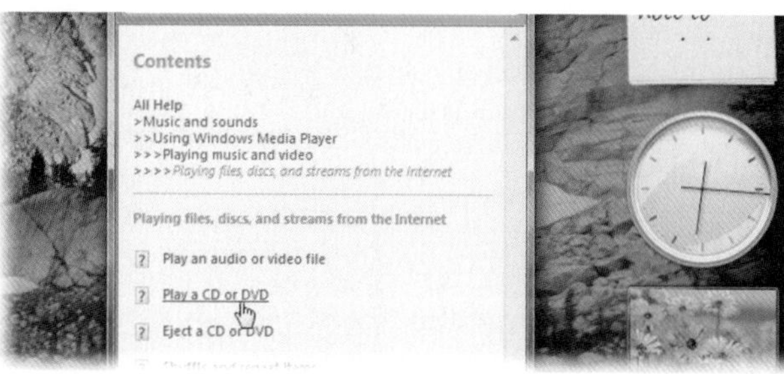

- This window explains the basics and tells you what you need in order to play a DVD movie or a music CD, but there's still more.
- Click on the **To play a CD or DVD** link and see what happens.
- This brings up detailed step-by-step instructions that explain how to play a CD or DVD, which should more than solve our query.
- If not, there is another live link underneath, and at the bottom there are some **See also** links that, when clicked, will take us to related topics.

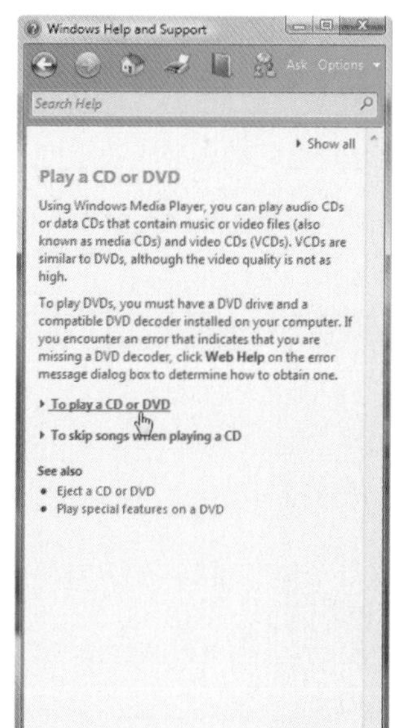

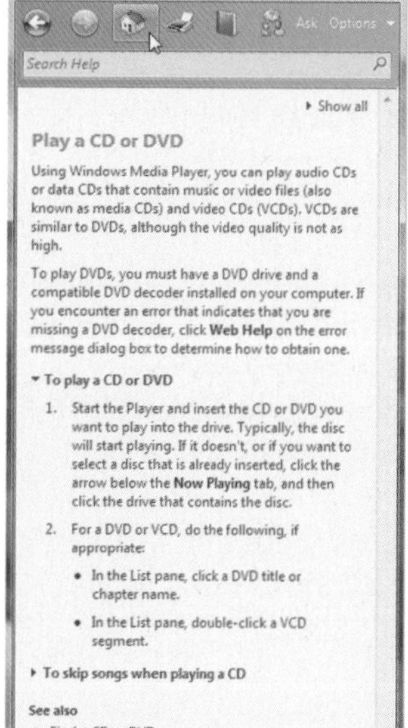

LETTING WINDOWS LOOK FOR HELP

- If you're not sure where to start, you can choose to ask Windows to find the answers for you.
- In the Help and Support page, click in the search box at the top, type in the subject, and hit the Enter key on your keyboard.

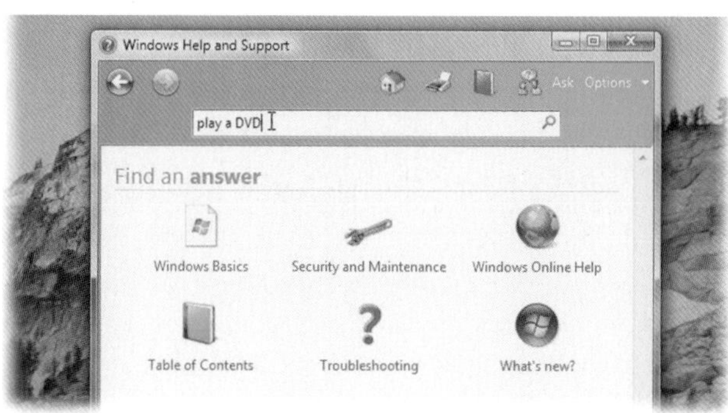

- Windows quickly brings back its best guesses for what you're after. In this example there are 30 entries that relate to our search term **play a DVD**. The first one looks good, so we'll click on this link.

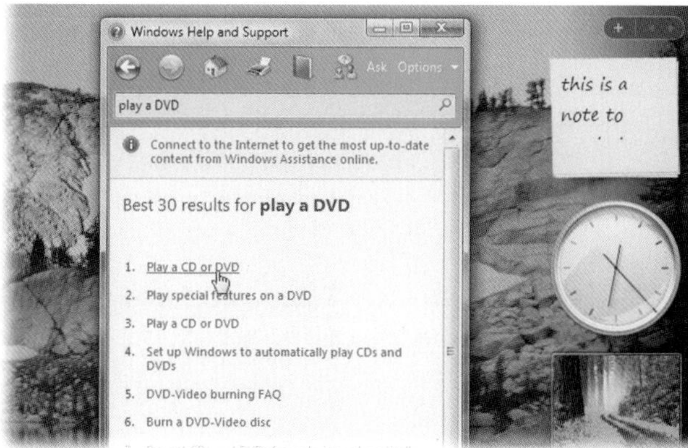

- Sure enough, we are taken to a section that contains general advice on playing a DVD on your Windows Vista PC, as well as a list of links that direct us to more detailed instructions.
- These include a link that applies directly to our search term, and clicking on this will certainly take us to the answer.

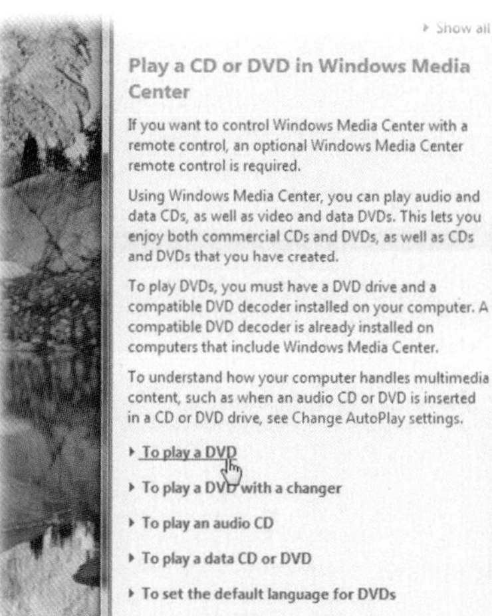

A Typical Program

One of the best ways to learn how Windows Vista works is to use one of the programs that's included. Although each program works slightly differently, they all have a lot in common.

Windows Calendar Basics

Windows Calendar is a new program, especially designed for Vista, that does a good job of organizing appointments and "to-do" lists for individuals, families, and even small businesses. In this section we'll use Calendar to create some typical appointments, schedule recurring events, and set an alarm as a reminder.

1 OPENING CALENDAR

- To open Windows Calendar, click the **Start** button once with the left mouse button and then choose **Windows Calendar** from the menu.

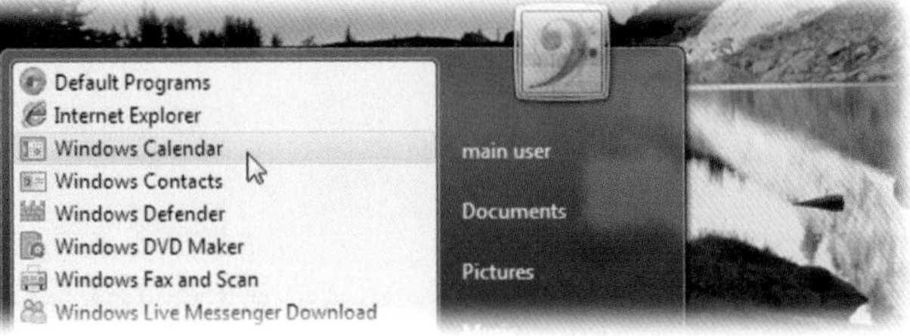

- Take a moment to look at the opening screen. The appointments window is in the middle; to the left there's a miniature calendar and a panel for multiple calendars and tasks; to the right is the **Details** pane.
- Click the arrow next to the **View** button and see what the different views look like. Then select the **Week** view.

In the ***Details*** *pane you can fine tune start and stop times for your appointments and tasks, and add reminder alarms*

● Here's the weekly view of the calendar program. To make sure that you're in the right place, click the **Today** button at the top. Notice that the current date is highlighted by a blue border.

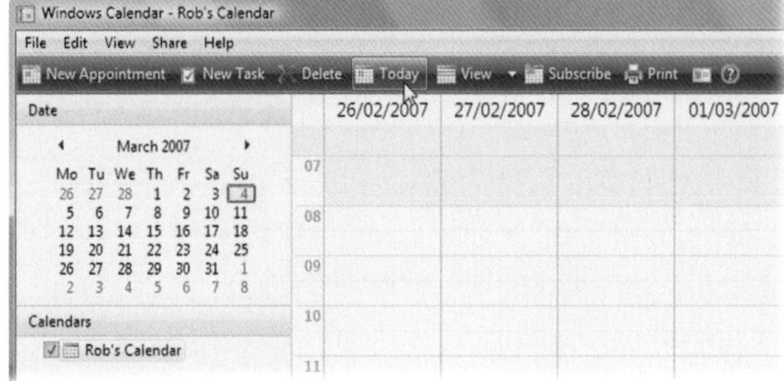

2 ADDING AN APPOINTMENT

● To add an appointment, move the cursor arrow into the column for today's date and double click at around the **12.30** point. Calendar creates a new block with the word **Appointment** already highlighted. You will see that that **Details** pane on the right now shows the time of this appointment.

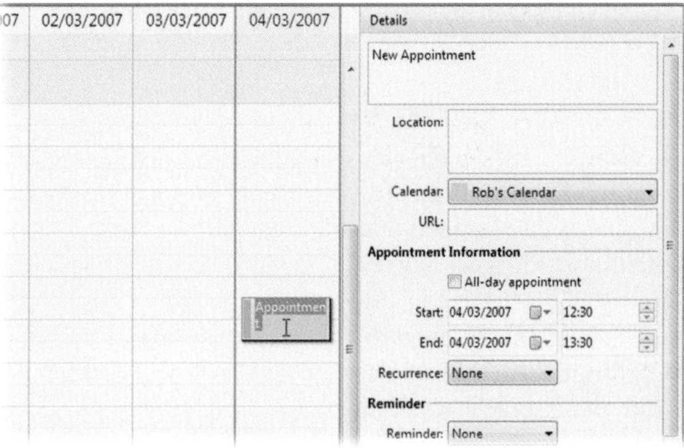

● Type in a name for the appointment–in this example, it's Sunday lunch. Calendar replaces the word **Appointment** with the text that you key in.

● An hour isn't long enough for Sunday lunch, so let's extend it. Move the cursor over the bottom of the appointment block and it will change to a double-headed arrow. Click and drag down to increase the period to a more realistic two and a half hours.

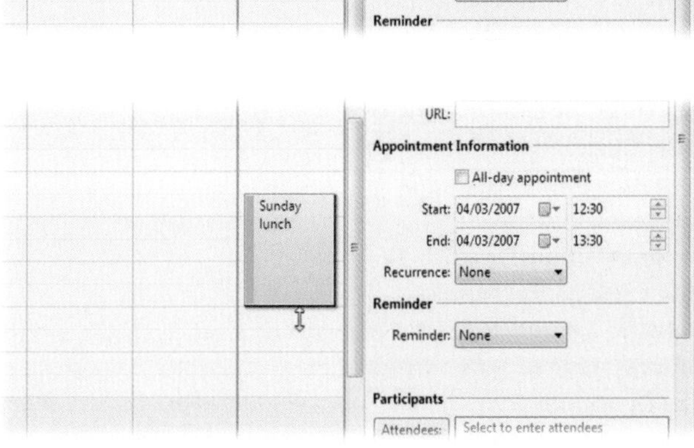

3 RECURRENCES AND ALARMS

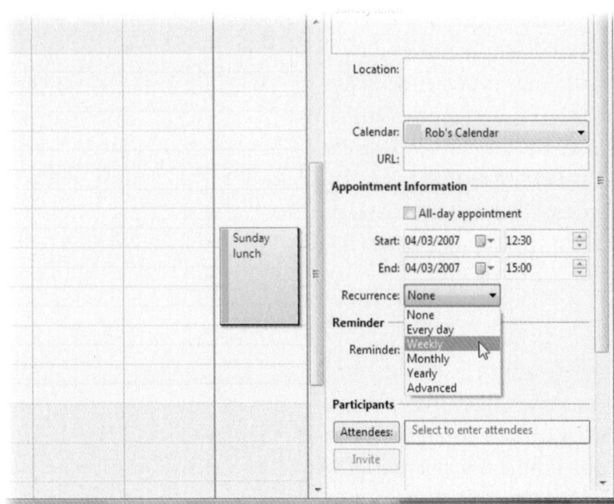

- We enjoy Sunday lunch every week at the same time, but instead of adding it to the calendar another 51 times, we can make the appointment recurring.
- Click on the **Sunday lunch** appointment to make sure it's selected and then click the arrow next to the **Recurrence** heading in the **Details** pane to open the drop-down list. Click on **Weekly** to select it.

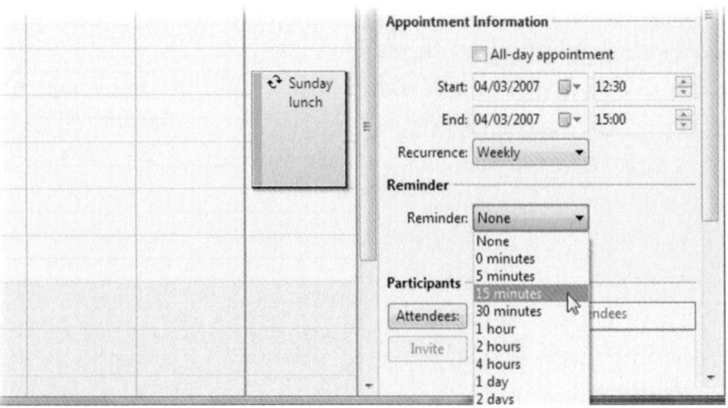

- Calendar now adds a little circular arrows icon to the appointment to indicate that it's a recurring event.
- If you're forgetful, you might want to add an alarm to the lunch appointment. Click on the arrow next to **Reminder** and choose **15 minutes** from the drop-down list by clicking on it.

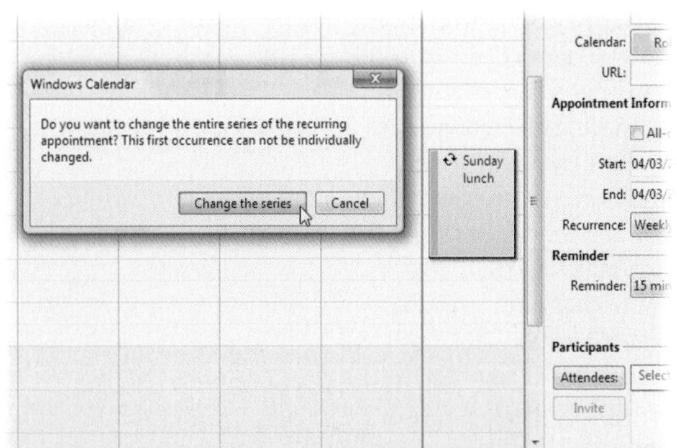

- Windows Calendar then asks you if you want to be reminded of all of the lunch appointments (although it asks the question in slightly strange computerspeak). Since your memory is unlikely to improve, click the **Change the series** button. This adds the alarm to every one of your Sunday lunch appointments throughout the year.

4 DIFFERENT TIMES AND DURATIONS

- To make appointments for the following week, move the cursor arrow over to the mini calendar on the left and click on the first day of next week–here it's Monday the 5th.

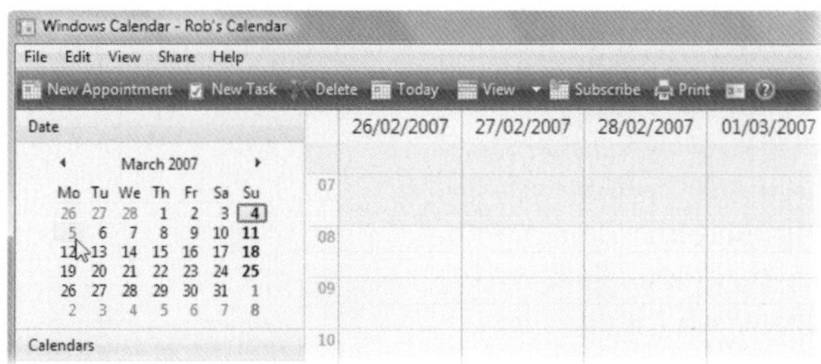

- To create a calendar appointment that runs for several days, double click as before, but this time be sure to position the cursor in the blue band at the top of the day in question. Unlike the other horizontal strips, this band has no time associated with it, because this is where Calendar stores day-long appointments.

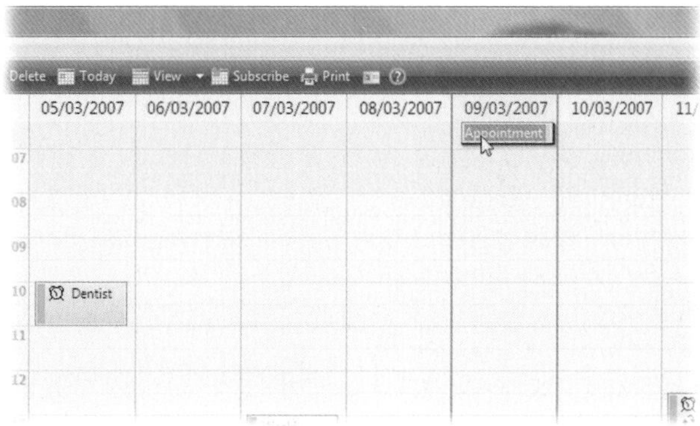

- Move the cursor over to the **Details** pane on the right. You will see that the **Start** date is correct (the appointment starts on the day we selected), but you'll need to set the **End** date.
- Open the drop-down list by clicking the arrow there and then select the correct date from the calendar that appears (in this example it's Sunday the 11th).

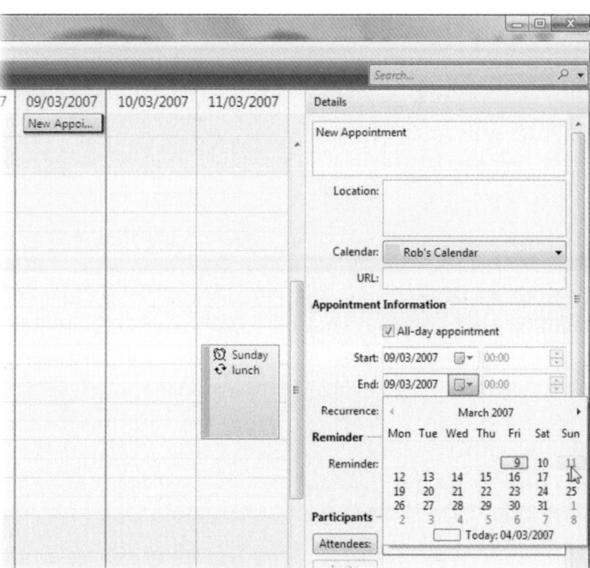

● Once you've set the end date, the appointment block in the calendar itself changes to reflect the new duration. The **New Appointment** block now stretches over two days of the weekend, and in the **Details** pane you'll see **New Appointment** at the top.
● Move the cursor to the end of these two words and then, holding down the left mouse button, drag left until both words are highlighted. You can now move the cursor away.

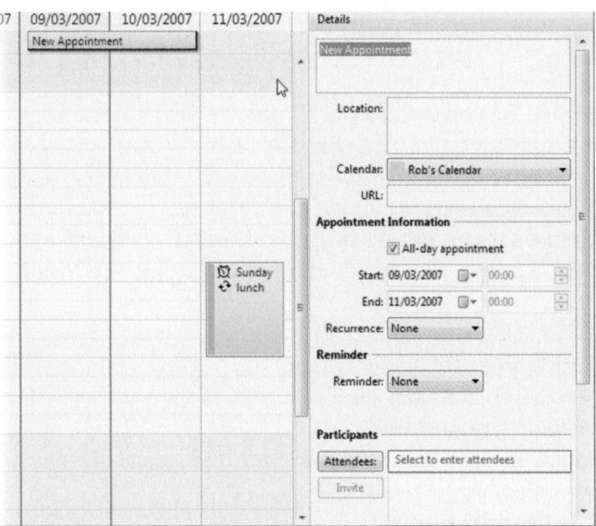

● With the words still highlighted, type in the name of the appointment (in this example it's **Weekend away**), and then click anywhere in the calendar with the left mouse button. The appointment block in the calendar now has a proper name–**Weekend away**.

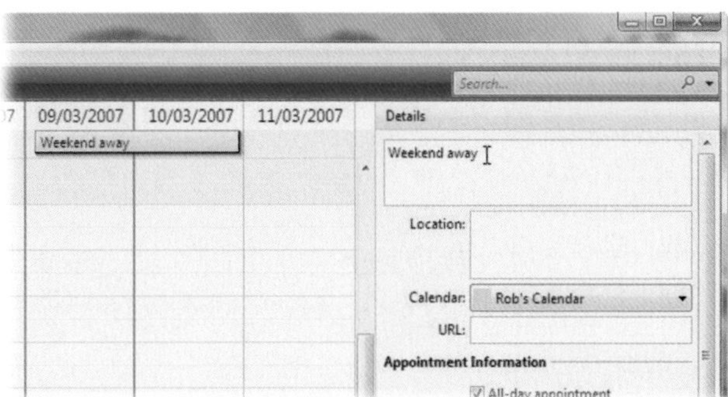

DELETING APPOINTMENTS AND TASKS

If plans change and you need to delete an appointment, Windows Calendar makes this easy. Just move the cursor over the appointment you want to delete and then click the right mouse button once. When the pop-up menu appears, select **Delete** by clicking on it and the appointment will vanish. To delete a task you can use exactly the same method. This same menu also offers a quick way to cut, copy, or rename an appointment or task.

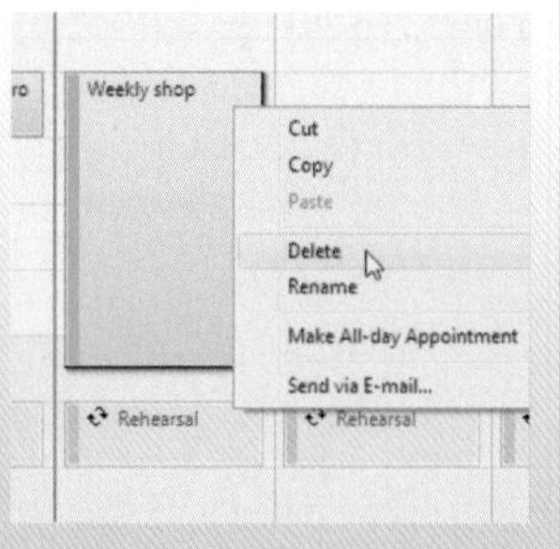

49 **Adding Tasks to the Calendar**

Managing Your Calendar

There will undoubtedly be times when arrangements change and you have to reschedule appointments, so you'll need to make these changes in your calendar. Meetings will sometimes overlap, and you'll need to be made aware of this. You will also want to include other kinds of task. In this section we'll look at how to manage these things, as well as showing you how to run two calendars at once.

CHANGING AN APPOINTMENT

- When you need to change the time of an appointment, the easiest way is to grab it with the mouse and move it.
- Click on the relevant appointment and–still holding down the left mouse button–drag it to the new time or date.
- You'll see a small open square next to the cursor, which tells you that you're moving an item.

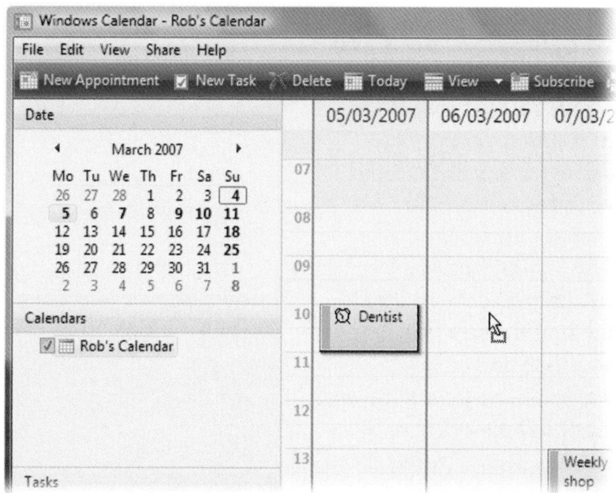

- When the cursor is over the new time slot in the calendar, release the mouse button and the relocated appointment appears in its amended position.

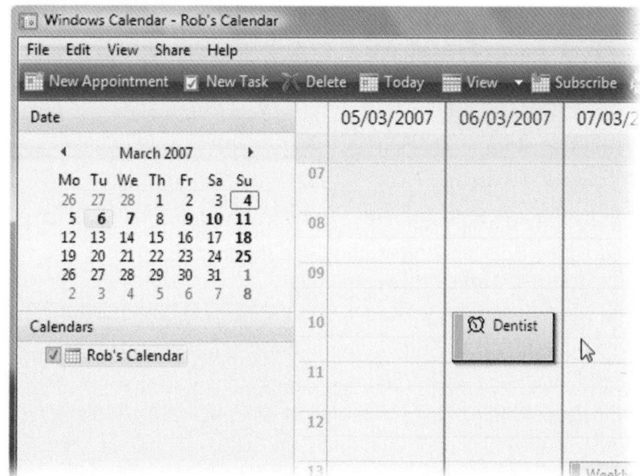

CONFLICTING APPOINTMENTS

● For the next example, we're going to view the calendar in the **Day** view.
● With an appointment on the relevant day selected, click on **View** on the button bar, and select **Day** from the drop-down menu.

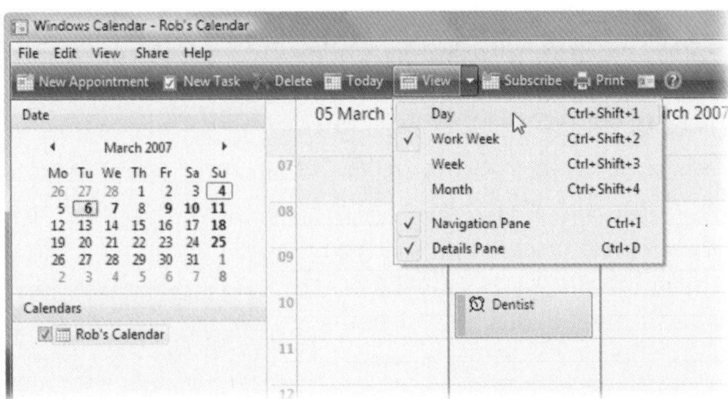

● Here's the Day view, and we can see that we have three appointments all starting at separate times.
● Unfortunately, the optometrist has just changed our appointment to 1pm, when we're meant to be picking up laundry on the other side of town!
● What happens when we click on **drop off spectacles** and drag it to a position an hour earlier?

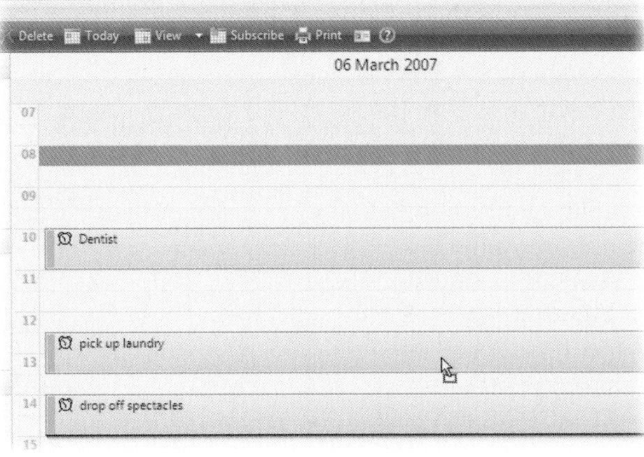

● When we let go of the mouse button, the moved appointment drops into place at the right time, but Calendar reduces the width of both overlapping appointments so they sit next to each other in the day planner. This alerts us to a conflict between the two appointments. It's simple and very effective.

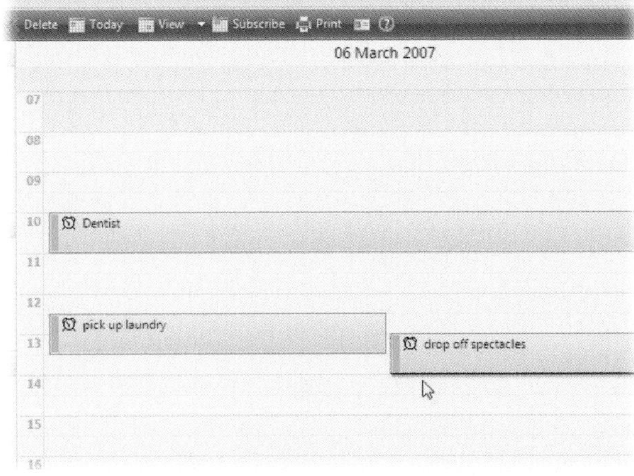

ADDING TASKS TO THE CALENDAR

- As well as appointments, Calendar also handles "to-dos" or tasks–jobs that have to be completed by a specific time or date.
- To create a task, left click once on the **New Task** button on the button bar.

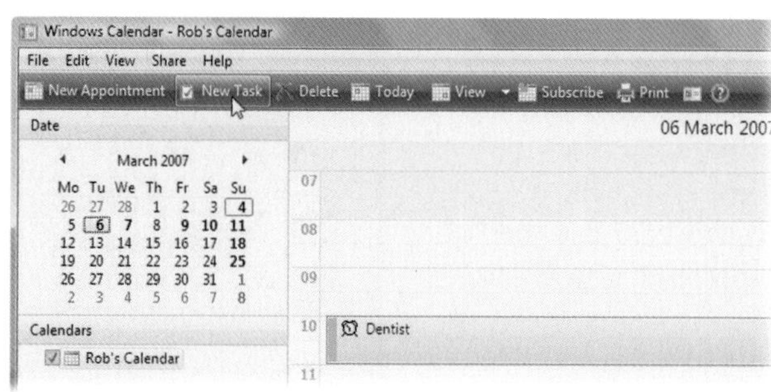

- Calendar creates a **New Task** in the **Tasks** pane on the left-hand side of the program window. Just like a new appointment, it highlights the words **New Task** ready for you type in your own description.

- Type in the name of the task and then click anywhere in the calendar to complete the action.

- Now let's look at the **Details** pane. By default, Calendar assumes that a task commences on the day it's created, so you can leave the **Start** date as it is.
- To alter the completion date, left click on the arrow next to the **Due date** box and choose a date from the little drop-down calendar that appears.
- You can add an alarm to a task in the same way as for an appointment.

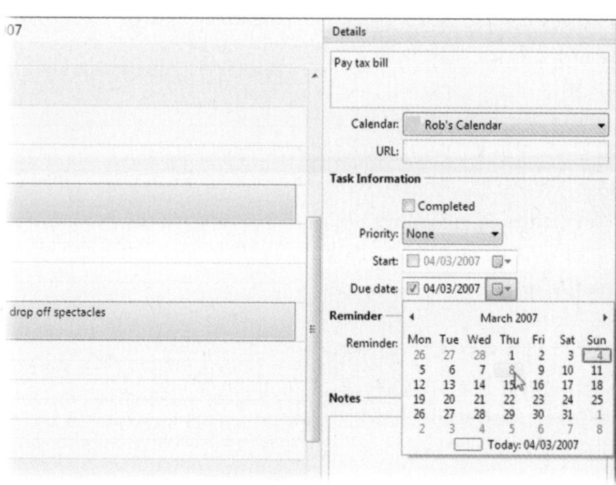

44 Recurrences and Alarms

ADDING A NEW CALENDAR

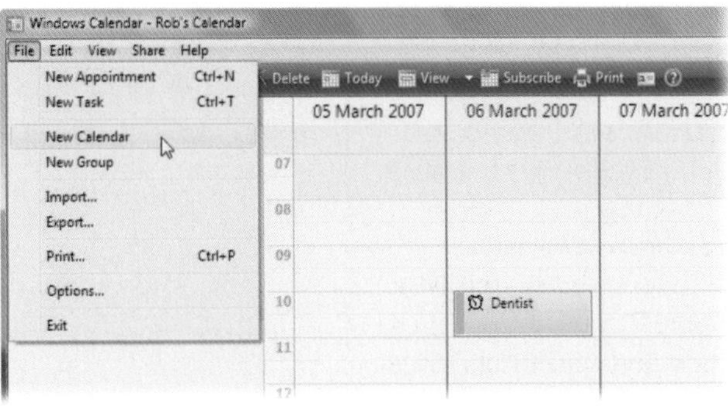

- Sometimes you need separate calendars for different aspects of your life, so let's create another.
- Click once on **File** at the top left of the screen with the left mouse button.
- Then choose **New Calendar** from the menu.

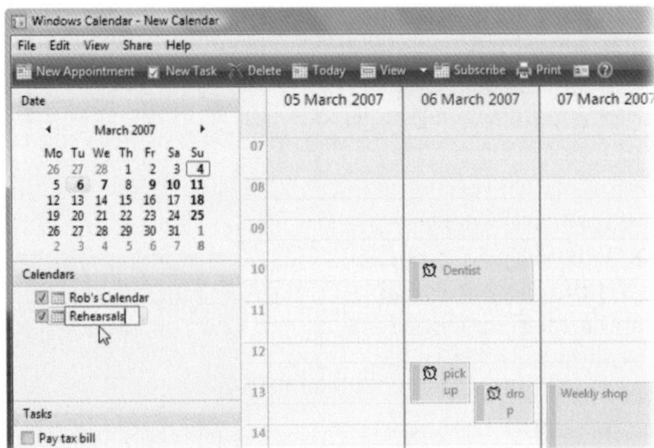

- A second calendar icon appears in the left-hand panel, highlighted for you to type in a name for it.
- This new calendar will be used to schedule all the events associated with organizing the forthcoming school play, so we'll call this calendar **Rehearsals**.

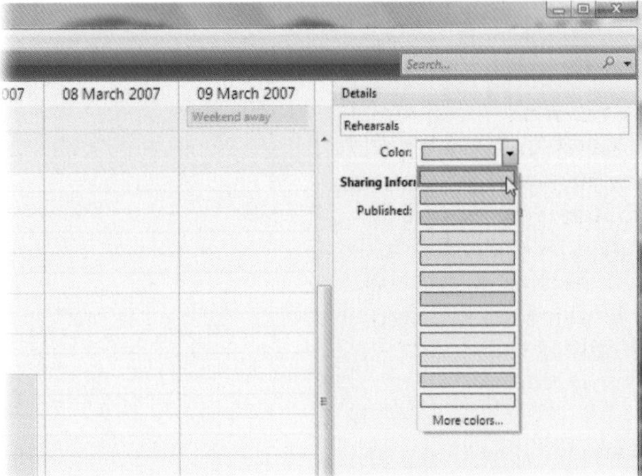

- We will be placing events for the school play in the existing pages, and we need to be able to distinguish between these events and those in our home life.
- With the **Rehearsals** calendar still selected, open the **Color** drop-down list in the **Details** pane on the right-hand side, and choose a new color for the new calendar. Pink will stand out beside the green.

WORKING WITH THE SECOND CALENDAR

- With the Rehearsal calendar still highlighted, double click in a time slot on the calendar to create a new appointment.
- Give it a name–this is an actual **Rehearsal**–and then click anywhere on the page to complete the action.
- There are now two kinds of appointment on the calendar–those in green from the original calendar and this pink one that we've just created.

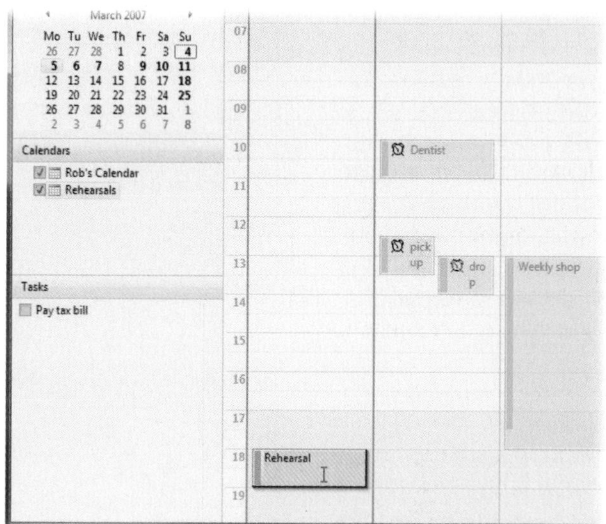

- Rehearsals take place at the same time every day, so select the new **Rehearsal** appointment and move the cursor to the **Details** pane.
- Open the drop down menu next to **Recurrence** by clicking on the arrow.
- Choose **Advanced** by clicking on it once.

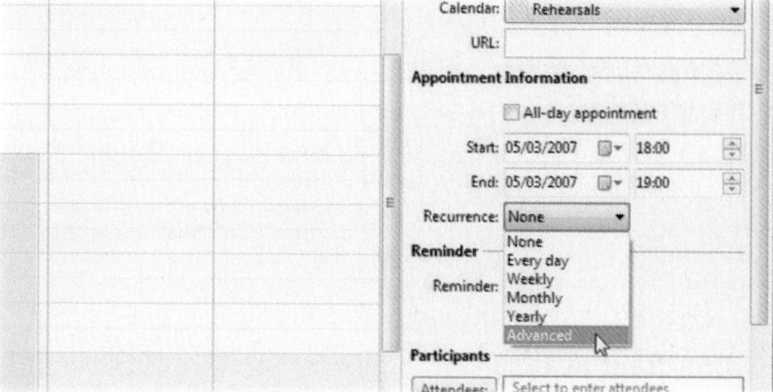

- When the dialog box appears, leave all the settings as they are except for one. We know the rehearsals will only last for another five days, so click the radio button next to **Until** to switch it on.

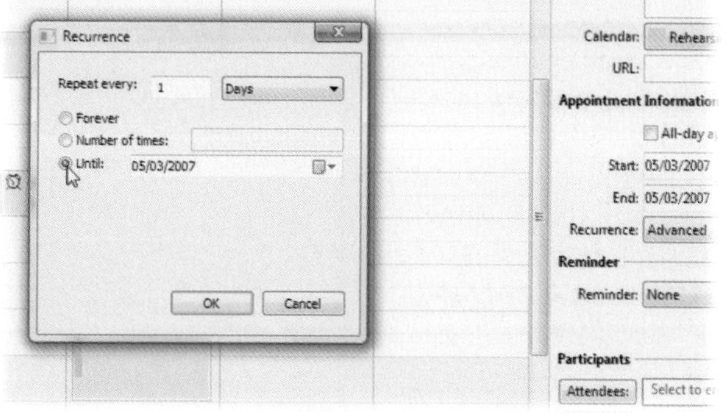

● At the right-hand end of the **Until** panel you will see a small arrow and calendar icon. Click on the arrow to open a drop-down menu.
● On the calendar that is revealed, select the last date in the appointment series by clicking on it once with the left mouse button.

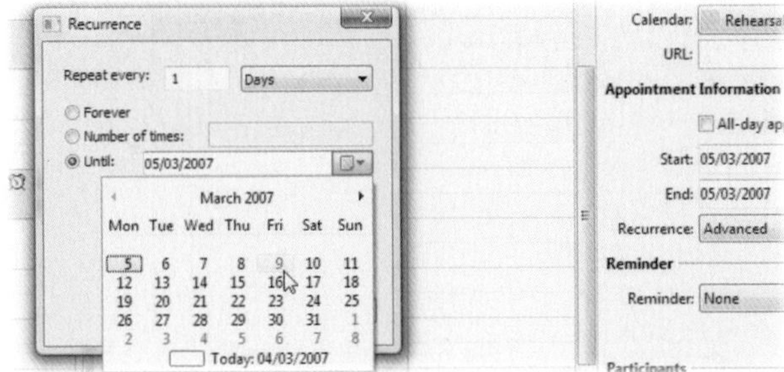

● Confirm the changes you've made to the series of appointments by clicking the **OK** button.

VIEWING A MONTH ON A SINGLE PAGE

● The dialog box vanishes, and we're back at the main calendar. The appointments we created in the original calendar are green, and those in the new Rehearsal calendar are pink. The color coding makes it easy to distinguish between them.
● To see a whole month's worth of appointments at the same time, click on the **View** button and choose **Month** from the drop-down menu that appears.

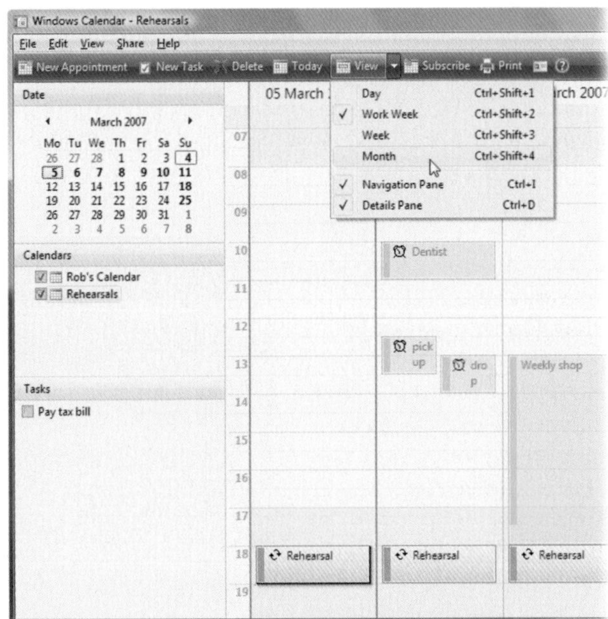

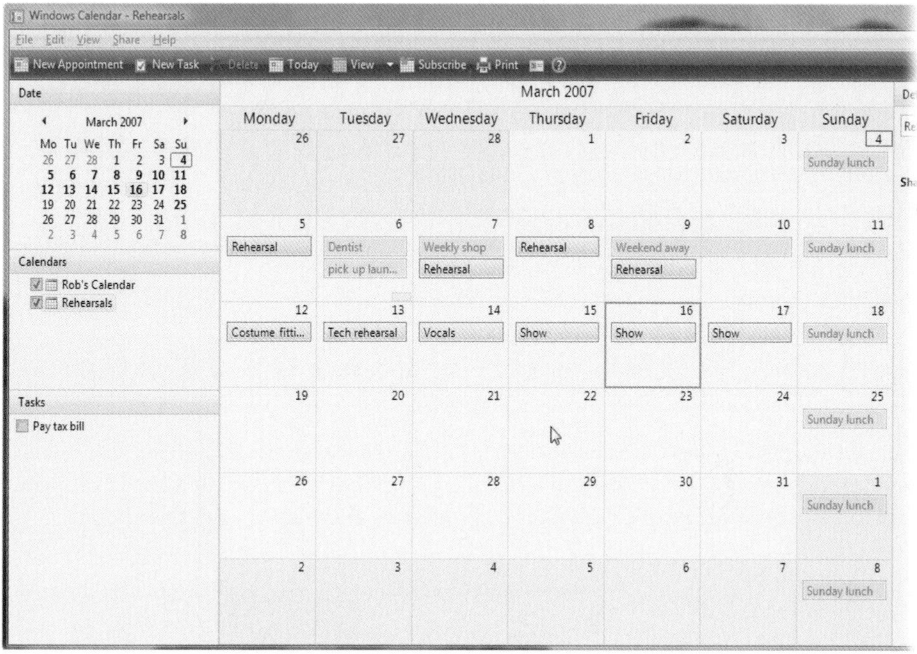

● The Month view gives a very clear overview of what needs to be done in the coming weeks, and multiple calendars have their uses in a busy home, or even in a school or small business.

● Each person in the family or the team can be given his or her own individual color so that events and meetings can be displayed side by side, helping everyone to organize their time and avoid conflicting schedules.

● If combining calendars like this gets too congested, you can always hide one or more of them.

● Click once on the check box next to the calendar you want to hide to remove the check mark. In this example, the original green calendar is now hidden. Replace the check mark, and the calendar returns.

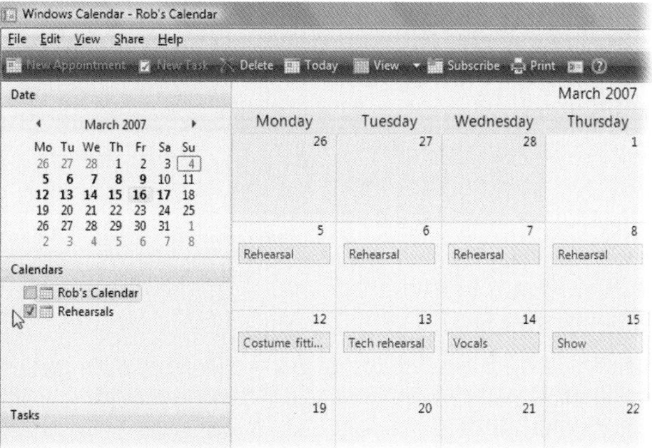

PERSONALIZING WINDOWS

In the same way you may like to personalize your real desk with a favorite photo or day-by-day calendar, you can change the way that Windows looks to suit your own taste.

CHANGING THE DESKTOP IMAGE

The new look of Windows Vista gives to a computer is one of its strengths, and when Vista is installed, Windows displays an attractive desktop background. However, if you want to change this, there's a range of great alternatives to choose from.

1 CHOOSING PERSONALIZE

- Click anywhere on the desktop with the right mouse button and then choose **Personalize** from the pop-up menu.

2 SELECTING THE OPTION

- The **Personalize appearance and sounds** dialog box opens. Here you can alter various visual and audio settings.
- To change the photo that Windows displays on your screen, click on **Desktop Background** once with the left mouse button.

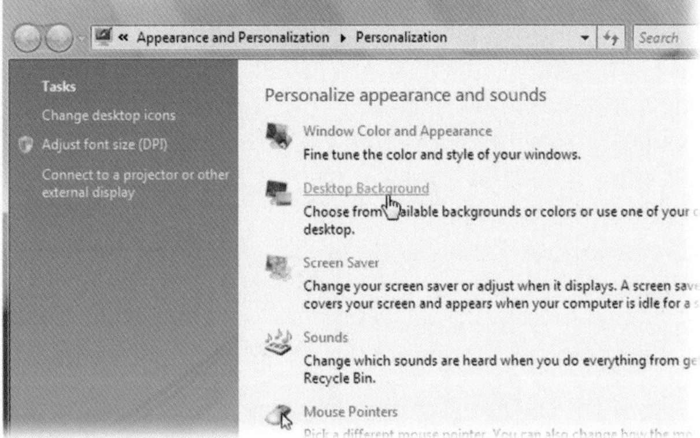

3 CHOOSING A BACKGROUND

- This dialog box displays a selection of photos and pictures that you can use as a background for your Windows desktop.
- Drag the slider on the scroll bar to reveal other photos in the dialog box.

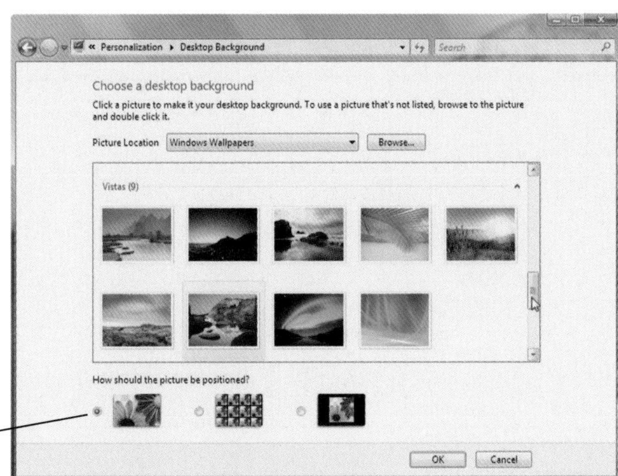

Here you can choose how to display the image–fitted to the screen, tiled, or centered

4 SELECTING THE IMAGE

- When you see one you might like, click on it and the desktop background will change to this image.
- When you find the one you want to use, click the **OK** button to confirm your choice, and the **Choose a desktop background** dialog box closes.

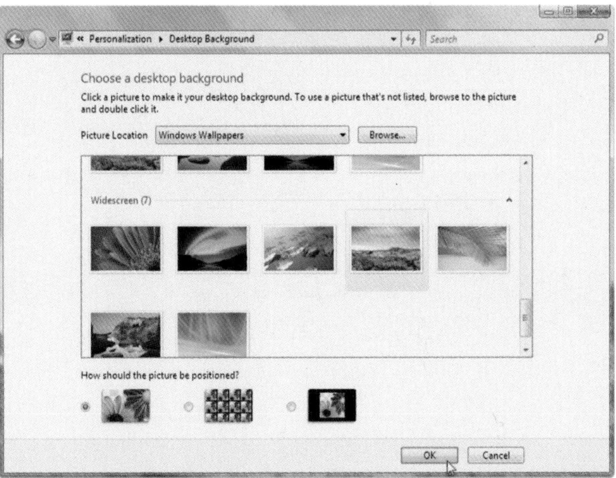

A CHANGE OF MOOD

Replacing the desktop background with one of the many alternatives can totally alter the appearance of your computer, so look through the choices and select one that suits you.

CHANGING THE WINDOWS COLOR

The color scheme that you see in the borders of open windows (such as the one below), in the Start menu, and in the Taskbar along the bottom of your screen is determined by the window color setting. You can alter this to suit your taste.

1 CHOOSING A STOCK COLOR

● In the **Personalization** dialog box that we have just seen [54], click once on **Window Color and Appearance**.

● The window that opens offers you a selection of stock colors. Click on any of these to see the effect in the border of the window.

● In the example below, **Teal** has been selected.

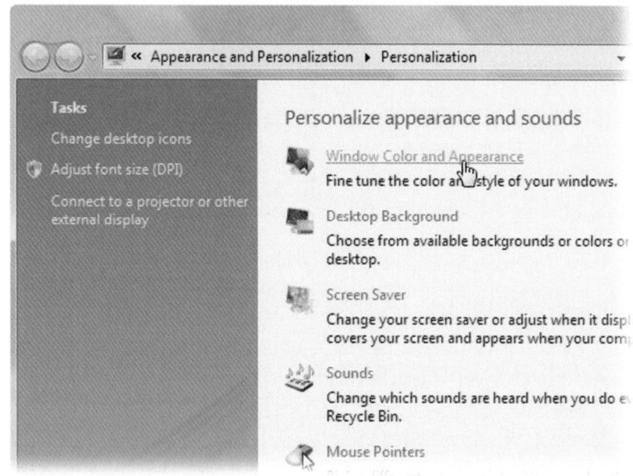

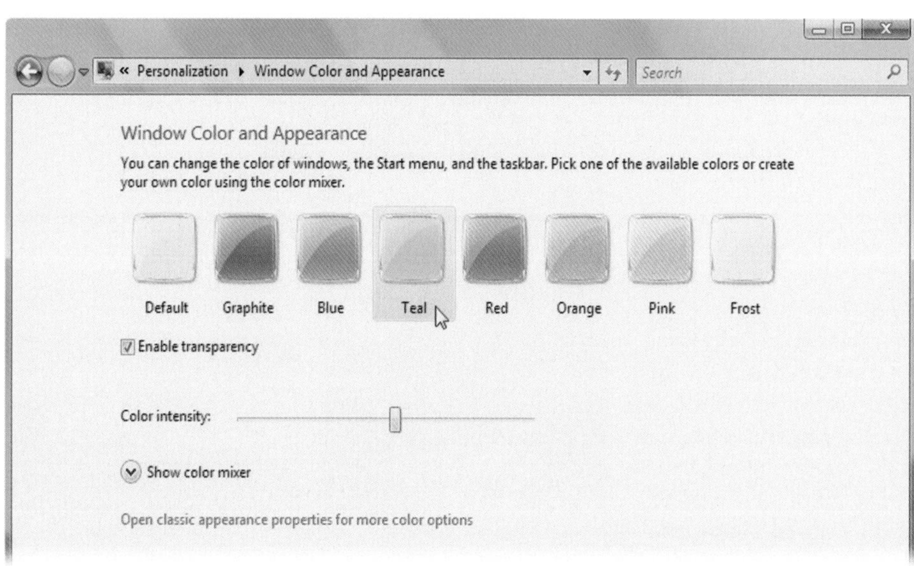

54 Choosing Personalize

2 MIXING YOUR OWN COLOR

- If none of the stock colors is to your taste, you can adjust the chosen color or create a new one.
- Click on the **Show color mixer** button to open the mixing tools.

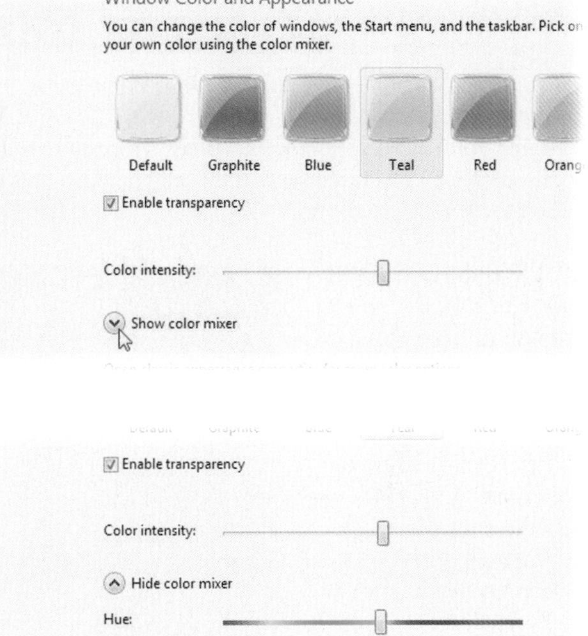

- In addition to the **Color intensity** slide bar, which was already visible, three more slider bars appear.
- Experiment with the **Hue**, **Saturation**, and **Brightness** by left clicking on each slider and dragging to the left and right.
- Watch the effects on the border of the window itself.

- You can fine tune the stock colors (here we have slightly darkened the Teal blue by just reducing the brightness) or create a totally new color using these tools.
- When the color is as you want it, click **OK**.
- You can return the screen to its original appearance at any time by opening this window and selecting the **Default** color.

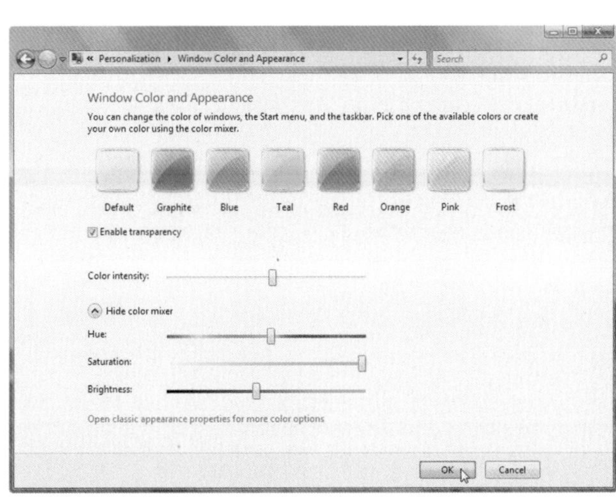

Desktop Icons

Personalizing means more than just changing the look of your screen. There are also practical changes that will make using your computer easier and improve efficiency. One way is to add icons to your desktop that provide shortcuts to the files, folders, pictures, and movies on your computer, as well as the hard drives.

1 OPENING ICONS SETTINGS

- By default, the only icon on the desktop is the **Recycle Bin**. We're going to add some more icons.
- In the **Personalization** dialog box, move the cursor over to the **Tasks** panel and then click once on **Change desktop icons**.

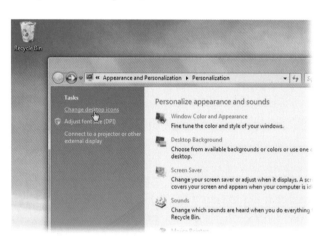

- The **Desktop Icon Settings** dialog box opens, listing the different icons you can have on your desktop and showing what they look like. You will see a tick next to the **Recycle Bin** because it is already on the desktop.
- Any of the other icons can be added to the desktop by clicking on the box next to the relevant icon title.

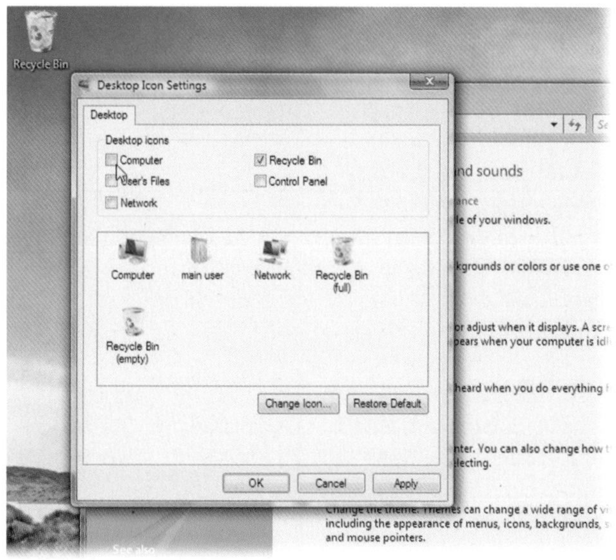

54 Choosing Personalize

2 SELECTING NEW DESKTOP ICONS

● The **Computer** and **User's Files** icons are probably the most useful. They give you easy access to your PC's hard disk and the files that you use most often. Instead of having to open the **Start** menu and find them from there, you'll always have them available on the desktop.

● To try them out, click on the boxes next to these and then click **OK**.

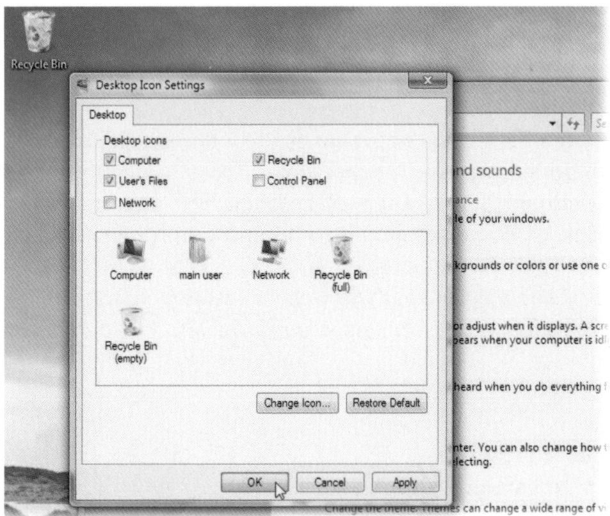

● The **Computer** and **User's File** (here called **main user**) icons appear on the left edge of the screen.

● Double clicking on these will immediately open their respective windows, allowing you to get to their contents quickly and easily.

ARRANGING DESKTOP ICONS

To change the size of the icons that Vista displays on the desktop, and to arrange them in different ways, click on the empty desktop with the right mouse button and choose **View** from the menu that appears. In the screen above, the icons have been "auto arranged"–they are lined up on an invisible grid, and Windows takes care of the order in which they appear on the desktop. Experiment by removing the check marks shown here to see how this affects the way your desktop icons are arranged.

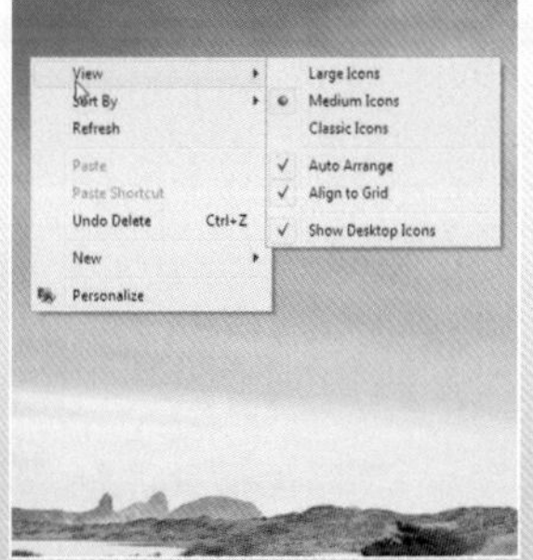

The Control Panel

Still on the subject of personalizing your PC, let's look at the Control Panel. This is the place where Windows Vista keeps many of its most important settings, some of which you will definitely need to change at some time, whether you want to set up parental controls, back up your hard disk, add or remove programs, or improve the security of your computer. We'll look at several of these Control Panel features in more detail at various points in the book, but here's a quick overview. To open the Control Panel, click the **Start** button and then choose **Control Panel**.

FEATURES KEY

❶ System and Maintenance
Check or improve your PC's performance, make backups, update Windows Vista.

❷ Security
Settings for keeping your PC safe from Internet intruders, spyware, viruses, and scams.

❸ Network and Internet
Control home networking and Internet settings, and manage Internet Explorer.

❹ Hardware and Sound
Adjust the settings of mouse, keyboard, printer, digital camera, scanner; adjust audio output; manage notebook battery life.

❺ Programs
Adjust program settings, delete programs, etc..

❻ Mobile PC
Visible only on notebook PCs, this helps users to gain a little extra performance or extend battery life.

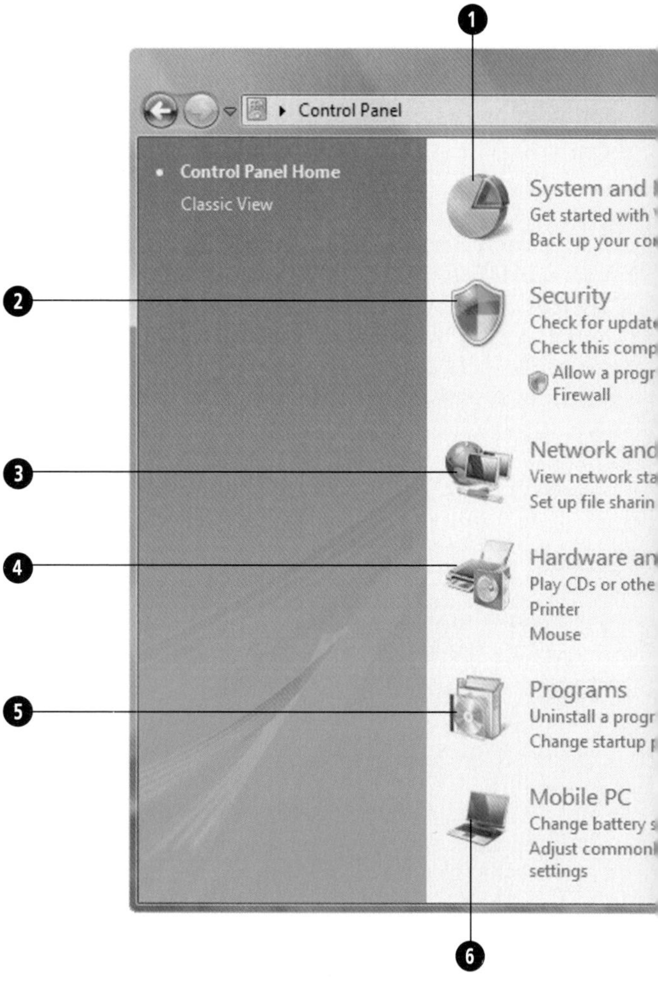

CLASSIC VIEW

If you've been using a previous version of Windows, you may be used to seeing the Control Panel contents displayed as individual icons. Vista will let you do that if you prefer. In the Control Panel, click the **Classic View** command in the left-hand column and each Control Panel program will be displayed as an icon.

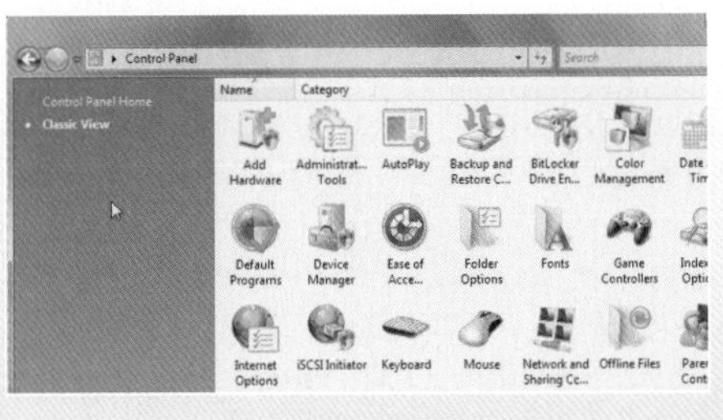

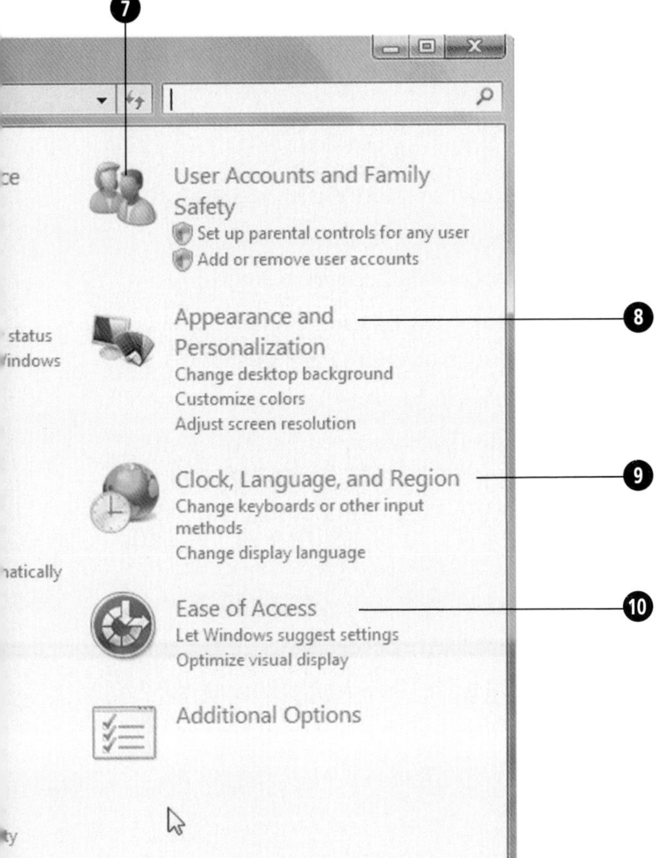

FEATURES KEY

❼ User Accounts and Family Safety
Set your PC up so that family members can use it safely. Keep an eye on what the kids are up to through the use of parental controls.

❽ Appearance and Personalization
Manage the way Windows looks and works from here.

❾ Clock, Language, and Region
Set time and date, specify time zone, add clocks for different zones, sort out localization issues, display language, currency, time, and date formats from here.

❿ Ease of Access
Windows has various ways of improving the display of information for the visually impaired; settings here can also help supplement sounds with visual clues for those who have impaired hearing.

FILES AND FOLDERS

WINDOWS VISTA ARRANGES EVERYTHING on your PC using a familiar, real-world model. So, just as a typical office keeps files inside folders inside other folders, so Windows does the same. Some folders are created automatically for you by Vista, and these are for handling common tasks like storing documents and photos. Others, you can create yourself as and when you need them. You can create and use as many files and folders as your PC can store–typically thousands upon thousands. In fact, a modern PC will almost never run out of space. Of course, this can be a problem in itself. How can you find anything among all those files and folders? In this chapter we'll look at how the system works, ways in which Vista helps you to stay organized, and how to find anything that's stored on your hard disk–even if you can't quite remember what it's called.

64 Exploring the System

72 Getting Organized

96 Shortcuts and Links

100 Searching for Items

Exploring the System

Like previous versions of Windows, Vista uses the familiar concept of files and folders to organize everything that's stored on your PC. Vista also introduces several new features that everyone will like.

Meet the Filing System

Windows offers a variety of folder views and ways of navigating the system, and here we look at some of the most useful ones. We start by getting acquainted with the "main user" folder window, so click on this folder on the desktop to open it.

FEATURES KEY

❶ Main User Folder
This is the actual folder that we're looking at. It's the "main user" folder that's created using the name you choose when you first set up Windows. Vista stores many of the files you use all the time in here.

❷ Folder Window
This window reveals the contents of the folder.

❸ Navigation Buttons
The Back and Forward buttons allow you to skip between folders you've already visited.

❹ "Breadcrumb Trail"
This tells you exactly how you got to the folder you're looking at.

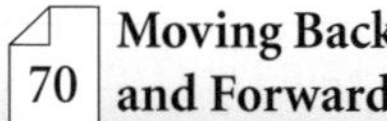
70 Moving Back and Forward

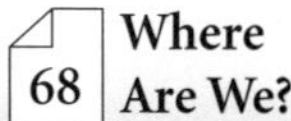
68 Where Are We?

WHERE DID THE MENUS GO?

If you've used Windows before, it may be a bit of a surprise to discover that Vista doesn't seem to have menus in its folder views any more. In fact, they are there, but they're turned off by default. To see the menus, press the Alt button on your keyboard once. The menus will stay in place until you press Alt again or click elsewhere on the screen.

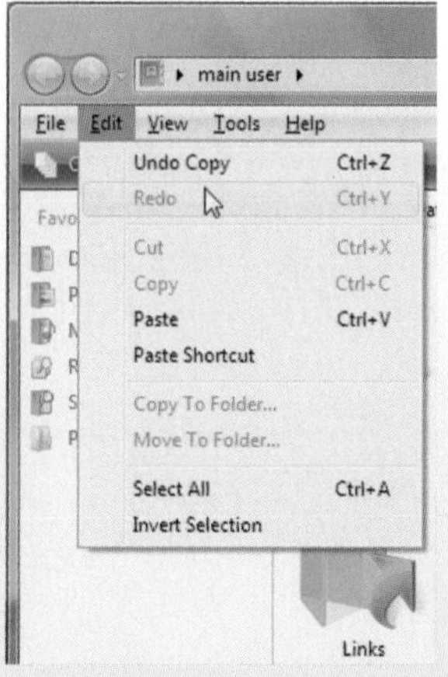

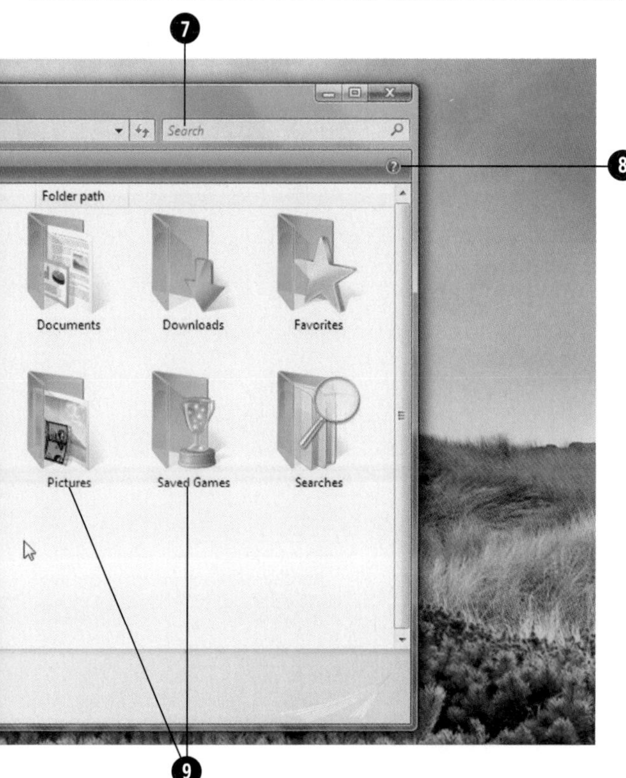

FEATURES KEY

❺ Views
This button provides various ways of looking at the items stored inside a folder.

❻ Burn
Vista lets you back up your data onto CD or DVD using the Burn button.

❼ Search
Vista's new search feature is everywhere, making it easier than ever to find files and folders that you've misplaced.

❽ Specific Help
Clicking this button launches Help that's specifically relevant to working with files and folders.

❾ Labeled Folders
Vista labels folders to help you identify their contents at a glance–these two are for storing pictures and games.

❿ Favorite Links
The Favorite Links pane lists those places on your PC that Windows thinks you'll be visiting most frequently so you can get to them more easily. You can add your own destinations to this list.

⓫ Organize
The Organize button controls the way basic information is presented in a folder window–for example, whether or not the list of Favorite Links appears on the left- hand side.

378 **Burning a Music CD**

99 **Creating New Favorite Links**

VIEWING FILES AND FOLDERS

Windows Vista offers a number of different ways to view your files and folders. Smaller icon sizes are useful if you've got lots of files and folders that you need to see at the same time or are working with a smaller screen and you want to pack in as much as possible. If you're short sighted or find the screen more difficult to read, then the larger icons are much more comfortable to work with.

SELECTING THE VIEWS MENU

● With the main user folder window open, start by moving the cursor to the arrow next to the **Views** button. Click once to open the drop-down menu.

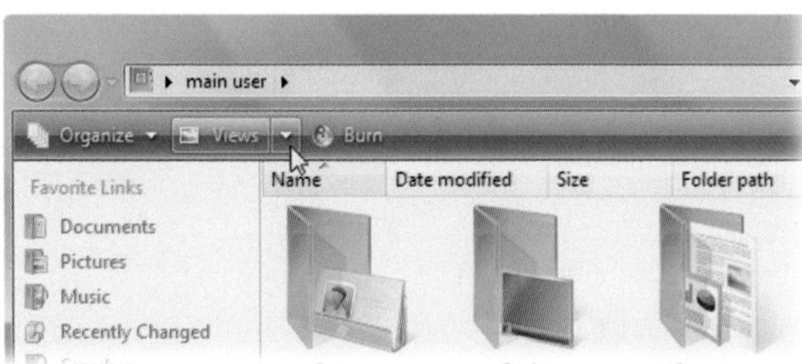

CHOOSING THE ICON SIZE

● This menu displays the different ways Vista includes to view your files and folders.

● To follow the sequence here, left click on the **Medium Icons** menu item.

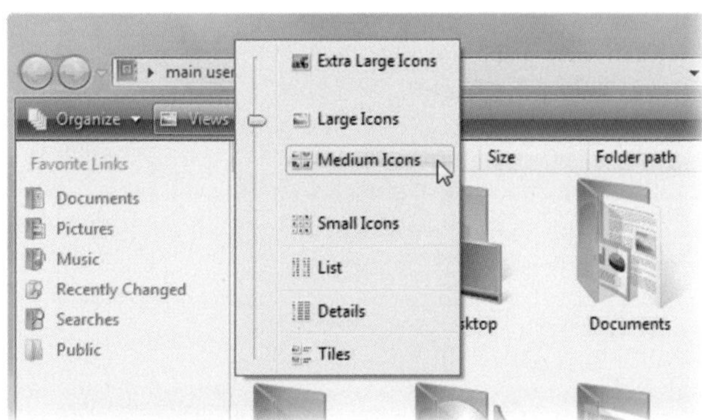

A SLIDING SCALE

In order to see the effects of choosing any of the various icon views, you can click on the slider shown in this menu and drag it up and down to see the icons decrease and increase in size dynamically. Using this method, you can choose an icon size that is in between those that are available by clicking.

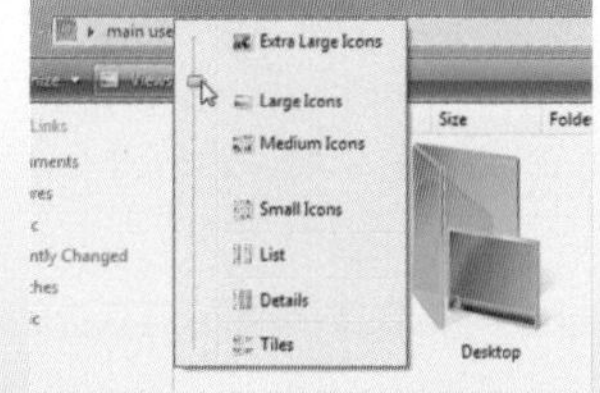

● Here's the result–the main user folder remains the same, but its contents are displayed with smaller icons. This view is useful when you want to display a large number of files and folders in a single window.

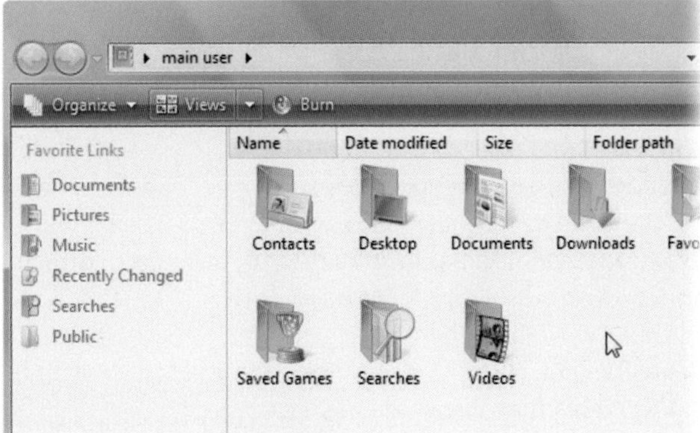

OPENING A SUB-FOLDER

● We are now looking at a group of folders inside the main user folder. From here we can open one of them and look inside.

● Move the cursor arrow over the **Documents** folder and then double click on it with the left mouse button.

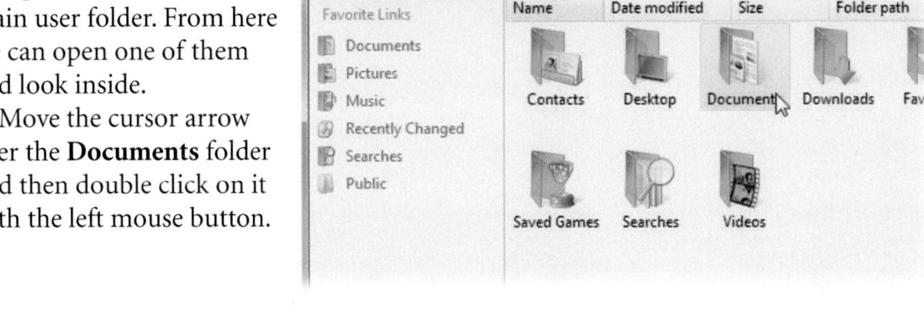

● This opens the Documents folder and, co-incidentally, shows another view with even smaller icons this time.

● You'll soon discover which style of view suits you best and it's very easy to switch between them if you change your mind.

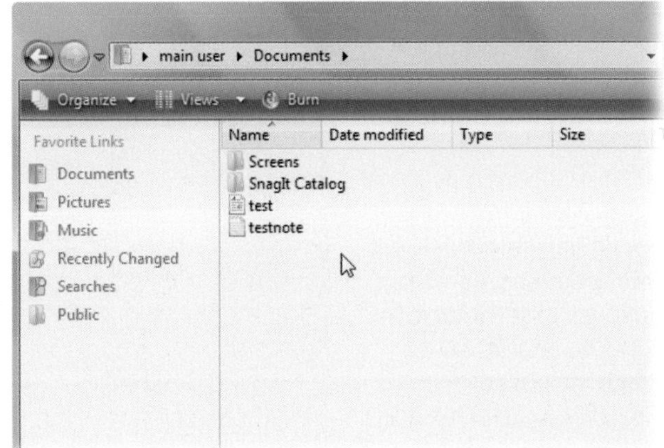

Moving between Folders

When you first start to use Windows, it's easy to keep track of your files, but as you use the system more and more, you'll start to develop your own way of storing the information you create. That necessarily means learning how to find your way around the system. If you're used to Windows, some of this will be familiar. If not, then it's worth taking the time to learn how to move around between folders.

WHERE ARE WE?

- The "trail" that Vista leaves at the top of the open window shows us that the folders and files listed are in the **Documents** folder, which is itself inside the **main user** folder.

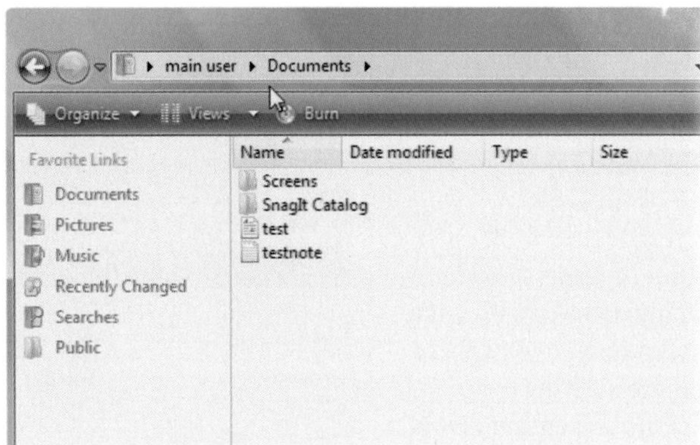

RETURNING TO THE MAIN USER FOLDER

- Clicking on the arrow next to **main user** opens a drop-down menu that lists the contents of the **main user** folder.
- You will notice that the title of the **Documents** folder is in bold type in the menu. This is because the Documents folder is open.
- From this menu we can open any of the folders in the main user folder by simply moving the cursor over a folder name and left clicking on it.

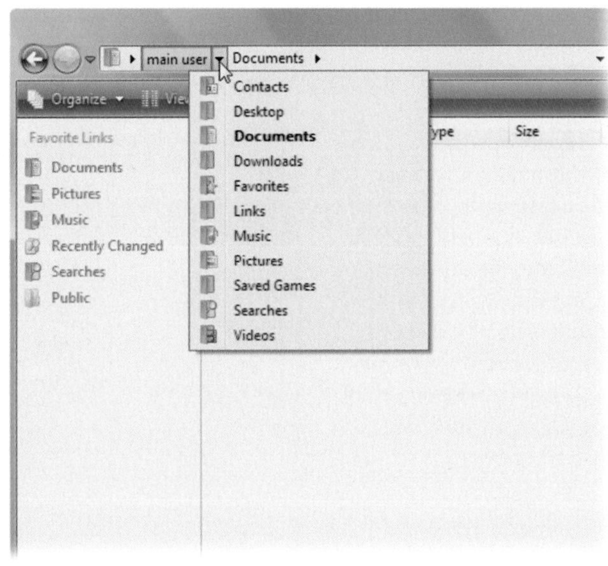

● With just two levels of folder open, the usefulness of navigating between them like this isn't immediately apparent, so let's explore a bit further.

● We have already created some files and folders within our Documents folder, and we're going to double click on the folder called **Screens** to open it.

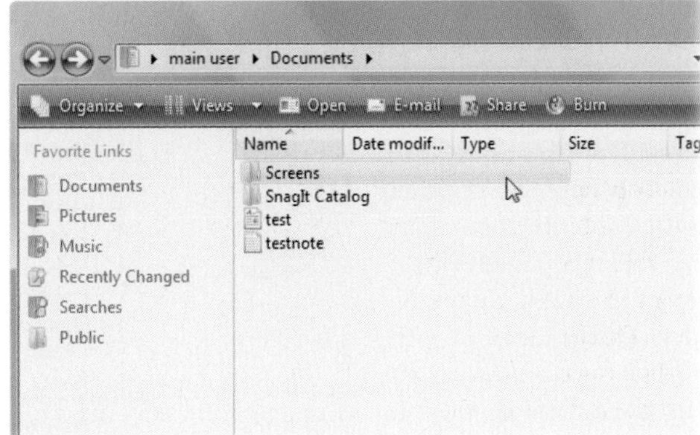

FOLDERS WITHIN FOLDERS WITHIN…

● This opens the Screens folder to reveal two further folders entitled Chapter One and Chapter Two.

● Here we're double clicking on **Chapter Two** to open that folder.

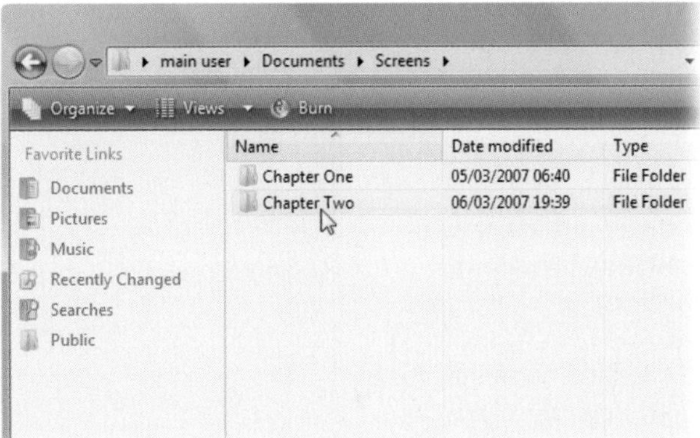

● Here we see the contents of that folder. The trail above the window shows us precisely where we are in the folder hierarchy.

● When we click the arrow to the right of **Screens** and open the drop-down menu, we see that the menu displays the two folders Chapter One and Chapter Two. The second item is emboldened because that is the open folder.

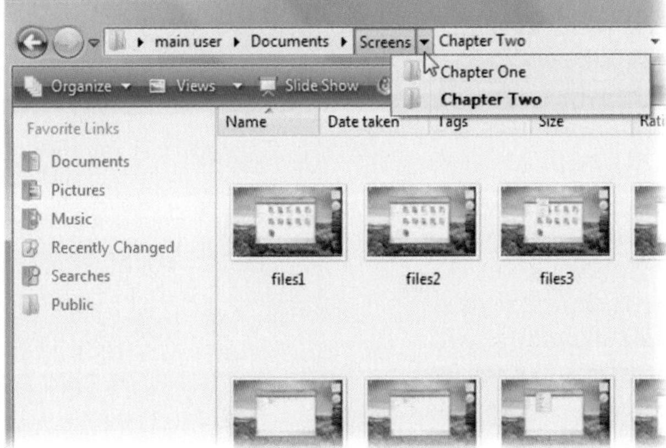

USING THE TRAIL TO NAVIGATE

- If we now click on the arrow to the right of the main user entry in the trail, the drop-down menu shows us the contents of the main user folder and highlights the folder that is currently open–**Documents**.
- Click once on this folder with the left mouse button.

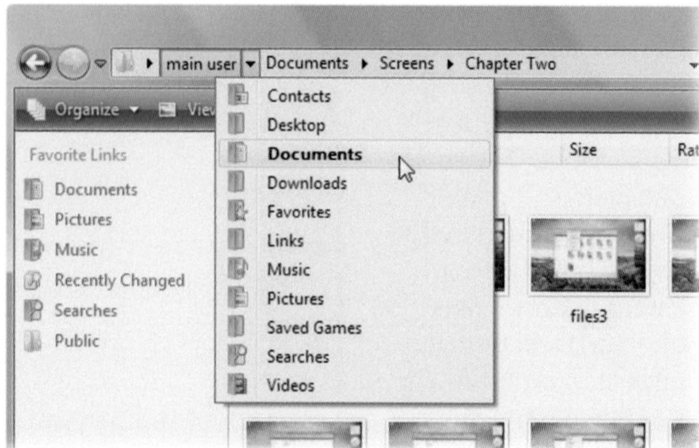

JUMPING UP THE HEIRARCHY

- Vista takes us from the open Chapter Two folder straight back to the Documents folder.
- If you've used previous versions of Windows, you'll realize what a great improvement this is on the old method of moving back up through the hierarchy folder by folder.

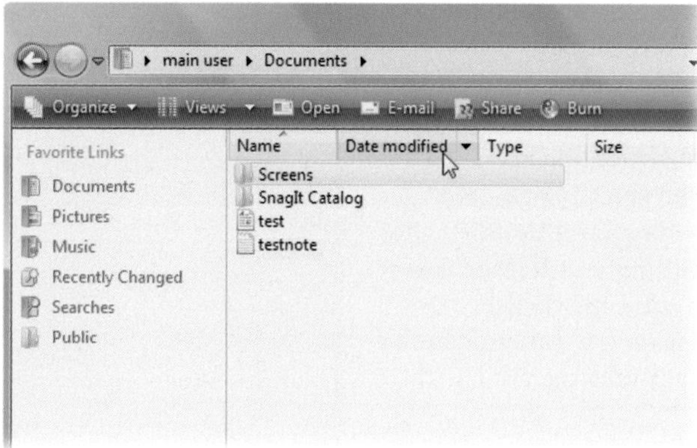

MOVING BACK AND FORWARD

- However, there's more. At the top of every Vista window are two buttons– Back and Forward. At this point, only the Back button is highlighted, or active. If we click the Forward button, nothing will happen. Click the Back button to see what happens.

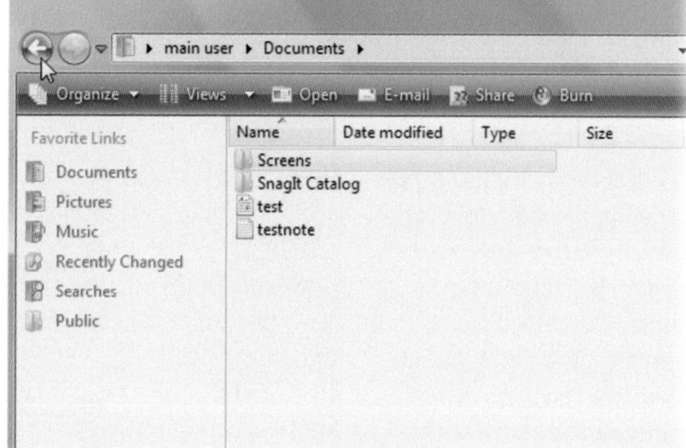

● As you can see, we've jumped back to the previous view–the Chapter Two folder–bypassing all the other folders in between. Now, because we've "stepped back" to a previous folder view, the Forward button is now also highlighted and thus, active. Having moved "back" we've got somewhere to move "forward" to.

● If we hover the mouse over the Forward button you'll see that it tells us it will take us **Forward to Documents**, the folder that we were previously viewing.
● If we hover it over the Back button, it indicates **Back to Screens**.

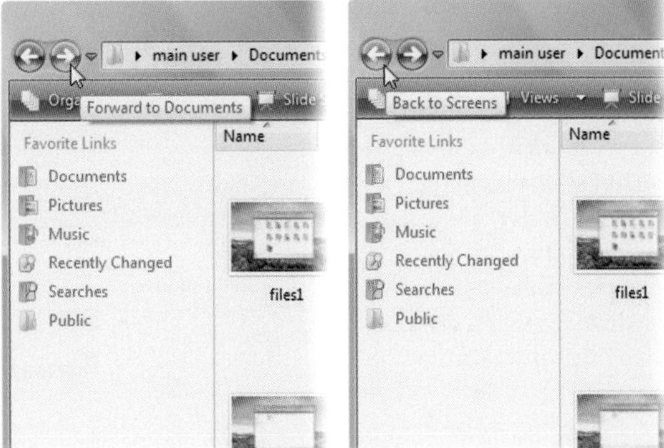

CONTEXT-SENSITIVE BUTTONS

If you look at the buttons above the different folders on these two pages, you'll see that they change depending on the kind of folder you're looking at. On this page for example, you'll see a **Slide Show** button, whereas on the opposite page that one is missing and there are **Open**, **E-mail**, and **Share** buttons instead. That's because Windows Vista is clever enough to understand a bit about what's in a folder and then display the buttons that are most appropriate to the content. Windows knows that the Screens folder on this page contains images, and therefore displays the Slide Show button.

GETTING ORGANIZED

In this section we will look at ways of displaying the contents of your PC, creating new files and folders, removing unwanted items, and copying and moving to keep things organized.

USING FOLDER LAYOUTS

One obvious way to see what is in a file is to open it, but this can be a slow way to view one individual file just to check whether it's the one you're looking for.

Windows Vista can display the contents of your PC in many different ways, and by using the Layouts menu you don't have to actually open a file to see what's inside it.

1 OPENING A NEW FOLDER

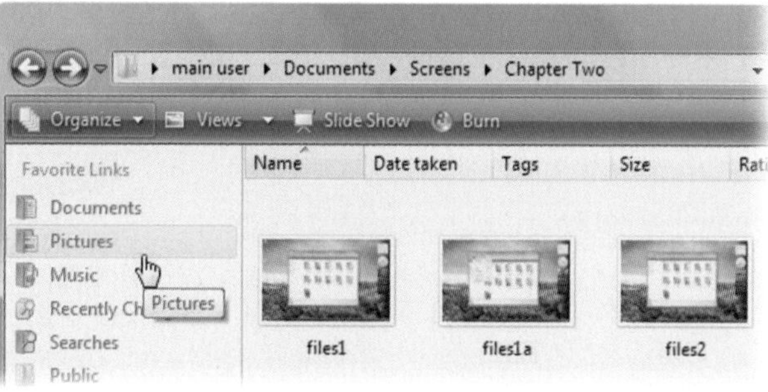

- Let's start by opening a different folder. Move the cursor arrow over the **Pictures** folder in the Favorite Links list on the left of the open window and click on it once with the left mouse button.

- This opens the Pictures folder where you'll see the **Sample Pictures** folder and any other folders that have been saved here.
- Double click on the **Sample Pictures** icon to open this folder.

2 VIEWING THE CONTENTS LIST

● Here we see the contents of Windows' Sample Pictures folder. The names are very descriptive, but wouldn't it be good to see what each picture actually looks like without having to open each one?

3 OPENING THE LAYOUT MENU

● Well, you can. Move the cursor arrow up to the **Organize** button above the Favorite Links list on the left of the main window.

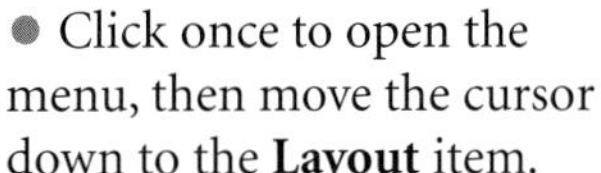

● Click once to open the menu, then move the cursor down to the **Layout** item.

● You will notice there's a small arrow next to it, pointing to the right. This indicates that there's a sub-menu here, which you can see just by leaving the cursor hovering over it. When the sub-menu pops out, click on **Preview Pane**.

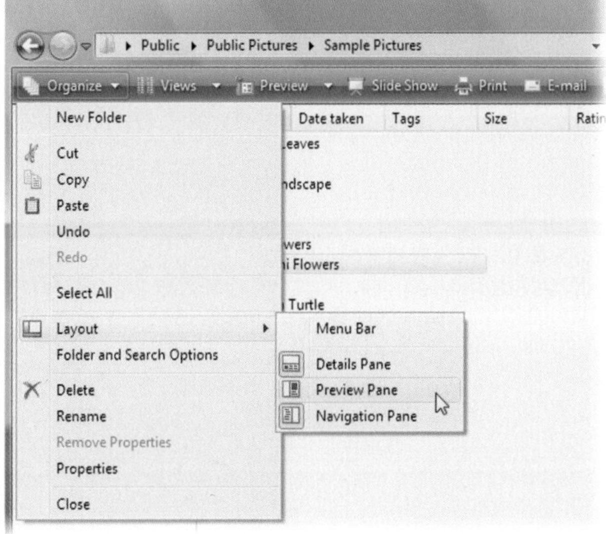

4 VIEWING AN IMAGE PREVIEW

● This adds a new pane–the Preview Pane–to the folder view on the right-hand side. Click on one of the names in the main window and you'll see a preview of what the picture itself looks like. These are the Frangipani Flowers.

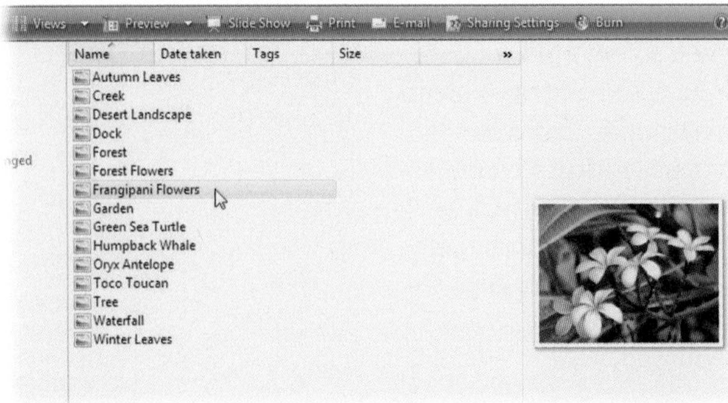

5 VIEWING DIGITAL MUSIC FILES

● You can use the Preview Pane on many different kinds of file–for example, on digital music files.

● Move the cursor arrow over to the Favorite Links pane again and this time click on the **Music** folder.

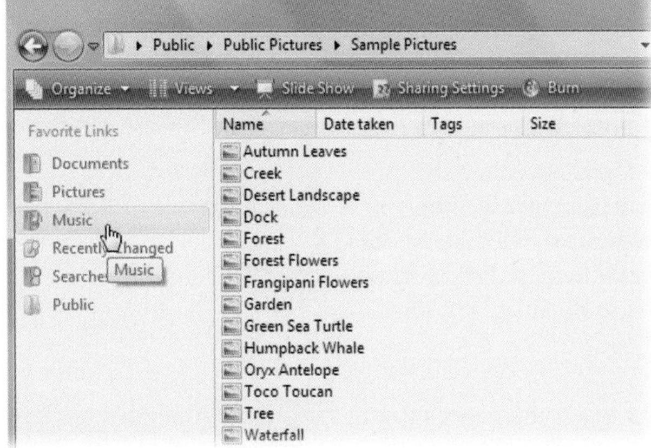

● When the Music folder opens, double click on the Sample Music folder to open that. This will display the selection of digital songs that is included free with Windows Vista.

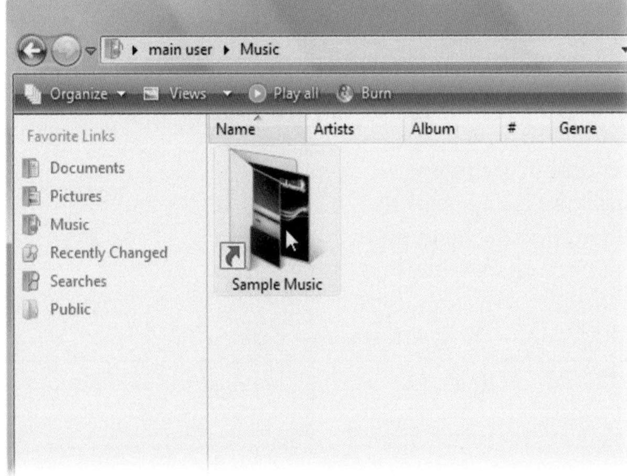

● Here are the songs. As you'll see later on ⎕, just double clicking on one of these will load the free Windows Media Player program and start the song, but there's an even easier way to hear the track using the Preview Pane.

● Move the cursor back to the **Organize** button and click once to open the menu. As before, move the cursor down to the **Layout** menu item and then, when the sub menu pops out, chose **Preview Pane**.

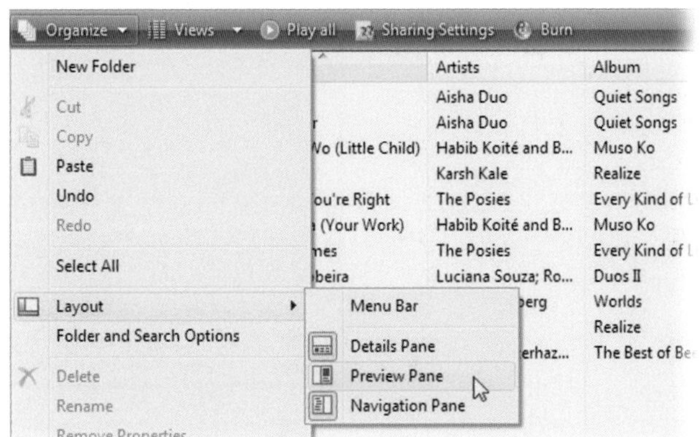

● Now click on one of the music files in the main window and see what happens in the preview pane on the right.

● You'll see the cover of the CD that the song is taken from, and beneath it there is a blue and white button. This is the Play button.

76 **Beyond Previewing Files**

● Move the cursor over the **Play** button so that it lights up, and then click it once with the left mouse button.
● After a second, the song begins to play (provided your computer's audio system is switched on). You can "audition" any sound on your PC in this way.

● The track will play all the way through, unless you click on the **Pause** button to halt it part way through.

BEYOND PREVIEWING FILES

The Preview Pane is great for determining the contents of a file, but there's no substitute for seeing the whole thing on the screen. You can do this by opening the program that was used to create the file in the first place, and then opening the file using Windows' **File** and **Open** menu commands. However, there's a quicker way. Simply double click with the left mouse button on the file you want to open. When you do this on a file such as one of the music tracks shown above, Windows finds the right program (in this case, it would be Windows Media Player), loads it, and then opens the song, which is then ready to play. Try double clicking on one of the sample music tracks, and then do the same with a text document, which will open in Notepad. Windows associates particular file types with certain programs, and generally knows which program to open when you double click on a file.

342 **Playing Your First CD**

Making a New Folder

As you start working with Windows Vista and its programs you'll certainly want to create your own system of folders to store all the letters, documents, spreadsheets, photos, movies, and other items that you create. In this section we'll show you how to make and locate new folders, as well as how to name them .

1 CHOOSING THE LOCATION

• To create a new folder in the Documents folder, move the cursor over to **Documents** in the **Favorite Links** pane and left click on it once to open the folder.

2 CREATING THE NEW FOLDER

• With the Documents folder now open, click the **Organize** button once and choose **New Folder** from the drop-down menu.

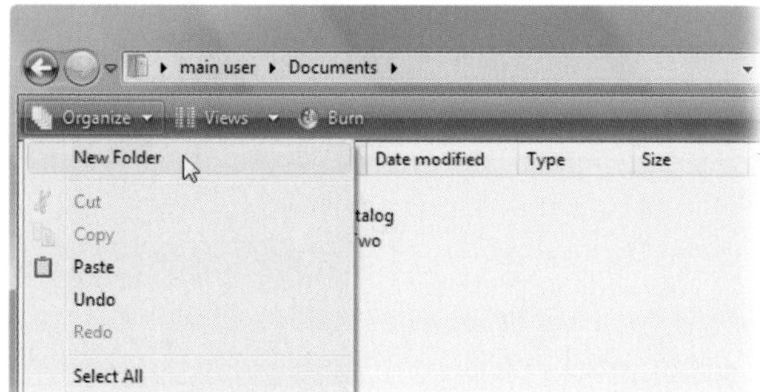

• When you let go of the mouse button, Windows creates a new folder inside the current folder.

• Because it's a new folder, it doesn't have a name, but Windows helpfully gives it a temporary **New Folder** tag and highlights it so you can give it a name for yourself.

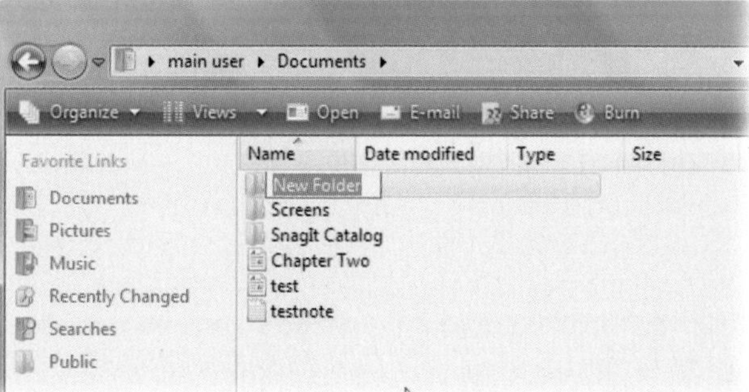

3 NAMING THE NEW FOLDER

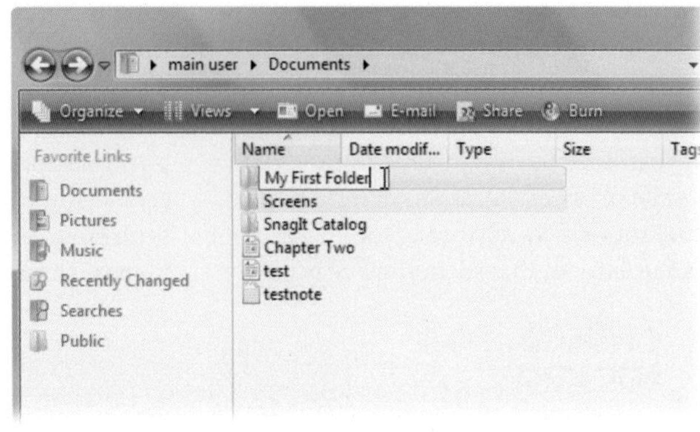

- When naming a folder, choose a name that has meaning for you or is part of a logical system.
- Just start typing the folder name and Windows automatically overwrites the temporary **New Folder** name. In this example we're calling it **My First Folder**.

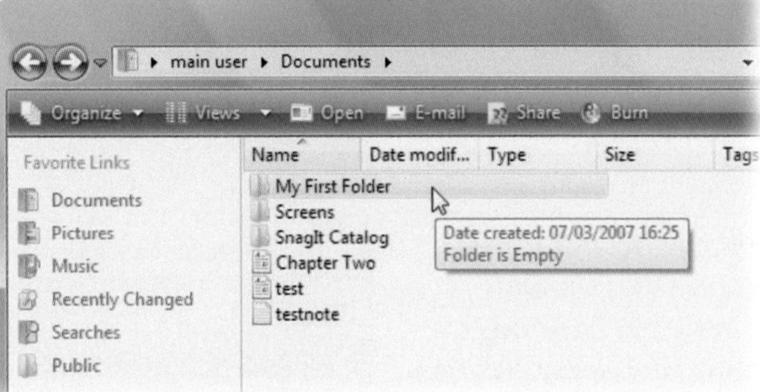

- When you've finished typing the name, click anywhere in the folder window to confirm it and you'll see the new folder name–**My First Folder**–in place. Let's look inside the folder by double clicking on the new name.

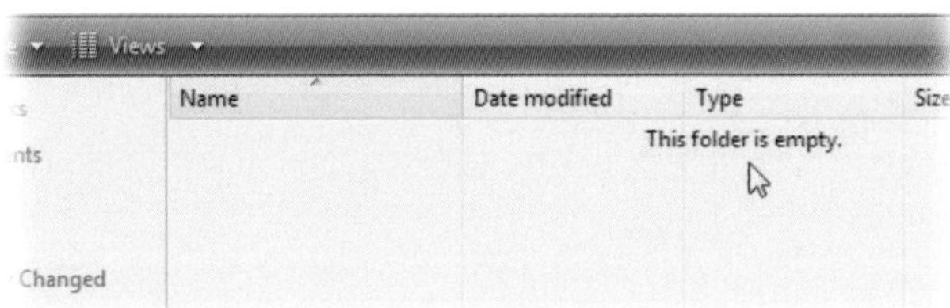

- Here's the inside of the folder. As we haven't stored anything in it yet, the folder is empty. We'll fix that in the next section.

RENAMING FILES AND FOLDERS

If you have given an item a name and want to change your mind, it is easy to rename it. Click once on the file or folder with the left mouse button. Wait for a second, and left click again. This highlights the file or folder name so you can just type in a new one over the top. When you've finished typing in the new name, click once with the left mouse button anywhere in the open window and the file or folder will now be renamed.

Making a New File

As you work on your computer, you will constantly need to create files, save and close them, and return to work on them at a later date. In this section we're going to create a simple file using the Notepad word processing program that comes free with Windows, store it in our new folder, and then retrieve it again.

1 OPENING NOTEPAD

- To open Notepad, begin by clicking the Start button to open the Start menu.

- Next, click the **All Programs** menu to open that. (Hovering the cursor over this menu will have the same effect.)
- In the All Programs menu, click the **Accessories** folder to open it.

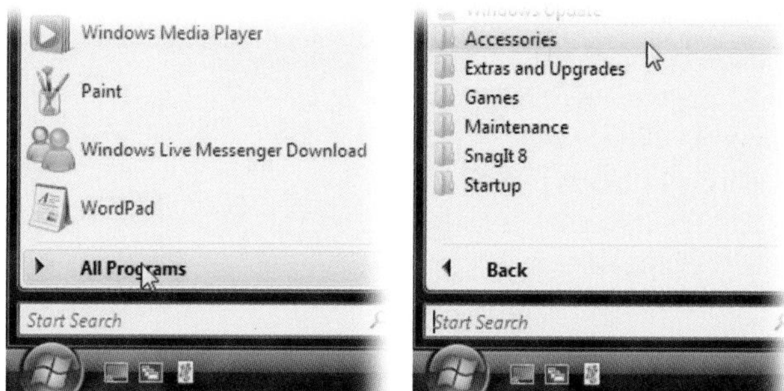

- In the Accessories folder, click the **Notepad** icon once with the left mouse button to launch the program.

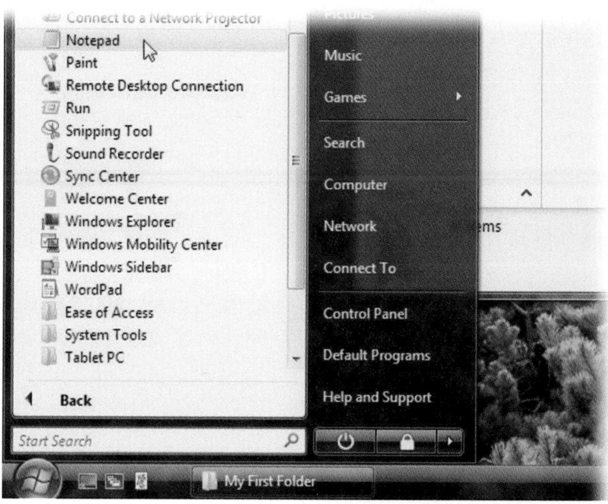

2 CREATING THE NEW DOCUMENT

● When Notepad opens, just click anywhere in the empty window and start typing. Type exactly what you see on the screen here, because we'll be using this text later in this chapter.

● When you've finished typing, move your cursor to the **File** menu.

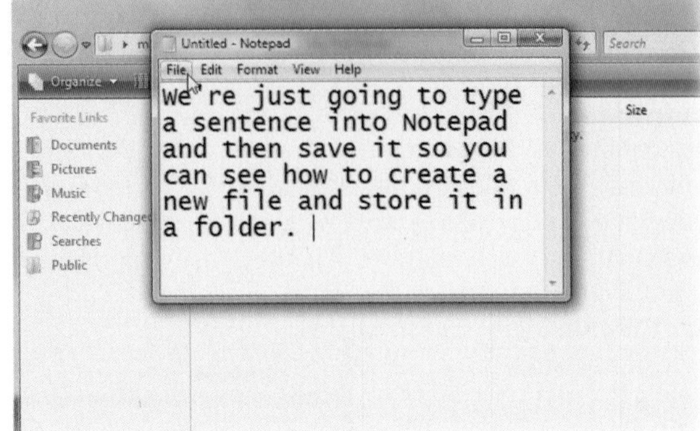

3 SAVING THE NEW DOCUMENT

● To save this document, click once on the **File** menu, and then choose **Save** from the drop-down menu.

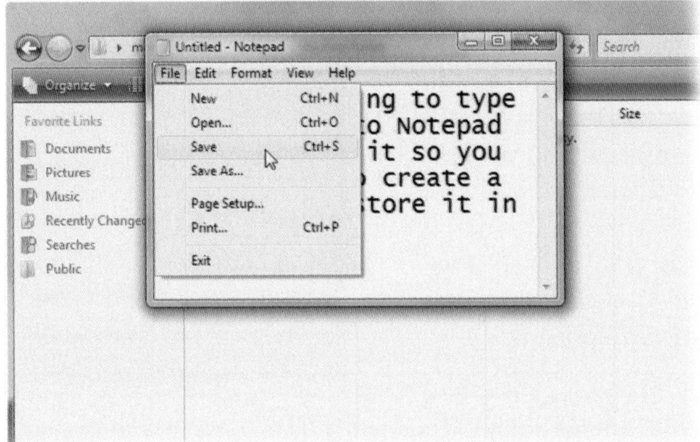

4 CHOOSING A LOCATION

● Notepad's **Save As** dialog box opens. By default, Notepad wants to save any new file in the Documents folder, but we want to save it inside My First Folder.

● Click on the arrow to the right of **Documents** in the "trail" we talked about earlier, and then pick **My First Folder** from the drop-down list.

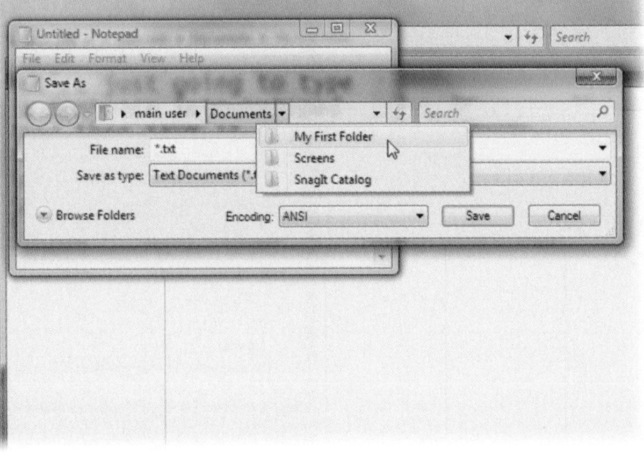

101 Searching for Content

70 Using the Trail to Navigate

5 NAMING THE NEW DOCUMENT

- The trail now points to **My First Folder**. Having told Notepad where we want to store the document, we now have to name it.
- Move the cursor into the box to the right of **File name** and click once with the left mouse button to highlight ***.txt**.

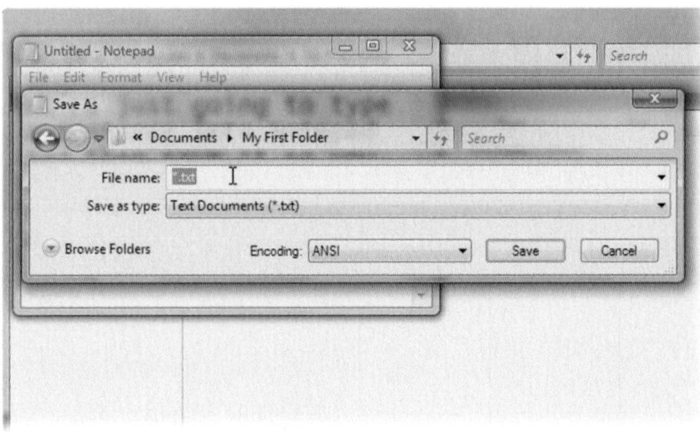

- Just start typing to replace the highlighted text that's currently there with a name for your new document–ours is called **my first document**. Then, click the **Save** button to save it into My First Folder.

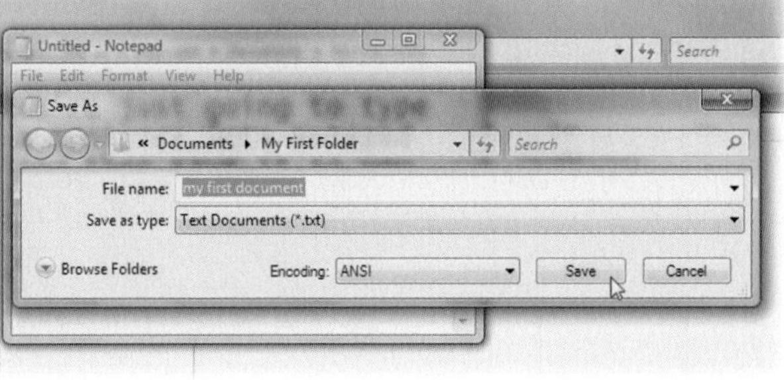

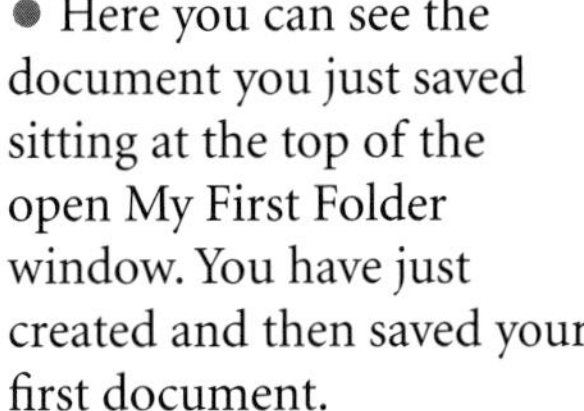

- Here you can see the document you just saved sitting at the top of the open My First Folder window. You have just created and then saved your first document.

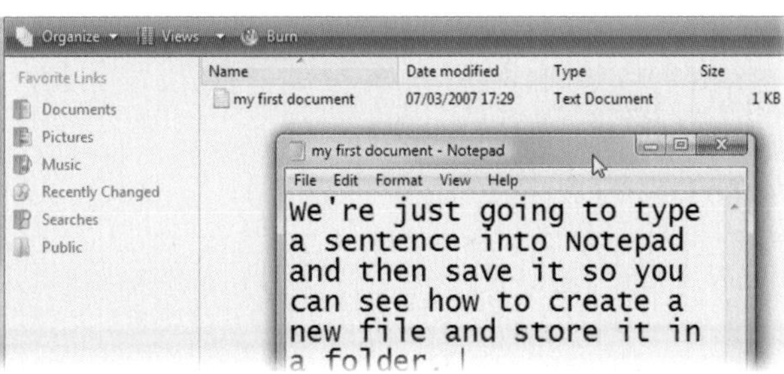

6 CLOSING NOTEPAD

- Close the Notepad program by clicking the little "x" at the top right-hand corner of the page.

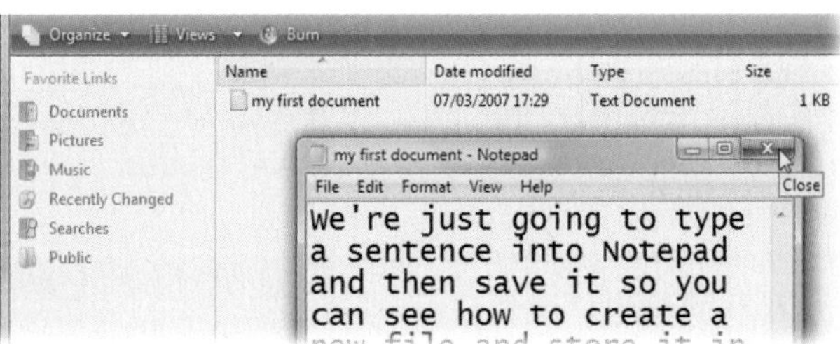

Retrieving a Saved File

To show how to find and open a file that has been saved, we are now going to retrieve the Notepad document that we just created. To open Notepad, follow the same steps as before–click **Start**, **All Programs**, **Accessories**, and then choose **Notepad**. A new, empty, untitled Notepad document will open on screen.

CHOOSING THE OPEN MENU

- When the empty Notepad window is open onscreen, click on **File** and then choose **Open** from the drop-down menu.

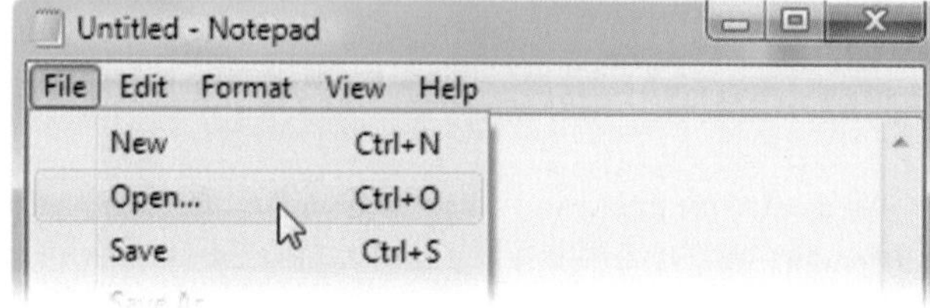

CHOOSING THE DOCUMENT

- Notepad displays its **Open** dialog box, looking much like a standard Windows folder view.
- Double click on **my first document** to open it (or click once on it and then click the **Open** button at the bottom of the screen).

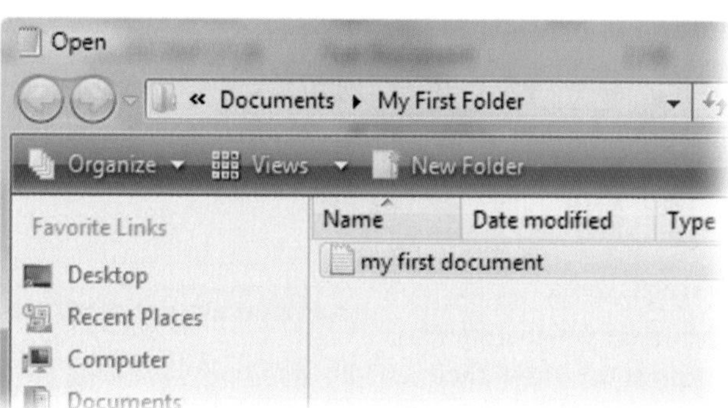

VIEWING THE OPEN DOCUMENT

- The document opens in Notepad, where you can carry on editing it and then save it again.
- This principle of opening a program, creating a file, working out where to store it, naming it, and then saving it so you can retrieve it later is the same for every single Windows program.

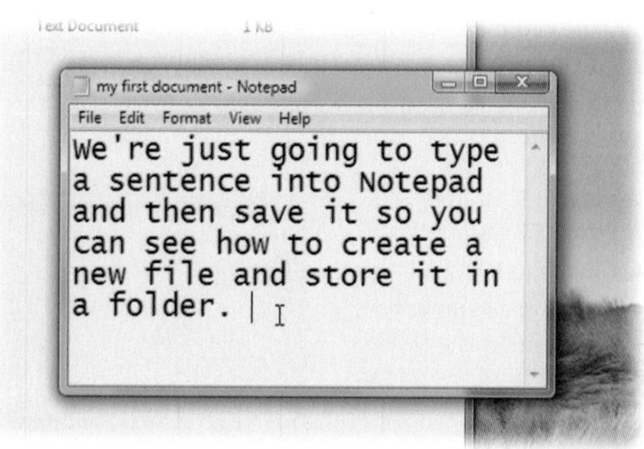

79 Opening Notepad

Deleting and Rescuing Files

When it comes to deleting files or folders, Windows has a fail safe system called the Recycle Bin. This is the place to which files are moved when you want to delete them, but items placed here can still be rescued. They stay safely in the bin–which is like another folder–until you decide to empty it. This is how it works.

DELETING A FILE

- We are going to delete the Notepad document that we created earlier.
- Click once on **my first document** with the right mouse button and then, when the drop-down menu appears, move the cursor down the menu to **Delete** and click on it.

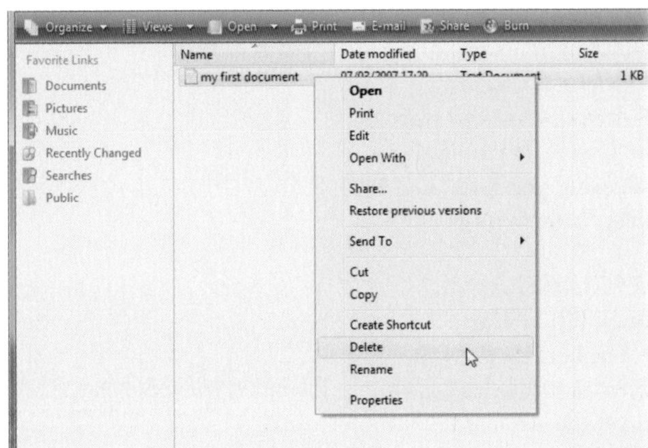

- Windows likes to make certain that you really want to delete something before it lets you go ahead, so you'll see this dialog box that asks **Are you sure you want to move this file to the Recycle Bin?** Click the **Yes** button to continue, and the file goes to the bin.

- This is how the Recycle Bin looks before and after you've deleted something. Just like a real bin, it's empty before and full after. Luckily, it will hold more than a normal bin!

VIEWING A DELETED FILE

- The Recycle Bin behaves much like a standard Windows folder, so if you want to see what's inside it, just double click on it with the mouse.
- Here we see **my first document**, inside the Recycle Bin. As far as Windows is concerned, the file's been removed from the system. If you look behind it, you'll see that **My First Folder** is now empty.

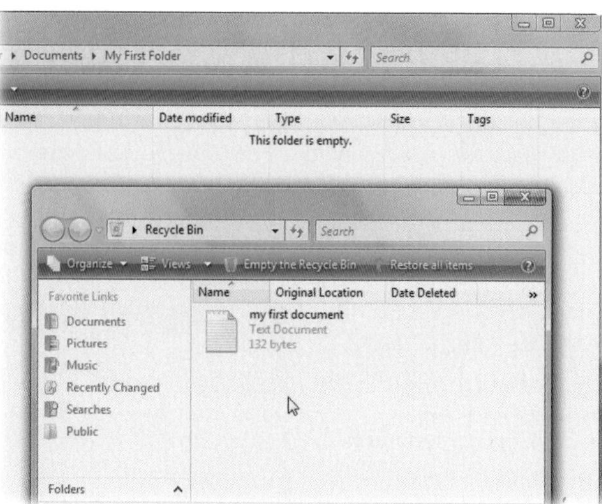

RESCUING A DELETED FILE

- The beauty of the Recycle Bin is that the deleted file can still be rescued if you realize later that you needed it–so long as you haven't emptied the bin.
- With the file highlighted, move the cursor up to the **Restore this item** button at the top of the window and click there once.

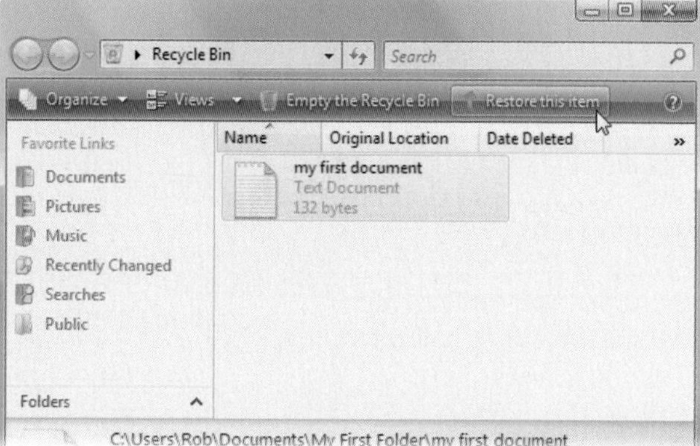

- Windows pops the file back into its original location on your PC, simple as that. Here you can see the file back in place in **My First Folder**. In front, the **Recycle Bin** folder is now empty again.

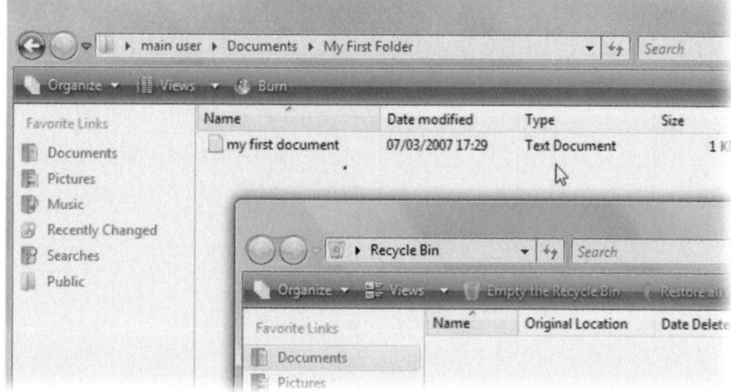

DELETING WITH DRAG AND DROP

● Drag and drop is one of Windows Vista's basic ways of working. We did this when we dragged the Notes gadget out of the Sidebar and dropped it onto the desktop with the mouse. Most of the items that you see on screen can be dragged and dropped.

● In My First Folder, left click on the document you just rescued, hold down the left mouse button, and start to drag it toward the still-open Recycle Bin window.

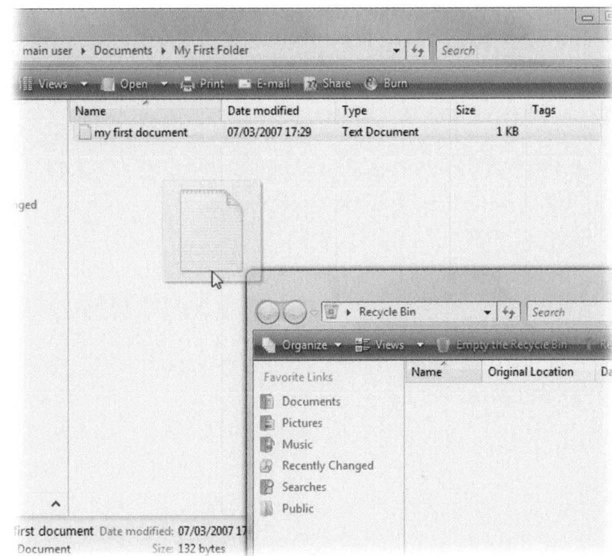

● As you drag the file into the Recycle Bin window, Vista displays a useful little tip that says **Move to Recycle Bin**, to help you keep track of what you're actually doing.

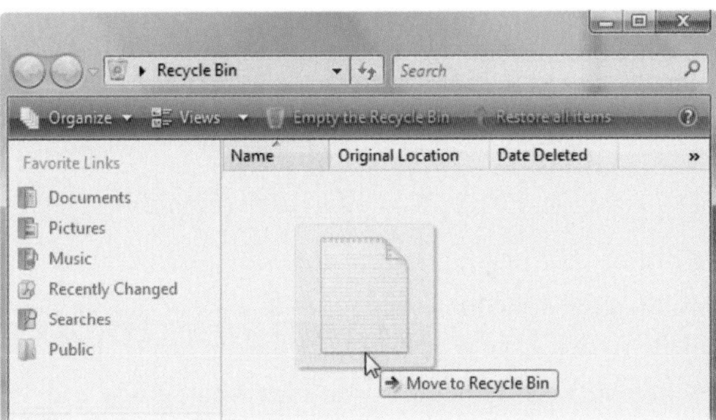

● When the file is fully over the destination folder, let go of the mouse button and drop the file onto the Recycle Bin window, as shown here.

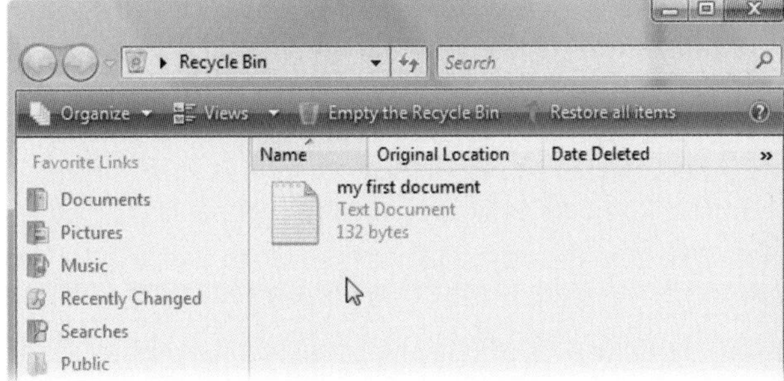

33 **Moving Gadgets To New Positions**

- If you want to rescue a deleted file, you can do so in exactly the same way.
- Click on the file you've just deleted and drag it out of the Recycle Bin window and up toward the My First Folder window.

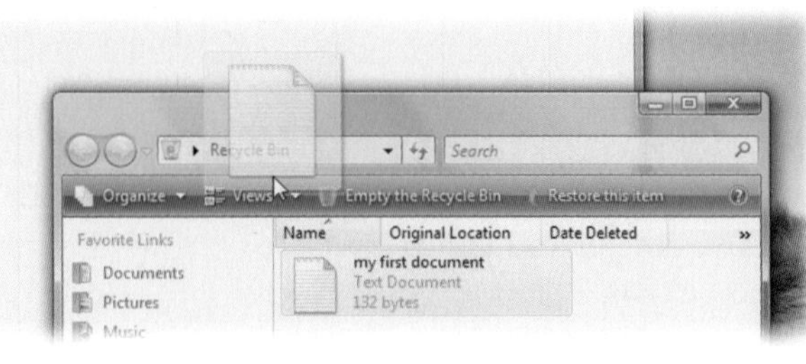

- Again, Windows displays a little tip telling you that the file is being moved into My First Folder.

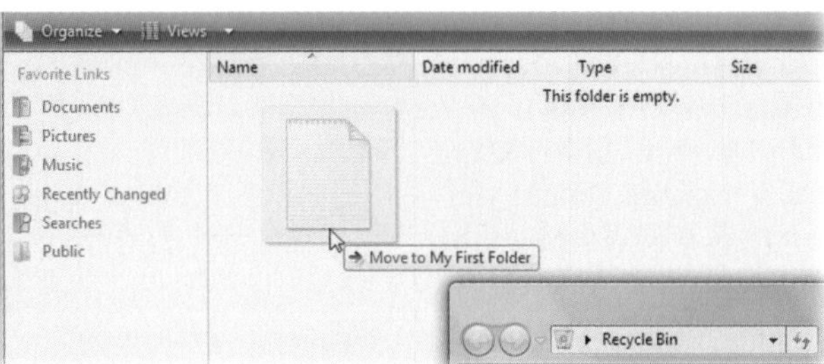

- When the file is within the **My First Folder** window, just let go of the mouse to drop it back into its original position.

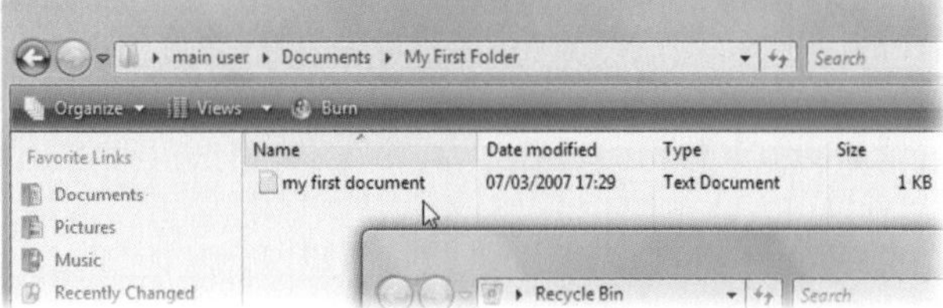

OTHER WAYS TO DELETE

Windows Vista provides two other ways to delete a file or folder. First, you can click on it with the cursor and drag it onto the **Recycle Bin**. As you do so, the bin will become highlighted and you'll see a little tip appear next to the cursor telling you that you're moving the file to the bin. When you delete an item by dragging and dropping it, Windows doesn't display a dialog asking if you're sure–it simply moves the file into the bin. Alternatively, click on the file you want to delete with the left mouse button and press the Del key on your PC's keyboard. Windows will ask if you're sure. If you are, click **Yes**.

MOVING AND COPYING

If you can see it in Windows, then you can probably click on it, and if you can click on it, you can probably drag it somewhere else. In this next section we'll show you how to move a file or folder, or several at a time, from one location to another, and how to copy files so that the same items can be in more than one folder.

LINING UP TWO WINDOWS

- To moves files from one folder to another, you may find it useful to have both windows open, side by side on the desktop.
- You should have My First Folder open already, so we'll open a second folder.
- Click on the Start button to open the Start menu.
- In the Start menu, find the **Pictures** menu item on the right-hand side and click on it once.

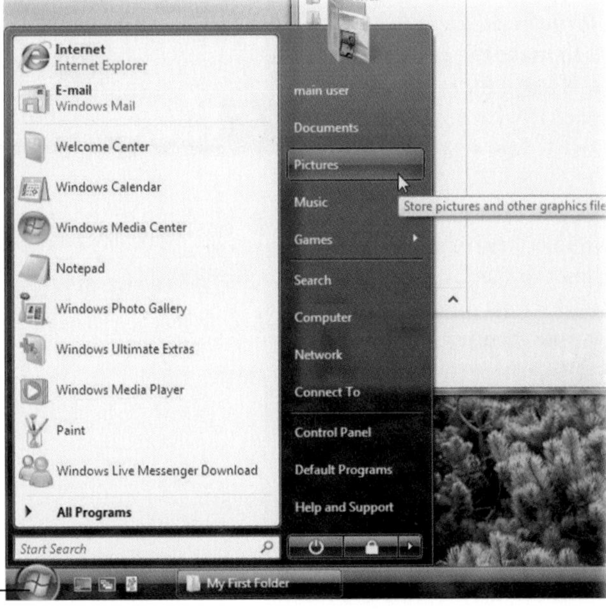

Open the Start menu by clicking on the Start button

- When the Pictures folder opens, move the cursor over the **Sample Pictures** folder inside it, and double click on it to open the folder.

- The Sample Pictures folder contains a good selection of photos we can work with–all supplied with Vista as standard.
- At the moment, the Sample Pictures window is on top of the My First Folder window, so it's going to be hard to drag and drop files between them.
- To make the task easier, we'll move the windows apart. Click once on the **My First Folder** window.

- Once the My First Folder window has been clicked, it comes to the foreground so that it's now on top of the Sample Pictures window.

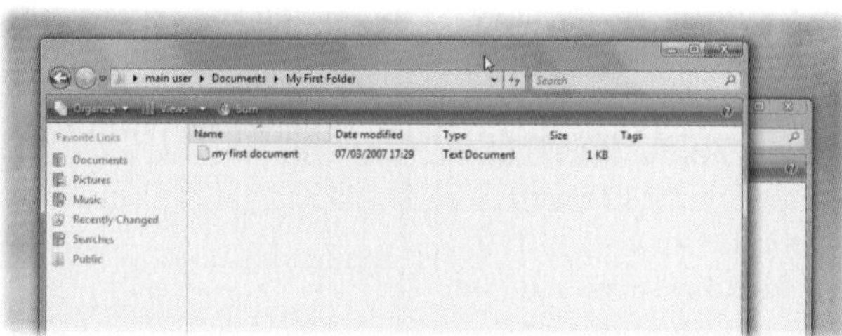

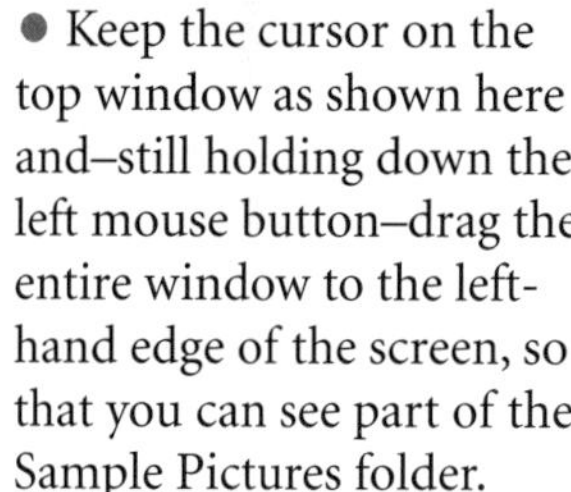

- Keep the cursor on the top window as shown here and–still holding down the left mouse button–drag the entire window to the left-hand edge of the screen, so that you can see part of the Sample Pictures folder.

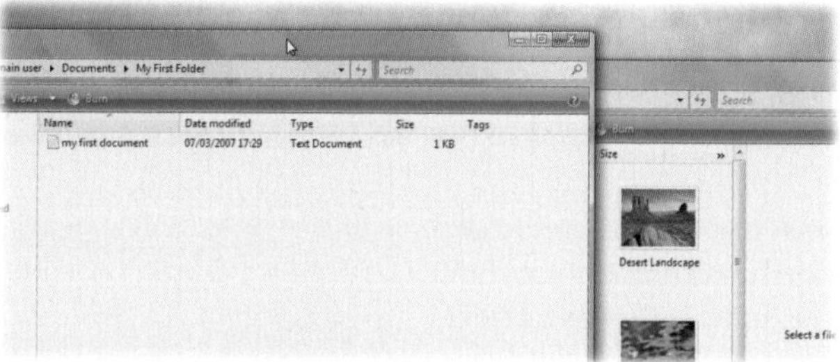

DO YOUR FOLDERS LOOK DIFFERENT?

If the appearance of the files in your folders is different from those you see here, use the Views menu in each window to change the view. Currently we are using the **Details** view in My First Folder, and the **Large Icons** view in the Sample Pictures folder. The Details view tells us each file's type and size.

66 **Viewing Files and Folders**

• Finally, click the Pictures folder to bring it to the foreground again, as shown here. You're now ready to start dragging files back and forth between the two open folders.

MOVING A FILE BETWEEN FOLDERS

• Now we're going to drag and drop an individual file from the Sample Pictures folder to My First Folder.
• Left click on one of the photos–in this example, it's **Autumn Leaves**–and, still holding down the left mouse button, start to drag it from one folder window to the other.

• As you move the file over the destination folder you'll see that Windows pops up a little message that confirms you're in the process of moving the file to **My First Folder**. Keep dragging until it is completely over the destination folder.

● Now let go of the left mouse button and the file will drop into the folder. You can see it here. At the same time, the destination folder moves in front of the source folder.

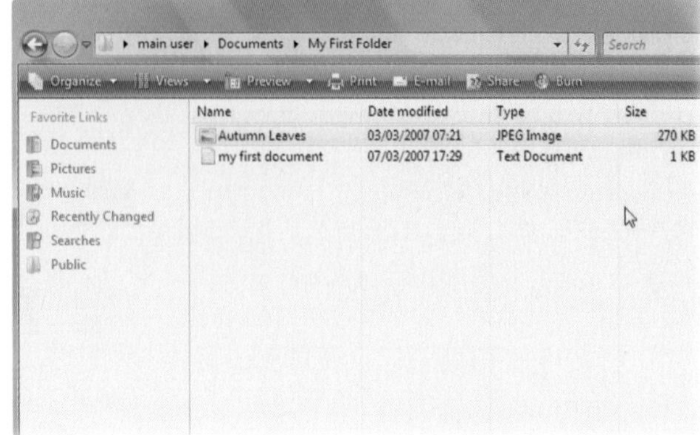

COPYING A FILE TO ANOTHER FOLDER

● You will often need the same file in more than one folder, so we are now going to copy the file back to the original folder.

● The process works in the same way as dragging and dropping, except that this time, you need to hold down the Ctrl key at the bottom left-hand corner of your keyboard.

● With this key held down, click on the **Autumn Leaves** file and drag it over the **Sample Pictures** folder.

● This time, as the file moves into the destination folder, the Windows pop-up message tells you the file is being copied, not moved and the message is preceded by a "+" sign instead of a small arrow.

● Below the moving file, you will also see a vertical black bar that indicates where in the destination folder the file will be located when you drop it.

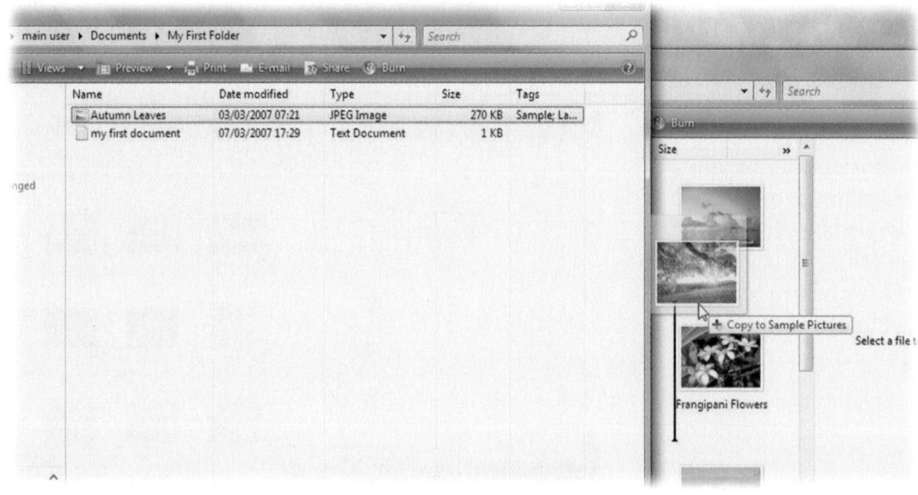

● Release the mouse button, and the Autumn Leaves picture appears back in the Sample Pictures folder. However, this time we can still see the file in My First Folder, which has now moved to the back. The file now exists in both locations. The first time, we moved the file, whereas this time we have copied it.

MOVING MULTIPLE FILES

● To move a sequence of photos, position the cursor at the extreme left of the main window in the Sample Pictures folder, hold down the left mouse button, and drag down and right.

● Windows draws out a rectangle, highlighting the three photos in a line at the top of the window.

● When all three are highlighted like this, let go of the mouse button.

● The three highlighted files will now behave as a single item.
● Move the cursor over any of the highlighted pictures, click and hold the left mouse button, and drag it onto the other folder.
● As you do so, Windows displays the number **3** on top of the picture you're dragging to indicate that, although we can only see one picture being moved, all three highlighted items are moving together.

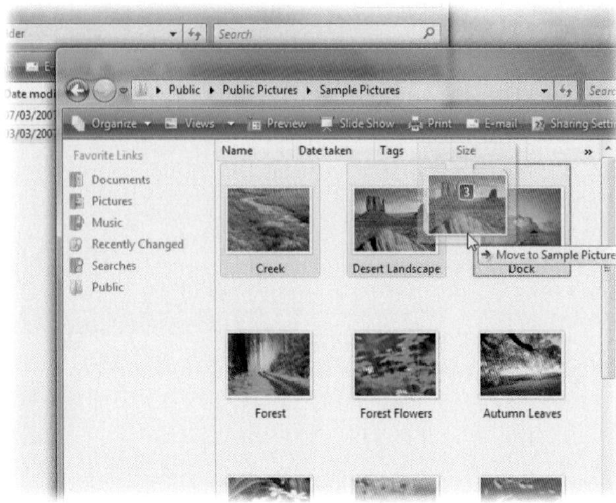

● As the picture (in fact, three pictures) are moved onto the destination folder, we again see the pop-up message that tells us what we're doing.
● The number **3** remains over the picture throughout the process.

● Release the mouse button and the three files appear in their new position in My First Folder. Being able to move multiple files like this means you don't have to laboriously drag files over one at a time.

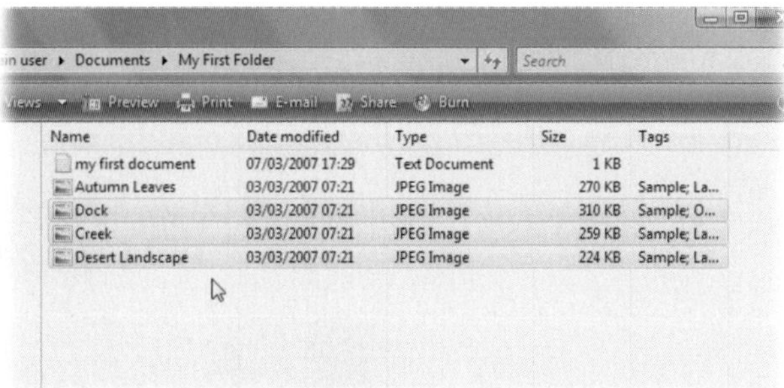

COPYING MULTIPLE FILES

- Copying multiple files works in the same way as copying single files.
- With the three files still highlighted and the Ctrl key held down, left click on one of the files and drag it out of the folder.

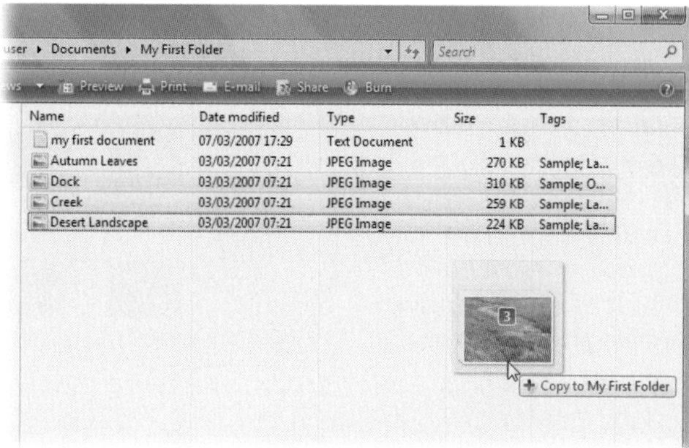

- As the picture moves over the destination file, Windows displays its message to show that we're copying the files into the Sample Pictures folder.
- It also displays the **3** to show that although only one picture is shown being dragged, there are actually three being copied across.

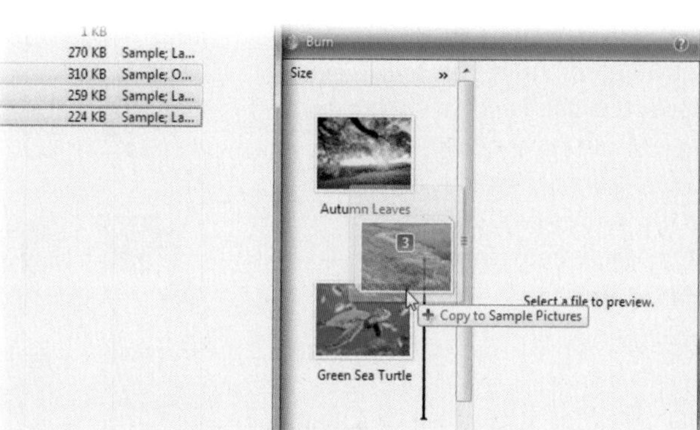

- When the mouse is released, the three photos appear in the Sample Pictures folder, but we can see that they are also still in My First Folder, from which they have been copied.

MOVING NON-SEQUENTIAL FILES

● We've seen how to highlight and move files that are stored sequentially, but what happens if you want to copy files that are scattered within a folder?
● Start by left clicking on the first photo that you wish to move.

● If you were to simply click on a second item, the first would cease to be highlighted, but if you hold down the Ctrl key and click on a photo on the next row down (in other words, one that is out of sequence), Windows highlights that one as well.

● Finally, still keeping the Ctrl key held down, click on a photo in the third row.
● You can see here that the three chosen photos are all highlighted, even though they are not next to each other in the folder.

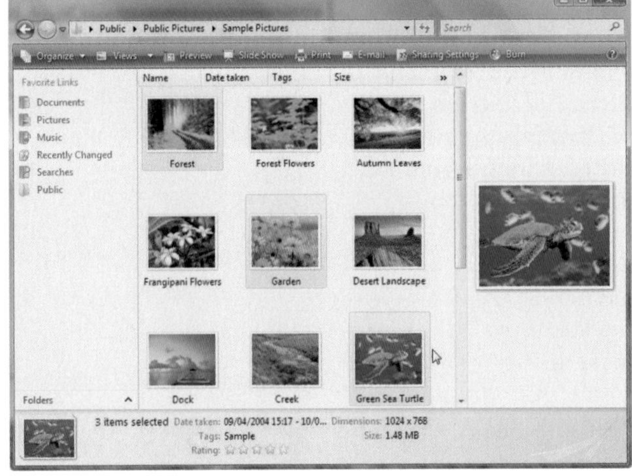

- Release the Ctrl key and then left click and hold on any of the three pictures.
- Now drag the photos out of the folder and they will behave just as the sequence of files did when we moved them to a new folder.

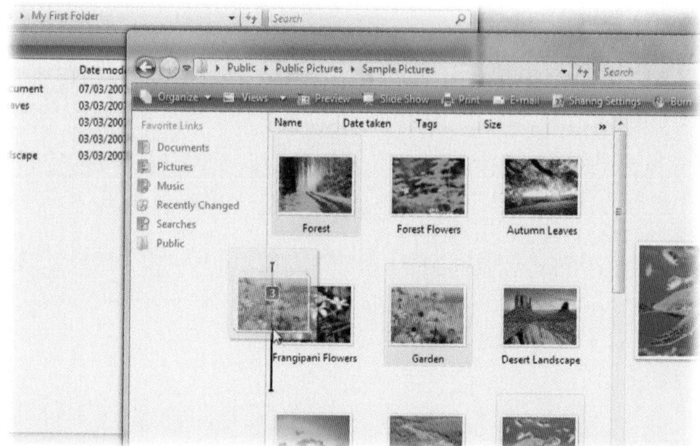

- Here are the files about to be dropped into the destination folder, again with the number **3** indicating that we are moving all three files at the same time.

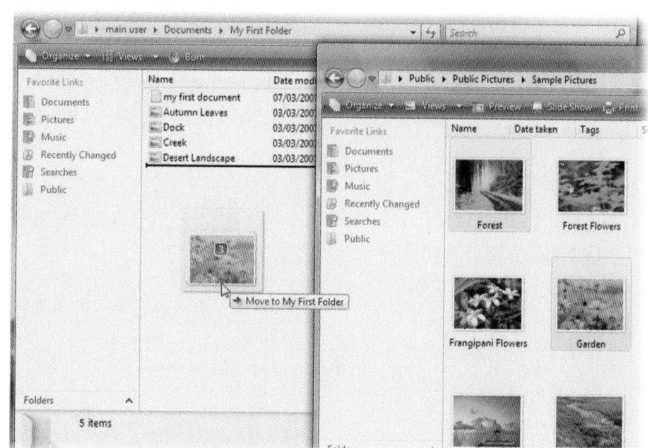

- When the mouse button is released, the moved photographs appear in their new position in the destination folder.
- You can drag and drop, move, and copy as many files as you like in exactly the same way. You can even move and copy groups of entire folders like this.

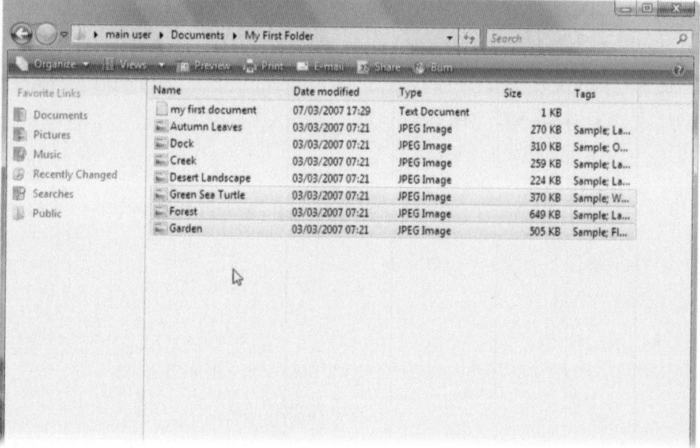

Shortcuts and Links

As you store more information on your PC, it becomes harder to find what you're looking for. Windows has a couple of clever tools to help you with this problem–Shortcuts and Favorite Links.

Creating Shortcuts

Any file, folder, or program on your computer can be opened by making your way to it through a sequence of menus, but for items that you use frequently, shortcuts offer a much quicker way. A shortcut is a link to the item, represented on your desktop by an icon. Clicking on the icon opens the file or program directly.

LOCATING THE CHOSEN ITEM

- Whether you intend to create a shortcut for a file, a folder, or a program, find the item on your computer.
- Here we have double clicked on the main user folder on the desktop, and then double clicked again on the **Documents** folder to open that. In that folder we can see **My First Folder**, which we created earlier. This is the chosen item.
- Click on this folder once with the right mouse button and a pop-up menu appears next to it.

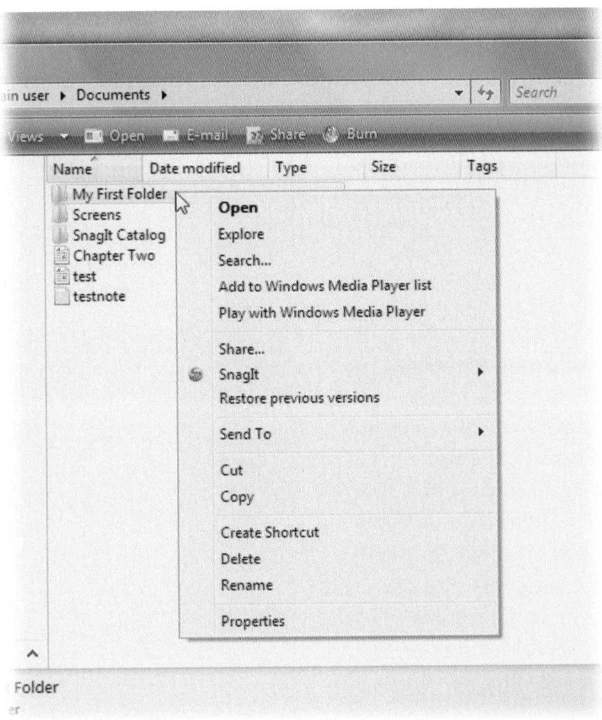

● Move the mouse down to the **Send To** menu, and a sub-menu pops out. (The small arrow at the right-hand edge of the menu indicates that there's a sub-menu attached to this.)

● Choose **Desktop (create shortcut)** by left clicking on it once.

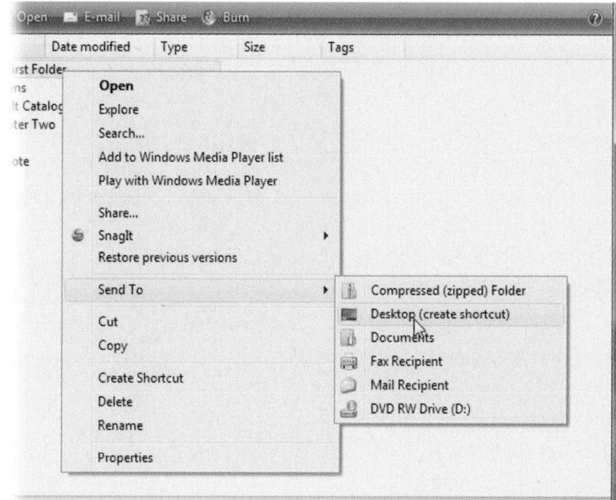

● Here's the result. A new icon, called **My First Folder - Shortcut**, is created on the desktop. The jaunty little arrow on the folder icon indicates that this is a shortcut that "points" to the folder, rather than being the actual folder itself. This allows you to keep the files and folders you create where they should be, in the Documents folder, but still have speedy access to them.

● Double click on the icon to open the folder.

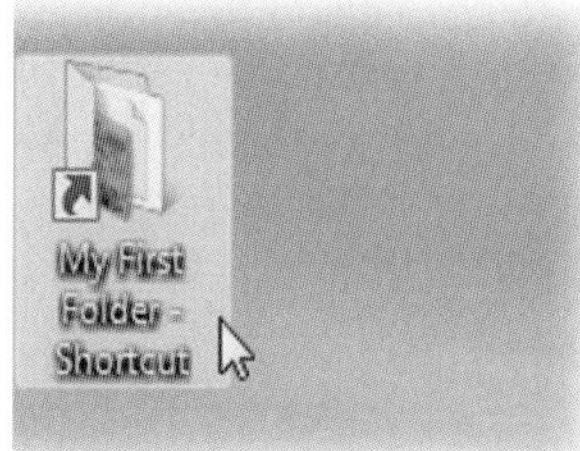

● My First Folder opens, ready for business. Creating shortcuts for folders you're using regularly like this saves you from having to spend time finding them when they're buried inside folders within other folders.

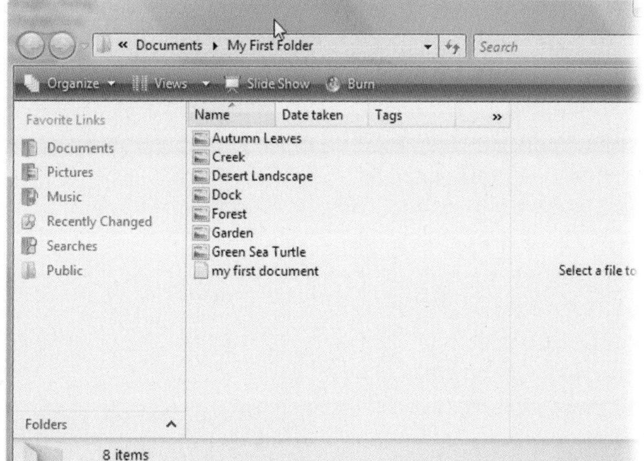

Using Favorite Links

To the left of every window you'll see a panel called Favorite Links. These are locations on your PC's hard disk that Windows thinks you'll be using often. You don't have to set them up–they just appear there. Here's how they work.

OPENING A FOLDER FROM A LINK

● Move the cursor over one of the links and then click on it with the left mouse button (in this example, we've clicked on the **Pictures** link).

● Windows opens the Pictures folder, just as if we'd navigated to it via the Start menu or by opening the main user folder first. In this way, Favorite Links work a bit like shortcuts.

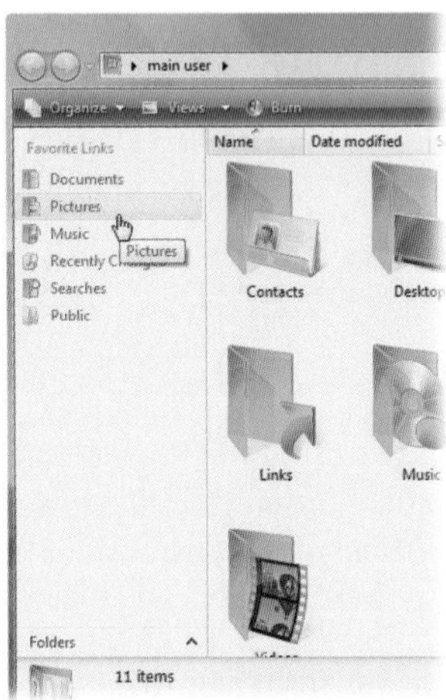

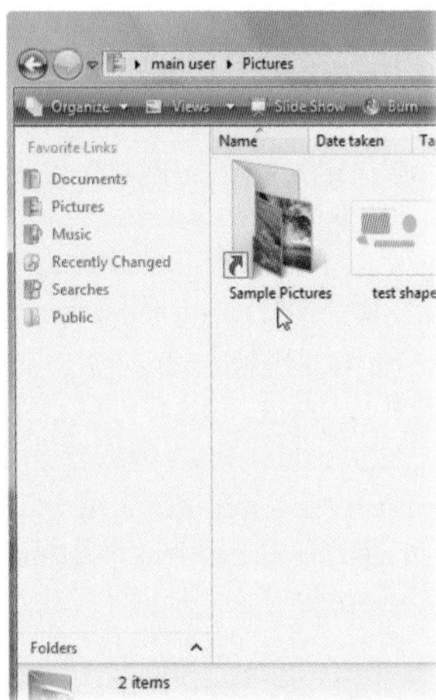

● Let's open another useful Favorite Link as a further example. Click on the **Recently Changed** link with the left mouse button.

● The **Recently Changed** folder is where Windows stores items you've been working on in the last few days, so this is a quick route to files that relate to current work or projects.

● Your folder is unlikely to look anything like this, as your files will be entirely different from these.

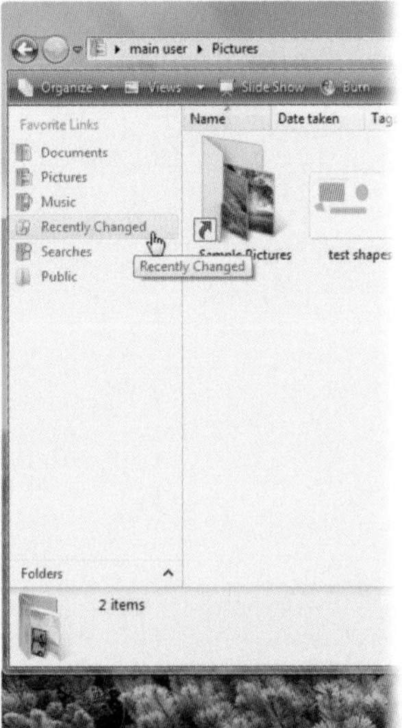

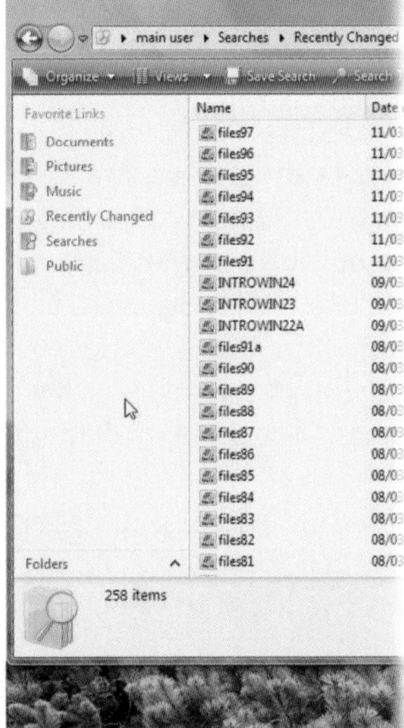

Creating New Favorite Links

You can add your own links to the Favorite Links list quickly and easily. As we're about to see, these links don't just work a bit like shortcuts–they are shortcuts. The difference is that they are readily at hand whenever you have a folder open.

OPENING THE LINKS FOLDER

- Move the cursor into the empty space beneath the list of Favorite Links, click there with the right mouse button, and choose **Open Favorite Links Folder** from the pop-up menu.
- Inside the Links folder there is a list of shortcuts, just like the one we created previously.

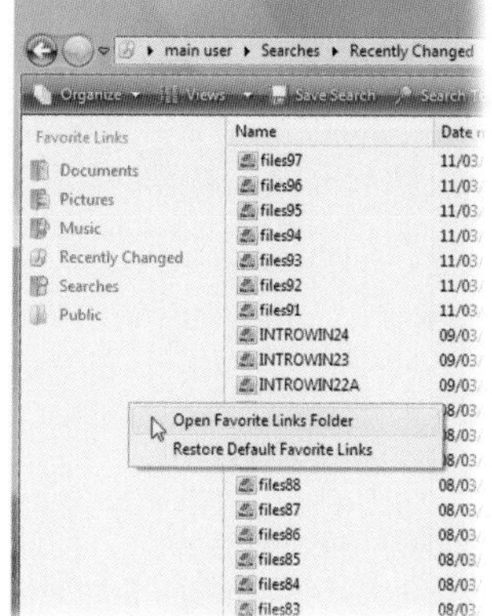

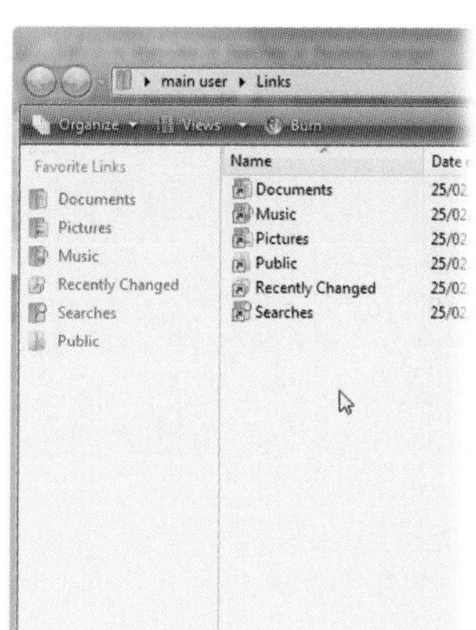

COPYING THE NEW SHORTCUT

- Since these are shortcuts, we can easily add to them the one we made earlier.
- Click on the **My First Folder** shortcut icon on the desktop and drag it into the open folder window. You are actually dragging a copy.

- When the icon is inside the folder window, release your mouse button and it drops into place in the list.
- It has also been added to the **Favorite Links** list in the left-hand panel, and it will now be available in every folder you open.

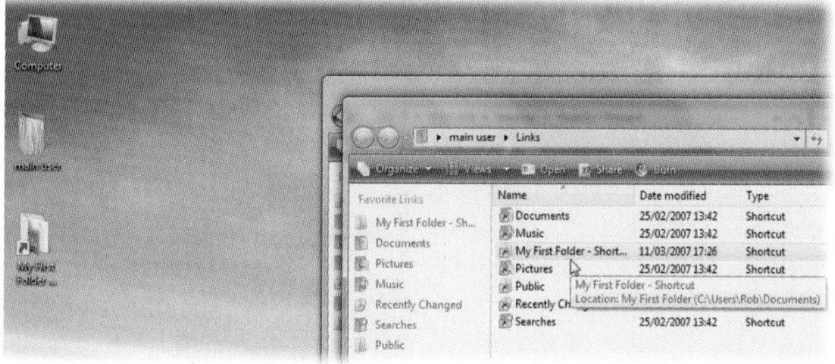

96 Creating Shortcuts

Searching for Items

Although you can use Shortcuts and Favorite Links to help keep things organized, there'll be occasions when things just go missing. That's when Windows Vista's Search features come to the fore.

Searching from the Start Menu

Here's how to find something directly from the Start menu, the most accessible search method, where you can look for an item by name or by content. We have kept the searches deliberately simple, just to demonstrate the principles involved.

OPENING THE START MENU

- Start by clicking the Start button. You will see a blinking insertion point in the **Start Search** box above the Start button.

KEYING IN THE SEARCH TERM

- We know there's a great photo of a dock stored somewhere on this PC but we can't remember where.
- We start typing in the word **dock**. As we do so, the letters appear in the Start Search box.
- As soon as we type the first letter, Windows starts to list all items that it thinks we may be looking for.
- Each successive letter refines the search further.

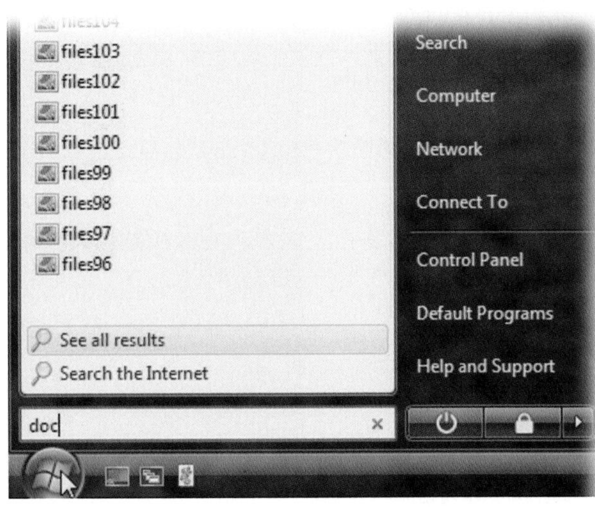

VIEWING THE SEARCH RESULTS

- The list of files and folders that Windows displays is in descending order of probability and, sure enough, there's a picture called Dock almost at the top of the list.
- Double click on the **Dock** file to open it.

- Windows recognizes that this file is a picture, and therefore launches the Photo Gallery program to open it.
- Sure enough, here's the photograph of the dock–the file we were looking for–displayed on the screen.

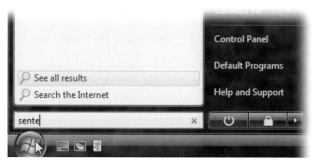

SEARCHING FOR CONTENT

- Windows can also look for text within documents. Earlier, we created a simple document using Notepad that included the word **sentence**. To find that document, click the Start button and begin typing the word **sentence**.
- The more letters you type, the fewer matches it will find. By the time we get to the fifth character, Windows finds just one document that matches our search, so we'll open it.

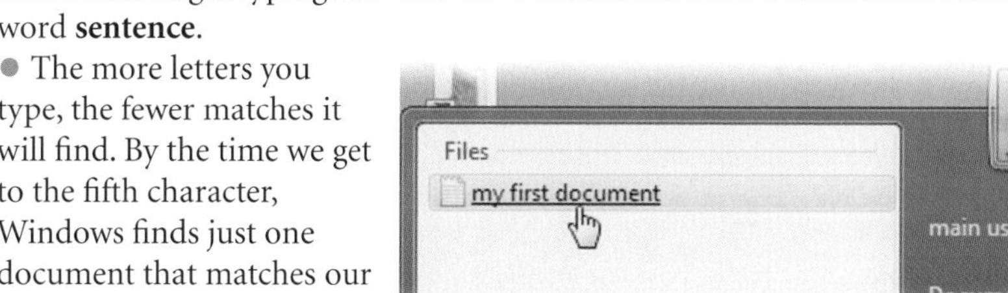

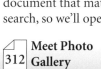

312 **Meet Photo Gallery**

79 **Making a New File**

- The Notepad document opens on the screen, clearly showing the word **sentence** in the text.
- This ability to look inside documents makes Windows Search a very powerful, and very helpful, feature.

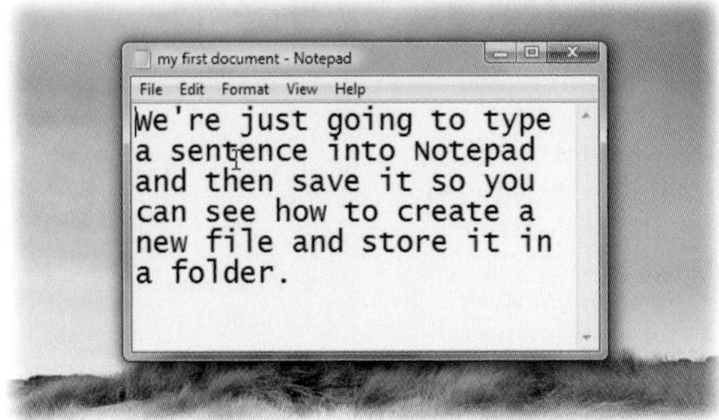

Searching From Within a Folder

As well as the search box in the Start menu, Windows also has the same facility inside every folder. This is especially useful if you've created a very large number of files. This method also enables you to refine your search using advanced features.

STARTING THE SEARCH

- Open any folder–here we've opened the main user folder by double clicking on it–and you'll see the search box at the top right corner.

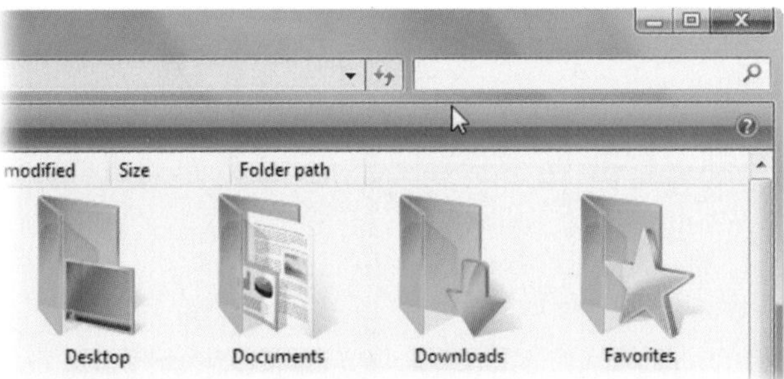

- Starting typing **sentence** into the search box again, and Windows starts to whittle down the number of possible matches.
- With four letters typed, the search results are down to just two possibilities–a document and a picture.

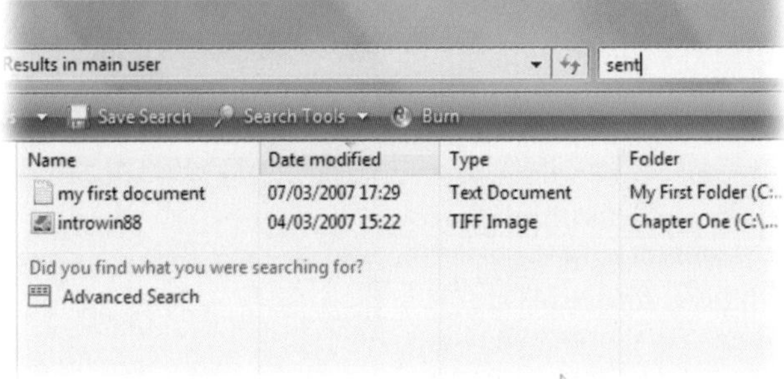

USING ADVANCED SEARCH METHODS

- In a more complex search with lots of different results it's sometimes necessary to use the **Advanced Search** feature, which appears under the results list.
- Click on it once with the left mouse button.

- This opens a whole new window on top of the search results. This Advanced Search window contains a range of search parameters. We're not going to investigate the use of all of them right now, but if you look along the top of the window you'll see that there are a number of ways to filter out results based on whether they are, for example, e-mails, documents, or pictures.

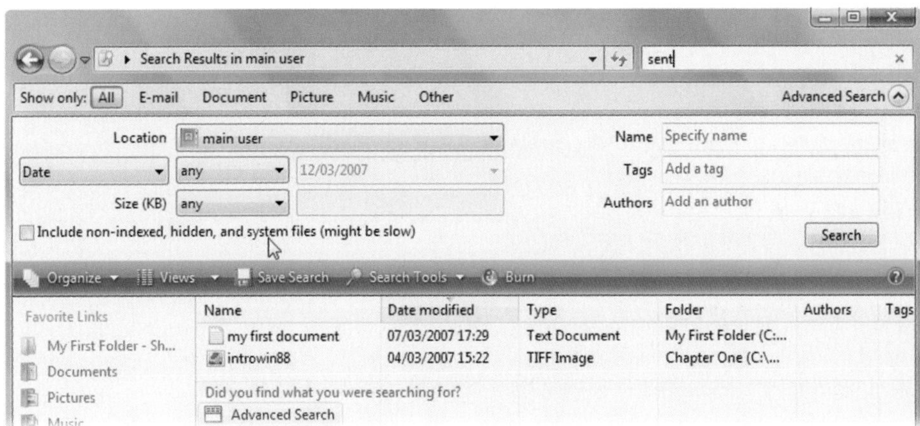

- We know that we are looking for a document, so we'll use the Advanced Search features to filter out everything else.
- Move the cursor over the **Document** button and the message **Show search results for documents** appears below the cursor.

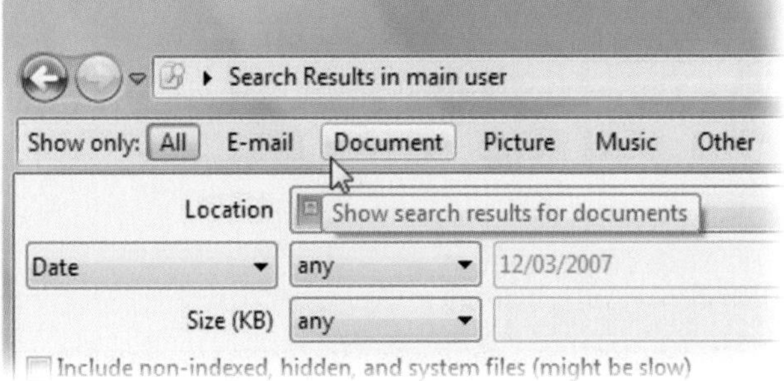

● Click the **Document** filter button and watch what happens.
● Windows removes from the list any results that are not documents, leaving us with the correct result.
● In the case of a large list of search results, this procedure is unlikely to leave you with just one choice, but it is a useful first step in narrowing the field.

SAVING THE SEARCH CRITERIA

● If we had used a wider range of the filters available in the dialog box, it might be worth saving these criteria in case we need to use them again. To do so, click on **Save Search**.

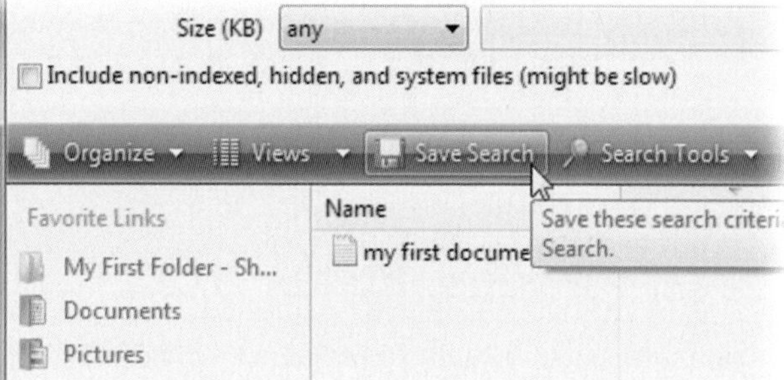

● A **Save As** dialog box opens, similar to those that we've looked at previously when saving a file. The box is already suggesting a name to give to the saved search by highlighting the original search term in the **File name** box.

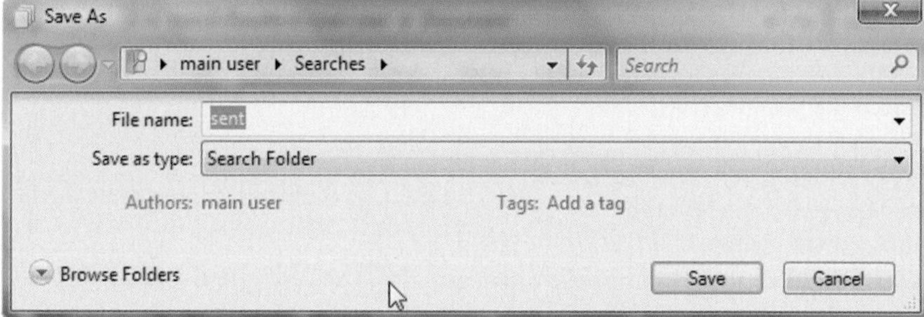

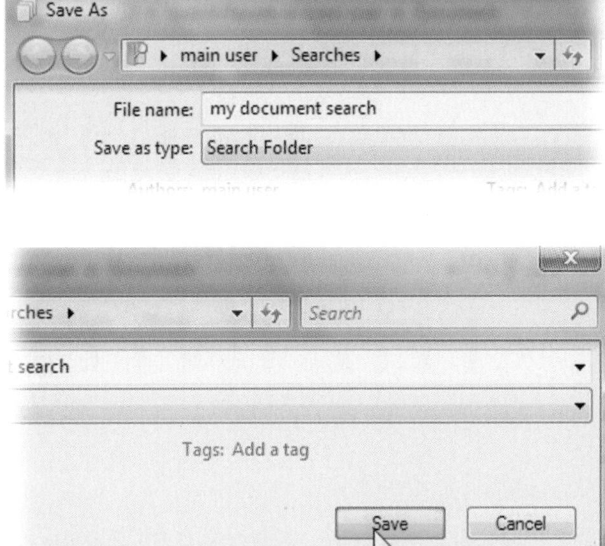

- Type in a name for the search that you're likely to remember in case you need to use it again. In this example the search is being given the name **my document search**.

- Then click the **Save** button to save the search. Now you can use the same search again later if you need to make a search based on the same criteria.

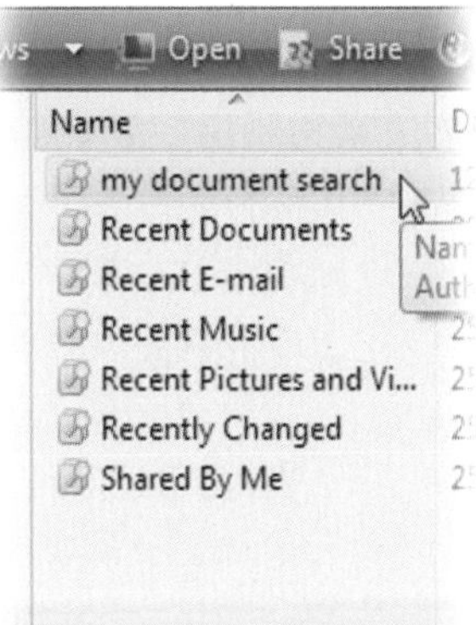

- To use that search again, you need to know where to find it. The answer is, in the **Favorite Links** list.
- With any folder open, click the **Searches** link in the left-hand panel.
- In the **Searches** folder you can see the search you just saved. Double click on it with the left mouse button to repeat the search.

FINDING SPECIFIC TYPES OF FILE

As well as searching for individual files, you can search for file types, such as documents created using Microsoft Word or pictures taken on a digital camera. Files created in Word are saved as **.doc** files, while most digital cameras save pictures as **.jpg** files. If you need to find all the Word documents in a folder, just type **doc** into the search box; to find digital images, type **jpg**.

USING THE INTERNET

ONLY TEN YEARS AGO most people who bought home PCs did so to play games, write letters, or do some simple bookkeeping. Now most people buy a home PC because they want to explore the Internet. This incredible network of computers, accessible by anyone for a very low cost, is home to billions of pages of information and entertainment. You can think of it as the world's biggest shopping mall and its largest library, a global dating service and friend-finder, a worldwide news service and homework helper, and a way for any individual to reach an audience of readers or listeners or customers anywhere in the world, from the comfort of their own homes. In this chapter you'll find out a little about this social and technological revolution and how you can make the most of it.

 108 Introducing the Internet

 114 Exploring the Internet

 132 Security Features

 140 Browser Plug-ins

 146 10 Great Sites

INTRODUCING THE INTERNET

In this section we'll talk you through what the Internet and the Web are, explain in brief how they work, and describe what you can expect to see on a typical webpage.

MEET THE WORLD WIDE WEB

When you hear someone talk about "surfing the Net," what they actually mean is that they're browsing webpages, either looking for information, goods to buy, music to listen to, or friends to chat with. What they're using is the World Wide Web.

WWW WHAT?

● The World Wide Web–from now on referred to as just the plain old "Web"–is an enormous collection of electronic "pages" that contain text, pictures, video, music, and animations stored on large, computers called web servers. What makes the Web tick–and allows everyone to use it–is the Internet, the global network that connects all of the web servers together. In other words, the Web is composed of interconnected digital content (such as text and pictures), and the Internet is the hardware that does all the connecting. It's more complex than that, of course, but that's the long and the short of it.

WHAT DO YOU NEED?

These days, most people use a broadband or ADSL connection to the Internet which is permanently "on" and shares your existing telephone line, so you can talk and surf at the same time, or your cable or satellite television connection. Typically, a single company supplies the unit that connects your PC to the Internet and you then pay a monthly fee for the service. If you've got a desktop and a notebook PC they can provide wireless equipment that allows the two machines to share the same Internet connection for about the same price, so you can surf the Web on a notebook PC from a garden chair! Some offer cheaper deals for slower connections or connections that are "capped" to prevent overuse (everything you do on the Web means an exchange of data, and that can be measured); more expensive deals allow faster speeds and unlimited use. It's still possible to use a telephone connection that dials in every time you want to use the Web or send e-mail (it's called dial up) but this is very slow and doesn't allow you to enjoy music or video; even pictures download at a snail's pace.

What's on the Web?

The pages of the World Wide Web offer information on just about every topic you care to imagine. Whether your interests include current affairs, astrophysics, golf, or Antarctic flora and fauna, somewhere there is certain to be a website devoted to that topic. The Web has always been the home of academic information, but in recent years it has also become an information base for public sector bodies, government departments and, most noticeably, commercial organizations.

Nonprofit organizations

News

Online games

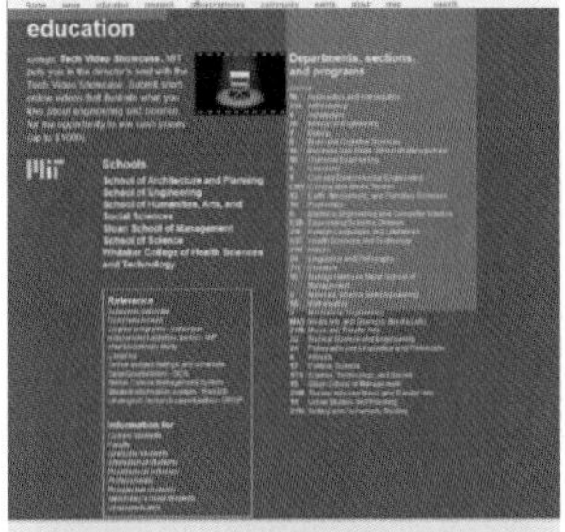

Research and education

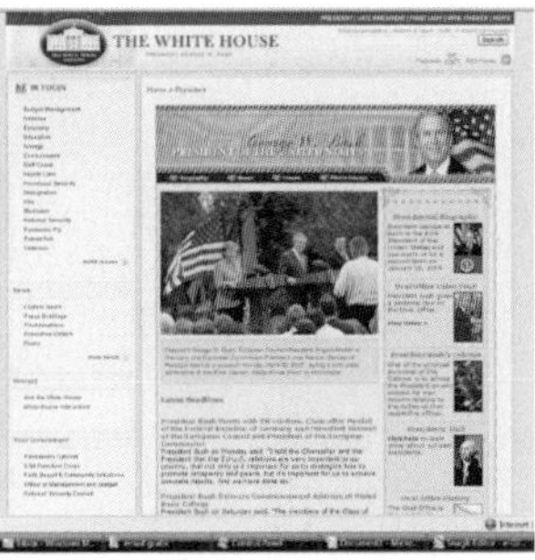

Government bodies

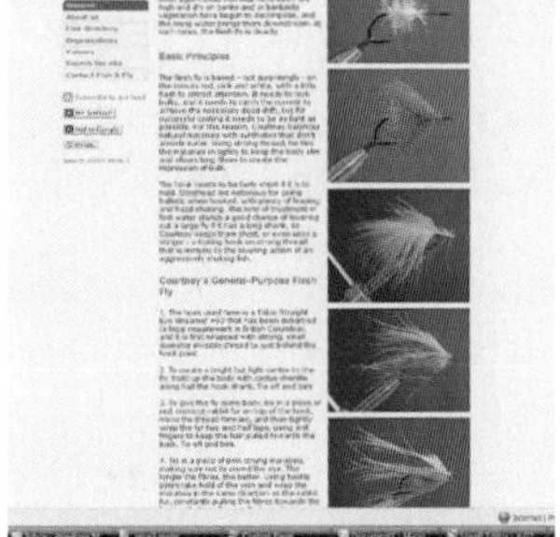

Sports and hobbies

SOMETHING FOR EVERYONE

Some webpages contain files you can transfer to your own computer to view or install. Others run programs within the page while you view. Some websites incorporate a catalogue of goods that you can search through and buy with a credit card, others host forums where visitors can exchange information, views, and opinions; you can bank online, research a homework project, design a t-shirt with your photo on it, buy music, get directions, see views of far-off places, get a weather forecast, find out what's on TV… In fact, if you can think of it, it's on the Web somewhere!

WHAT'S ON A WEBPAGE?

When the Web started, pages contained only text and very basic formatting, and they offered very little in the way of design. Today's webpages are a world away from those early pioneers, and many sites now aspire to be multimedia extravaganzas. As well as text, hyperlinks to other pages, and images, a typical webpage is likely to incorporate sophisticated graphics and may include video clips, sound sequences, and interactive animations. You may even be able to play miniature software programs knows as "applets" on the page. Most will include some form of hyperlink contents list, as well as "back" and "home" buttons, so you can easily visit other parts of the site and can move directly to the opening page of the website.

GRAPHICS

- A well-designed website can be a showcase for the graphic designer's skills.

HYPERTEXT LINKS

- Use hypertext links, or "hyperlinks", to go to other relevant sites.

TEXT

- Text within a page can be copied, pasted, and saved to your hard disk.

PHOTOGRAPHS

- Images on a webpage can also act as hyperlinks.

MULTIMEDIA FILES

- These can be sound, video, or interactive animations.

DOWNLOAD FILES

- Webpages can contain files to transfer to your own computer to view or install.

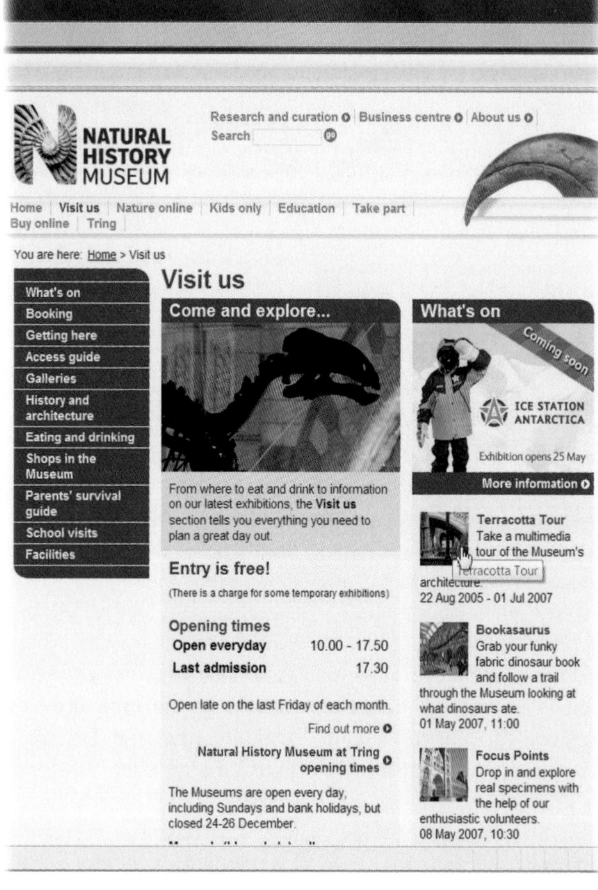

111 What Are Hyperlinks?

WHAT ARE HYPERLINKS?

- Web resources (all the digital content you see on webpages) are connected together by means of hyperlinks, which are like automatic cross-references embedded in the page.
- A hyperlink is usually a piece of text or a button, but can also be a picture or an animation. When you click on it in your web browser, it opens another part of the webpage you're looking at, a different page within the website you're visiting, or a page on a totally different website.
- In this way, a few clicks can you take you from trout in New Zealand to nuclear physics in Massachusetts, via endangered snow leopards in India and sailor's knots in Iceland.

HOW CAN YOU TELL?

- How do you know what's a hyperlink and what isn't?
- Simple–the cursor arrow changes to a little pointing hand to indicate that you're hovering over a hyperlink, whether it's an image or a piece of text.
- Textual hyperlinks are often distinguished by being blue and underlined.

I KNOW I'VE BEEN HERE BEFORE!

- Once a hyperlink has been used, if you return to the same page you may find that it has changed color.

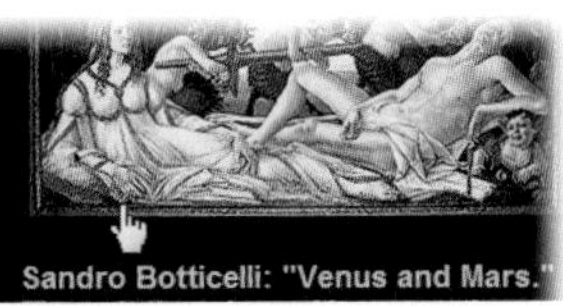

www.cafevenus.com/ - 5k - Cached - Si

Venus and Mars
Sandro Botticelli: "Venus and Mars." The
satyrs honk horns and play about Mars,
www.windows.ucar.edu/tour/link=/mytholo
gods_n_goddesses/Venus/Venus_and_M

» Venus and Mars in the enterpris

www.cafevenus.com/ - 5k - Cached - Si

Venus and Mars
Sandro Botticelli: "Venus and Mars." The
satyrs honk horns and play about Mars,
www.windows.ucar.edu/tour/link=/mytholo
gods_n_goddesses/Venus/Venus_and_M

» Venus and Mars in the enterpris

IS THE WEB SAFE?

Like most exciting places in the real world, the Web has some areas that are unsavory and unsuitable, especially for young people. We've devoted a whole chapter to using your computer safely, so we won't detain you here. Suffice it to say that the dangers are avoidable, and most people use Internet Explorer to wander round the Web without any problems at all.

WHAT'S A WEB BROWSER?

A web browser is a program that's clued in to the way in which webpages are designed, and it works with the underlying technologies they use in order to display the content properly and in an attractive way. There are a few different web browsers, but the one we'll be using in this book is Internet Explorer 7.0, which comes free with Windows Vista. It's got everything you need to start exploring the Web and, as you'll see in this chapter, Internet Explorer has been designed to help you find your way around the Internet and keep you safe while you're finding your feet.

198 Staying Safe

Understanding Web Addresses

Web addresses are known as URLs. This stands for Uniform (sometimes Universal) Resource Locator. URLs are made up of two distinct parts: a protocol and a domain name. The protocol, the first part of the URL, tells the web browser what type of site it is contacting–a website, a file transfer site, or a secure website, for example. In this case the protocol is http, standing for Hypertext Transfer Protocol, the standard for web communications. The second part, the domain name, is like a street address–it tells the web browser where to go to find the site.

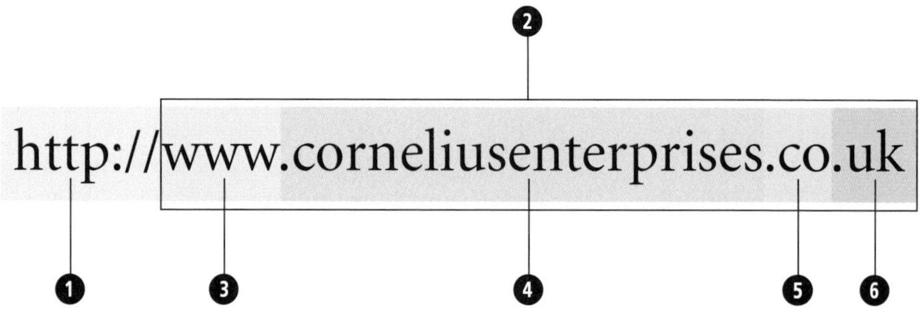

THE DIFFERENT PARTS OF A WEB ADDRESS

1 Protocol
Most web addresses begin with http://. This stands for Hypertext Transmission Protocol. This protocol is used to transfer ordinary webpages over the internet. Other protocols you are likely to encounter are ftp:// (file transfer protocol) and https://. This protocol is used on "secure" websites, for sending and receiving sensitive information safely.

2 Domain Name
The domain name has several parts and is mapped to an Internet Protocol (IP) address.

3 www
The vast majority of web addresses have www (standing for World Wide Web) as the first part of the domain name.

4 Host
This part of the domain name is a name chosen by the owner of the website and can be, for example, a company name.

5 Type of Site
This part of the domain tells you what type of site the website is. For example, .co or .com stand for commercial sites; .gov for government organizations; .org for non-profit organizations; and .edu or .ac for educational sites.

6 Country
Websites other than US sites also have a country code. UK denotes a website based in the United Kingdom.

Finding the Right Address

Of course, nearly every company or institution has a web address now, and they're always happy to give it to you, but what about those addresses you don't know? Once you understand a tiny bit about how the Web works, the names of some websites are so obvious you can guess them. Others need researching.

TAKING A CHANCE

Nearly all web addresses begin with "www" followed by a name with no spaces, followed by a suffix such as ".com" (a commercial organization), ".org" (usually a non-profit organization), or ".ac" or ."edu" (an academic institution); elsewhere, countries outside the US use their own suffixes– ".uk" for the UK, ".es" for Spain, ".au" for Australia, and so on. So, if you wanted to find the web address for Ford, a good first guess would be **www.ford.com**.

MAKING A SEARCH

Alternatively you can use one of the Web's search engines, which are a bit like telephone directories for websites. The most famous of these is Google, at www. google.com. Once you're there, type **Ford** into the search box, press Enter on your keyboard, and there's Ford's website, at the top of results list.

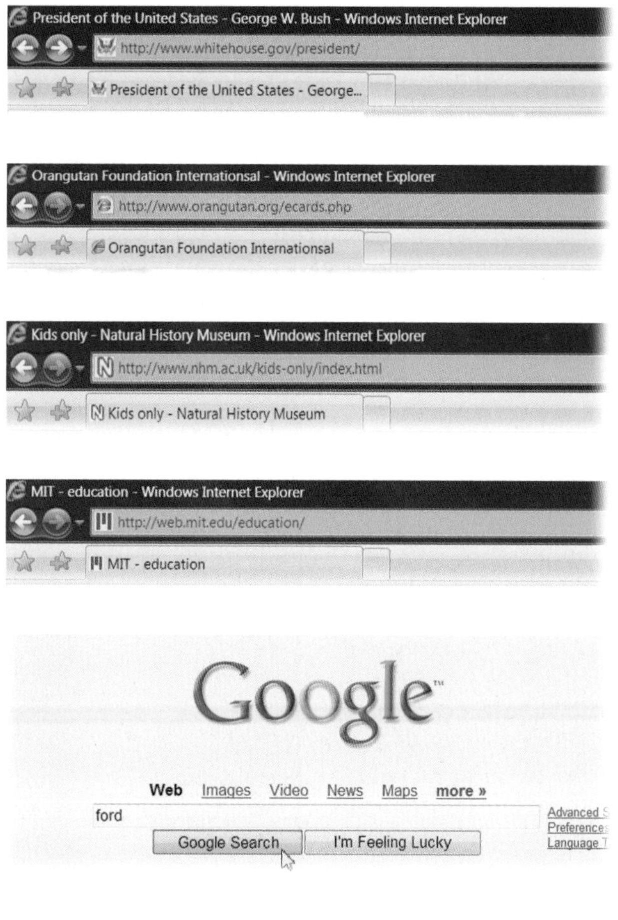

EXPLORING THE INTERNET

If you want to start exploring straight away then, provided you have an Internet connection and an account with a service provider, Vista has everything you need to begin your adventure.

INTRODUCING INTERNET EXPLORER

Internet Explorer 7.0 is a program that comes free with Windows Vista and lets you browse the web. It has all of the controls you need to navigate successfully round this enormous electronic world and can help you find what you're looking for, as well as remembering favorite websites so you can re-visit them easily. We'll start by opening Internet Explorer, the program that most people use to browse webpages.

LAUNCHING INTERNET EXPLORER

- Click the Start button to open the Start menu.

- Windows assumes–probably correctly–you'll be using Internet Explorer a lot of the time and you'll be opening it frequently, so it pins it to the top of the Start menu for easy access.
- Slide the cursor up to the icon and click on it once with the left mouse button.

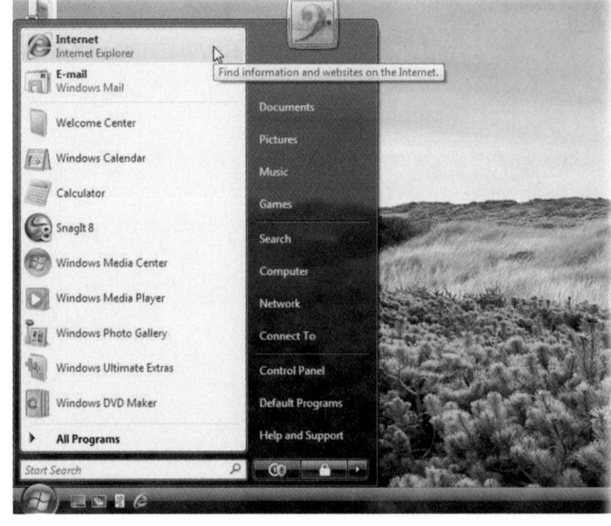

● The Internet Explorer window opens, displaying the webpage that is selected as the "home page" within the program. By default, this page is preset to be the MSN (that's Microsoft Network) home page for your country, so this webpage will appear when you first open Internet Explorer.

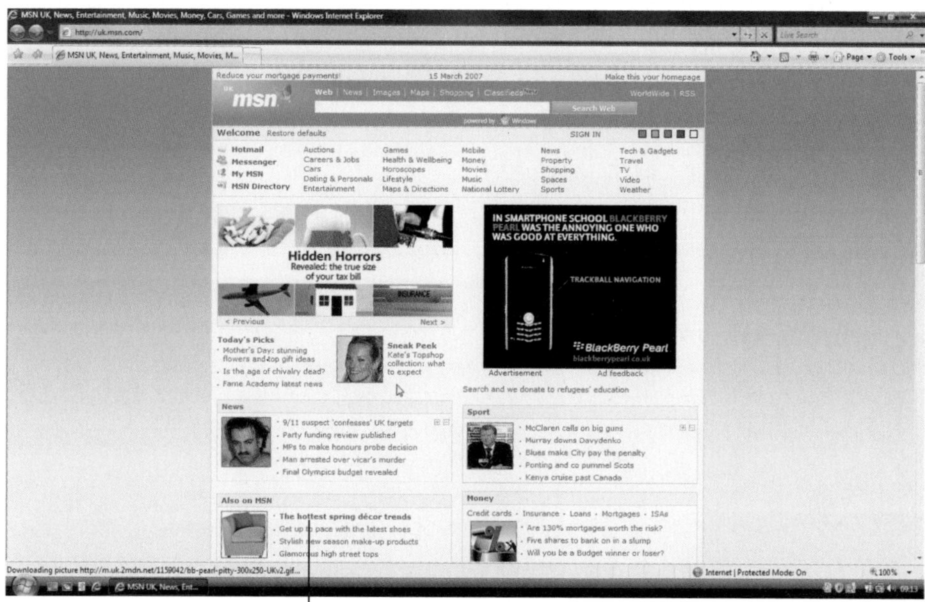

The actual content of the MSN home page changes continuously, so the page that you see on screen will not look exactly like this one.

ALTERNATIVE BROWSERS

Although Internet Explorer is used by most web surfers, there are a number of alternative browsers, of which the main two contenders are Firefox and Opera. However, many of the competitive advantages that these featured over Internet Explorer have disappeared with the advent of the new version of Internet Explorer for Vista and, unless you have a specific reason for doing otherwise, there's currently no compelling reason to switch to another browser. Make your own mind up by visiting **www.getfirefox.com** and **www.opera.com**.

The Internet Explorer Window

Internet Explorer is a web browser, a program that enables you to find your way around the world wide web, to go directly to websites when you know their addresses, and to keep track of where you've been. The browser recognizes links within webpages–text and images that connect to other pages–and takes you from page to page with a mouse click. A variety of buttons ranged along the top of the web browser screen allow you to move back and forth through sequences of visited webpages, and to compile lists of favorite sites that you want to revisit regularly.

FEATURES KEY

❶ Title Bar
This shows the name of the webpage you're looking at.

❷ Address Line
This is where you type the address of the website you want to go to.

❸ Current Tab
Internet Explorer can open more than one website at once, so it also puts the site name here on the tab.

❹ New Tab
Clicking here will open a new blank page so you can go to a second website using the Address line and load that alongside the first site.

❺ Refresh and Stop
If a website gets "stuck" when it's trying to load, click Stop first and then Refresh to try and load the page again.

❻ Search Box
Type a search term in here and click the magnifying glass icon to search for it.

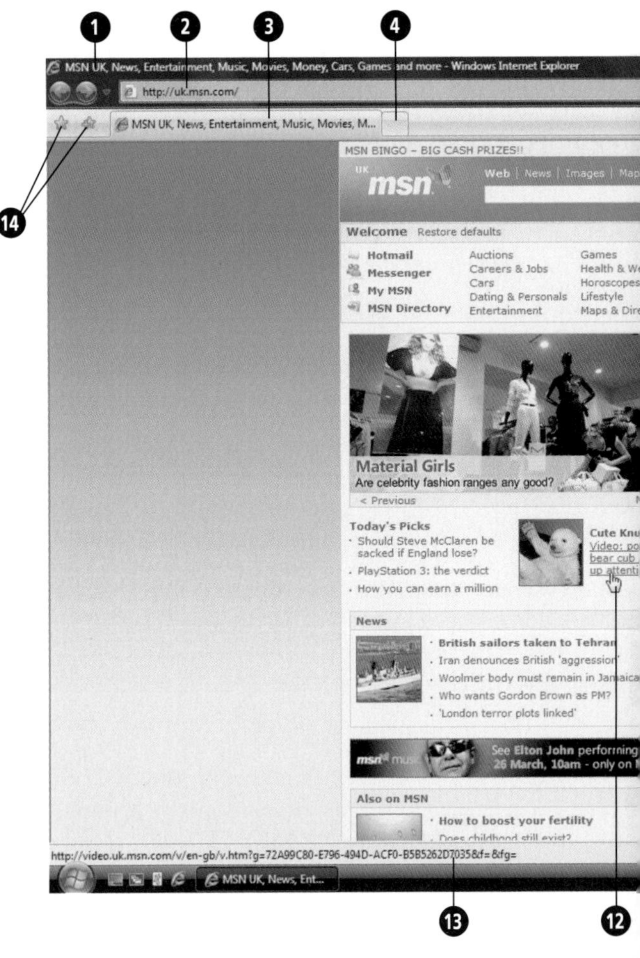

THE BUTTON BAR

Looking at them from left to right, these buttons take you back to your home page (and offer the opportunity to change the home page), allow you to keep track of websites that change their content regularly, print a webpage, control how the page is displayed, change your settings, and get help.

FEATURES KEY

❼ Button Bar
See The Button Bar (left).

❽ Scroll Bar
Most websites are "tall and thin," so you need to drag the scroll bar down with the cursor to see the rest of them.

❾ Website Search Box
Many sites include their own search boxes that enable you to search the particular website or the Internet.

❿ Zoom
Click here to zoom in or out of a website to make it larger or smaller on the screen.

⓫ Security Settings
Internet Explorer displays its current security level here; by default, this is switched on.

⓬ Hyperlink
When the cursor hovers over a hyperlink it changes from an arrow to a pointing hand.

⓭ Status Bar
When you hover the cursor over a link, the actual web address that it points to is displayed here–this one is for a video of the seal pup that the cursor is pointing at.

⓮ Favorites
These two buttons open and control the list of your favorites. These are websites that you return to regularly; storing their addresses here is more convenient than typing them in anew each time.

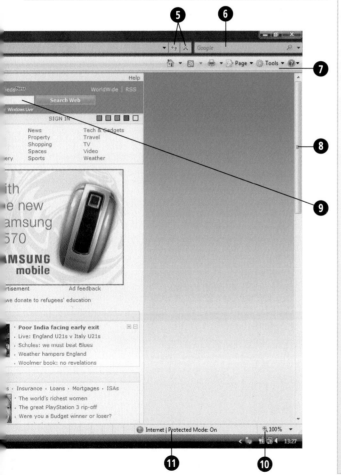

Changing Your Home Page
19

BASIC NAVIGATION

Using the web is all about finding your way around successfully. Right from the start, Internet Explorer is on hand to help you navigate through the billions of pages currently available online. In this section we'll demonstrate how to move between two different webpages using Internet Explorer's simple controls.

1 USING HYPERLINKS

- With the cursor in a blank area of the webpage, we see that it has the traditional arrow shape.
- When we move it over this piece of text, next to the picture of the model Kate Moss, we see it turn into a pointing hand. This indicates that this text is a link that will open another webpage when we click it.
- So, let's click it.

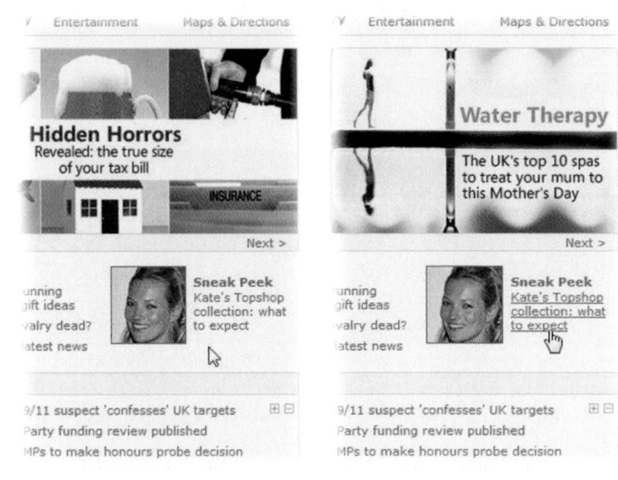

- Here's the new webpage. In this example, it's still part of the MSN site, but it's clearly a completely different page. If you imagine the link on the previous page was the listing on a magazine's contents page, this page is the actual article.

2 BACK AND FORWARD

● We've already spent some time exploring the Back and Forward buttons in Windows folders, and here they are again. To move back to the previous webpage, just move the cursor arrow up to the Back button and click it once.

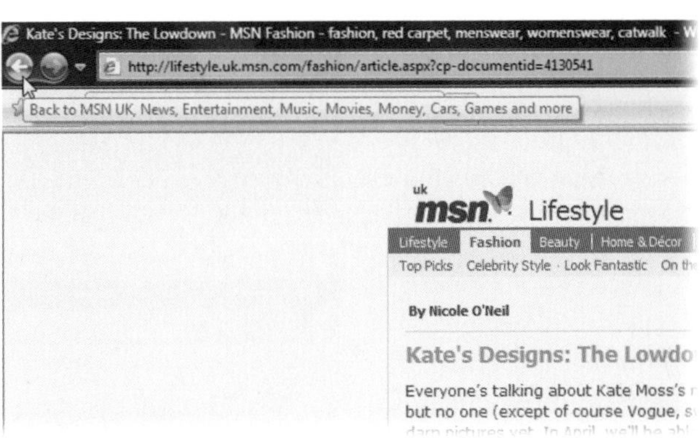

● Here we are, back at the original webpage. Notice too that the Forward button is now highlighted, meaning that it's become active. That's because having opened a second page we now have two pages to move back and forth between.

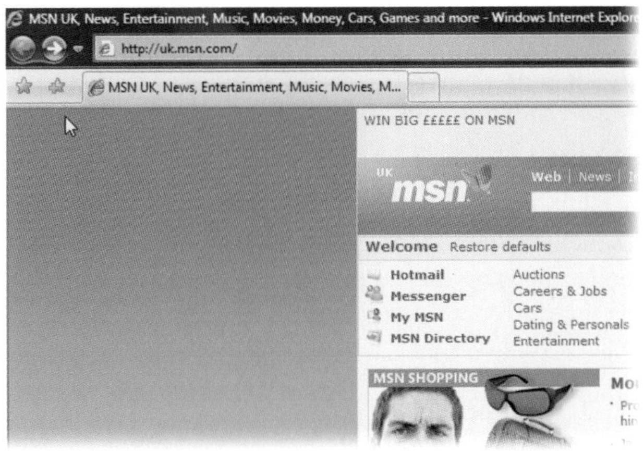

CHANGING YOUR HOME PAGE

The choice of which website to have as your home page is a personal one. It may be that MSN suits you fine, but you may find that you would rather have a search engine, or a home page that gives you direct access to a variety of webpages. To change the home page, go to the chosen website and then click the arrow next to the home page button in the button bar. Click on **Add or Change Home Page**. In the dialog box that appears, click on the radio button next to **Use this webpage as your only home page**. Then click on **Yes**.

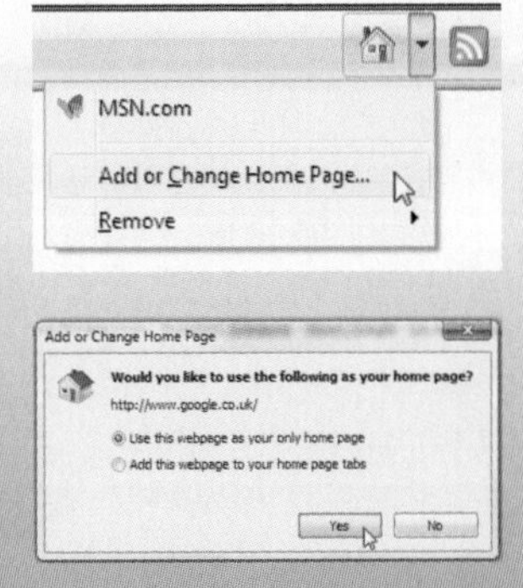

70 **Moving Back and Forward**

148 **www.Google.com**

156 **www.Netvibes.com**

3 VISITING RECENT PAGES

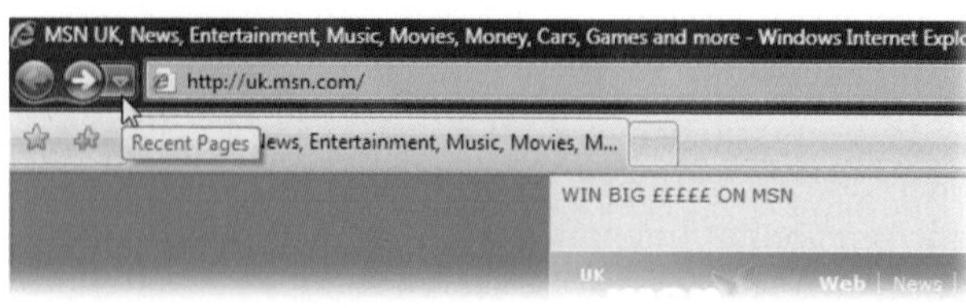

● Notice too that there's another button next to the Forward button. Move the cursor over this and click it.

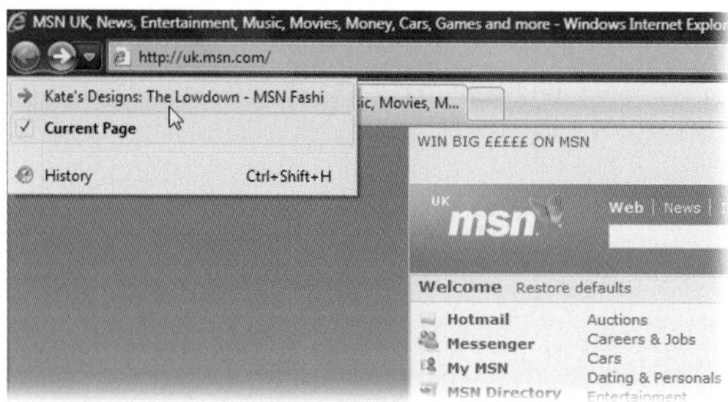

● This opens the **Recent Pages** drop-down list. Here you can see the current page along with the other page we visited. To open that second page again, move the cursor down to its entry in the menu and click it once.

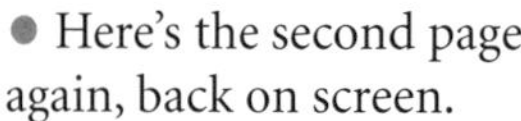

● Here's the second page again, back on screen.

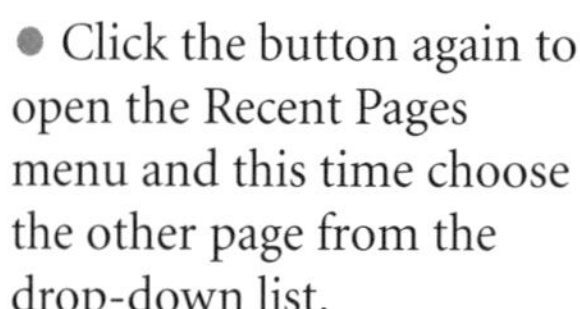

● Click the button again to open the Recent Pages menu and this time choose the other page from the drop-down list.

● Here we are back at the first page again. As we'll discover, Internet Explorer has a host of features that are designed to help you find your way around the web, but these are the ones you'll use most often.

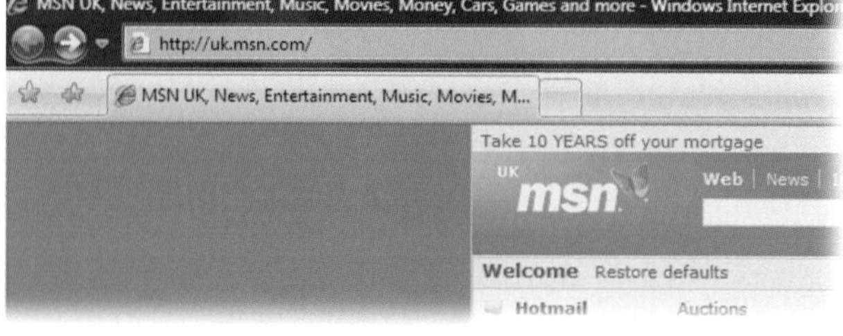

TABBED BROWSING

Older versions of Internet Explorer could only open one website at a time. With IE version 7.0 for Vista, however, you can open several sites at once, courtesy of the tabs feature. Each open webpage has a tab at the top, rather like those in a card index, and these stand next to each other along the top of the page. This means you can keep sites that you refer to frequently over the course of the day open all the time, which is much more convenient than having to keep loading them up when you need them. To open any particular webpage you need only click on its tab.

1 OPENING A NEW TAB

- To begin, move the cursor up to the **New Tab** button just to the right of the MSN tab at the top, and click once.

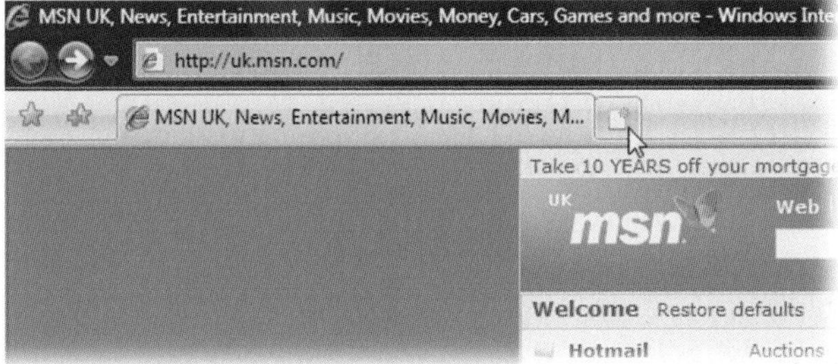

- Internet Explorer opens up a new empty window with some explanatory text about tabs and how they work. Have a quick read and then move the cursor up to the line above the tabs where Internet Explorer has highlighted **about:Tabs**. This text describes the content of the browser tab and is called the address line because this is where you'll type in the addresses of websites you know and want to visit.

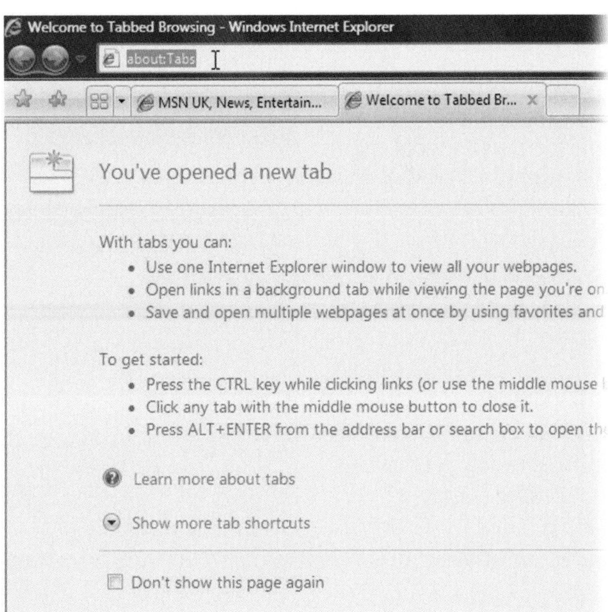

2 OPENING A NEW WEBSITE

● Type **www.nasa.gov** into the address line at the top of the window.
● Then press the Enter← key to go to the website.

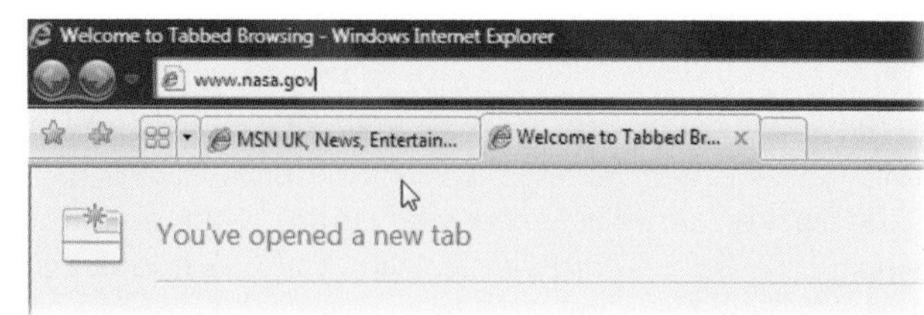

● After a moment the NASA website loads into the new space on your screen. Here's what the NASA home page looked like on the day we visited.

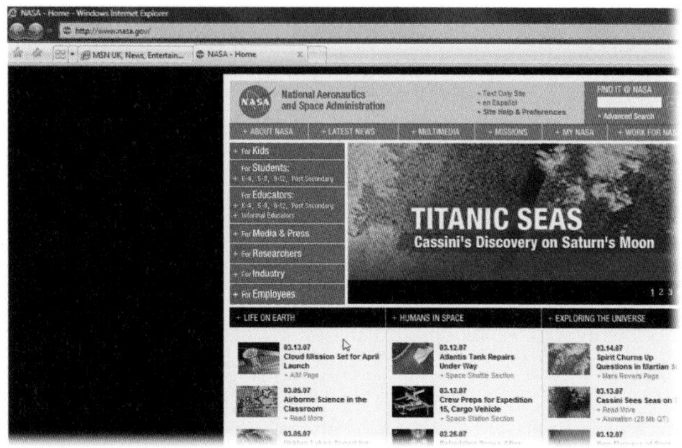

3 FLIPPING BETWEEN SITES

● There are now two tabs along the top of the screen– one for NASA and one for the original MSN website.
● You can now switch between the sites by clicking on their respective tabs.
● Click the MSN tab now, and we are back at the MSN site, with the NASA site tab still visible.
● We can switch back and forth between the two sites at any time simply by clicking on the tabs at the top of the screen.

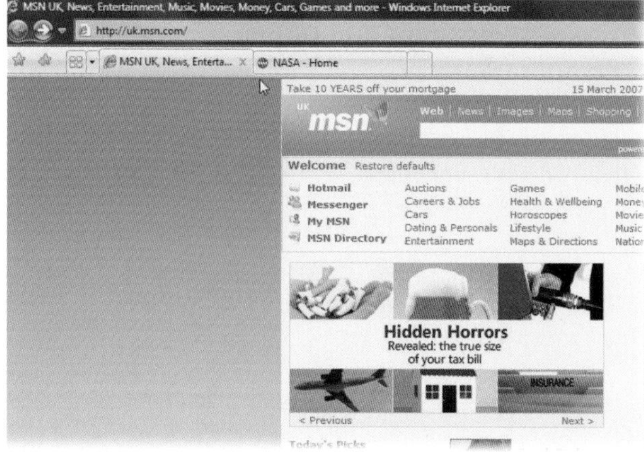

4 ADDING MORE WEBSITES

● To create some more tabs, click the New Tab, type in **www. cnn.com**, and press Enter↵.

● Repeat the process for **www. amazon.com** and **www.wikipedia.org**.

● There should now be five tabs along the top of the main browser window, each one with the name of the website it relates to clearly visible. The site on screen is Wikipedia, the free online encyclopedia that anyone can edit.

● We can switch to any of the other tabbed websites by clicking on its tab, but now a new button has appeared to the left of the tabs. This is the Quick Tabs button, which offers us even easier, and clearer, access to all the tabbed websites.

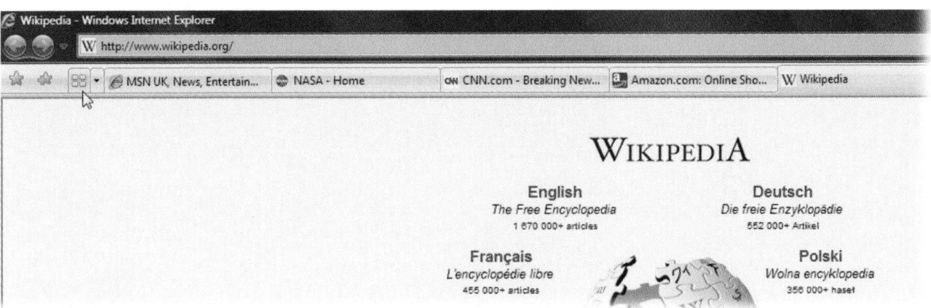

5 USING QUICK TABS

● Clicking the Quick Tabs button opens up a miniature version–often called a thumbnail–of each of the websites that are open in the web browser.

● This view is extremely useful if, for example, you're researching a topic or switching between several online shopping sites and trying to compare prices for a particular item.

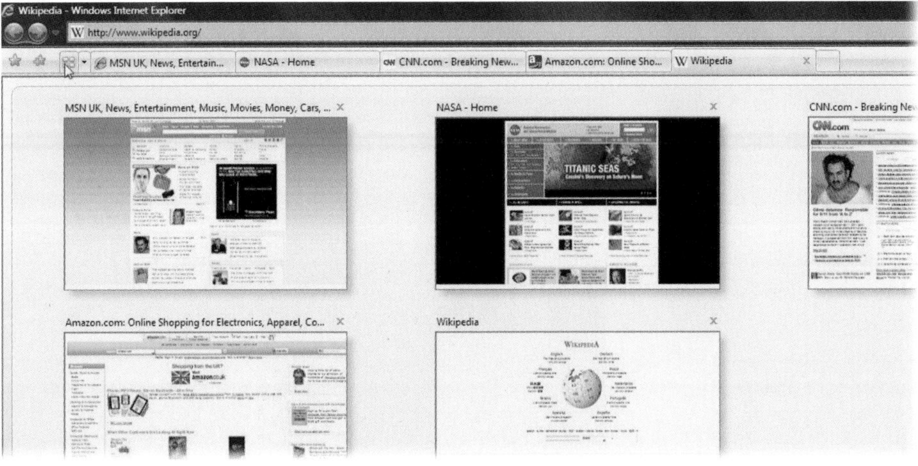

162 **www.Wikipedia.org**

● To make use of this feature, move the cursor over one of the thumbnails.
● The cursor changes into a pointing hand, indicating the thumbnail is a link that you can click.
● Click on the thumbnail.

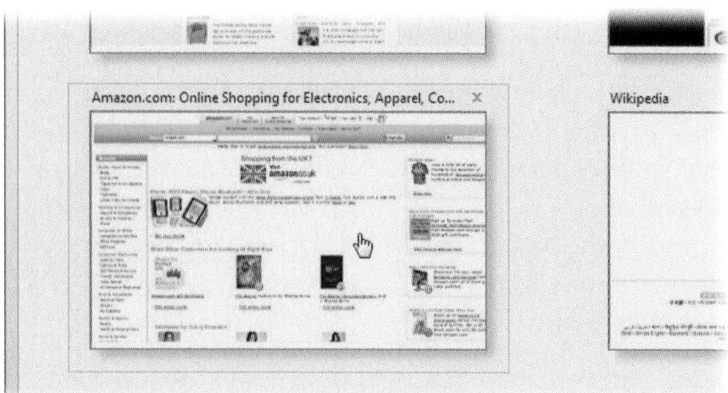

● The webpage expands to fill the screen and the other thumbnails disappear.
● To display them all again, simply click the Quick Tabs button again. This facility is available whenever you have more than two tabs.

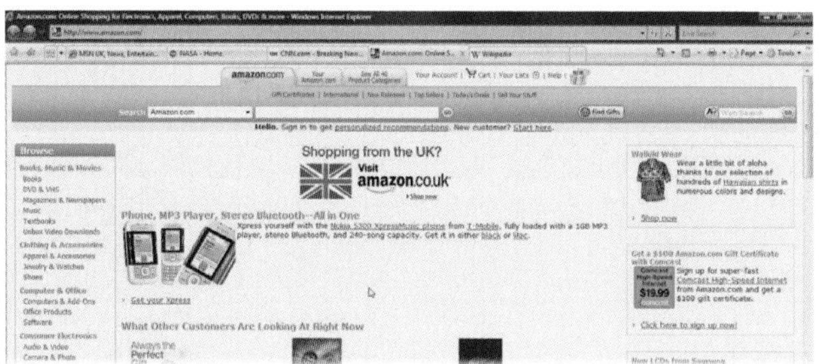

Using Favorites

Sometimes you'll come across a website that you'll need to return to or just know you're going to visit again and again. If that's the case, you can add it to your list of "favorites" so it's easy to visit whenever you want to with just a click of a button.

1 ADDING TO THE FAVORITES LIST

● Start by switching to a site you'd like to add to your favorites. We're going to choose NASA.
● With the webpage on screen, click on the button second from the left on the button bar. The button has a little gold star with a green "+" sign on it.

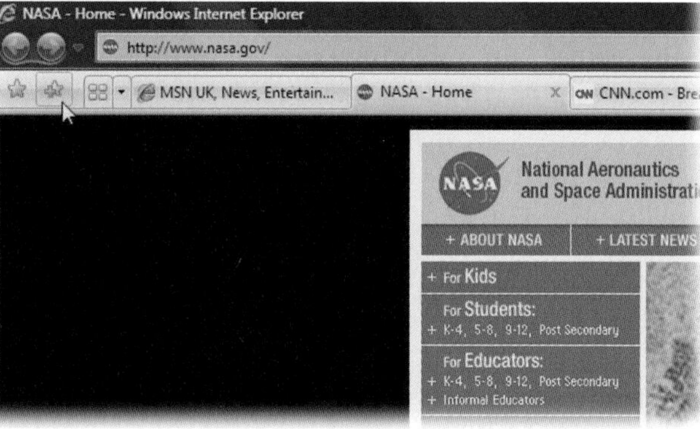

● This opens a menu with several options on it for organizing those websites you'd like to visit regularly. Choose the first option–**Add to Favorites**–by clicking there once with the left mouse button.

● The **Add a Favorite** dialog box appears. Unless you want to re-name the website for your own reference (rarely necessary), you can leave all the settings as they are and simply click the **Add** button.

● With the page safely stored in the favorites menu, click on the little "x" on the tab to remove the website from your browser.
● For the other open websites, bring each one to full screen, add it to the favorites list, and then close it in this same way.

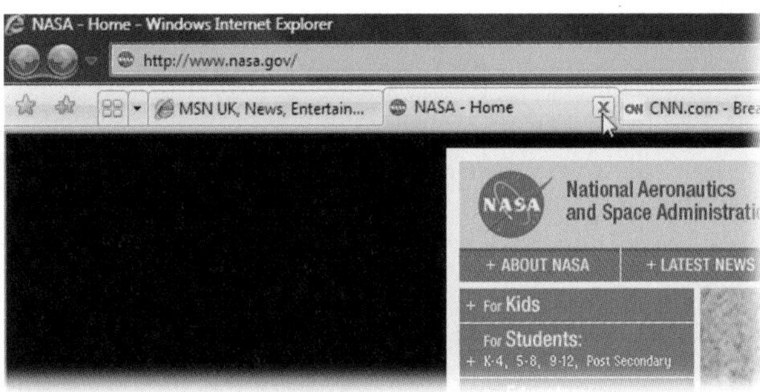

2 FINDING A FAVORITE SITE

● To go to a website that is saved on your Favorites list, start by clicking on the Favorites button–it's the one at the far left end of the button bar with a little gold star on it.

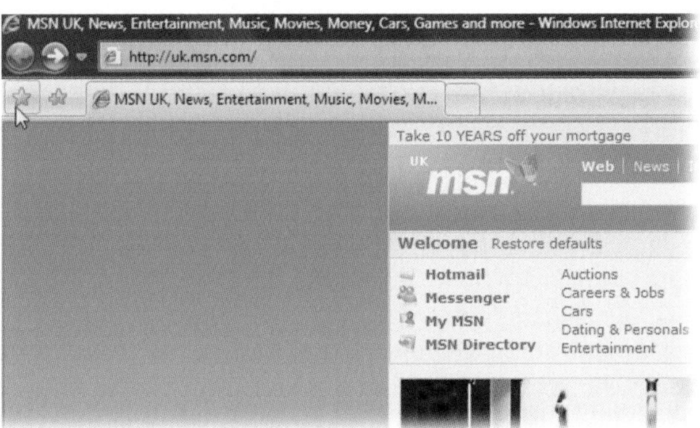

● To open the menu, click the button. Now you can see entries for the websites we were looking at a few pages ago, all neatly arranged on the menu.

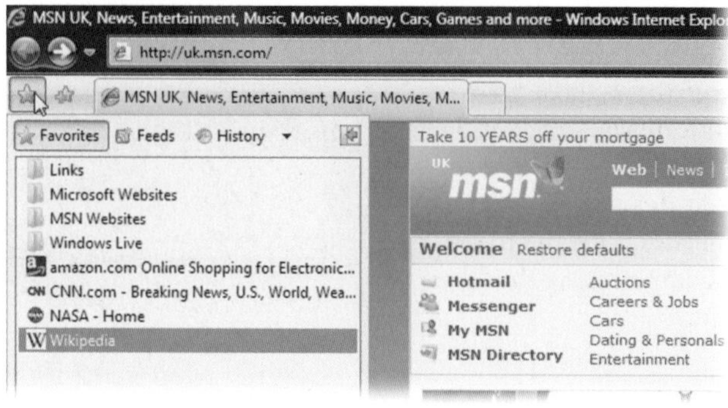

3 OPENING A FAVORITE

● Slide the cursor down to the website you'd like to visit again–we're going for NASA. If you now click on the website name, it will replace the site that you're currently looking at.

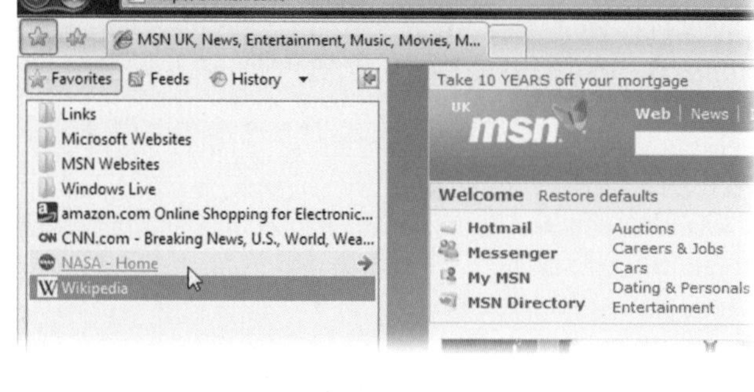

4 OPENING IN A NEW TAB

● However, you can also open the chosen site in a new tab so that you can flip between it and the currently open website.

● Slide the cursor along to the right and click on the little arrow.

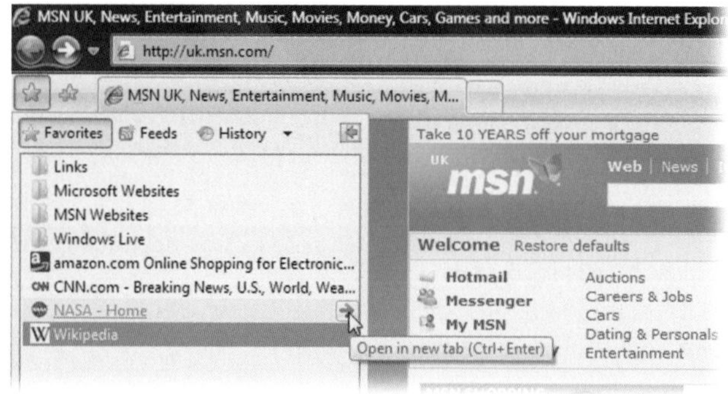

● A new tab has appeared for the NASA website.

● Move the cursor over to the new tab and click on it to switch to that website.

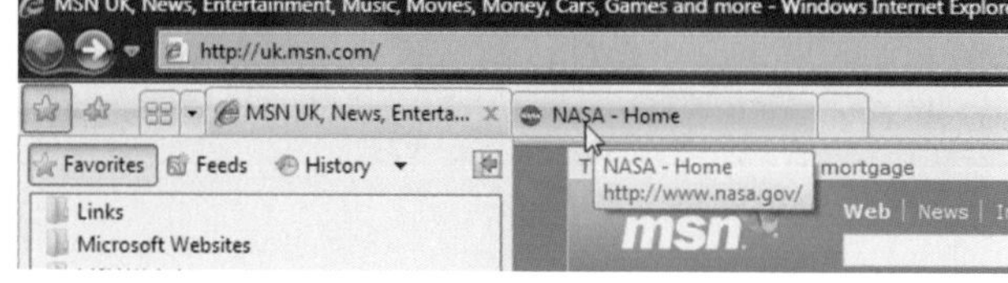

● Two things now happen. The main window switches to the new website, moving us from MSN to NASA, and at the same time the Favorites menu disappears.
● You can get the menu back by clicking the "star" button again.

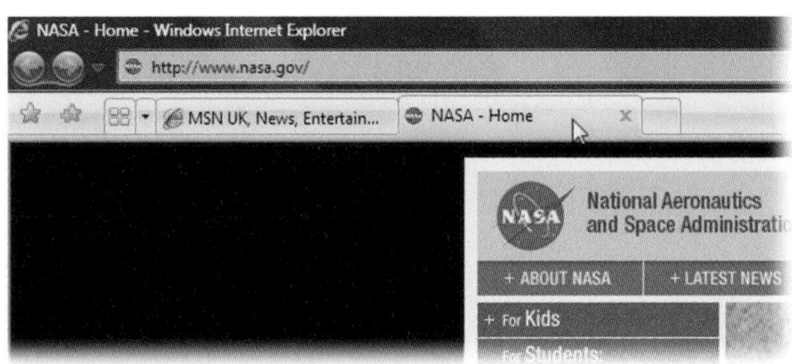

5 KEEPING FAVORITES OPEN

● Alternatively, you can keep the Favorites menu open. Click the star button to open the menu, and then click once on the small button on the right with the green arrow on it.

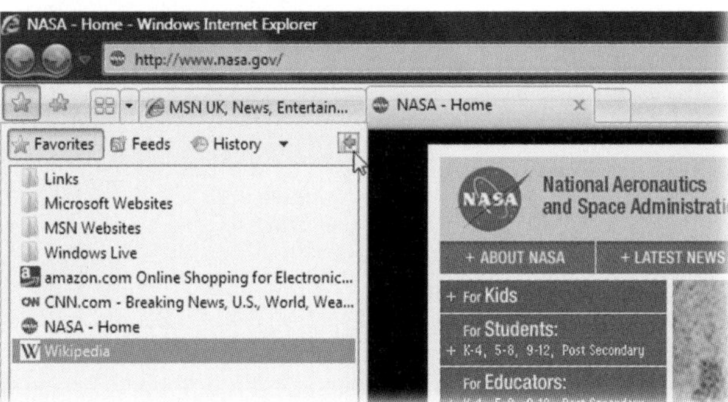

● This now pins the Favorites menu open until you unpin it again by clicking the "x" that has taken the place of the little green arrow. This is useful, especially on a wide-screen monitor that has plenty of width to play with.
● To prove it won't close, switch back to the other open website by clicking on the other tab.

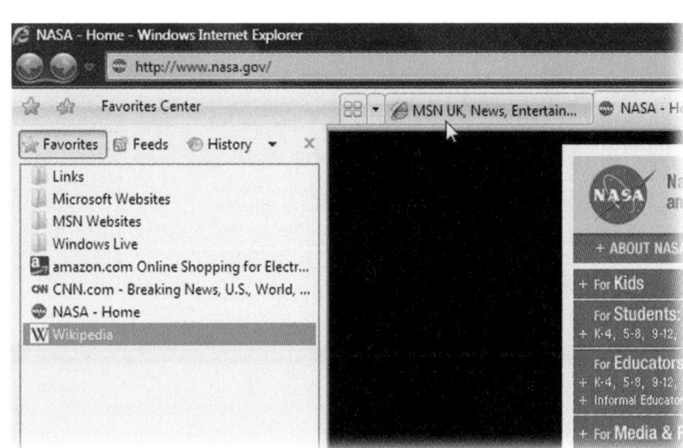

● Here's the original webpage, but this time the Favorites menu has remained open, so you can have immediate access to it.

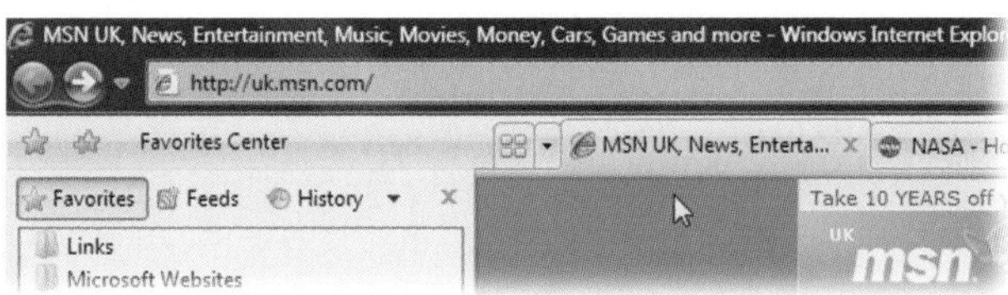

FINDING WEBSITES

We've looked at how you can jump straight to a website if you know its address or are prepared to have a guess. However, what happens when you don't know exactly what you're looking for, or are after something that has many different possible interpretations? That's when you need some help from a search engine.

1 SEARCHING WITH LIVE SEARCH

● You can often find what you're looking for by using the search feature that's built into Internet Explorer. It's called **Live Search** and it sits in a little box at the top right-hand corner of the browser window.

● In order to find anything, you have to tell Live Search what you're looking for by typing in a search term, so start by clicking in the empty Live Search box.
● The box goes blank, and you have a flashing insertion point.

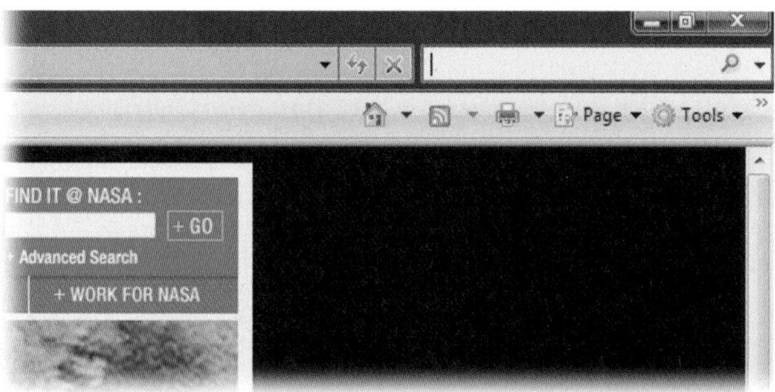

● Type in the word **Colorado** and then slide the cursor along to the magnifying glass icon.
● Click on this, and Live Search sets off and to find websites whose content corresponds with whatever you've typed into the box.

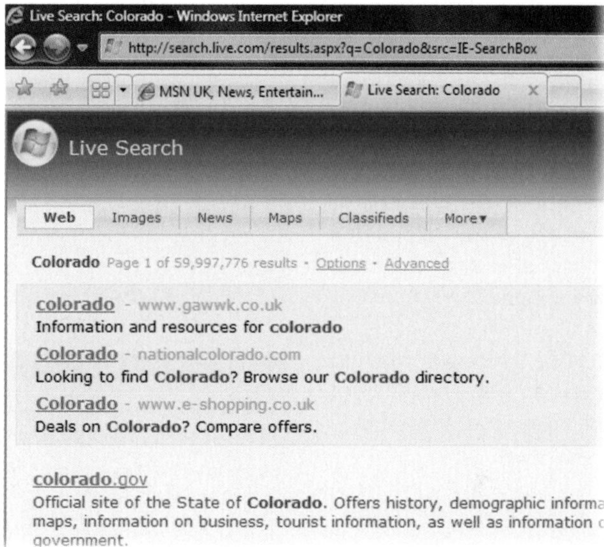

- After a few seconds (or longer, depending on the speed of your Internet connection) Live Search returns a list of results.
- In this example, Live Search tells us it managed to find nearly *60 million* websites with information related to Colorado.
- Each entry in the list has a title, a web address, and a brief summary describing what's on the site.
- Above the main list, in a tint panel, you will see a short list of commercially sponsored results.

2 OPENING A FOUND WEBSITE

- The first website in the main list looks a good bet, so we'll click on that.

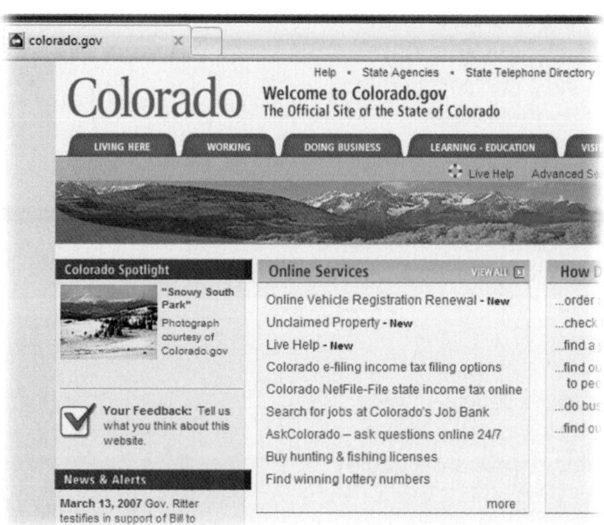

- The **.gov** suffix tells it's probably an official site and, sure enough, the state website for Colorado opens in your browser.
- You can start to explore it by using the links and other navigational tools we've already looked at.
- If it turns out not to be the website you're after, just click the Back button and try another of the results.

119 Back and Forward

3 CHANGING TO GOOGLE SEARCH

● There are alternatives to the Live Search tool we just used, so let's look at the most famous–Google ☐.
● Click on the arrow to the right of the magnifying glass tool to open the drop-down menu.

● Slide the cursor down the menu and left click once on the **Find More Providers** menu item.

● The Microsoft webpage that opens lists all kinds of different search engines and directories.
● The ones in the left-hand column are general web search providers, and they include the most popular of these–Google.

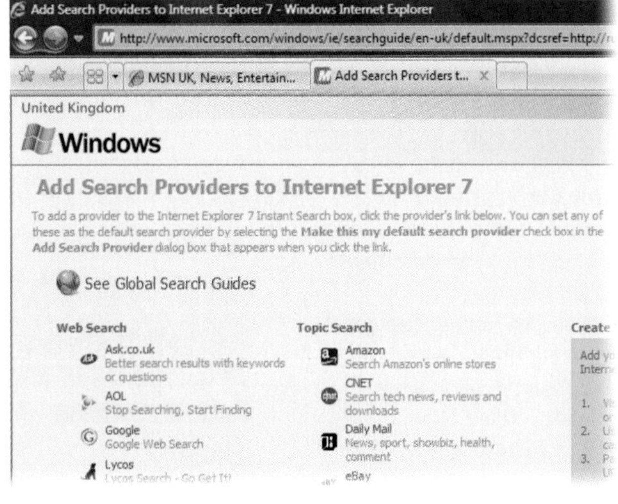

● Move the cursor over to the entry for Google and, when it turns into a pointing hand, click it once with the left mouse button.

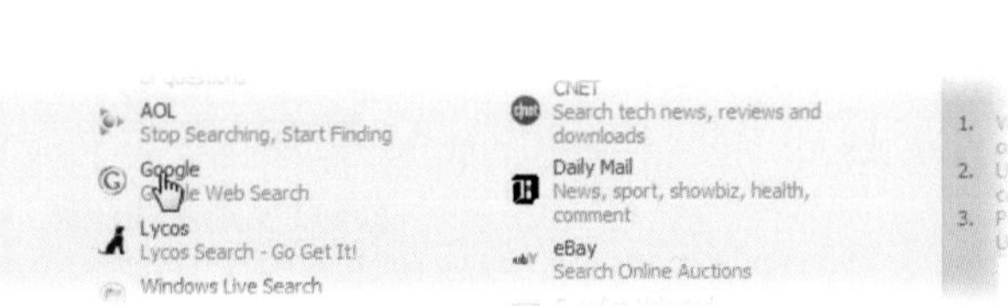

☐ 148 **www.Google.com**

- Windows pops up a dialog box asking you if you want to make Google your default search provider.
- Click in the empty box with the left mouse button to put a tick there.

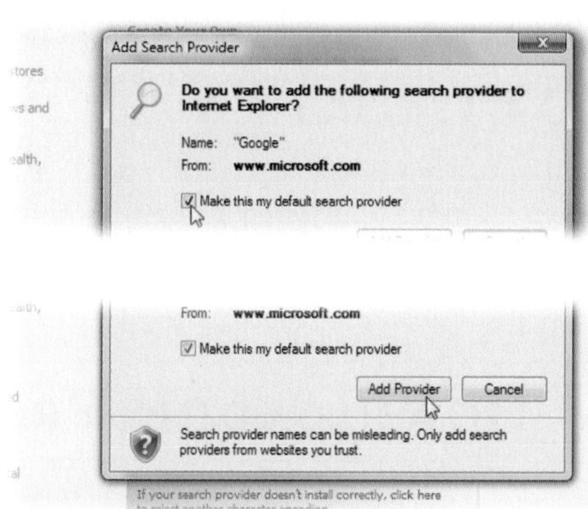

- To confirm that you actually want to make Google your default search provider, click the **Add Provider** button at the bottom of the dialog box.

4 USING GOOGLE SEARCH

- Click on the magnifying glass, and the search is now made by Google instead of Microsoft's Live Search.

- And here is the first page of results, this time as found by Google. Again, the search engine lists the most likely results at the top.
- You can see that **colorado .gov** is again at the top, and the site name has changed from blue to purple, indicating that Internet Explorer knows we have already visited the site.

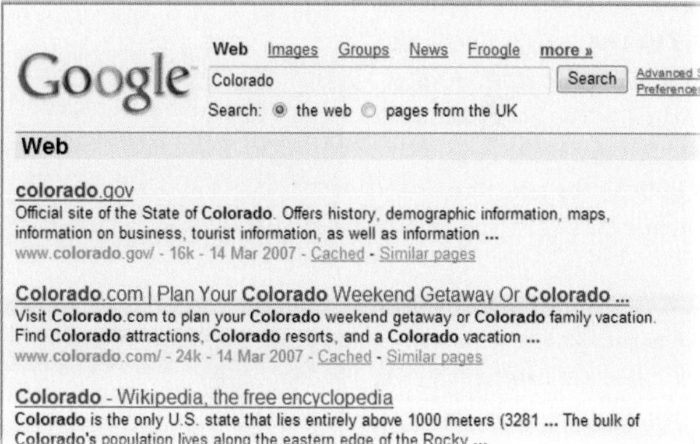

- On the right-hand side of the window, Google tells us that it found 177 million results in four hundredths of a second!

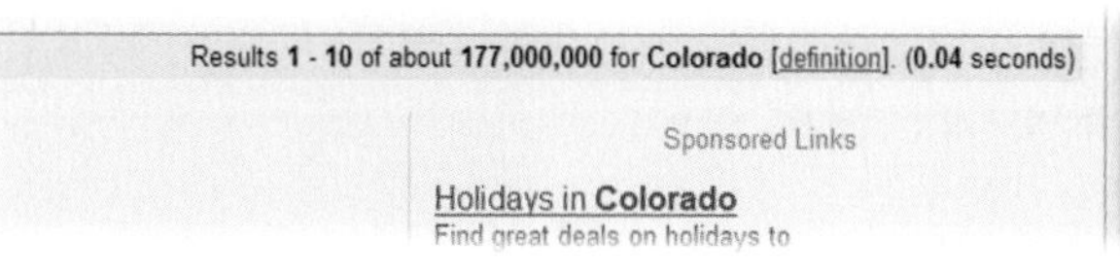

Security Features

Sadly, the web has its unpleasant side. Fortunately, Internet Explorer includes a number of features that offer some protection against unsafe downloads, irritating pop-ups, and rip-off sites.

Downloading Programs

Most programs used to come on CDs that you installed at home, but many are now available to download from the Internet. When Internet Explorer detects something it feels is suspicious, it will tell you by displaying a message in the Information Bar. By default, it plays safe by warning you when you're about to download a program, and it tries to let you know exactly what you're installing.

- We'll start by trying to download a program that we want to install. We know the site address, so we'll go to it using the Address Bar at the top of the window.
- Click there once to highlight the text that's already there.

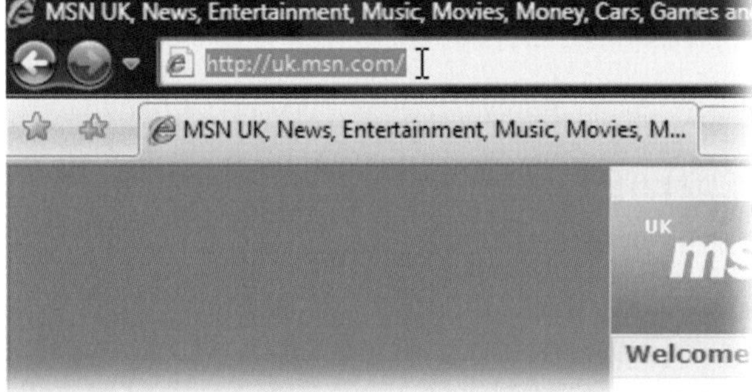

- Into the address line type **www.picasa.com**. This is the name of a free program from the people behind Google, and it makes a great job of tidying up and organizing digital photos.
- Press Enter to display the Picasa website.

- Here's the Picasa website, which explains a bit about the program itself and what it can do.
- In order to use Picasa you must download it to your PC and then set it up.
- The first thing to do is click on the **Download Picasa** link with the left mouse button, like this.

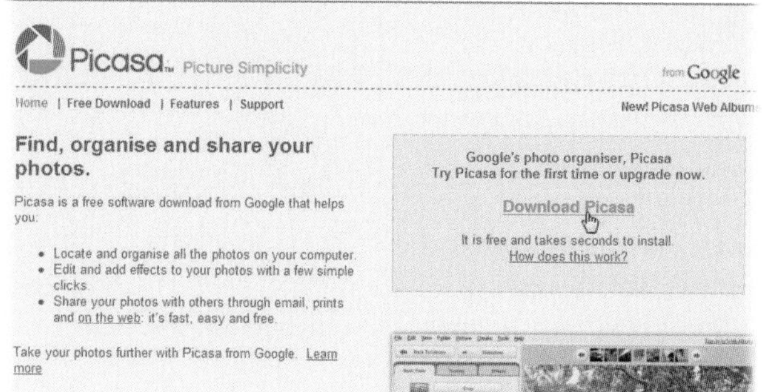

2 INFORMATION BAR WARNING

- Internet Explorer jumps into action immediately and displays a dialog box drawing your attention to the **Information Bar** at the top of the screen, which is alerting you to something.
- Click the **Close** button.

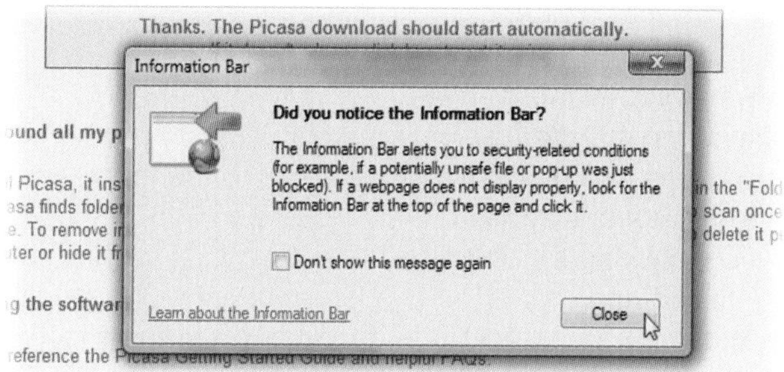

3 EXAMINING THE BAR

- The Information Bar is a little notification strip that appears above the main browser window and displays a message every time Internet Explorer thinks a website might be up to something suspicious.
- In this instance it's displaying the following:

To help protect your security, Internet Explorer blocked this site from downloading files to your computer. Click here for options....

- When you first start to use Internet Explorer you'll get a lot of messages like this. That's partly because it's set up to be safe rather than sorry, and partly because it can't yet tell the difference between a program that you've asked for and is perfectly safe and one that you haven't asked for and is trying to install itself sneakily when you're not looking in order to damage your PC or collect information about you.
- Click the Information Bar to continue.

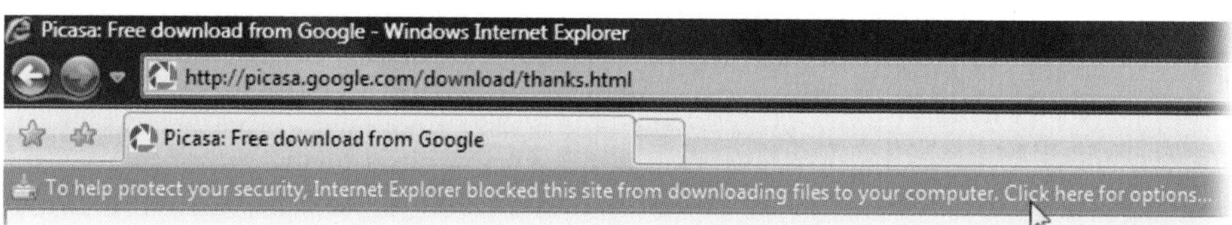

4 INFORMATION BAR MENU

- Windows displays a menu that caters to all levels of experience.
- If you know what you're doing, you can just click the **Download File** option.
- To find out more, click on **What's the Risk?**.

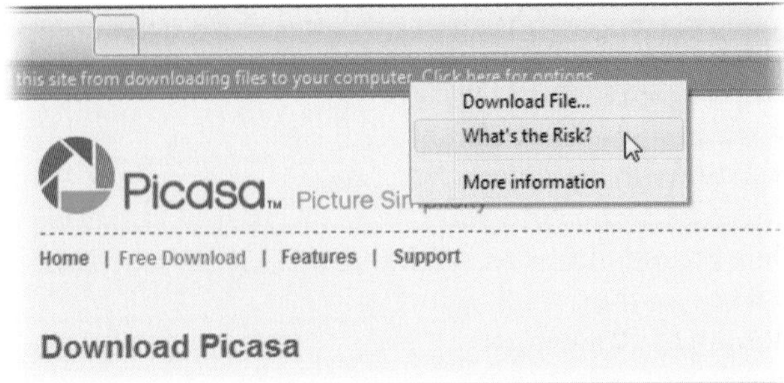

5 GETTING HELP AND SUPPORT

- This Help and Support window appears. Windows help is context-sensitive, so everything here is worth reading as it specifically covers blocking files from downloading.
- When you've finished reading, click the little "x" at the top right-hand corner to close the window.

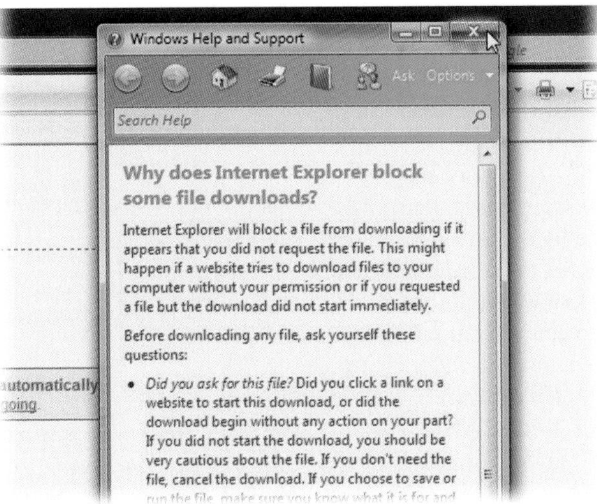

6 DOWNLOADING THE PROGRAM

- We've returned to the main browser window.
- Having read through the Help window, and knowing that Picasa comes from a reputable source (Google), we intend to proceed.
- Click the Information Bar again with the left mouse button and, when the menu appears, choose **Download File**.

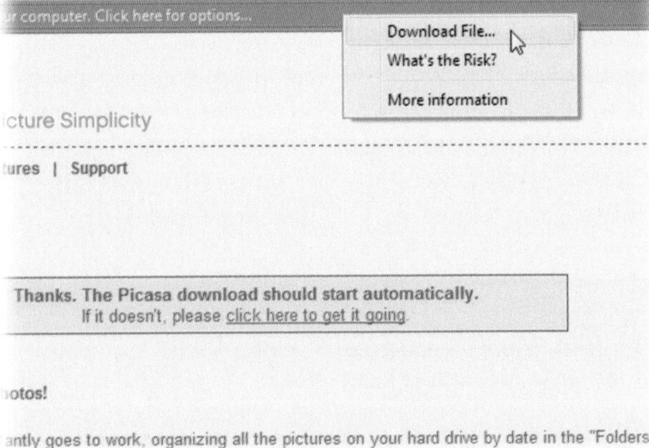

- Windows displays the **File Download - Security Warning** dialog box.
- This asks you if you want to **Run**, **Save**, or **Cancel** the download. (It also repeats the warning about the potential dangers of downloading files.)
- Click the **Save** button.

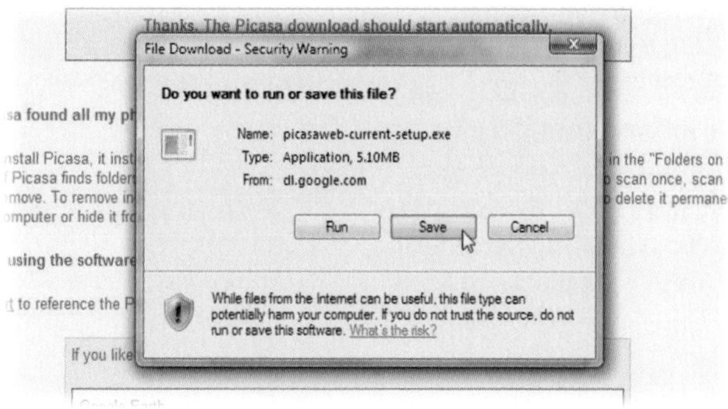

- Having told Windows that you want to save the file, it now needs to know where you want to save it.
- By default, Windows likes to keep all your downloads in the same place to make them easier to keep track of, so unless you have a specific reason for doing so, you shouldn't change any of the settings here.
- Click the **Save** button to begin downloading the file.

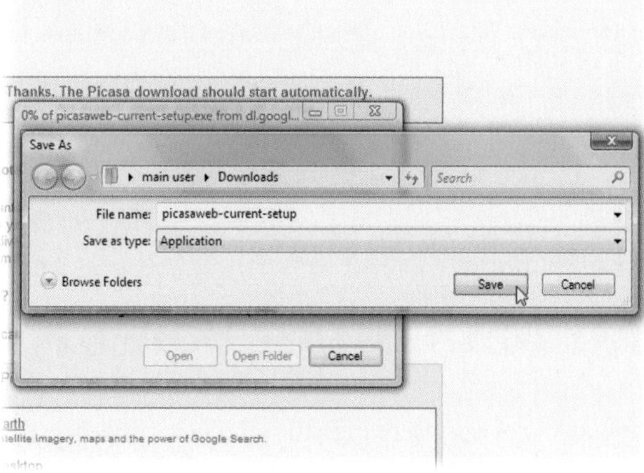

- After some behind-the-scenes activity, Windows begins the download. If you have a fast connection like this one, the program will be copied to your PC in a few minutes.
- You can track how the download is coming along by following the green progress bar as it travels from left to right across the dialog box.

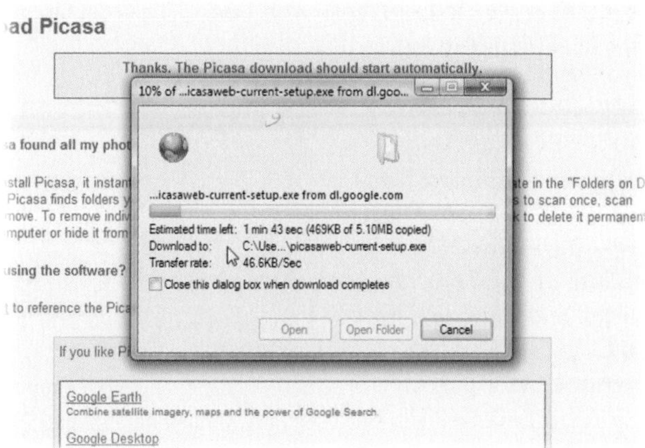

● When Windows has finished downloading the file it will display the **Download complete** dialog box and the green progress bar will run all the way over to the right. Click the **Close** button to finish the process.

PROGRAM INSTALLATION

Once a program has been downloaded to your PC you still need to install it before you can actually use it. In this section we are concerned only with Internet Explorer's security features, and do not cover installation, but details of how to install Picasa can be found in Chapter 7, Enjoying Your Photos .

MANAGING POP-UP WINDOWS

Some websites use annoying little windows called pop-ups that appear on screen while a webpage is open. Some of these promote products and services or invite you take part in surveys and competitions. Other websites use pop-ups as important information and navigation tools. Internet Explorer can help you manage pop-ups so you get to see the ones you want and can avoid the ones you don't.

OPENING A WEBSITE WITH POP-UPS

● As an example, we'll go to a website we know uses pop-up windows.

● Click on the Favorites button and then click once on CNN to open that website's home page .

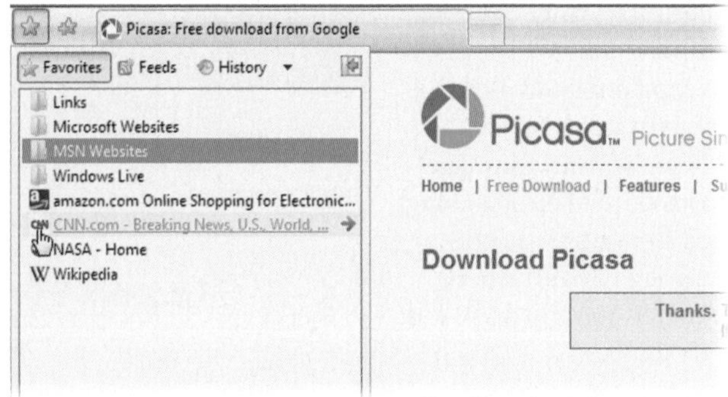

310 Enjoying Your Photos

● As soon as the page loads, Windows displays the **Information Bar** dialog box. Click the **Close** button.

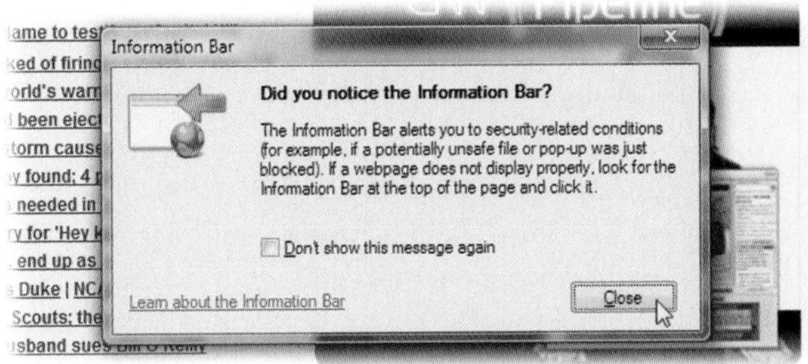

THE POP-UP HAS BEEN BLOCKED

● The Information Bar tells you the pop-up has been blocked. This is Internet Explorer's default position, erring on the side of safety.

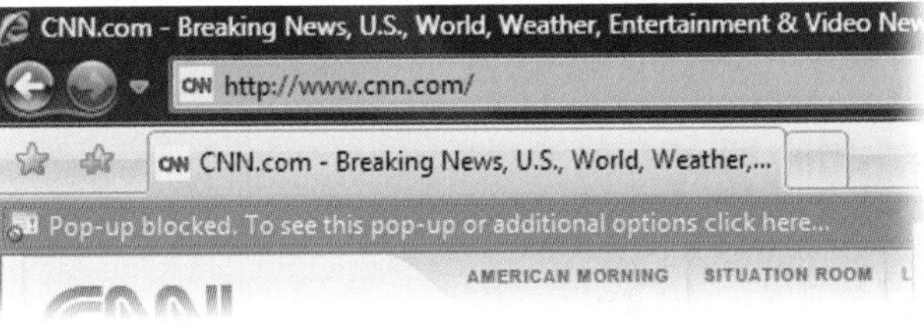

ALLOWING POP-UPS TEMPORARILY

● Click on the Information Bar with the left mouse button to open the menu and choose to **Temporarily Allow Pop-ups**. This gives you a chance to check out that everything's OK.

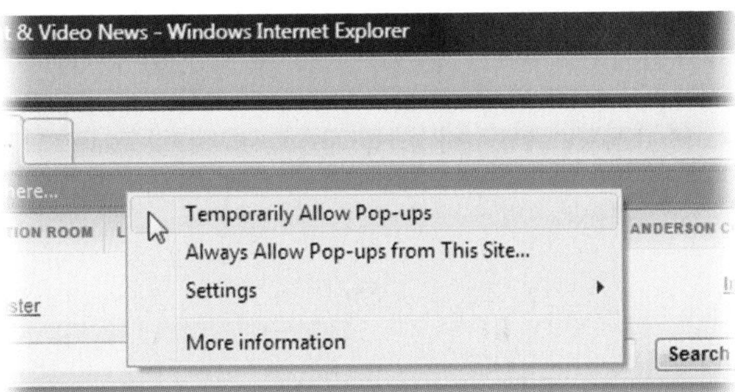

VIEWING THE POP-UP

● The website immediately displays a pop-up window that wasn't visible before.

● In this case, it's perfectly harmless–indeed, it's helpful–but in many cases, pop-ups like this are just plain annoying and the web browser's ability to hide them is very welcome.

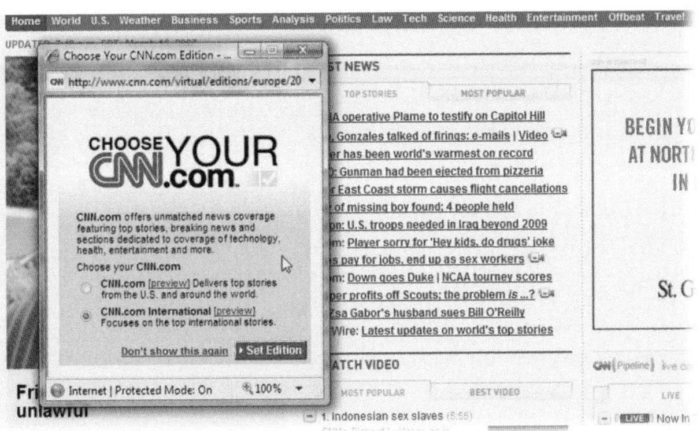

PHISHING WEBSITES

In recent years a phenomenon known as "phishing" or "spoofing" has become more common. This is when a website (and sometimes an e-mail message) pretends to be something it isn't, in order to extract private information from you or trick you into downloading a program that will secretly spy on your PC's activities, gathering information about the sites you visit; some can even tell what you're typing! Internet Explorer comes with a Phishing Filter that can help with this.

1 OPENING THE TOOLS MENU

- For this example it doesn't matter which website you're looking at, but to follow this sequence exactly, click the Back button until you're looking at the Picasa website.
- Now move the cursor up to the **Tools** button and click there once with the left mouse button.

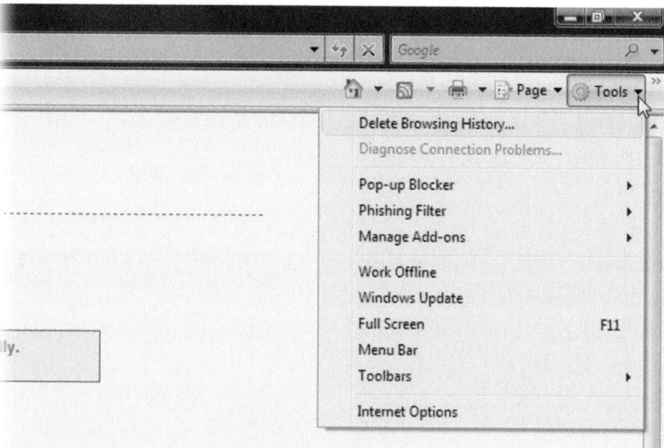

2 CHOOSING THE PHISHING FILTER

- Move the cursor down the menu to the **Phishing Filter** entry and let it hover there for a second.
- The small arrow at the end of the bar indicates that there's a sub-menu, and after a moment it opens automatically.

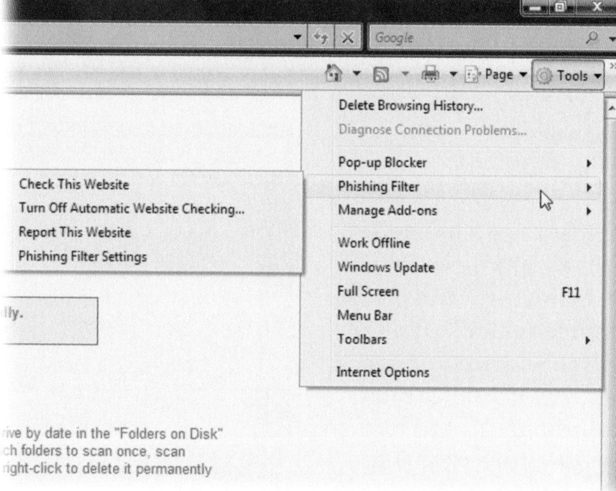

3 CHECKING THE WEBSITE

- By default, Internet Explorer automatically checks each website you visit against a list of those it knows to be suspect.
- However, if you have your own suspicions, you can check for yourself by clicking the **Check This Website** menu option with the left mouse button.

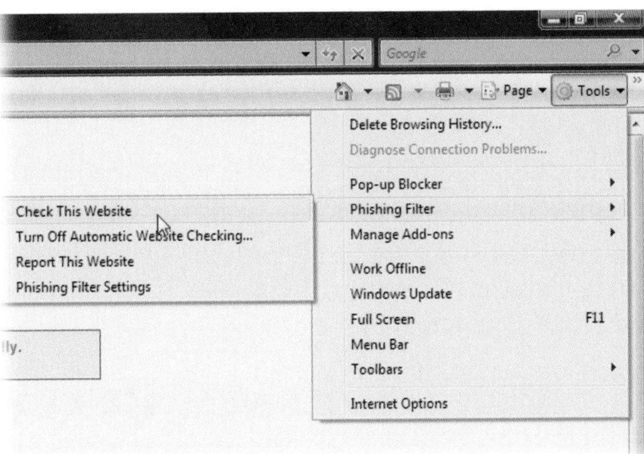

- Internet Explorer then displays a dialog box asking you if you want to have the current site checked against a list of known phishing websites. Sharing your suspicions like this is completely anonymous.
- Click **OK** to send details of the website to Microsoft for checking.

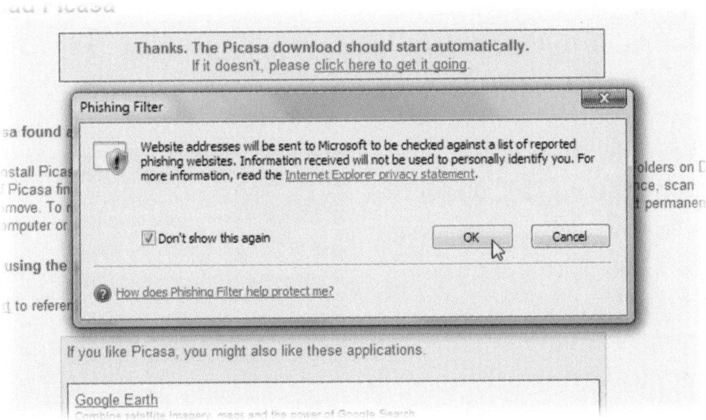

4 REPORTING BACK ON THE WEBSITE

- Of course, the Picasa site is perfectly legitimate, so Microsoft returns a message saying it can't find it on the list of suspicious websites.
- To find out more about how this feature works click the **How does Phishing Filter help protect me?** link at the bottom of the box.
- Otherwise, click **OK** to close the dialog box.

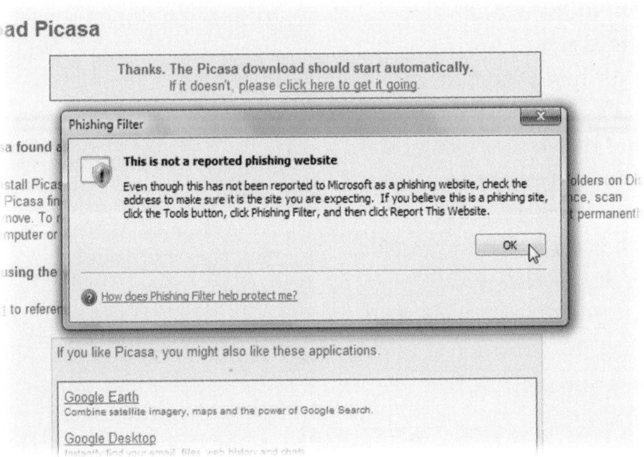

Browser Plug-ins

Website developers often use additional technology in their pages that requires you to download and install extra programs called plug-ins. In this section we'll look at a typical example.

Flash Player

Flash is one of the most commonly used technologies on the web, and it's highly likely that, sooner rather than later, you'll come across a site that uses it to run onscreen animations. Fortunately, it's what web experts call a "mature" product–one that is tried and tested–and therefore it's easy and safe to find, install, and use.

OPENING A SITE REQUIRING FLASH

- Not all websites require the Flash Player, which is a program used mainly to create animations and interactive menus, but we'll open one that does.
- Click once in the address line at the top of the browser window to highlight what's there.

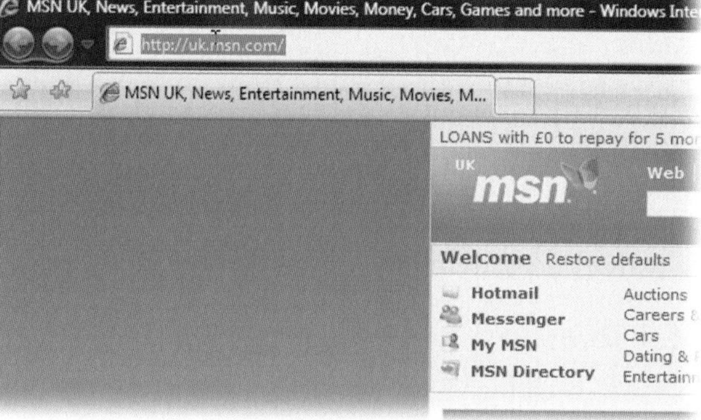

- Type the address of the website we want to visit into the address line. It's **www.nationalgeographic.com**–the site of the internationally renowned magazine and TV channel.
- Then press Enter.

WHEN A WEBSITE REQUIRES FLASH

- When a website uses a Flash animation, it checks to see if your web browser already has the necessary plug-in. If it can't find the plug-in, it displays a message to alert you.
- Here, the message is subtle, but it's there, together with a button offering a free download of Flash Player.
- Left click once on the button to get Flash Player.

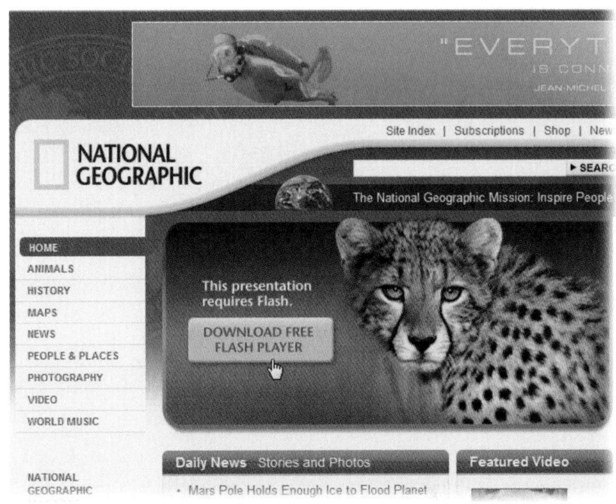

DOWNLOADING FLASH PLAYER

- Typically, you'll now see another smaller window open in your web browser displaying the website of Adobe, the company that makes Flash Player.
- Move your cursor over the **Download now** button and click it once with the left mouse button.

VISITING THE DOWNLOAD CENTER

- This takes you to another part of the Adobe website.
- Click the **Download Now** button.

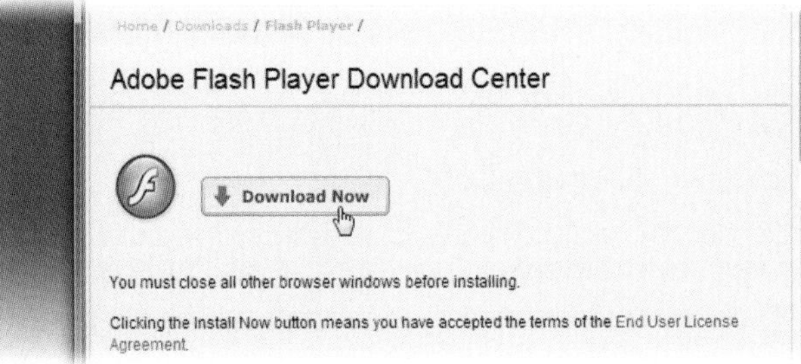

THE INFORMATION BAR DIALOG

- You're about to download a program, so Internet Explorer gets concerned and displays a dialog box directing us to the Information Bar.
- Proceed by clicking the **Close** button.

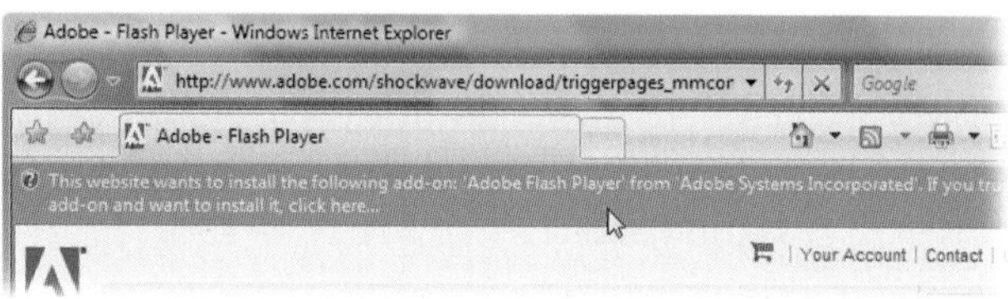

- Move the cursor up to the Information Bar and then click there once with the left mouse button. This allows the installation process to continue.

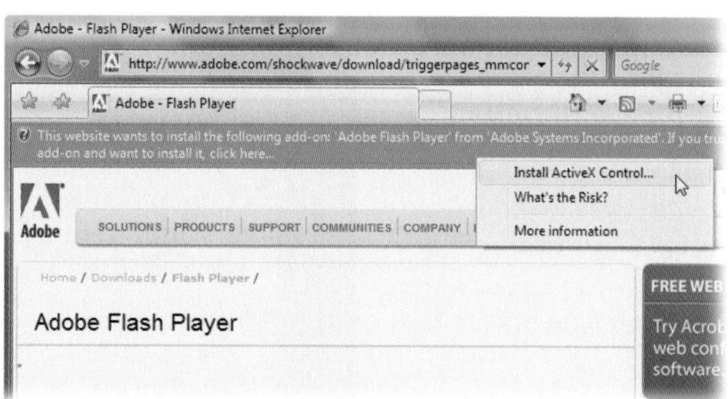

- When you click the Information Bar, Internet Explorer opens a menu.
- Left click once on the first menu item–**Install ActiveX Control**. (This sounds very serious, but you're simply telling Internet Explorer to go ahead and download the free Flash Player.)

USER ACCOUNT CONTROL DIALOG

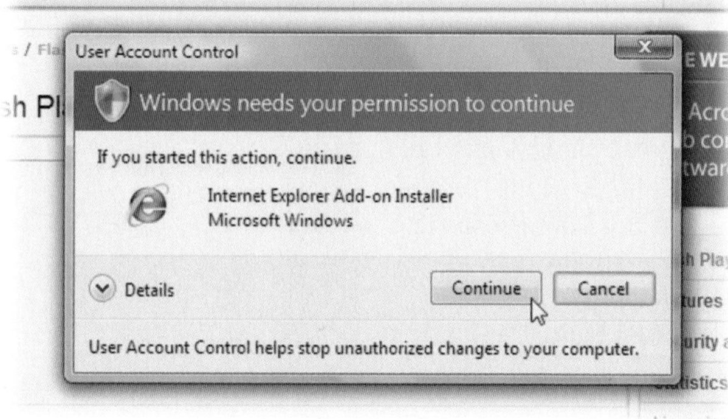

- Windows then displays the **User Account Control** dialog box. This appears every time you try to do anything that could fundamentally change your Windows setup.
- Click the **Continue** button to accept the download and proceed.

SECURITY WARNING

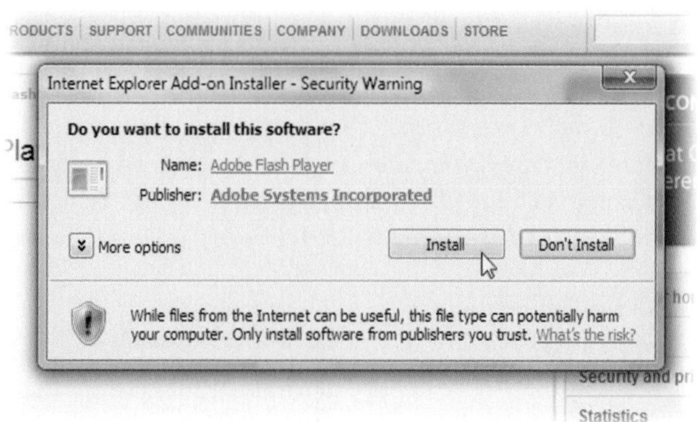

- Those dialog boxes keep on coming. This one–the **Add-on Installer Security Warning** dialog–asks if you really want to install the new software.
- We're confident that the Flash Player won't harm our system, so we're going to click the **Install** button.

DOWNLOADING AND INSTALLING

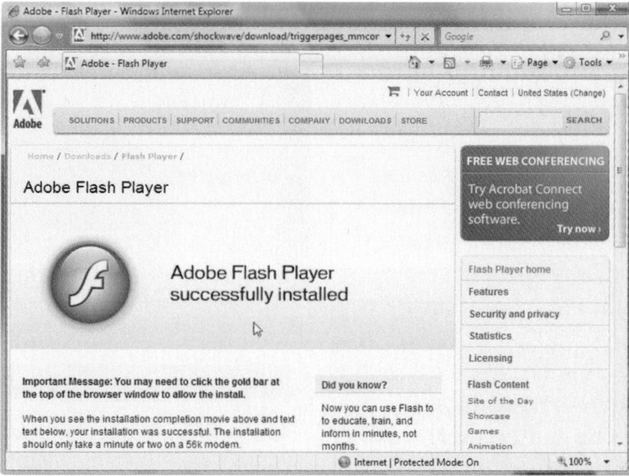

- The program downloads and installs itself. You don't have to do anything; it all happens behind the scenes. This is typical of the way browser plug-ins such as Flash Player install themselves.
- When it's done, an onscreen animation tells you **Adobe Flash Player successfully installed**.

TOO MUCH FLASH?

Sometimes a website overdoses on Flash and slows everything up. Fortunately, like all extras for Internet Explorer, Flash can be turned on or off to suit you. With Internet Explorer loaded, click the **Tools** button and choose **Managing Add-ons** and then **Enable or Disable Add-ons**. In the **Manage Add-ons** dialog, highlight **Shockwave Flash Object** and then click the **Disable** radio button. Click **OK** to confirm your choice. You can switch Flash back on by re-enabling it from the same dialog box.

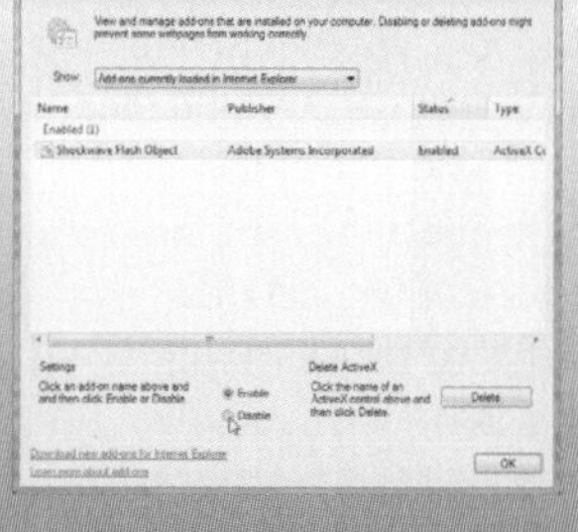

USING FLASH PLAYER

Once it's installed, you rarely have to do anything to use the Flash Player. Internet Explorer detects that a website uses Flash and loads the player. The Flash part of the site detects that the player is present and starts playing. It's as simple as that.

CLOSING THE TOP WINDOW

● Close the Adobe webpage by clicking the "x" at its top right-hand corner.

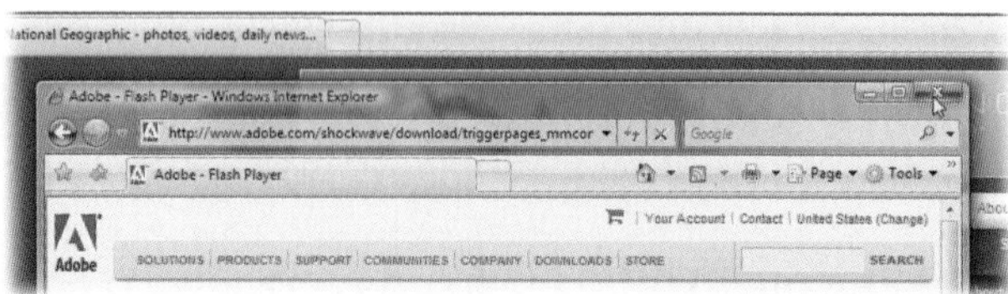

REFRESHING THE WEBSITE

● Back at the original website, you can see that it's still asking you to download the Flash Player - that's because it doesn't realize you've already done it.

● To solve this, click on the Refresh button, the double arrow button to the right of the address line, to reload the National Geographic website into your browser.

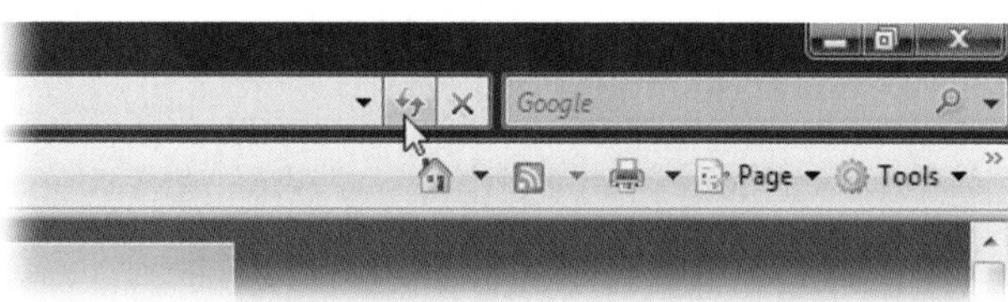

● Here's the website after it's been refreshed. Now it recognizes we've installed the Flash Player and it loads in the animation. The static image of a cheetah is replaced by a slide show.

● Having downloaded Flash Player, your browser will run Flash animations on the websites you visit.

PLUG-INS YOU MAY ALSO NEED

QUICKTIME

Developed by Apple, this is widely used by websites for playing back video. It's particularly popular with movie companies, and many trailers that you find on the web will require QuickTime in order to play them back. A free version can be downloaded from: **www.quicktime.com**

REALPLAYER

Some media companies that broadcast radio shows or play video clips on their websites use a technology from a company called RealNetworks. What's clever about the RealPlayer is that instead of getting you to download a video or sound file and then play it when it's stored on your PC, it keeps the content on the web server and streams it from there. This benefits the provider because it keeps the content (which is usually copyrighted) secure, and it benefits the user because the content starts playing almost straight away–you don't have to wait to download it.
The player program is free from: **www.real.com**

ZIP

What started life as a specific program–PKZIP–has become a generic term for compressing and decompressing files. "Zipping" has a number of advantages. Imagine you have 10 photos that you want to download to your PC. Ordinarily, you'd have to get each one separately and wait for it to download. If those photos have been compressed into a single archive they've been made smaller (which makes them quicker to download) and combined into a single file (which means you only have to download one thing). All you then need is something on your PC that can extract the compressed photos from the file and re-instate them as separate individual photos you can look at. Windows Vista has this feature built in, so if you need to download a file that has a name like FILE. ZIP, then you can go ahead. There are free programs that have more features that you may find useful at a later stage.
Get a free Zip program from: **www.7-zip.org**

ADOBE READER

So that you can see complex documents without having the software that created them, website creators use special software to prepare the documents so that you can read them using Adobe Reader.
It's a very useful free program that you'll use time and time again.
Go to: **www.adobe.com**

ADOBE SHOCKWAVE

Originally, Shockwave served much the same purpose as Flash (see elsewhere on this page) but now it has come to be used more for creating games that you can run directly from websites.
Get it from: **www.adobe.com/products/**

10 Great Sites

It's not easy to pick 10 sites from the millions on the web, but these sum up the diversity that exists–from professional and commercial sites to content generated by ordinary PC users.

The Pick of the Web

There are literally millions of websites, but now and again one comes along that changes the way people use or experience the web and creates a whole new genre or business that others then follow. Here's our selection of 10 of the very finest websites that you can find. We've picked them from various categories to give you a broad sense of what's on offer. Some are commercial, some are quirky, some you may have heard of, others you won't have come across, but all are worth visiting.

PUTTING TOGETHER THE TOP 10

- We wanted to highlight particular areas in our choice, so we have included:
- Commercial sites such as Amazon and eBay, both enormously successful international operations that have transformed buying and selling.
- Co-operative sites such as Wikipedia and VideoJug, where ordinary people from all over the world are contributing both their academic knowledge and their practical experience to benefit others.
- Communal sites such as YouTube and Flickr, where individuals can post videos and photos of their day-to-day lives, as well as special events, holidays, and so on.
- Cool sites with cutting edge technology, either in an obvious way such as Microsoft's 3D aerial mapping or in a behind-the-scenes way that we almost take for granted, like Google's brilliant searching.

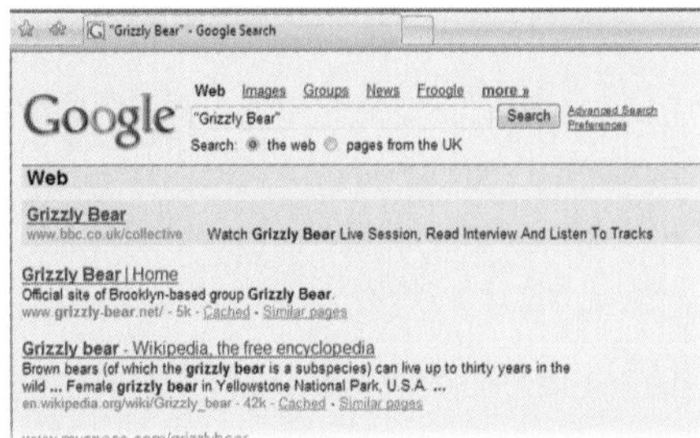

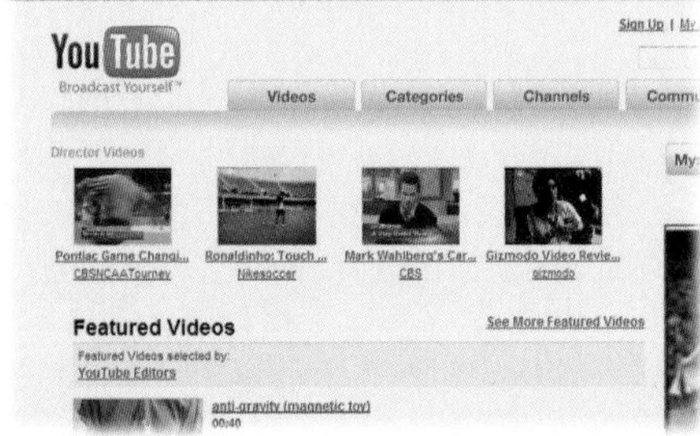

home | pay | register | site map
Start new search
Buy
Sell
My eBay
Community
Help
Hello! Sign in/out.
Whatever it is...you can get it on
Search eBay.com | Search eBay Express
"grizzly bear"
All Categories
Search
Specialty Sites
eBay Express
eBay Motors
eBay Stores
eBay Business
Half.com
Apartments on Rent.com
StubHub Tickets
Put More Spring
In Your Step
Espadrilles
It's FREE!

Hello. Sign in to get personalized recommendations. New customer? Start here
Shopping from the UK?
Visit
amazon.co.uk
The Secret Hardcover by Rhonda Byrne

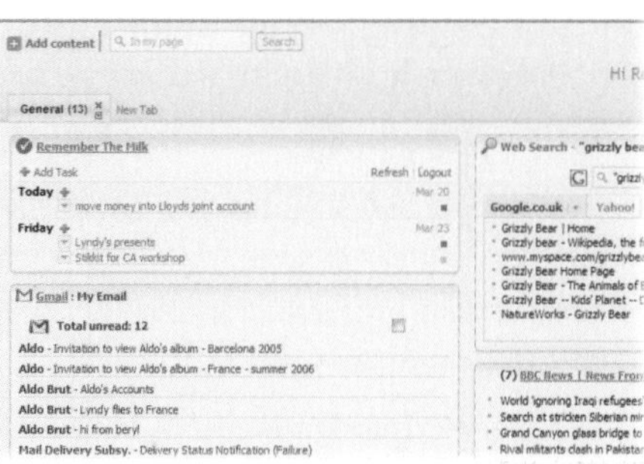
Add content
General (13)
New Tab
Remember The Milk
Add Task
Refresh | Logout
Today
move money into Lloyds joint account
Friday
Lyndy's presents
Stikkit for CA workshop
Web Search
Google.co.uk
Yahoo!
Grizzly Bear | Home
Grizzly Bear Home Page
NatureWorks - Grizzly Bear
Gmail : My Email
Total unread: 12
Aldo - Invitation to view Aldo's album - Barcelona 2005
Aldo - Invitation to view Aldo's album - France - summer 2006
Aldo Brut - Aldo's Accounts
Aldo Brut - Lyndy flies to France
Aldo Brut - hi from beryl
Mail Delivery Subsy. - Delivery Status Notification (Failure)

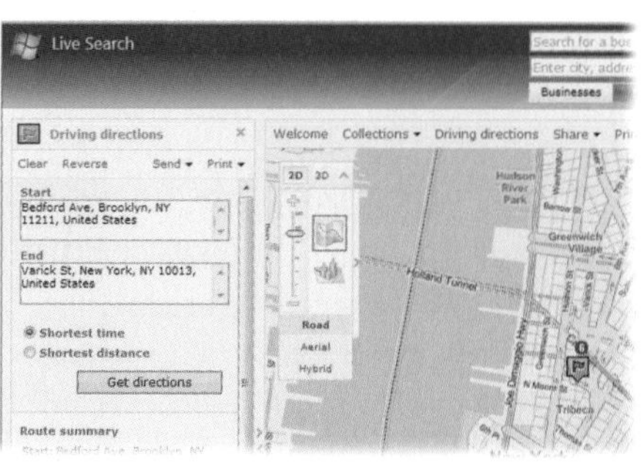
Live Search
Businesses
Driving directions
Clear
Reverse
Send
Print
Start
Bedford Ave, Brooklyn, NY 11211, United States
End
Varick St, New York, NY 10013, United States
Shortest time
Shortest distance
Get directions
Route summary
Welcome
Collections
Driving directions
Share
Road
Aerial
Hybrid
Holland Tunnel
Greenwich Village
Tribeca

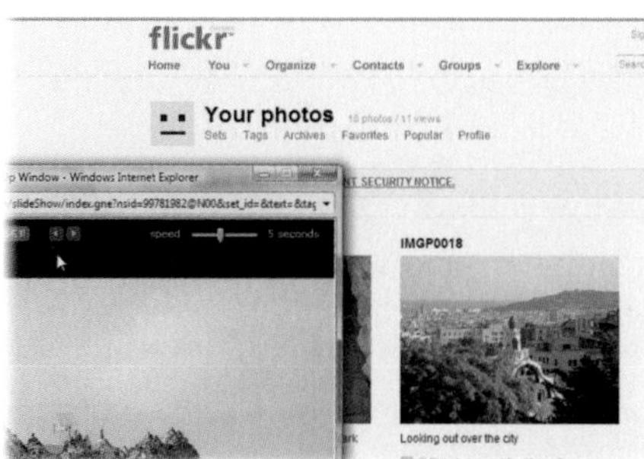
flickr
Home
You
Organize
Contacts
Groups
Explore
Your photos
Sets
Tags
Archives
Favorites
Popular
Profile
IMGP0018
Looking out over the city

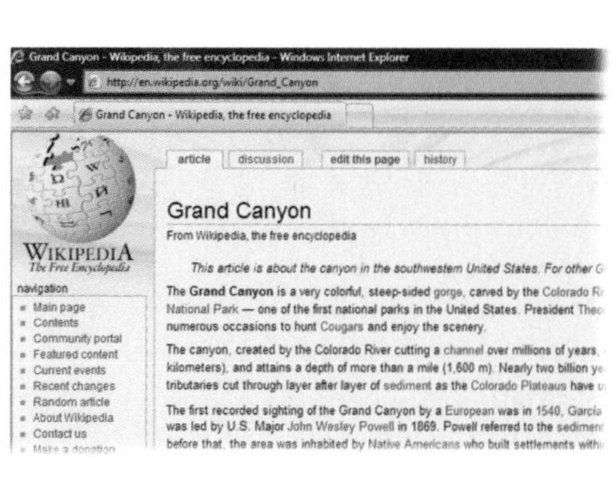
Grand Canyon - Wikipedia, the free encyclopedia - Windows Internet Explorer
http://en.wikipedia.org/wiki/Grand_Canyon
article
discussion
edit this page
history
Grand Canyon
From Wikipedia, the free encyclopedia
WIKIPEDIA
The Free Encyclopedia
navigation
Main page
Contents
Community portal
Featured content
Current events
Recent changes
Random article
About Wikipedia
Contact us

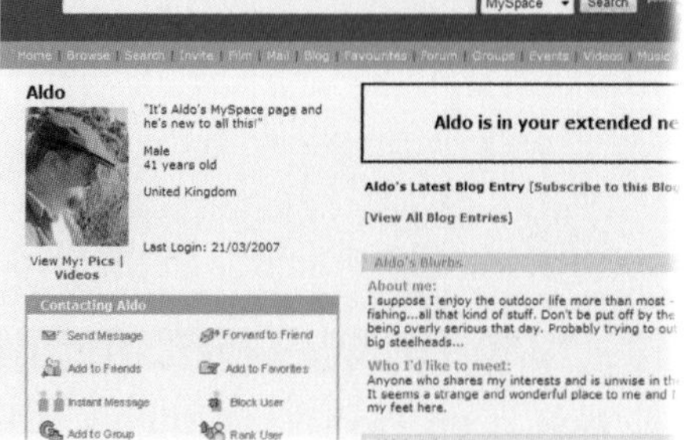
MySpace
Search
Aldo
"It's Aldo's MySpace page and he's new to all this!"
Male
41 years old
United Kingdom
Last Login: 21/03/2007
View My: Pics | Videos
Contacting Aldo
Send Message
Forward to Friend
Add to Friends
Add to Favorites
Instant Message
Block User
Add to Group
Rank User
Aldo is in your extended ne
Aldo's Latest Blog Entry
[View All Blog Entries]
About me:
Who I'd like to meet:

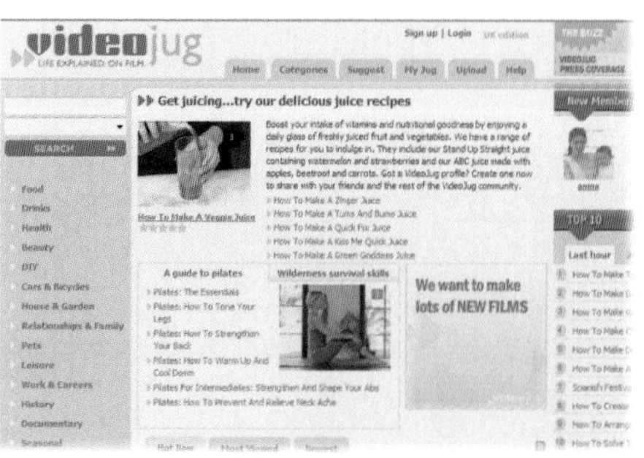
videojug
Get juicing...try our delicious juice recipes
A guide to pilates
Wilderness survival skills
We want to make lots of NEW FILMS

WWW.GOOGLE.COM

Google takes its name from the mathematical term for a one followed by 100 zeroes–a Googol. The reasoning behind the name was to give its many users some idea of the vast amount of information that Google is able to search. Google's simplicity, speed, and superior search features have made it the world's favorite way to find things on the web, and the company behind it has now branched out into online word processing, calendars, spreadsheets, route maps, real time chat, 3D virtual mapping, and much, much more. Using the search term **"Grizzly Bear"**, let's take a look at the features that make Google such a hit with web users.

FEATURES KEY

❶ Search Box
Type whatever you're looking for here in the search box. Using double quotes like this makes Google search for the whole phrase instead of both words individually.

❷ Images Link
Click the Images link and Google will search for pictures of your selection.

❸ Links
These links lead to other Google services, for example, Groups where you can chat to other people about grizzlies, News where you can read news stories about grizzlies, and Froogle where you can shop for grizzly merchandise.

❹ Advanced Search
This link lets you refine your search. For example, you can specify websites in English that have mentioned grizzlies in the last three months.

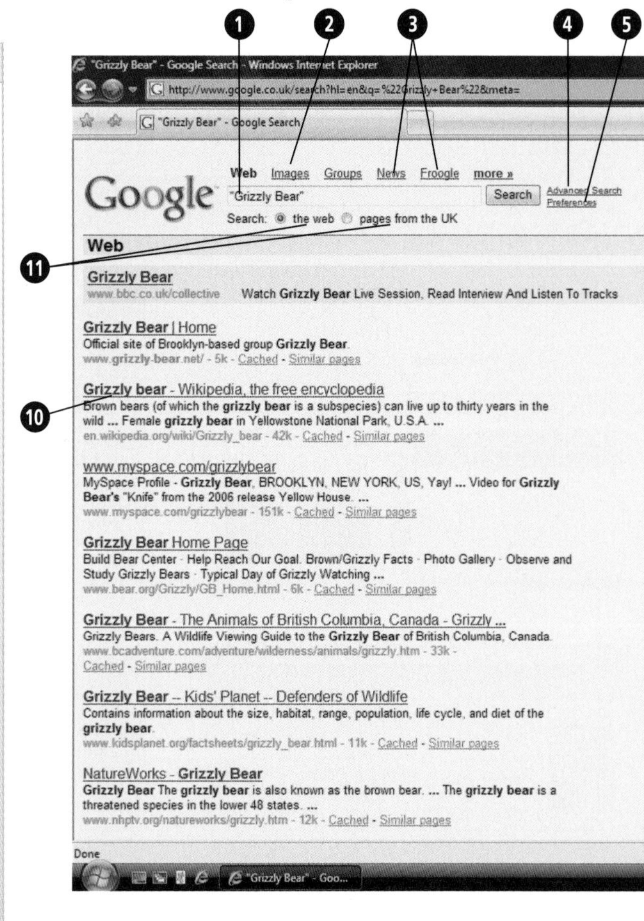

IMAGES

Google now searches more than two billion images, so the chances are that Google will be able to find a picture of your chosen subject. Bear in mind, however, that copyright laws apply–just because you can find an image doesn't mean you can then use it as if it were your own.

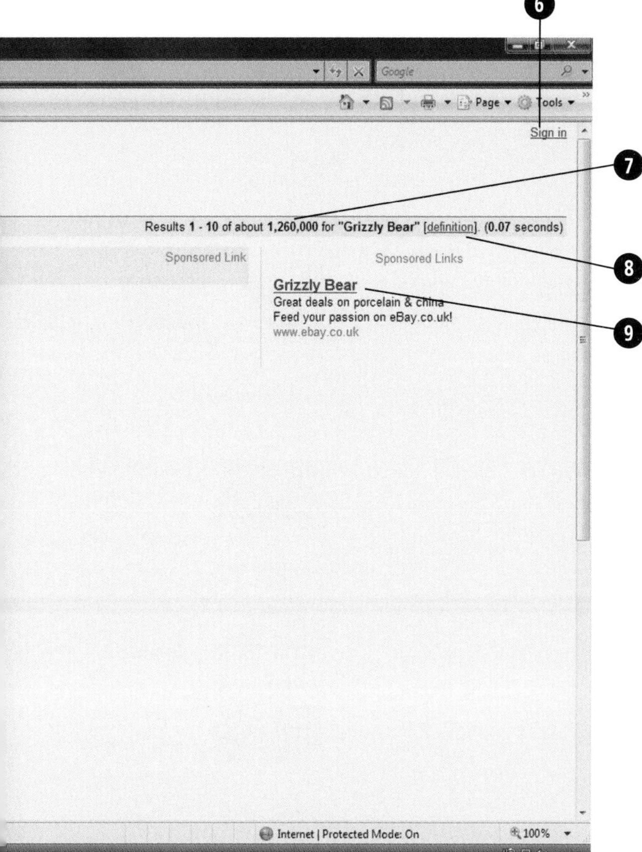

FEATURES KEY

❺ Preferences Link
The Preferences link can be used to personalize your Google page. For example, use it to change the number of results per page it retrieves.

❻ Google Account
To use other Google services, such as e-mail or live chat, you have to create a free Google account. Click on this link to sign into an account.

❼ Search Results
Google tells you how many websites it has matched to your search text. Here it displays the first 10 results for about 1,350,000!

❽ Definition
*Clicking the **definition** link opens another website that offers a range of definitions for your search text.*

❾ Sponsored Link
This is an advert that Google thinks carries a product or information that's relevant to your search.

❿ Results
Google lists the results of your search here and displays a clickable heading that will take you to the site, a brief description, and the address of the website.

⓫ Search Choices
Using these radio buttons, you can choose to search all the web or more local pages.

www.YouTube.com

YouTube lets you upload videos and then store them in its huge computers for free–a simple idea that's turned into a worldwide phenomenon in only a few years. Once loaded onto its computers, YouTube indexes videos in such a way that visitors can find and then watch them as many times as they like–again for free. It's been hit by copyright problems (people have been uploading films and TV shows) but it's the content generated by users that makes YouTube one of our 10 must-see sites. You can also create your own "channels" like a TV station and subscribe to those created by others. This is 21st-century TV at its very best.

FEATURES KEY

❶ Thumbnails
When the YouTube website appears, it shows a selection of video clips that you can play straight away by clicking on the selected thumbnail picture.

❷ Tabs
Click these tabs to browse videos by category–for example Music, or News and Politics–or by channels that, according to YouTube "focus on the latest work of favorite artists or topical themes."

❸ Sign Up
*Click the **Sign Up** link to create a YouTube account. It's free, and you'll need to join in order to upload videos, create playlists of favorite videos, leave comments for others to read, and so on. Click the **My Account** link to review and amend your account details.*

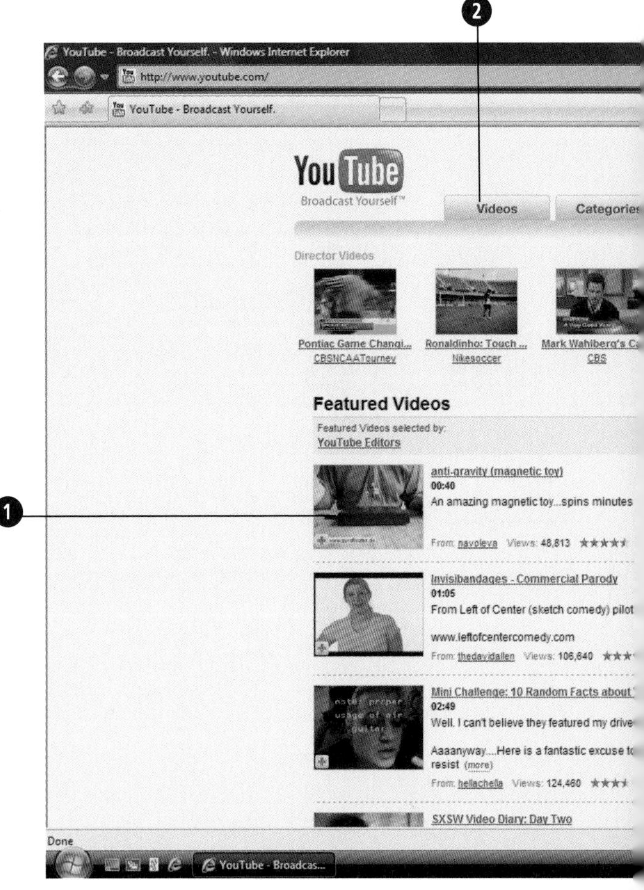

A TYPICAL YOUTUBE VIDEO

Actually there's no such thing. For example, this six-minute video consists of a number of still photos of Noah, a man who took a photo of his own face every day for six years and then strung them together to make a video. In this simple yet powerful video, you'll see him grow older before your eyes.

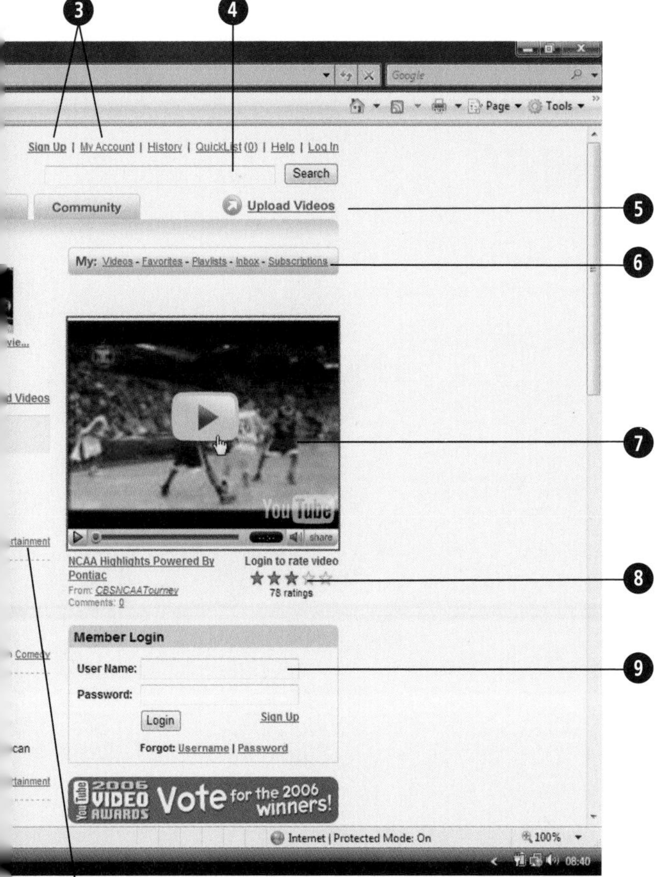

FEATURES KEY

❹ Search
Search for videos here. For example, typing in ***"Grizzly Bear"*** *returns a selection of videos that include real grizzlies as well as a band called Grizzly Bear.*

❺ Upload
Members can upload their own videos to YouTube by clicking this link. You should never upload video unless you own the copyright.

❻ Favorites
Members can click on this toolbar to access their favorite videos, playlists, manage their subscriptions to YouTube channels, etc..

❼ Playback
Click the large arrow in the middle of the video window to play back the video. Use the controls under the window to pause and resume videos.

❽ Ratings
Members can rate videos using a five-star system.

❾ Member Login
Members sign in here by typing in their user name and password.

❿ Category Links
Each featured video comes from a particular category– for example, Entertainment or Comedy. Click on this link to open a page of videos from the selected category.

WWW.EBAY.COM

This is one of the web's biggest success stories, both in terms of the number of people who use the service and the amount of money it makes. The idea is beautifully simple–you post items on the site that you want to sell (anything from computers to houses, teddy bears to CDs); visitors then bid on these items in an auction. Auctions are time-limited and eBay offers various clever ways of bidding that don't require you to sit at your PC all day, trying to outbid other people. Sellers pay a small percentage of the final sale price to eBay, while buyers don't pay any fees. Buyers can give feedback on sellers, so that untrustworthy sellers can be earmarked.

FEATURES KEY

❶ Home, Pay, Register
Home takes you to eBay's front page. Pay takes you to your account to pay for a successful bid. Register takes you to an online form where you can sign up as a member.

❷ My eBay
***My eBay** is where the website stores your settings. Here, you can also watch items for news of the latest bid.*

❸ Community Link
This takes you to a series of webpages where you can join in eBay-related discussions.

❹ Search
Type in a search word to find items for sale.

❺ Live Help
*Click the **Live Help** link and you can find solutions to eBay-related problems by typing your question to a support technician who's waiting to help.*

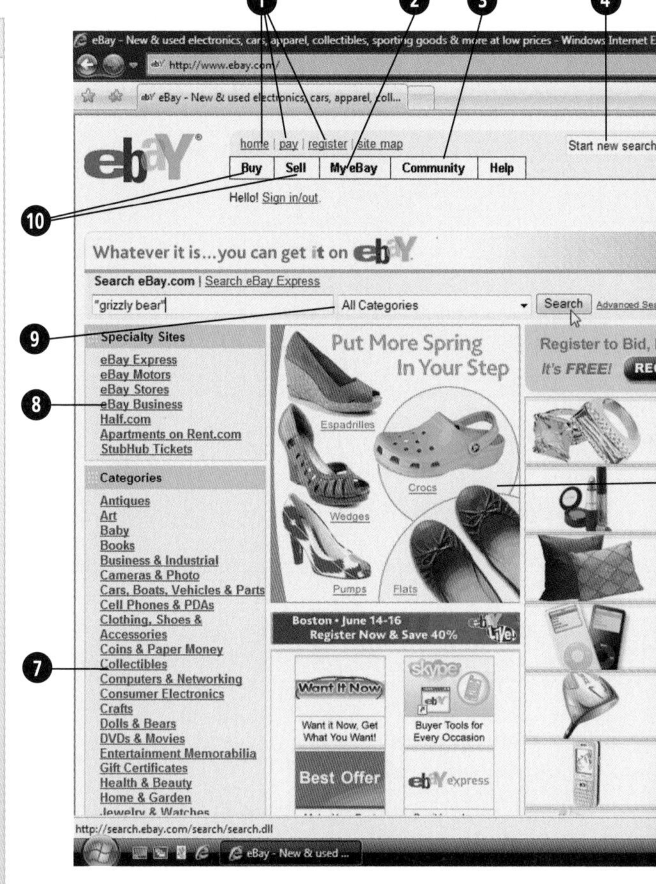

A TYPICAL EBAY AUCTION

Here's an item up for auction on eBay. Most include a photo and display the current bid. Many have a **Buy It Now** price that, if met, ends the auction. There's also a **Watch this item** link; click on this to add the item to your My eBay screen so you can return later to see the current price. Only bid on those items that you're prepared to buy–if you win an auction, you're under an obligation to complete the contract and pay for the item.

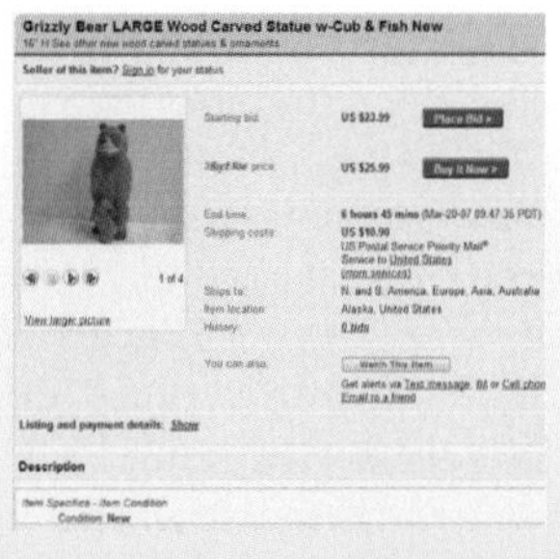

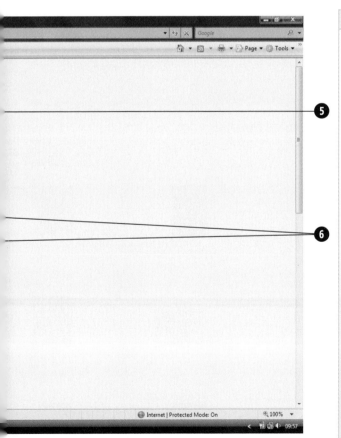

FEATURES KEY

❻ Goods Categories
All of these pictures are links to eBay categories where you'll find goods for sale, either new or second-hand.

❼ eBay's Categories
These are eBay's main product categories.

❽ Specialty Stores
eBay has proven so successful that a range of sub-sites have grown up around it, each one specializing in a particular product area.

❾ Drop-Down List
Next to this search box there's a drop-down list of eBay's categories so you can choose to search for something in one of them, rather than the entire site.

❿ Buy/Sell
Once you've registered, clicking one of these links takes you to the relevant part of the website.

www.Amazon.com

Probably the Internet's favorite shop, Amazon gets it right by keeping it simple. It offers a vast selection of goods at very competitive prices, a generally efficient tracking and delivery service, and a website that's easy to use. You have to sign up to buy items from Amazon, but this is easy and free. Goods for sale range from books and DVDs to consumer electronics and computers, and the company is now also offering services such as DVD rentals by post. Amazon customers can write reviews of the products they've bought and their no-nonsense ratings are a generally good guide if you're uncertain about the suitability of a particular product.

FEATURES KEY

❶ Search
Click here to search the Amazon store.

❷ Recommendations
Once you've signed up to Amazon and done some shopping, click here to see product recommendations based on what you've bought.

❸ Account Details
Clicking this link lets you review your account details, for example, payment details.

❹ Shopping Cart
*Click the **Cart** link to see what is currently in your electronic shopping cart.*

❺ Lists
This link is for making lists of items you'd like to buy, as a reminder to yourself or to share with friends–as a wedding gift list, for example.

❻ Help
If you need any help with your shopping, click here.

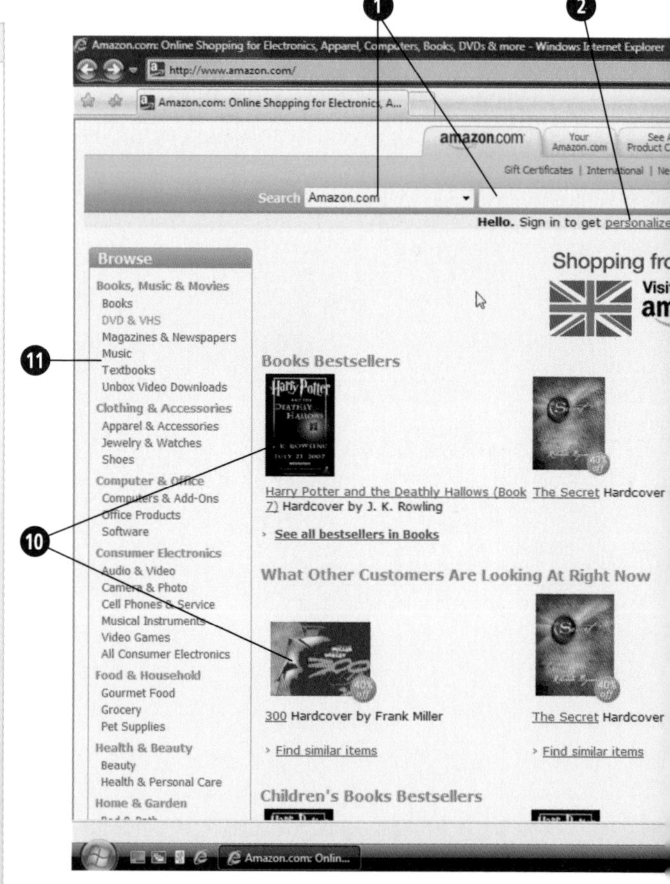

AMAZON LISTINGS

Here's a typical listing for a product on Amazon–a DVD box set. This particular product has a five star rating, based on nearly 3,000 customer reviews. Purchasers can add the set to a shopping list or pop it straight into their shopping cart; they can get it gift wrapped, see how long it'll take to deliver, see extra pictures of the product, or scroll down the webpage to read some of the product reviews written by other Amazon customers.

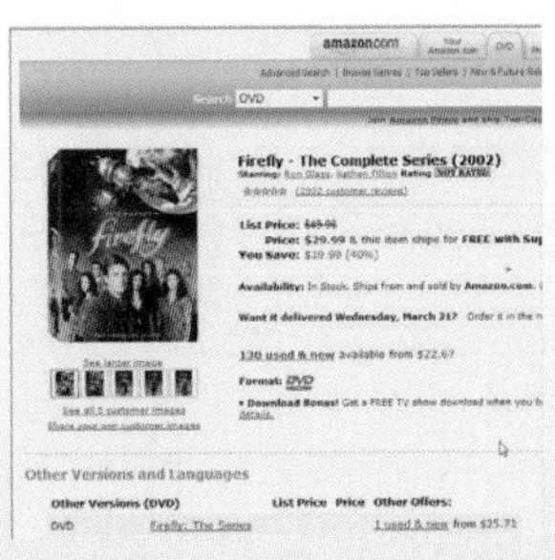

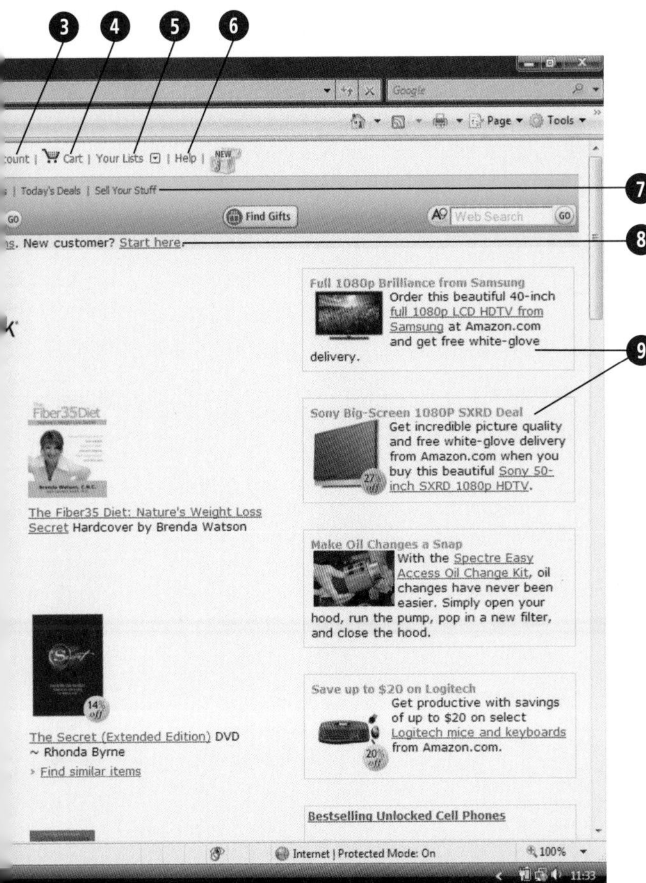

FEATURES KEY

❼ Links
This series of links takes you to webpages that help you personalize your shopping.

❽ Start Here
If you've never used Amazon before, click the ***Start Here*** *link for an introduction to the world of online shopping.*

❾ Promotions
Amazon highlights examples of products that it's currently promoting.

❿ Features
Every day Amazon features particular products on its front page. Clicking the image will open a page that displays the product in more detail and includes price, reviews, details of special offers, and so on.

⓫ Amazon Store
Click on any of these categories to display that part of the Amazon store.

WWW.NETVIBES.COM

When you first load your web browser in the morning, the page that loads each time is usually called your home page. Often it'll be the page of the company that sold you your PC or the company that makes the operating system you use. You can change this page so that instead you see the front page of your favorite newspaper or TV show, or you can use Netvibes to create your own, unique home page. Netvibes is made up of modules that you can pick and choose yourself–you can download news from your favorite service or radio station, have your own calendar, see your e-mails as they arrive, and keep a check on the latest movie trailers, all from a single page–Netvibes.

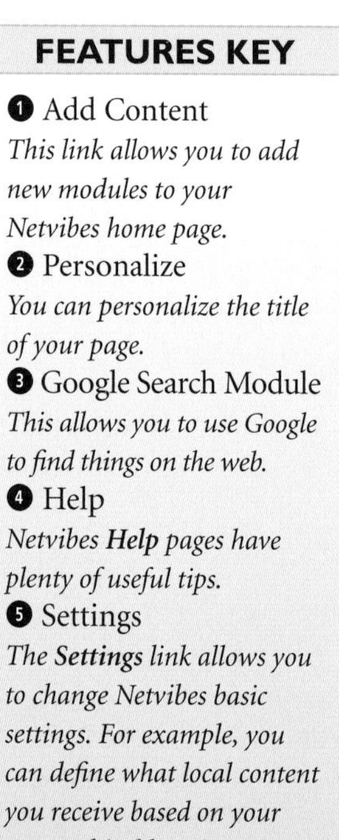

FEATURES KEY

❶ Add Content
This link allows you to add new modules to your Netvibes home page.

❷ Personalize
You can personalize the title of your page.

❸ Google Search Module
This allows you to use Google to find things on the web.

❹ Help
*Netvibes **Help** pages have plenty of useful tips.*

❺ Settings
*The **Settings** link allows you to change Netvibes basic settings. For example, you can define what local content you receive based on your geographical location.*

❻ Sign Out
When you've finished for the day, sign off here.

❼ Search Module
This is the Netvibes image search module.

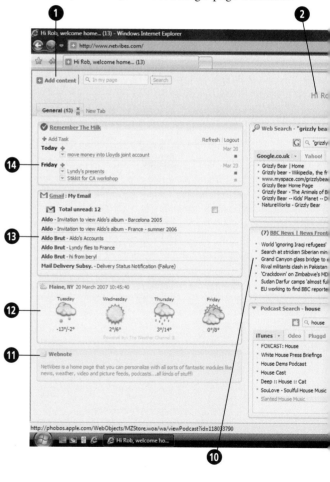

ADDING MODULES

There are nearly 700 Netvibes modules on offer, any of which you can add to your Netvibes home page for free. These include calendars, games, news feeds, calculators, clocks, maps, stock tickers, and many more. Make any of these a part of your Netvibes home page with a few simple mouse clicks.

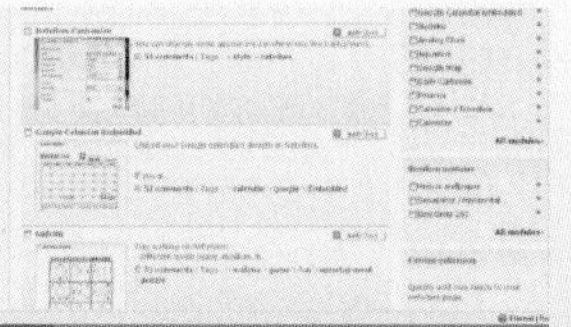

FEATURES KEY

❽ Apple Module
This is the Apple Movie Trailers module, which keeps an eye on Apple's website and notifies you whenever new movie trailers appear.

❾ Podcast Search Module
Podcasts are radio shows that you can download and listen to whenever you like.

❿ BBC Headlines
These are headlines from the BBC website. There are hundreds of different news "feeds" like this available, and it is easy to add any of them to your home page.

⓫ Sticky Note
Here's a neat little sticky note module that you can use to jot down notes, telephone numbers, and such like.

⓬ Weather Module
The weather module displays an easy-to-understand graphic of the next four days weather, which can be modified to suit your geographical location.

⓭ Google Mail
If you have a free Google Mail e-mail account, you can check your e-mail from inside your Netvibes home page–you don't have to go to Google's webpage.

⓮ To-Do List
This is a neat calendar/task organizing list.

www.Local.Live.com

This website offers a fascinating glimpse into the future of modern mapping. It has great street level maps that you can use to wander around your own–and other peoples'–neighborhoods. You can use it to get detailed directions from A to B that are written in a simple style, as well as finding local attractions and amenities such as bars, restaurants, and theatres. However, the real fun starts when you explore the 3D views. Microsoft has assembled a vast collection of detailed aerial photos. These can be invaluable if are moving house and want to have a snoop around the neighbors' gardens, or if you're unsure of the layout of a particularly tricky intersection.

FEATURES KEY

❶ Search
Search for a specific kind of business here.

❷ Location
Type in the name of the location you want Local.Live to display here.

❸ Help
Click here for help on using Local.Live.

❹ Sign In
Signing up to Local.Live is free by clicking here.

❺ Options
Change Local.Live's settings from here. For example, you can change the setting so that when you revisit the website is will always show the last location you visited.

❻ Main Window
This is the main map window. Use the controls to zoom in and out, change views, or move to a different destination.

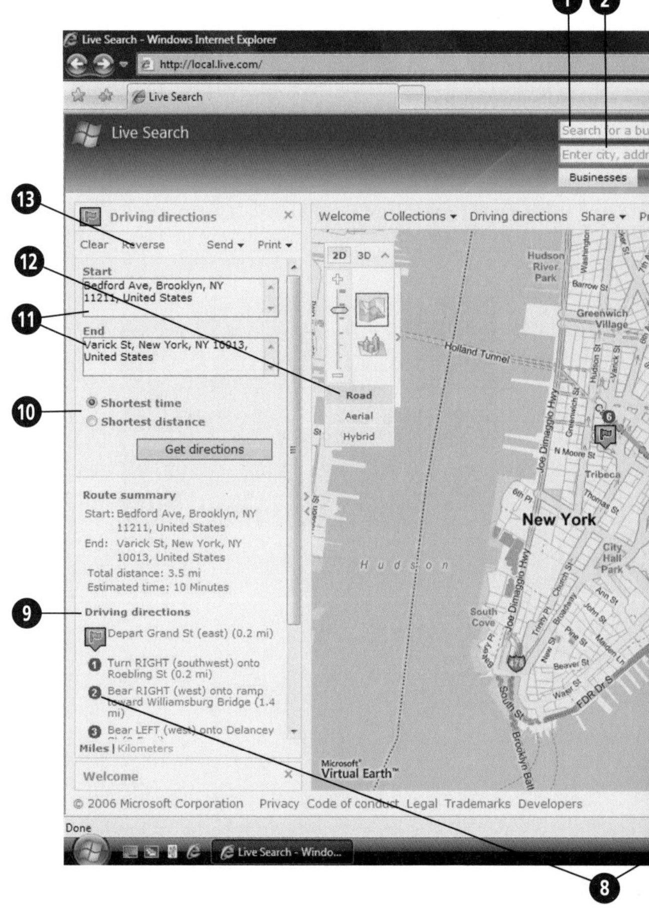

MEET THE NEIGHBORS

Here we've switched to Local.Live's 3D view and zoomed right in to the building at the end of the route we mapped below on the main map (see the little red flag on the roof?) You can use the **N**, **S**, **E**, and **W** controls in the panel to rotate round the view so you can see the building from all sides.

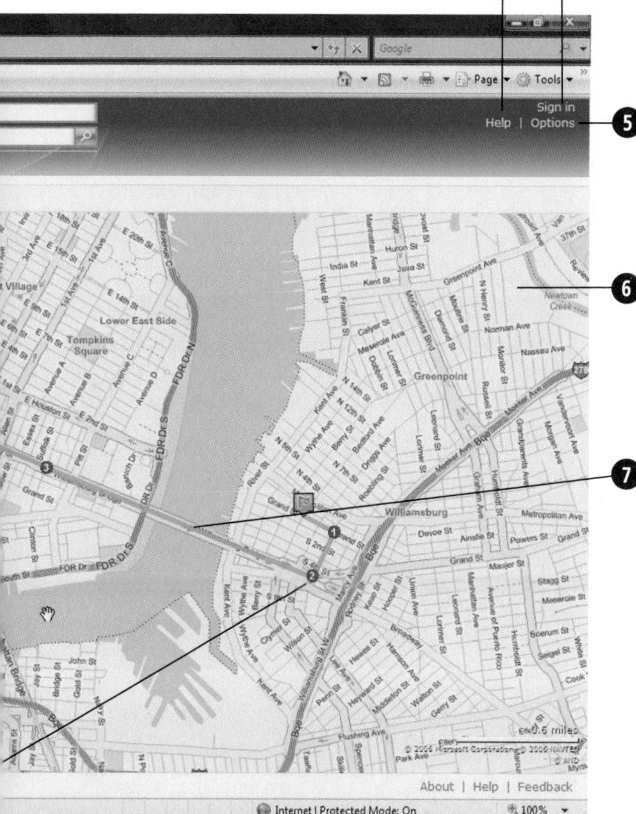

FEATURES KEY

7 Route Finder
Here we're using Local.Live as a route finder to plot our way from Brooklyn to central New York–the route is marked out in blue.

8 Waypoints
When Local.Live creates a route it automatically inserts waypoints at various major turns or intersections.

9 Directions
Local.Live puts the actual written driving directions on the left of the map window.

10 Plotting
You can choose between plotting the shortest distance (as the crow flies) or the shortest time, which may involve traveling further in terms of miles.

11 Start/End
Local.Live displays both the start and end points of the journey.

12 View
Local.Live offers multiple styles of views. This is the Road view. There is also an Aerial view, which shows the topology as if photographed straight down from an airplane, and a Hybrid view, which combines map and photo styles.

13 Reverse Link
Click the Reverse link to re-plot the journey backward.

WWW.FLICKR.COM

Although followed by a number of other competing services, Flickr was the first to offer Internet users a place to store and show their digital photos for free. The idea behind Flickr is simple–rather than having to create CDs or DVDs of your photos and then post them to friends and family, you can upload them to Flickr and then invite people to have a look at them; if they find photos they like, they can download them to their own PCs, print out hard copies, and so on. Flickr has many excellent features, including slideshow features, and you can add tags to photos to make it easier for visitors to find your pictures. Best of all, Flickr is free.

FEATURES KEY

❶ Your Photos
These links allow you to play with your photos in different ways. For example, you can organize them into sets, look at photos by date, or see which are the most popular.

❷ You/Organize
***You** takes you to the page seen here–the main space for your photos–while **Organize** lets you create sets out of individual photos.*

❸ Other Links
*The **Contacts** link helps you to stay in touch with friends and share your photos. The **Groups** link takes you to an area where people have created photo groups with others that share their interests. The **Explore** link takes you on a tour of Flickr.*

❹ Search
Search Flickr for photos by typing in a keyword here.

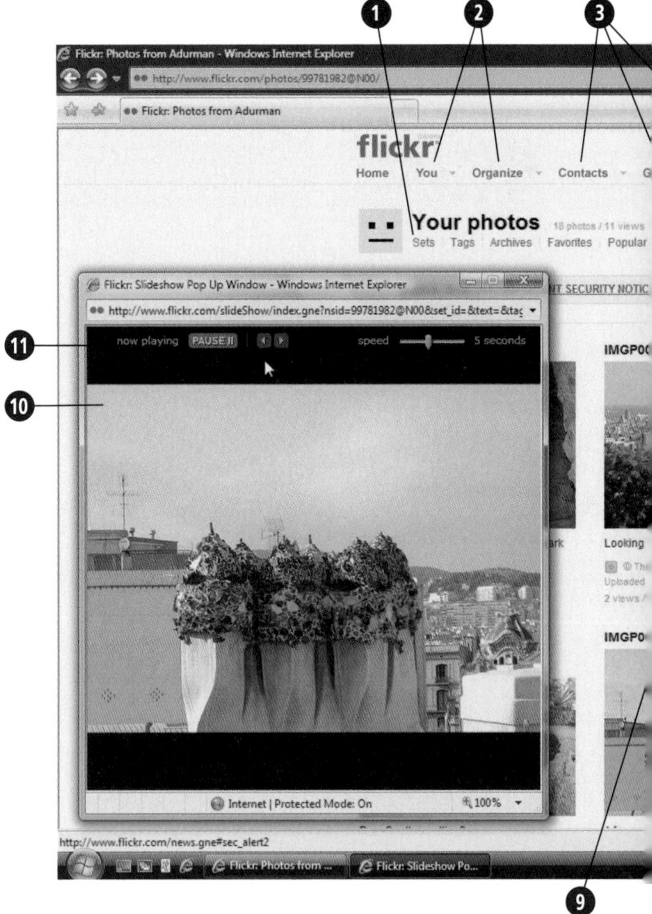

TAGS ARE EVERYWHERE

Tags are crucial to the way that Flickr works. Here, we've gone to the main Flickr webpage and opened the drop-down list next to the **Explore** button and chosen **Popular tags**. We've then picked Japan from the list. As a result, thousands of photos with the tag **Japan** are displayed.

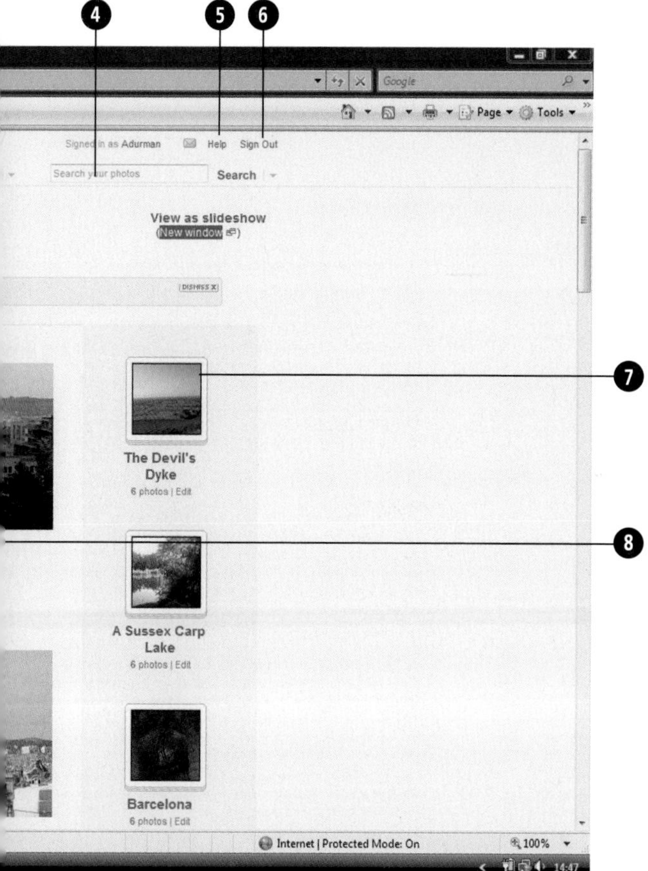

FEATURES KEY

❺ Help
Click here to access Flickr's help pages and Frequently Asked Questions.

❻ Sign Out
Click here to sign out.

❼ Sets
*These are photo sets created by this user. You can create a set by using the **Organize** link, typing in a name for the set, and then dragging your photos into the set with the mouse.*

❽ Caption
This caption was typed in by the person who uploaded the photo to Flickr.

❾ Basic Information
This tells you when the photo was uploaded, how many times it's been viewed, whether anyone's left a comment about it, whether it's public or private.

❿ Slide Show
Here's a Flickr slide show in action. Left to itself, Flickr will play back all the photos in a set, showing each one for five seconds before moving on to the next.

⓫ Controls
These are the controls for the slide show. Visitors can use the controls to pause playback or alter the length of time that each individual photo is displayed.

WWW.WIKIPEDIA.ORG

Wikipedia is an online encyclopedia comprising more than six million articles in over 250 different languages. It's searchable and features millions of internal and external links to other articles and websites, but what makes Wikipedia stand out is that anyone can edit it. You can simply go to an article in the website and make changes to the text, add new sections, original photos, maps, links to external websites, etc.. Wikipedia survives on goodwill and the good-natured policing of the thousands of people who contribute the articles–and is a fabulous example of how people all over the world can pool their knowledge for the greater good.

FEATURES KEY

❶ Discussions
There are often lively disagreements between Wikipedia "editors," so the website provides a page "behind" each article where contributors can discuss–or defend–their changes.

❷ Edit This Page
*Click the **edit this page** link to open the entire entry.*

❸ History
*Click the **history** tab to see a detailed list of the revisions made to this article since it was first created.*

❹ Article
This is a typical Wikipedia article, about the Grand Canyon in the United States. The blue text denotes hyperlinks that, when clicked, will open a different article elsewhere in Wikipedia.

❺ Sign In
Sign up to Wikipedia here.

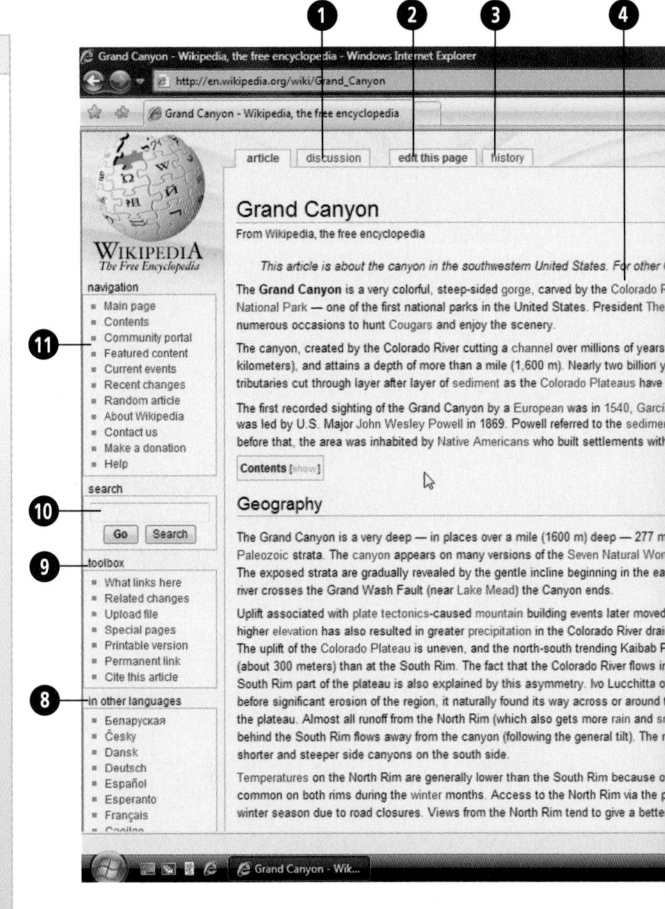

EDIT YOURSELF

Here's the Wikipedia editing window in action. The text for the Grand Canyon article is in the middle of the screen. Wikipedia uses brackets, dashes, and full stops as codes to produce special formatting for things such as headings, links, and pictures. These may seem strange at first, but you'll soon get used to them. Some of these formatting functions are incorporated into the toolbar that runs along the top of the editing window–if you've used Microsoft Word this kind of toolbar will be familiar.

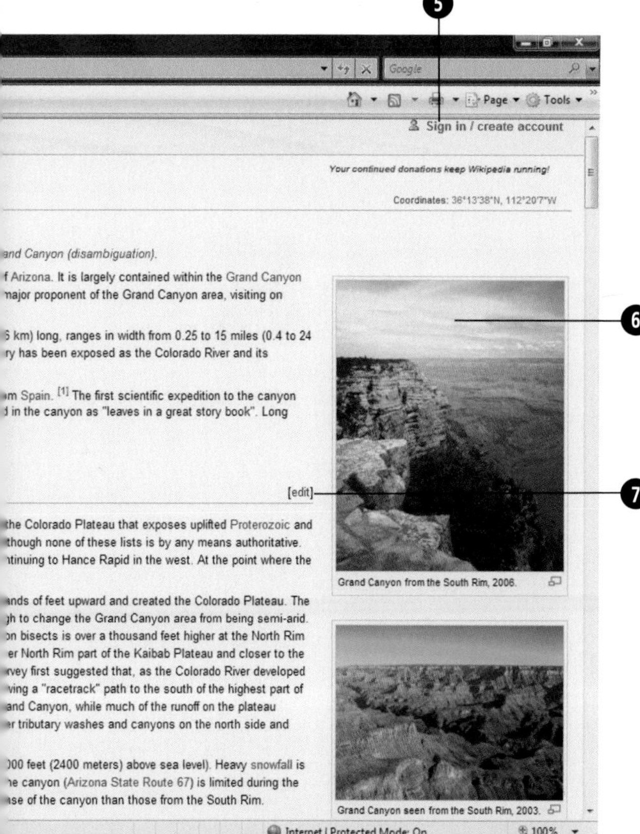

Grand Canyon from the South Rim, 2006.

Grand Canyon seen from the South Rim, 2003.

FEATURES KEY

❻ Enlarge
Click to enlarge the photo.

❼ Edit
Clicking on the edit button to open the editing window.

❽ Change Language
You can click here to change the language of the article you're reading.

❾ Toolbox
*The **toolbox** provides a number of utilities that you'll find helpful if you're contributing to Wikipedia, including the ability to upload files.*

❿ Search
The search box lets you find things quickly and easily.

⓫ Navigation
Here you'll find Wikipedia's highlights–lists of recently changed articles, special features on new content, and detailed instructions on how you can contribute.

Introducing Word 260

www.MySpace.com

This is the website that inspired the so-called social networking revolution. By positioning itself as a place on the web where you can make friends–rather than say, a dating site–MySpace attracted all kinds of people who'd normally shy away from that kind of online meeting place. Then, by giving members the tools to create an interesting page with photos, music, slide shows, video, text, and so on, MySpace also attracted everyone who wanted a presence on the web, but didn't know–or care– enough about it to create their own website. It's a double whammy that has seen MySpace become one of the most popular destinations on the web.

FEATURES KEY

❶ Search
*Looking for someone on MySpace? Type his or her name into this box and then click the **Search** button.*

❷ Specific Search
Click here to open the drop down menu and make your search more specific.

❸ Blog
If the person is keeping an online diary (web log or "blog"), it will appear here.

❹ About Me
This is where you tell people a little bit about yourself.

❺ Friends
This is the heart of MySpace–your friends. Make friends by going to someone else's MySpace page and inviting them to be your friend.

❻ Photos
Click on any of your friends' photos to go to their MySpace page.

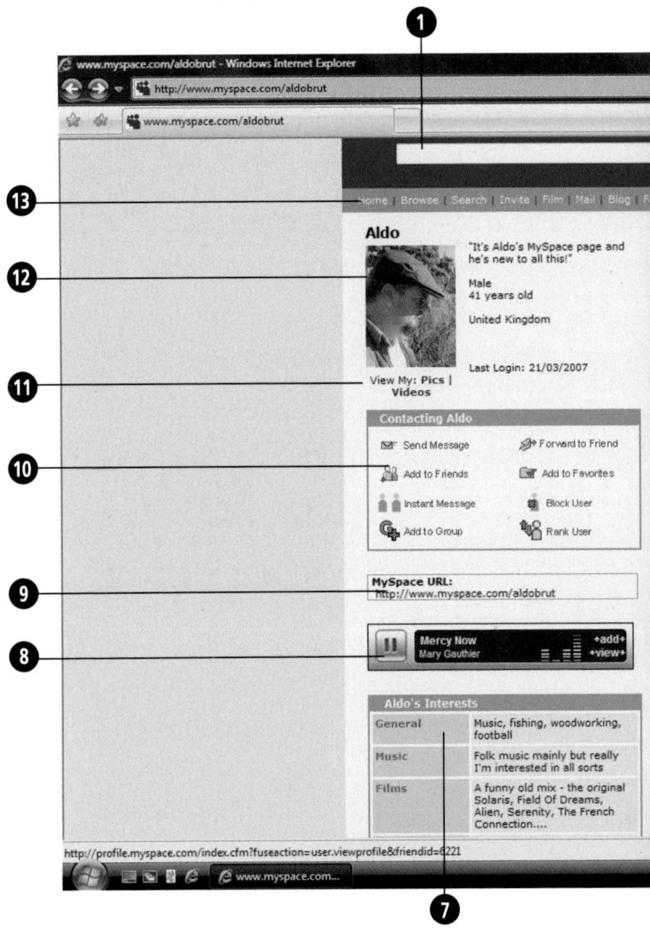

CREATING YOUR MYSPACE PAGE

MySpace provides all the tools you need to build your own page. This screen shows the electronic forms that each user fills in to create his or her page. As well as text, you may want to add background images, video clips, photos and slide shows, and all sorts of other visual fun.

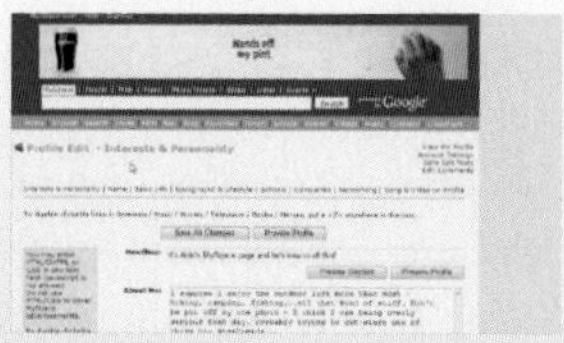

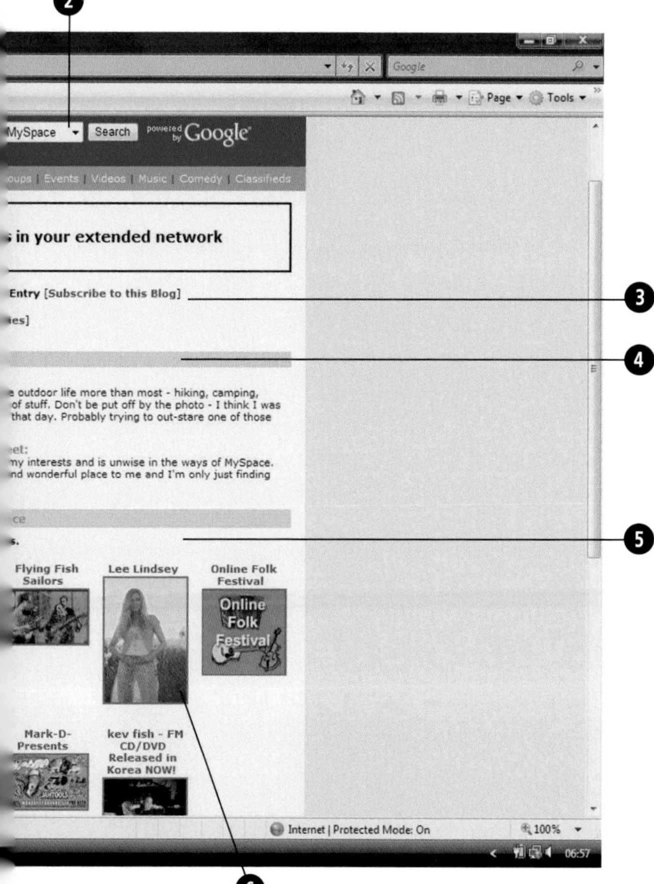

FEATURES KEY

❼ Description
Here's where you tell visitors about your likes and dislikes, interests, and hobbies.

❽ Media Player
This is the MySpace media player. It plays a song in the background that people can listen to when they visit your MySpace page.

❾ Direct Link
Want someone else to be able to go straight to your MySpace page? This is the address they need to type into the address line on their web browser.

❿ Contact
The ***Contacting…*** *box contains all the commands you need to add friends, send them messages, rank them, and send them instant messages. You can also block MySpace users from here.*

⓫ View
Visitors can click here to look at any photos or videos that you may have uploaded.

⓬ Brief Description
Here's the photo and brief description of this user.

⓭ Useful Commands
This menu bar contains many useful commands for using MySpace. You can browse users at random or by criteria, invite friends to join MySpace, or even look for a job or a house!

WWW.VIDEOJUG.COM

The web is an extraordinary resource for those seeking information, but it can also help with more practical, everyday problems, like how to fix a dripping tap, arrange flowers in a vase, or choose a camera. The Video Jug site has collection of "how-to-do" online videos, which you can search or browse by category. You can play videos back as many times as you like, and many also have instructions that you can print out. Some videos are produced by experts, while others have clearly been made by enthusiastic amateurs. In fact, anyone who signs up to Video Jug can upload their own videos and share with the world a skill or technique that they've learned.

FEATURES KEY

❶ Search
Type in a keyword and Video Jug will search its entire library for videos that match.

❷ Tabs
The tabs along the top allow you to browse Video Jug's content by category, suggest new topics or videos, upload your own, and create your own "channel" of favorites.

❸ Sign Up
Sign up to Video Jug here. It's free. Members can also download videos to their iPods or PlayStation Portables.

❹ New Member
When you join Video Jug, you may see yourself here as one of the new members.

❺ Charts
These are Video Jug's charts– looking at what other people find interesting can often lead you to content you hadn't previously considered.

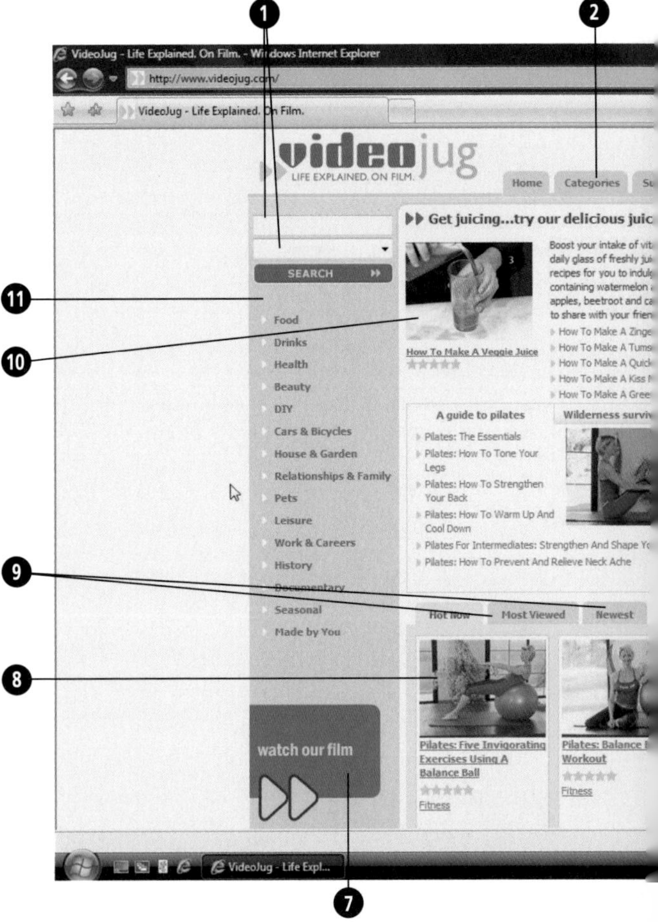

A DRIPPING TAP

Here we've gone to the DIY category, selected plumbing, and chosen a video that tells us how to fix a dripping tap. The little player window has all the controls you need to play the video clip–you can pause to take notes, for example–and you don't need any special software to play the videos.

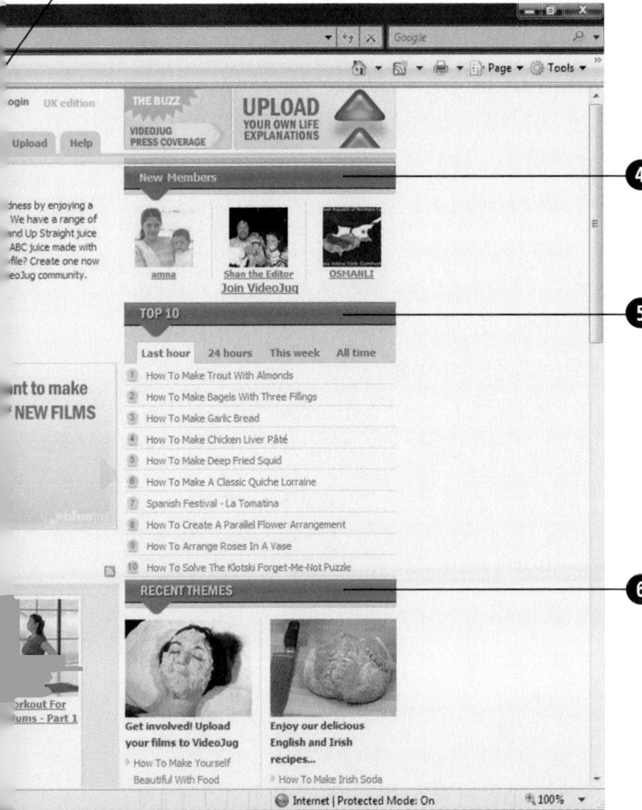

FEATURES KEY

6 Themes
Along with categories, Video Jug puts different video clips together based on themes. Again, you may find inspiration by looking here rather than searching or browsing through the categories listed elsewhere on the front page.

7 Promotional Video
Click here to watch a promotional video that explains the thinking behind Video Jug.

8 Highlights
*Every day the site highlights a different set of videos, labeling them as "**hot.**" Simply click on it to select.*

9 Most Viewed/Newest
Click the tabs here to explore the newest videos and also those that have been viewed most often.

10 Main Story
Every day Video Jug picks one video clip as it's lead–a bit like the main story in a magazine. Click the picture to start playing the video back on your PC.

11 Main Categories
These are Video Jug's main categories. Clicking on one of the titles here will open any sub-headings; for example, clicking DIY opens Doors, Electrical, and Plumbing.

USING E-MAIL

E-MAIL HAS BECOME such a part of our lives that many of us rarely use any other means of sending written messages, pictures, or computer documents. Almost instant and virtually cost free, electronic communication over the Internet allows us to keep in touch with friends and family, colleagues and business contacts wherever we are in the world, and wherever they are. In this chapter we look at the key features of Windows Mail, the e-mail program that's installed with Vista. As well as showing you how to compose and send e-mails, we explain how to deal with incoming mail, keep it organized, and avoid having an inbox full of junk mail. In the last section we look at some simple ways to customize your messages to reflect your personal style.

170 INTRODUCING MAIL

176 CREATING E-MAIL

184 INCOMING E-MAIL

194 PERSONALIZED E-MAIL

INTRODUCING MAIL

Windows Mail is one of the applications that make up the Windows Vista suite of programs. It offers all the features you need to be able to send and receive electronic mail over the Internet.

WHAT WINDOWS MAIL CAN DO

Windows Mail provides a gateway to the world of electronic mail. It allows you to send and receive electronic mail messages, and to include all kinds of digital files, such as images, text documents, hypertext links to websites, and even complete programs, in your outgoing mail. It also provides the organizational system for filing incoming e-mail, and the facilities for you to record and store all your email addresses and personal contact details in the form of an electronic address book.

OPENING WINDOWS MAIL

- Windows assumes that Mail is one of the programs you'll be using frequently, so you will find it in the top section of your Start menu.
- To open Mail, click on the Start button and then click on **Windows Mail**. The Mail window will open.

- In the unlikely event that Windows Mail is not pinned to the top section of your Start menu, click on **All Programs** and select Windows Mail from the list of programs. The Windows Mail window will open.

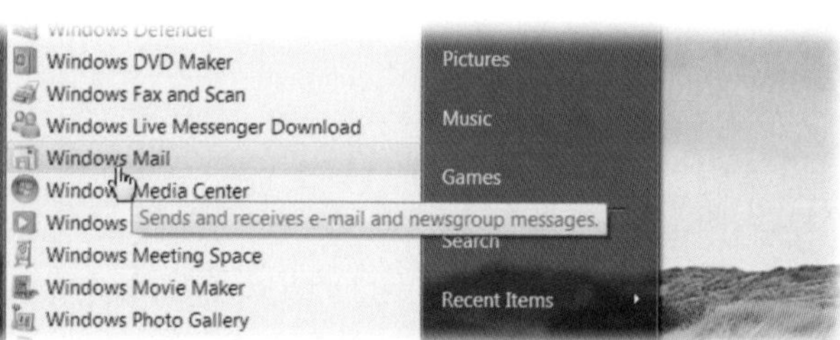

THE WINDOWS MAIL INBOX

This is the window that you will see each time you open Mail–the Windows Mail Inbox. This is where you will manage your e-mail communications. From here you will go online to send mail out and collect your incoming mail, read it, move it to folders that you have created, or delete it. Here you can also start the process of creating a new e-mail and replying to, or forwarding, e-mails that you've received.

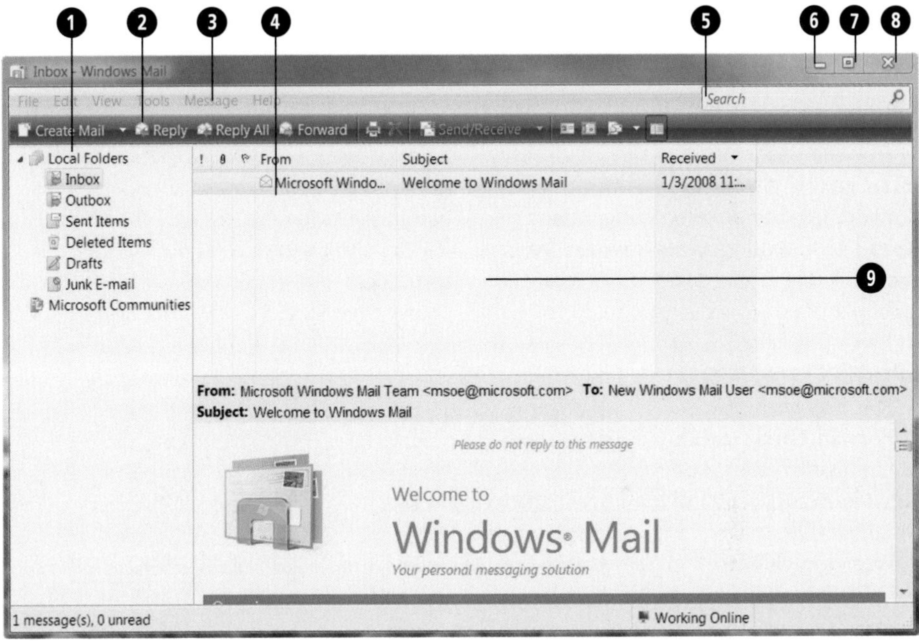

FEATURES KEY

❶ Folder List
These are the folders in which e-mails can be filed. New folders can be added.

❷ Toolbar
These are the tools for creating and replying to e-mails, as well as sending and receiving.

❸ Menu Bar
Provides access to a range of drop-down menus.

❹ Contents Panel
Displays a list of the titles of all e-mails in the selected folder.

❺ Search
Type a search term into this panel to find a specific e-mail or newsgroup message.

❻ Minimize

❼ Maximize

❽ Close

❾ E-mail Preview Panel
Displays the text of an e-mail selected in the Contents Panel.

OPENING WINDOWS MAIL FOR THE FIRST TIME

The very first time you open Windows Mail, a Windows "wizard" may open–the start of a sequence of step-by-step dialog boxes to open an e-mail account. If you have all the information you need (see below), then go ahead. Otherwise, click **Cancel**. When you have the necessary information, open your new e-mail account by following the steps shown here.

OPENING AN E-MAIL ACCOUNT

In order to send and receive e-mail, you need a computer running an e-mail program, or "client," such as Windows Mail, an Internet connection, and an e-mail account with your Internet Service Provider (ISP). Setting up the account requires certain information that you can only get from your ISP so, before starting the process, make sure you have all the details listed below. You may find that your ISP is willing to talk you through the setting up process by phone.

WHAT DETAILS DO I NEED TO KNOW?

- You don't need to understand these questions or the answers, but every letter in the answers has to be correct.
- What type is the incoming e-mail server? The answer will probably be POP3 or IMAP.
- What is your e-mail password? Your ISP needs to know this during setup. You can change it to a personal choice later.
- Does the server require authentication?
- What is the address of your ISP's incoming (POP3) mail server?
- What is the address of your ISP's outgoing (SMTP) mail server?
- What will your e-mail address be? You need to agree this with your ISP.

STARTING THE PROCESS

- To open your first e-mail account, or subsequent accounts, start by clicking on **Tools** in the menu bar.
- Select **Accounts** from the drop-down menu by clicking on it.

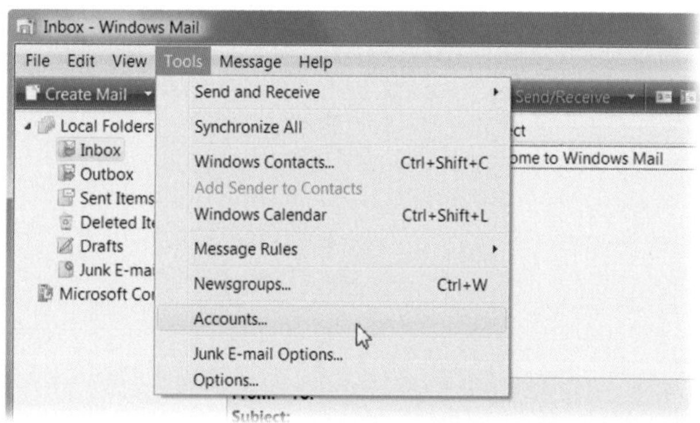

ADDING AN ACCOUNT

- The **Internet Accounts** dialog box opens. You want to add an account, so click on the **Add** button.

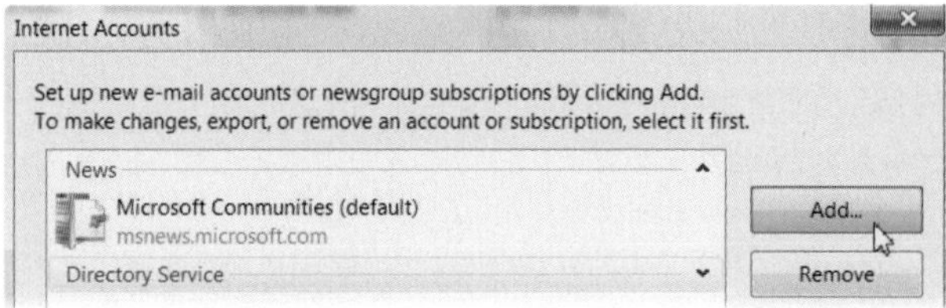

SELECTING AN ACCOUNT TYPE

- You are now asked to select an account type.
- Click on **E-mail Account** and then click on **Next** at the bottom of the box.

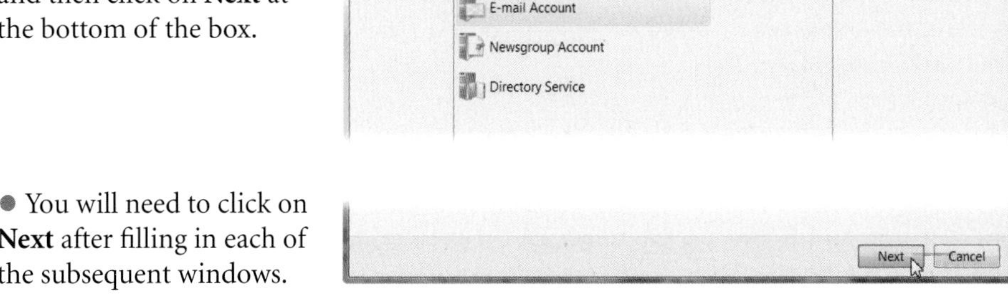

- You will need to click on **Next** after filling in each of the subsequent windows.

FILLING IN THE DETAILS

- A sequence of windows now begins, in which you are asked to input the details that we looked at earlier. Key in your name as you wish it to appear on your outgoing mail.

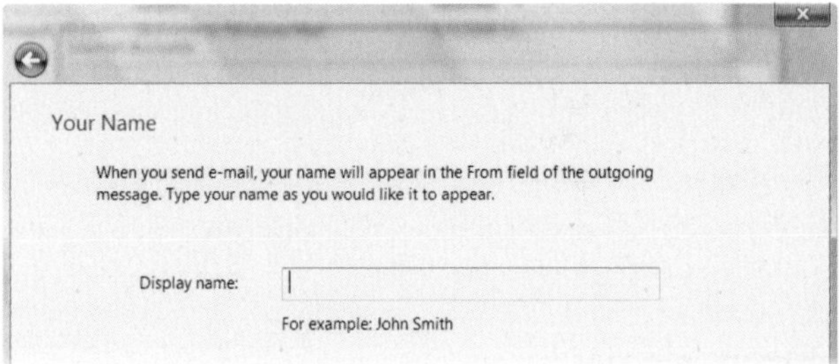

- Key in the complete e-mail address that you have agreed with your ISP.

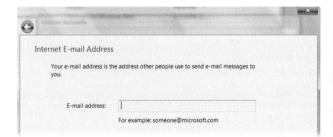

SETTING UP THE E-MAIL SERVERS

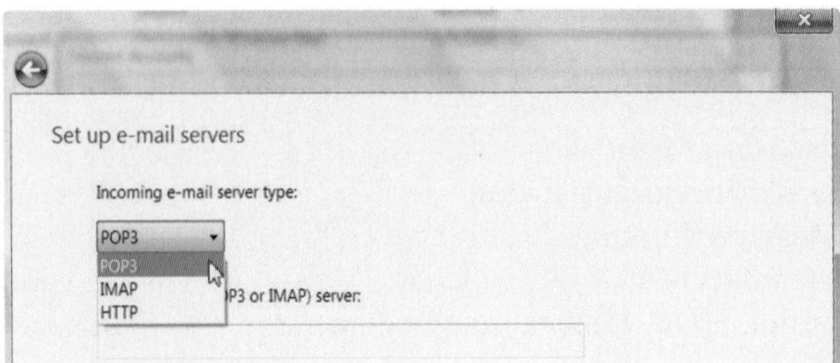

● Click on the small arrow to the right of the first panel and, from the drop-down menu, select the type of your ISP's incoming e-mail server.

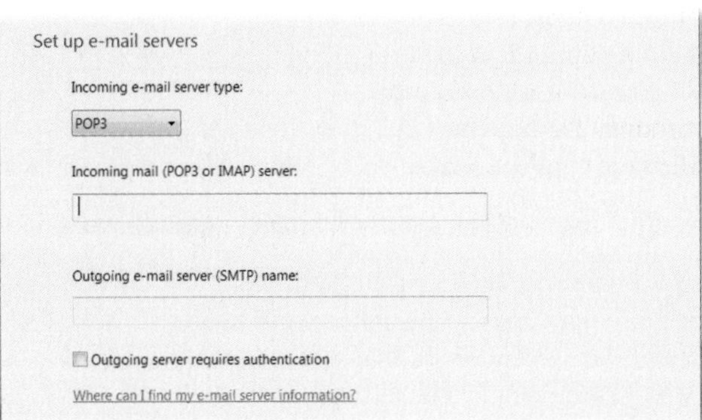

● In this same window, type in the address of the incoming mail server.

● Fill in the details of your ISP's outgoing e-mail server.

● If the outgoing server requires authentication, place a checkmark in the box by clicking on it.

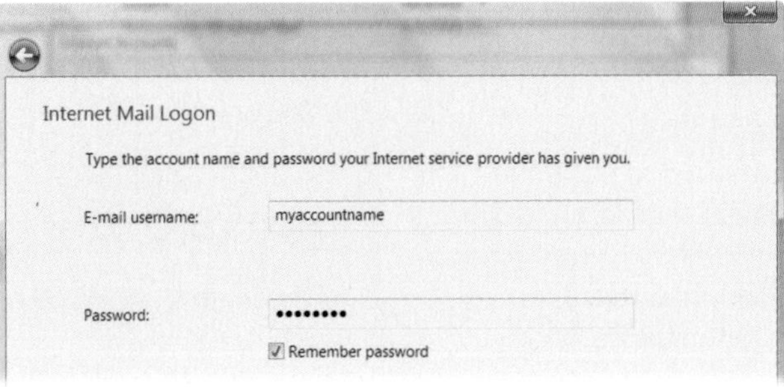

● You will have discussed your email address/user name and your password with your ISP. Fill in these details here.

● If you are not concerned that others may gain access to your e-mail, you can choose to have Mail remember your password.

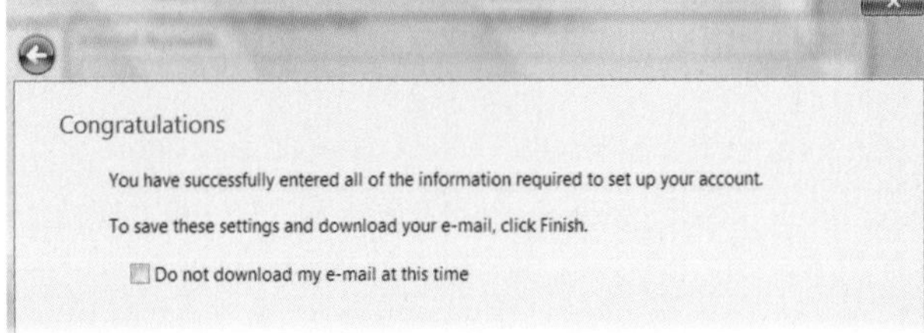

● The Wizard congratulates you on setting up your e-mail account.

● Click on the **Finish** button in the bottom right-hand corner of the window to complete the process and return to the Mail Inbox.

The New Message Window

E-mail messages are composed in the **New Message** window, which is opened from the **Inbox** by clicking the **Create Mail** button on the toolbar. An e-mail message is made up of several parts. The "header" contains the address(es) of the recipient(s) and the subject of the message. The "body" contains the message itself.

OPENING THE NEW MESSAGE WINDOW

● From the **Inbox**, click on the **Create Mail** button in the toolbar. The **New Message** window opens.

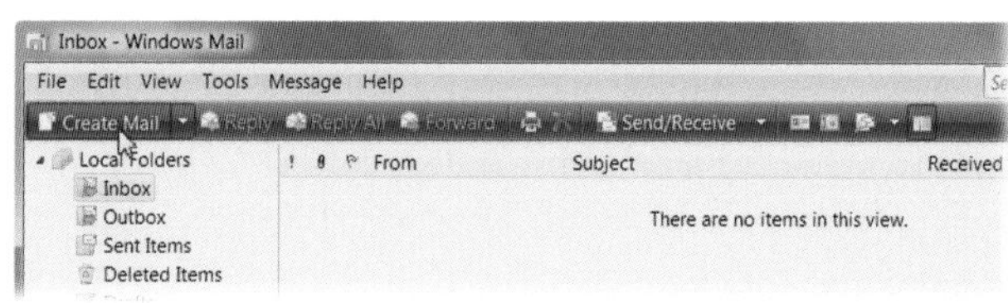

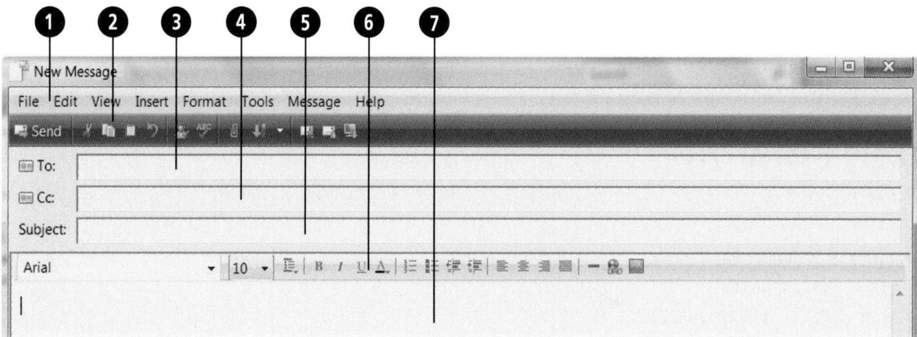

FEATURES KEY

❶ Menu Bar
Provides access to a range of drop-down menus.

❷ Toolbar
This provides buttons for editing text; for checking spelling; for attaching files; for sending and prioritizing the message.

❸ The To: field
This contains the e-mail address of the recipient of the message.

❹ The Cc: field
This contains the e-mail addresses of people to whom you would like to send "carbon copies" of the message. You can send to as many people as you wish.

❺ The Subject: field
This contains the subject of the message, so that people can tell at a glance what your message is about.

❻ Formatting Toolbar
This offers some of the standard word-processing features to enable you to align text, choose the font and style, and add bullet points.

❼ Message Body
This is where you type the text of the message. It acts as a normal word-processing window.

CREATING E-MAIL

In this section we look at writing an e-mail, formatting the text, adding attachments, addressing your message, saving it to send later, and sending it on its way.

COMPOSING A MESSAGE

If you have any experience of a word-processing program such as WordPad or Microsoft Word, you will find that composing a message in Mail is very similar. Many of the tools are exactly the same, and the formatting toolbar (see opposite) will be familiar to anyone who uses other Microsoft programs.

KEYING IN AND FORMATTING TEXT

- Click once in the message body area to create an insertion point, and then type in your message.
- The words will "wrap" when they reach the end of a line. Use the Enter key to start a new line.

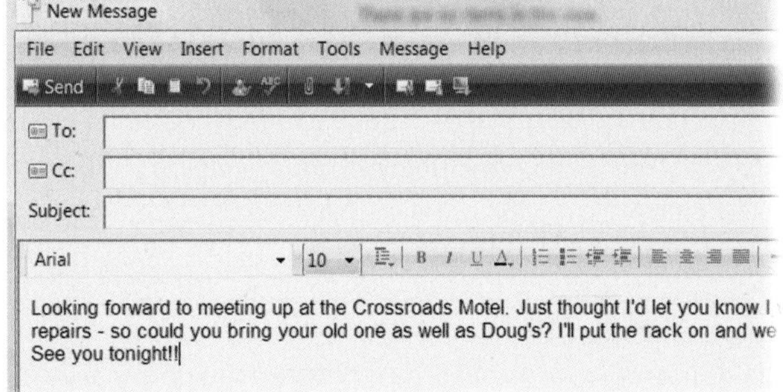

- To change the text style, drag the cursor across the selected text to highlight it, and then click on, for example, the **Bold** and **Italic** buttons.
- Click off the highlighted text to see the effect these changes have had.

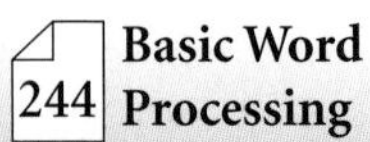
Basic Word Processing 244

Introducing Word 260

THE FORMATTING TOOLBAR

Once text has been selected, this toolbar can be used to make changes to the font, font size, font style, and color; numbered and bulleted lists can be created; the text can be indented by varying amounts; the text can be aligned with either side of the page, with both sides, or centered; and horizontal lines, hyperlinks, and images can be inserted.

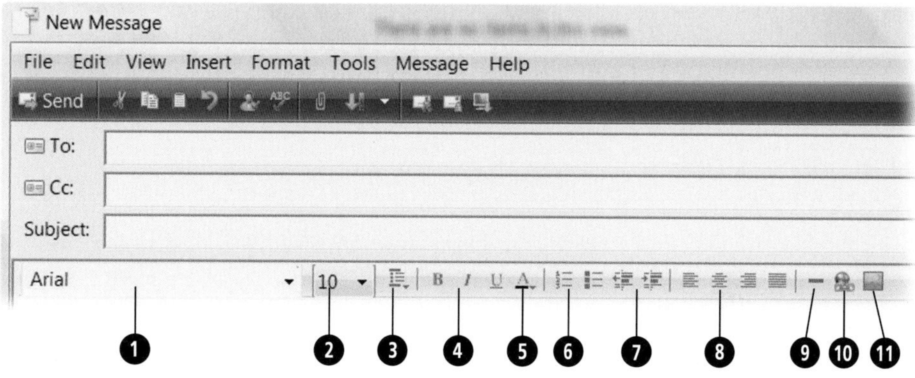

FEATURES KEY

❶ Font
❷ Font Size
❸ Paragraph Style
Provides a range of pre-set paragraph styles.
❹ Font Style
Clicking on these three buttons changes the regular font to bold, italic, or underline.
❺ Font Color
❻ Numbered and Bulleted Lists
❼ Decrease/Increase Indent
❽ Alignment
Use these buttons to range text left, center it, range it right, or justify the text.
❾ Insert Horizontal Line
❿ Create a Hyperlink
⓫ Insert Picture

PARAGRAPH STYLE FORMATTING

● Click on the **Paragraph Style** to see this drop-down menu. Selecting any of these options will apply the particular style to the selected paragraph.

● A paragraph is selected simply by clicking in it with the mouse cursor.

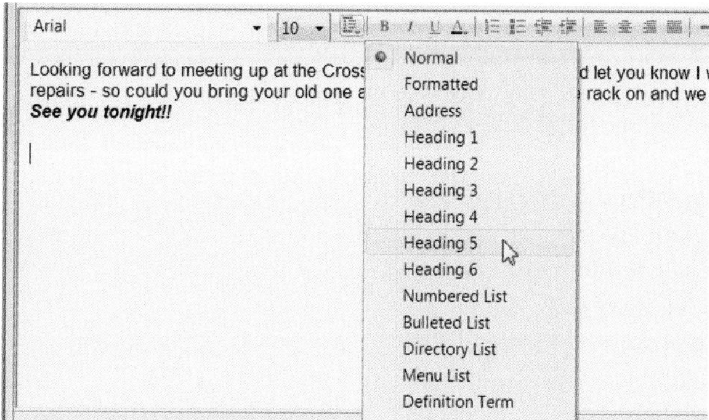

Adding an Attachment

As well as the text of an e-mail message, you can also send files. These files are "attached" to your message. Attachments can include word-processing documents, images, sound or video files, and even computer programs. When you send an attachment, your computer copies the file and sends it with the message–the original stays on your computer. You can send more than one file with a message. Alternatively, you can insert the contents of the file into the message body itself.

ATTACHING A FILE TO AN E-MAIL

- Whatever kind of file you want to attach to your e-mail, click once on the **Attach File To Message** paper clip icon.

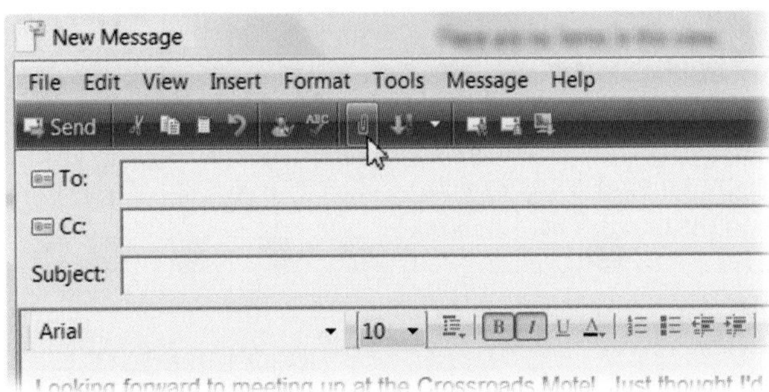

- In the **Open** window that opens, navigate to the file– in this case we are attaching an image.
- Attaching large files increases the size of the message and the length of time it takes to download, so check the file size.
- To do this, hover your cursor over the image to bring up the information. (Alternatively, right click on the file, select **Properties** from the pop-up menu, and view the information in the **General** tab.)
- Anything under 500KB will not cause a problem.

• To attach the file, select it by clicking on it once (the file name will appear in the **File name** panel) and then click on the **Open** button at the bottom of the window. Alternatively, simply double click on the image.

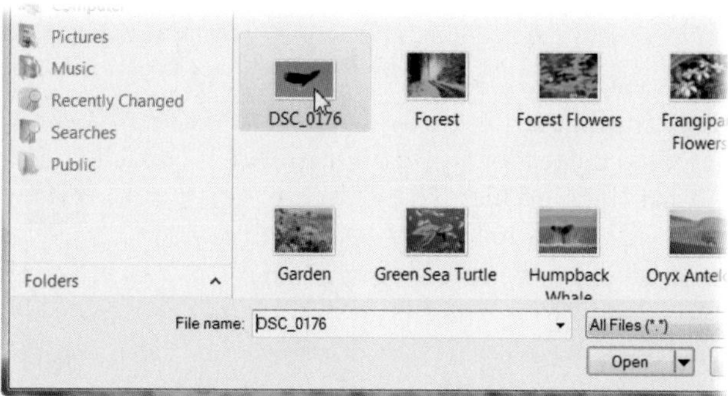

• The **Open** window closes, and in the **New Message** window you will see that a new **Attach** panel has appeared in the message header. This displays the type, name, and size of the attached file.

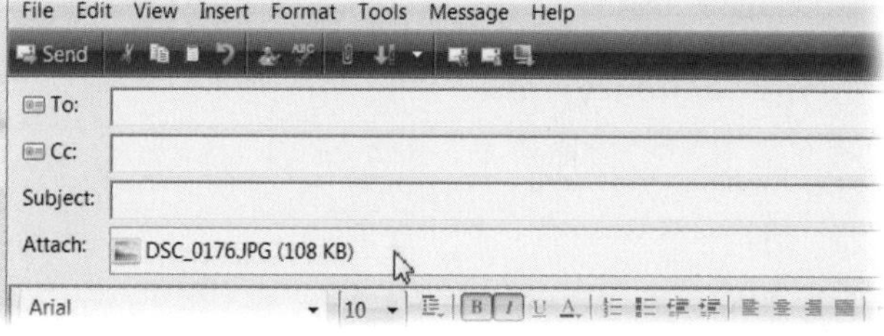

REMOVING THE ATTACHMENT

• If you change your mind, you can easily remove the attachment.

• Right-click on the file name in the **Attach** panel, and select **Remove** in the pop-up menu.

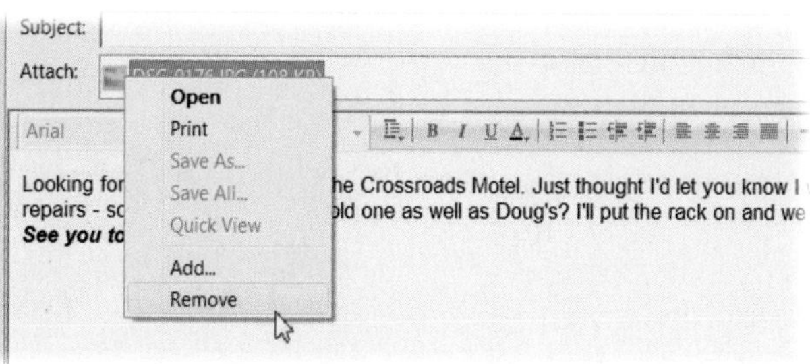

INSERTING A FILE IN THE E-MAIL

• Instead of sending the image as an attachment, it is possible to insert it in the body of the e-mail itself.

• To do this, click on **Insert** in the menu bar, and select **Picture** from the drop-down menu.

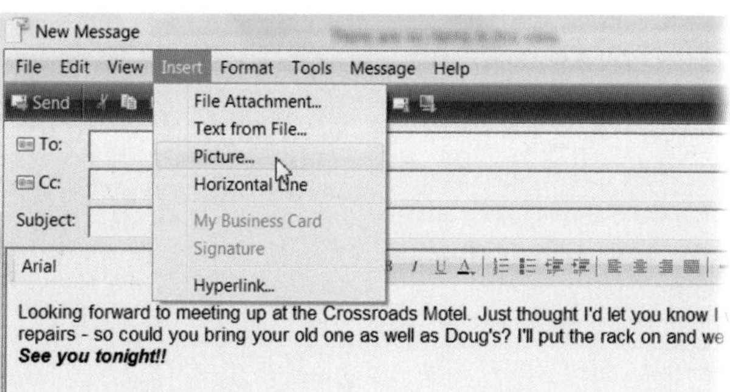

● Windows takes us to our pictures, and here we select the image, just as we did when attaching it [see page icon].

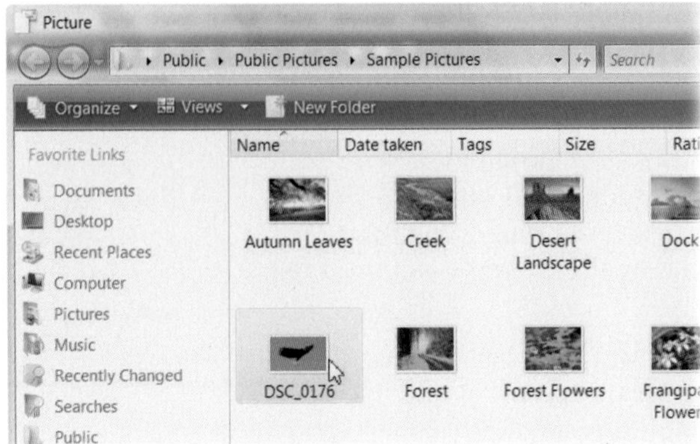

● As we can see, the image is inserted in the body of the e-mail.

● It appears where the insertion point was, so click at the end of your text when you start the process to make sure the insertion point–and therefore the picture–is not positioned in the middle of the message.

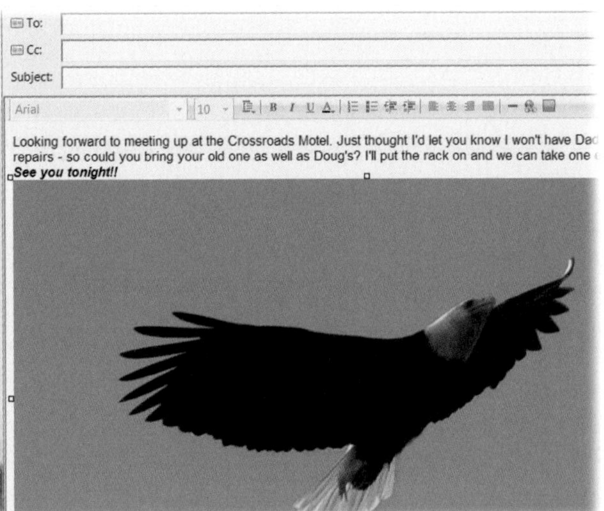

REMOVING THE ATTACHMENT

● If you change your mind about an inserted file, right click on the file itself, and select **Cut** in the pop-up menu that appears.

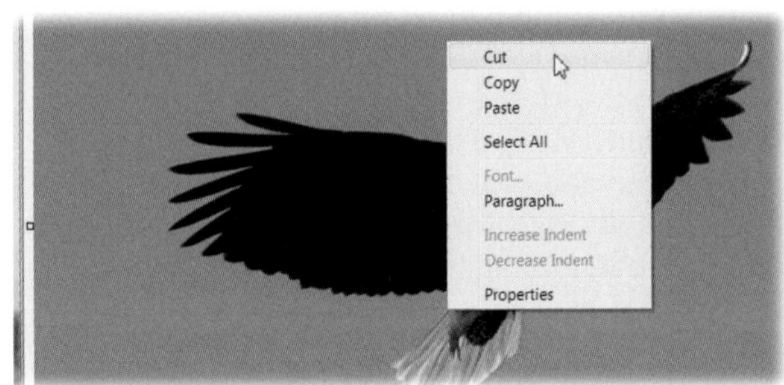

178 **Attaching a File to an E-mail**

Addressing an E-mail

When you have composed a message and added any attachments, the final step before sending it is to add the e-mail address of the recipient(s). Unlike ordinary letters, you can send a single electronic message simultaneously to as many people as you want by simply including all their e-mail addresses in the address field. It is important when addressing a message to make sure that you spell and punctuate the address exactly. If any characters are wrong, or spaces creep in, the message will not be delivered to its destination because the address simply won't be recognized.

TYPING THE RECIPIENT'S ADDRESS

- Click in the **To:** field of the message window, and type in the recipient's e-mail address.

- If you wish to include more than one e-mail address in the **To:** field, type a semicolon or a comma, then a space, and then the next e-mail address.

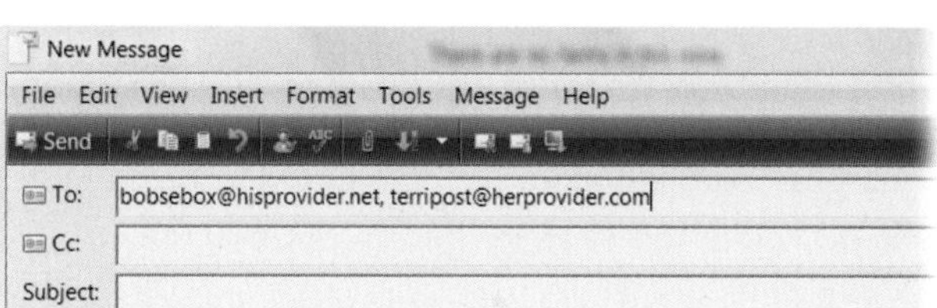

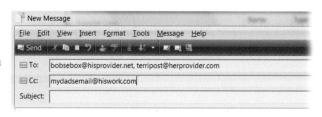

SENDING COPIES OF YOUR E-MAIL

To send a "carbon copy" to one or more people, click in the **Cc:** field in the message header and then type in their e-mail address.

COMPLETING THE SUBJECT LINE

To let the recipient know what the e-mail is about, key in a brief summary in the **Subject:** field. This then appears in the title bar.

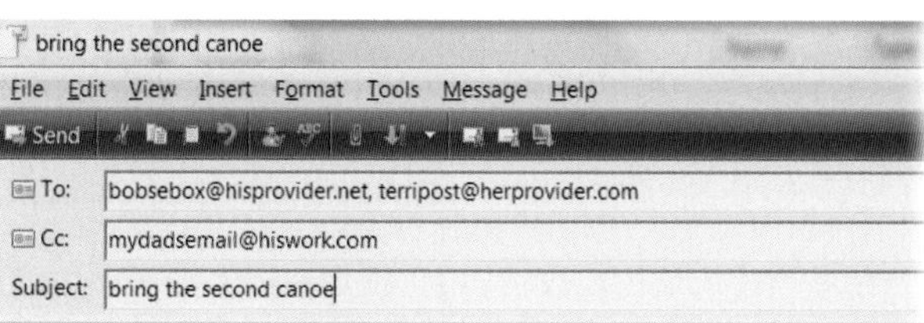

Saving and Opening a Draft

You can stop composing a message and save it to be completed at a later date in the same way that you can save any other computer file. Saved messages are known as "drafts," and they are saved in the **Drafts** folder in Mail.

SAVING A MESSAGE AS A DRAFT

- While you have your message on the screen, click on **File** in the menu bar and then click on **Save** in the drop-down menu.

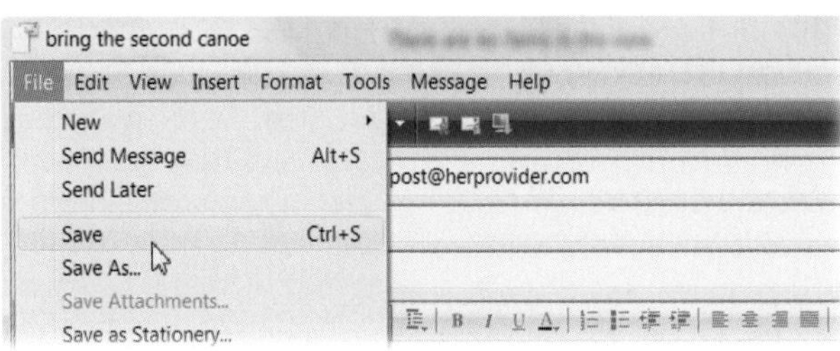

- Your message is saved as a draft in the **Drafts** folder, and the number **1** appears next to **Drafts** in the folder list on the left-hand side.
- You can now close the message window by clicking on the **x** in the corner.

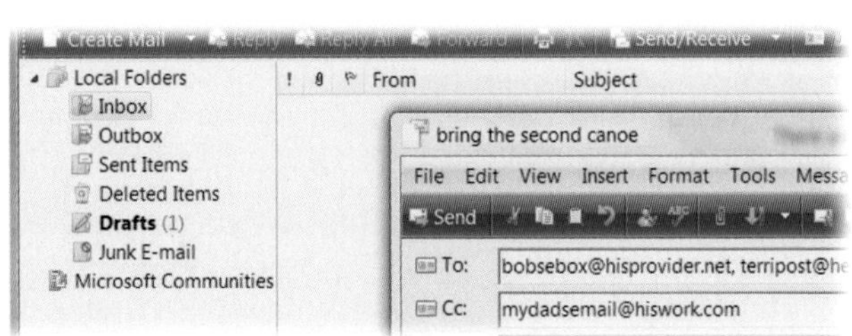

OPENING A DRAFT MESSAGE

- To continue writing the message, click on the **Drafts** folder to see the contents.

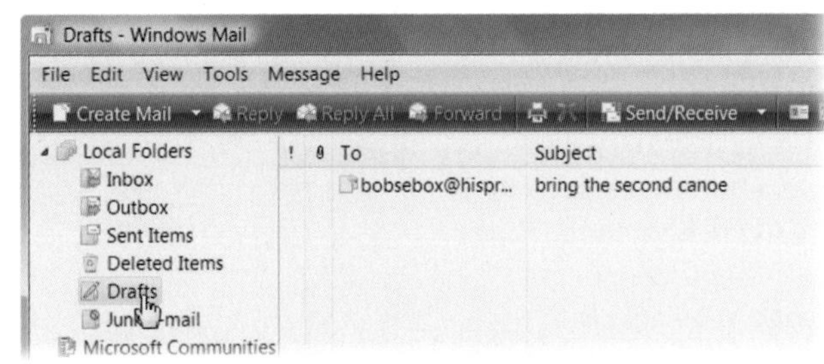

- Double click on the title of the message to reopen it and continue composing.

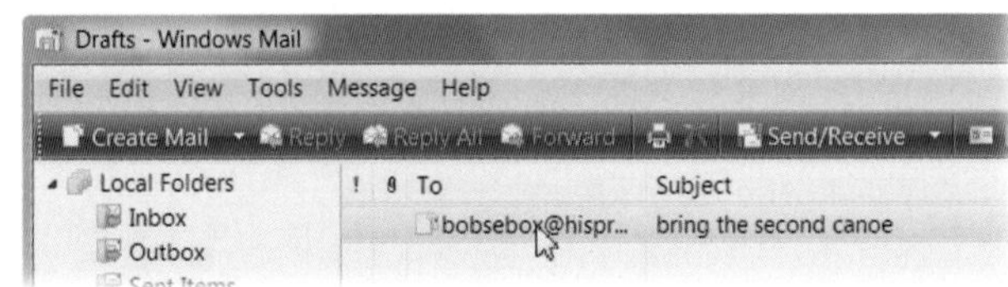

SENDING YOUR E-MAIL

Outlook Express offers several options when sending: you can send a message at once or send it later. For example, you can use Send Options to keep copies of messages, or to record automatically the addresses of people who write to you.

SENDING YOUR E-MAIL RIGHT AWAY

- To send a message, click the **Send** button on the toolbar. If you are online, it will be send immediately.
- If you are offline, it will be stored in the **Outbox** until you go online again.

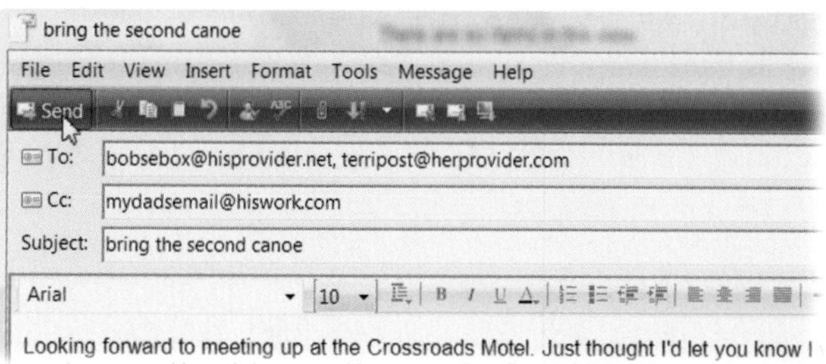

SENDING LATER

- If you have finished a message, but do not want to send it immediately, click on **File** in the Menu bar and select **Send Later**. The message will be saved in your **Outbox**.

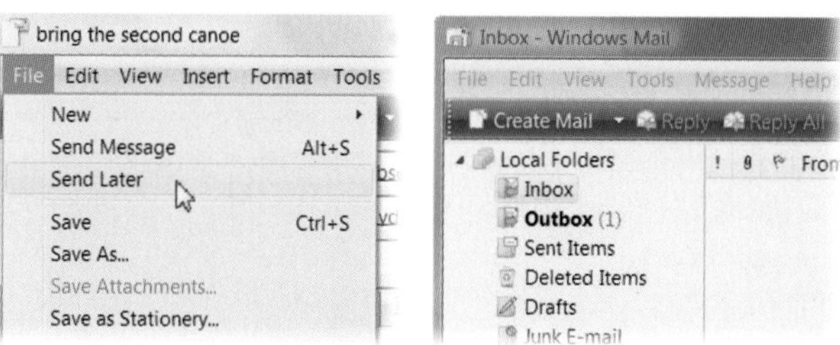

- When you want to send the saved message (and receive incoming mail ◻), go to the toolbar and click on **Send/Receive**.

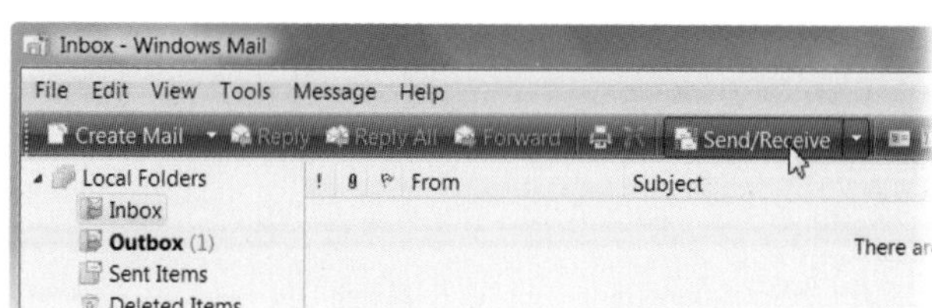

WORKING OFFLINE

If you pay for the time you spend connected to the Internet, you may wish to compose your e-mails "offline." To do this, click on the **File** menu in the Windows Mail window and select **Work Offline** from the drop-down menu. To go online, go to the same menu and deselect **Work Offline**.

Receiving E-mail 184

Incoming E-mail

Once you are familiar with Windows Mail and have sent your first e-mail, you'll be eager to receive replies. This section tells you about receiving and managing incoming messages.

Receiving New Mail

When you launch Windows Mail, it may automatically go online, check your mail server for any incoming mail, and download new messages into your **Inbox** so that you can read them. (This depends on settings in the **General** tab of the **Options** in the **Tools** menu, which you can change.) Whether this happens or not, there are several methods that you can use to check for new mail while you are online. To try them out, first open the Inbox by clicking the **Inbox** icon in the Folders list.

USING THE MENU TO RECEIVE E-MAILS

- To check your e-mails, first click on **Tools** in the Menu bar and choose **Send and Receive** from the drop-down menu.
- From the submenu that appears, choose **Send and Receive All**.
- If you don't wish to send messages from your **Outbox** at the same time as checking for new ones, choose **Receive All**.

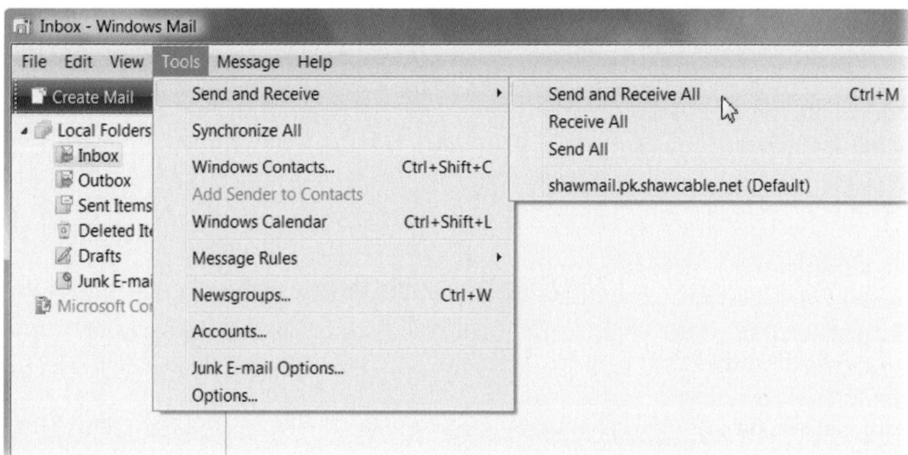

• Note that you must be connected to the Internet to receive mail. If you are trying try to collect mail while offline, you will be prompted to go online.

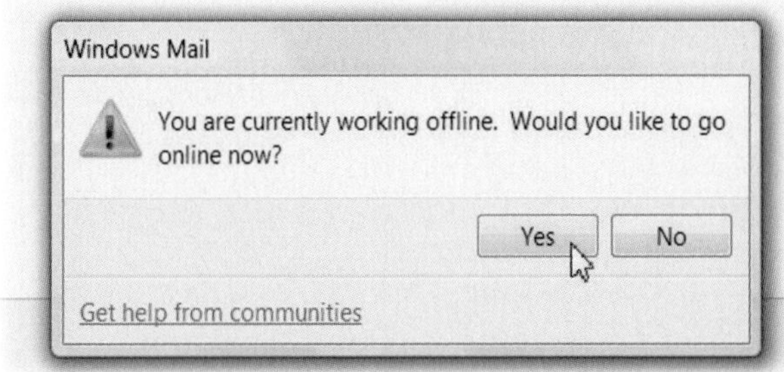

USING THE SEND/ RECEIVE BUTTON

• Click the **Send/Receive** button on the main toolbar.
• If you click on the arrow to the right of the button, you will be given the same options as those in the **Tools** sub-menu.
• You will see from the drop-down menu that you can also use the keyboard shortcut Ctrl M.

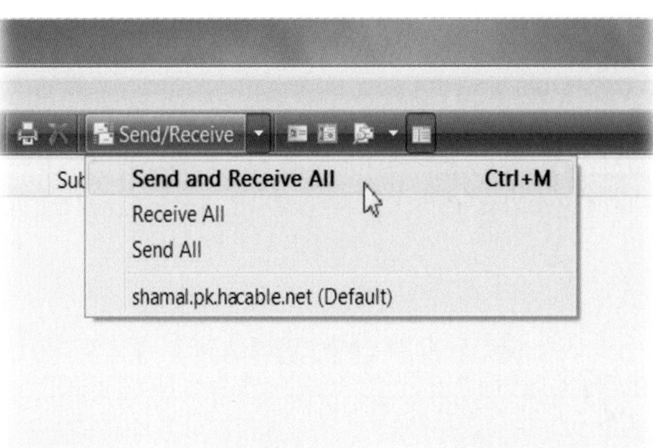

READING INCOMING MESSAGES

All your incoming e-mail arrives by default in the **Inbox**, which stores and lists all your incoming messages. There are several ways in which you can read your incoming mail. To try them out, click on the Inbox icon on the **Folders** list to open the **Inbox**.

OPENING A MESSAGE

• New, or "unread," messages appear in bold type, and the number of unread messages is displayed next to the **Inbox** icon in the **Folders** list.

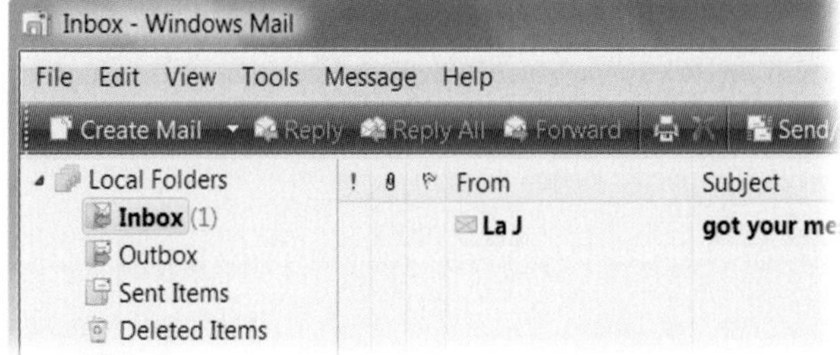

● In the **Inbox** message list, select the message you want to read by double clicking on it.

● Alternatively, you can select the message by clicking on it once with the mouse, and then pressing the Enter↵ key to open the message.

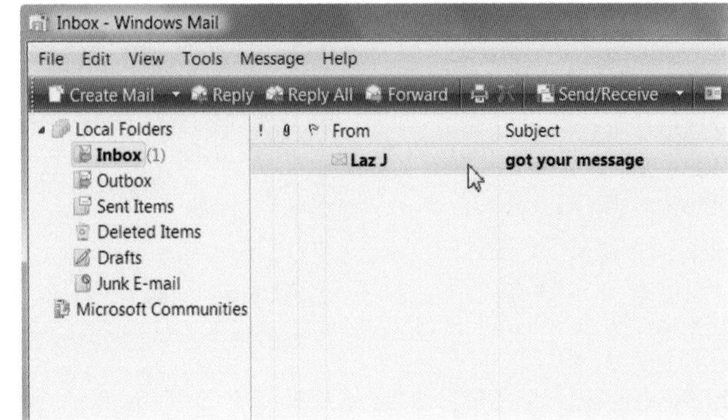

● The contents of the open e-mail are displayed in the bottom half of the message window.

From: Laz J <la.j@saw.ca> To: crotes.eyes@saw.ca
Subject: got your message

Thanks for the e-mail. We'll bring the second canoe. Se
Bob and Terri

Responding to Messages

There are several ways of responding to an incoming e-mail. You may want to reply to the sender directly, or to all the recipients of the message, or you may wish to forward the message to someone else, perhaps including a brief note of your own. You may want to print the message, or you may not want to respond at all, but just move the message to a new folder and keep it for reference. Windows Mail provides for all of these actions, and they can be done from the message window.

REPLYING TO THE SENDER

● In order to reply to a message, it must first be selected, so start by clicking on the message title.

● To reply directly to the sender, click the **Reply** button on the toolbar.

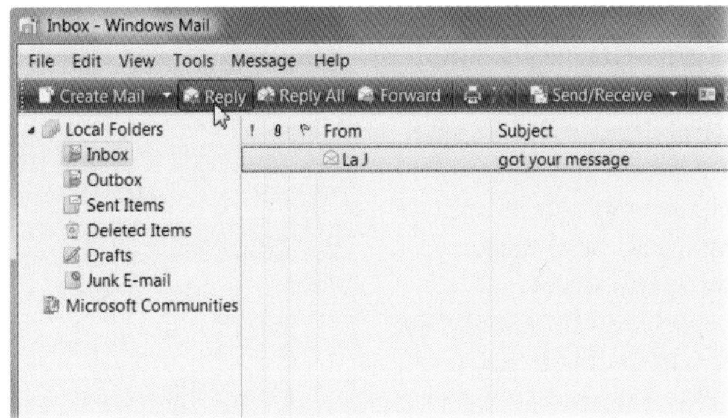

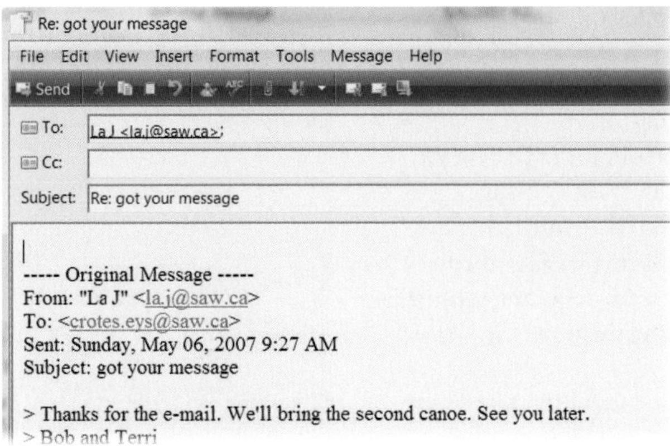

● A message window opens with the contents of the sender's message included, and his or her e-mail address inserted in the **To:** field.
● The insertion point is already at the top of the message body, so type your response and then send it by clicking on the **Send** button in the top left corner of the window.

REPLYING TO ALL

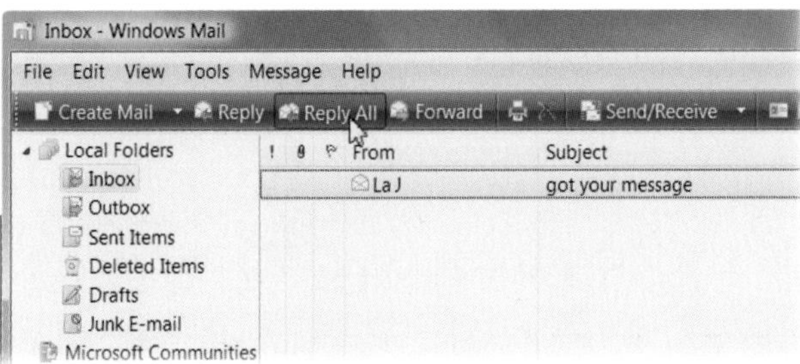

● If the message was sent to several people, you can reply to all of them at the same time by clicking the **Reply All** button on the toolbar. All the recipients' addresses will then be listed in the address fields.

FORWARDING MESSAGES

● To send the message onward to one or more people, click the **Forward** button on the toolbar.

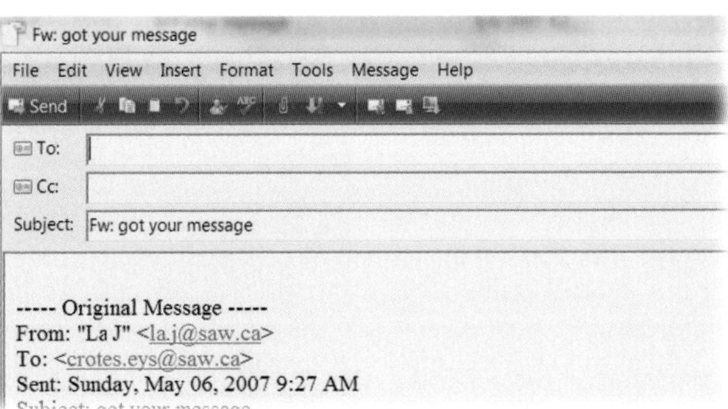

● A message window opens with the contents of the sender's message included, but the address field will be blank and the insertion point will be in the **To:** field.
● Type in the recipient's e-mail address and add any remarks of your own at the top of the message before clicking on **Send**.

PRINTING THE MESSAGE

● To print out the message, click on the **Print** button in the toolbar.

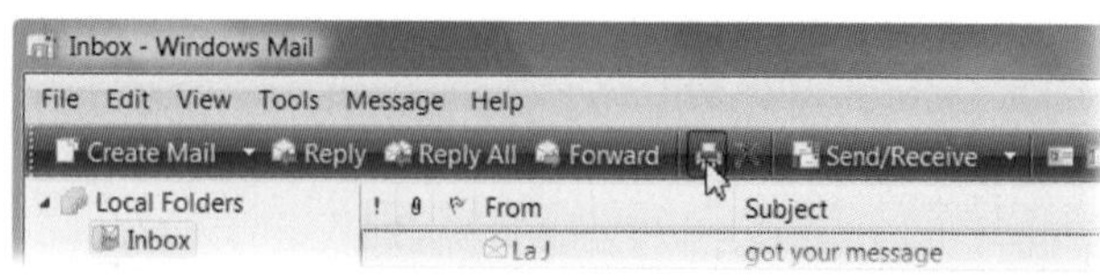

● The **Print** dialog box appears. Make your selection from the options available here (you may wish to print several copies, for example), and then click on **Print**.

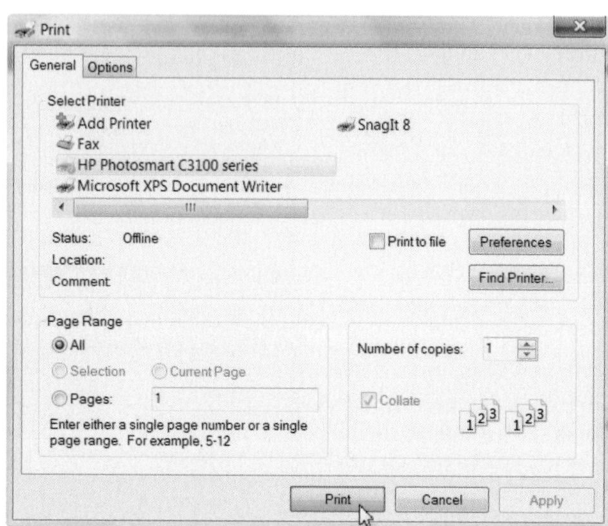

MANAGING YOUR E-MAIL MESSAGES

There is more to e-mail than just receiving and reading, composing and sending messages. If you become an active e-mail correspondent, before long your **Inbox** (and **Sent Items** folder) will be full to overflowing. Unwanted messages will need to be deleted, and you'll find it useful to create new mail folders for storing messages that are to be kept. This section shows you how to keep your e-mail tidy.

DELETING MESSAGES

● To delete a message from the message list, click on the message title and then click on the **Delete** button on the toolbar.

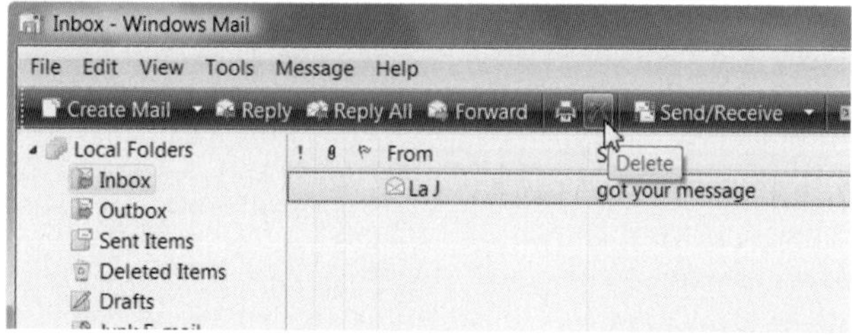

● Alternatively, right click on the message title and select **Delete** from the drop-down menu.
● The message is removed from the message list and transferred to the **Deleted Items** folder.

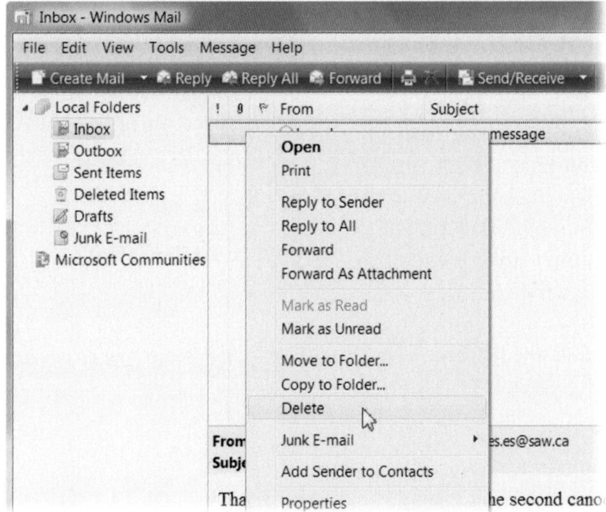

CREATING A NEW FOLDER

● In order to organize your incoming mail, you will need to create extra folders.
● To do this, right click on the **Local Folders** icon at the top of the Folders list and select **New Folder** from the drop-down menu.

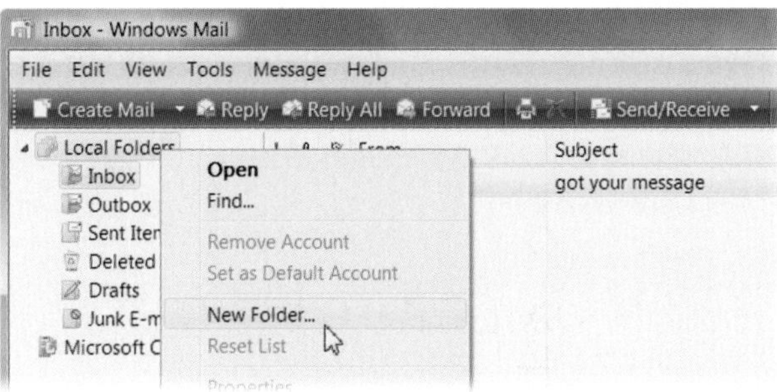

● In the **Create Folder** dialog box that appears, key in a name for the new folder. By default it will be created in **Local Folders**.
● Click on **OK**.

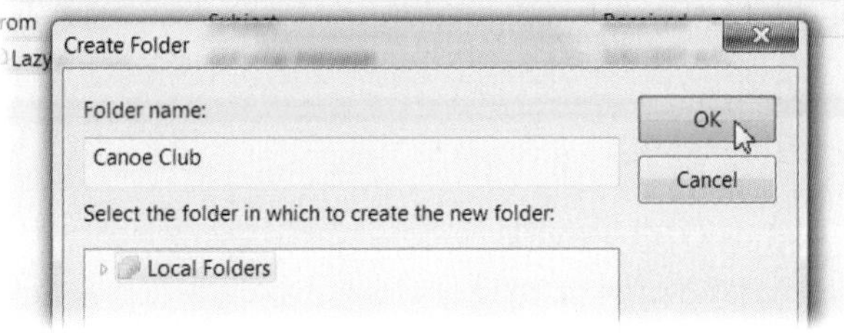

● The new folder appears in the Local Folders list.

STORING MESSAGES

● To move an e-mail message into a folder, simply click on the message title, drag it over the destination folder, and release the mouse button.
● A small file icon will accompany the cursor as you do this.

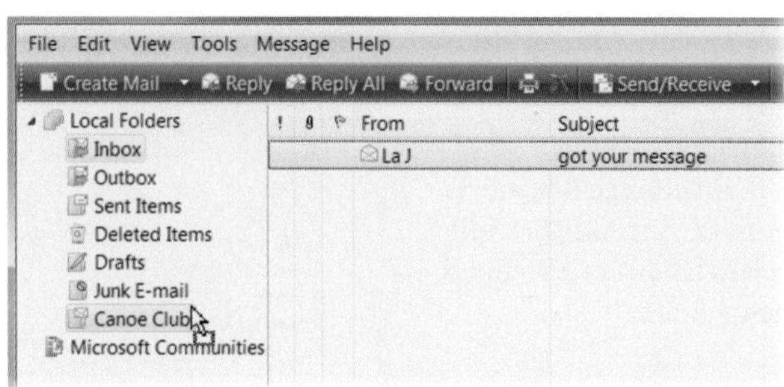

MOVING MESSAGES BETWEEN FOLDERS

● To move a message from one folder to another, open the source folder to view its contents by clicking on it.
● Drag the message over the destination folder and release the mouse button.

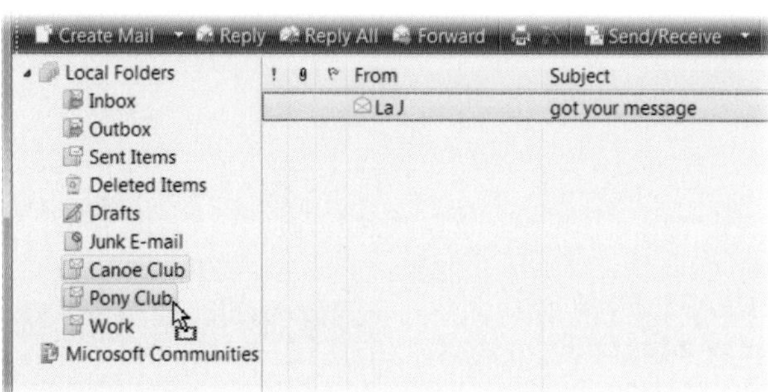

AVOIDING JUNK E-MAIL

One of the few downsides of the e-mail system is the vast amount of unsolicited e-mail that can bombard the average user, some of it with malicious intent. Fortunately, Windows Mail contains built-in safeguards, and you can adjust the program settings to filter out as much or as little of this as you wish.

INCOMING JUNK E-MAIL

● Your first brush with junk e-mail will probably be a **Windows Mail** dialog box alerting you to possible junk or phishing e-mail.
● Click on **Open Junk E-mail Folder** to take a look at what has arrived.

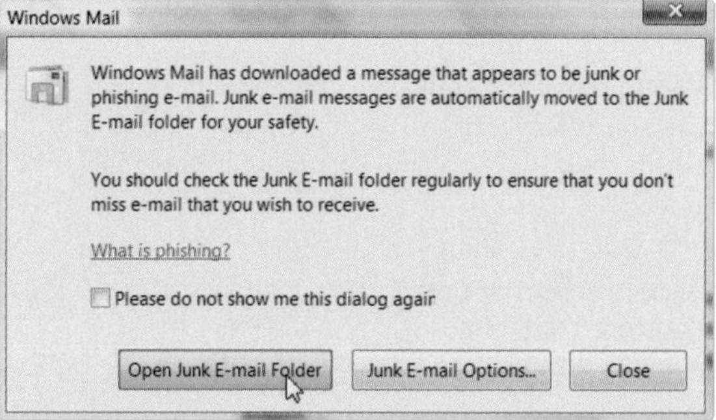

- If a particular message in your **Junk E-mail** folder looks suspicious, do not open it.
- Right click on the message title and then select **Delete** from the pop-up menu that appears.

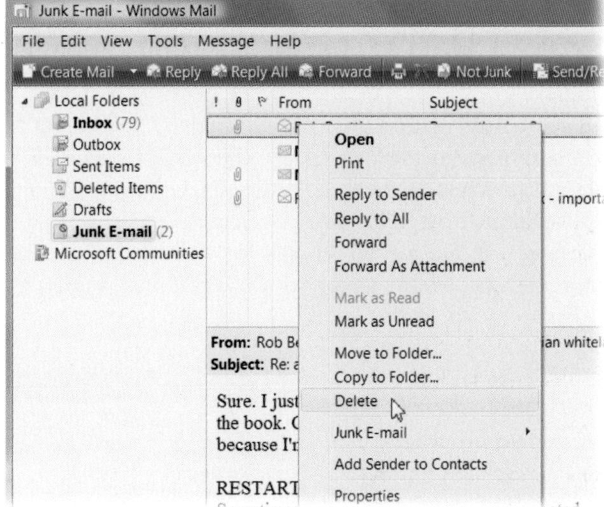

- If you know the sender, and Windows Mail is just being oversensitive, right click on the message title and select **Junk E-mail** from the drop-down menu.
- Then select **Add Sender to Safe Senders List** from the submenu that appears.

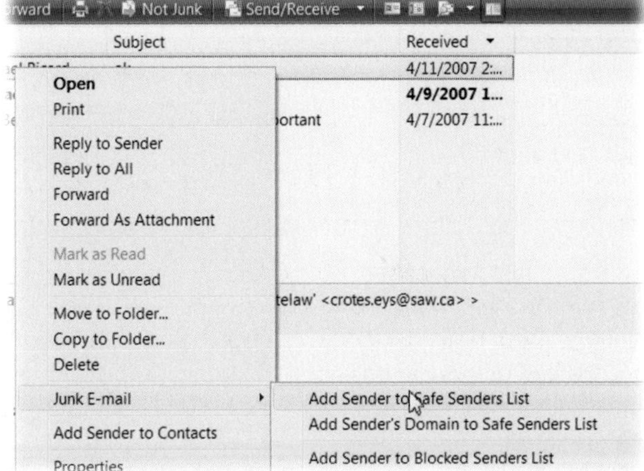

- Windows Mail pops up a confirmation box.
- Click **OK**.
- From now on, mail from this sender will no longer be sent to the **Junk E-mail** folder, but will go to your **Inbox** as normal.

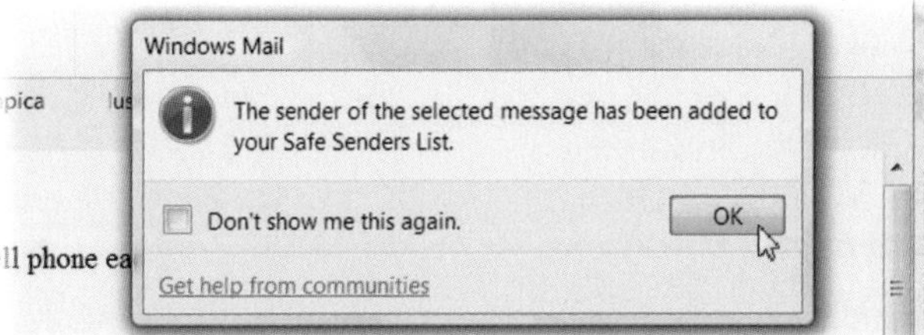

Customizing Junk E-mail Settings

Windows Mail contains a host of settings that determine how the program operates. For most of these, the default settings need not be altered, but in the case of e-mail blocking you may want to choose for yourself. If you want to keep your level of protection high, which will block a certain amount of "safe" mail, you may wish to place all your regular correspondents on your Safe Senders list, for example. Conversely, if you choose a low level of protection, each time you receive unwanted mail, you should add the sender to the Blocked list.

JUNK E-MAIL OPTIONS

- To check out what your junk e-mail settings are, and to adjust them if you want to, click on **Tools** and select **Junk E-mail Options** from the drop-down menu.

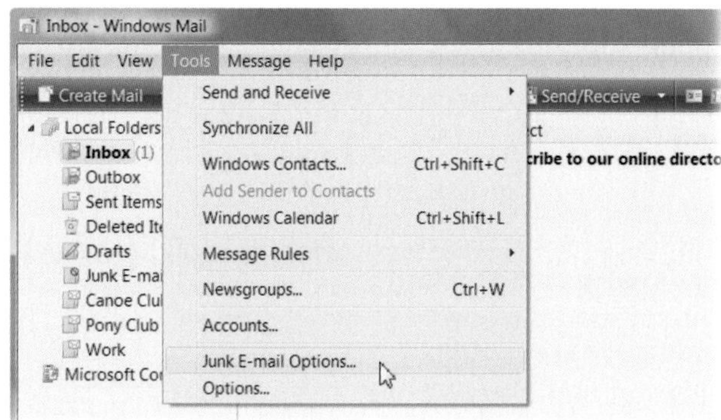

- In the **Options** tab you can select the level of junk e-mail protection that Windows Mail will provide.
- There is a balance to be achieved between filtering out too much and too little. If junk e-mail does not seem to be a problem for you, you may find that **Low** is the right setting for you.

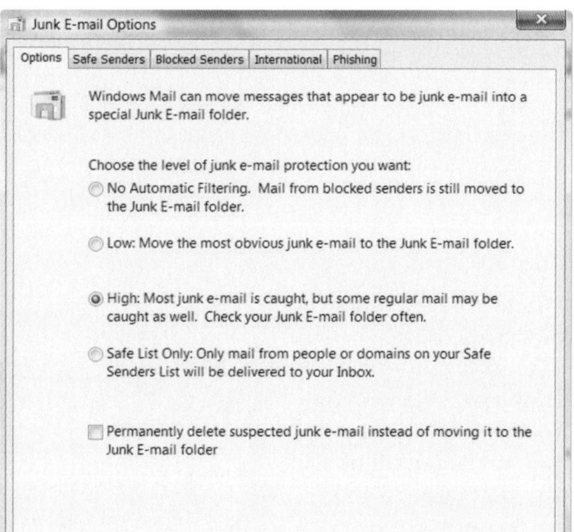

● In the **Safe Senders** tab, you can view addresses already on the list and also add ones whose e-mails we don't wish to have blocked.

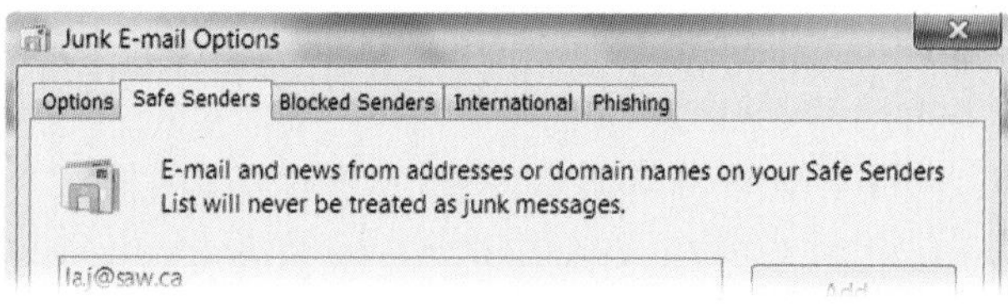

● Just as Safe Senders can be added to the list by right clicking on a message title and making a selection from the drop-down menus, Blocked Senders can also be added this way.

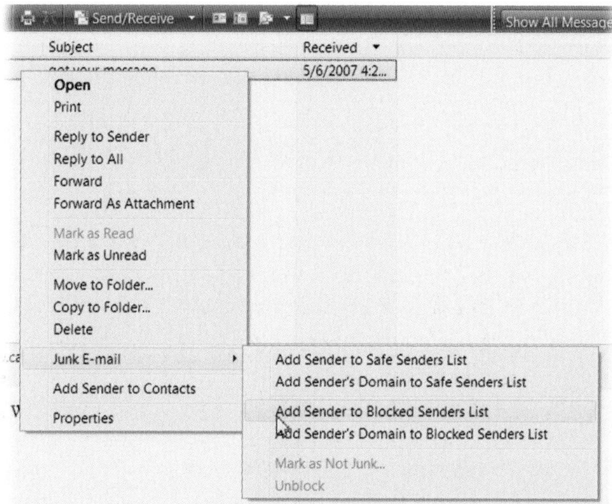

● The list of Blocked Senders can be viewed and amended under the **Blocked Senders** tab of the **Junk E-mail Options** dialog box.

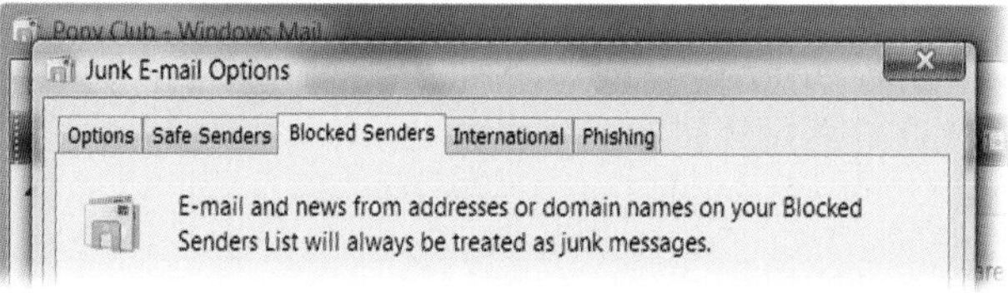

● The **Phishing** tab gives you the choice of having your Inbox protected against potential Phishers, and by default this option is checked.

● Click on the **What is phishing?** link for a succinct explanation.

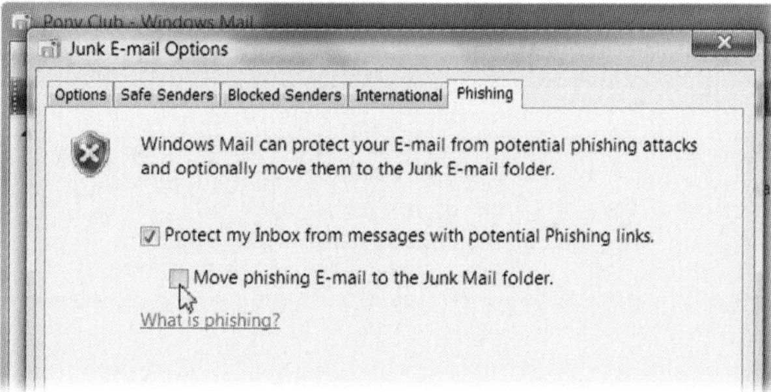

Personalized E-mail

Just as a good old-fashioned letter can be on classy, hand-made, watermarked headed notepaper, so an e-mail can be customized to reflect the personality of its sender.

Using Signatures

If you usually like to finish your messages in a certain way, for example, including your name, job title, or contact details, an e-mail "signature" saves you typing the same details every time you write a new message. A signature consists of a line or two of text that can be automatically inserted at the foot of an e-mail message.

CREATING A SIGNATURE

● To create a signature, start by clicking on **Tools** and selecting **Options** from the drop-down menu.

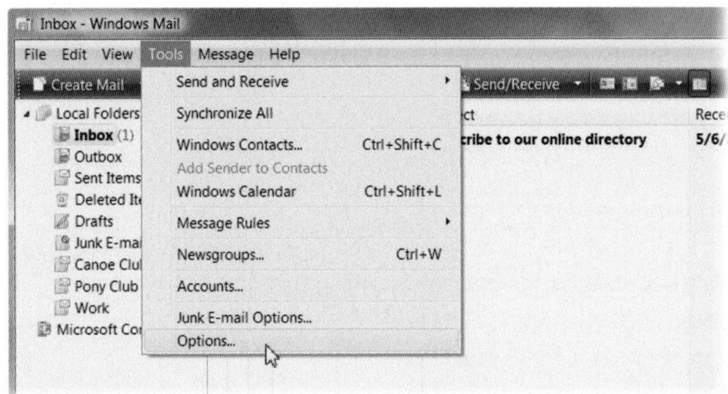

● In the **Options** dialog box, select the **Signatures** tab and click on **New**.

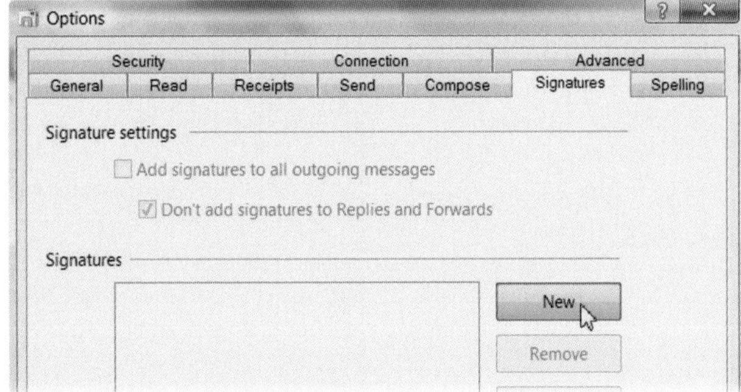

- In the **Edit Signature** text box, type in the details that you wish to see at the foot of each e-mail message.
- Place a checkmark next to **Add signatures to all outgoing messages** and click **OK**.

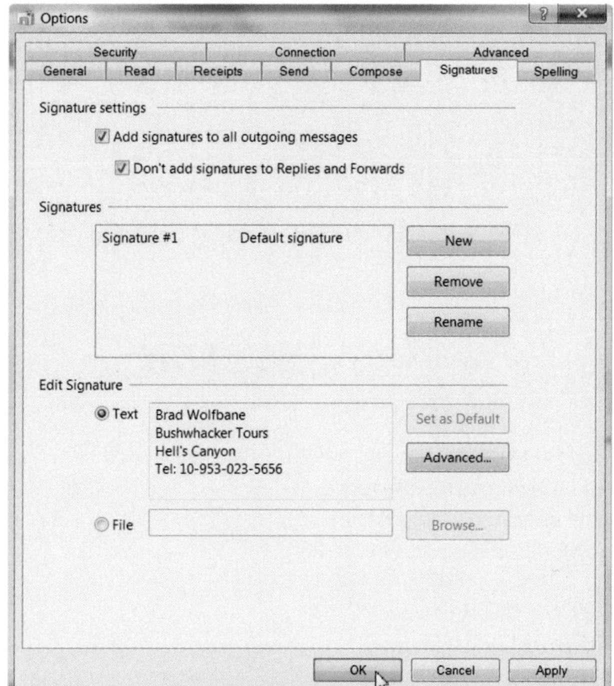

- Now when you click on **Create Mail** and open a **New Message** window, these details will automatically appear in the message body.
- As you type in your text, your contact details remain at the foot of your message.

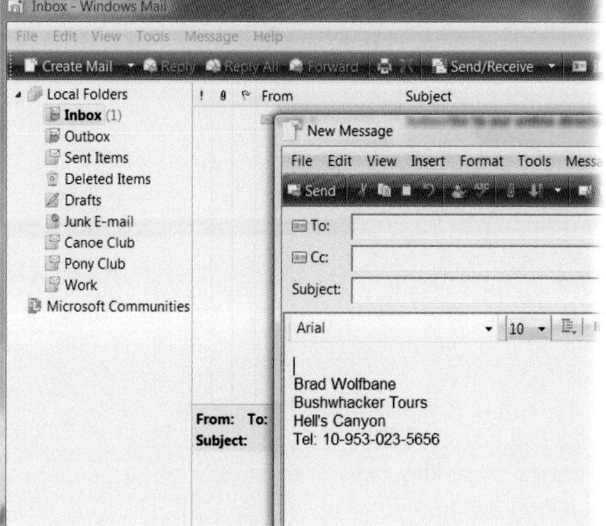

USING BACKGROUNDS

If you've ever received an e-mail with a brightly colored background and you've wondered how it was done, here's the answer. Used with care, the backgrounds available in Windows Mail can add flare to your messages. Used recklessly, they can render your message totally illegible, so make your choices wisely.

OPENING THE OPTIONS

- Click on **Create Mail** to open a **New Message** window, and click on **Format** in the menu bar.
- Select **Background** and then click on **Picture** in the submenu that appears.

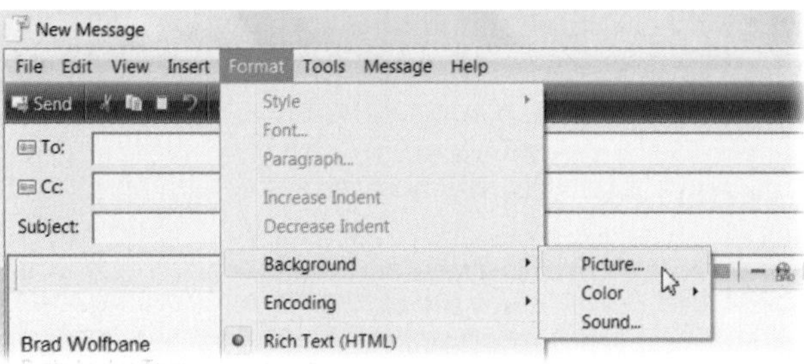

- In the **Background Picture** dialog box, you can browse your hard PC for images to use as a background, but there is also a pre-made selection.
- Click on the arrow to the right of the **File** panel to bring up the list of choices.
- Slide your cursor up the list and select one by clicking on it.
- Click on **OK** to confirm your choice of background.

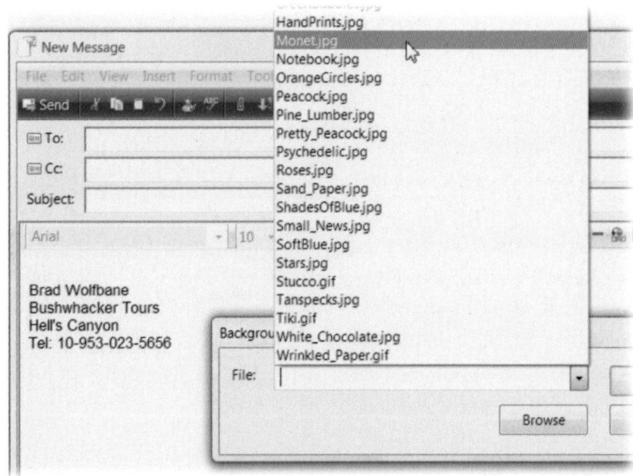

- Your message now has this background.
- To remove it, repeat the steps and delete the file name from the **File** panel in the **Background Picture** dialog box.

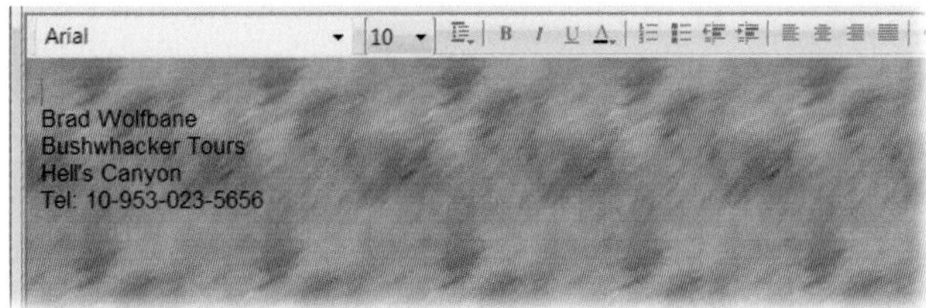

USING STATIONERY

Windows Mail's collection of stationery provides more than just a background. Each type of stationery also brings with it a font color, to give your e-mail a co-ordinated look. Here we deal with a single message, but stationery can be set for all new messages by using the **Compose** tab in the **Options** in the **Tools** menu.

OPENING THE STATIONERY WINDOW

- Click on **Message** in the toolbar, select **New Message Using**, and then choose **Select Stationery** from the submenu that appears.

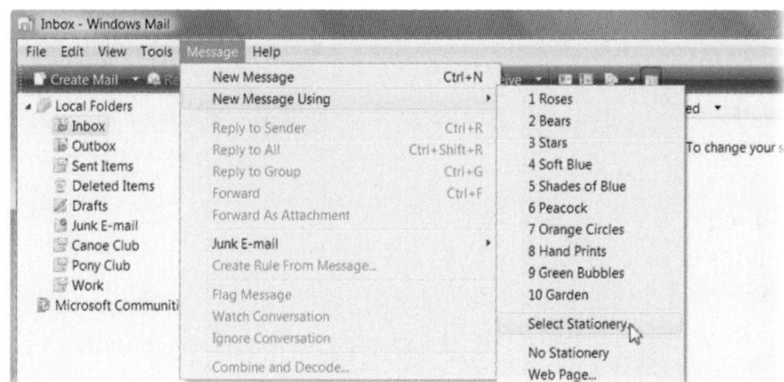

SELECTING YOUR STATIONERY

- In the **Select Stationery** window, click on any of the listed options and you will be able to see what it looks like in the **Preview** pane. If you can't see a preview, make sure the **Show preview** option is checked.
- Click on **OK** to confirm your selection.

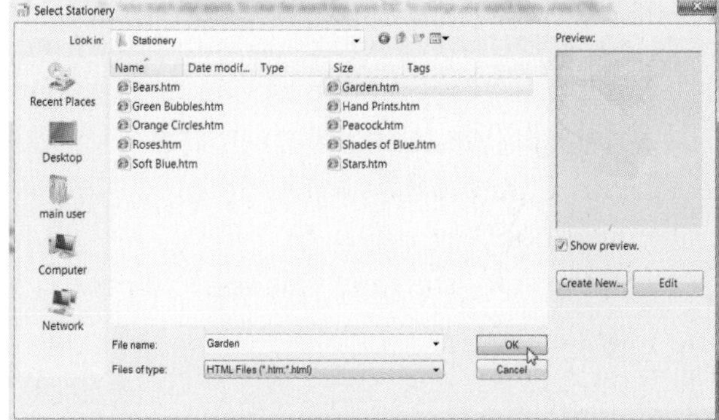

VIEWING THE EFFECT ON THE PAGE

- The **New Message** window opens, and the message is in the style of your chosen stationery.
- As you can see, the text of the signature is now in a matching color.

STAYING SAFE

YOU'VE PROBABLY HEARD a lot about the potential dangers that lay in wait for PC users–scams, online stalkers, identity theft, and much more. So, just how real are these threats? Are you and your family in genuine danger, or is it being exaggerated by those who stand to gain by selling you solutions to problems that you'll probably never encounter? Here, we'll outline the dangers and show you how Windows works to help you avoid them. We'll also look at the extra software you need–to protect against viruses, specifically–and how it works.

200 What To Expect

206 Windows Update

212 Windows Firewall

216 Malware Protection

230 Sharing Your PC Safely

What To Expect

If you look after your PC, then your PC will look after you. Keep it up to date, keep away from the less well-lit corners of the web, and don't extend more trust to strangers than you would in real life.

The Dangers

The sad fact is that there are people out there who want to pester you with junk get-rich-quick schemes, steal from you, con personal information out of you and then sell it to others, or who just want to vandalize anything they can. In this respect, the electronic world isn't so different from the real one, and, just like the real world, there are millions of us who go about our business every day without any problems at all. The dangers are there, but they're manageable–with a little help.

PHISHING

● Phishers are simply 21st-century con artists who try and trick you into revealing private information, such as your bank account details. Their preferred tool is e-mail, and they'll usually target you with a message that looks as if it came from a financial institution. Banks, though, will never e-mail you asking you to go online and re-enter your user name and password. Similarly, ignore e-mails thanking you for an order you haven't made or claiming "your loan request has been processed" when you haven't asked for one.

Dear Barclays Online banking customer,

Barclays Protection Department requests you to start the client details confirmation procedure. By clicking on the link at the bottom of this letter you will get all necessary instructions how to start and complete the confirmation procedure. The following steps are to be taken by all customers of the Barclays Online banking.

Barclays Protection Department apologizes for the inconveniences caused to you, and is very grateful for your cooperation.

To start the confirmation procedure, click the following link:
http://barclays.co.uk/procedureid0732100211/client.html

Copyright © 2007 Barclays Bank PLC. Registered in England. Registered No: 1026167.

This is a typical fake e-mail, designed to persuade you to reveal your user name and password so they can be used to gain access to your bank account.

MALWARE

- This is the umbrella term for all of the nasties that PCs can catch–viruses, worms, and trojans. The most common way to get infected is to receive an e-mail from someone–often, but not always, someone you don't know–that has a file attached. This file may be masquerading as a photo or document, but actually contains a small program that copies itself secretly to your PC and then goes about its business. Malware can make a PC run very slowly, it can spy on the websites you visit, it can attach itself to every e-mail you send and spread to everyone in your address book; it can even damage or destroy your files. The other common ways to become infected are: clicking a link in an e-mail that takes you to a phishing site; using illegally copied software; or playing pirated films and music.

VIRUS, WORM, OR TROJAN?

- A virus cannot infect your PC unless you run it or open it. Viruses can't spread by themselves and need people to help them by passing them on unwittingly, usually attached to e-mails. They vary in severity from displaying a stupid message to deleting your files.
- A worm can spread without any human intervention, using the communications network built into every PC in order to replicate itself over and over again. A worm can infect your address book, sending itself to every address on your computer, thereby spreading its destruction. Worms can overload entire computer networks and bring them to their electronic knees.

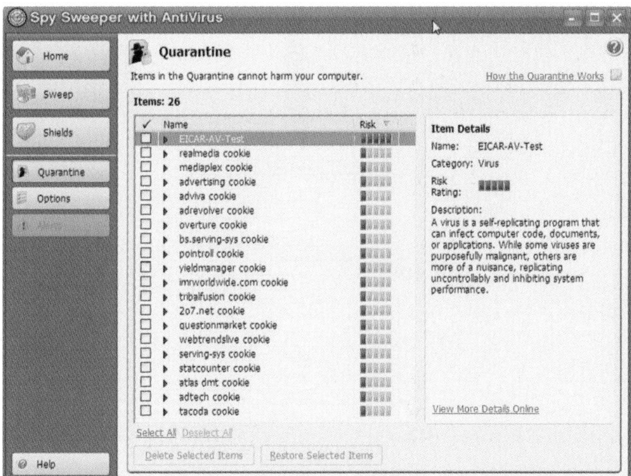

Antivirus and antispyware programs such as Spy Sweeper can "catch" a potential threat trying to copy itself to the PC, and can scan the PC for viruses and spyware and then quarantine them.

- A trojan doesn't spread like a virus or a worm, but usually arrives in the guise of a program you asked for or at least one that looks safe or useful. It then sits there doing nothing until the time comes for it to activate. Trojans can be merely irritating or they can cause real damage. More recently they've also been known to open a secret door in your firewall so that hackers can infiltrate your system.

BEWARE OF FRIENDS BEARING GIFTS!

Although most PCs get infected via e-mail or the web from complete and troublesome strangers, it can also happen courtesy of a friend or colleague who's either not as careful or just not as savvy about security as you are. If you're accepting any kind of file from someone else, whether it's on floppy disk, CD-ROM, DVD, Zip disk, or USB stick, you should always run it through your virus checker first to make sure that it's clean and safe before loading it onto your computer. It's important to remember that some kinds of malware can remain dormant for weeks or even months on end before activating, so you won't always know that there's something wrong right away.

SPAM

- This is simply electronic junk mail. Like real junk mail it promises you the earth–cheap software and pharmaceuticals, get-rich-quick-schemes, online gambling, performance enhancing products, and so on; sometimes these e-mails will also include links to seedy websites.
- Some spam e-mails seem very polite and ask you to reply if you'd like to be taken off their mailing list. However, you should never reply to spam. By doing so, you tell the spammer that they've reached a real address. They will sell it on to other spammers, and you'll get many times more junk than before. Just delete spam without opening it.

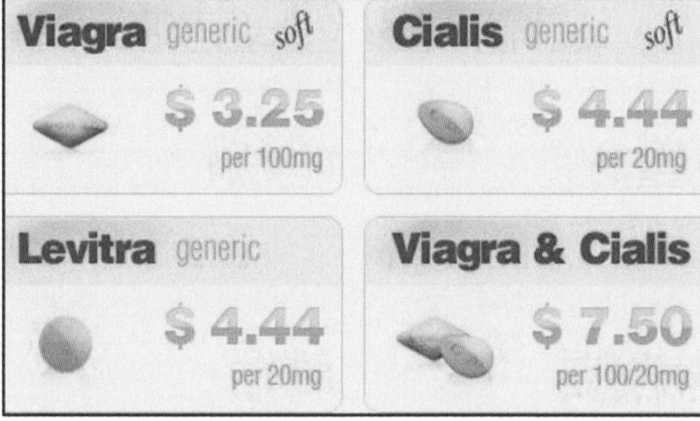

SPYWARE

● Some people think spyware is just another kind of malware, but it's different enough to warrant its own category. It infects a PC just like malware, but then sits there "listening." It may record the keystrokes you type or the websites you visit with a view to stealing passwords or simply to help an unscrupulous advertiser find out about the kinds of things you're interested in so they can bombard you with pop-up adverts.

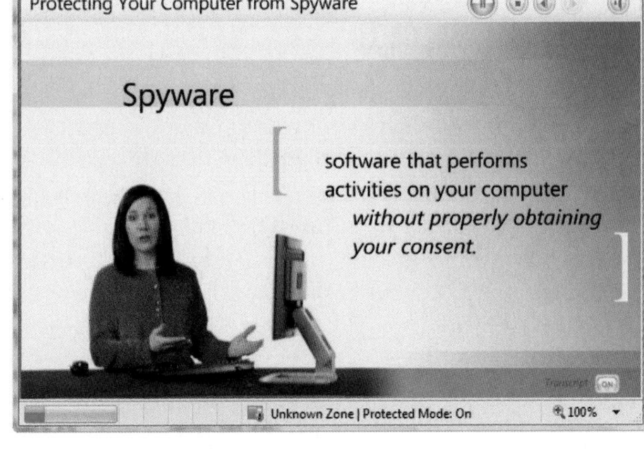

For handy video tutorials about about spyware, ***go to www. microsoft.com/athome/security/videos/default.mspx.***

SOFTWARE VULNERABILITIES

● Despite what the authors would have us believe, software isn't perfect, and sometimes unscrupulous users can find these imperfections and take advantage of them.

● This is particularly true of the operating system itself–Windows–and the web browsing program Internet Explorer.

● What is the solution? As we'll explain later on, you need to keep your software up to date.

THE APPLE ALTERNATIVE

Apple's advertising campaigns make considerable play of the fact that people who own Apple Macs don't have to worry about viruses as much as the people who own PCs. By and large, this is certainly true. However, the reason isn't necessarily because Macs are more secure than PCs. Rather, it is because there are many millions more PCs in the world than there are Macs. If you're a malicious virus writer, you'll want to infect as many computers as possible with your handiwork. It therefore makes more sense to target the largest potential audience, and that's PC users running Microsoft Windows.

Windows Update
206

THE SECURITY CENTER

Just as you wouldn't leave your front door open at night, and your wallet, car keys, and address book on the table on the hallway, you shouldn't leave the electronic doors open on your PC. Fortunately, Vista has plenty of ways to help you keep things safe and secure, and Microsoft has thoughtfully gathered them all in one place–in the Security Center. Here, we'll have a closer look at this feature.

OPENING THE CONTROL PANEL

- To explore Vista's Security Center, begin by clicking the Start button to open the Start menu.

- When the menu opens, slide the cursor arrow up and right to the **Control Panel** entry. To select, click on it once with the left mouse button.

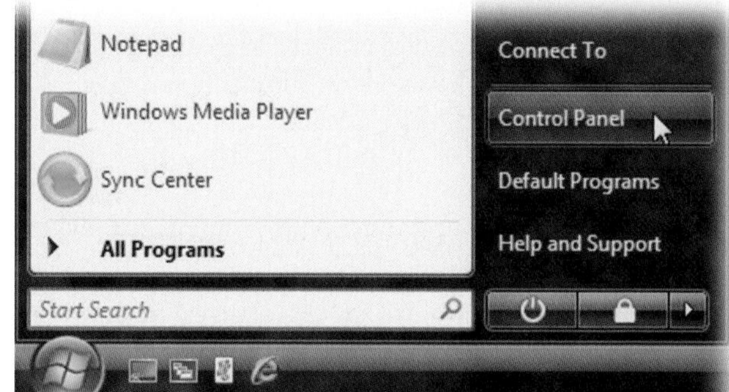

CHECKING THE STATUS OF YOUR PC

- When the Control Panel opens, find the **Security** section and then look underneath for the **Check this computer's security status** link. Move the cursor over it so it changes to a pointing hand, and then click to select.

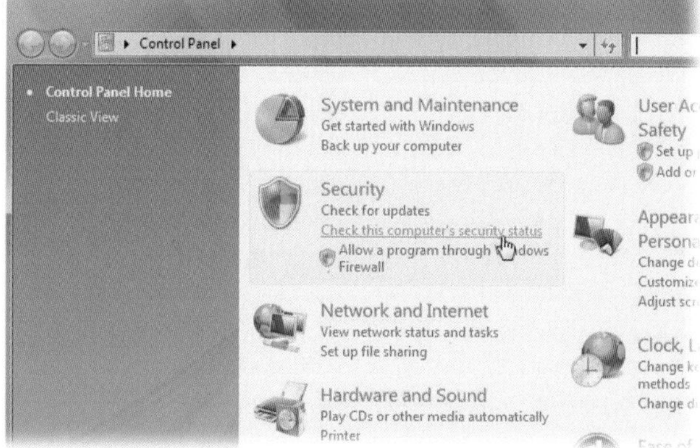

THE SECURITY CENTER WINDOW

• This is the heart of Windows' security settings and programs. At first sight, it doesn't look like much fun, but once things are set up correctly, you won't need to spend much time in the Security Center at all because it's been designed to virtually run itself.

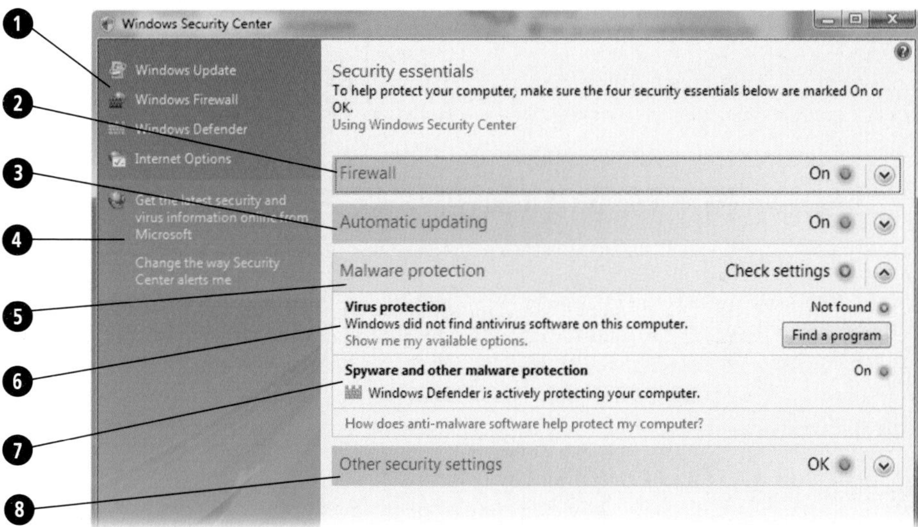

WINDOWS SECURITY CENTER

❶ Key Links
When clicked, these links open windows directly onto the key components in the Windows Security Center.

❷ Firewall
Windows Vista includes a firewall designed to keep hackers out. Here, Security Center indicates that the Firewall is switched on.

❸ Automatic Updating
Similarly, Automatic Updating is switched on–this means that Windows will regularly connect to a Microsoft website, look for important updates, and then download and install them. You don't have to do anything.

❹ Latest Information
These settings alter the way that the Security Center displays its warnings. There is also a link connecting to a Microsoft website that has information about new virus threats.

❺ Malware Protection
Malware Protection is flagged as orange, for caution.

❻ Virus Protection
Here it notes that it's been unable to detect any virus protection on this PC. This is normal. Windows Vista doesn't include any antivirus software, so we'll have to install some.

❼ Windows Defender
Vista includes a program called Windows Defender–it can sniff out uninvited programs that are spying on the way you use your PC and get rid of them for you. Security Center tells you it's switched on.

❽ Other Security Settings
These settings, which include the User Account Control, are also giving us the green light.

216 **Malware Protection**

Windows Update

Windows is constantly updated by Microsoft. Most of the time this happens automatically but, in some cases, updates are considered useful rather than crucial, requiring the do-it-yourself approach.

Installing Updates Manually

Unless you specifically request otherwise–and we recommend that you don't–security updates are handled automatically by Windows. You may not even notice the little icon appear in the Notification Area telling you that an update is being installed. Occasionally, however, you may be able to improve the performance of your PC by downloading an update yourself, as in the following example.

1 STARTING WINDOWS UPDATE

- With the Windows Security Center still open, move the cursor over the **Windows Update** link on the left so it changes into a hand and click once.

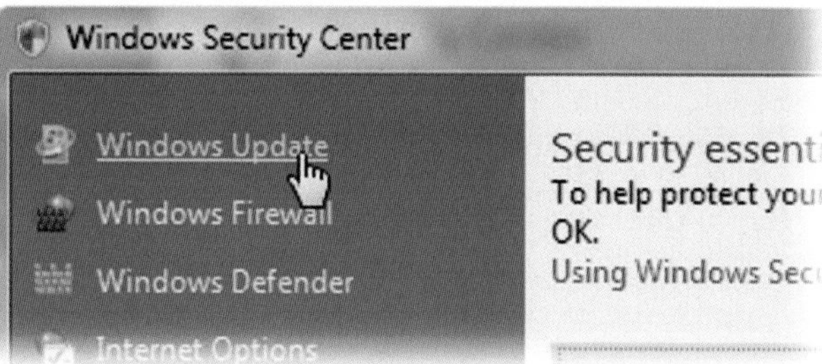

- Windows tells us that we're up to date in terms of necessary bug fixes and security, but notes that there are 20 optional updates available. Let's have a look at them by clicking the **View available updates** link. (If Windows says it can't display any updates–see the Going Online box opposite).

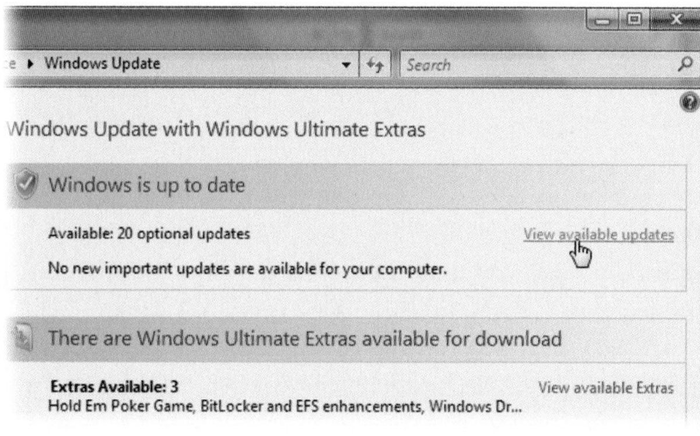

2 VIEWING AND SELECTING

- Windows displays a list of current updates that are available for this PC and this version of Windows.
- In this example, we're going to download the video update for our notebook PC, so check this item by clicking in the checkbox next to it.

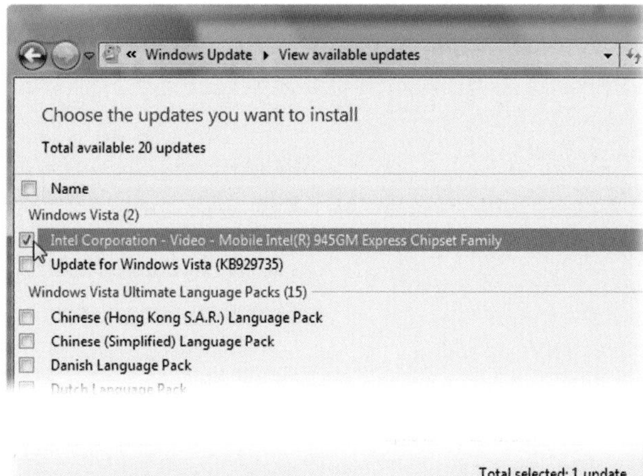

- Move the cursor down to the **Install** button and click it once with the left mouse button.

3 DOWNLOADING AN UPDATE

- Windows pops up the **User Account Control** dialog box and asks if you really want to download the update. It's fine, so just click **Continue**.

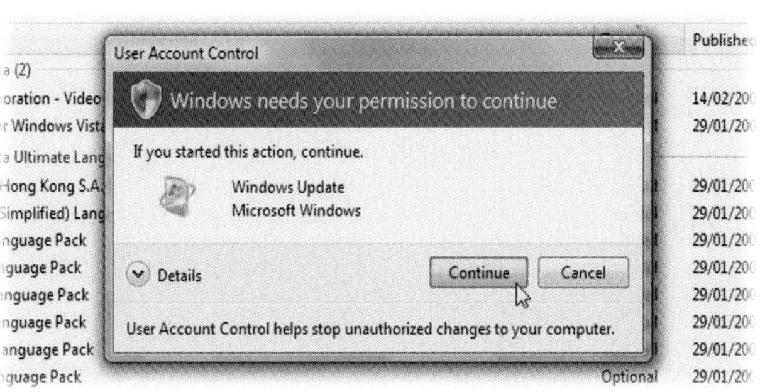

- Here's the update coming down. The progress bar moves from left to right to indicate how the download is coming along.

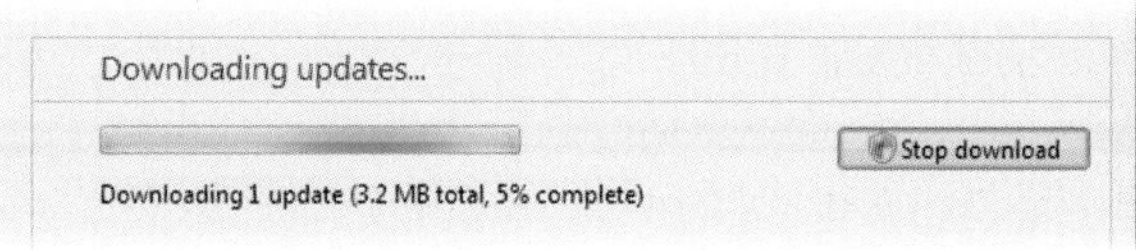

GOING ONLINE

Windows keeps its updates on the web, so if you can't see them it may be because you have a dial-up Internet connection rather than broadband. If that's the case, you will need to connect to the web before you download any updates. Once you are connected, go back to Starting Windows Update and try again.

4 INSTALLING THE UPDATE

- When the download is complete, Windows will install it, and your PC may re-start itself. When the process is finished, you'll return here and Windows will display a message that says **The updates were successfully installed**.

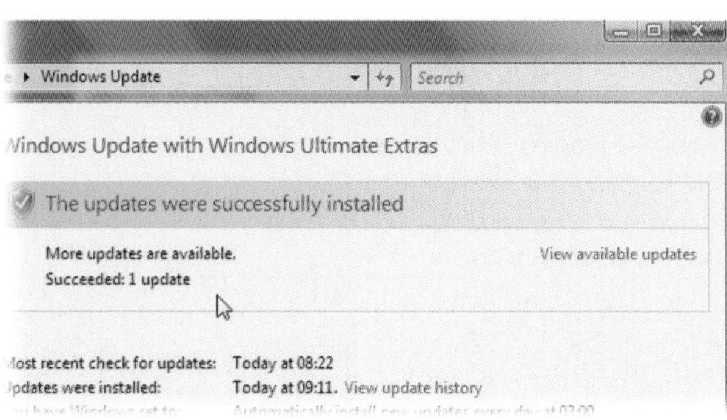

5 VIEWING THE UPDATE HISTORY

- You can check what you've just updated, as well as seeing how busy Windows has been behind the scenes, by clicking the **View update history** link on the left of the window.

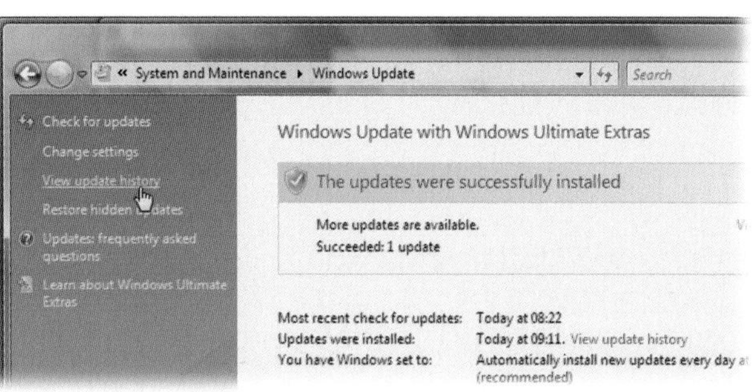

- Here's the list of updates that have been installed since this PC was first switched on. You can see that they're variously labeled **Important**, **Recommended**, and **Optional**. When you're done, click the Back button.

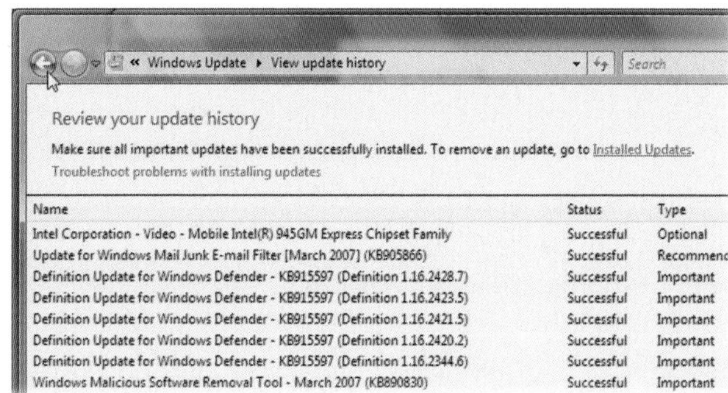

WINDOWS UPDATE NOTIFICATIONS

When Windows Update is set to automatic, a little message like this will sometimes pop up from the Notification Area. Click on the message and follow the instructions to install the update.

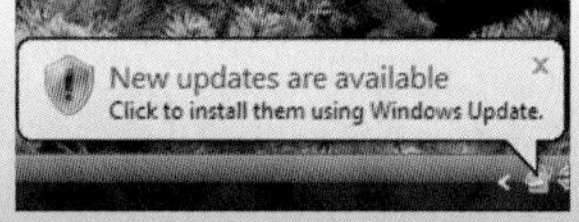

27 The Notification Area

CHANGING UPDATE SETTINGS

Windows takes a guess at when and how often you would like to check for updates. However, the schedule it picks might not be your preferred choice. This section shows you how to change the time at which updates are installed on your PC.

1 THE SETTINGS WINDOW

● Back at the Windows Update window, move the cursor over to the left and click once on the **Change settings** link.

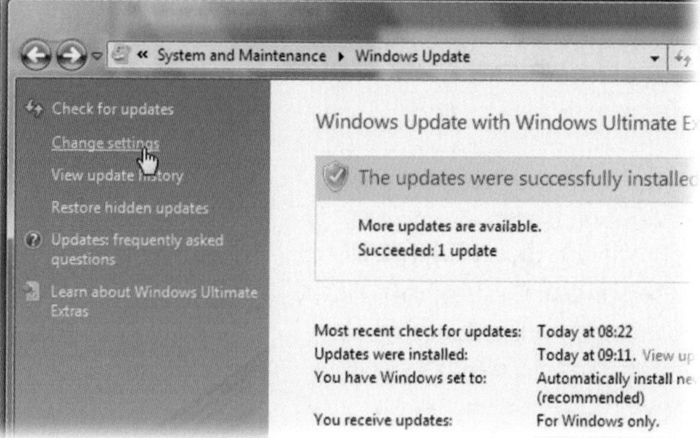

● Here you can see that Windows is set to **Install updates automatically (recommended)**. This is the recommended setting and, unless you have a specific reason for doing so, you shouldn't need to change it. You may, however, want to alter the actual schedule–at the moment it's set to look for and install new updates every day at 3.00am.

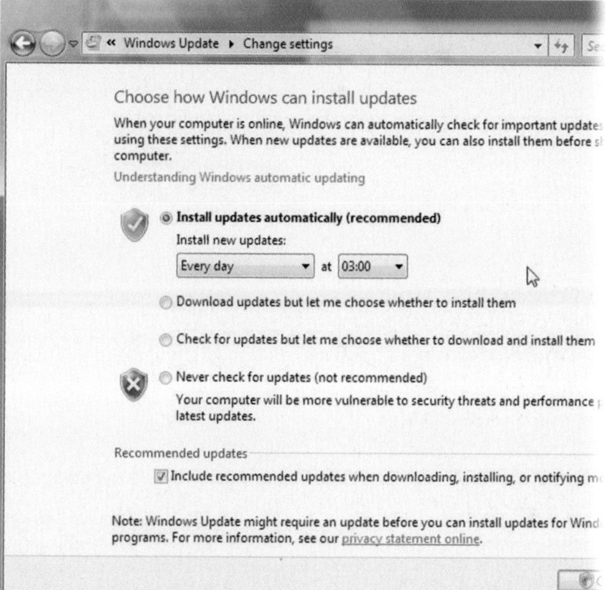

2 CHANGING THE UPDATE SETTINGS

- We want to install updates every day, but would prefer to check at a different time, when we're sure the PC will be switched on. So, place the cursor over the drop-down list arrow and click once to open.

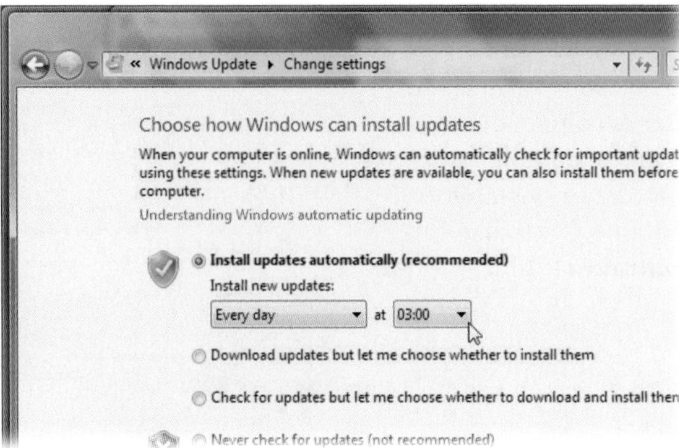

- Slide the cursor down the list until you find a time when you'd like to run the updates. We're going to choose 18:00 (6.00pm) because it's at the end of the day when we're finishing work, but the PC will still be switched on.

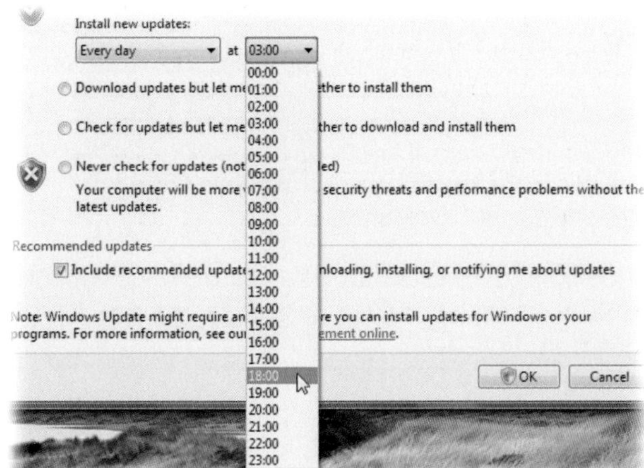

- Here you can see we've changed the time of the daily update download to the more convenient time of 18:00. Click the **OK** button to continue.

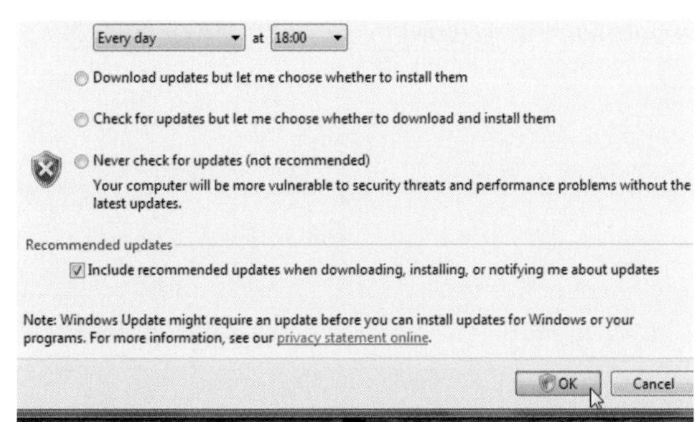

● Because we're changing something to do with the way Windows works, the **User Account Control** dialog box pops up and asks if we're sure we want to continue. Click the **Continue** button.

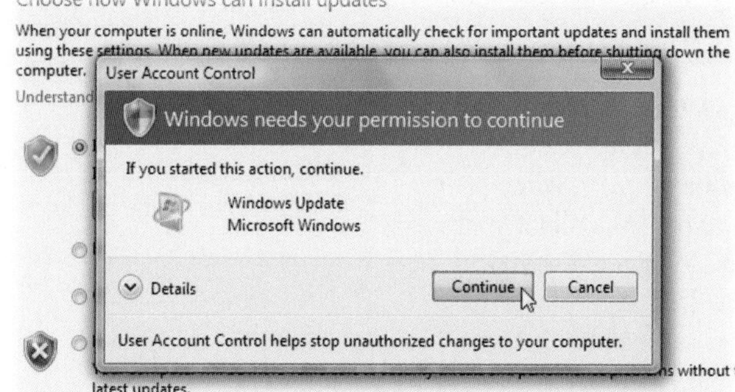

3 GETTING HELP WITH UPDATES

● If you'd like to know more about how Windows Updates work and what they do, click on the link on the left called **Updates: frequently asked questions**.

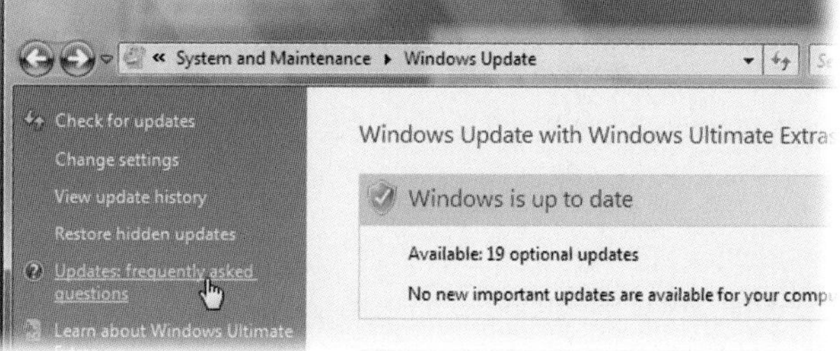

● Windows displays a context-sensitive help window that answers the kinds of questions that most new users will ask about updates. When you've finished, click the "x" to close the help window.

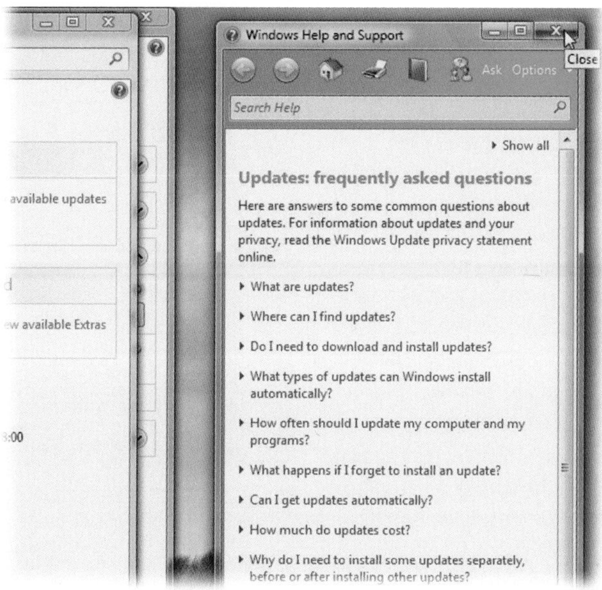

Windows Firewall

Windows Firewall acts a kind of electronic gatekeeper for the web, distinguishing between safe communication that should be allowed and suspect communication that needs to be blocked.

Configuring the Firewall

Firewall's default settings should do the job for most people the majority of the time. However, you'll occasionally find a program that needs to communicate through the firewall and, without a little adjustment, Windows won't let it. So, to make the program work properly for you, you may have to change Firewall's settings.

1 WINDOWS SECURITY ALERT

- The first time you meet Windows Firewall may be when you see a dialog box like this. In this example, we've downloaded a program called NoteZilla, an excellent notes program, and it has tried to open the firewall to accept incoming network connections, which doesn't sound like a very good–or secure–idea.

- If you're new to all this, you won't necessarily know what to do for the best, so click the **What are the risks of unblocking a program?** link to see if that helps.

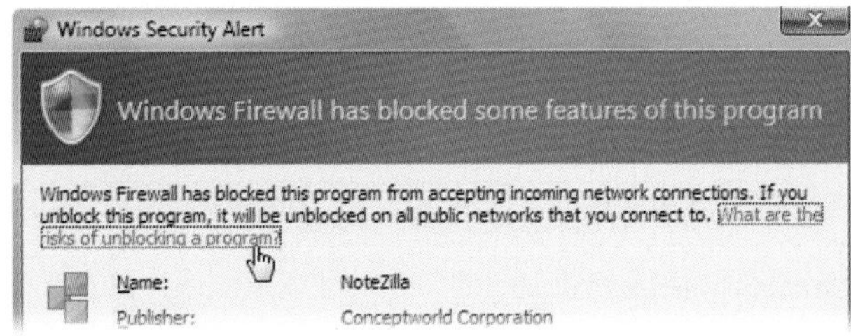

- The help on offer here is rather general and doesn't really solve our dilemma– whether to block or unblock the Notezilla program. Click the "x" to close the help window.

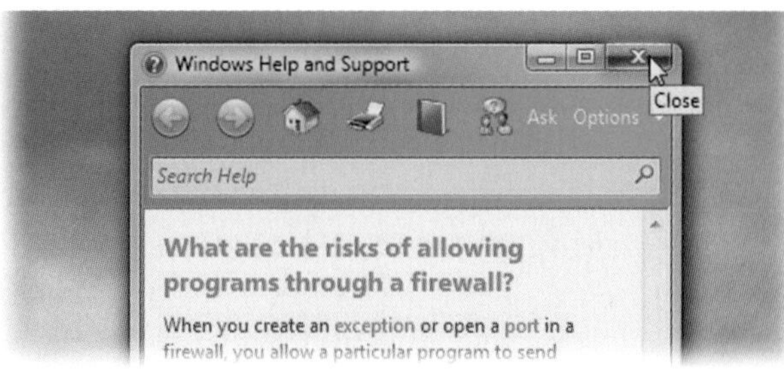

- In most circumstances, it is best to err on the side of caution, and that's what we're going to do here by clicking on the **Keep Blocking** button.

2 CREATING AN EXCEPTION

- Sometimes, you'll find that the way Windows Firewall blocks a program prevents it from working properly. If that's the case, you'll have to create what's called an exception. Go back to the Security Center again and click on **Windows Firewall**.

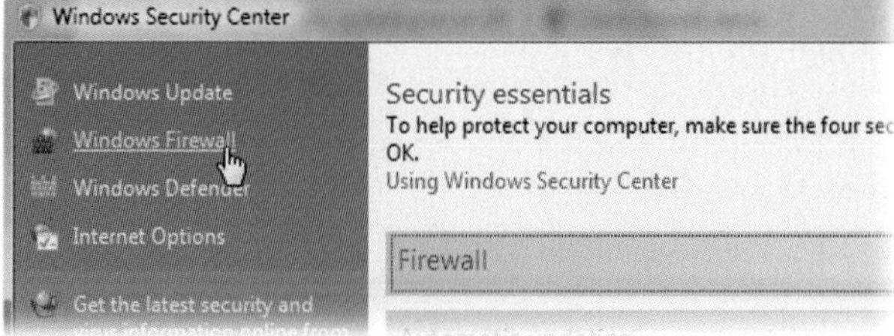

- When the Firewall window opens, click the **Change settings** link.

● When the **User Account Control** dialog box appears, click the **Continue** button.

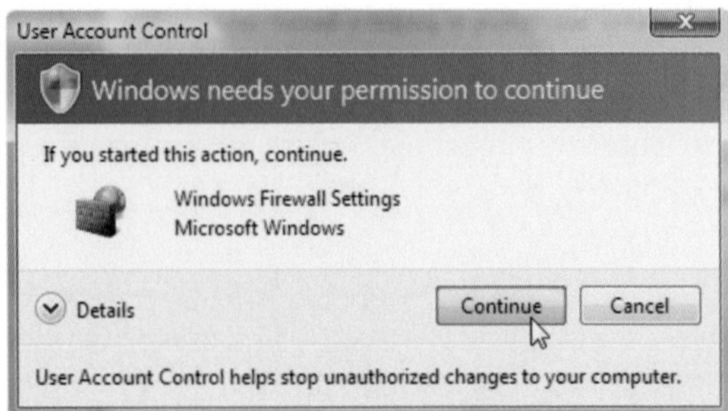

● This opens the **Windows Firewall Settings** dialog box where you can make changes to the way that the firewall interacts with Windows programs. Click on the **Exceptions** tab at the top to open another part of the dialog box.

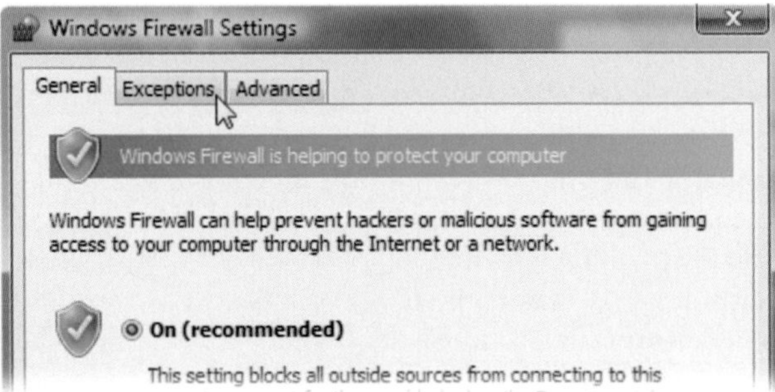

● Here's the list of Exceptions–programs or services that Windows allows to receive data through the firewall. To include the program we're using we'll need to click on the **Add program** button.

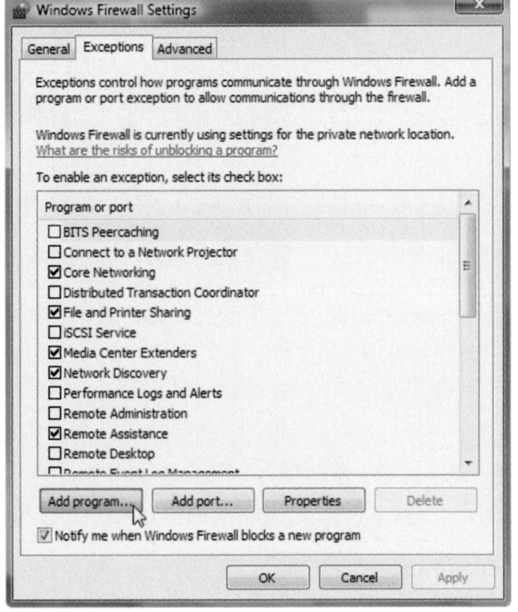

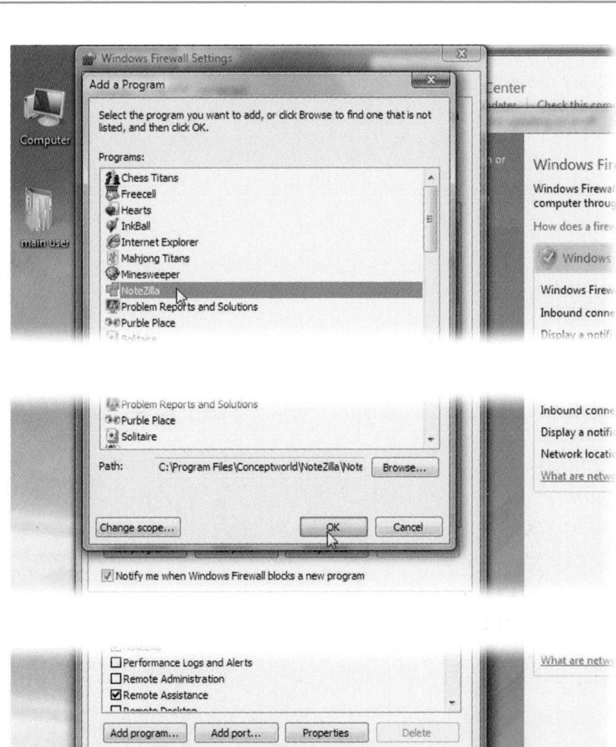

• NoteZilla, the program that we want to use, is displayed in the list of programs. Click on it once with the left mouse button.

• Click the **OK** button to confirm the changes and add this particular program to the list of Exceptions.

• The list now appears and we can see that the program we added–Notezilla–is now included in the list and has a little tick in the box next to its name, indicating that the Exception rule is active. If we want to temporarily stop the Exception later on, we can come back here and remove the tick. Click the **OK** button to finalize your changes and return to the Windows Firewall window.

OUTBOUND CONNECTIONS

Although Windows Firewall can stop programs from trying to "call out" through the firewall to other computers or networks, this feature is turned off by default. Keep your antivirus and antispyware software up to date and run it regularly and you should be OK. However, if you want to find out more about how to block outbound connections from your PC, open the Control Panel and choose **System and Maintenance**, then scroll down and click the **Administrative Tools** heading. When the window opens, double click the **Windows Firewall with Advanced Security** shortcut. When the **User Account Control** dialog appears, click **Continue** and that will open the advanced settings window. Click **Help** to find out more. Only change the settings here if you know what you're doing or have experienced help.

Malware Protection

Malware–viruses, worms, trojans, and spyware–can compromise a home PC and result in anything from sluggish performance to a huge loss of data. The only solution is to take steps to protect your PC.

Getting Protected

Windows Vista includes a firewall and antispyware software, but it doesn't come with any virus protection software. This is something you must sort out for yourself as soon as possible. If you ignore the dangers and continue to surf the web, send and receive emails, download and run programs, etc., you will get caught out.

FINDING AN ANTIVIRUS PROGRAM

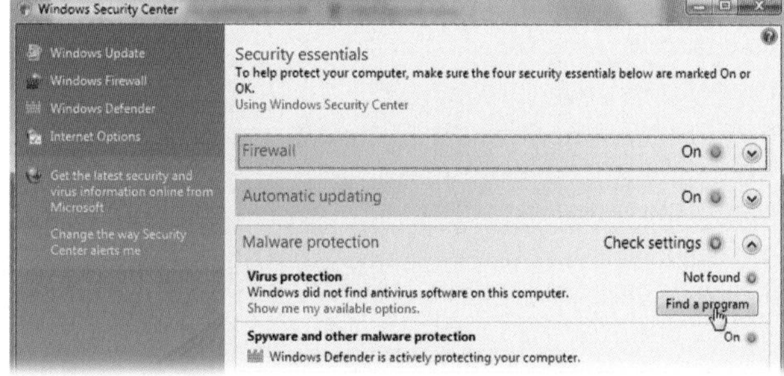

- Navigate to the **Windows Security Center** again and find the **Malware Protection** heading. Underneath that is a button labeled **Find a program**. Click it once with the left mouse button.

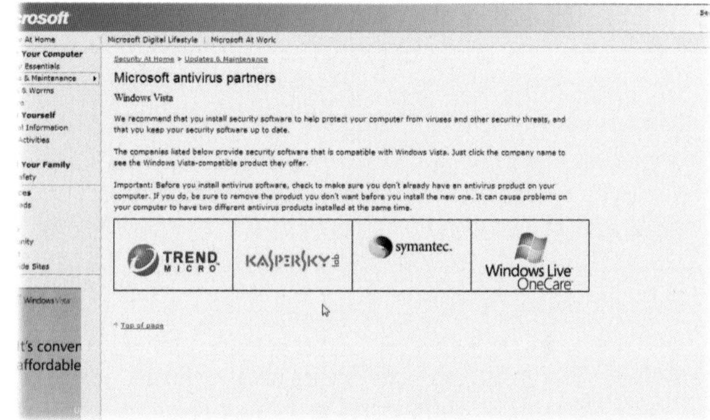

- This opens Internet Explorer and navigates to a website that has details of various deals Microsoft has done with antivirus software vendors. All of these are products that work with Windows Vista.

● You'll see that one of the options here is something called **Windows Live OneCare**. Click on this to investigate further.

● This opens a new window that describes the benefits of OneCare–a kind of all-in-one maintenance and security package from Microsoft. There's even a free 90-day trial if you wish to check out the product. For now, click the '**x**' to close this browser window.

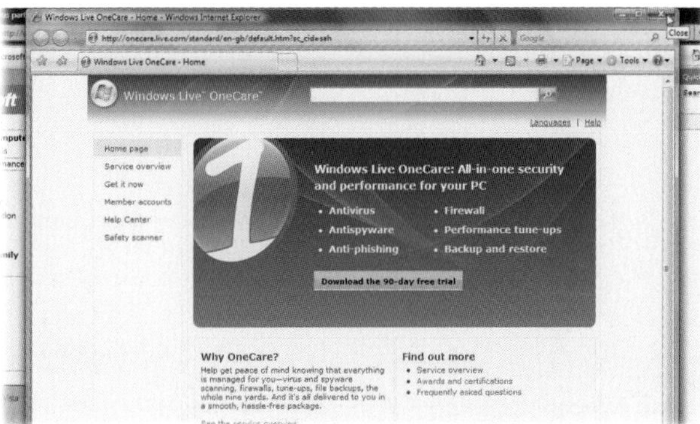

● Back at the original web site, let's have a look at one of the other offerings. This one's from Symantec, a well known and well respected vendor of security software. Click on the icon to open its web site.

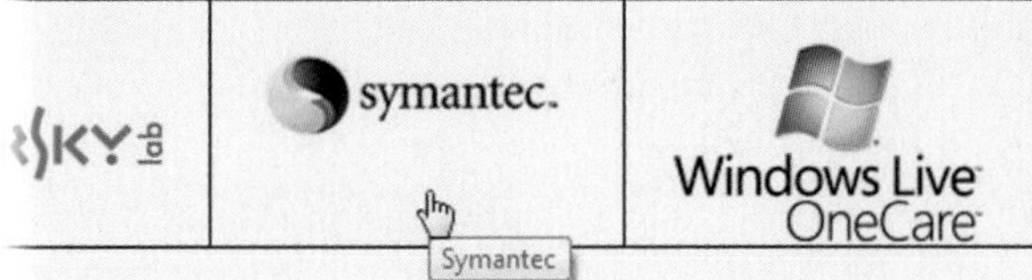

TWO INTO ONE WON'T GO

When it comes to firewalls, antivirus, and antispyware software, it's very important that you don't run two different products at the same time. The two will compete with each other and both try to run the show, bumping into each other, causing false alerts, slowing down your PC, and generally fouling everything up. Their behavior may actually make you less, rather than more, secure. You should always uninstall one antivirus program before you install a new one; if your antivirus software includes a firewall or antispyware software, turn off the Windows equivalents.

● Again, you can see that Symantec offers a free 90-day trial, enabling you to download and check out the program. As Vista becomes more popular, many more programs and services are likely to come onstream. Click the 'x' to close the browser window.

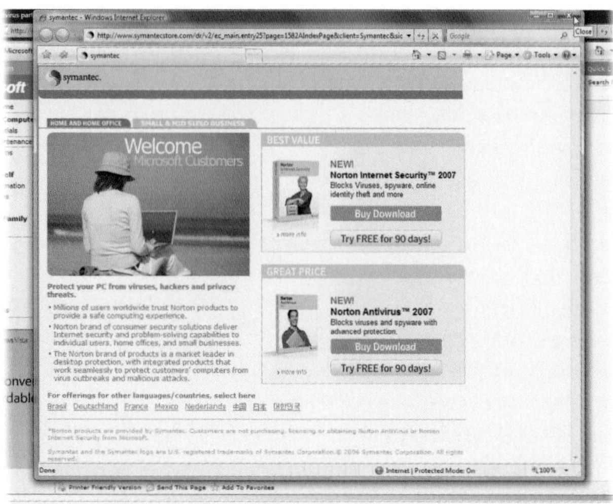

A Typical Antivirus Program

Most antivirus programs also include either antispyware software or a firewall, or both. This is problematic for the typical Windows user because, while we need the antivirus software, we don't need the other two because Vista already provides them. So, the first thing we need to do is set up our antivirus software and then, as we've mentioned before, make sure we're only running one of each of everything else.

THE HOME SCREEN

● Every antivirus program has a screen that looks something like this. All the basic information you need to know–what protection is running, how up to date it is, when your PC was last scanned, and so on–is collected in one easy-to-read window. This one belongs to Spy Sweeper with AntiVirus, the program we'll be using as an example in this chapter.

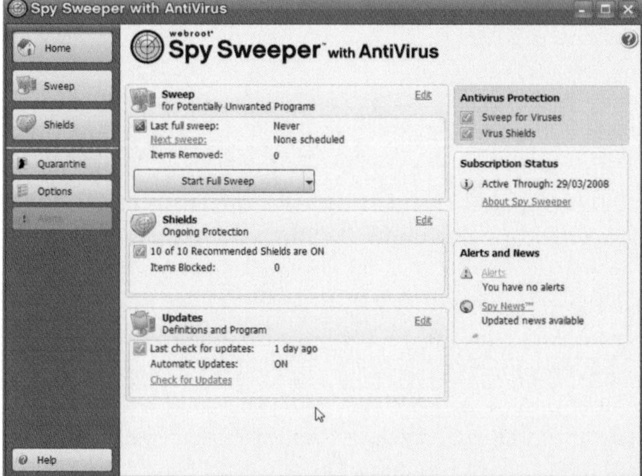

CHECKING FOR UPDATES

- All security software needs to be updated regularly so that it can deal with new threats as they arise. Remember, new malware is being produced and circulated all the time. Here, we're clicking the **Check for Updates** link.

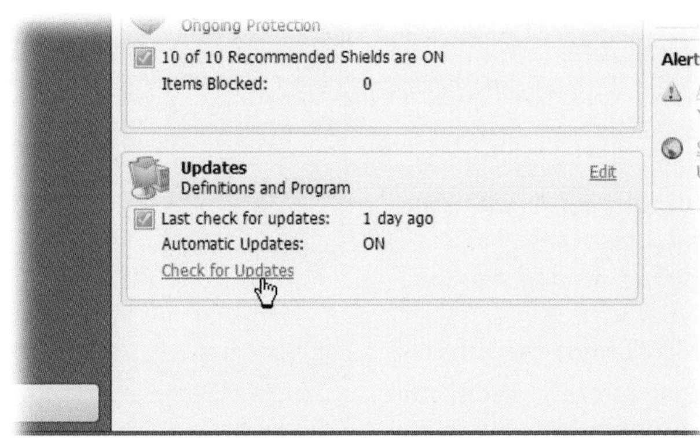

DOWNLOADING UPDATES

- The Spy Sweeper antivirus program goes off and checks its website to see if there are any updates presently available. If there are, Spy Sweeper downloads them automatically and then integrates them into its database of known threats–this is the only way that a security program can keep protecting you properly. Here you can see that Spy Sweeper is telling us that we're protected from 172,031 threats.

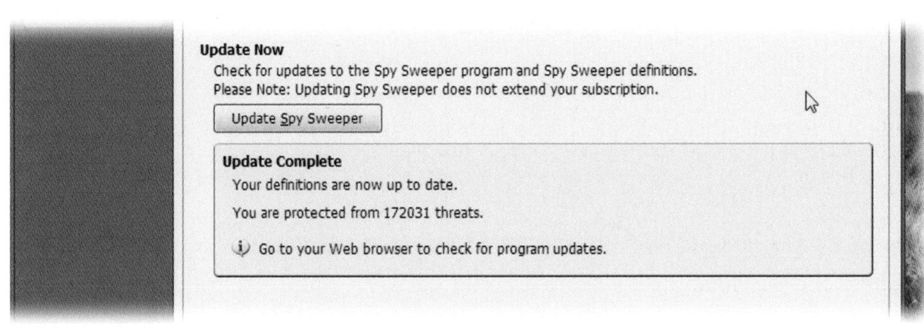

STANDALONE SAFETY

The only alternative to implementing proper protection is to run your PC in complete isolation, using only the programs that came with it (or shrink-wrapped commercial ones from a store), never connecting to the web, and never plugging in a storage device from someone else, for example, a floppy disk or a CD. Although this will keep your PC safe from malware, it means you'll be missing out on many of the experiences that make personal computing so rewarding. Our recommendation? Invest in some decent antivirus software and keep it up to date.

READY TO START SCANNING

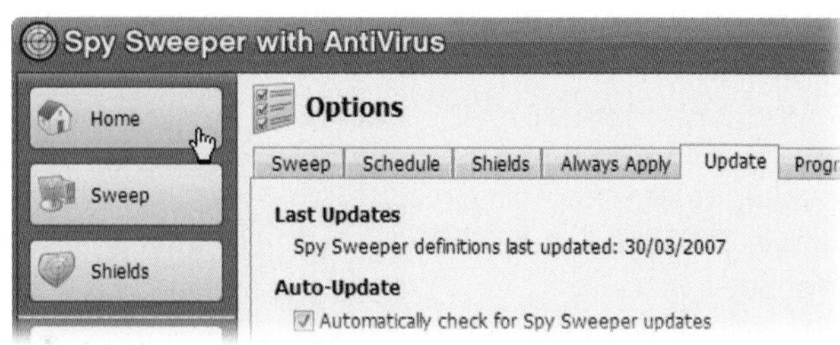

● Most antivirus programs use simple web-style navigation buttons to move around. Here, clicking the **Home** button will take you back to the main screen.

● Here we are back at the main screen. Next, before we can scan our PC for the first time to see if we've picked up any unwelcome "guests," we need to resolve any potential conflicts between this antivirus program and Windows' own protection.

Turning Off Windows Protection

The antivirus program we're using here is Webroot's Spy Sweeper with AntiVirus. As its name suggests, it includes an antispyware component, but no firewall, so we can leave the Windows firewall on, but we should turn Windows Defender off so that it doesn't conflict with the antispyware that's included with Spy Sweeper.

CHECKING THE SECURITY ESSENTIALS

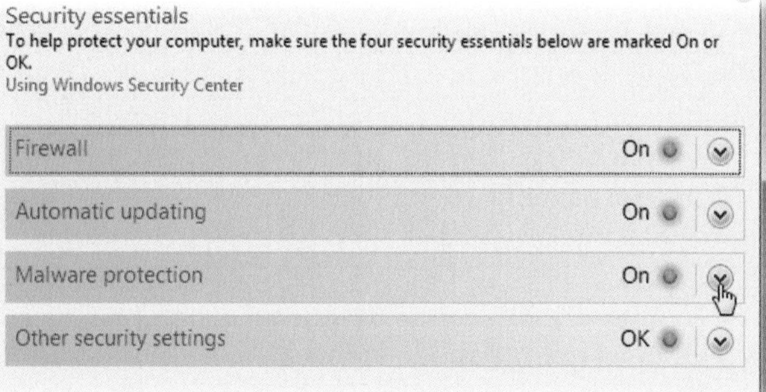

● Go back to the Windows Security Center. You'll see that all the lights are now green. That's because Windows knows that we now have an antivirus program installed. Click on **Malware protection** to look at things more closely.

- Athough Windows has registered our antivirus software (**Spy Sweeper with AntiVirus reports that it is up to date and virus scanning is turned on**), it's also telling us that both Windows Defender and Spy Sweeper are turned on. This is not a good idea, so we should turn Defender off.

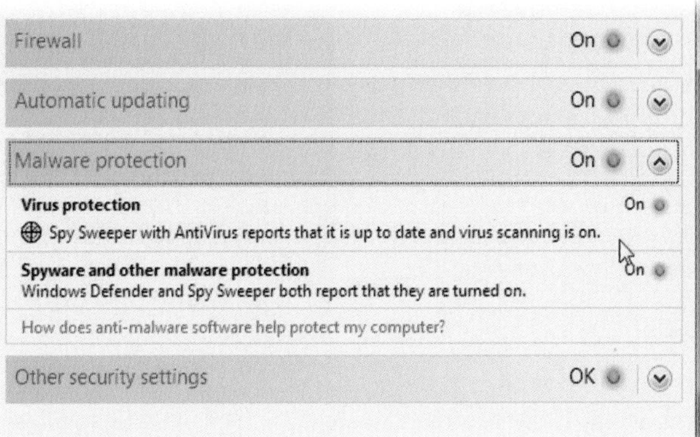

OPENING WINDOWS DEFENDER'S SETTINGS

- Move the cursor over to the **Windows Defender** link on the left and click on it once.

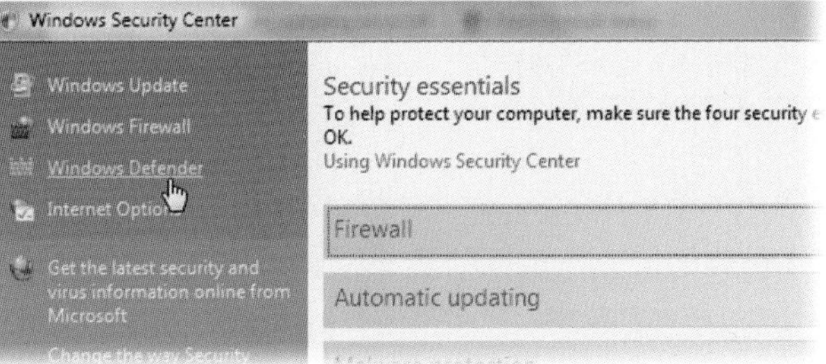

- When the Defender window opens, move the cursor to the **Tools** link in the top row of commands and click it with the left mouse button.

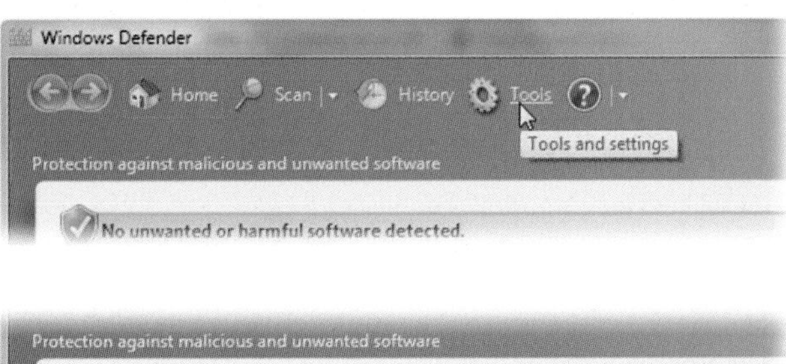

- At the next screen, move the cursor to the **Options** link and click it.

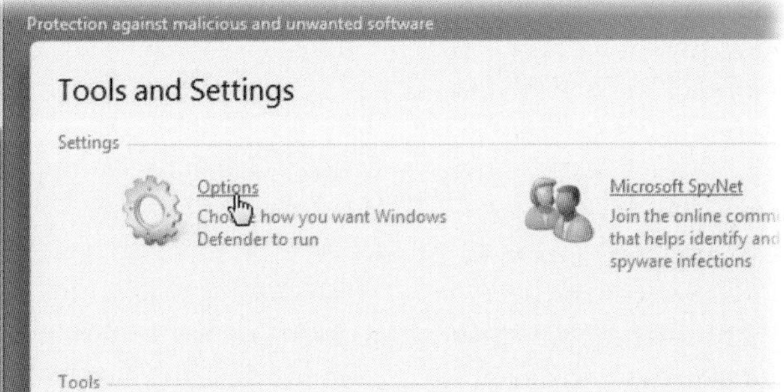

- When the Options window opens, grab the slider with the cursor and–still holding down the left mouse button–start to drag it down.

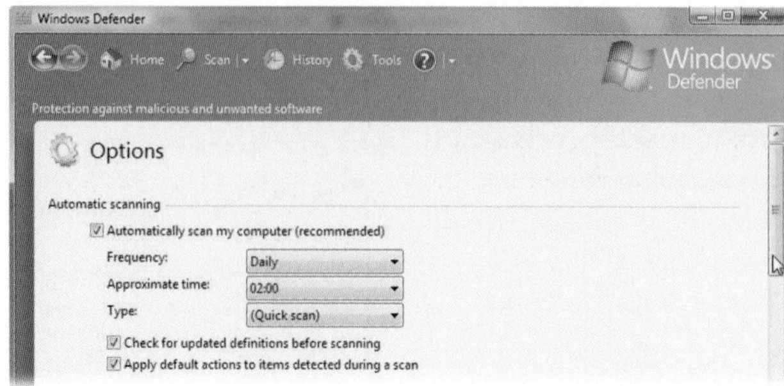

- Right at the bottom of the window you'll come to the **Administrator options**. Here, there's an option to **Use Windows Defender**, which is currently ticked.

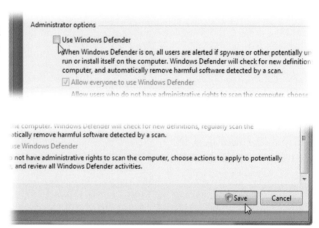

TURNING OFF WINDOWS DEFENDER

- Click there once with the left mouse button to remove the tick and turn Windows Defender off.

- Click the **Save** button to confirm your changes.

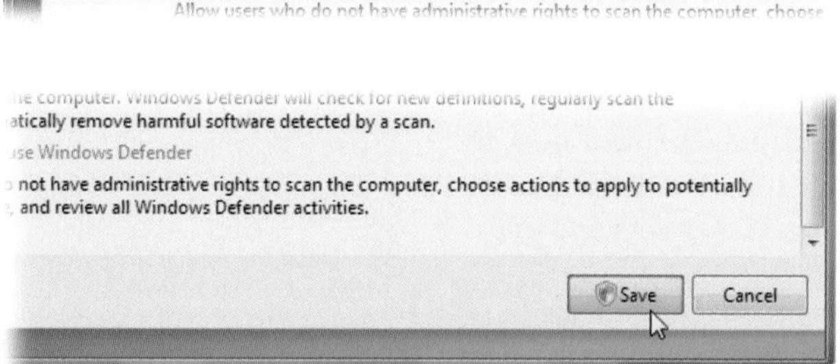

TURNING OFF WINDOWS FIREWALL

If, after installing your antivirus software, the Security Center window tells you that you have two active firewalls, you should turn off Windows Firewall. To do this, go to the Security Center and click the **Windows Firewall** link. In the next window, click the **Turn Windows Firewall on or off** link. Click **Continue** in the User Account Control dialog box. In the next dialog box, click the empty radio button next to **Off** and click **OK** to confirm.

● When the **User Account Control** dialog box appears asking if you're sure you want to make this change, click the **Continue** button.

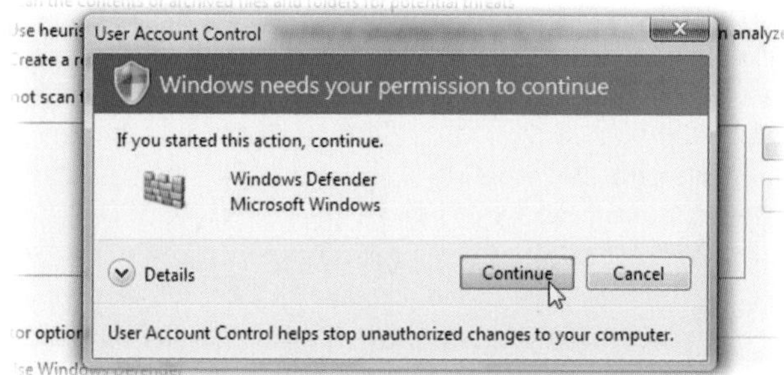

● Windows then displays a warning telling us the **Windows Defender is turned off**. This is fine, so click the **Close** button.

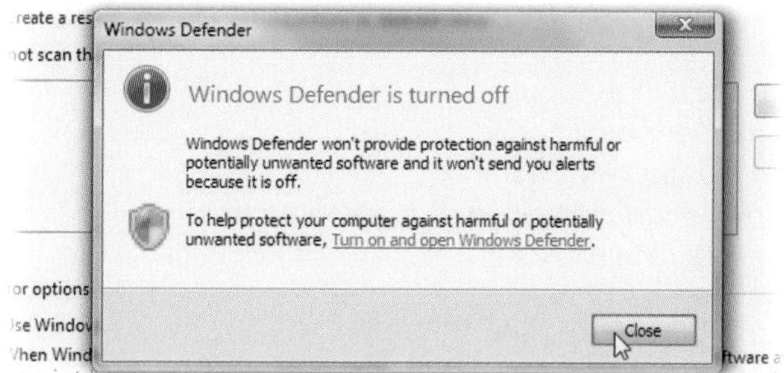

● This returns us to the Security Center where Windows now reports that Spy Sweeper is protecting the computer from spyware and other malware. Notice too that all the lights in the window are still showing green, despite the fact that Defender is now turned off.

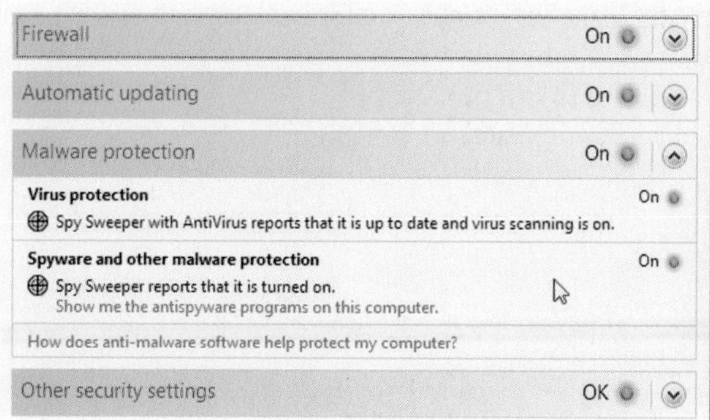

POP-UP MESSAGES

Many antivirus programs display little pop-up messages over at the bottom right of the Windows desktop, in the Notification Area, like this.

Your First Scan

In order to protect your PC from security threats, antivirus and antispyware programs (from here on called antivirus programs) need to scan the files stored on your PC. Once they've done that, they can report back on any potential problem and deal with it. When you first set them up, you'll often have to do the first scan manually. Thereafter, you can schedule the scan to run automatically on a regular basis.

RUNNING A MANUAL SCAN

You'll usually run this from the main page of the antivirus program and there'll usually be a choice of different levels of scan. Just like cleaning a house, you can choose how thorough you want to be, and the program will usually offer some kind of guidance. As a rule of thumb, go for a thorough scan the first time, and once a week from then on. The full scan will take a little longer, but will delve into the darkest corners of your PC to search for potential problems. We're using Spy Sweeper with AntiVirus for this, and although your program may look different, it will have similar features and work in broadly the same way.

CHOOSING A SCAN TYPE

- Click the arrow on the **Start Full Sweep** to open the drop down menu.

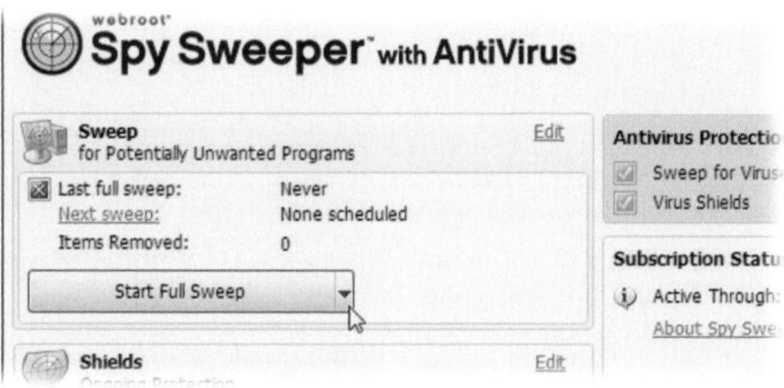

- As you can see, Spy Sweeper offers three types of scan. As a rule you should pick the most thorough one, especially for your first scan. We're going to select **Start Full Sweep**.

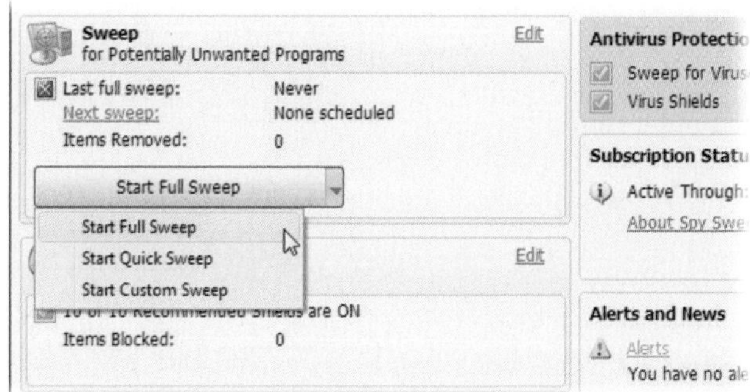

RUNNING THE SCAN

- Clicking the **Start Full Sweep** button like this begins the scan.

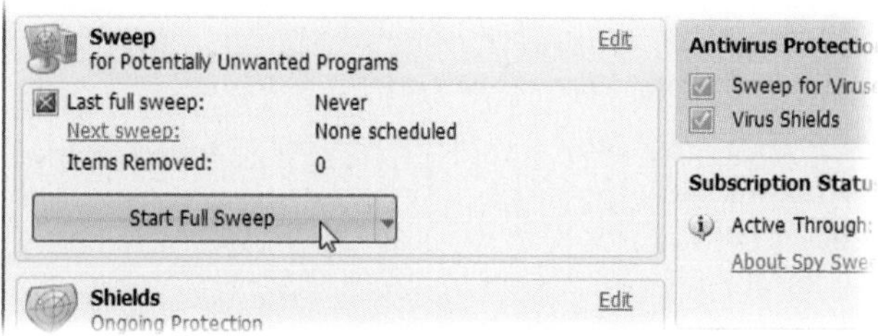

- When the scan starts, you'll usually see something like this–a progress bar that moves from left to right, indicating how far through the process you are. There'll also usually be some kind of status message–here it's indicating the number of items it's found and how much time has elapsed since the scan started.

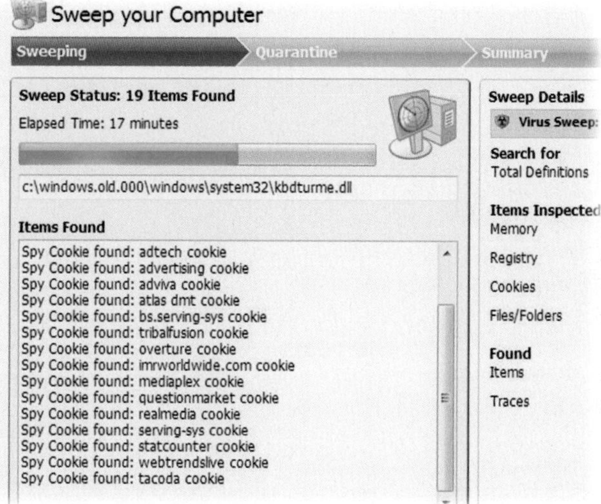

READING THE RESULTS

- At the end of the scan, your program will tell you what it found. There may be nothing to report; at other times, there'll be a genuine threat; most of the time it'll find items of low level risk, like the ones shown here. These aren't viruses–they're "cookies" and they're used by websites to track visitors' habits and preferences when they're browsing the web.

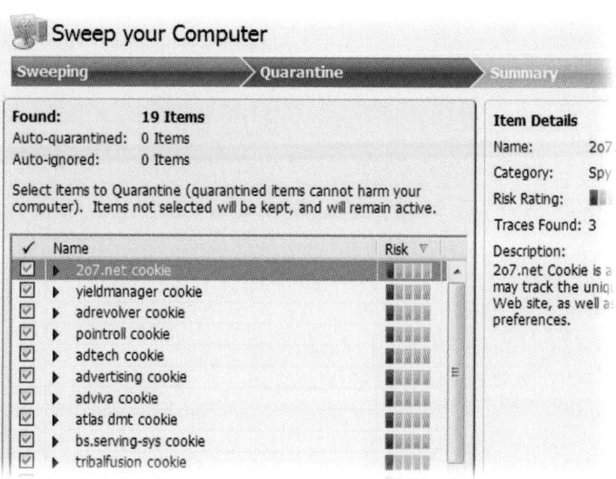

● Many antivirus programs will offer more information about individual items they've found in a scan. Here we've highlighted the first item in the list and are clicking on the **View More Details Online** link.

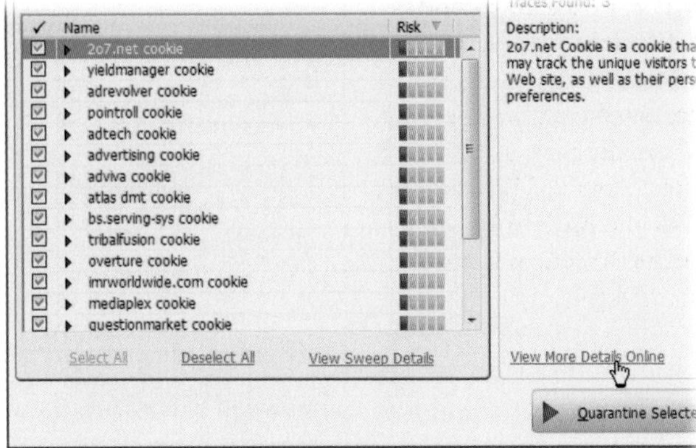

● Here's what the website has to say. Advice regarding low level threats can often be pretty equivocal, leaving you to make up your own mind.

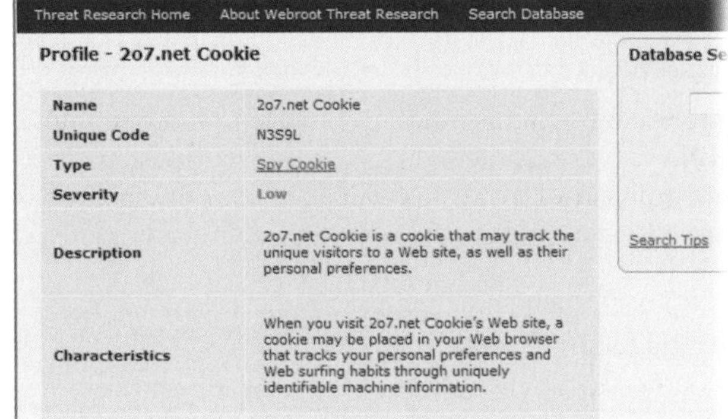

QUARANTINING THE SUSPECT FILES

● Many cookies are used to store useful information (like your preferences when you visit a website) but others are there to keep an eye on which sites you visit and then report back, helping to build up a profile of your Internet activities. So, we're going to quarantine these 19 items by clicking the **Quarantine Selected** button.

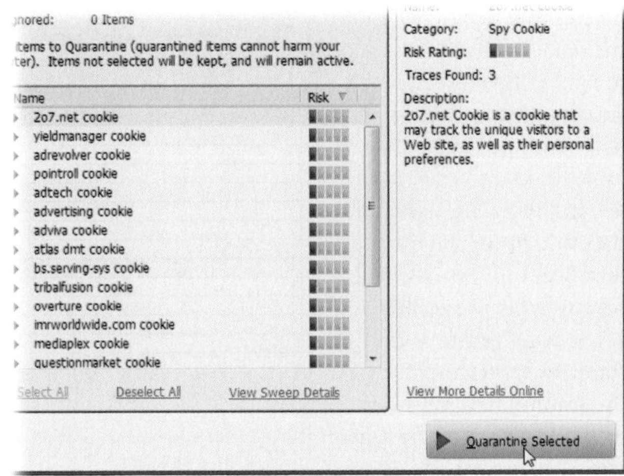

● It only takes a second before Spy Sweeper reports back that it's put all 19 items into quarantine where they can no longer affect your PC. We can now click the **Back to Home** button to return to the main page.

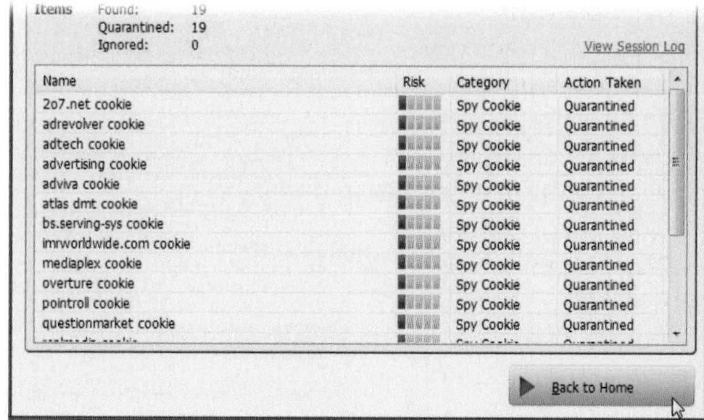

SCHEDULING FUTURE SCANS

The best way to keep your PC free from malware is to make sure that your antivirus software is up to date and to scan your PC on a regular basis. The antivirus program should be set to update itself automatically, but you may need to create a schedule for regular scans. We'll look at how to do that here.

OPENING THE SCHEDULE

● Somewhere on the main screen of your antivirus program there should be an option to schedule when the next system scan is due to run. In Spy Sweeper, we simply click the **Next sweep** link like this.

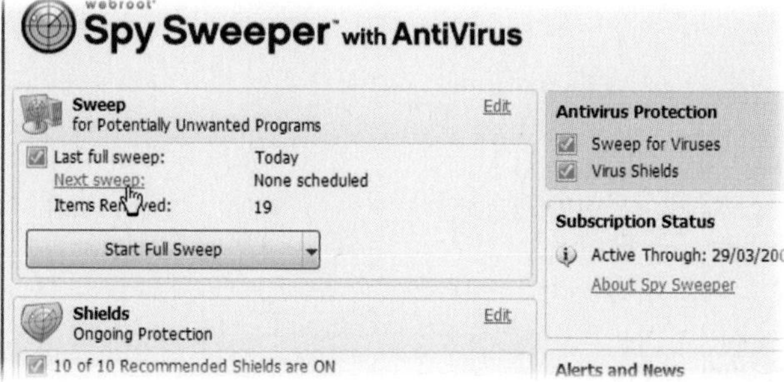

● This opens the Schedule page which is currently empty because we haven't set any scheduled scans up yet. Before we continue though, we're going to click the **About Schedules** link to see if that can offer any friendly guidance.

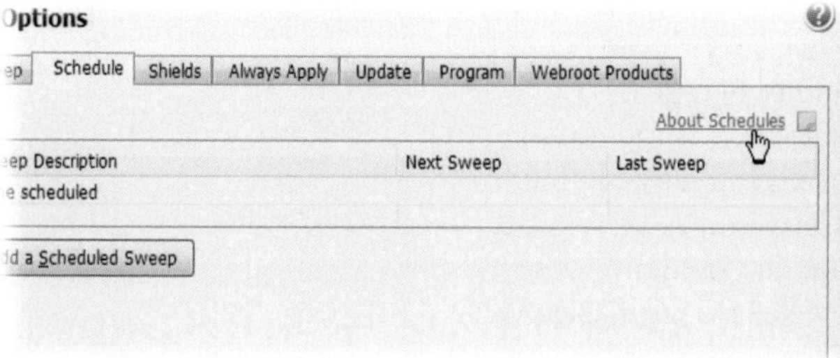

● The resulting screen is helpful and recommends that we scan once a week at least. Click the '**x**' to close the tip.

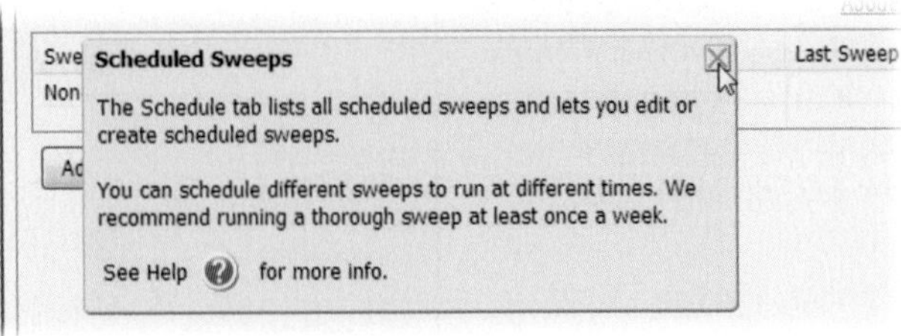

CREATING A NEW SCHEDULED SCAN

● When the tip closes, we can click the **Add a Scheduled Sweep** button.

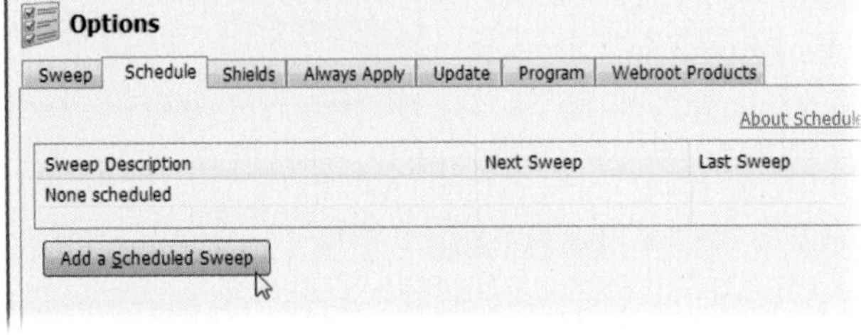

● This opens the **Schedule Wizard**. We're going to leave the settings here as they are because we want to do a thorough scan once a week. Notice that the Full Sweep here will also scan any external drives that may be plugged into our PC. Clicking **Next** takes us to the next screen.

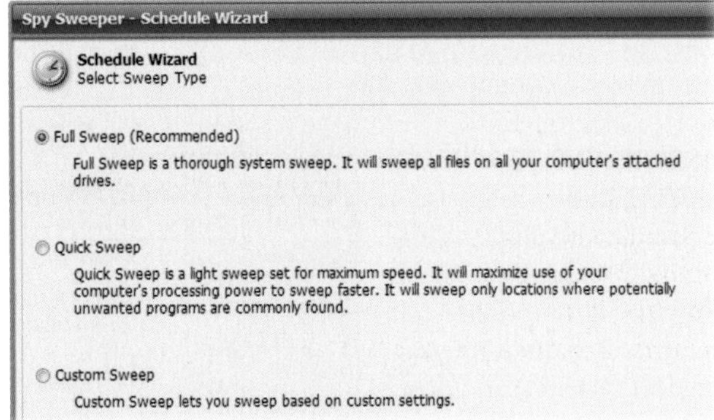

● The schedule looks pretty good as it is–it's set to run every Monday at 5.00pm. However, we'd like to change the time so that it runs later in the day, when we're more likely to have finished using the PC. To adjust the time, move the cursor to the drop-down arrow and click on it.

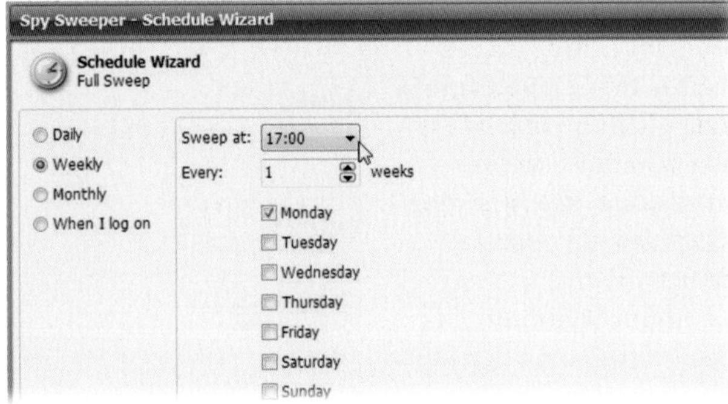

• When the drop-down list opens up, select a different time from the options there. We are going to choose 18:00, or 6.00pm.

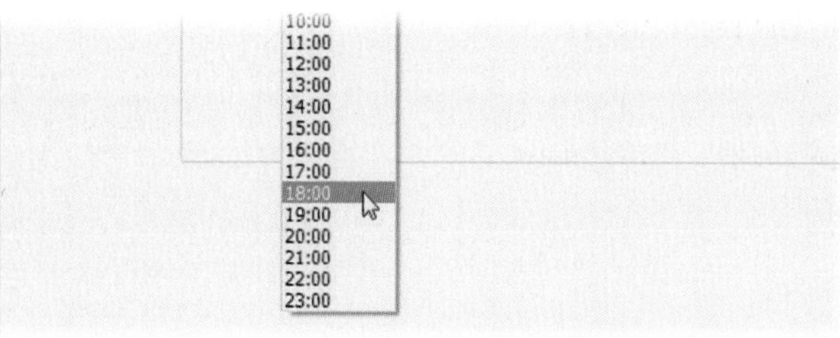

• Having chosen the new time for the scheduled scan, we can review the other options to make sure that they're correct.

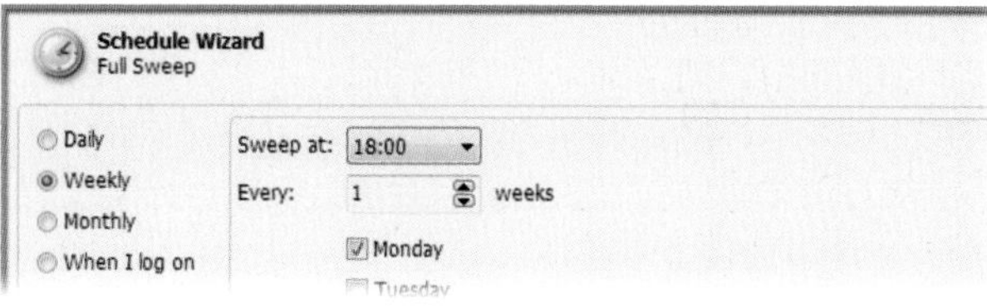

• Since all is well, we can just click the **Finish** button to conclude.

• Here's the finished scheduled scan. If we want to edit it in the future, we can double click on it. Now though, we can click the **Home** button to return to the main Spy Sweeper page.

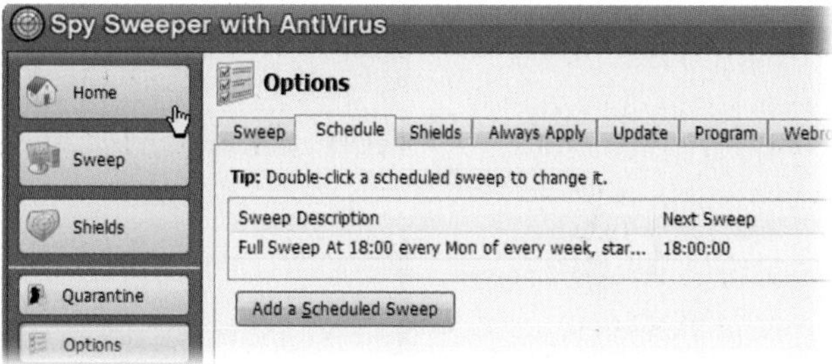

• You can see that the program reports not just that we did a full sweep today, but also that one is now scheduled to run automatically. This is the scheduled scan that we just created.

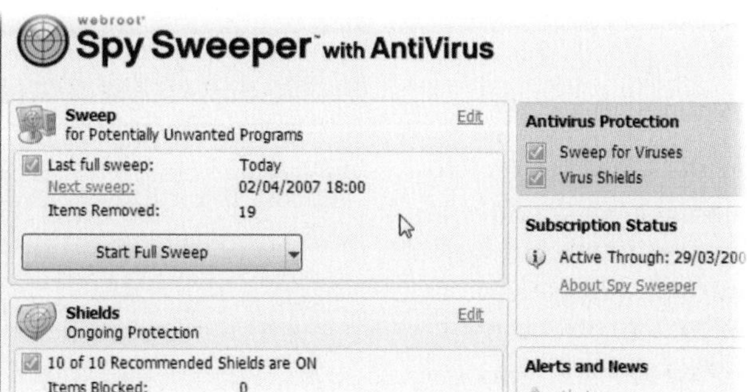

Sharing Your PC Safely

Creating an account password ensures a basic level of security, and you, as the main user, can set up other accounts so that several people can share the same PC safely.

Password Protection

Having made the effort to protect your PC from electronic intruders, it makes sense to protect it from old fashioned ones as well. Even if you aren't storing highly sensitive information on a computer, you still don't want anyone else nosing around your system, perhaps changing settings by mistake or accidentally removing something. The easiest way to prevent this is to create a password for your account.

1 OPENING USER ACCOUNTS

- Begin by moving the cursor to the Start button and clicking there once.

- Next, select **Control Panel** from the Start Menu.

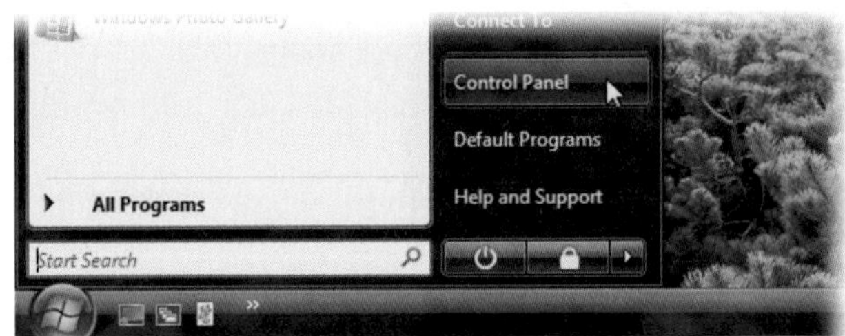

- When the Control Panel window opens, locate the **User Accounts and Family Safety** heading and click on it once with the left mouse button.

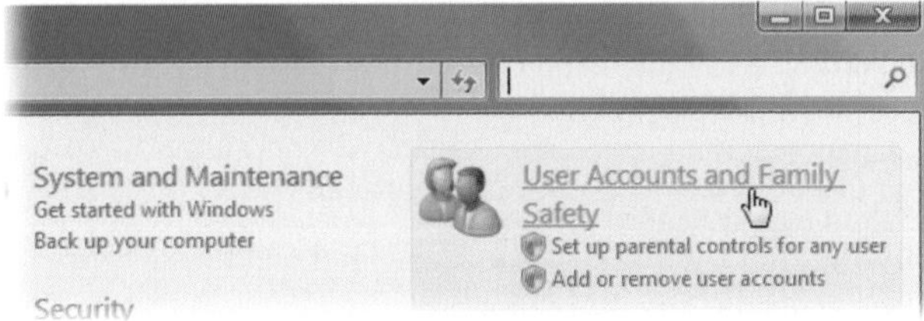

● When the next window opens, find and click on the **Add or remove user accounts** link.

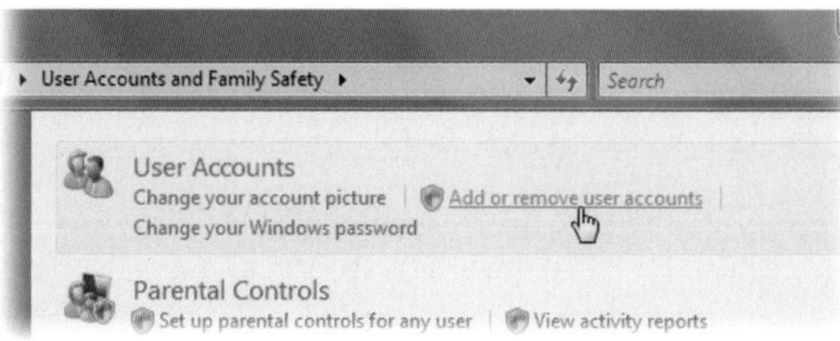

● We're about to alter Windows' system settings, so the **User Account Control** dialog appears asking for permission to carry on. Click the **Continue** button.

2 OPENING MAIN USER ACCOUNT

● This opens the **Manage Accounts** window. As you can see, Vista starts with two accounts–the **main user** and a **Guest** account, which is currently turned off. We want to add a password to the main user account, so click on that.

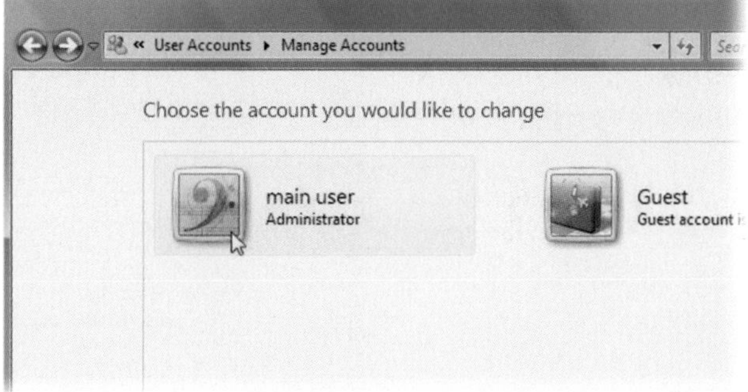

3 CREATING A PASSWORD

● Windows presents several different options down the left-hand side, some of which we'll explore in a short while. For now though, we're going to click the **Create a password** link.

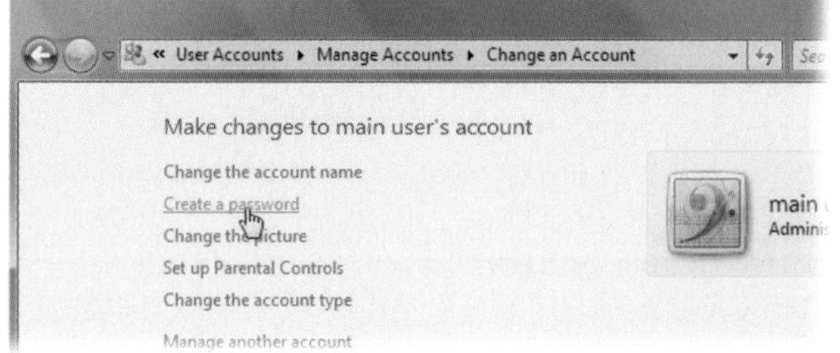

- Windows is going to ask us to type in a password, confirm it by typing it in again, and also to type in a password hint. Start by clicking in the first **New password** box.

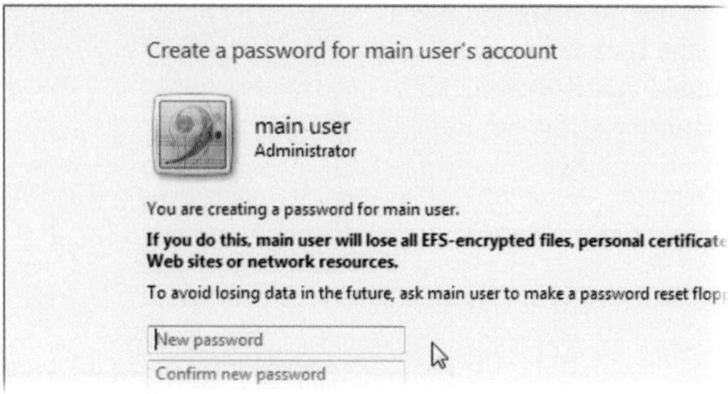

- Type in your password. If you want to know how to create a good one, see A Strong Password (below). You can see how secretive Windows is. As you type the password, the characters are changed into black dots.

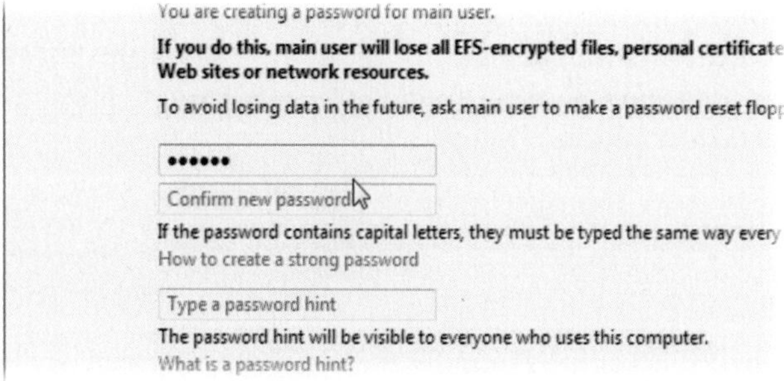

- Next, click in the box underneath with the cursor.

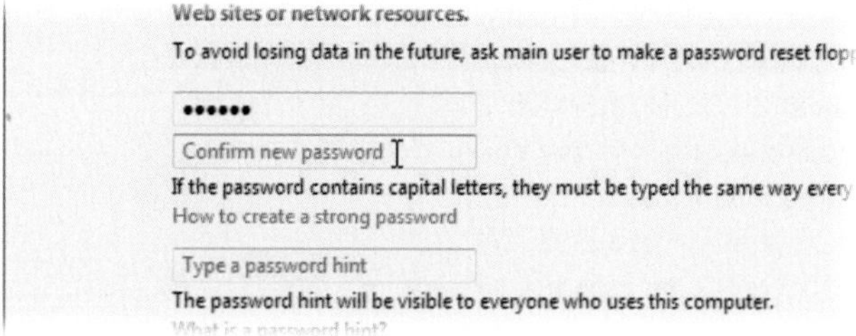

A STRONG PASSWORD

In order to create a strong password that can't easily be guessed, make sure it doesn't include your name, any complete words, is different from passwords you use elsewhere, and includes letters in both cases, numbers, and symbols found on the keyboard. Then, make sure you don't write it down and leave it somewhere near the computer. If you are worried about forgetting your passwords, consider getting a program for storing passwords. Visit http://keepass.info/ to find a good, free password program.

● Type the password in again. It must be exactly the same both times–if it isn't, Windows will display an error message.

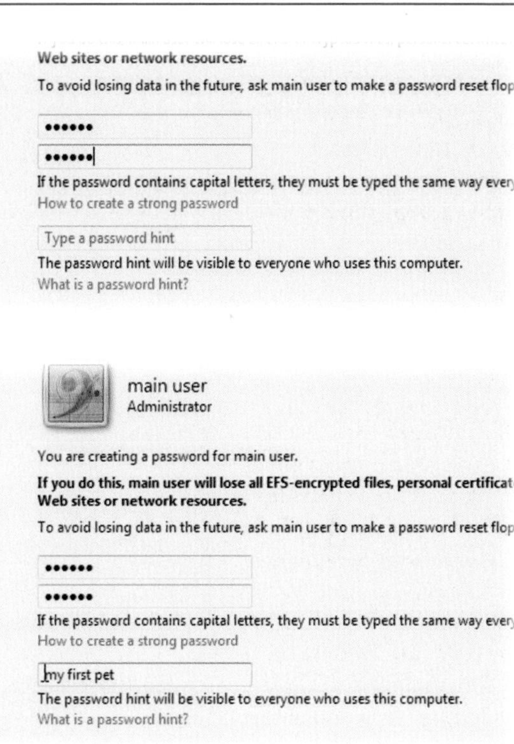
Web sites or network resources.
To avoid losing data in the future, ask main user to make a password reset flop
••••••
••••••
If the password contains capital letters, they must be typed the same way ever
How to create a strong password
Type a password hint
The password hint will be visible to everyone who uses this computer.
What is a password hint?
main user
Administrator
You are creating a password for main user.
If you do this, main user will lose all EFS-encrypted files, personal certificat
Web sites or network resources.
To avoid losing data in the future, ask main user to make a password reset flop
••••••
••••••
If the password contains capital letters, they must be typed the same way ever
How to create a strong password
my first pet
The password hint will be visible to everyone who uses this computer.
What is a password hint?

● Click in the password hint box and type in a phrase that will help you to remember your password in case it slips your mind at a later date. People often use the name of their pet or their mother's maiden name, but a strong password shouldn't be quite so easy to guess!

● When you've finished, click the **Create password** button to confirm your new password.

to everyone who uses this computer.
Create password
Cancel

● Now, back at the **Change an Account** window, you can see that the main user account is now labeled **Password protected**. From now on when you switch the machine on in the morning, Windows will ask for this password.

ccounts ▸ Change an Account
Search
user's account
main user
Administrator
Password protected

SETTING UP SEPARATE ACCOUNTS

If more than one person uses your PC, you can share it more efficiently by setting other people up with their own accounts. As the main user, you keep certain privileges (for example, only you can install new software or make changes to system settings), but they have their own account and their own wallpaper, color scheme, icon arrangements, etc.. Vista will also keep your files separate, so there's no danger of someone else accidentally over-writing important documents.

OPENING A NEW ACCOUNT

● At the Manage Accounts window, simply click on the **Create a new account link** as we're doing here.

● You now need to choose an account type and give it a name. It's nearly always best to create **Standard user** accounts for other people, as this prevents them from installing or uninstalling programs and making changes to the system. By default, Windows selects **Standard user** whenever this window opens. Click in the **New account name** box to continue.

● Let's imagine this account is for a teenage girl named Alice. We'll type her name into the new account box. Be careful to spell it correctly.

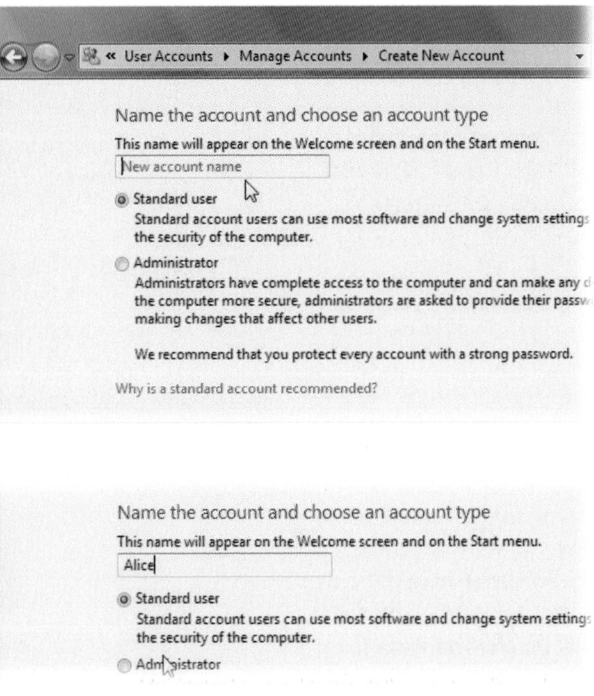

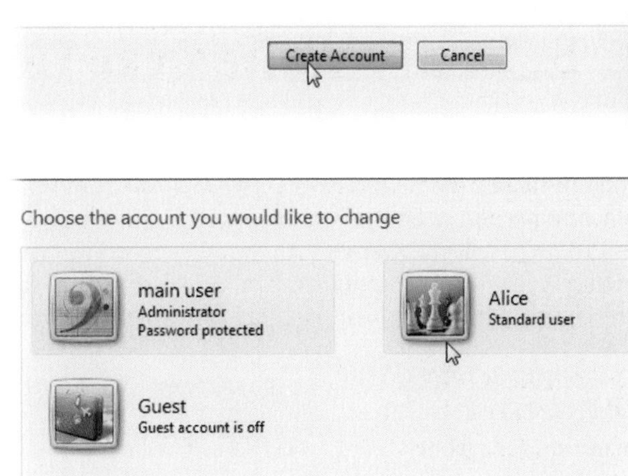

- To make the new account for Alice, move the cursor down and click the **Create Account** button.

- Here's the new account– **Alice**, **Standard user**. Alice's account is accompanied by a photo of chess pieces. However, we know she's not a big chess fan, so let's go ahead and modify the picture for her by clicking on her name once with the left mouse button.

- In the next window you'll see a number of different settings that we can change. For now, click the **Change the picture** link with the left mouse button.

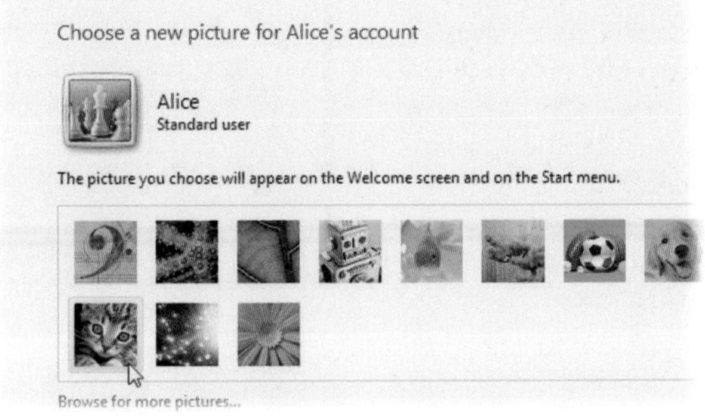

- Choose another picture from the selection shown here. We're going to select the kitten picture by clicking on it once.

- Click the **Change Picture** button and Alice's personal picture changes from the chess pieces to the kitten.

USING PARENTAL CONTROLS

One of the most useful things about user accounts is that the main user–i.e. you–can exercise a lot of control over the way that other people use your PC. This is particularly helpful when it comes to preventing children and adolescents from doing what they shouldn't or straying where it's not appropriate–a particular concern when youngsters are surfing the net. Windows Vista gathers a selection of ring fencing tools together in the Parental Controls section, and that's our next stop.

1 OPENING PARENTAL CONTROLS

- You should still be looking at the account that we have just created, which means all of the controls are available down the left of the window. Click **Set up Parental Controls** to continue.

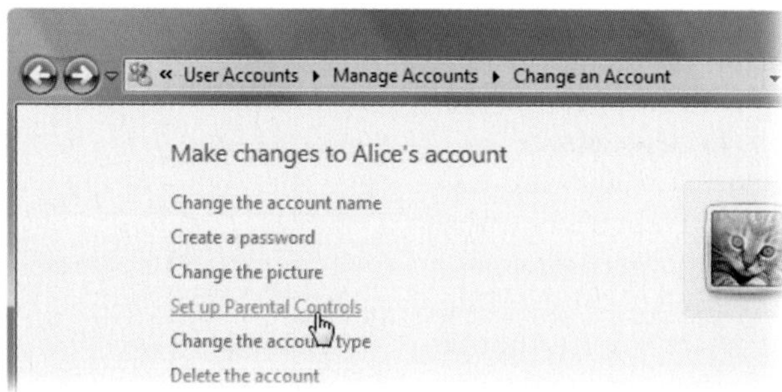

- When the **User Account Control** dialog appears, click **Continue**.

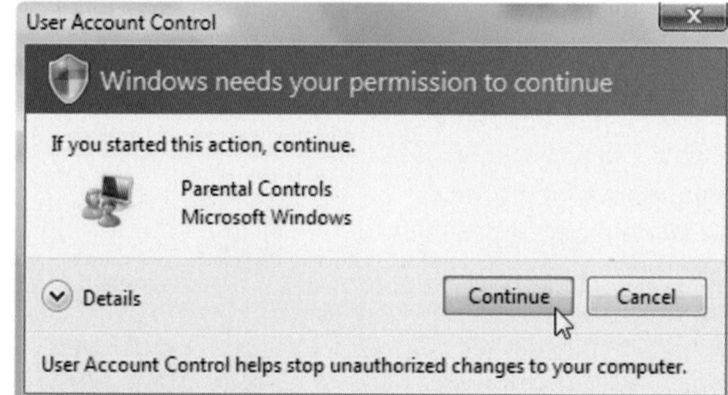

- Next, select the account to which you want to add controls. In this case, we want to add parental controls to the newly created Alice account.

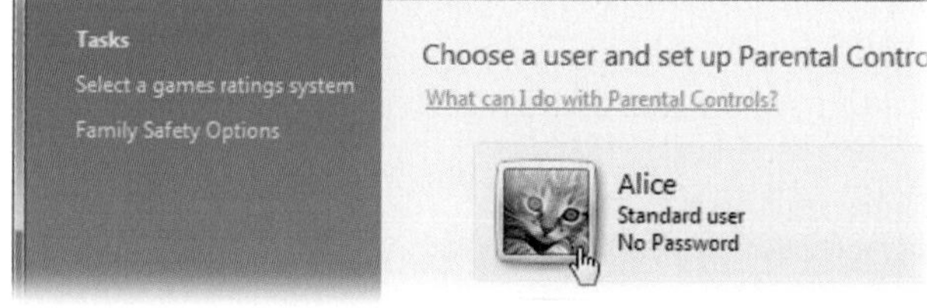

2 IMPLEMENTING CONTROLS

- This is the main **Parental Controls** window. You can see that the controls are currently switched off.

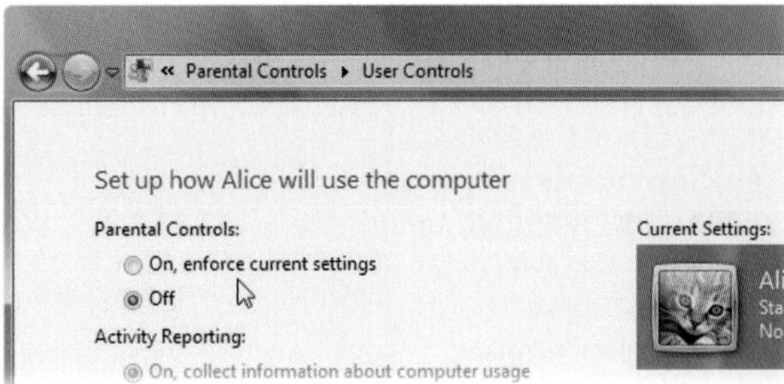

- To turn Parental Controls on, move the cursor to the empty radio button at the top (the **On, enforce current settings** button) and then click there with the left mouse button.

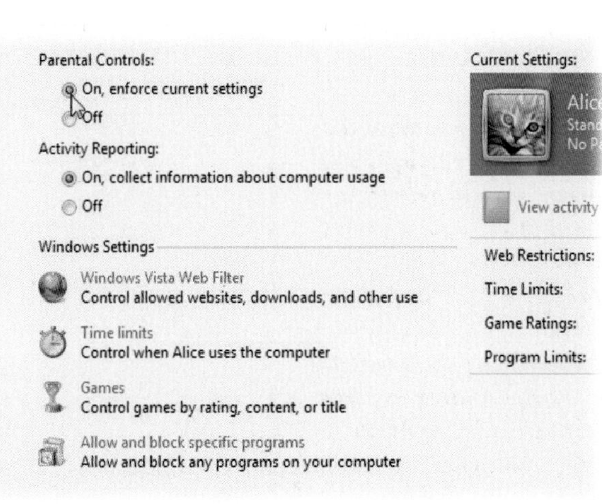

- One of the things that parents and other carers are most concerned about is what kids get up to when they're surfing the web, and Vista's Parental Controls can really put your mind at rest on this issue.
- To start putting controls in place, click on the **Windows Vista Web Filter**.

3 LIMITING WEBSITE ACCESS

● By default, the **web restriction level** is set to **Medium**, as we can see from the radio button in the middle of this screen, but to demonstrate how powerful this feature is, we're going to be a bit Draconian with Alice's account so she can only visit a single website. Move the cursor to the checkbox next to the **Only allow websites which are on the allow list** link.

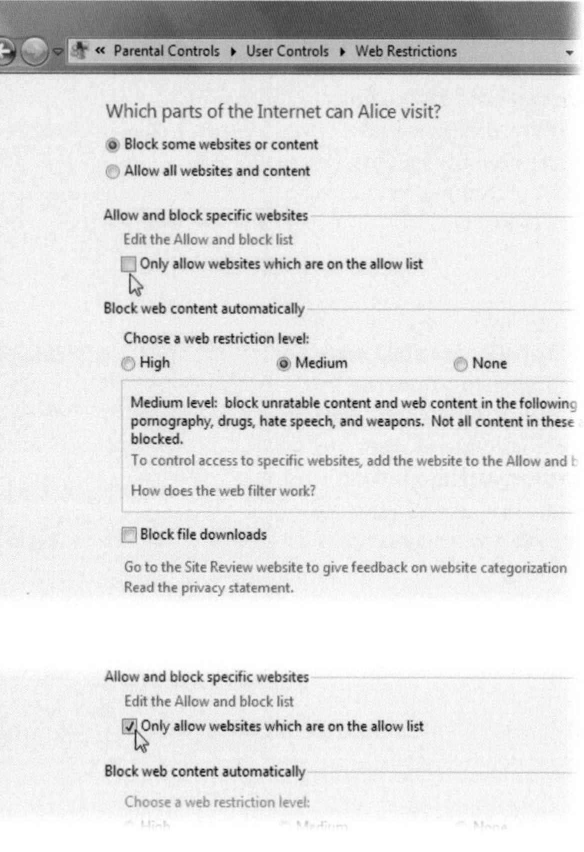

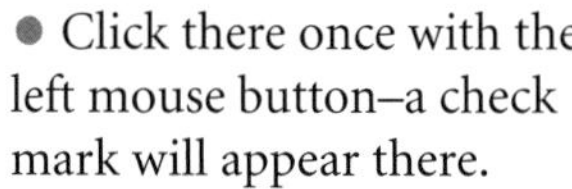

● Click there once with the left mouse button–a check mark will appear there.

Allow and block specific websites
Edit the Allow and block list
Only allow websites which are on the allow list
Block web content automatically
Choose a web restriction level:

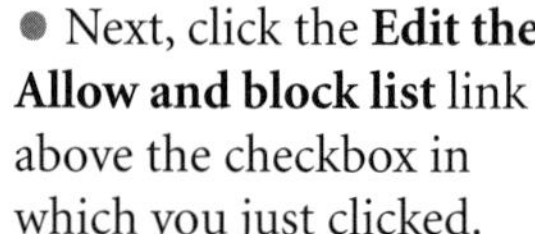

● Next, click the **Edit the Allow and block list** link above the checkbox in which you just clicked.

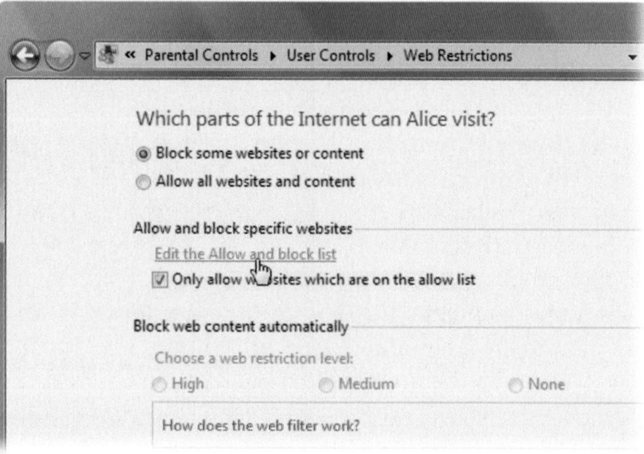

4 ALLOWING WEBSITES

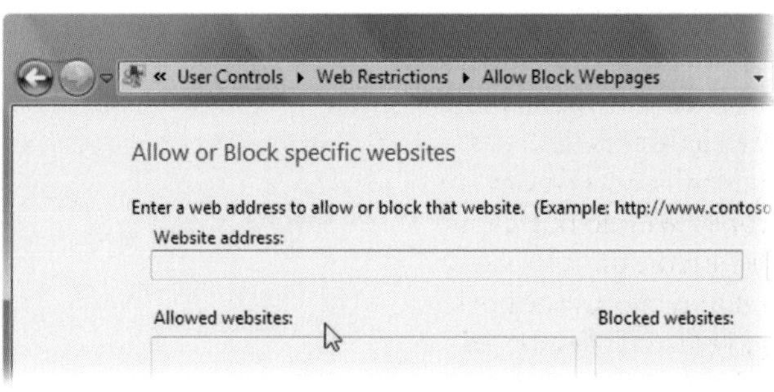

● In the **Allow or Block specific websites** dialog box you can type in the address of any specific website that this person is allowed to visit.

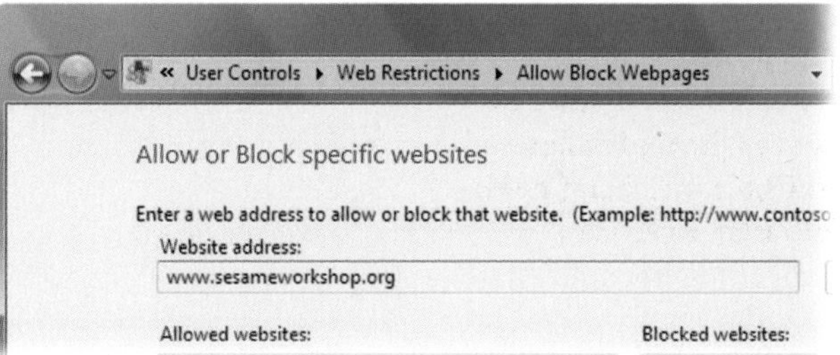

● Type the address of a website into the empty box at the top–in this example we're going to key in **www.sesameworkshop.com**, home of the world famous Sesame Street.

When you've finished typing in the address, check it's spelled correctly and then click the **Allow** button.

SETTING A TIME LIMIT

Windows Vista has the answer for those children who spend too much time at their computers. The program allows the main user to specify the times of day and the days of the week when other account holders are allowed to access the web. For example, you might want to limit the amount of time your teenager spends online to an hour a night, and only between 6.00pm and 7.00pm. After that time period Windows will automatically log them off, whether they like it or not. You'll find this under Parental Controls.

- The Sesame Street website now appears in the **Allowed websites** box on the left–this is the list of websites that Alice is allowed to visit.
- You can also block a specific site by typing in its address and clicking on the **Block** button.

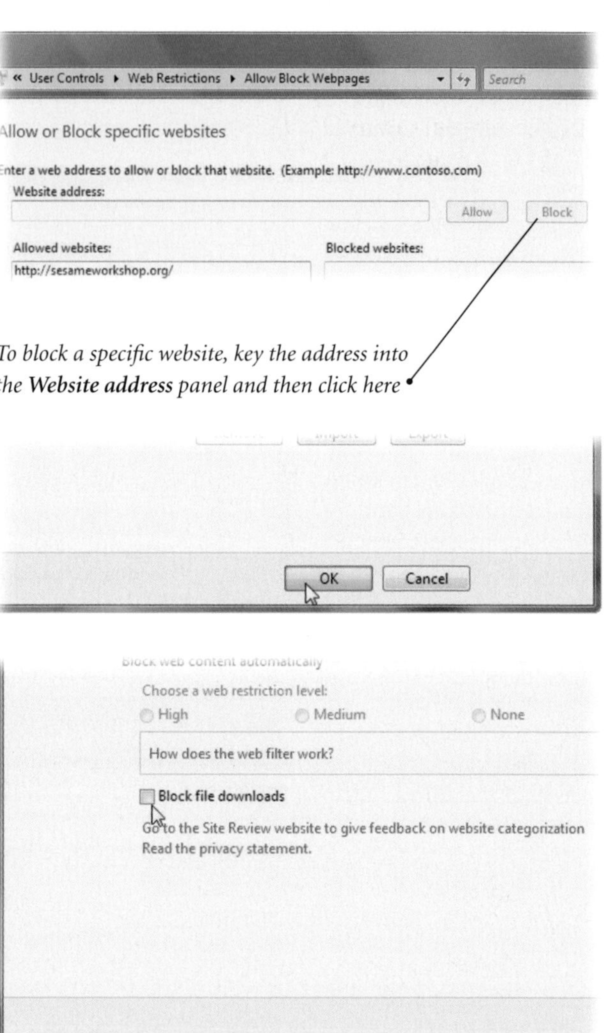

To block a specific website, key the address into the ***Website address*** *panel and then click here*

- We're just going to show you the principle of site blocking, so we'll leave it at that and click the **OK** button to confirm our changes.

5 BLOCKING FILE DOWNLOADS

- We are back at the main Web Restrictions window and we now want to prevent Alice from downloading any files. Youngsters are often less suspicious and can be tricked into downloading things they shouldn't. Move your cursor to the **Block file downloads** button.

GAMES RATING

Just in the same way that movies are rated, to give parents some idea of their content, there are also ratings for computer games. Windows Vista has a feature that allows you to block specific games by name or only play games that, for example, have a Universal rating (suitable for all). To use this very helpful feature, go to the Parental Controls **Tasks** panel.

- Click in the empty box once to put a tick there and switch on file blocking. With the Parental Control settings as they are now, Alice can now only visit a single Internet site, and she is barred from downloading any files.

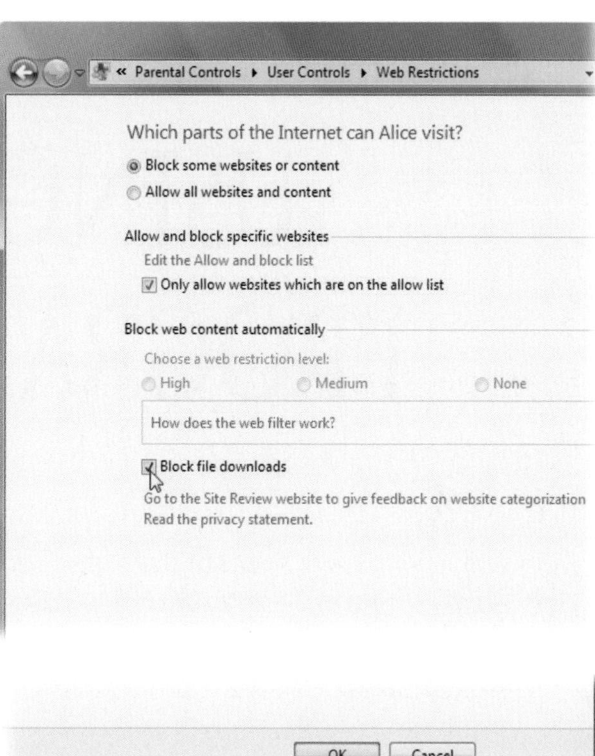

- Finally, click **OK** to confirm your changes.

VIEWING ACTIVITY REPORTS

When you use Parental Controls for particular user accounts, Vista will keep an eye on what those account users are doing. Vista will then present the results in a report, so you can see when the user logged on to the PC, or if anyone has tried to access a banned website or attempted to download a file, and so on. You will be reminded about these activity reports by a little message window that pops up above the Notification Area.

USING PROGRAMS

AS WE HAVE ALREADY SEEN, there is a wealth of software included with Windows Vista. Much of it is media-orientated, but there is also a useful word-processing program called WordPad. In this chapter, we take a look at how to use WordPad, as well as introducing you to a selection of other programs that you may choose to install–Microsoft Word for advanced word processing, Microsoft Excel for creating spreadsheets, and Family Tree Maker, a genealogy program designed to help you investigate and chart your family history. These are all powerful programs, and our aim here is just to demonstrate their basic functions and get you up and running if you invest in any of these.

244 Basic Word Processing

260 Introducing Word

278 Introducing Excel

298 Genealogy Software

Basic Word Processing

In this section we're going to look briefly at how a basic word processing program works, enabling us to create, edit, and save a text document using various fonts and formats.

This Is WordPad

We've already looked at Notepad, the simple note-writing program that comes with Windows Vista. WordPad, which is included with Windows Vista, is the next step up. WordPad documents can include complex formatting (using a range of fonts, text styles and colors, line spacing, indented paragraphs, bulleted lists etc.), and you can also embed pictures and other documents within a WordPad document. Many of the basic operations in WordPad are the same as those in Microsoft Word.

OPENING WORDPAD

- Click on the Start button to open the Start menu.

- Move the cursor to **All Programs**, and either hover there or click on it to view the full program list.

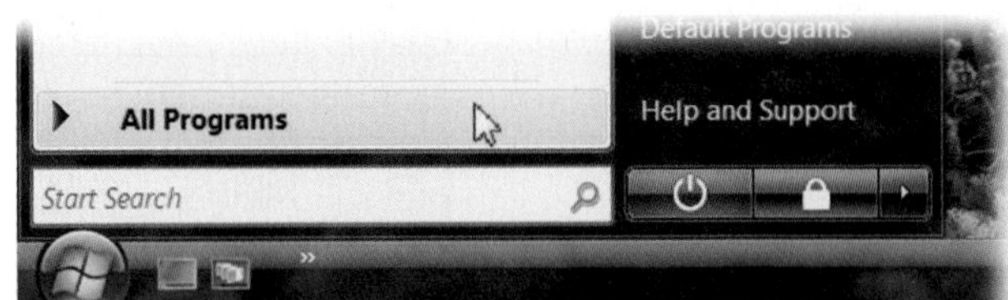

- Select **Accessories** from the program list by left clicking on it once.

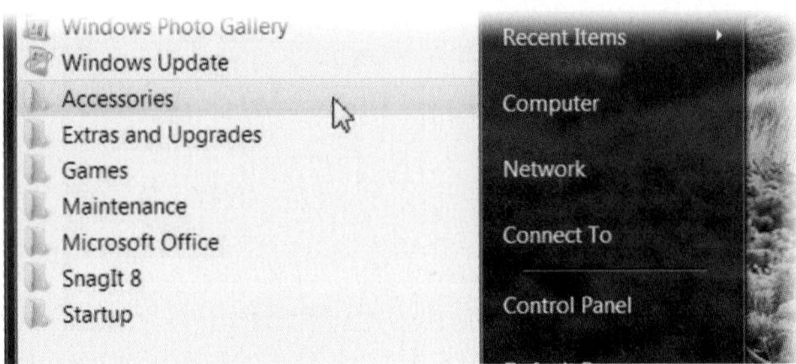

79 **Making a New File**

260 **Introducing Word**

● In the list of Accessories, click on **WordPad** to open the program.

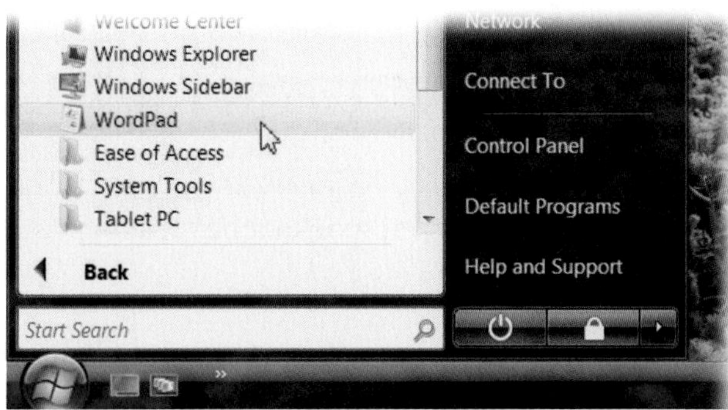

THE WORDPAD WINDOW

● The WordPad program opens, giving you an open empty document ready to start typing. The controls that run along the top of the document window provide the tools to save and open documents, and to change the look and position of the typed text.

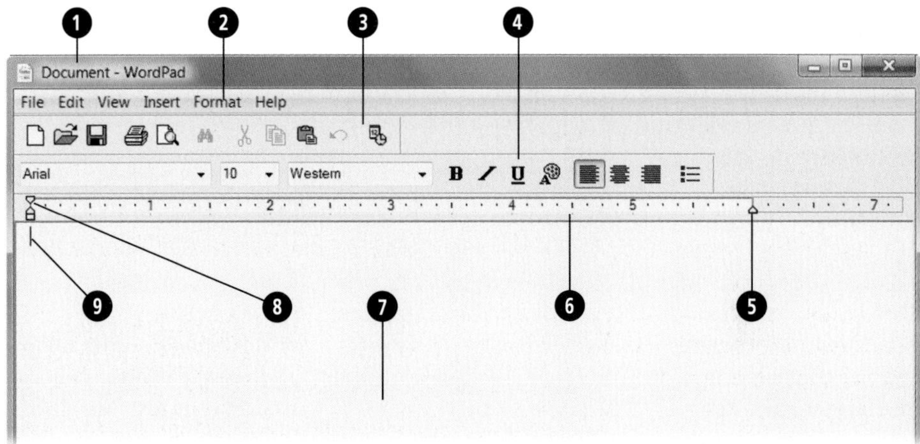

FEATURES KEY

❶ Title Bar
Displays the document title.

❷ Menu Bar
Contains the main menus.

❸ Toolbar
Contains the main buttons for actions on files and text.

❹ Format Bar
Contains the main layout options.

❺ Right Indent Button
Used to set right indent.

❻ Ruler
Displays indents and margins.

❼ Document Area
This is where your typed text appears.

❽ Left Indent Button
Used to set left indent.

❾ Insertion Point
Typed text appears here.

KEYING TEXT INTO THE DOCUMENT

● As you type, the flashing cursor, or insertion point, moves along ahead of the typed letters.

Document - WordPad
File Edit View Insert Format Help
Arial
10
Western
Dear Bob and Terri,

Insertion point ahead of text

● When you reach the right-hand edge of the page, the text automatically runs over onto the next line, or "wraps."

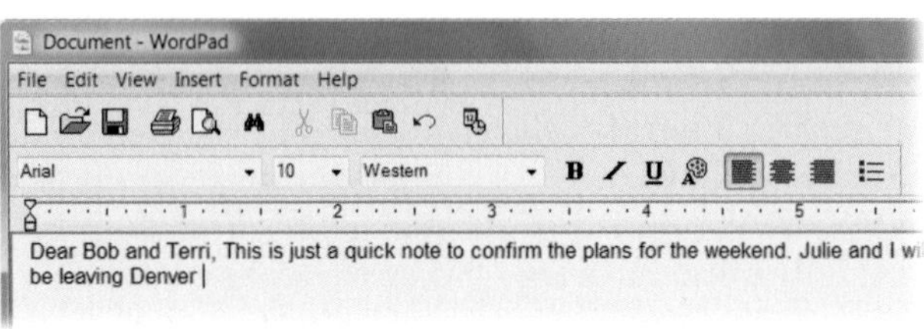
Document - WordPad
File Edit View Insert Format Help
Arial
10
Western
Dear Bob and Terri, This is just a quick note to confirm the plans for the weekend. Julie and I wi
be leaving Denver

● Pressing the Enter key will start a new line of text (or introduce a line space if you press it twice), but you only need to do this if you want to start a new paragraph.

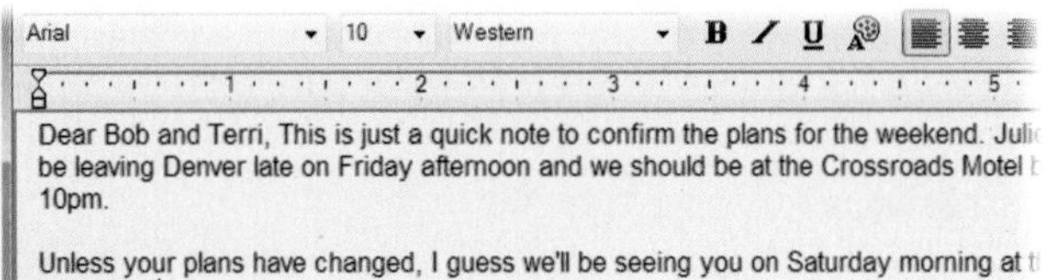
Arial
10
Western
Dear Bob and Terri, This is just a quick note to confirm the plans for the weekend. Juli
be leaving Denver late on Friday afternoon and we should be at the Crossroads Motel
10pm.
Unless your plans have changed, I guess we'll be seeing you on Saturday morning at t
campsite.

● When your typing has filled the space of the document area, the page will move up a line at a time as you add lines.

● As soon as the text exceeds the document area, a scroll bar appears down the right-hand side of the window to allow you to scroll up and down through the document.

● You can also move up and down the document using the mouse wheel.

After about 5 miles, the road crosses a bridge over Black Creek. The logging road goes off to the left just before the road turns sharp right after the bridge.There's a sign (41 Main), but it's easy to miss.
Stay on 41 Main for about 12 miles. It's real rough in places, so keep it slow, especially if you've got Doug's canoe on the rack!
When you see the turning for Seymour Lake and Brown's Bay, you've got about 3 miles to go to the Stella Lake junction.
Just before the turning, there's a large clearing on the right - there's usually some big machinery parked there. The road rises, and as you come over the top, the trail to Stella Lake is immediately on your right.
It looks worse than it is. The first few hundred yards has some nasty boulders, and it's steep, but then it levels out and the going's good.

Scroll bar appears when the page is filled with text

INSERTING TEXT IN THE DOCUMENT

● Once there is text on the screen, you can click anywhere in the text to move the insertion point to a new position.

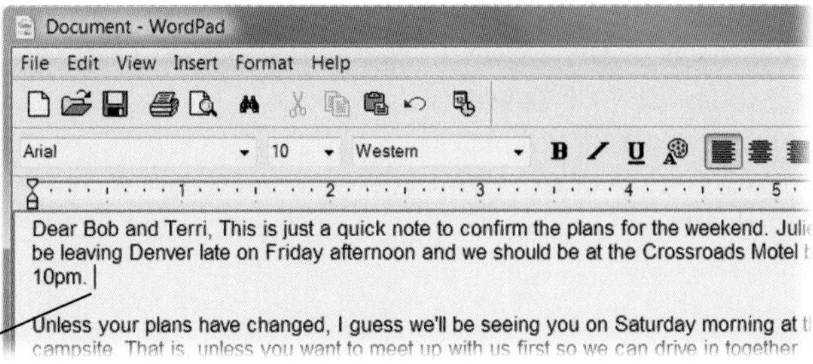

Insertion point positioned here

● Any text that you type will then be inserted in that position on the page.

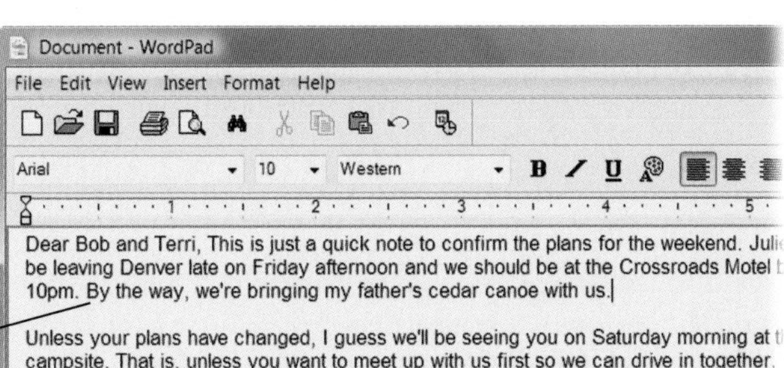

Typed text appears here

SELECTING TEXT

● Before text on the page can be manipulated in any way, it needs to be selected, or highlighted, so that WordPad knows which text to act on, whether it's an individual letter, word, sentence, or paragraph, or all the text in the document.

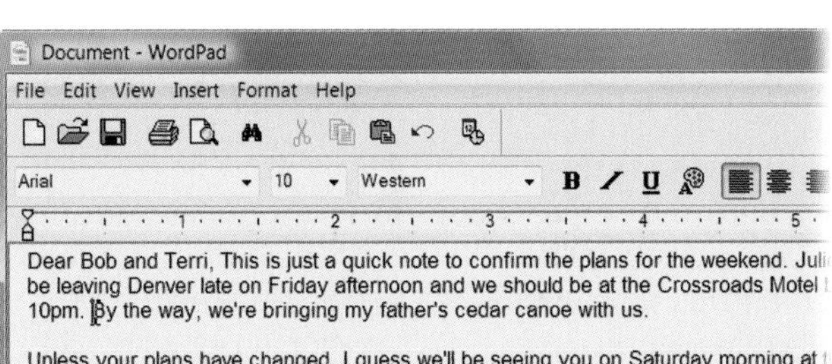

● WordPad has a range of ways of doing this, using the keyboard or the mouse, but the most commonly used method is to left click at the start of the chosen text, drag to the end of the text, and release the button.

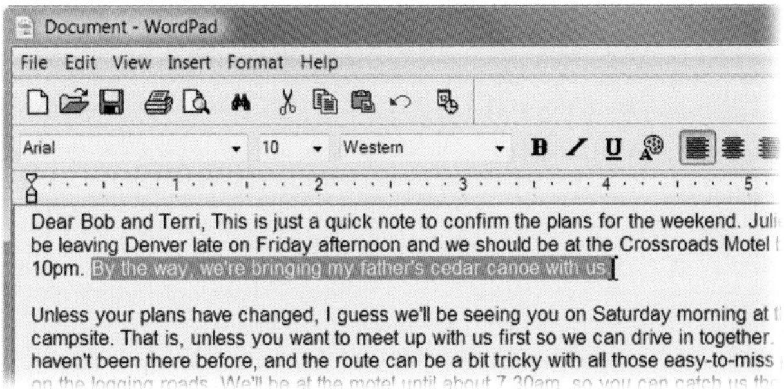

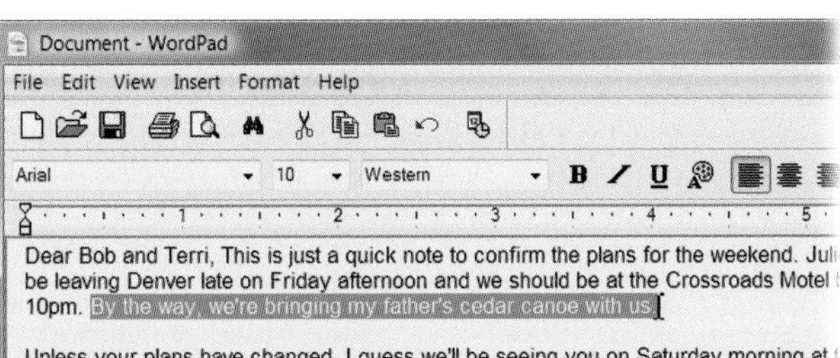

● To select all the text in a document, go to the **Edit** menu and choose **Select All** from the drop-down menu. As you can see in the menu, the keyboard shortcut to do this is Ctrl **A.**

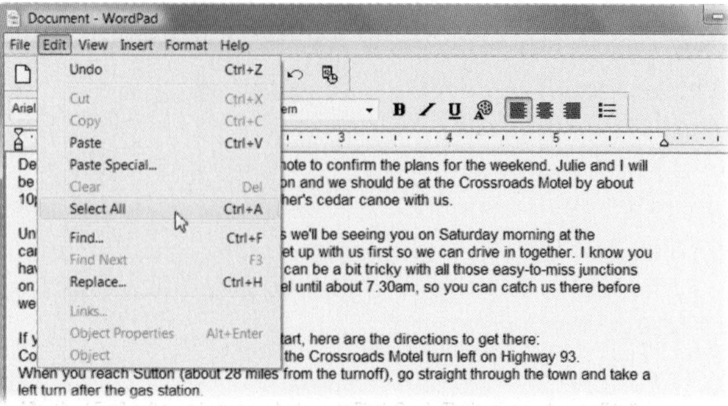

MANIPULATING TEXT

Much of the strength of a word processor –and the reason that typewriters are gathering dust in lofts or rusting in landfills–lies in the fact that with a program like this, text can be edited, replaced, copied, moved, deleted, and printed repeatedly. Once a piece of text has been selected, it can be manipulated using drop-down and pop-up menus, toolbar buttons, or keyboard shortcuts.

CUTTING TEXT

● With the text selected, click on **Edit** in the menu bar at the top of the screen.

● From the drop-down Edit menu, select **Cut** by clicking once on it.

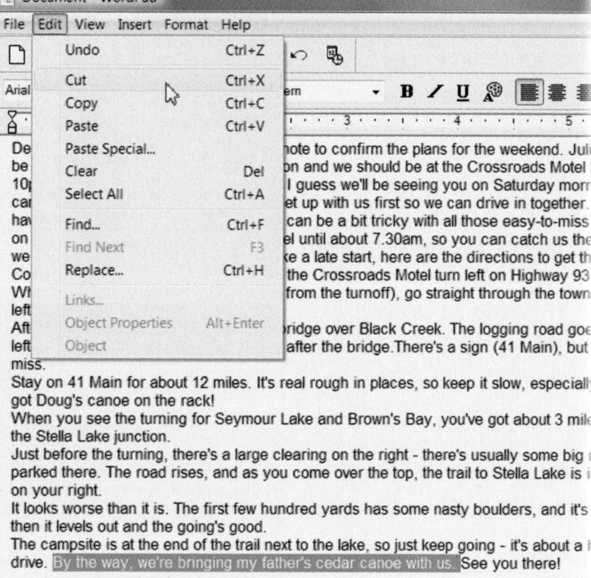

- Your block of text will disappear, but it is not lost. The text ahead of it moves back to take its place.

Stay on 41 Main for about 12 miles. It's real rough in places, so keep it slow, especiall
got Doug's canoe on the rack!
When you see the turning for Seymour Lake and Brown's Bay, you've got about 3 mil
the Stella Lake junction.
Just before the turning, there's a large clearing on the right - there's usually some big
parked there. The road rises, and as you come over the top, the trail to Stella Lake is
on your right.
It looks worse than it is. The first few hundred yards has some nasty boulders, and it's
then it levels out and the going's good.
The campsite is at the end of the trail next to the lake, so just keep going - it's about a
drive. See you there!

PASTING TEXT

- Position the insertion point where you want the text to reappear.

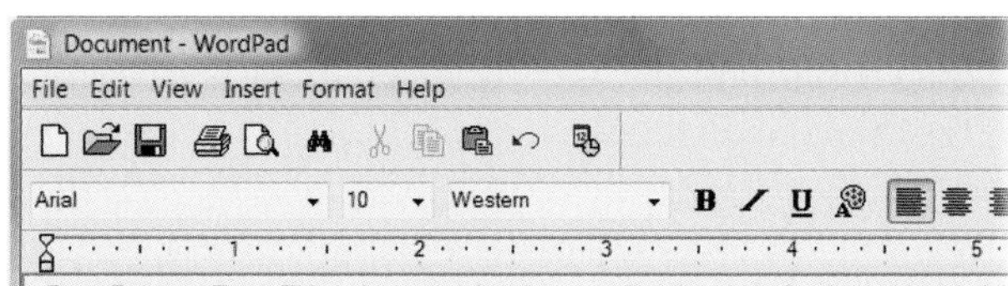

Insertion point has been positioned here

- Click on **Edit** in the menu bar, then on **Paste** in the drop-down menu.

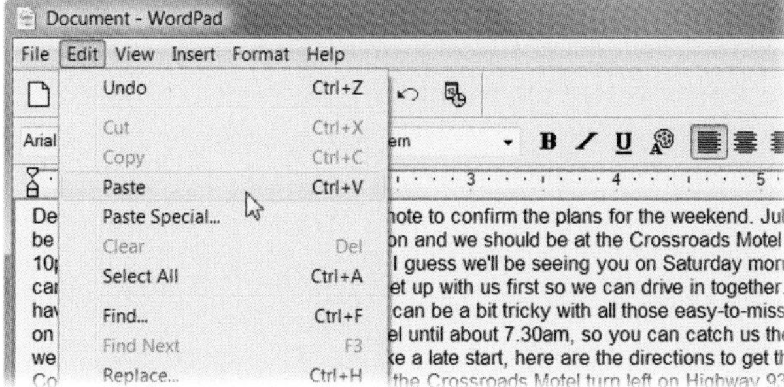

- The text is pasted back into your document exactly where you want it.

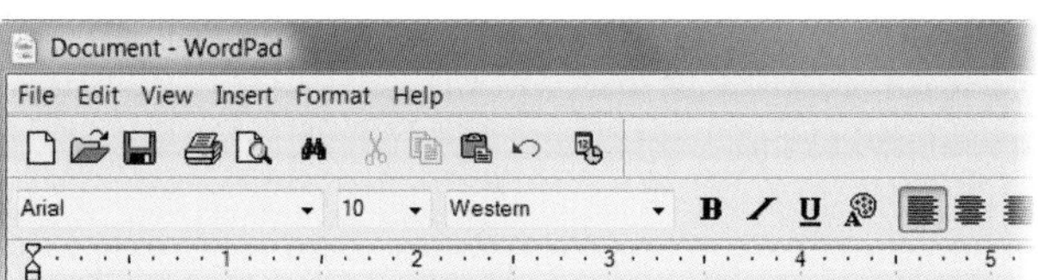

Document - WordPad
File Edit View Insert Format Help
Arial
10
Western
Dear Bob and Terri, This is just a quick note to confirm the plans for the weekend. Juli
be leaving Denver late on Friday afternoon and we should be at the Crossroads Motel
10pm. By the way, we're bringing my father's cedar canoe with us. Unless your plans
changed, I guess we'll be seeing you on Saturday morning at the campsite. That is, un
want to meet up with us first so we can drive in together. I know you haven't been there
and the route can be a bit tricky with all those easy-to-miss junctions on the logging ro
be at the motel until about 7.30am, so you can catch us there before we leave. If you
ahead or make a late start, here are the directions to get there:
Coming from the south, when you reach the Crossroads Motel turn left on Highway 93
When you reach Sutton (about 28 miles from the turnoff), go straight through the town
left turn after the gas station.
After about 5 miles, the road crosses a bridge over Black Creek. The logging road goe

The cut text reappears pasted in the new position

COPYING TEXT

You may want to copy a block of text to a new location while leaving the original block in its old position. To do this, simply follow the cutting and pasting procedure detailed above, but when you come to cut the text, select **Copy** instead of **Cut** in the **Edit** menu. The original block of text will stay where it is, but you can paste copies of it wherever you want.

MOVING TEXT USING DRAG AND DROP

- With the chosen text selected, place the mouse cursor over the block of highlighted text.

- Hold down the left mouse button and drag the cursor to the position in the document where you want the text to appear.
- You will see a small rectangular text icon at the tail of the cursor arrow as you move it.

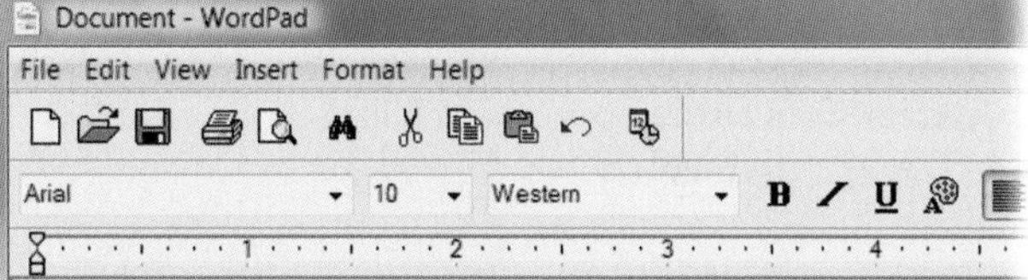

- Now release the mouse button, and the text appears in the new location.

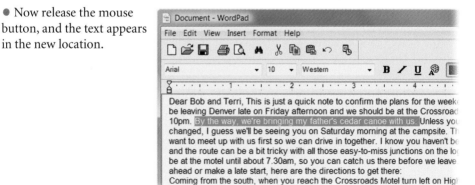

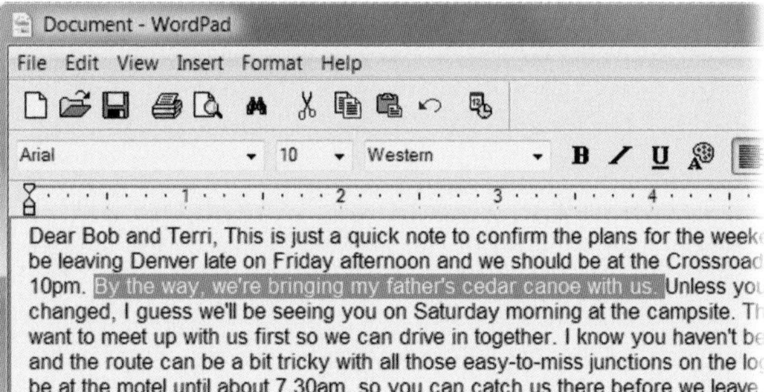

CORRECTING ERRORS AS YOU TYPE

- You have misspelled a word as you are typing.
- To remove the misspelled word, press the ← Bksp key to remove one letter at a time until the mis-typed letters are gone.
- The retype the word correctly and continue.

CORRECTING EARLIER ERRORS

- When a misspelled word is higher in the text than the insertion point, click at the end of the error to relocate the insertion point.
- Then delete and replace in the same way as above.

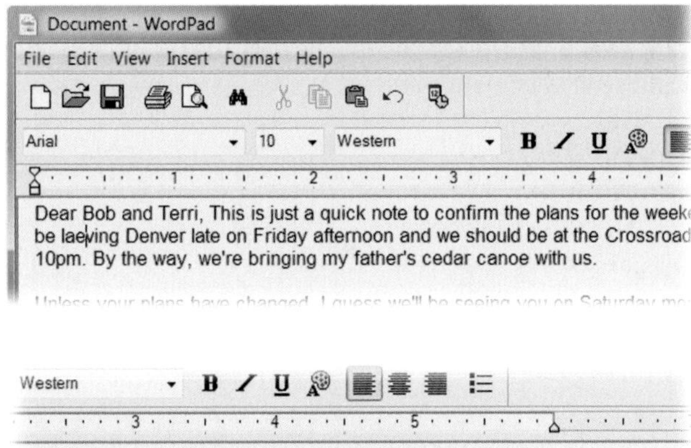

REPLACING TEXT

- To replace a block of text with new text, select the text by dragging the cursor along it to highlight it.
- Then simply type in the new text, which will replace the highlighted text.

VANISHING POINT

You will notice that when you have selected and highlighted a block of text, there is no longer an insertion point in your WordPad window. What has happened is that the block of selected text becomes one very large insertion point. It is important to be careful at this point, because if you press any character key while your text is selected, the entire block will disappear and be replaced by whatever you type.On the plus side, this provides an easy way deliberately to delete large amounts of text. Highlight all the text that you wish to delete and press the ←Bksp key to make it all disappear.

ENHANCING THE TEXT

Another great strength of a word-processing program is the power it offers to have the text looking just the way you want. It allows you to control every aspect of the font appearance, as well as the position of each paragraph of text within the page. Here we look at using the Format menu and the Format Bar to change the font, font size, font style and optional effects, as well as color.

CHANGING THE FONT

- With the text selected, click on the **Format** menu button.
- From the drop-down menu, select **Font**.

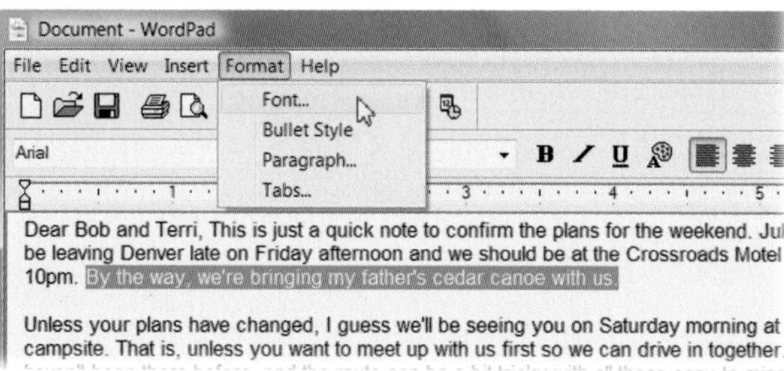

- The **Font** dialog box appears. Here you can use make your choices of font, font style, font size, font effects, and font color all in one go.

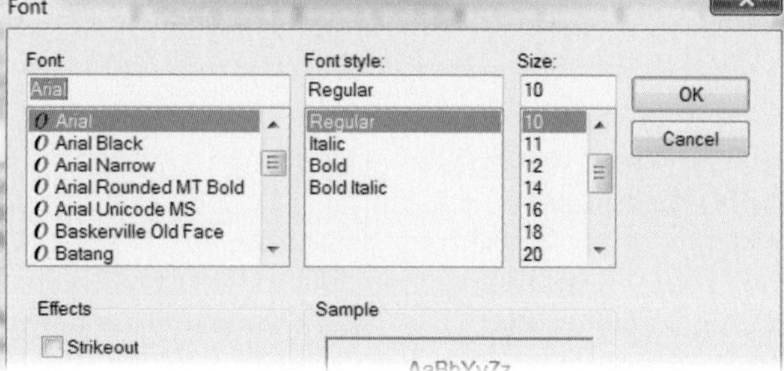

CHOOSING A FONT

- Use the scroll bar next to the Font box to run through the list and find the font you want. Here we are selecting **Blackadder ITC**.
- You will see that text in the **Sample** panel changes to this new font.

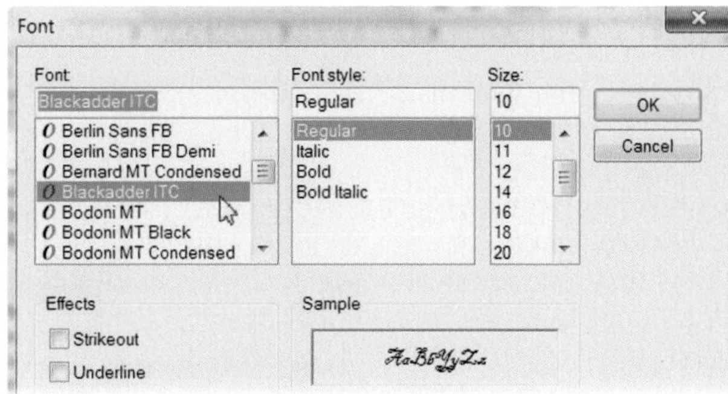

CHANGING THE FONT STYLE

- From the list of styles we are selecting **Bold**. Again, the **Sample** text changes.

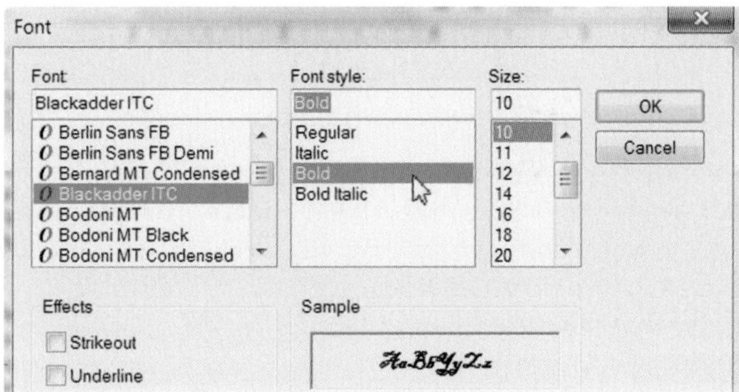

CHANGING THE FONT SIZE

- In the **Size** panel, we are selecting **20** point as the size for our highlighted text.

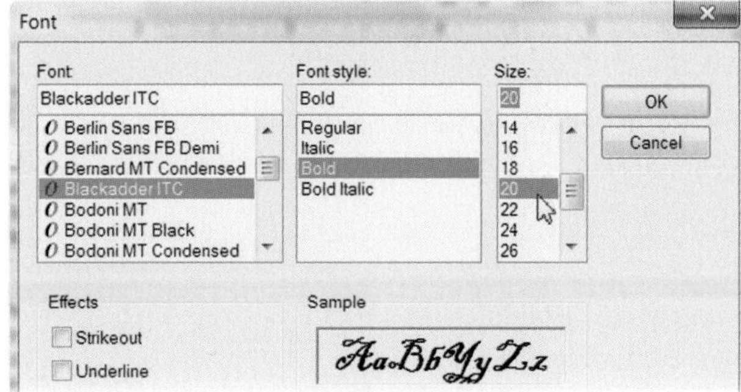

OPTIONAL FONT EFFECTS

- **Strikeout** and **Underline** font effects are available by clicking in the relevant check boxes.

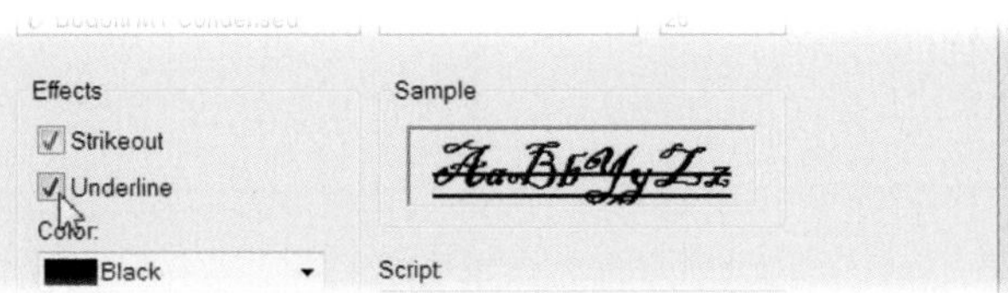

CHANGING THE FONT COLOR

● To change the color of the font from the standard black, click once on the arrow at the right-hand end of the **Color** panel.
● Slide your cursor down the pop-up palette to highlight the color of your choice, and click to select it.

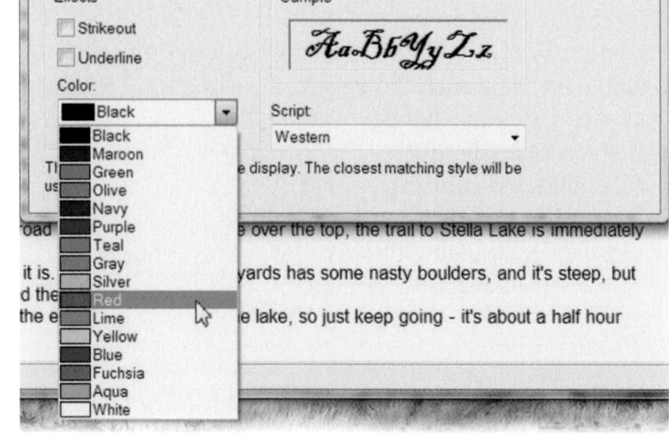

● The sample text now shows how the highlighted text in your document will appear with these choices.
● If this is what you want, click **OK** to confirm.

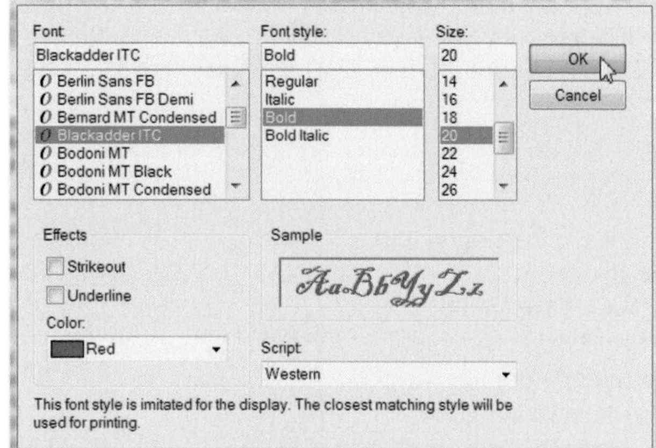

● You return to the WordPad page. The selected text will still be highlighted, so click anywhere in the document to deselect, and the text appears as you've defined it.

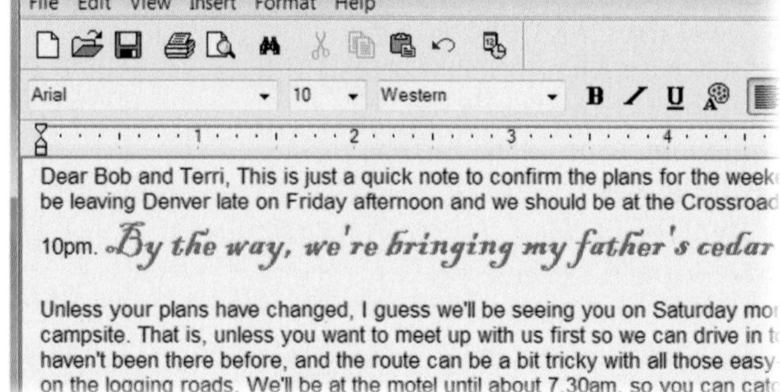

WHOOPS!

There will be times when you change your mind about substantial changes that you've made to a document and confirmed, or you simply make a mistake. Don't panic. The Undo button in the toolbar will solve the problem. A single click will restore the text to the way it was before you made the change. Successive clicks will take you back step by step.

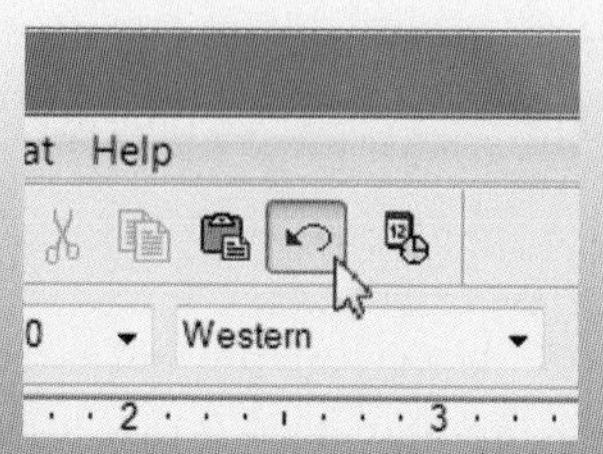
at Help
Western

Changing the Layout

The text in your WordPad document–all of it or just individual paragraphs–can be set to align with the left or right edges of the page, to be centered on the page, or to be indented. Text can also be set as a bulleted list.

CHANGING THE TEXT ALIGNMENT

- Select all the text or click in the single paragraph to be changed.
- Then click on the **Format** menu button, and select **Paragraph** from the drop-down menu.

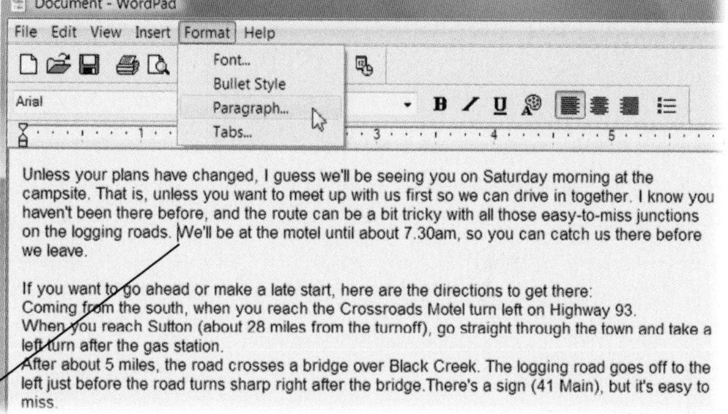
Document - WordPad
File Edit View Insert Format Help
Font...
Bullet Style
Paragraph...
Tabs...
Arial
Unless your plans have changed, I guess we'll be seeing you on Saturday morning at the campsite. That is, unless you want to meet up with us first so we can drive in together. I know you haven't been there before, and the route can be a bit tricky with all those easy-to-miss junctions on the logging roads. We'll be at the motel until about 7.30am, so you can catch us there before we leave.
If you want to go ahead or make a late start, here are the directions to get there:
Coming from the south, when you reach the Crossroads Motel turn left on Highway 93.
When you reach Sutton (about 28 miles from the turnoff), go straight through the town and take a left turn after the gas station.
After about 5 miles, the road crosses a bridge over Black Creek. The logging road goes off to the left just before the road turns sharp right after the bridge.There's a sign (41 Main), but it's easy to miss.

Simply clicking in the chosen paragraph selects it for changes

- In the **Paragraph** dialog box, click on the arrow at the right-hand end of the **Alignment** panel, and select the **Right** option.
- Click **OK** to confirm your selection.

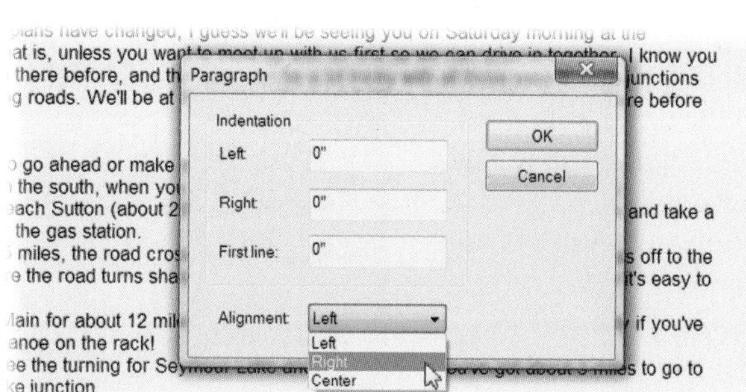
Paragraph
Indentation
Left 0"
Right 0"
First line: 0"
OK
Cancel
Alignment Left
Left
Right
Center

- **Right** now appears in the **Alignment** panel.
- Click **OK** to confirm your selection.

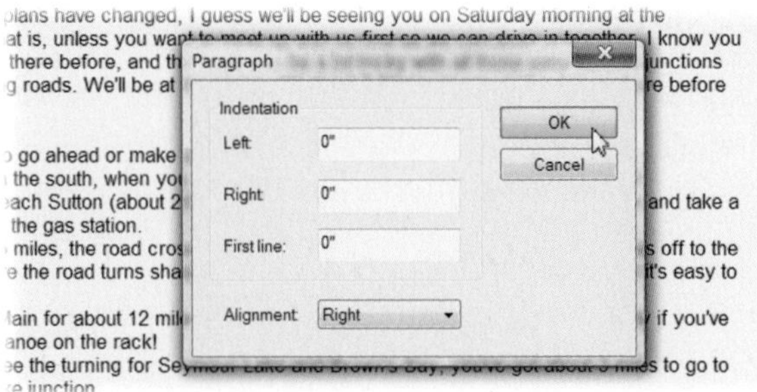

- Click off the highlighted text, and the paragraph is now aligned with the right-hand edge of the page.
- Centering the text and aligning it with the left-hand side are achieved by selecting the **Center** and **Left Alignment** options.

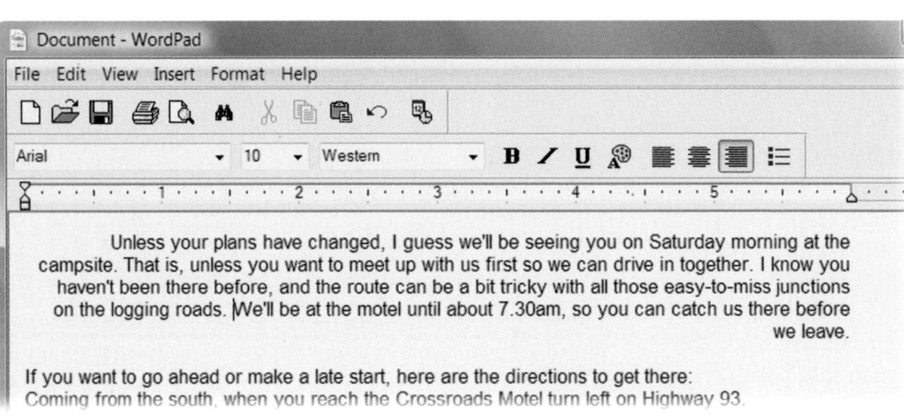

INDENTING TEXT

- To indent a paragraph from one or both sides of the page, select the paragraph, open the **Format** menu again, and choose **Paragraph** to open the dialog box.
- Here, we have returned the previous paragraph to Left alignment and selected it again by clicking in it.

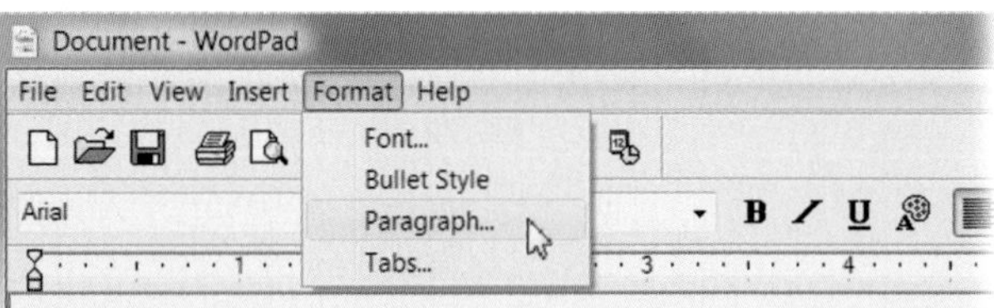

- We're going to indent the left- and right-hand sides by 1 inch, and indent the first line of the paragraph by half an inch *less*, so we highlight the text in the **Left**, **Right**, and **First line** panels in turn and type in **1**, **1**, and **-0.5**.
- Click **OK** to confirm.

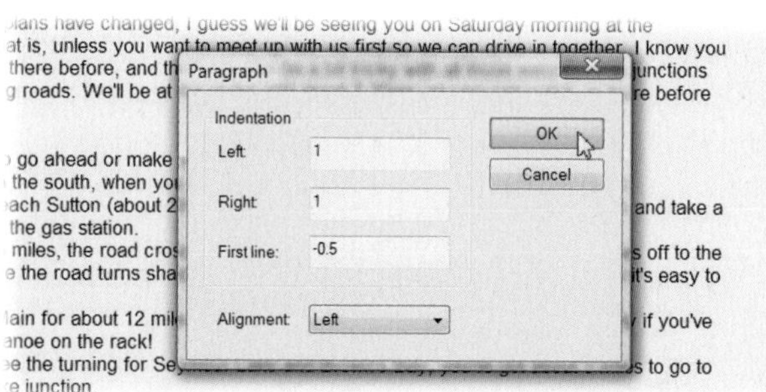

- When the dialog box closes, you will find the text is now indented from the page edges by one inch on both sides, and the first line is indented by half an inch.

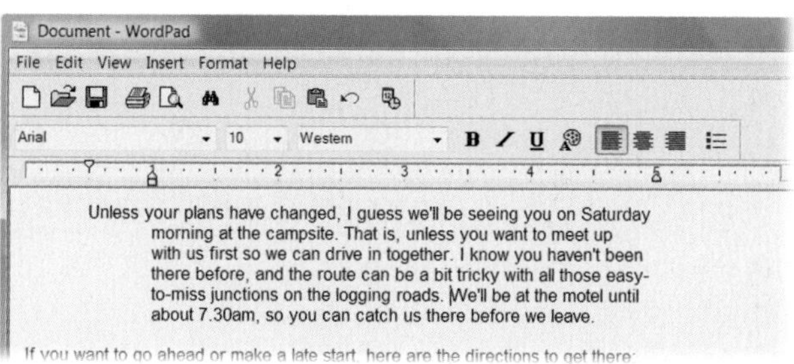

CREATING A BULLETED LIST

- To indent lines of text and mark each line with a bullet, start by highlighting the text.
- Again, open the **Format** menu, but this time select **Bullet Style**.

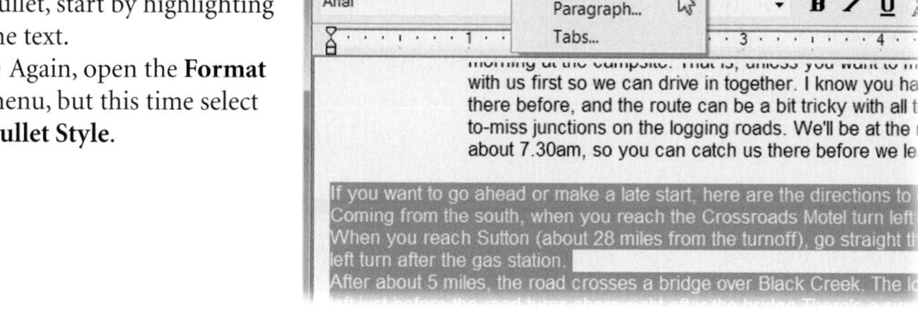

- You now have a list of bulleted entries.
- Note that if you leave lines spaces between entries, each line space will also be marked with a bullet.

USING THE FORMAT BAR

● Almost all of the text formatting that we have looked at can be achieved by using the Format Bar that runs across the top of the document area.

● Simply highlight the relevant text and then either click on the arrow next to the **Font** or **Font Size** panels and select from the drop-down list, or click on the appropriate button.

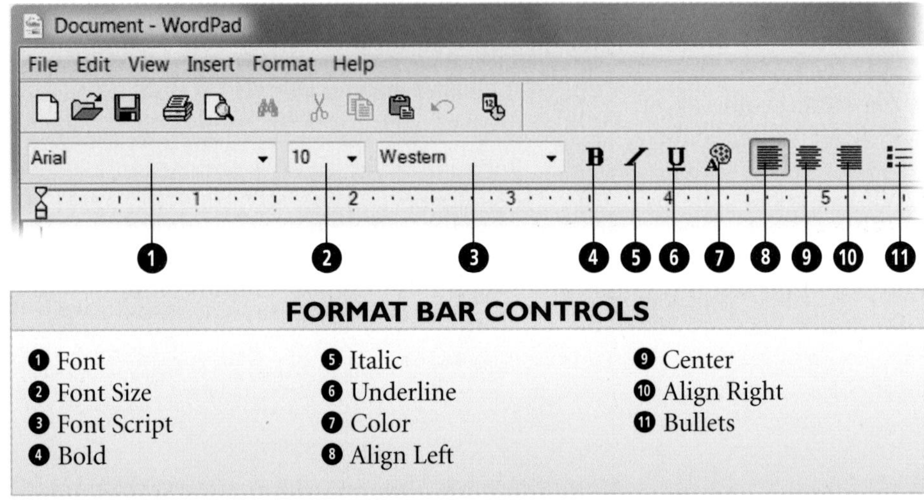

FORMAT BAR CONTROLS

1 Font
2 Font Size
3 Font Script
4 Bold
5 Italic
6 Underline
7 Color
8 Align Left
9 Center
10 Align Right
11 Bullets

OPENING, SAVING, AND PRINTING FILES

The File menu allows you to create, open, or save WordPad documents, save one with a new name, or print the document. Keyboard shortcuts are available for most of these, and there is also a row of shortcut buttons beneath the menu bar.

OPENING A NEW FILE

● To open a new WordPad file, click on the **File** menu and then on **New**. You can also hold down the Ctrl key and type **O**, or click on the New icon on the toolbar.

● You will be asked to choose a new document type, and whether you wish to save the current file.

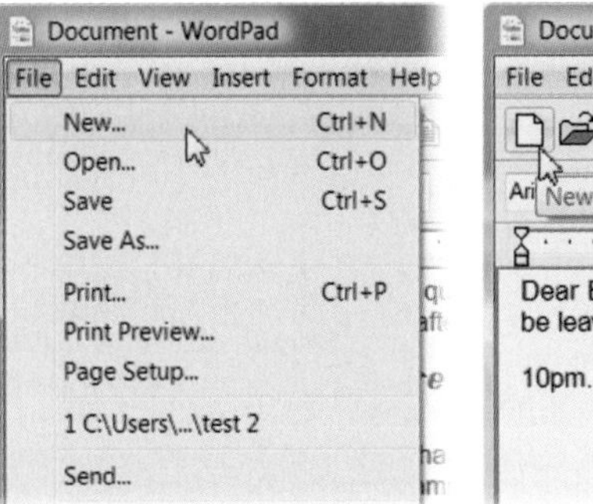

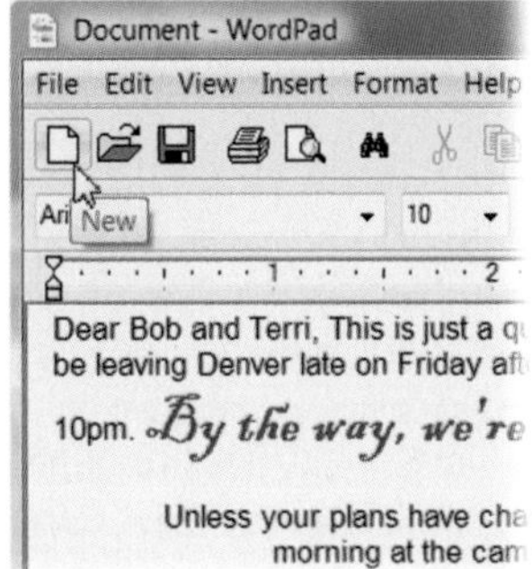

OPENING AN EXISTING FILE

● To open an existing WordPad file, click on the **File** menu and then on **Open**. You can also hold down the Ctrl key and type **O**, or click on the Open icon on the toolbar.

● You will then be asked to navigate to the chosen file.

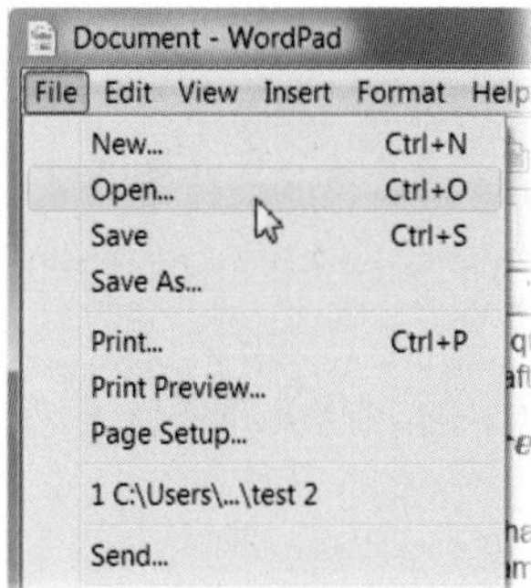

SAVING THE CURRENT FILE

● To save the current WordPad file, click on the **File** menu and then on **Save**. You can also hold down the Ctrl key and type **S**, or click on the Save icon on the toolbar.

● The first time the file is saved, you will be asked to choose a name for it and a location in which to save it.

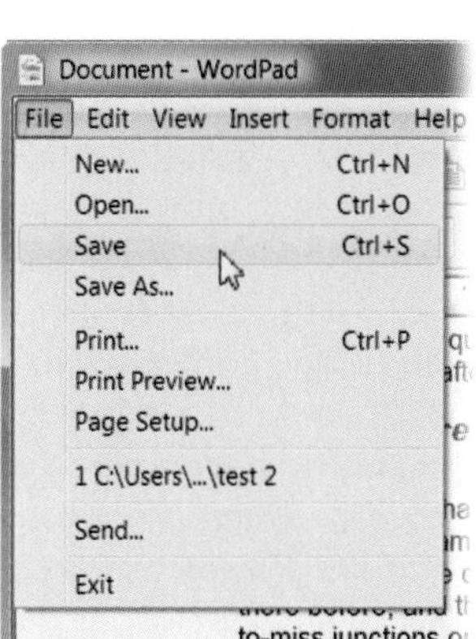

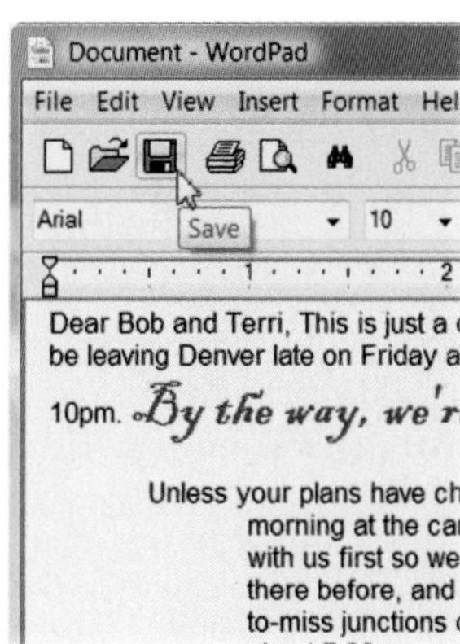

SAVING A FILE UNDER A NEW NAME

● To save the current WordPad file under a new name (which you may wish to do so that the original file remains unchanged), click on the **File** menu and then on **Save As**.

● Just as when you save a file for the first time, you will be asked to choose a name for it and a location in which to save it.

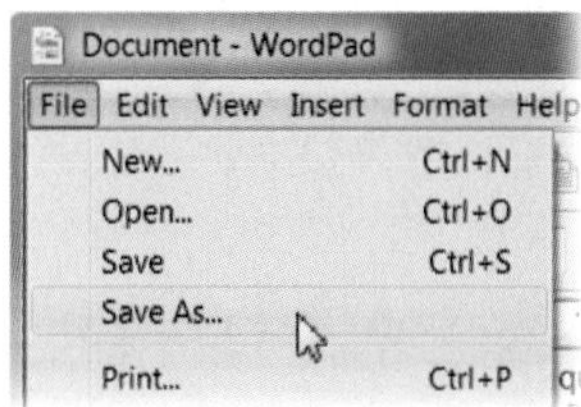

PRINTING THE FILE

● To print the current WordPad file, click on the **File** menu and then on **Print**. You can also hold down the Ctrl key and type **P**, or click on the Print icon on the toolbar.

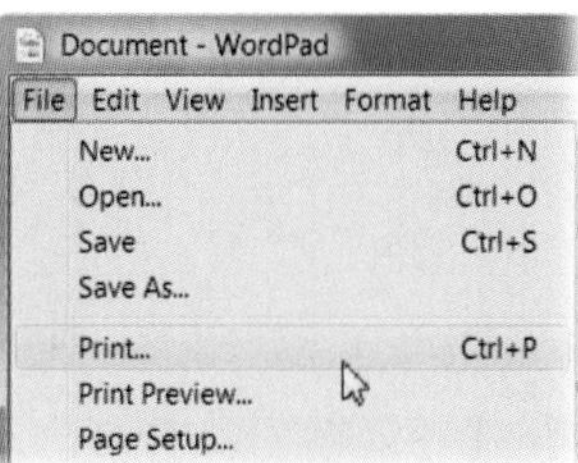

INTRODUCING WORD

If WordPad is Notepad's big brother, then Microsoft Office Word 2007 is the clan chief. This section provides an overview of this powerful program's main formatting features.

WHAT CAN WORD DO?

The features contained in Word make it one of the most flexible word-processing programs available. Word can be used to write anything from shopping lists to large publications that contain, in addition to the main text, illustrations and graphics, charts, tables and graphs, captions, headers and footers, cross references, footnotes, indexes, and glossaries. The program can also check spelling and grammar, check text readability, search for and replace text, import data, perform calculations, and provide templates for many types of document, from memos to webpages.

LAUNCHING WORD

Word launches just like any other program running in Windows. With the Windows desktop onscreen, you can launch Word as the only program running or you can run it alongside other programs, allowing you to exchange data back and forth between different applications.

LAUNCHING BY THE START MENU

- Place the mouse cursor over the Start button and left click to open the Start menu.
- If Word is on your Start menu, click on it to launch the program. If not, click on **All Programs** and select **Microsoft Office Word 2007** from the list of programs, or select **Microsoft Office**, and then Word.

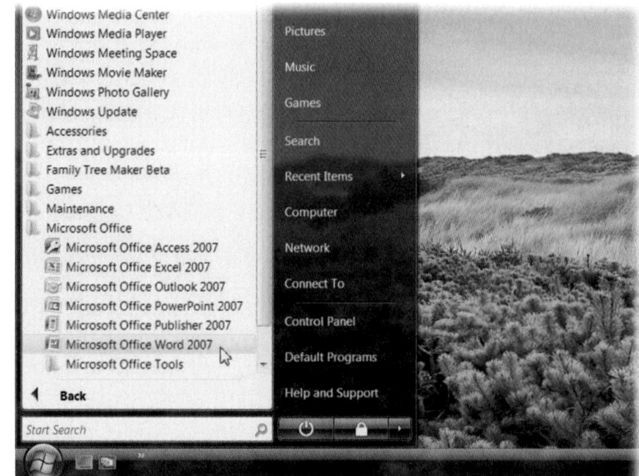

LAUNCHING BY A SHORTCUT

- You may already have a desktop icon for Word, which is a shortcut to launch the program. If so, click on the icon to open the program.
- The Microsoft Word window opens.

Manipulating Text

As the basics of keying in, selecting, editing, copying, deleting, and pasting text are the same in Word as they are in WordPad, these are not covered in this section.

WHAT IS A WORD DOCUMENT?

In its very simplest form, a Word document is a sequence of characters that exists in a computer's memory. Using Word, a document can be edited, added to, and given an almost infinite variety of layouts. Once a document has been created, it can be saved, duplicated, printed, published on the web, or sent as an e-mail.

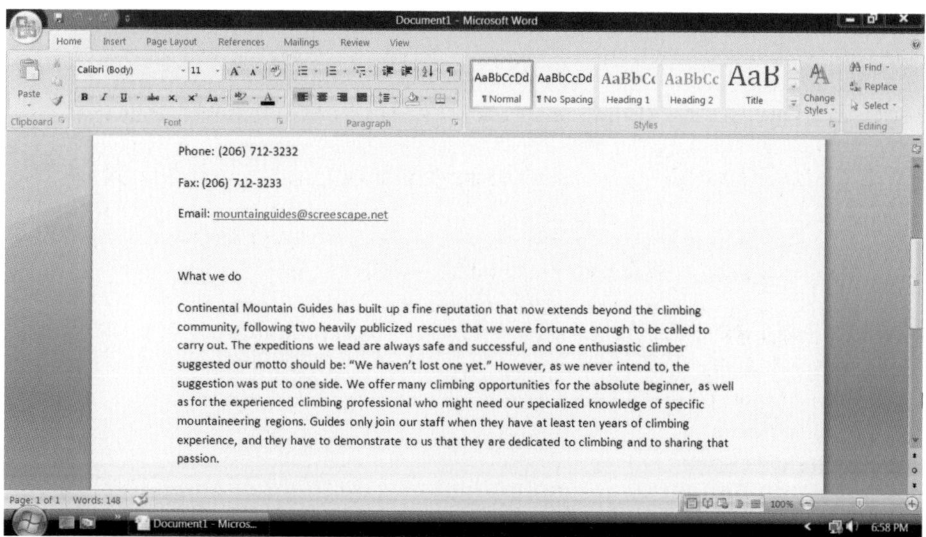

OBTAINING WORD

Microsoft Office Word 2007 is best bought as part of one of the various Microsoft Office 2007 packages that include such programs as Excel, Access, Outlook, and Powerpoint. If you'd like to try it out before you spend the money, download a free 60-day trial version from the Microsoft website first.

THE WORD WINDOW

At first glance, Word's document window may look like a space shuttle instrument display, but you'll soon discover that similar commands and actions are grouped together. This "like-with-like" layout helps you to understand quickly where you should be looking on the window for what you want. Have the window open, and experiment as you read through the details of the controls. The precise appearance of the window will vary depending on the resolution at which your monitor is set. In this particular screen shot, we have deliberately used a low resolution to maximize the size of the elements for clarity. At a higher resolution, the range of options is seen in more detail, as you will see in the subsequent pages.

FEATURES KEY

❶ Office Button
Used to carry out actions such as opening, saving, or printing your document.

❷ Home Tab
Contains the most commonly used text formatting commands.

❸ Quick Access Toolbar
A handy set of tools that can be customized to suit.

❹ Other Tabs
Clicking on any of these brings up a specific ribbon of commands.

❺ Minimize Word

❻ Restore Word

❼ Close Word

❽ Word Help
Click here for online help and advice from Microsoft.

❾ View Ruler
Clicking here brings a ruler into view along the top of the document.

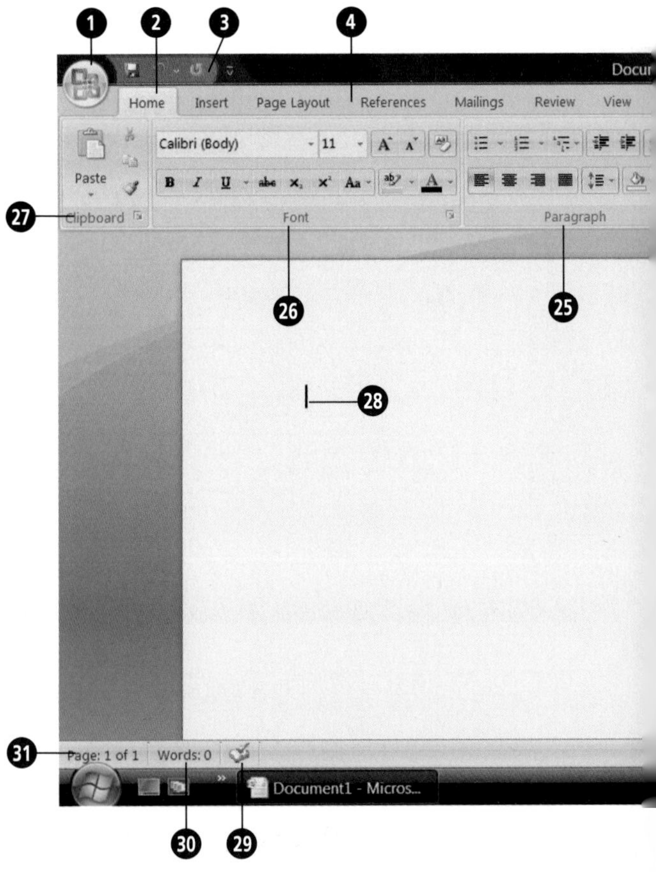

WORD'S RIBBON TOOLBAR

Word 2007 provides the easiest access yet to all the tools and controls needed to produce professional quality documents. This is achieved by using the Ribbon toolbar, part of Microsoft's Fluent User Interface, located along the top of the document window. The Ribbon consists of several tabs that relate to different aspects of the Word document, and within each tab the commands are grouped in a logical fashion. The **Home** tab, which is selected here, contains most of the common text formatting tools and commands.

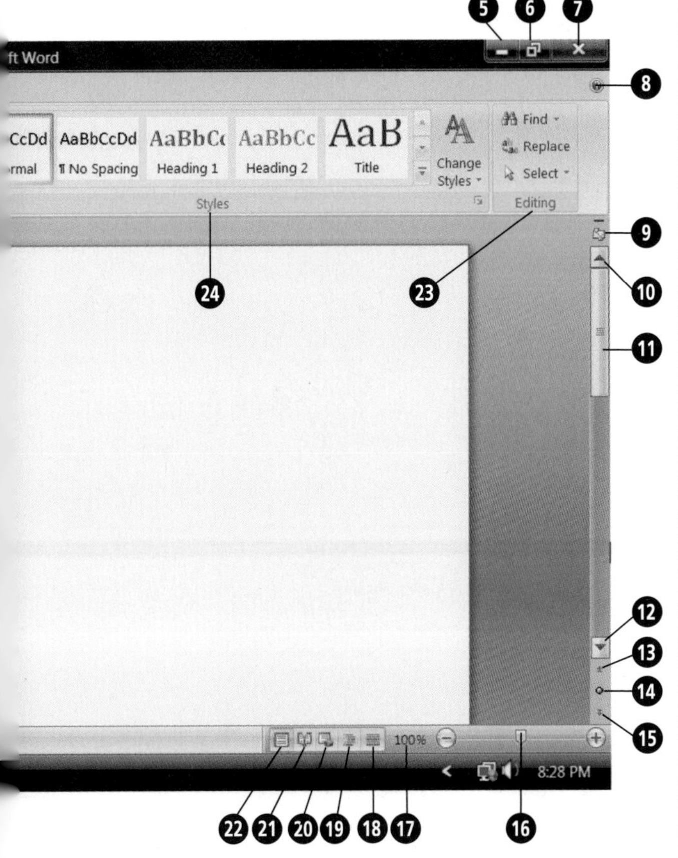

FEATURES KEY

⑩ Scroll-up Arrow
Moves up the document.
⑪ Scroll Bar Box
Moves text up or down.
⑫ Scroll-down Arrow
Moves down the document.
⑬ Page-up Button
Shows previous page of text.
⑭ Select Browse Object
Opens browse options menu.
⑮ Page-down Button
Displays next page of text.
⑯ Zoom Slider
Sliding this button to left and right alters the magnification of the page.
⑰ Zoom Button
Click here to open the Zoom dialog box.
⑱ Draft View
⑲ Outline View
⑳ Web Layout View
㉑ Full Screen Reading
㉒ Print Layout
㉓ Editing Group of Commands
㉔ Styles Group of Commands
㉕ Paragraph Group of Commands
㉖ Font Group of Commands
㉗ Clipboard Group of Commands
㉘ Insertion Point
Typed text appears here.
㉙ Proofing Button
㉚ Word Count
㉛ Page Indicator

The Office Button

If you're used to earlier versions of Word, you may be wondering where the controls to open, save, and print files have gone. The answer is here–behind the Office button–and there are many other useful commands and shortcuts in here as well.

USING THE OFFICE BUTTON

- Simply click on the button to open the menu.
- The left-hand list has all the file commands that we have seen in WordPad, as well as commands for preparing the document for distribution, sending it by e-mail, and publishing it to a blog. All the documents you have opened in the recent past are listed in the right-hand side of the panel, and clicking on any of these will take you directly to that document.

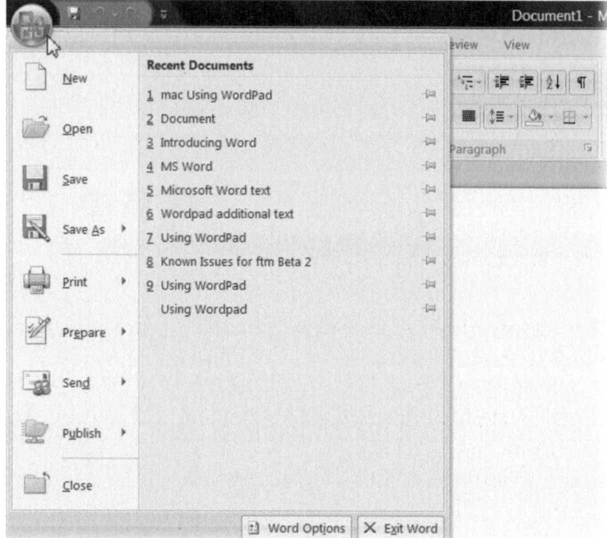

- Hover your cursor arrow over each of the menu buttons in turn to see the range of options that each one offers. The **Save As** menu, for example, gives you a wide range of formats in which you can save the document, including compatibility with older versions of Word.

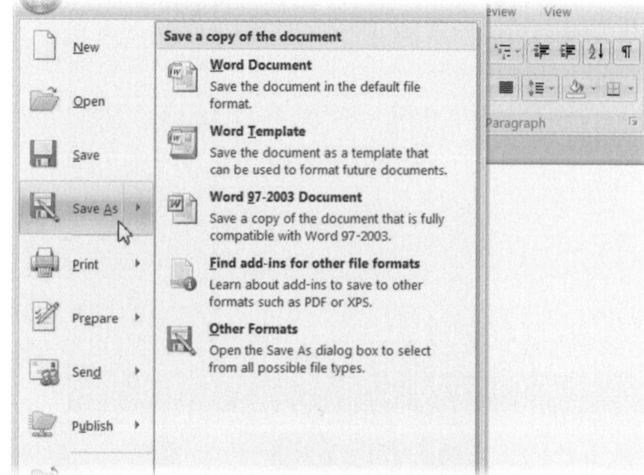

The Quick Access Toolbar

Located to the right of the Office Button, the Quick Access Toolbar contains, by default, some controls that you may need often–the **Save** command, for regularly saving your work, and the **Undo** and **Redo** commands for undoing an unwanted change and redoing it when you change your mind again.

CUSTOMIZING THE TOOLBAR

- Clicking on the arrow to the right of the toolbar opens the **Customize** menu, in which you can add a range of other commands that you may find useful.

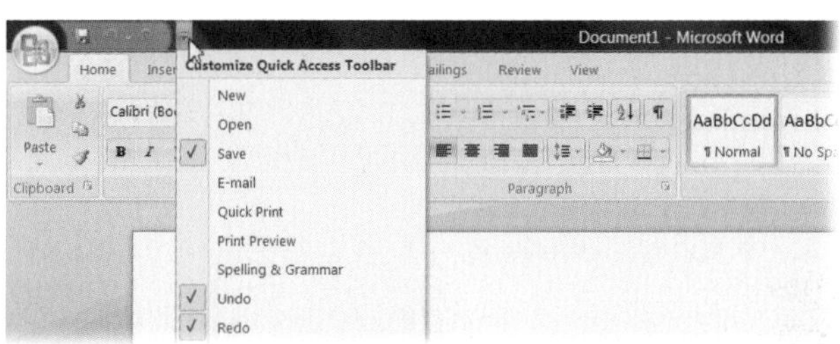

- Any of the buttons on the Ribbon can be added to the Quick Access Toolbar simply by right clicking on the button (here we have clicked on **Bold**) and then selecting **Add to Quick Access Toolbar** from the drop-down menu.

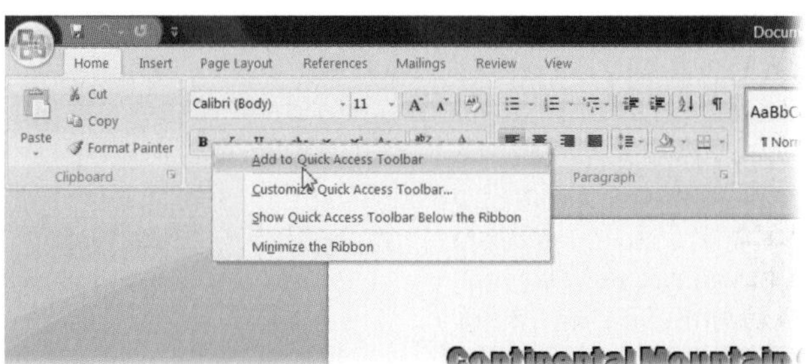

- To remove the button from the menu, right click on it and select **Remove from Quick Access Toolbar**.

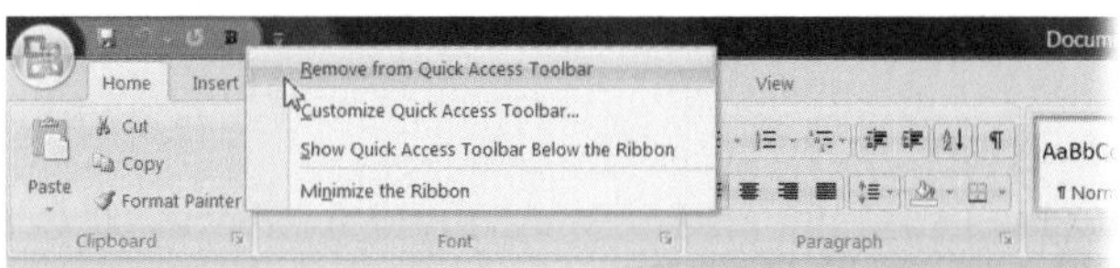

- To move the Quick Access Toolbar even closer to your text area click on **Show Below the Ribbon**.
- It now appears below the Clipboard tools.

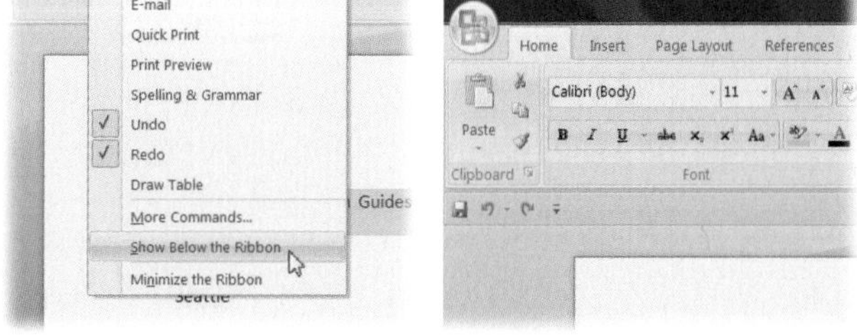

263 **Word's Ribbon Toolbar**

The Home Ribbon

This is likely to be the Ribbon that you have open above your document most of the time, for it is here that you will find the menus and buttons that enable you to copy, move, and delete text, as well control the appearance and position of all text elements. Here we'll look at each group of controls in the Home Ribbon in turn.

THE CLIPBOARD

● The **Clipboard** has all the controls for cutting, copying, and pasting text. They're all available when a piece of text is highlighted.

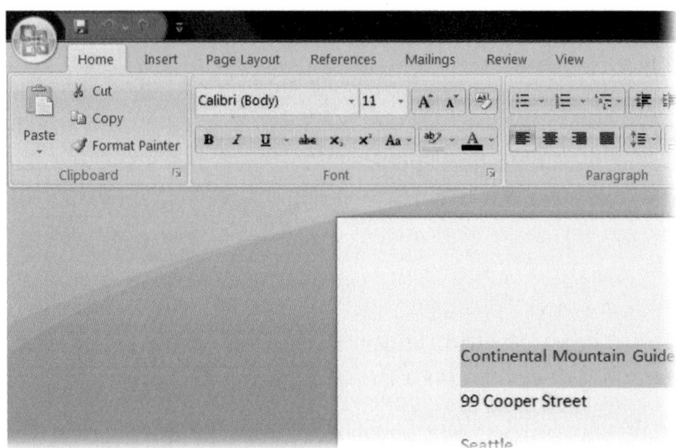

● Clicking on the scissors icon will cut the highlighted text, while clicking on the duplicated page icon will copy text.

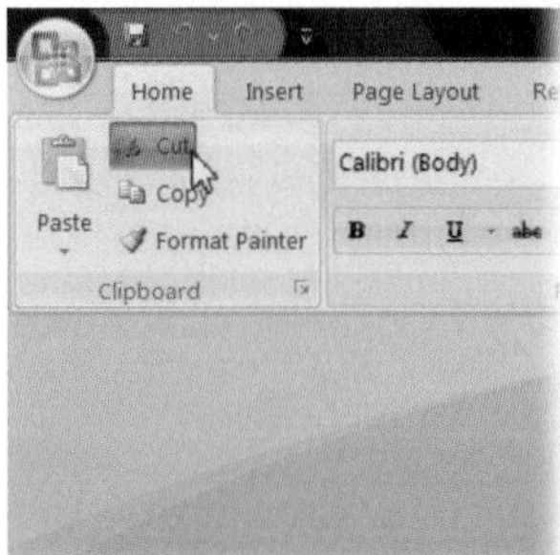

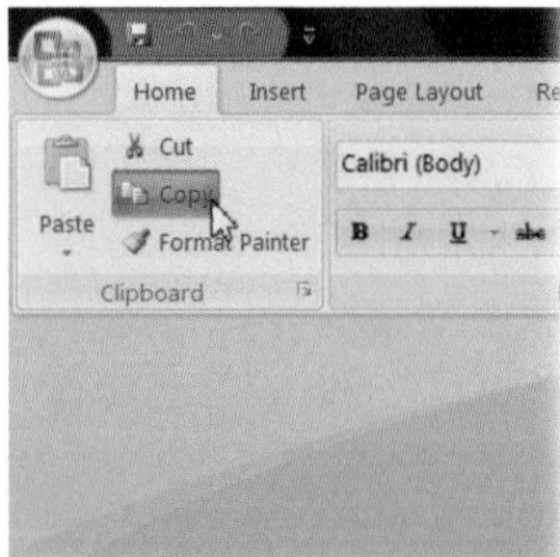

SCREEN TIPS

You don't need to memorize all the buttons in the toolbars. Simply roll the cursor over a button and wait–a screen tip appears telling you the function of that button. The tip will also tell you if there's keyboard shortcut available and what it is.

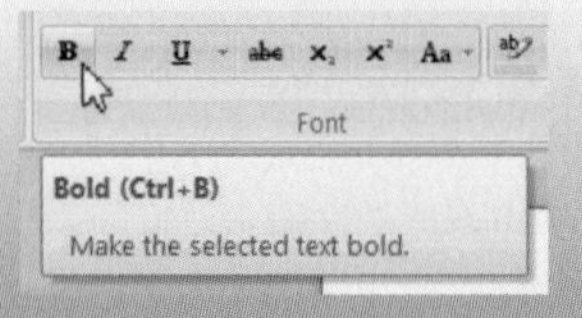

● With your insertion point in the desired position in the document, clicking on the clipboard icon will paste the text into the document.

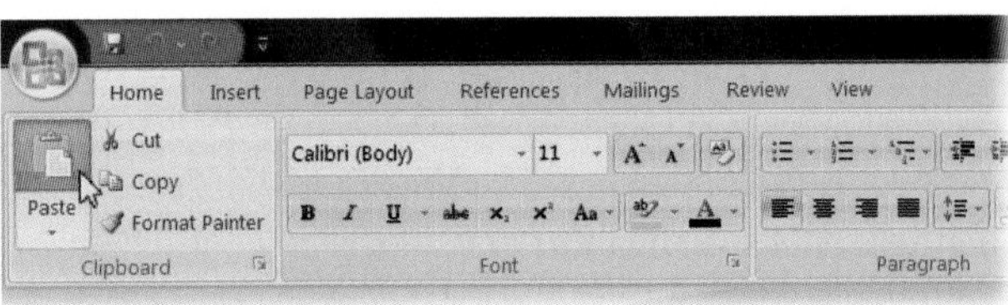

● Clicking on the arrow below the **Paste** command opens the possibility of **Paste Special**.

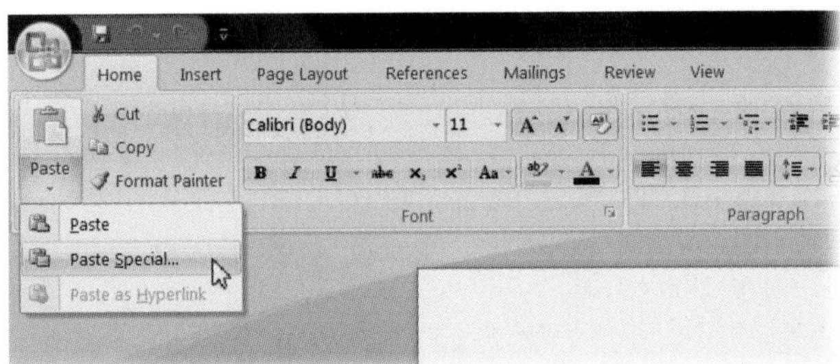

● If you select this, you can then choose the format in which the selected text (or graphic) is to be pasted.

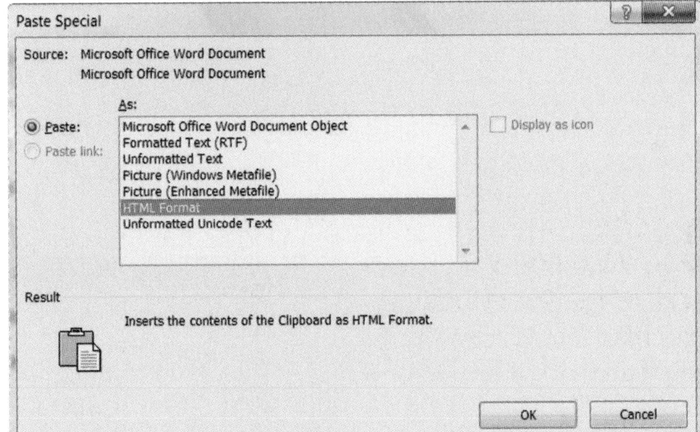

MULTIPLE CLIPS

● Any text that is cut or copied is placed in the clipboard for future use.

● Click on the small button next to **Clipboard** to view the clips.

● The clipboard opens, showing the text that has been cut or copied.

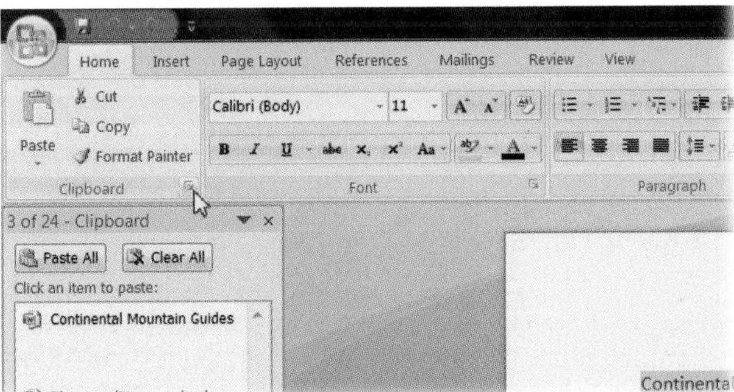

● Clicking on any of these entries will paste that piece of text into the document in the current insertion point position, and this can be done repeatedly.

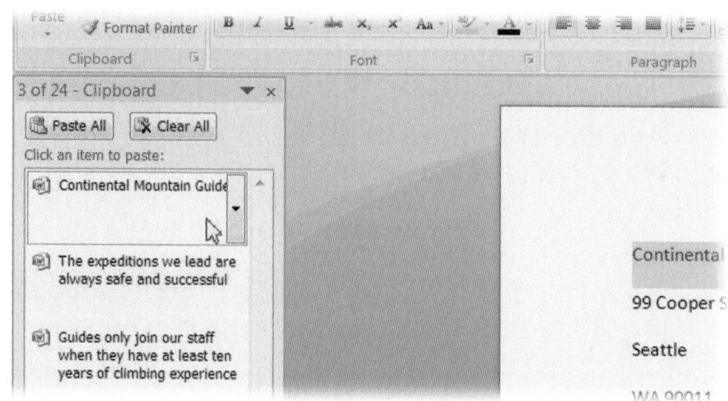

THE FONT GROUP

● As the name suggests, these are the tools to help you enhance the look of your text, by choosing the font, font size, style, and color.

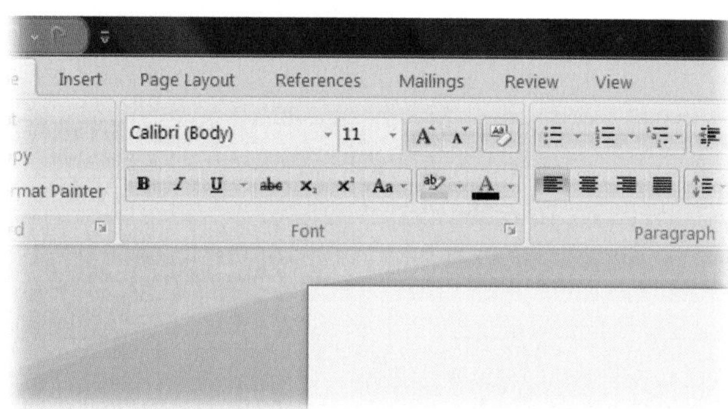

● To change the font, select the text you wish to change and click on the arrow next to the current font name.

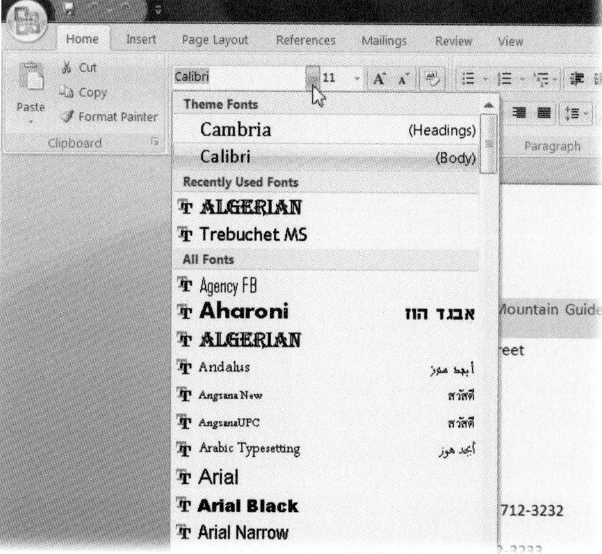

● Use the scroll bar to move up and down the list. As your cursor hovers over each font, the selected text shows how it would look.

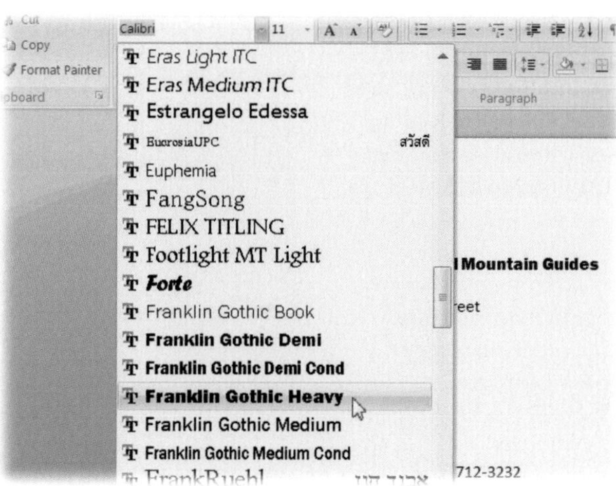

● Select the font you want by clicking on it, and the selected text will appear in that font.

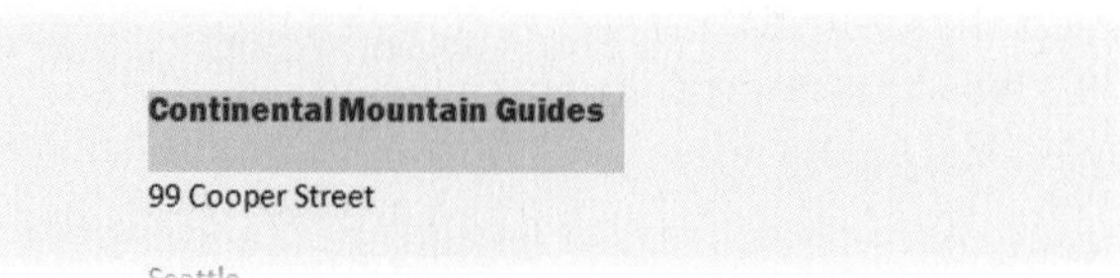

● To change the font size, click on the arrow next to the font size, and select a new size by clicking on it.

● The size of the font can also be increased or decreased by 2 points at a time by clicking on the **Grow Font** or **Shrink Font** buttons.

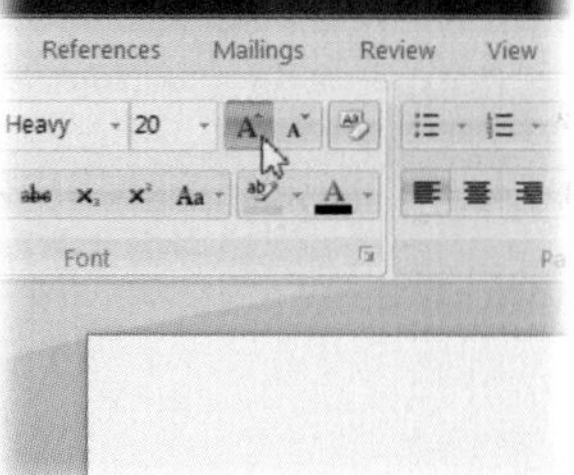

- To change the font style, click on one of the style buttons. From left to right, these change the font to **Bold**, **Italic**, **Underline**, **Strikethrough**, **Subscript**, **Superscript**, or change the case of the lettering.
- Clicking on the arrow next to the **Underline** button reveals a range of underline styles, from which we're choosing one.

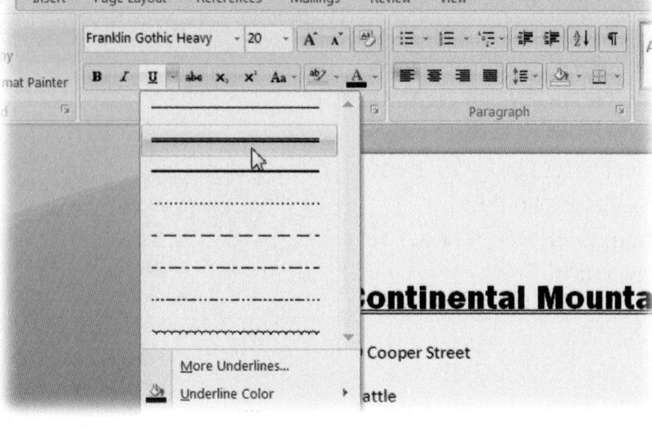

- Clicking on the **Text Highlight Color** button makes the selected text look as though it has been marked with a highlighter pen.

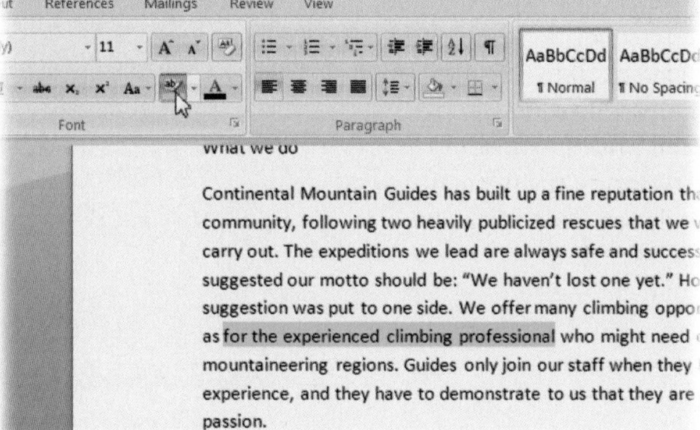

- Click on the arrow to the right of it to display the drop-down color palette and select a new color for the highlighter.

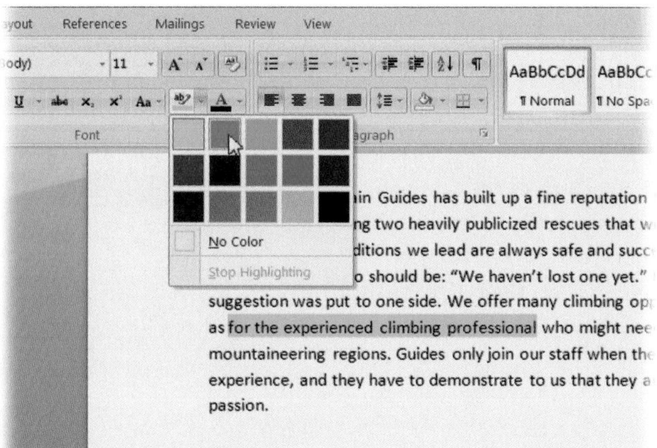

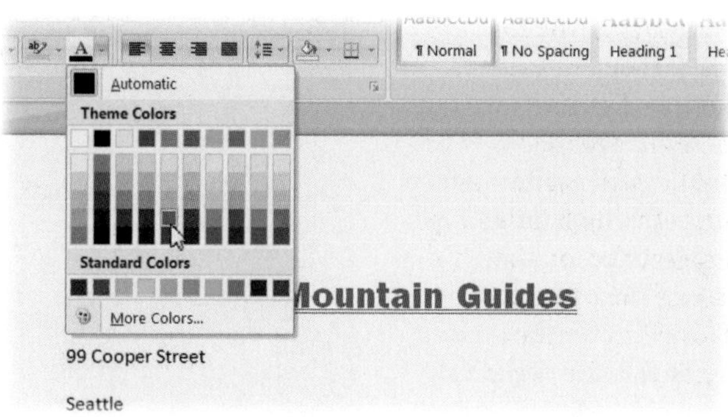

- To change the color of selected text, click on the arrow next the **Font Color** button and select a color.
- Once a color has been selected, clicking the **Font Color** button will now change selected text to this new color.

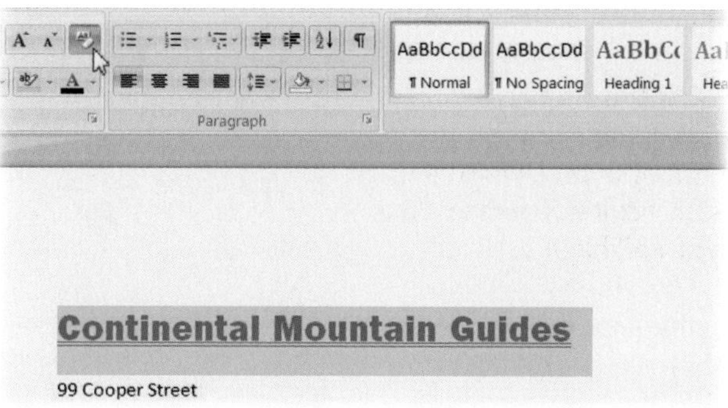

- The final button in the Fonts group is **Clear Formatting.** With the text selected, clicking here removes all the formatting that we have just applied.
- In this case, it would return it to the normal body text style with which we started.

ALL IN ONE

- All of the Font commands are available in a single dialog box that opens when you click on the button at the bottom right of the Font group panel.

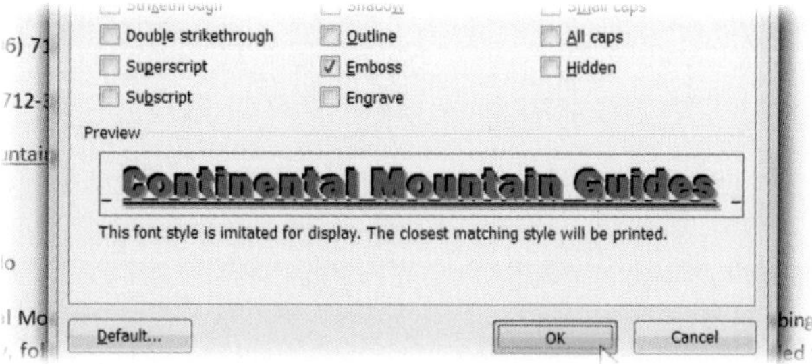

- Scroll through the **Font**, **Font style**, and **Size** lists to make your choices, and place a check mark in the boxes to choose from an extended range of **Effects**.
- Click on **OK** to confirm your selection.

HELP IS CLOSE AT HAND

● Font management is made even easier by Word 2007's mini toolbar, which appears whenever you highlight text.
● Just leave your cursor hovering over the highlighted text and this selection of commands from the **Font** and **Paragraph** (see below) groups floats into view.
● Click on any of these to implement a change.

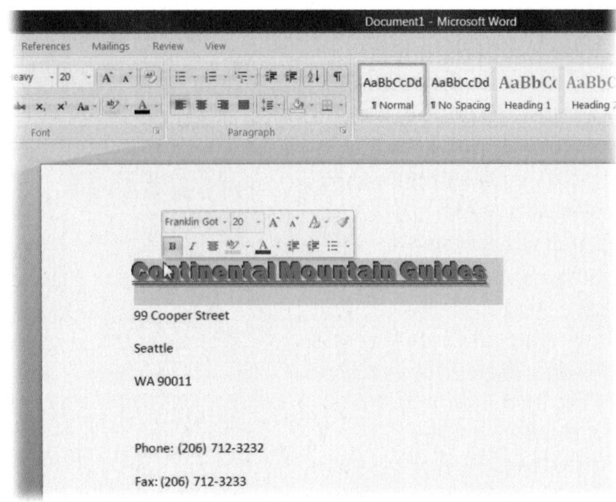

THE PARAGRAPH GROUP

● This set of commands enables you to alter the position and spacing of individual paragraphs of text, as well as sorting text entries into alphabetical order, creating colored backgrounds, and placing text within a border.

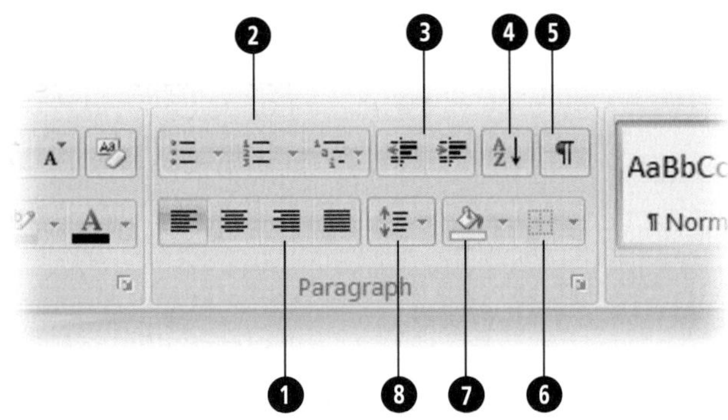

FEATURES KEY

❶ Alignment
These buttons are used to align selected text with the left-hand margin, to center it, align it right, or justify it with both margins.

❷ Lists
Click on one of these to create a bulleted list, numbered list, or multilevel list.

❸ Decrease/Increase Indent
To indent selected text, click the right-hand button. The left-hand button decreases the indent.

❹ Sort Text
Click here to sort the lines into alphabetical order.

❺ Show/Hide
Click here to make formatting marks visible or to hide them.

❻ Borders
Click the arrow to the right of this button to create a border.

❼ Shading
Use this button to select a color and create shading.

❽ Line spacing
Click this button to change the spacing between selected lines of text.

THE PARAGRAPH DIALOG BOX

- Clicking on the small button at the bottom right of the Paragraph group opens the **Paragraph** dialog box.
- This box gives you control over alignment, indents, and spacing.
- A second tab opens the **Line and Page Breaks** dialog box.
- Click on **Tabs** to open the Tabs dialog box.

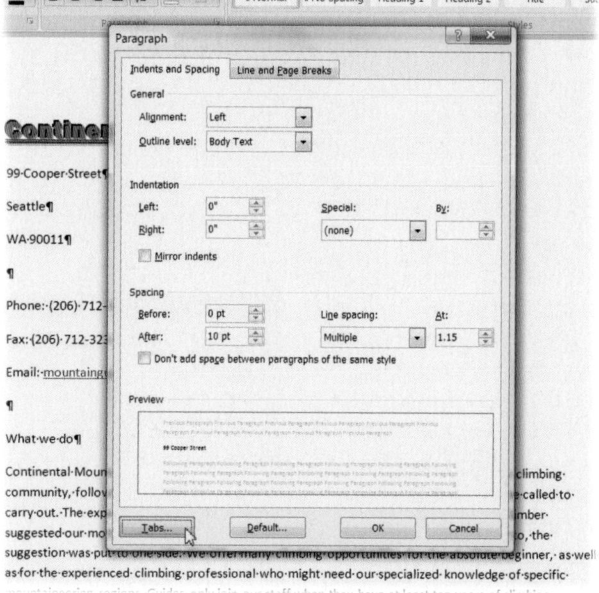

- Here you can set the position and type of tabs that will respond to the Tab key on your keyboard.

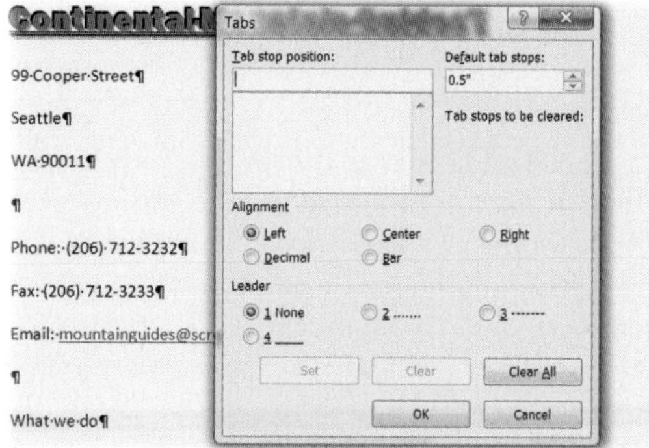

THE EDITING GROUP

- The **Styles** group deserves a section to itself, so we're jumping to the far right-hand end of the Ribbon now, to the **Editing** group of commands.

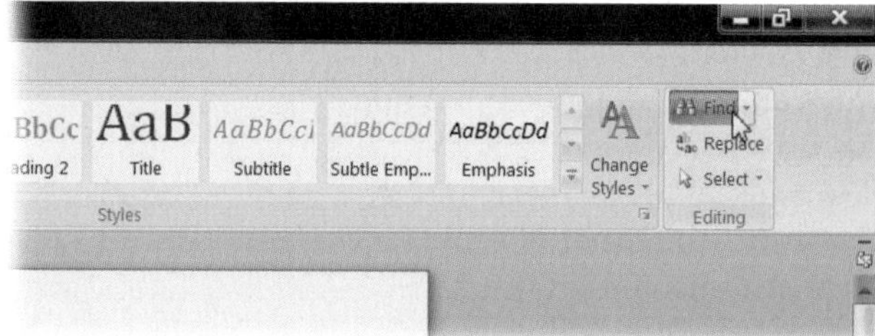

● The top two buttons open the **Find and Replace** dialog box where, by using the relevant tab, you can find a piece of text within the document, replace with another piece of text, or go to a specific element in the document.

● The **Select** button allows you to **Select All** the text (just as if you had used the keyboard shortcut Ctrl A), to select objects, or to select text that has the same formatting as the text that you have previously highlighted.

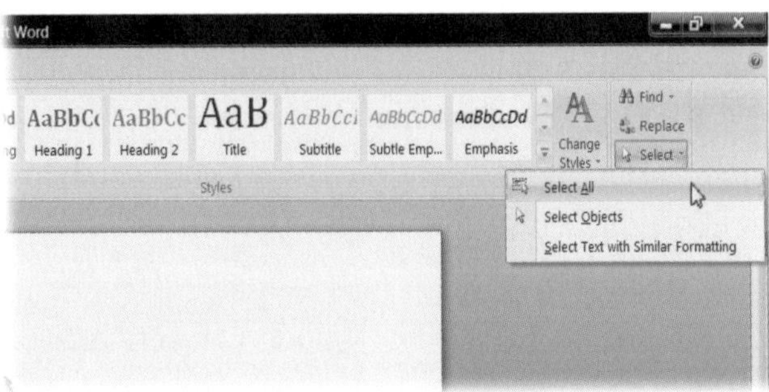

Styles and Style Sets

So far we have been looking at all the tools that enable you to amend the various aspects of fonts and layout one by one, but Word has a handful of trump cards to play. The **Styles** group in the **Home** tab of the Ribbon toolbar is a palette of ready-made looks that you can apply to the various levels of text in your document. Whatever changes you may have made to a piece of text, applying a **Style** will over-ride them all and introduce this coherent look.

SELECTING STYLES

● With our heading highlighted, **Normal** is the style highlighted in the Styles group. This is the default style for all text in a document, even if–as we have done–you make piecemeal changes to the look of the text.

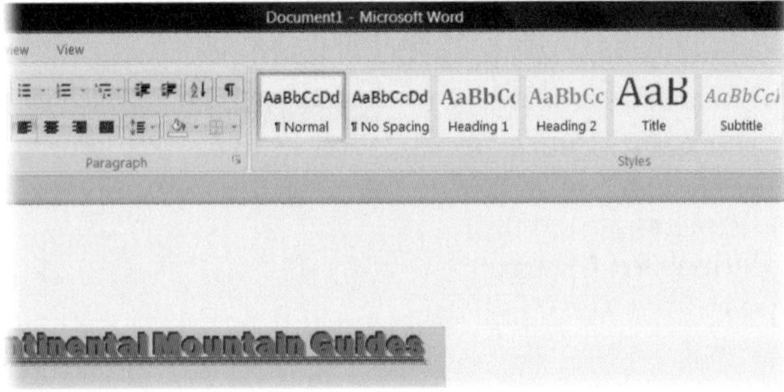

- Clicking on the downward-pointing arrow at the right-hand end of the **Style** opens the full palette.

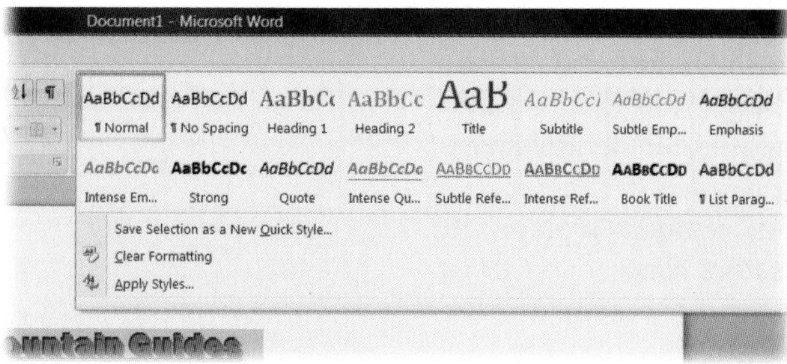

- Now watch what happens as we roll the cursor over a different style. Our heading loses all of the styling that we have added and adopts the look of the chosen Style.

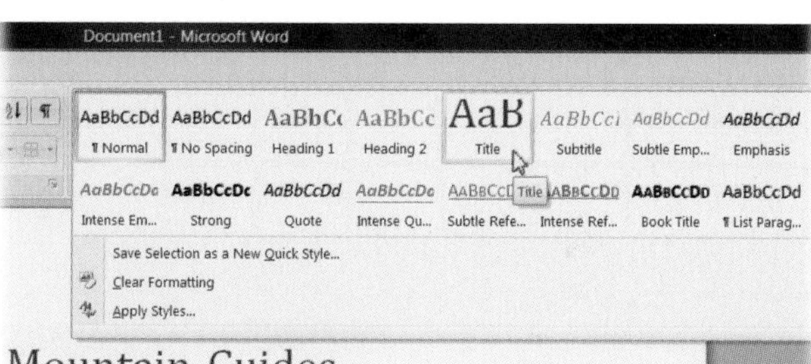

- We've now clicked on this Style to change the heading to **Title** style, and we've also selected a new style for each of the sections of text in the document. This is the result.

Continental Mountain Guides

99 Cooper Street
Seattle
WA 90011

CHANGING STYLES

- All the styles we have used from the palette are in a single family This is the default family, and it uses a few fonts in a small range of layout options and a limited range of colors. All of this can be changed.
- Click on the **Change Styles** button and select **Style Set**.

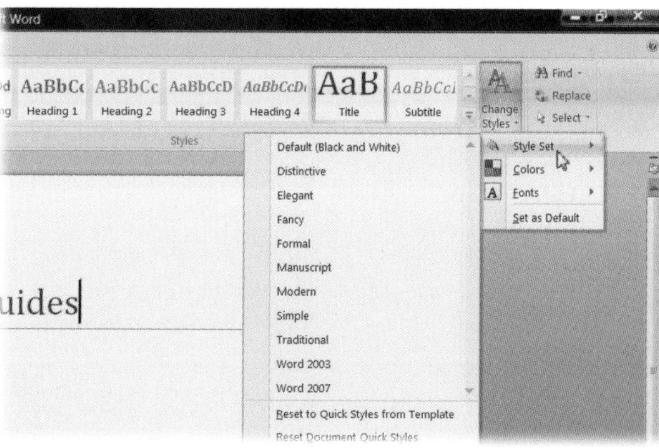

• Move the cursor down through the list so that you can see the effect that each style set has on the layout and colors of the text. In this example, we have chosen **Fancy**.

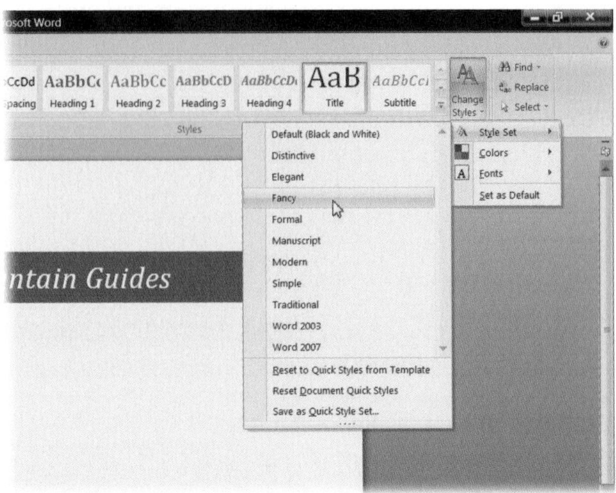

• Now click again on the **Change Styles** button and select **Colors**. Choosing from this list of palettes determines the range of colors that will be used. Here we're selecting **Flow**.

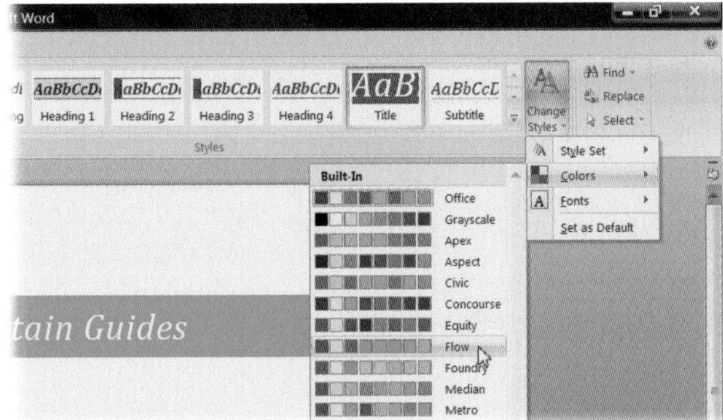

• Do the same to select a font group. Again, we have chosen the **Flow** set.

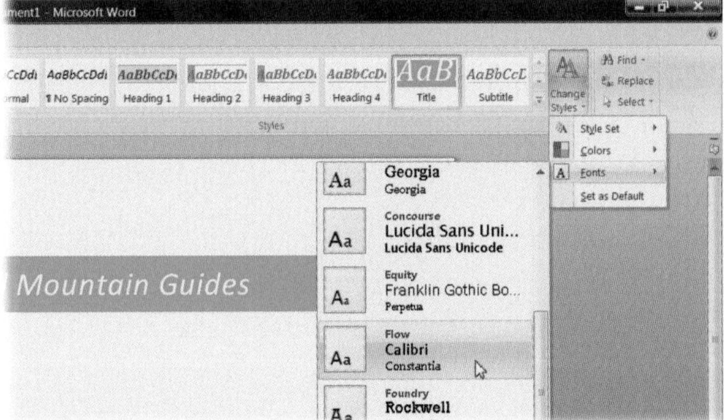

● Now the page has a completely different look, made up of sets of design elements that are provided by Word. It's a quick way to bring a professional feel to your documents.

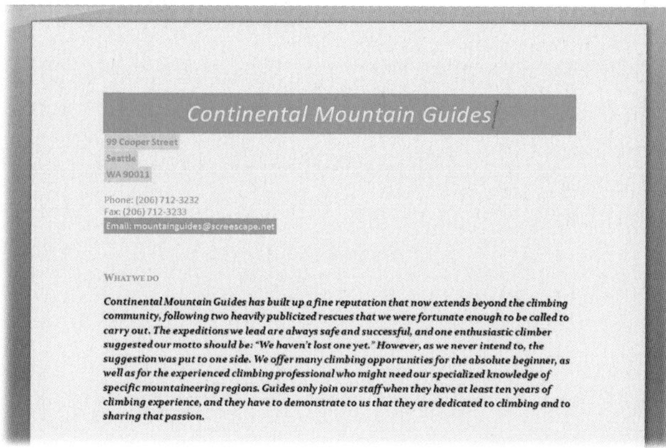

USING THE THEMES TAB

● Word has yet another design card up its sleeve– this time in the **Page Layout** tab of the Ribbon toolbar. Here you'll find the tools to adjust many aspects of the page and the text, including the margins, columns, and spacing, but we are going to take a look at the far left-hand end.

● Clicking on **Themes** delivers a palette of complete make-overs for your document–colors, fonts, and effects– and all in one package. Any graphics will be given the same coherent look, such as this SmartArt illustration that we have imported using the **Insert** tab.

● Each of these elements can also be chosen separately if you prefer. To do this, use the **Colors**, **Fonts**, and **Effects** buttons in this group.

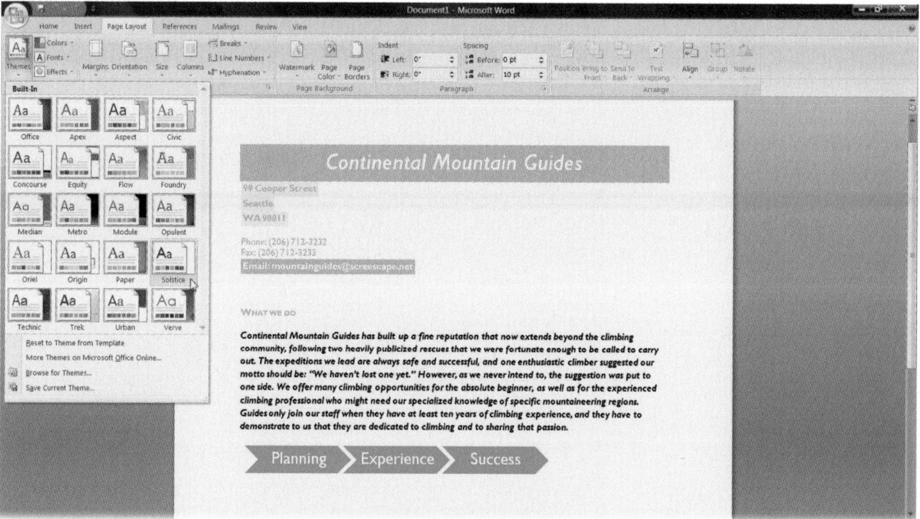

INTRODUCING EXCEL

Excel is a spreadsheet program, designed for storing and manipulating numerical data, carrying out complex calculations, and presenting the data visually.

WHAT CAN EXCEL DO?

Storing spreadsheet data is only the beginning as far as Excel is concerned. The wide range of features it contains lets you manipulate and present your data in almost any way you choose. Excel can be used as an accounts program; it can be used as a sophisticated calculator capable of utilizing complex mathematical formulas; it can also be a diary, a scheduler, and much, much more. Excel has many of the capabilities of Microsoft Word, using fonts, colors, borders, and text formatting to present textual and numerical information in a clear and professional style. Data can be also be presented in highly visual ways using Excel's wide range of pre-designed graphs and charts.

WHAT IS A WORKSHEET?

- At the heart of Excel is a two-dimensional grid of data storage spaces called a worksheet (right).
- This is where you input the data that you want to store, manipulate, or analyze. The individual spaces are called cells.
- To begin with, all the cells are empty. As you enter data into the cells, you build and develop the individual worksheets.

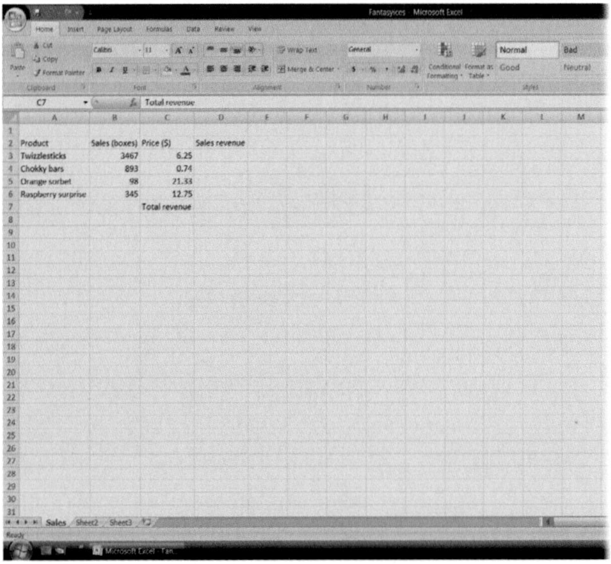

LAUNCHING EXCEL

Like Word, Excel 2007 is part of the Microsoft Office 2007 suite of programs. Various editions of Office 2007–containing different combinations of the Office programs–can be bought off the shelf or online. A free 60-day trial that includes Excel can be downloaded from the Microsoft Office website.

LAUNCHING WITH THE START MENU

- Once Office has been installed on your PC, you can launch Excel by clicking on the Start button to open the Start menu, and then clicking on **All Programs**.
- In the All Programs list, click on **Microsoft Office**, and then select **Microsoft Office Excel 2007** by clicking on it twice.
- The Excel window will appear onscreen.

LAUNCHING WITH A SHORTCUT

- If there is already a shortcut icon for Excel 2007 on your desktop, open Excel by double clicking on the icon.
- The Excel window will appear onscreen.

THE EXCEL WINDOW

When Excel launches, the window that appears on your desktop will be called Book 1–Microsoft Excel. The main part of the screen is the worksheet–a grid of blank rectangular cells. Letters and numbers label the columns and rows of the grid, and each cell has a unique address, such as A1, that specifies its position on the grid.

Along the top of the screen runs the Ribbon toolbar, which, if you've read the previous section ☐, will look very familiar. The left-hand end of the Home ribbon, shown here, contains the very same tools that are found on the Word toolbar. Many of the commands found in the other ribbons are specific to Excel.

FEATURES KEY

❶ Office Button
Click here to carry out actions such as opening, saving, or printing your document.

❷ Home Tab
Contains the most commonly used text formatting commands.

❸ Quick Access Toolbar
A handy set of tools that can be customized to suit your needs.

❹ Other Tabs
Clicking on any of these brings up a specific ribbon of commands.

❺ Minimize Excel

❻ Restore Excel

❼ Close Excel

❽ Excel Help
Click here for online help and advice from Microsoft.

❾ Minimize Window

❿ Close Window

⓫ Restore Window

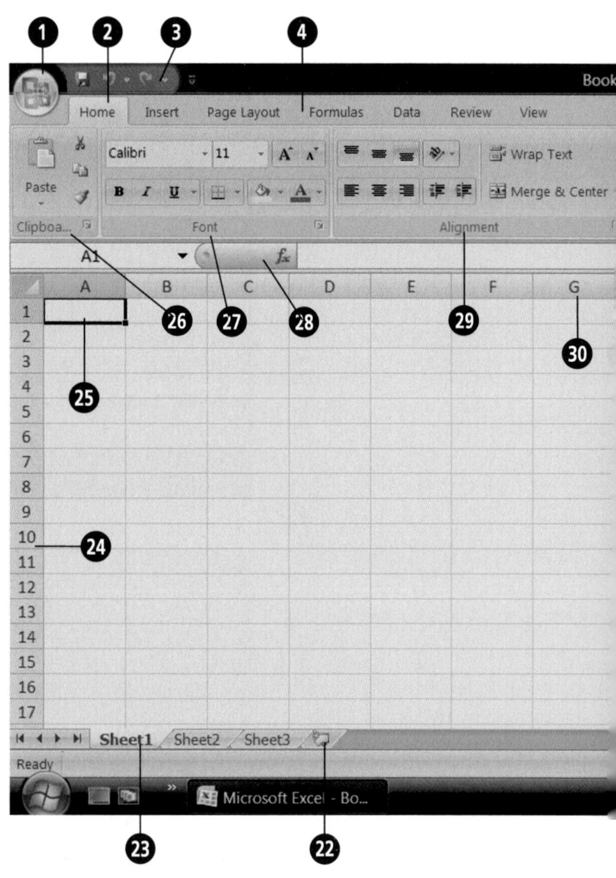

SCREEN RESOLUTION

The precise appearance of the Excel window will vary depending on the resolution at which your monitor is set. In this particular screen shot, we have deliberately used a low resolution to maximize the size of the elements for clarity. You will probably want to use your monitor at a fairly high resolution. To set this, click on **Adjust screen resolution** in the Control Panel, under the **Appearance and Personalization** heading.

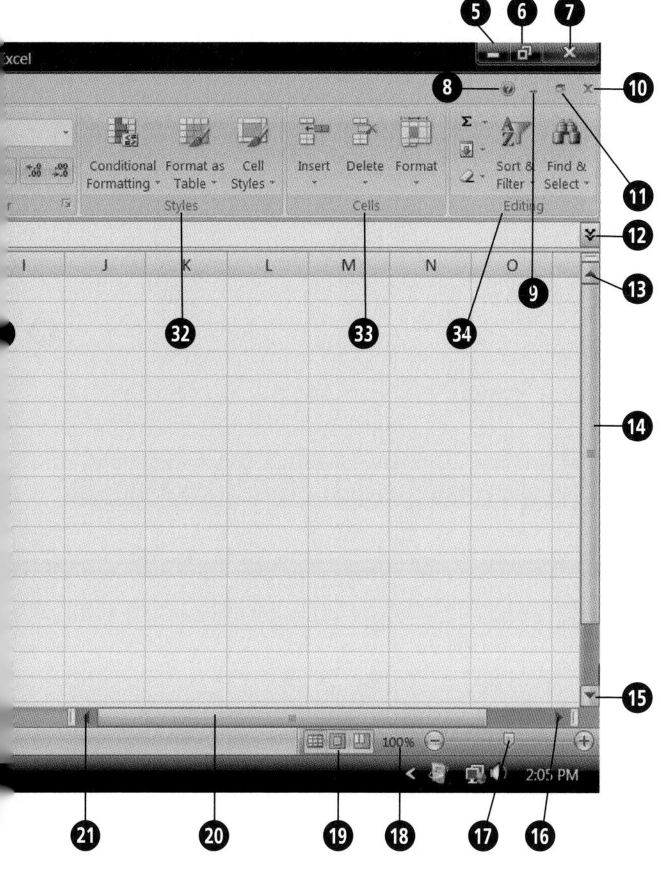

FEATURES KEY

⓬ Expand Formula Bar
⓭ Scroll-up Arrow
Moves up the document.
⓮ Scroll Bar Box
Moves text up or down.
⓯ Scroll-down Arrow
Moves down the document.
⓰ Scroll Right Arrow
Moves across the document.
⓱ Zoom Slider
Alters the magnification of the page.
⓲ Zoom Button
Opens zoom menu.
⓳ Views Buttons
⓴ Scroll Bar Box
Moves page left and right.
㉑ Scroll Left Arrow
Moves across the document.
㉒ Insert Worksheet
㉓ Worksheet Title
㉔ Row Numbers
㉕ Active Cell
㉖ Clipboard Group of Commands
㉗ Font Group of Commands
㉘ Insert Function
㉙ Alignment Group of Commands
㉚ Column Letters
㉛ Number Group of Commands
㉜ Styles Group of Commands
㉝ Cells Group of Commands
㉞ Editing Group of Commands

NAMING, SAVING, AND FINDING FILES

Anything you create using Microsoft Excel is stored on your computer as a file called a workbook. A workbook contains one or more separate worksheets. When you first start up Excel, you are presented with an unused workbook called Book1. This contains blank worksheets, initially labeled **Sheet1**, **Sheet2**, and **Sheet3**.

1 RENAMING A WORKSHEET

- You can switch between worksheets by clicking on the tabs at the bottom of the workbook window. To begin with, the worksheets are all blank.

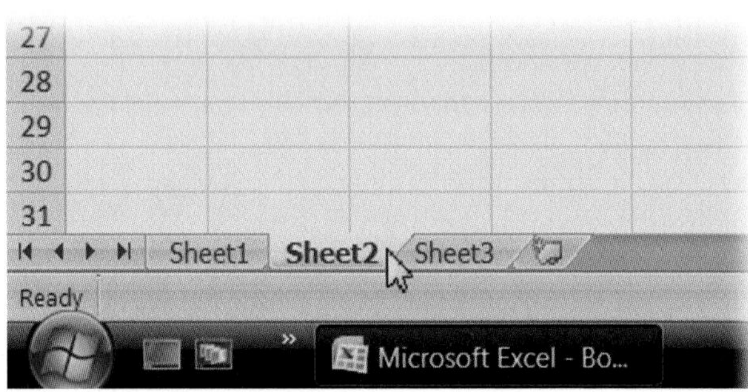

- Once you put data into a worksheet, you should give the worksheet a short name to indicate what it contains. As all worksheets start with a default name (such as Sheet1), you are actually renaming the worksheet. Here's how to do it.

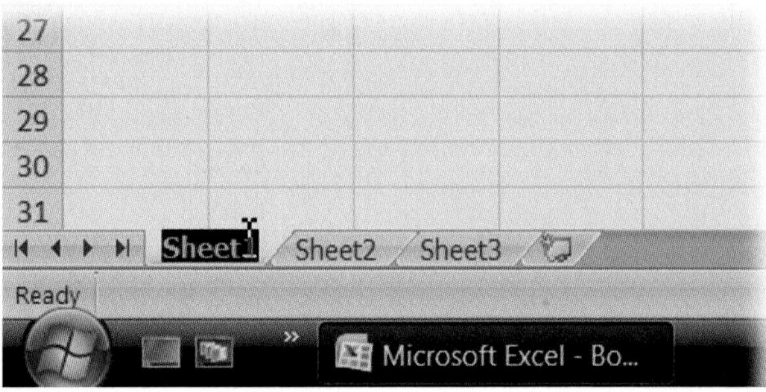

- Double-click on the existing name, so that it becomes highlighted.
- Type the new name and press Enter.

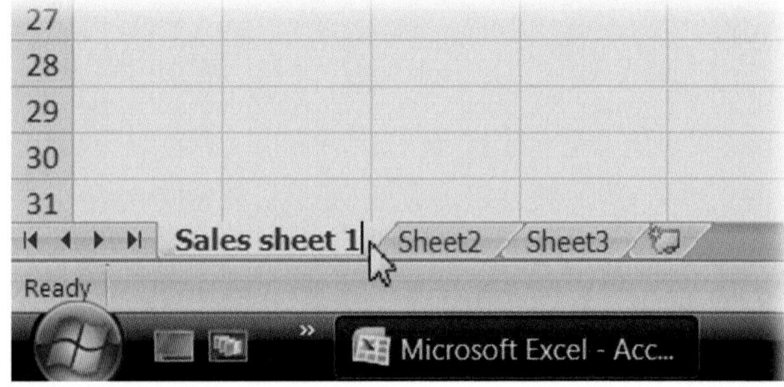

2 SAVING AND NAMING

● You should save your work frequently to your hard disk. When you save in Excel, you save the whole workbook containing the worksheet(s) you have been developing.
● The first time you save a workbook, you should name it (actually rename it) at the same time.
● Click the Office button and choose **Save As**, and select Excel Workbook–the default format.

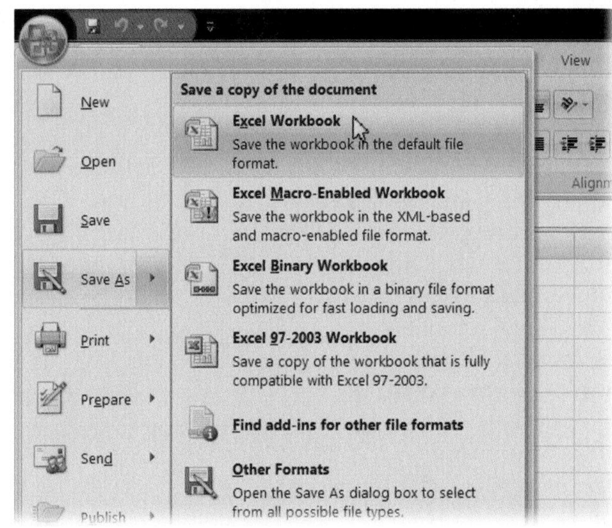

● The **Save As** dialog box appears. Your workbook will be saved in the folder displayed here, unless you navigate to another folder.
● In this instance, accept the displayed folder, but remember where the workbook is being saved.
● In the **File name** box, type the name you would like to give the workbook, and then click on the **Save** button at the bottom right.

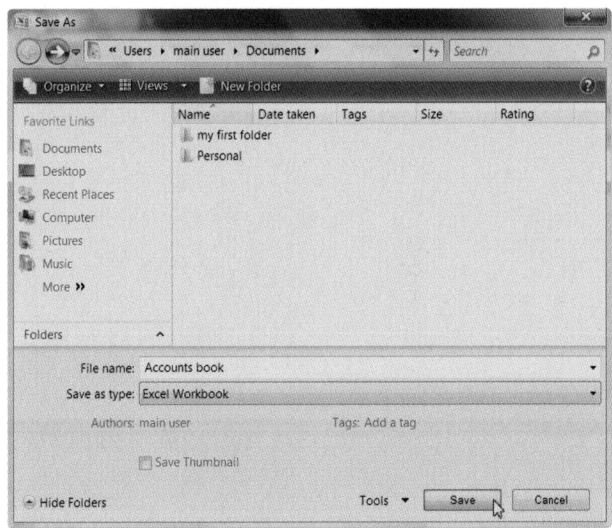

● On subsequent occasions when you want to save the workbook, just click on the **Save** button in the Quick Access Toolbar, or use the keyboard shortcut Ctrl S.

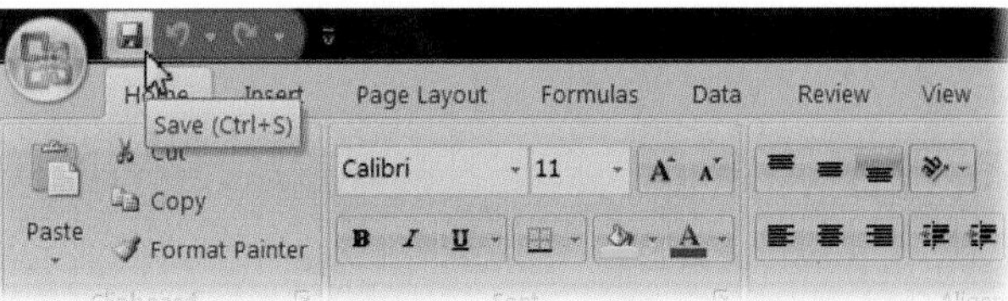

3 CLOSING A WORKBOOK

● Click the **Close Window** button at the top right.

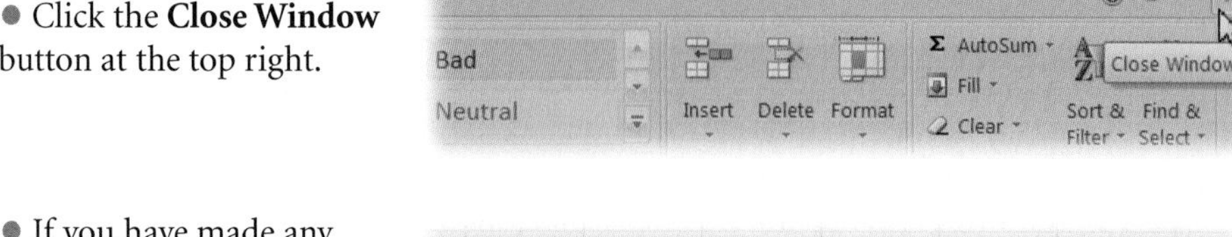

● If you have made any changes since your last save, a box appears asking whether you want to save the changes. Click **Yes** if you wish to save changes.

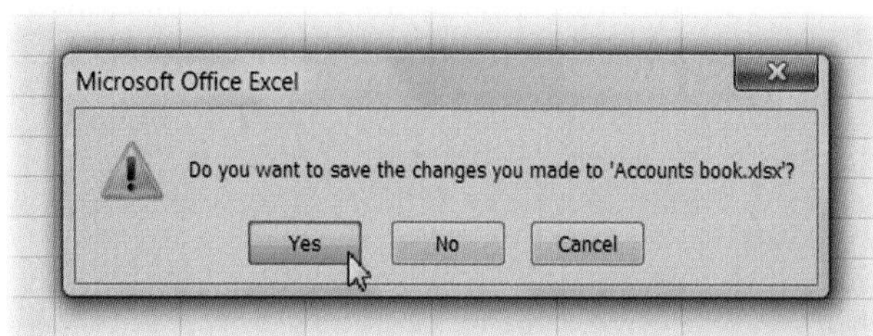

4 OPENING A NEW WORKBOOK

● Click on the Office Button and select **New**. You can also select recent Excel documents from here.

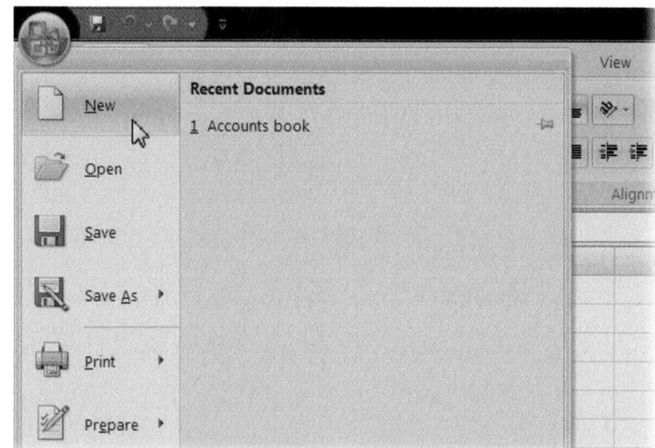

5 OPENING A SAVED WORKBOOK

● In the Office Button drop-down menu, click on **Open** to select.
● In the **Open** dialog box, click on the workbook you want to open, and then click on **Open** at the bottom right of the box.

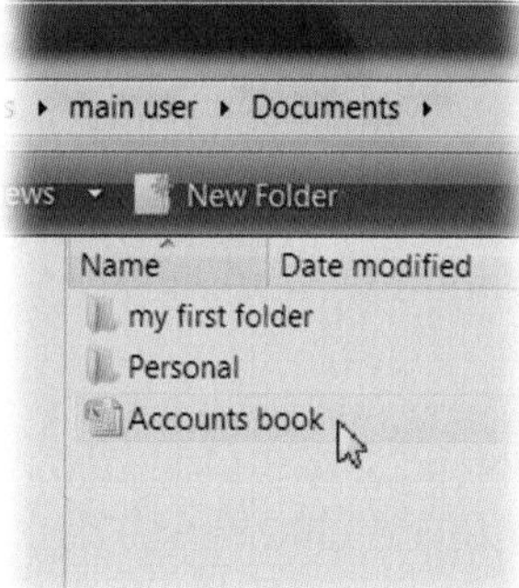

SELECTING WORKSHEET CELLS

Before performing any operation in Excel, such as typing data into cells, coloring cells, or deleting them, you need to choose the cells on which you are going to perform the action. This process is called cell selection. You can select a single cell, a horizontal row or vertical column of cells, or several rows or columns. You can also select a block of cells, or several separate blocks. When a group of cells is selected, they will appear within a black border with a blue tint, except for the "active cell," which remains white. Anything you type will appear only in the active cell, but other actions, such as coloring or deleting, will apply to all the cells in the selected area.

SELECTING A SINGLE CELL

- Move your mouse pointer over your chosen cell and click the left mouse button.
- The black border round the cell indicates that it is selected, and this is now the active cell.

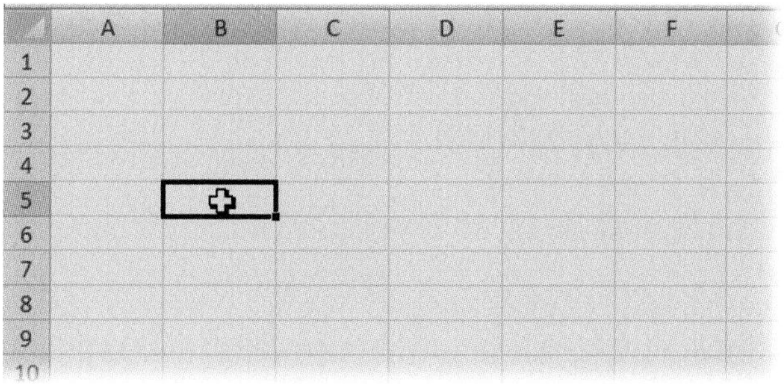

SELECTING A SINGLE COLUMN

- Click on the column header button at the top of your chosen column.
- Click and drag across the header buttons of several columns to select them all.

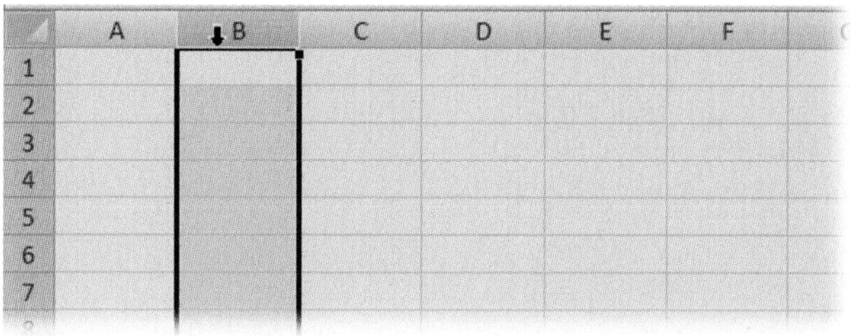

SELECTING A SINGLE ROW

- Click on the row header button to the left of your chosen row.
- Click and drag down the header buttons of several rows to select them all.

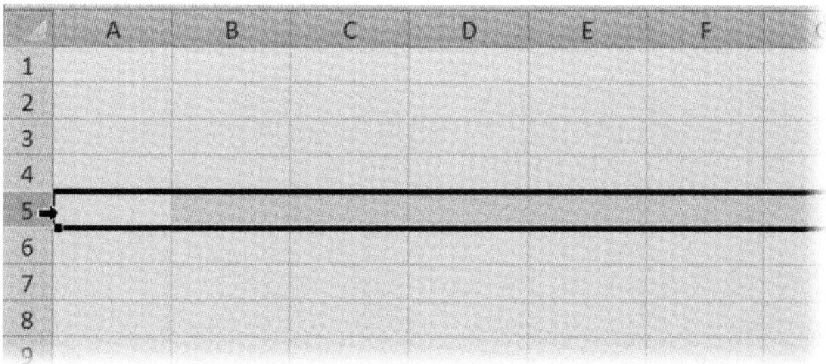

SELECTING A BLOCK OF CELLS

• Click on a cell at one or end or corner of the block you wish to select.

• Hold down the Shift key and drag the pointer to the opposite end or corner of the block to highlight all the cells in between.

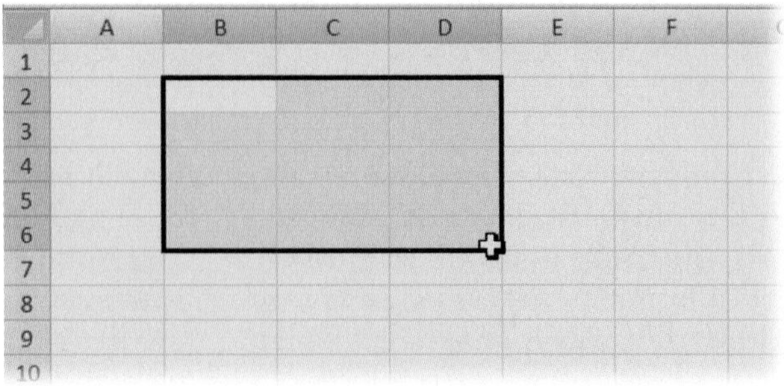

SELECTING SEVERAL BLOCKS

• Holding down the Ctrl key, click and drag to select a block, and then repeat for subsequent blocks, which will all remain selected.

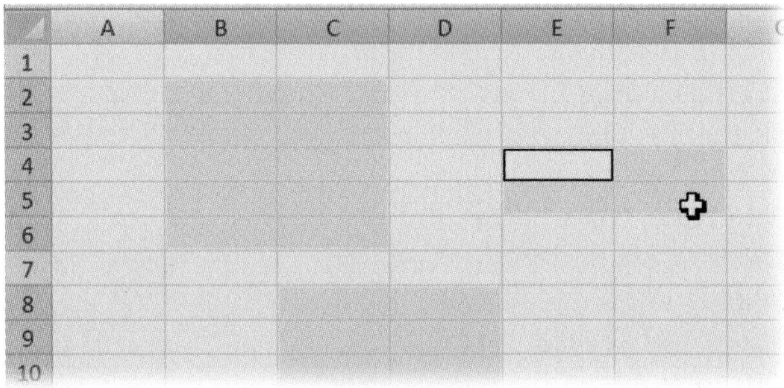

SELECTING THE WHOLE WORKSHEET

• The small square in the top left corner of the worksheet is the **Select All** button.

• Click here to select all the cells in the worksheet. Cell A1 will be the active cell.

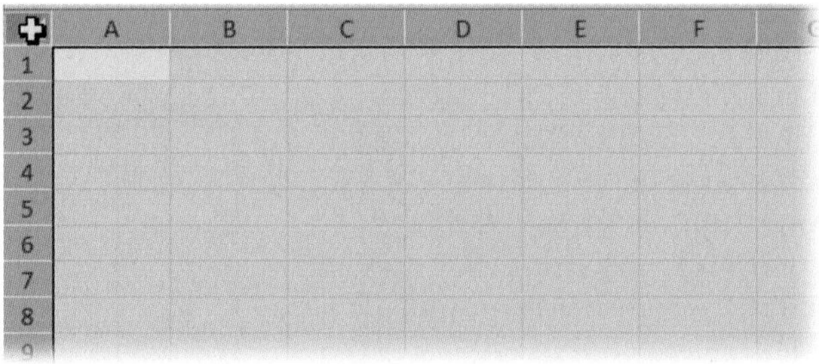

• Alternatively, use the keyboard shortcut Ctrl A; in this case, the active cell will be the cell that was active before all the cells were selected.

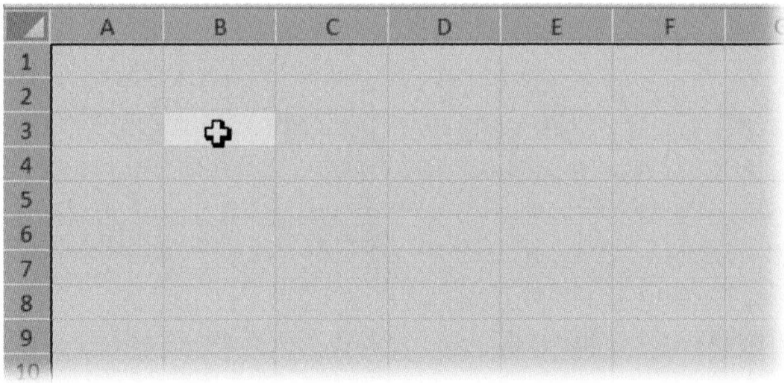

Entering Text

There are three categories of data that you can put into a worksheet–text, numbers, and formulas. Worksheets usually take a tabular form, and text is used most often as labels for the table's rows and columns. It makes sense to enter these text labels first, in order to provide a structure for the numerical data and formulas. To demonstrate the principles, we are using the simple example of a sales worksheet for a small business. It may be helpful to follow our worked example step by step.

SELECTING THE FIRST CELL FOR TEXT

- Click on cell A2 to select this cell. Cell A2 is now the active cell and anything you type on the keyboard will appear in this cell.
- Note that A2 appears in the name box at the top left of the worksheet.

TYPING IN THE TEXT

- To follow this example, type the word **Product**.
- Note that the insertion point stays just to the right of the last letter you typed, marking where the next letter you type will appear.

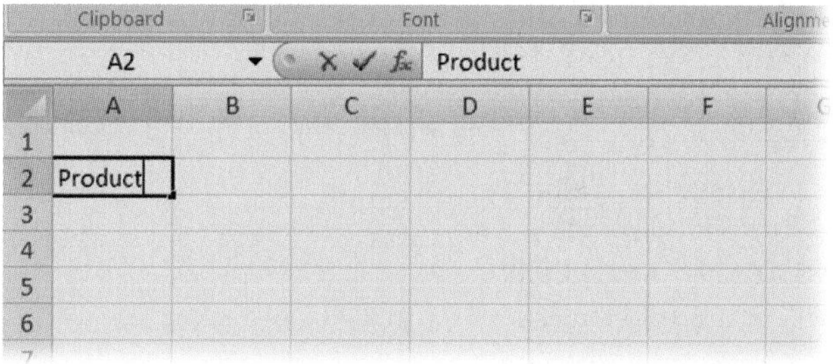

COMPLETING THE ENTRY

- Once you have typed your text, press Tab. This completes the data entry into the cell, and the active cell now moves down a single cell to A3. Further entries can be made in the same way.

CREATING COLUMN HEADINGS

- To add column headings for the numerical data, select the cells B2 to D2. Type **Sales (boxes)**, which appears in the current active cell, B2.

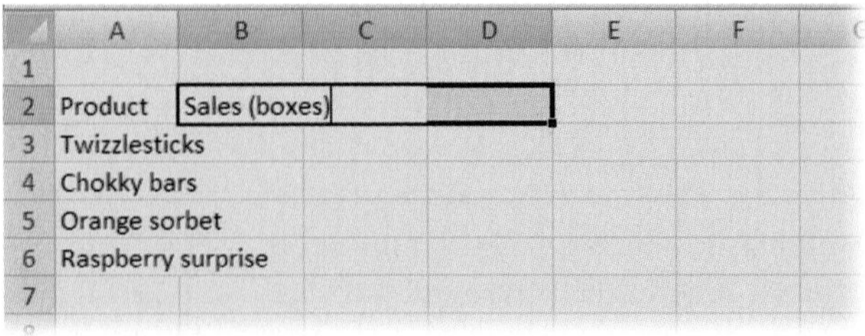

- Complete the entry by pressing the Tab key. This time, the active cell moves one cell to the right.
- Type **Price ($)** into C2, press the Tab key, and type **Sales Revenue** into D2.

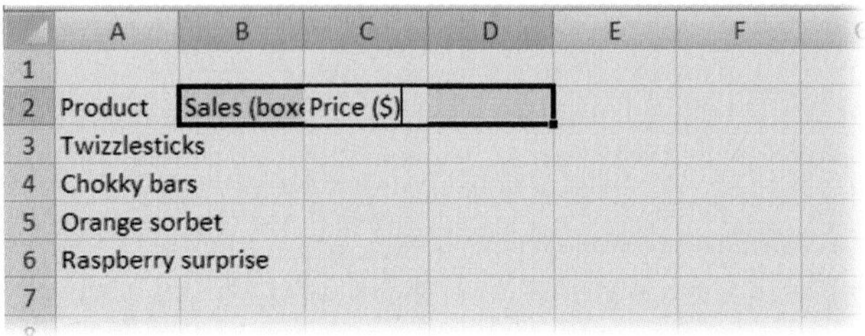

ADDING FURTHER LABELS

- Select cell C7, and type in **Total revenue**.

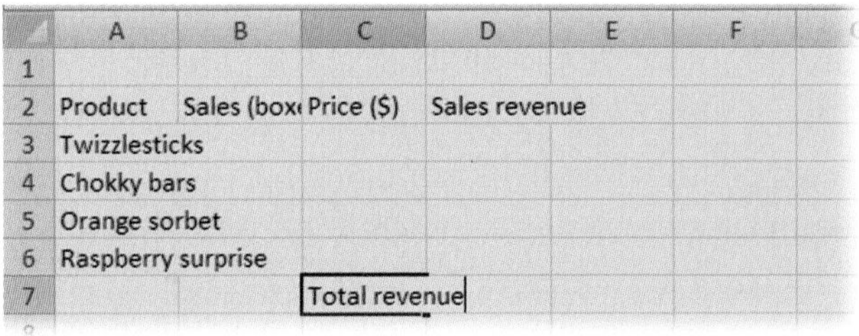

ADJUSTING THE COLUMN WIDTHS

- There are some quick methods for adjusting the widths of columns to fit cell data. For this example:
- Move the mouse pointer over the line that divides column headers A and B. The pointer should form a bar with arrows pointing to either side.

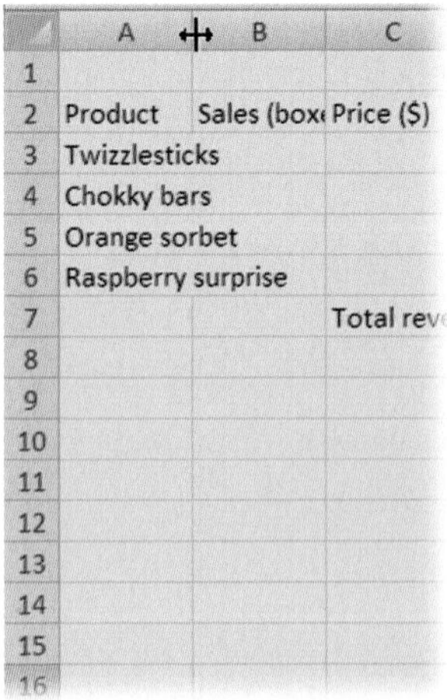

TYPING ERRORS

If you mistype a letter, press the ← Bksp key on your keyboard to delete the last letter you typed. If you want to start the data entry into a cell from scratch, press the Esc key at the top left of your keyboard. Even if you have completed entering data, it's easy to change data later.

285 **Selecting a Single Row**

● Click and drag the mouse pointer to the right. A dotted vertical line shows the position of the new column divider.
● Drag this line to the right of the words **Raspberry surprise**, and the column widens to that extent.

	A	B	C	D	E	F
1						
2	Product	Sales (box	Price ($)	Sales revenue		
3	Twizzlesticks					
4	Chokky bars					
5	Orange sorbet					
6	Raspberry surprise					
7		Total revenue				
8						

● With the mouse pointer on the line that divides column headers B and C, double-click the mouse.

	A	B	C	D	E	F
1						
2	Product	Sales (box	Price ($)	Sales revenue		
3	Twizzlesticks					

● This method automatically widens column B to display the longest line of text in that column. Now widen columns C and D.

	A	B	C	D	E
1					
2	Product	Sales (boxes)	Price ($)	Sales revenue	
3	Twizzlesticks				
4	Chokky bars				
5	Orange sorbet				
6	Raspberry surprise				

Entering Numbers

Numerical values include integers (whole numbers), decimal numbers (such as 3.25), fractions, monetary amounts, percentages, dates, and times. Excel applies various rules to detect whether a string of characters constitute a numerical value and, if so, what type (integers, date, time, etc.). If Excel recognizes the typed-in expression as a numerical value, it will align it ranged right in the cell.

ENTERING WHOLE NUMBERS

● Just click on the cell in which you wish enter the number.
● In this example, click on cell B3 and type in any whole number.

	A	B	C	D	E
1					
2	Product	Sales (boxes)	Price ($)	Sales revenue	
3	Twizzlesticks	3467			
4	Chokky bars				
5	Orange sorbet				
6	Raspberry surprise				
7			Total revenue		
8					

NUMBER FORMATS

The way in which a number or numerical expression is displayed in a cell is affected by what format that cell has. By default, cells have a "general" number format. When you type any numerical expression into a cell that has this "general" number format, Excel analyzes what type of expression it is and then displays it in an appropriate standard way, usually, though not always exactly, as it is typed. For example, an integer will be displayed an an integer, a date will be given a date format, and so on.

- Press Enter↵ to complete the entry.
- Now enter further whole numbers (less than 1,000) into cells B4 to B6, pressing Enter↵ after each entry.
- These numbers represent the sales of boxes of the company's other products.

	A	B	C	D	E
1					
2	Product	Sales (boxes)	Price ($)	Sales revenue	
3	Twizzlesticks	3467			
4	Chokky bars	893			
5	Orange sorbet	98			
6	Raspberry surprise	345			
7			Total revenue		
8					
9					
10					

ENTERING DECIMALS

- You enter decimal numbers into cells just as you would write them. Simply type a period to represent the decimal point.
- Here we are have typed in a range of prices in the cells C3 to C6, pressing Enter↵ each time to move to the cell below.

	A	B	C	D	E
1					
2	Product	Sales (boxes)	Price ($)	Sales revenue	
3	Twizzlesticks	3467	6.25		
4	Chokky bars	893	0.74		
5	Orange sorbet	98	21.33		
6	Raspberry surprise	345	12.75		
7			Total revenue		
8					
9					
10					
11					
12					

IS IT A NUMBER?

Excel interprets various sorts of expression (not just strings of digits) as numerical values. For example $43, or 43%, or 4.3, or 4,300, or 4.3E+7 (standing for 43,000,000) are all recognized as numerical values. Both -43 and (43) would be recognized as negative or debit numbers.

FORMULAS AND CALCULATIONS

For even the simplest Excel worksheets, you will soon want to use formulas. A formula returns (calculates and displays) a value in a cell based on numbers you supply it with, arithmetic operators (such as plus or multiply), and cell references (the numerical values held in other worksheet cells). Much of the power of the Excel program derives from the use of cell references in formulas, because if you decide later on to change a value in a referenced cell, all formulas in the worksheet that depend on that reference are automatically recalculated.

MULTIPLYING TWO CELL VALUES

- For a cell to contain the result of multiplying the values of two other cells, you can type an = sign into the cell followed by the addresses of the two cells, separated by the multiplication operator: *.
- Here we want cell D3 to contain the revenue from Twizzlesticks sales. This is the sales figure (cell B3) multiplied by the price per box (cell C3). So, select cell D3 and type: =B3*C3.

SUM | =B3*C3

	A	B	C	D	E
1					
2	Product	Sales (boxes)	Price ($)	Sales revenue	
3	Twizzlesticks	3467	6.25	=B3*C3	
4	Chokky bars	893	0.74		
5	Orange sorbet	98	21.33		
6	Raspberry surprise	345	12.75		
7			Total revenue		
8					
9					
10					
11					
12					
13					
14					
15					
16					
17					

- Press Enter↵, and you will see the result of the calculation displayed in D3.
- Now select D3 again and look at the Formula bar above it. There is now a difference between what D3 actually contains (which is a formula, as shown in the Formula bar) and what is displays (the value that is calculated by that formula).

D3 | =B3*C3

	A	B	C	D	E
1					
2	Product	Sales (boxes)	Price ($)	Sales revenue	
3	Twizzlesticks	3467	6.25	21668.75	
4	Chokky bars	893	0.74		
5	Orange sorbet	98	21.33		
6	Raspberry surprise	345	12.75		
7			Total revenue		
8					
9					
10					
11					

FORMULAS USING THE MOUSE

- Instead of typing, you can use the mouse to help you construct formulas. Here we'll enter the formula =B3*C4 into cell D4.
- Select cell D4 and type the = sign.

SUM | =

	A	B	C	D	E
1					
2	Product	Sales (boxes)	Price ($)	Sales revenue	
3	Twizzlesticks	3467	6.25	21668.75	
4	Chokky bars	893	0.74	=	
5	Orange sorbet	98	21.33		
6	Raspberry surprise	345	12.75		
7			Total revenue		

- Now click on cell B4. D4 now contains the expression:=**B4**.

	A	B	C	D	E
1					
2	Product	Sales (boxes)	Price ($)	Sales revenue	
3	Twizzlesticks	3467	6.25	21668.75	
4	Chokky bars	893	0.74	=B4	
5	Orange sorbet	98	21.33		

- Type an asterik (*) and then click on cell C4.
- Finally, press Enter.

	A	B	C	D	E
1					
2	Product	Sales (boxes)	Price ($)	Sales revenue	
3	Twizzlesticks	3467	6.25	21668.75	
4	Chokky bars	893	0.74	=B4*C4	
5	Orange sorbet	98	21.33		

COMPLETING THE FORMULAS

Now use either entry method to enter the formulas:=B5*C5 into cell D5 and: =B6*C6 into cell D6. The results of these formulas appear in the cells.

D7

	A	B	C	D	E
1					
2	Product	Sales (boxes)	Price ($)	Sales revenue	
3	Twizzlesticks	3467	6.25	21668.75	
4	Chokky bars	893	0.74	660.82	
5	Orange sorbet	98	21.33	2090.34	
6	Raspberry surprise	345	12.75	4398.75	
7			Total revenue		

QUICK CALCULATIONS

Excel can be used for one-off calculations. If you want to perform a quick calculation and you don't have a calculator, you can use any cell in Excel instead. Suppose you want to add 23 to 31 and multiply the result by 27. Select a blank cell and type: =(23+31)*27, then press Enter. If you don't want to leave your calculation on display, you should then clear the cell.

ADDING VALUES IN SEVERAL CELLS

● To add together the values in several cells, you could type in an addition formula. For example, to calculate the sum of the values in cells D3 to D6, you could key in the formula =D3+D4+D5+D6.

● However, when the cells are adjacent in the same row or column, there is a quicker method. Excel has built-in tool to do this. It is called **AutoSum**.

● In cell D7, we want to put the sum of the revenues generated by the individual products, held in cells D3 to D6. To do so, select cell D7, and then click the **AutoSum** button in the **Editing** group on the Home ribbon.

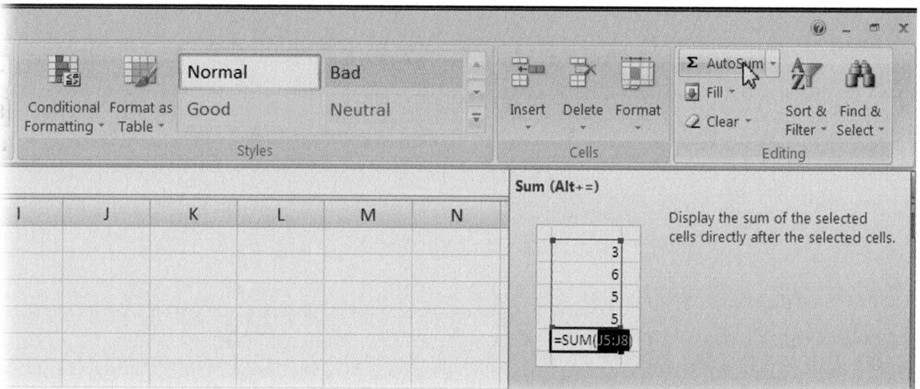

● A flashing border appears around cells D3 to D6, and the term: **=SUM(D3:D6)** appears in cell D7 and in the formula bar. This indicates that a function (a special type of formula) called SUM, is adding the values in cells D3 to cell D6.

A	B	C	D	E	F
	Sales (boxes)	Price ($)	Sales revenue		
icks	3467	6.25	21668.75		
ars	893	0.74	660.82		
orbet	98	21.33	2090.34		
y surprise	345	12.75	4398.75		
		Total revenue	=SUM(D3:D6)		
			SUM(**number1**, [number2], ...)		

MATH OPERATORS

The five math operators available are:
+ (addition),
- (subtraction),
* (multiplication),
/ (division), and
^ (raising to the power).
These follow the standard order of operations, which can be overruled only by using brackets. If you want to subtract A2 from 5, and then multiply the result by B2, you should type: =(5-A2)*B2.

● Press Enter ↵, and the figure for total revenue appears in cell D7.

A	B	C	D	E	F
	Sales (boxes)	Price ($)	Sales revenue		
ticks	3467	6.25	21668.75		
bars	893	0.74	660.82		
sorbet	98	21.33	2090.34		
ry surprise	345	12.75	4398.75		
		Total revenue	28818.66		

ADDING STYLE

Even the most elementary worksheet may benefit from some basic formatting to help clarify which parts are headings and which are data, and to improve the overall visual attractiveness of the worksheet. The formatting features and toolbars in Excel are just as extensive as those in Word. In fact, they are virtually the same.

FONTS AND COLORS

● As in Word, these commands control the look of the text and numbers. Here we are selecting a new color for the product lines. The palette that we are offered is the standard Office palette.

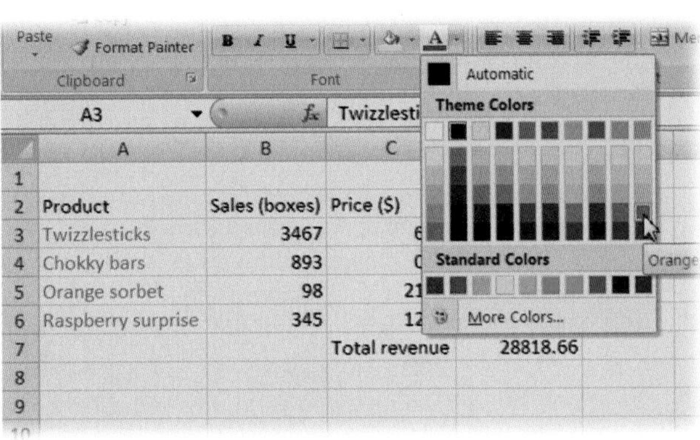

	A	B	C	D
1				
2	Product	Sales (boxes)	Price ($)	
3	Twizzlesticks	3467	6	
4	Chokky bars	893	0	
5	Orange sorbet	98	21	
6	Raspberry surprise	345	12	
7			Total revenue	28818.66
8				
9				

● Here we have colored the text and figures, and changed some of the fonts to distinguish between headings, products, sales figures, unit prices, and sales revenue.

Paste | Format Painter | Clipboard | Font | Alignment | J16

	A	B	C	D	E
1					
2	Product	Sales (boxes)	Price ($)	Sales revenue	
3	Twizzlesticks	3467	6.25	21668.75	
4	Chokky bars	893	0.74	660.82	
5	Orange sorbet	98	21.33	2090.34	
6	Raspberry surprise	345	12.75	4398.75	
7			Total revenue	**28818.66**	
8					

The Font Group 268

USING THEMES

- Clicking on the **Page Layout** tab brings up this range of commands, including the **Themes** that we saw in Word.
- As you roll your cursor over each of the **Built-In** Themes in turn, you will see the text and numbers in your worksheet take on the fonts and colors that make up that particular theme.

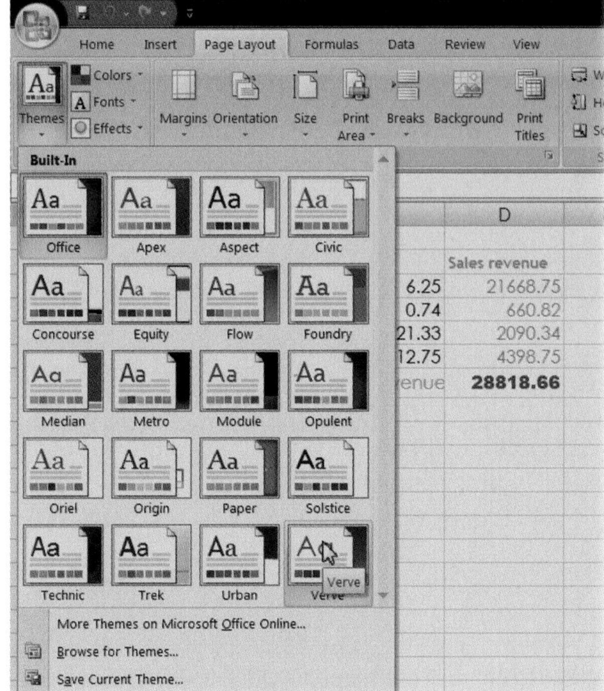

- Choosing another theme, such as **Verve**, changes the font selections and the color palette, to give a completely new look to the worksheet.
- The appearance can be further fine tuned by using the **Colors**, **Fonts**, and **Effects** buttons in the **Themes** group to alter individual elements.

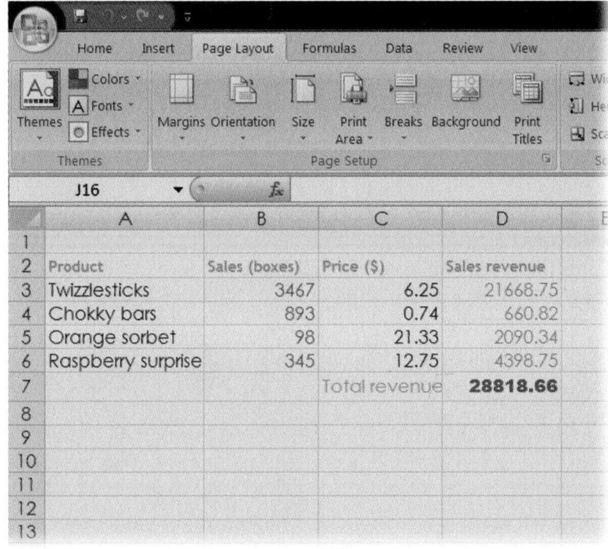

	A	B	C	D
1				
2	Product	Sales (boxes)	Price ($)	Sales revenue
3	Twizzlesticks	3467	6.25	21668.75
4	Chokky bars	893	0.74	660.82
5	Orange sorbet	98	21.33	2090.34
6	Raspberry surprise	345	12.75	4398.75
7			Total revenue	28818.66
8				
9				
10				
11				
12				
13				

277 **Using the Themes Tab**

CHARTS AND GRAPHICS

As well as being a powerful spreadsheet program, Microsoft Excel offers a wide range of facilities that allow you to show numerical data in the form of two- and three-dimensional charts. Here are just a couple of simple examples.

SELECTING THE RELEVANT DATA

- To show the products' relative contributions to the revenue stream by using a pie chart, begin by selecting cells A3-A6, and then, with the Ctrl button held down, selecting cells D3-D6.

	A	B	C	D	E
1					
2	Product	Sales (boxes)	Price ($)	Sales revenue	
3	Twizzlesticks	3467	6.25	21668.75	
4	Chokky bars	893	0.74	660.82	
5	Orange sorbet	98	21.33	2090.34	
6	Raspberry surprise	345	12.75	4398.75	
7			Total revenue	**28818.66**	

SELECTING A CHART TYPE

- Access to the charts is through the **Insert** ribbon, so click on the **Insert** tab to see the range of options.
- Now click on **Pie** and select an exploded **3-D Pie** chart from the options.

- The data is now presented as a 3-D pie chart. The products are color coded and labeled, and the colors are those from the Verve palette, which we selected earlier.

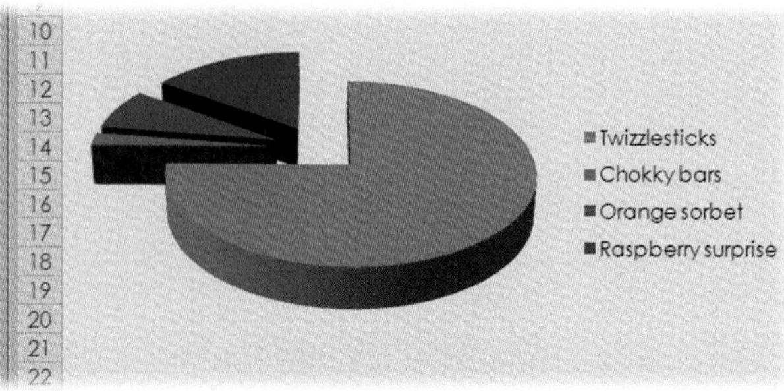

FINE TUNING THE CHART

● As soon as a graphic of any kind is selected, the **Design** ribbon (visible in the bottom screen shot on this page), appears, and here we can choose a more elaborate chart layout.

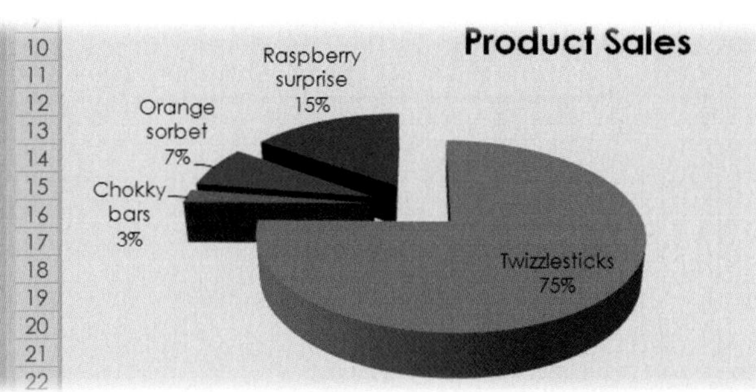

DISPLAYING DATA AS A BAR CHART

● A bar chart is ideal for comparing sets of figures, and here we are charting the relative sales of two ice cream lines by selecting the data, clicking on the column tool, and selecting **3-D Column** graph.

● The result, presenting the figures in a visually clear way, can be seen below.

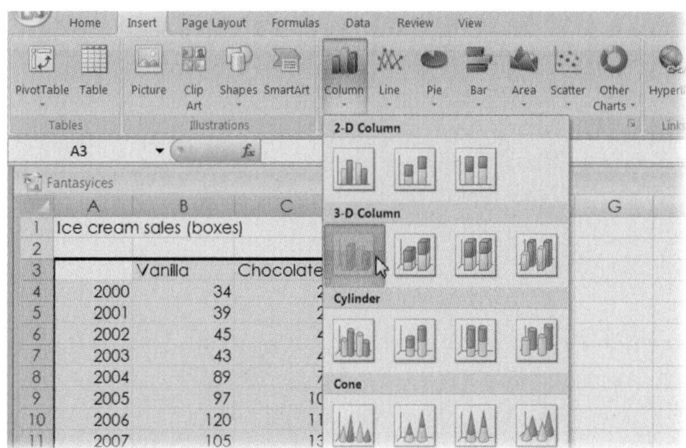

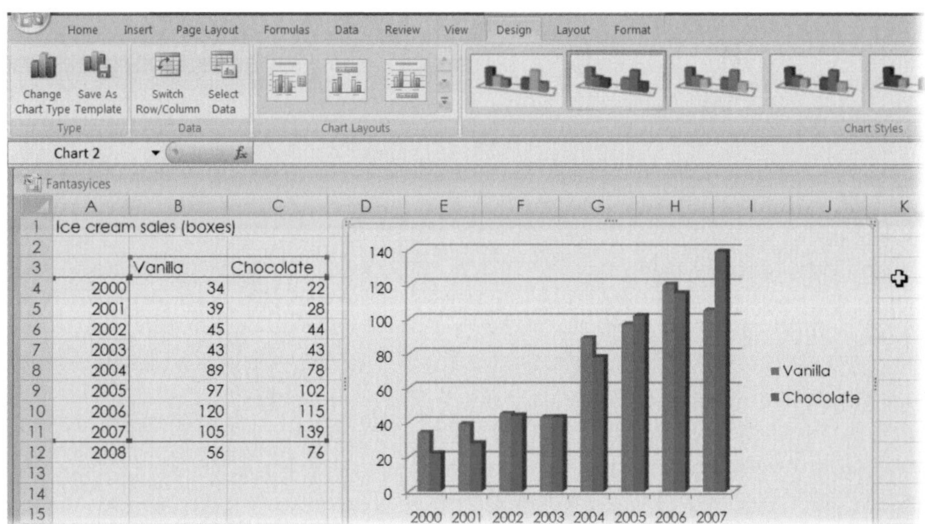

Genealogy Software

Family history and genealogy are fascinating subjects, and with the right Internet resources and the software to record and organize, delving into your ancestry has never been easier.

Why Use Software?

The art and science of constructing a family tree used to require worldwide travel, visits to public records offices, reams of paper, countless index cards, and hundreds of hours of painstaking work. The advent of the Internet and specialized genealogy software such as Family Tree Maker have made the research, recording, organization, and presentation of data much quicker and a whole lot simpler.

WHAT IS FAMILY TREE MAKER?

- FTM is effectively a database program into which you put all the information you can gather about your family.
- This information can then be viewed and added to in a host of useful ways.
- Direct links between the program and specific websites mean you can search the globe for further information and take the results directly into your family tree.
- A range of templates make it possible to present your family history page by page in many exciting ways.

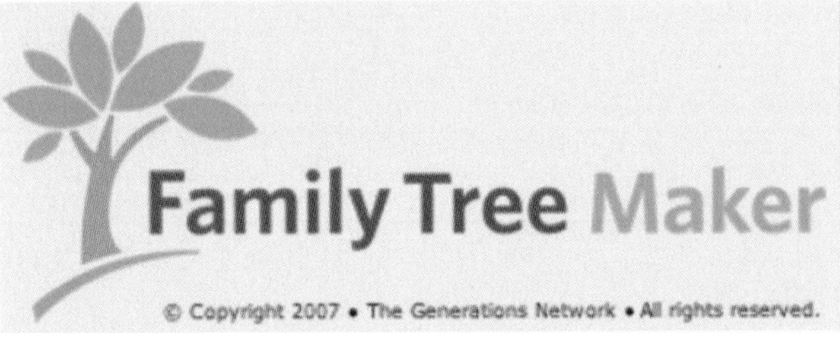

Family Tree Maker
© Copyright 2007 • The Generations Network • All rights reserved.

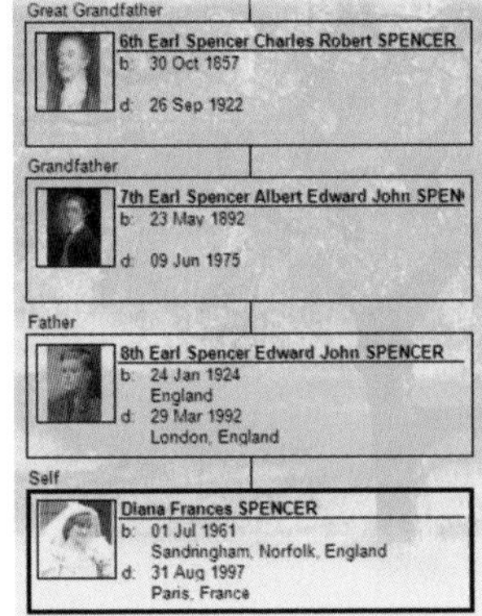

GETTING STARTED

When you first open Family Tree Maker, you are given the **Plan** view, with a **New Project** window ready for you to start creating. Here you have the choice of starting a new project by inputting information about yourself, importing a family tree that you have already created in a previous version of FTM or another genealogy program, or going online to find an existing family tree.

INPUTTING INFORMATION

- As soon as you have input your details, your family name becomes the project name, and you can choose a location for the project on your hard disk. Click on **Continue** to move to the next stage.

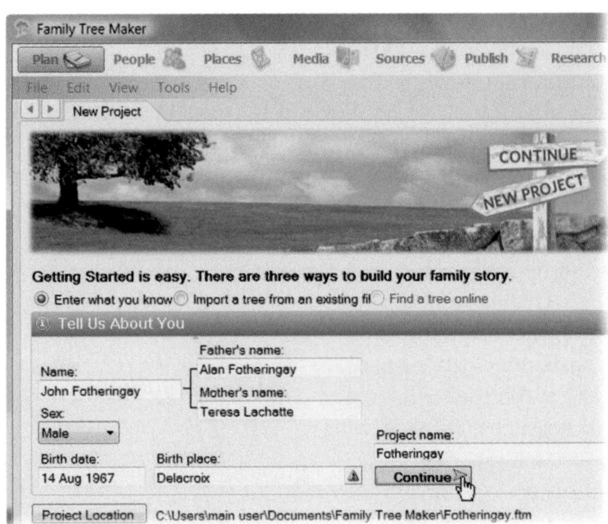

ADDING PEOPLE

- The **People** window opens in the **Family** view. This window invites you to add details of your spouse and grandparents.
- Clicking in any of these panels opens a box into which you can type the name of the person to be added to the family tree.
- Each time a panel has been completed, click on **OK** to confirm.

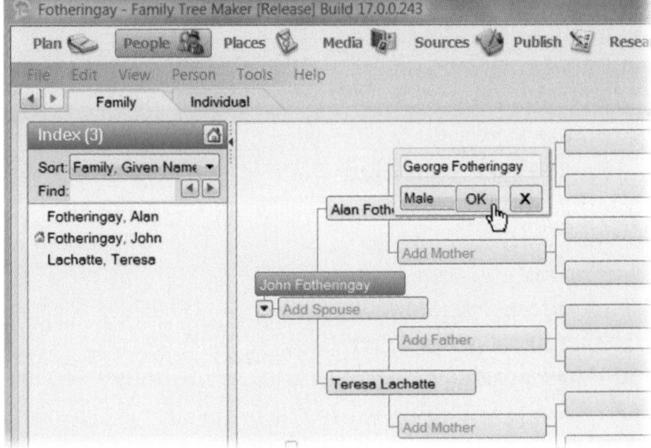

- As each person is added, so the panels for members of earlier generations become available. We are now able to fill in the name of John's great grandfather.
- With this entry selected, this individual is now featured in the right-hand panel, where you can add all the information available to you concerning the person's sex, birth, death, and marriage.

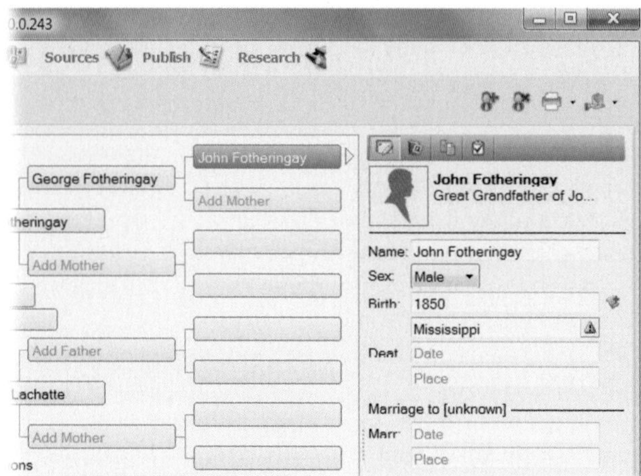

ADDING SOURCES

- When a text panel is selected, a **New source** icon appears next to it.
- This feature allows you to link every new piece of information with the source from which it came, so that you can keep track and return to the source if you need to.
- Clicking on the icon brings up a menu in which you can select **Add New Source** or **Link to Existing Source**. Here we are selecting the first.
- The **Add Source** dialog box opens, and here you can record precisely where the information came from, whether it was a legal document or a conversation with Aunt Jemima.

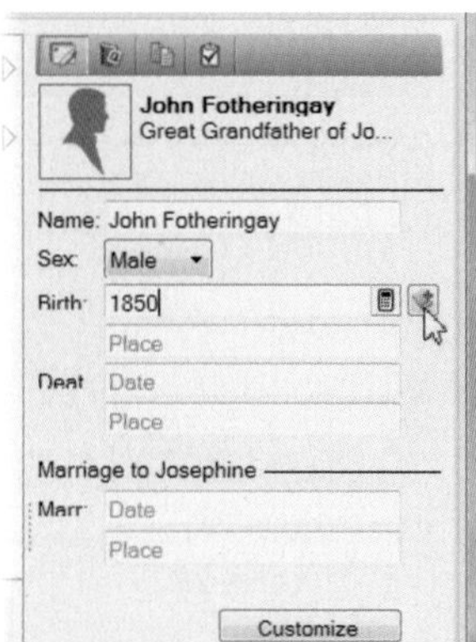

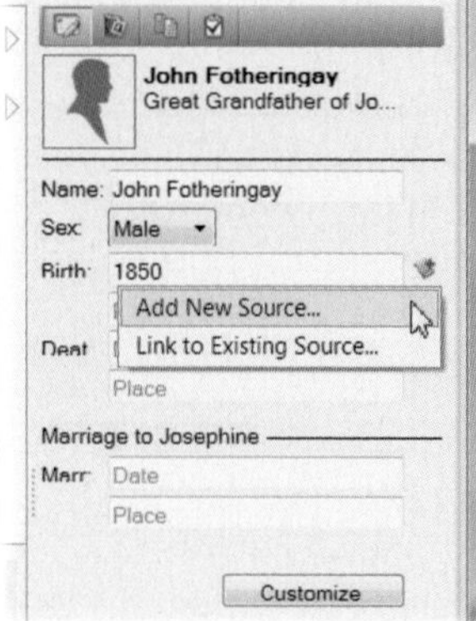

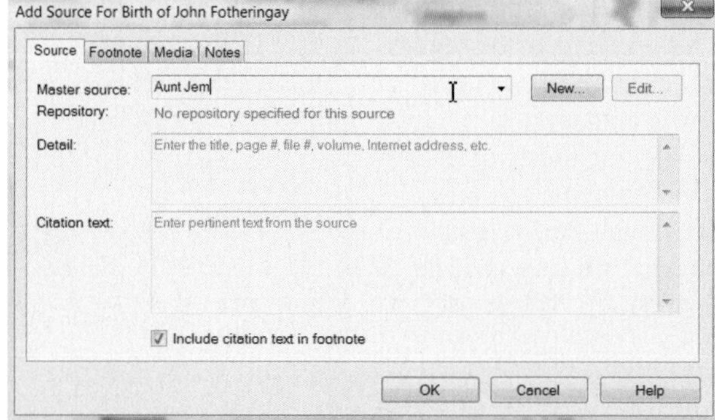

● Clicking on the **Media** tab allows you to navigate to any forms of media that relate to this source. It could be a scanned image of the legal document, or it could be a photo of your informant. Whatever the case, it can now be linked to the information concerning John Fotheringay's birth.

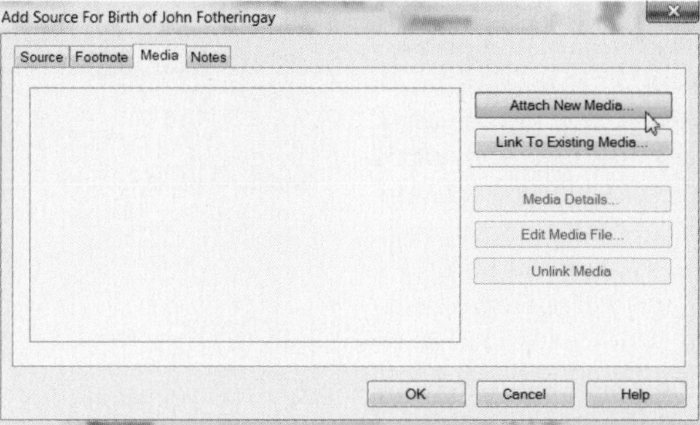

● The **Notes** tab opens a text document in which you can record notes about the source of your data.

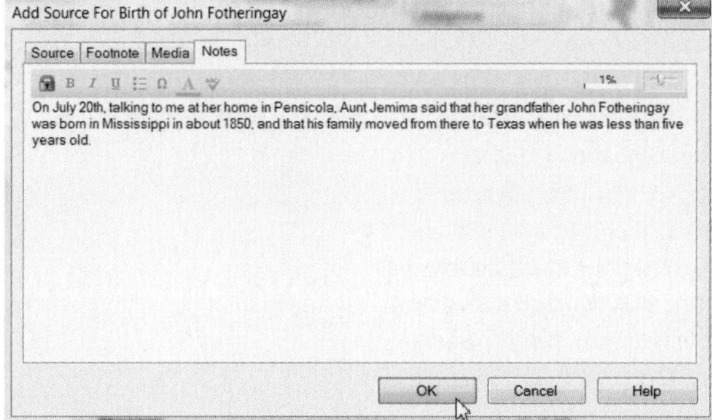

● In the bottom half of the window, additional information about this person's wife and any other children can be added.

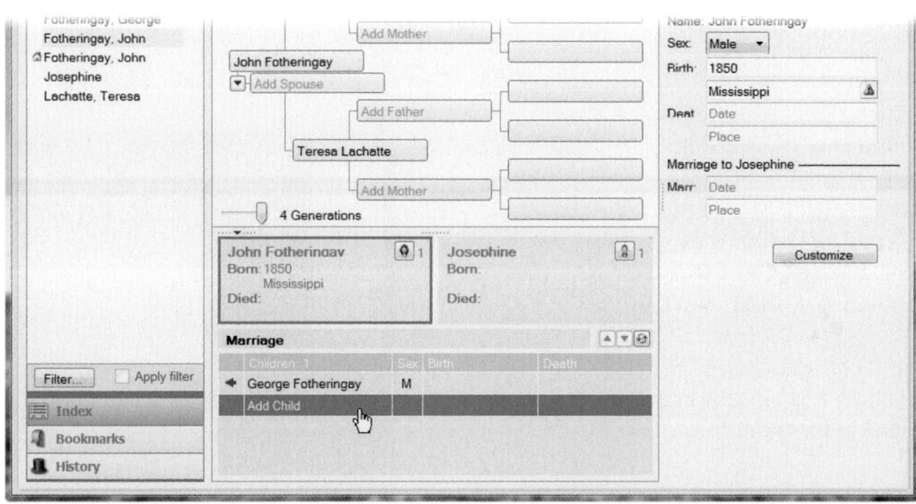

● The individual is also added to the list of people in the left-hand panel, and already these can be sorted according to several criteria by clicking on the arrow to the right of the **Sort** panel.

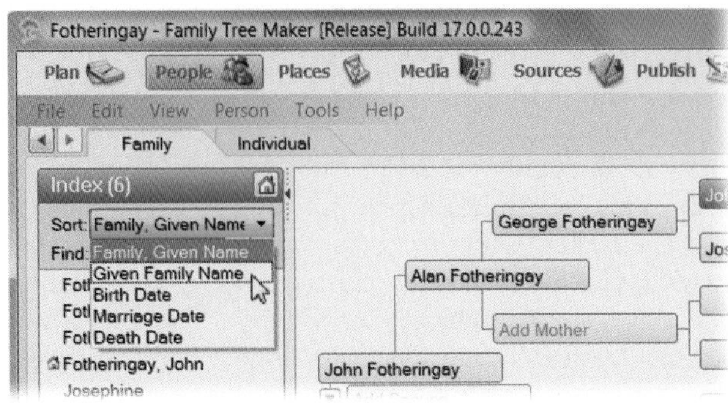

LOOKING AT PLACES

● Clicking on the **Places** button at the top of the screen brings up the **Manage Places** window. So far we have only input two place names, but clicking on either of these brings up a map showing its location.

● The right-hand panel (not shown here) lists all the people in your chart associated with the place.

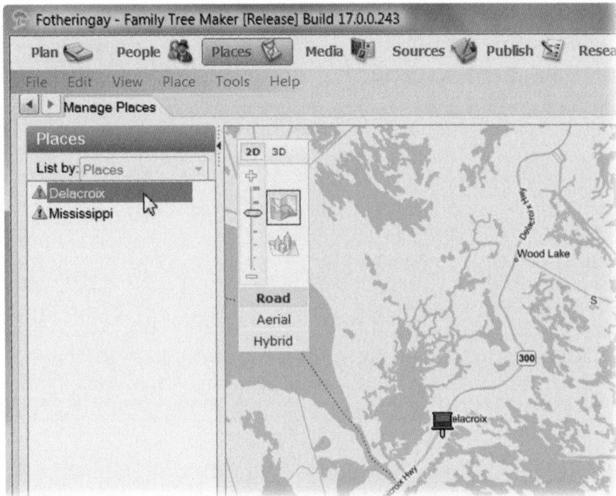

● Using the slider, we can zoom in on the location, and we can also select an **Aerial** satellite view or an interesting **Hybrid** view that superimposes the road map on the satellite view.

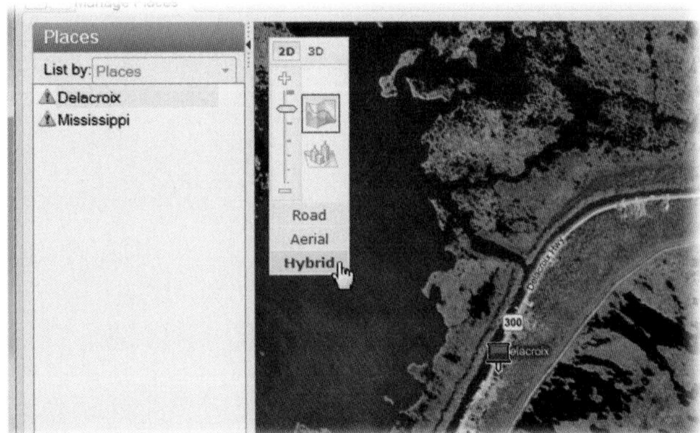

Online Research

If you hadn't already guessed, we've just been online. Family Tree Maker doesn't include a detailed map of every location, but when you click the **Places** button it does one of the things it does so well–it goes to the Internet. The map that we saw is supplied courtesy of Microsoft Virtual Earth™. Family Tree Maker will also automatically search the largest online collection of family history information–Ancestry.com–for your ancestors, based on the information in your project.

STARTING THE ONLINE SEARCH

- With John's Great Grandfather, John, selected in the pedigree chart, we've skipped to the right-hand end of the toolbar and clicked on the **Research** button, which gives us the **Search** window.
- In the left-hand panel, we've selected **Ancestry.com**, one of the MyFamily.com websites, and we're clicking on **Search**.

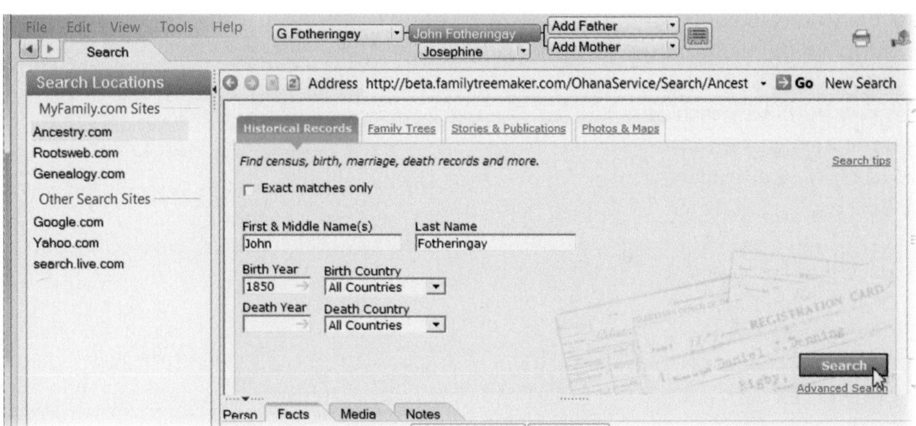

- Within seconds we have a list of results, and the top one is the **1880 United States Federal Census.** We'll click on this entry to see more.

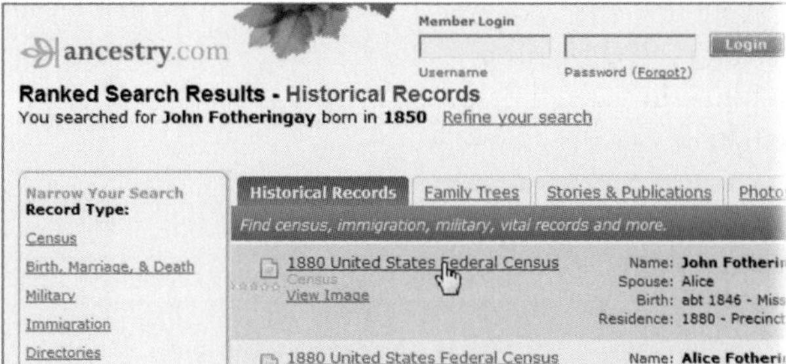

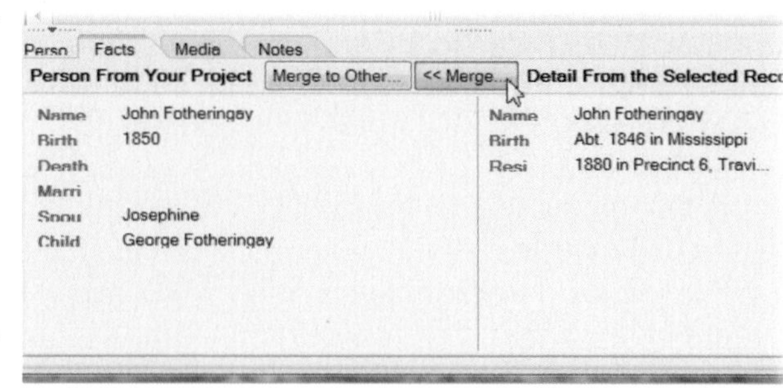

● The details that appear in the bottom right-hand panel can be merged with the information we have in the project if we wish, or we can sign up for a free account with ancestry.com for more extensive records. Let's see what happens if we choose to merge.

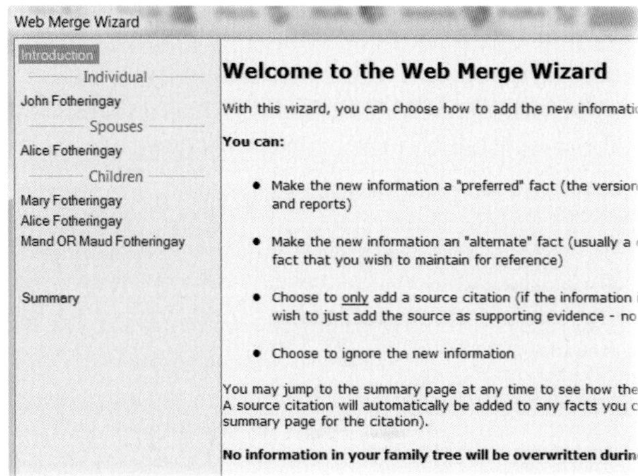

● The **Web Merge Wizard** offers us a range of choices of how we would like to treat this information, depending on whether or not we feel it refers to the right person or conflicts with what we already know. ● We can choose to add this new information to our records without losing any details that we already have.

DELVING DEEPER

● If we choose to open a free trial account with ancestry.com, further census information appears, including, in this case, the person's occupation.
● We are also given the option of viewing an image of the original page of the 1880 census, so we're clicking on this.

- The page appears on the screen, and we can scroll up and down the census page to see details of all this person's neighbors.
- We can also choose to save it by clicking on the **Save** button.

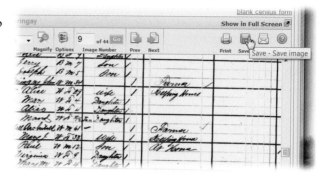

- The **Save Options** dialog box asks you where you would like to save it. We're clicking on the **Save to your computer** radio button, and then clicking on **OK** to confirm.

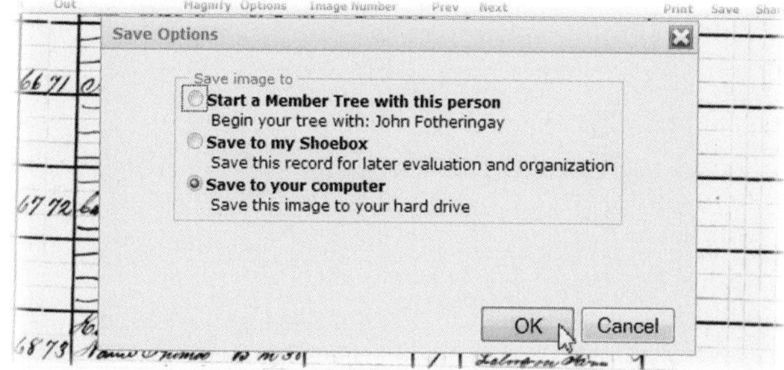

- The **Save As** dialog box asks us where we want to save the image of the page, and what we want to name the file. When these details are complete, click on **Save**.

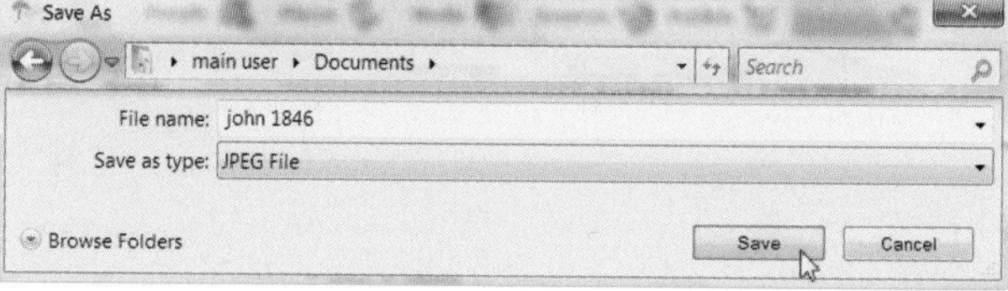

- We feel this is an important document, and we'd like to link it to the person we think it refers to.
- To navigate to this individual's personal file, start by clicking on the **People** button in the toolbar.

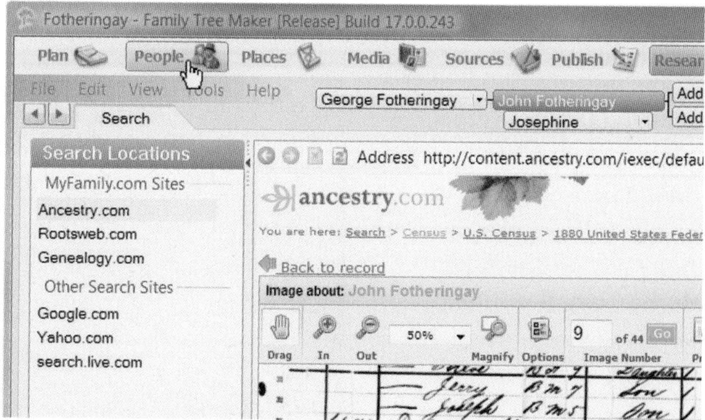

● This returns us to the family pedigree. Now, with **John Fotheringay** selected, click on the **Individual** tab to view the facts that we have about him.

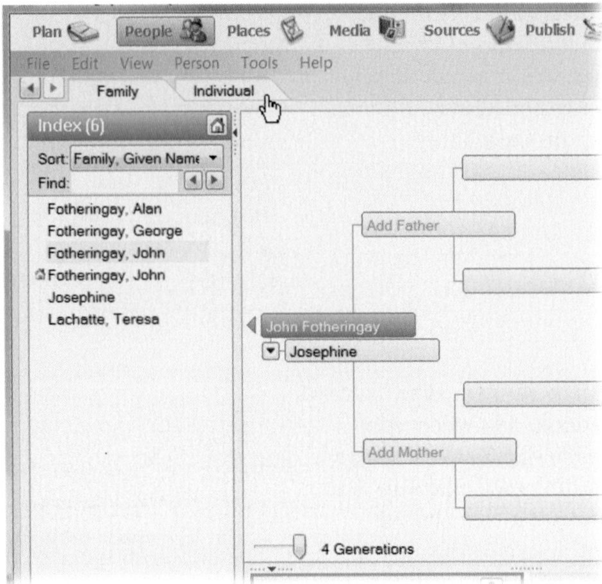

● Here we see the data that we input, together with additional information from our web search.

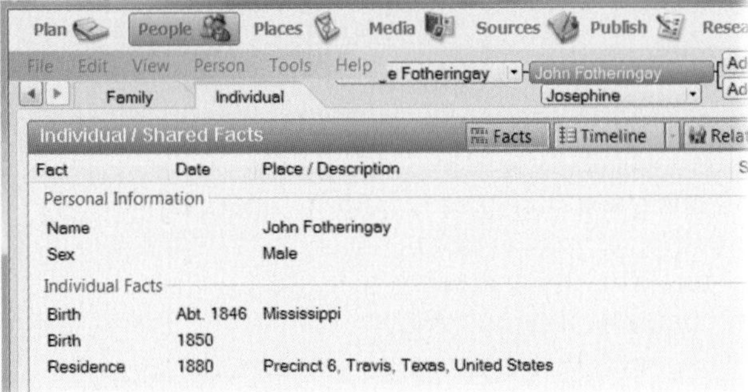

● The bottom panel of the same window contains the **Person**, **Notes**, **Media**, and **Tasks** tabs.

● Select the Media tab, and then click on the **Add Media** button in the top left corner of the panel.

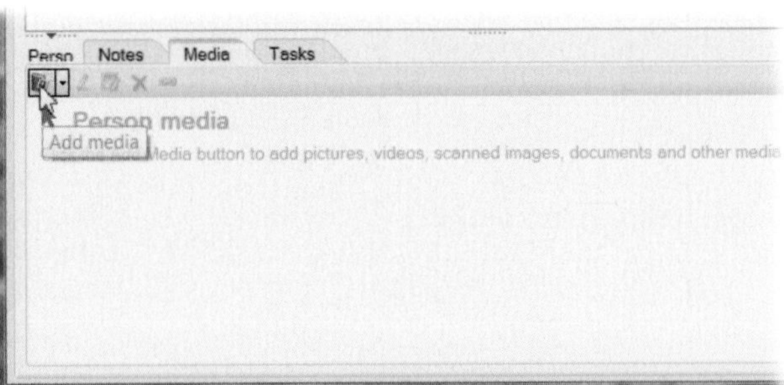

● The **Select media item** dialog box opens. Here we select the item we want (the image **john 1846**), and then click on **Open**.

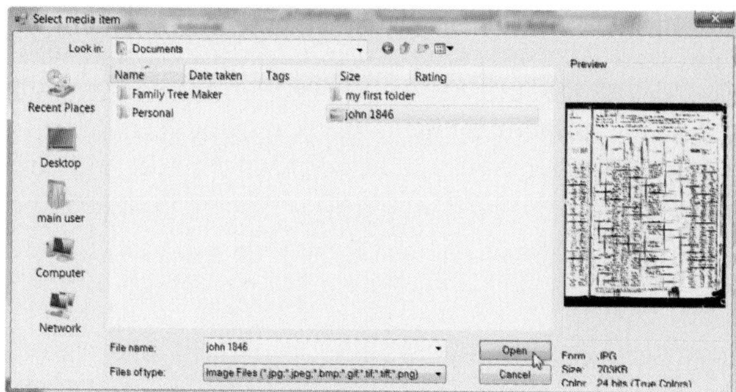

● In the **Copy files to media folder** dialog box we have the option of linking directly to the image we have saved, or making a copy before linking.
● We are choosing to create a copy of the image in the media folder.

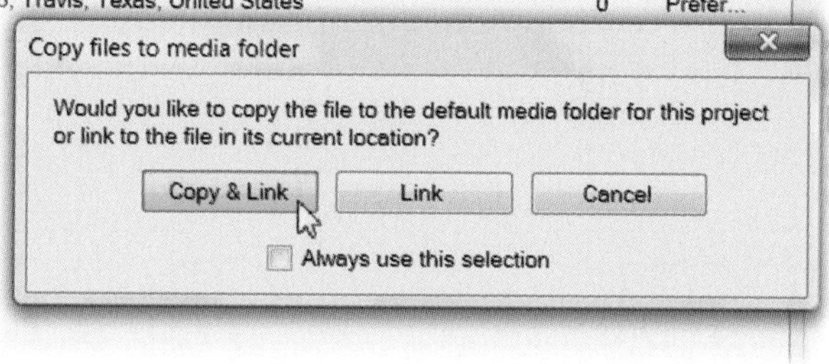

● The file appears in the Media panel, and clicking on it opens the image in a **Media Detail** window. In this window you can rotate and size the image, as well as writing a caption, filling in the date, and writing a detailed description.

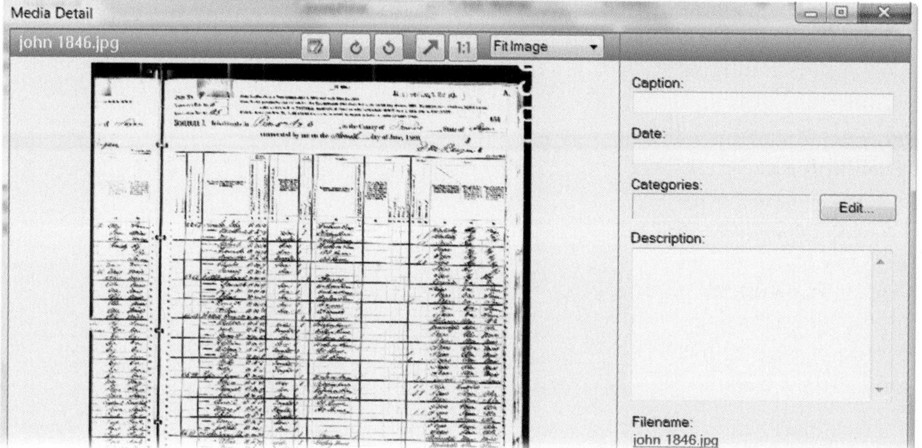

● When we return to this individual's file and click on the **Timeline** button, we can see a chronological list of our facts pertaining to this particular person. The toolbars and the right-hand panel allow us to add or delete people and data, and to cite the sources for the information that we have gathered and recorded.

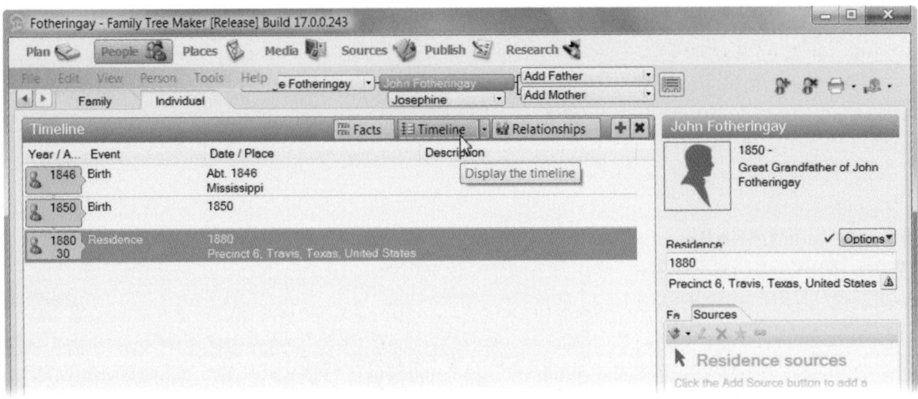

"Publishing" Your Family Tree

In the **Publish** area of Family Tree Maker, you can really make your family's past come to life. Here you can turn all the data you have collected–the information, the sources, the photos, and documents–into charts and reports using ready-made templates that you can then print out and use to present your own family history.

PUBLICATION TYPES

● Click on the **Publish** button in the toolbar to see the range of chart templates available in which to present your genealogical data.

● These are listed in the left-hand panel under the heading **Publication Types**.

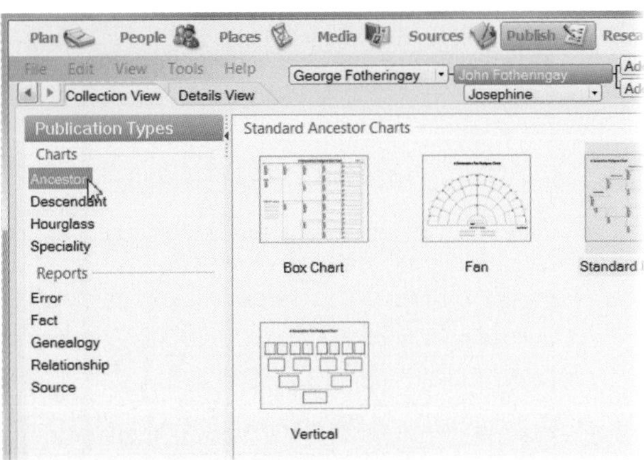

• The **Standard Pedigree** in the **Ancestor** group of **Publication Types** presents the information in a simple branching tree diagram, but in the right-hand panel we are given detailed control over the layout of the chart and the kinds of data we wish to include in it.

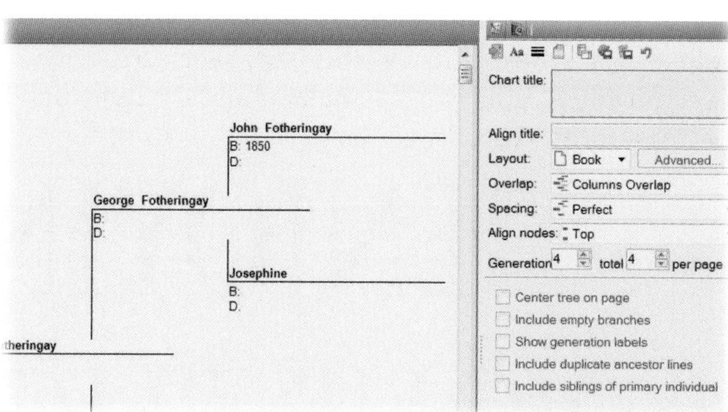

• In the **Relationship Chart**, if we select any two people in our family, Family Tree Maker helps us to draw the inter-generational connections between them.

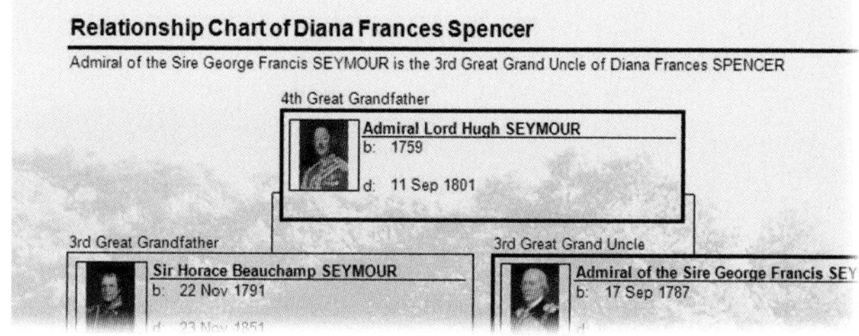

• Media items such as portraits and photographs can be included in the illustrated chart.

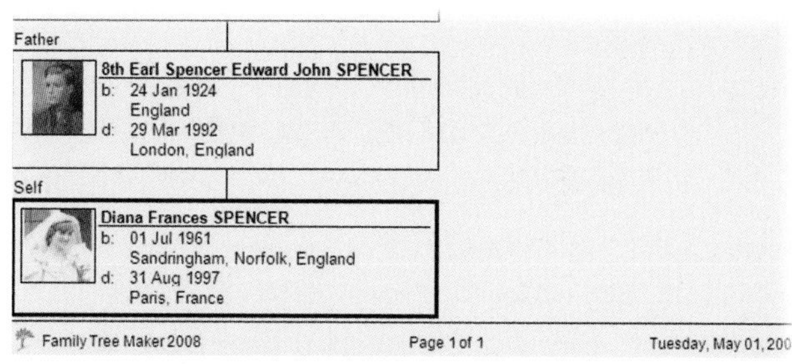

TAKING IT A STEP FURTHER

If you choose to subscribe to ancestry.com, you'll find a new application there called Ancestry Press. This allows you to export your data and images and, by using a variety of templates, to design your own, professional quality, book. The software gives you the facilities to crop and enhance images, edit text, and select design elements. You can print out all your pages at home or choose to have them professionally printed and bound. Using Ancestry Press, you can also create presentation charts for family members.

ENJOYING YOUR PHOTOS

PHOTOGRAPHS USED TO BE DISPLAYED IN ALBUMS or stuffed in old shoe boxes, but in today's digital age, we can do so much more with them. A modern PC has the capacity to store literally thousands of digital images, and here they can be viewed, organized, improved, and manipulated, sent by e-mail, printed, and copied onto CD or DVD. If your computer is running Vista, you already have a program–Windows Photo Gallery–that will help you do all this and more. In this chapter, we look at how to import digital images onto your computer, and how to make the most of them using this powerful program. We also look at a way of putting your photos on the Web for all the world to see.

312 MEET PHOTO GALLERY

322 ORGANIZING YOUR PHOTOS

330 IMPROVING YOUR PHOTOS

334 SHARING YOUR IMAGES

Meet Photo Gallery

Photo Gallery is a new addition to Windows and it is the ideal program for viewing and organizing your digital images, especially if you have a large collection on your PC.

Photo Gallery's Key Features

While Windows Vista provides everything you need to import digital images and store them on your PC's hard disk, Photo Gallery provides the means to bring your digital collection to life. Using a simple and intuitive toolbar, you can view your images in many different ways–from thumbnails to a professional slide show–as well as using Photo Gallery image-enhancing capabilities to improve the quality of your photos. Above all, Photo Gallery helps you organize your photographic memories simply and clearly so that you can always find the one you want, either for yourself or to send to friends and family.

OPENING PHOTO GALLERY

- Click on the **Start** button to open the Start menu.

- From the Start menu, click on **Windows Photo Gallery** to open the program.
- If Photo Gallery does not appear on your Start menu, click on **All Programs** and select **Windows Photo Gallery** from the list.

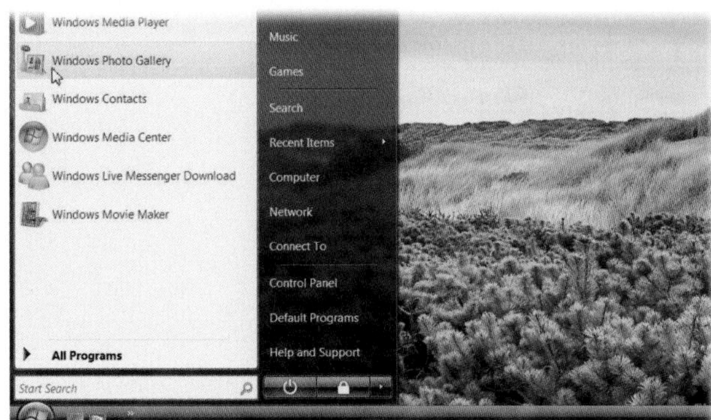

THE PHOTO GALLERY WINDOW

● **Windows Photo Gallery** window opens onscreen. Unless you have already imported images into your Pictures folder, the Photo Gallery window will display the sample pictures and videos that come with Vista. On the left-hand side, you will see a list of folders and the tags and dates that have been used to organize access to the images.

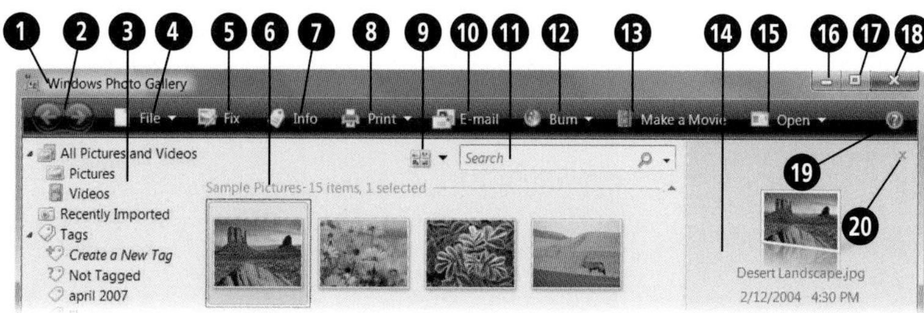

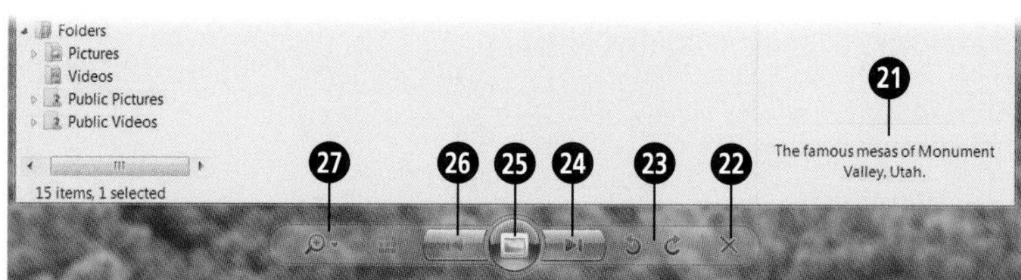

FEATURES KEY

❶ Title Bar

❷ Back/Forward Buttons
Take you back and forth through sequences of images.

❸ Navigation Pane
Takes you to groupings of images using the tags and dates that have been applied.

❹ File Menu
Use to carry out actions on files and folders, and to adjust settings.

❺ Fix Button
Opens image-editing tools.

❻ Gallery
Displays current selection.

❼ Info Button
Opens info pane when it is closed or hidden.

❽ Print Button

❾ Thumbnail Menu
Click here to choose a thumbnail view, group or sort the images, or open a table of contents.

❿ E-mail Button
Click here to attach a file to an e-mail.

⓫ Search

⓬ Burn Button
Create data disc or video DVD.

⓭ Make a Movie
Opens Windows Movie Maker.

⓮ Info Pane
Displays details of the selected image.

⓯ Open

⓰ Minimize

⓱ Maximize

⓲ Close

⓳ Help

⓴ Hide Info Pane

㉑ Caption

㉒ Delete

㉓ Rotate Buttons

㉔ Next

㉕ Play Slide Show

㉖ Previous

㉗ Zoom Button

322 **Adding a Tag**

327 **Dating the Image**

IMPORTING IMAGES

Photo Gallery gives you the opportunity to start organizing your images even before you import them. Here we will look at copying images from a digital camera or a CD onto your hard disk and starting to apply Photo Gallery's tags. Windows Vista is set up to recognize a digital camera when connected with a USB cable.

COPYING FROM A DIGITAL CAMERA

- Connect your camera to your PC using a USB cable.
- The **AutoPlay** window opens. If it does not, you may need to install the software that comes with your camera.
- Select **Import pictures** from the list of options.

- The **Importing Pictures and Videos** window opens.
- Take this opportunity to tag all the photos that you are about to import by keying in a suitable label in the **Tag these pictures** panel.
- The **Options** link in the bottom left-hand corner provides an opportunity to change the import settings. For now, we will leave these at their default setting.
- Click on **Import**.

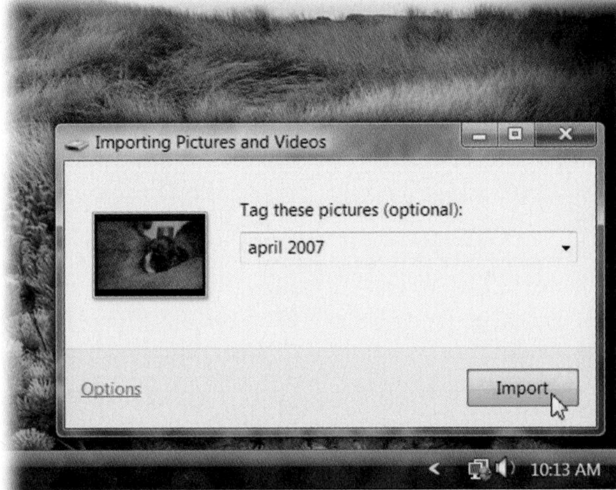

317 Import Settings

● You can follow the process of the import by watching the progress bar that is displayed.

● When the import is complete, **Windows Photo Gallery** opens automatically to display a gallery of all the **Recently Imported** images. Each of these pictures carries the tag that we added when we imported them, and that new tag now appears in the list of tags in the navigation pane on the left-hand side.

New tag

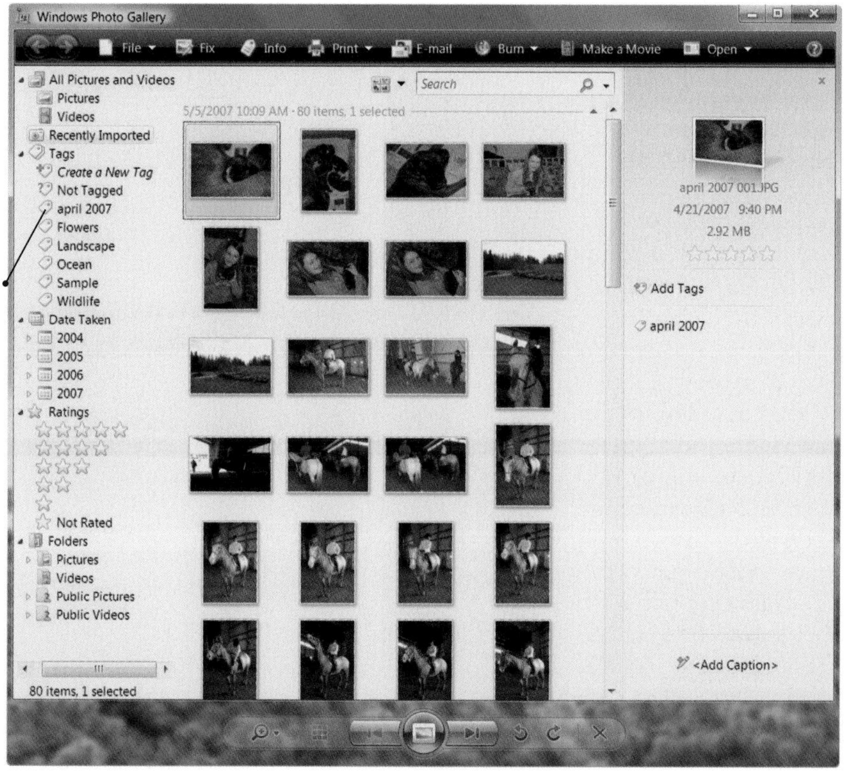

COPYING FROM A CD

- Place your photo CD in your PC's CD tray and close the tray. The **AutoPlay** window opens.
- Click on **Import pictures** to start the process.

- The **Importing Pictures and Videos** window opens. Key in a tag that applies to all the pictures in the CD. Click on **Import**.

- The **Importing Pictures and Videos** window displays the progress of the importing process.

- When the import is complete, Windows Photo Gallery opens automatically to display a gallery of all the **Recently Imported** images.
- The new tag can be seen in the navigation pane.

Our new tag has been added to the list in the navigation pane

IMPORT SETTINGS

- When you start to import the pictures, the **Importing Pictures and Videos** window appears. Clicking on the **Options** link opens the **Import Settings** dialog box. Here you can change the settings for the device you are using, whether it is a camera or a CD/DVD. You can choose a location in which to store the pictures, determine the folder name, and control other options.

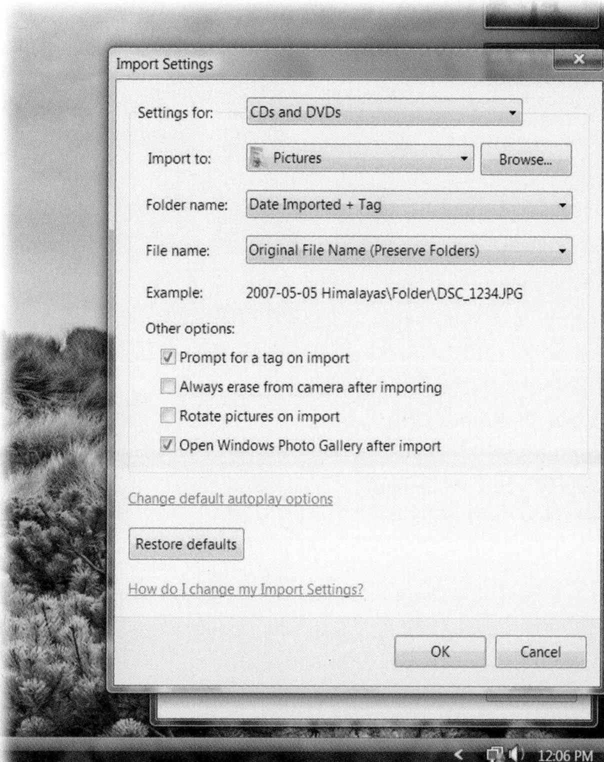

Viewing Your Photos

Now that we have a large number of images in our Pictures folder, it's time to see how Photo Gallery can help us to view them. This program has the power to show you every picture on your computer in a single gallery or, once you have organized your collection ☐, it will find and display that one image you were seeking.

VIEWING THE PHOTO GALLERY

- Once your images have been imported, the Windows Photo Gallery will display them as thumbnail images.
- The first image in the sequence is selected and this image appears in the info pane, together with information about it. We will look at adding more information to individual images in the next section.

- As you slowly roll your cursor over each picture, an enlarged thumbnail version appears, with the image details displayed beneath it.

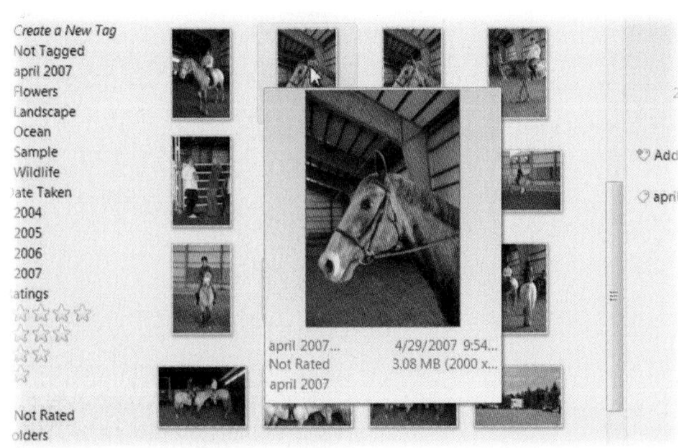

322 Getting Organized

● To view the image in a larger format, double click on the thumbnail in the gallery and the picture opens in its own window with its own info pane.

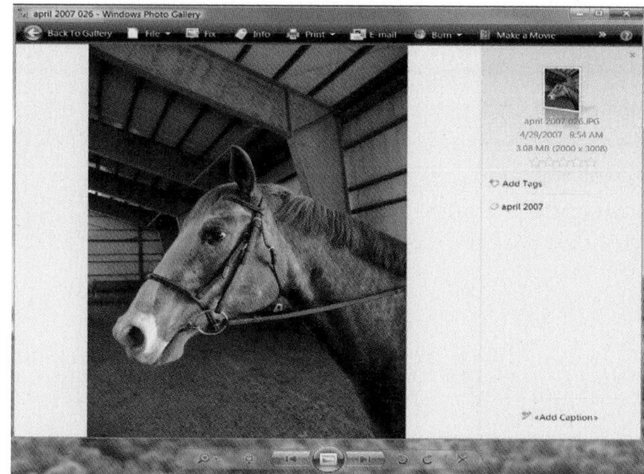

● Using the controls at the bottom of the window, click on the **Next** button to move through the images in the gallery in sequence.

RUNNING A SLIDE SHOW

● To run through all the images in the gallery as a full-screen slide show, click on the central **Play Slide Show** button.

● To control the way in which the slide show runs, right click anywhere on the screen and choose from the options in the pop-up menu.
● Click on **Exit** to close the slide show.

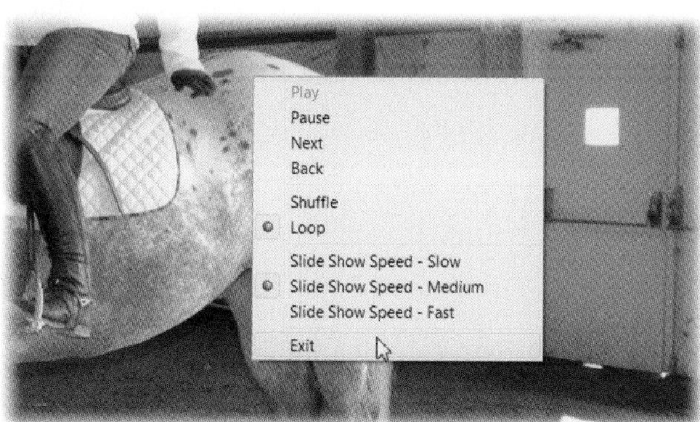

ZOOMING IN ON AN IMAGE

- To enlarge an image, click on the magnifying glass icon at the left-hand end of the controls and a slider bar will appear.

- To zoom in on the image, use your mouse to drag the slider upward.

- To see areas of the image that are out of the frame in this enlarged view, place your cursor anywhere on the picture, hold down the left mouse button, and drag the picture.

DELETING AN IMAGE

● To delete an unwanted or poor quality image, such as this particularly under-exposed one, click on the red cross icon at the right-hand end of the controls.

● The **Delete File** dialog box appears asking you to confirm that you wish to delete the image. If you are sure, click on **Yes**.

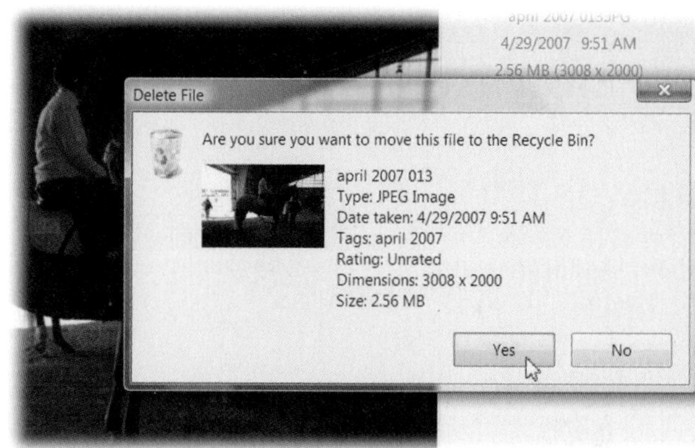

RETURNING TO THE GALLERY

● When you have finished viewing the images in a large format, click on the **Back to Gallery** arrow at the top left of the window to return to the gallery and the thumbnail views of your photos.

ORGANIZING YOUR PHOTOS

If you've ever tried to find a particular picture among the hundreds on your hard disc, you'll know how hard this can be. Photo Gallery comes to the rescue by attaching searchable information to every one.

USING TAGS

Tags are at the heart of Photo Gallery's clever way of organizing your photos. By attaching a key word or phrase to each one of your photos, you can then search for all images that share a particular tag. In the previous section, we put a single tag on all the images we imported. Now we will add more detailed information.

ADDING A TAG

- Before a tag can be added, you need to select the image.
- To select a single image, simply click on it.

- To add a tag to your image, click on **Add Tags**.

- Type the new key word(s) into the text panel. Press Enter to add the tag. Here, we have typed in the word **cordoba**.
- You can add as many tags as you wish to any image by repeating this process.

TAGGING A SEQUENCE

- To select a sequence of images, click on the first one, hold down the Shift key, and click on the last one. The info pane shows that six images have been selected here.

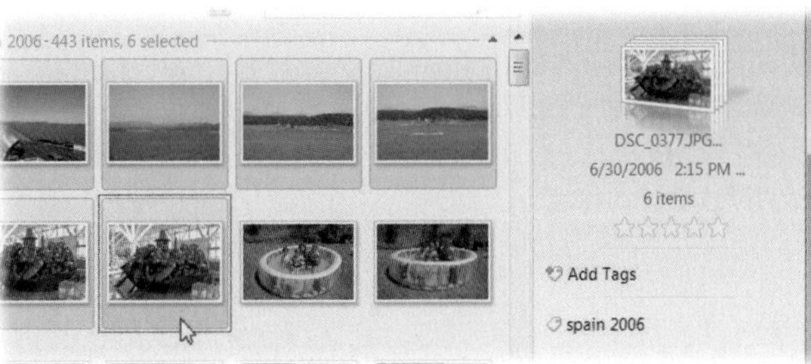

- To add a tag to all six images, click on **Add Tags**.

- Type the new key words into the text panel. Press Enter to add the tag.

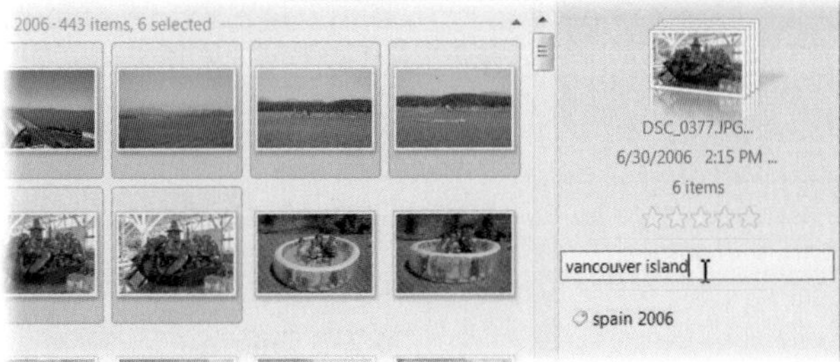

SELECTING SEPARATE IMAGES

• Photos that need the same tag may not be in sequence. To select them, click on the first image and then, holding down the Ctrl button, click on each of the others. They are all selected.

• Now when we add a tag, it will be added to all of these images.

USING THE SAME TAG

• Now that we have created tags, Photo Gallery offers them to us whenever we click on the **Add Tags** panel.
• To use one from this list, simply slide your cursor over it and click to select.

SELECTING ALL THE IMAGES

- To select all the images in a gallery, click on the area behind the images.
- The info panel shows how many images there are in the gallery.

- Now type Ctrl A and all the images are selected, as you can see in the Info pane. Tags can be added to all these at the same time.

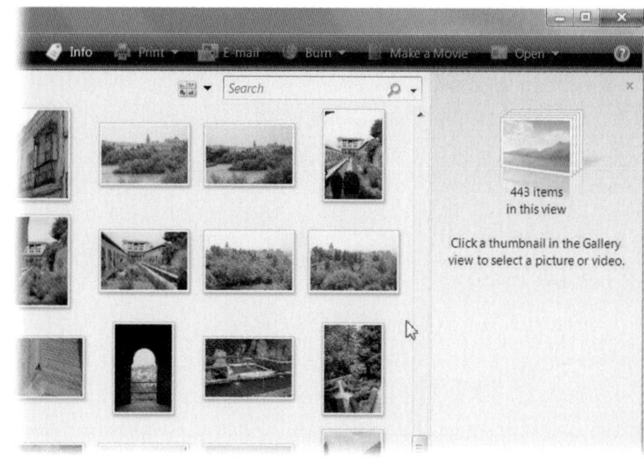

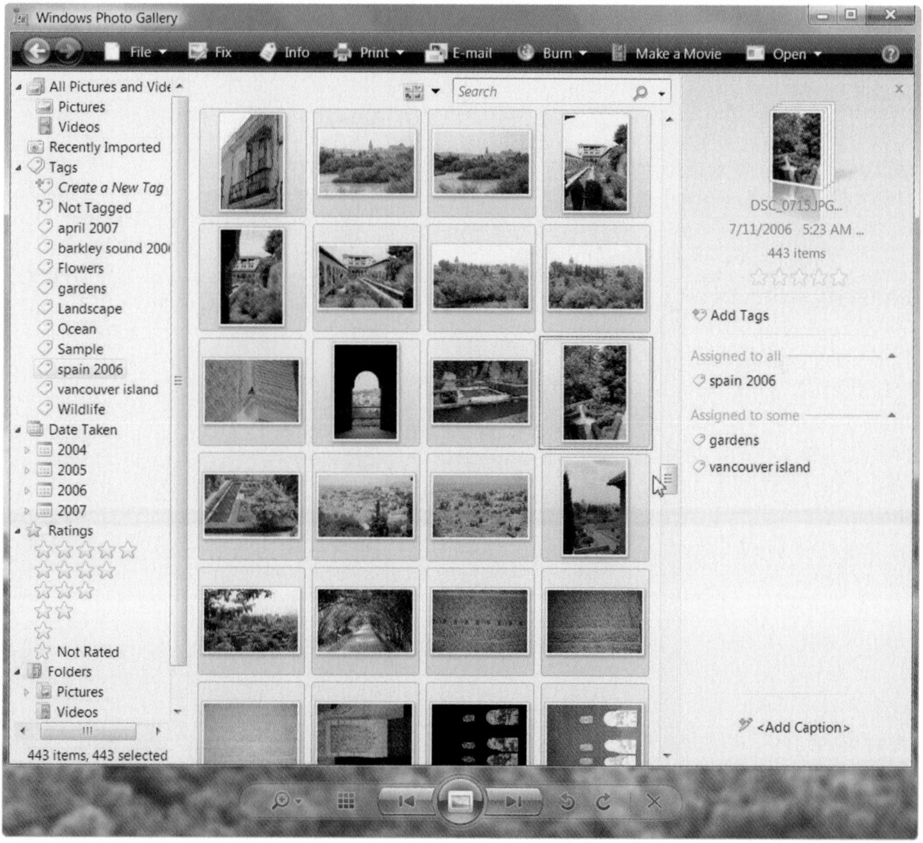

TAGGING AN IMAGE THE QUICK WAY

● To tag an image without having to type anything, simply click and drag the image onto the tag in the Navigation pane that you want to apply. The tag is added automatically.

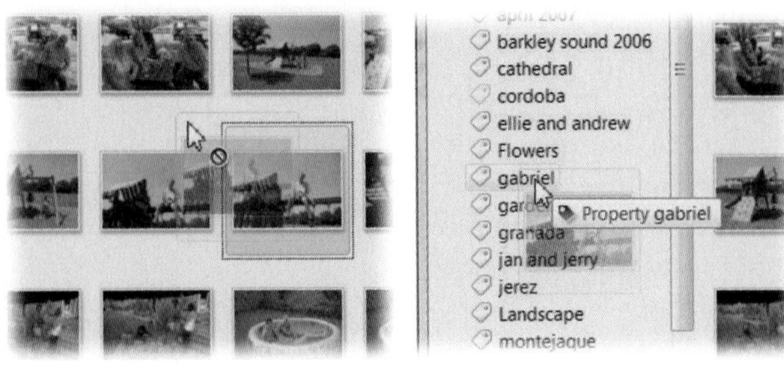

EDITING AND DELETING TAGS

There will be times when you to wish to alter a tag that you have created. You may also want to remove a tag that has been applied to a particular image, or even get rid of a tag that you have created but no longer find useful at all. This is what to do.

EDITING A TAG

● To edit a tag, simply right click on it in the Navigation pane and select **Rename** from the pop-up menu. Type in a new name over the highlighted text.

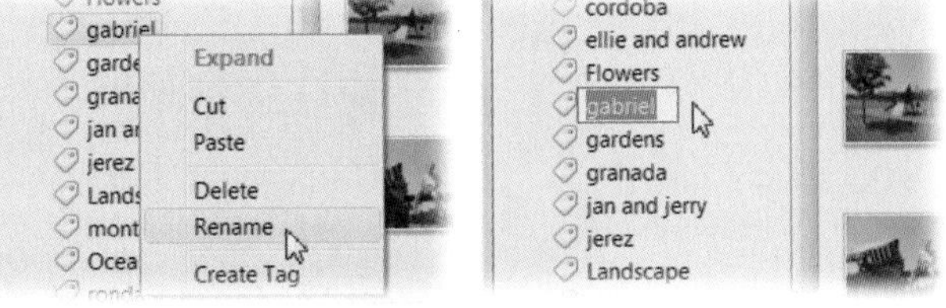

REMOVING A TAG

● To remove a tag from a single photo or a group of photos, select the image(s), right click on the tag in the Info panel, and click on the **Remove Tag** button that appears.

DELETING A TAG

● To delete a tag completely, right click on the tag in the Navigation pane and select **Delete** from the pop-up menu that appears.

Rating and Dating Your Images

No matter how great a photographer you may be, not all your images have the same wonderful quality or mean as much to you. Photo Gallery lets you apply a personal rating system to each of your images, so that you can easily go to your best and most important pictures at the click of a button.

GIVING YOUR IMAGE A RATING OUT OF 5

- To judge a picture, you really need to see it large, so start by double clicking on the image to see it full size.
- To check it out further, use the zoom slider at the left-hand end of the controls or, if the mouse has a wheel, zoom in using that. You will notice that this image has several tags.
- To give this image a rating, place the cursor over the highest star rating you wish to assign, and click on that star. We are giving this picture of a bald eagle a four-star rating.

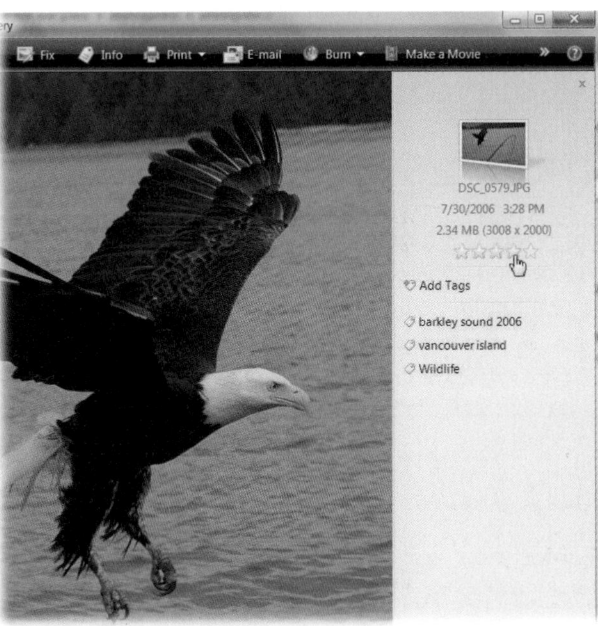

DATING THE IMAGE

- Most digital cameras automatically date a photo when it is taken, and this information stays with the image when it is imported onto the PC. However, if the image has no date, click in the date panel to open the drop-down calendar and navigate to the date you wish to set.

ADDING A CAPTION TO AN IMAGE

● In order to attach more descriptive information to an image, click on **Add Caption** at the bottom of the info pane.

● Write your caption in the text panel.

● When you return to the Gallery view and select this image, you will find that this caption appears at the bottom of the Info pane.

FILTERING YOUR PHOTOS

So what is the purpose of adding tags, dates, and ratings to our images? These are the means by which Photo Gallery will search and sort your digital collection to group the images you want into custom-made galleries. You can search for images that have a specific combination of tags to sharpen the focus of your search.

COLLECTING A GROUP OF IMAGES

● We want to find any images of wildlife on Canada's Vancouver Island.

● To begin our search, we want to make all our images available, so we are clicking on the **Pictures** folder at the top of the Navigation pane.

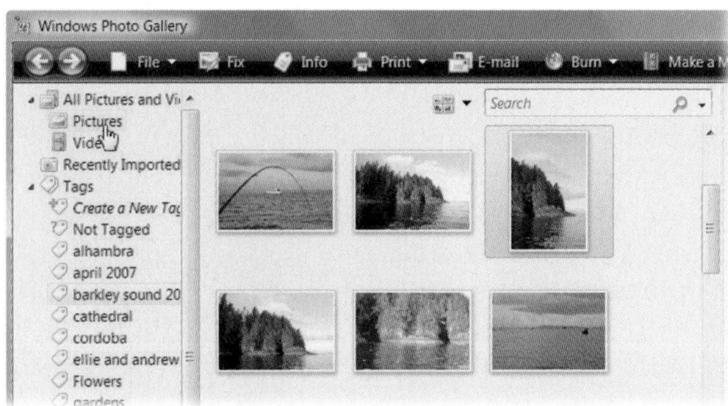

- To search for all images that share a single tag, click on that tag in the Navigation pane. Here we are clicking on **Wildlife**.

- All the wildlife items on our hard disk now appear in the Gallery.

FILTERING THE IMAGES

- If we now key another tag into the **Search** panel, we can filter the images in the current gallery.
- As we key in **vancouver island**, images that do not have the Vancouver Island tag are filtered out. Only our images of Vancouver Island wildlife remain.

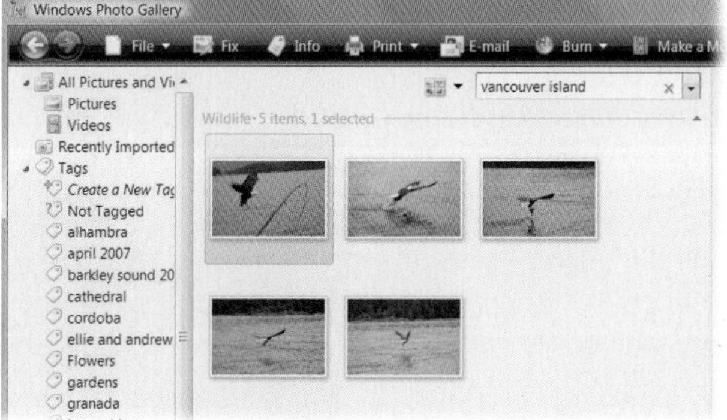

IMPROVING YOUR PHOTOS

The Fix menu offered by Photo Gallery contains the tools to overcome the most common problems encountered by the amateur photographer, and to add some interesting effects.

USING THE FIX MENU

Your digital images are now safely on your PC, and they're tagged and organized. However, some of them probably require some minor adjustments to ensure that they're looking their best. The **Fix** menu offers a range of simple adjustments that allow you to improve the exposure, the color, and the crop of your images.

STARTING THE PROCESS

- Select an image by clicking on it and then click on the **Fix** button at the top of the screen.

- The image opens full size in its own window. In place of the Info pane you will see a list of useful image-editing tools.
- **AutoAdjust** is a shortcut route to improving the color and exposure of the image. To select, click on it.

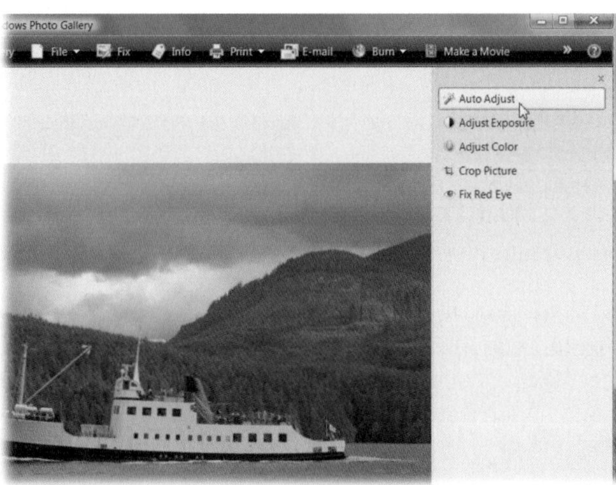

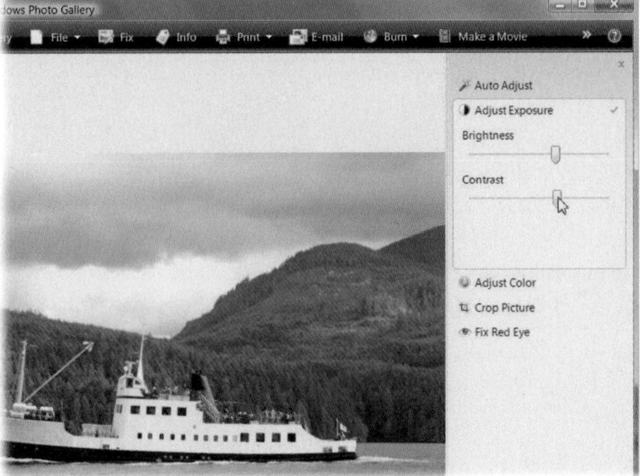

● Clicking on **Adjust Exposure** displays slider bars for **Brightness** and **Contrast**.
● Experiment with these to adjust the image.

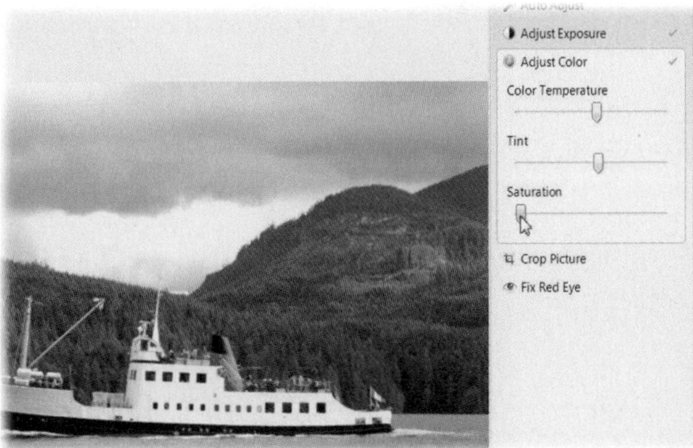

● Clicking on **Adjust Color** reveals a further three slider bars that control **Color Temperature**, **Tint**, and **Saturation**. These can produce some interesting effects but should be used with subtlety. Dragging the **Saturation** slider all the way to the left will produce a black and white image.

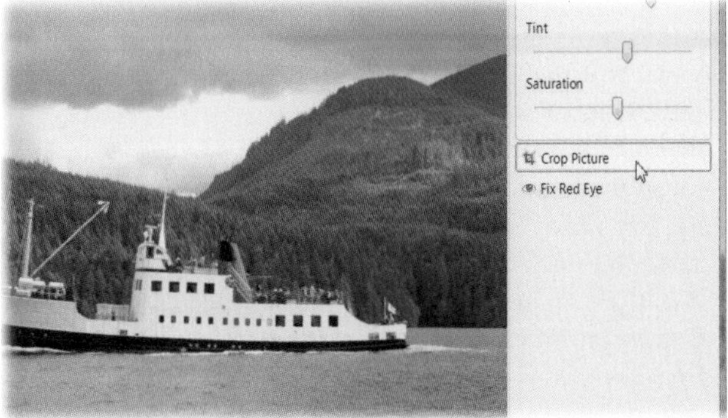

● Many images benefit from being cropped, either to remove unnecessary background detail and focus on the subject matter, or simply to enlarge the subject. Click on **Crop Picture** to begin the process.

- This produces a marquee on the image, which can be dragged into a new position with the mouse.
- Dragging on the corner points or the mid points of the sides will change the shape, size, and proportions of the marquee.

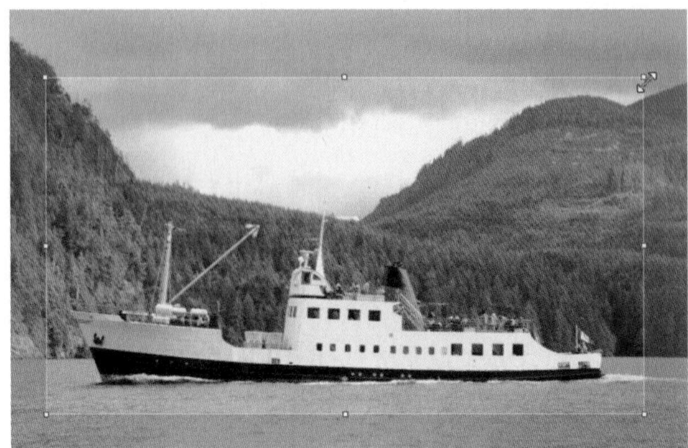

- Click on **Apply**, and the area outside the marquee will be cut off when you apply the crop.

REVERTING TO THE ORIGINAL

When you return to the Gallery after using the **Fix** menu to alter an image, the enhanced image will be saved, but this does not mean that your original has been lost. To retrieve it, double click on the enhanced image in the Gallery and then go to the **File** menu. Select **Revert to Original**. A **Revert to Original** dialog box will ask you whether you are sure that you wish to revert, as all the changes you have made will be lost. You cannot keep the original and the enhanced version, so you may wish to copy any image before you start to fix it.

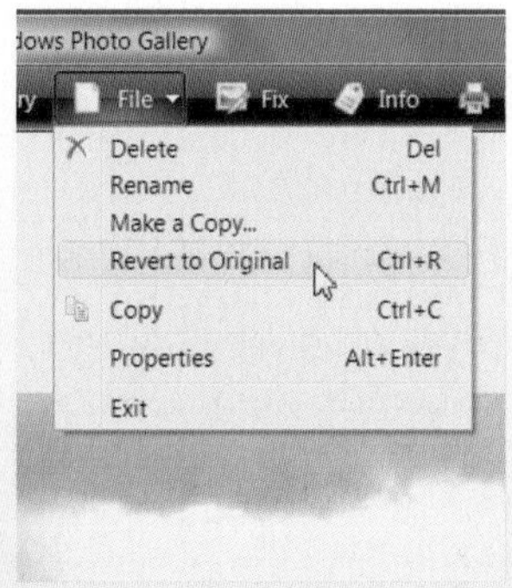

- If you are not satisfied with the outcome, click on the arrow to the right of the **Undo** button and select the **Undo Crop** menu option.
- You will see that it is possible to undo any or all of the changes that you have made from this menu.

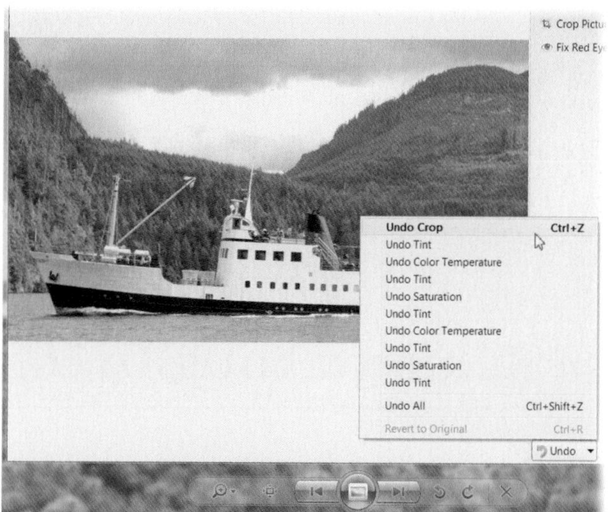

GOING TO EXTREMES

- If you are not a slave to realism, the **Fix** tools can be used to create some wonderful otherworldly effects. It can be surprising how much potential is hiding in any picture.
- Playing with exposure and color adjustments can change the whole mood of the picture.

FIXING RED EYE

Although many modern digital cameras can overcome the problem, the reflection of flash light off the back of the retina can still produce unattractive pictures of red-eyed people and animals. The **Fix Red Eye** tool at the bottom of the **Fix** list can take care of this. The key to success is to zoom in as far as possible on the red pupil before clicking on the tool and following instructions.

Sharing Your Images

Now it's time to share your images with your family and friends by sending them copies of your favorites. You can even show the world your photos on the Internet.

Burning Your Images to Disc

If you have a new computer running Vista, it's fairly certain that you have a disc burner. Windows Photo Gallery assumes you have, and has the tools you need to gather a collection of images and burn them straight to disc at the click of a mouse.

SELECTING IMAGES

● Using the tabs in the Navigation pane, bring your chosen images into the Photo Gallery.

● Now highlight the images you want to send to your friends or family, either by selecting them individually, or by clicking on the background and typing Ctrl A to select them all. Click on the **Burn** button at the top of the window and select **Data Disc**.

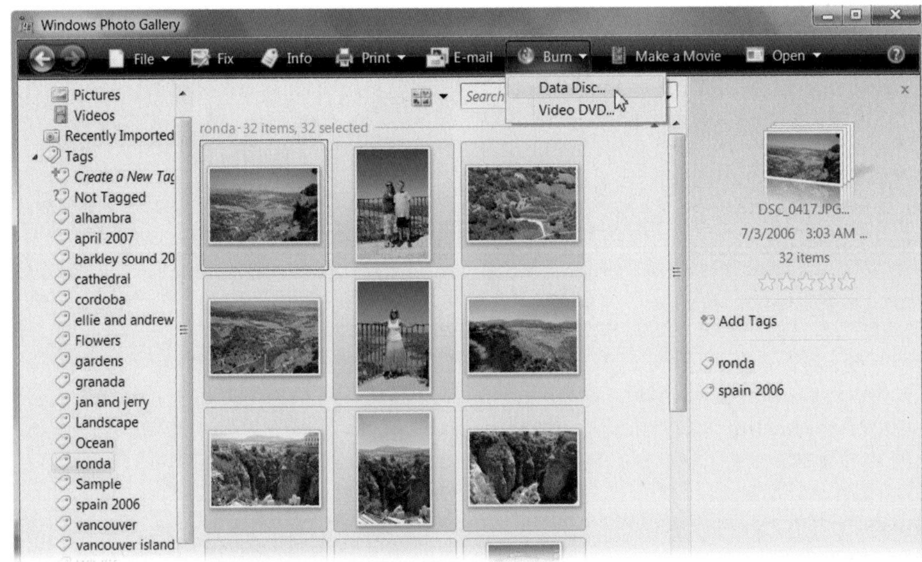

BURNING THE DISC

- The **Burn to Disc** dialog box opens and asks you to insert a writable disc into the drive.
- Place a blank writable CD or DVD in the drive tray and close it.

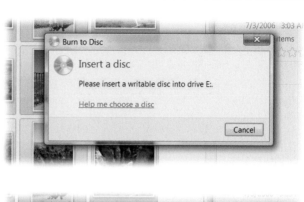

- You are now asked to choose a title for the disc. Today's date is written in as the default title, and this is highlighted.

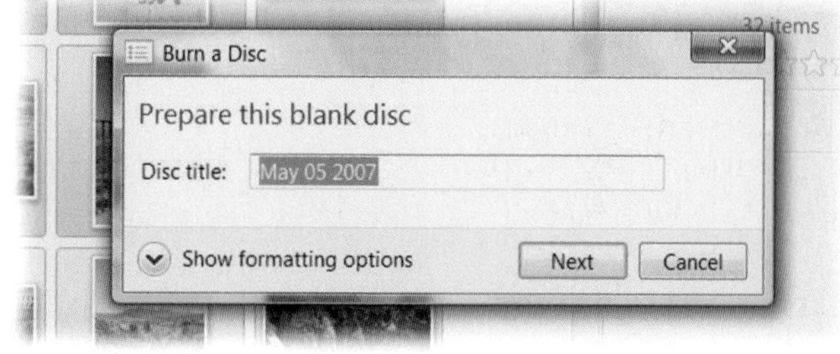

- Just type in the title you would like. Keep it short, as you can only use a limited number of characters.
- Click **Next** to continue.

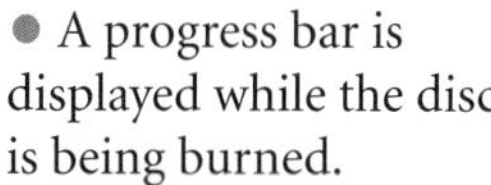

- A progress bar is displayed while the disc is being burned.

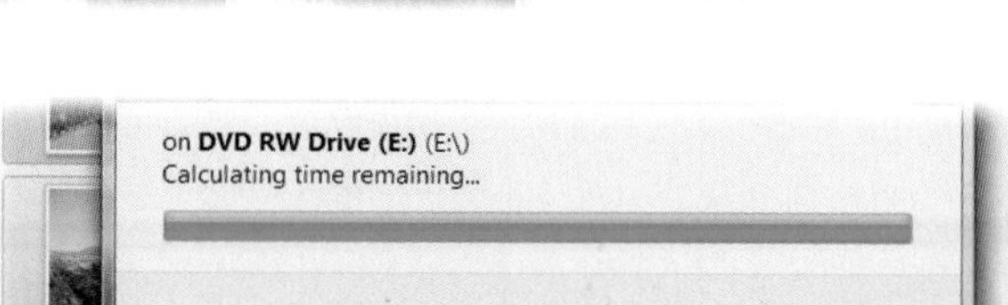

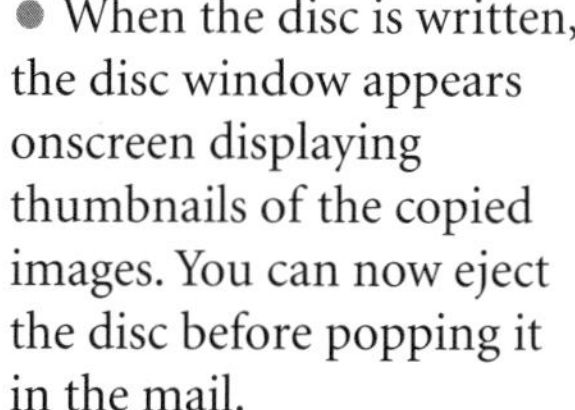

- When the disc is written, the disc window appears onscreen displaying thumbnails of the copied images. You can now eject the disc before popping it in the mail.

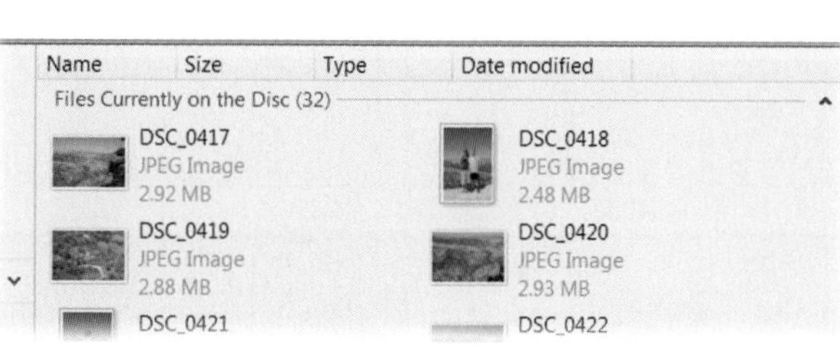

MAKE YOUR OWN SCREEN SAVER

If you'd like the pleasure of displaying your own images as your PC's screen saver, Windows will work with Photo Gallery to do just that. You can even use the Photo Gallery tags to determine precisely which images will appear.

SCREEN SAVER SETTINGS

- Click on **File** and select **Screen Saver Settings** from the drop-down menu.

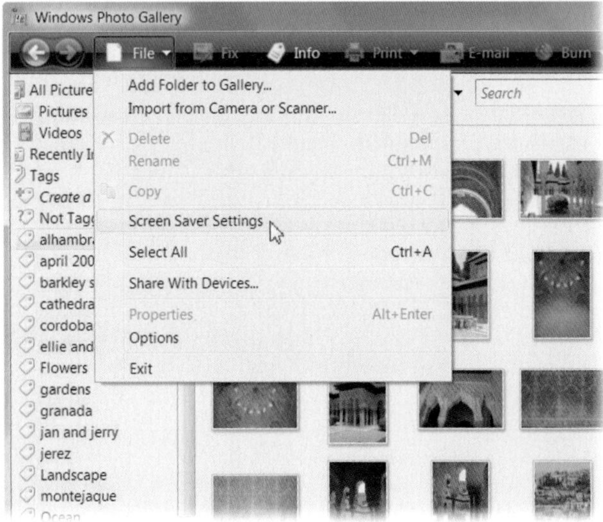

- Click on the **Screen saver** name and select **Photos.** Then click on the **Settings** button.

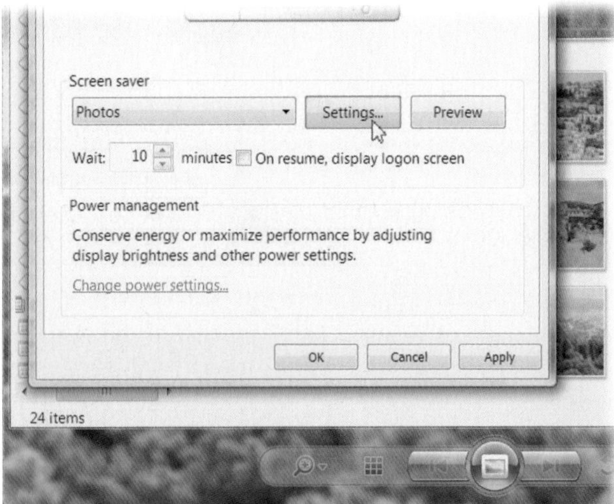

- In the **Photos Screen Saver Settings** dialog box, click on the **Use all pictures and videos from Photo Gallery** radio button.
- Then type in the name of any tag you wish to apply and click on **Save**.

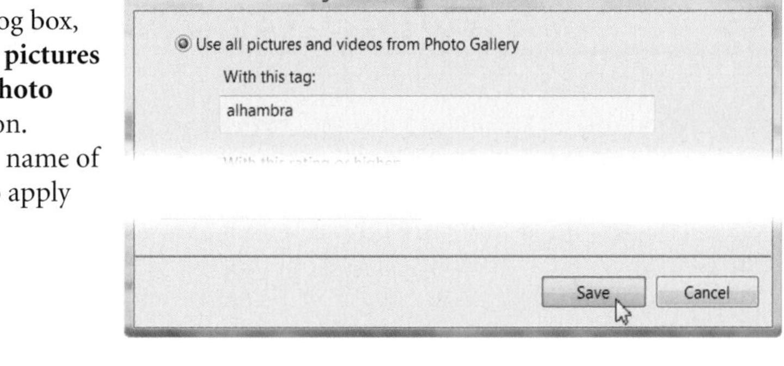

- You can then watch a preview of your handiwork before clicking **OK** to return to Photo Gallery.

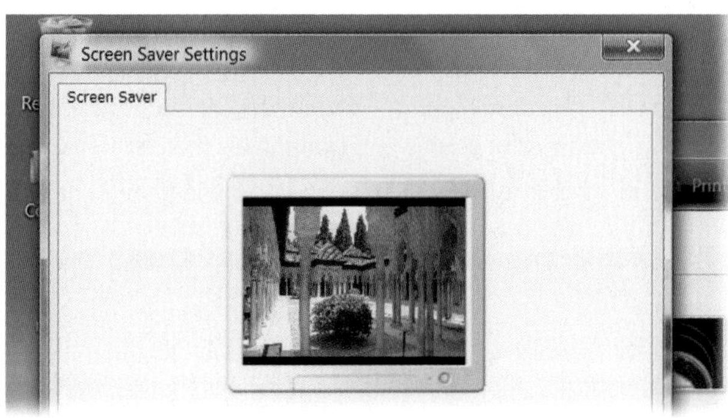

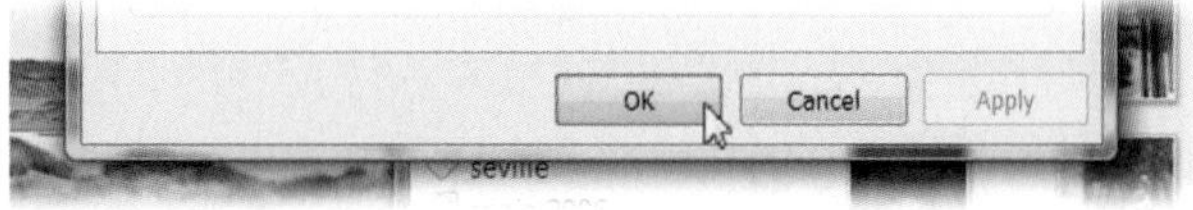

E-MAILING IMAGES

We have seen how to attach an image file to an e-mail in Windows Mail, but you can also send an image by e-mail directly from within Photo Gallery simply by using the handy button in the toolbar. Keep an eye on the sizes of the files if you are sending several at a time. Click on the images that you want to send to select them, and then click on the **E-mail** button at the top of the screen. In the **Attach Files** dialog box you can choose the size at which you wish to send the image. Smaller files are of a lower quality, but will download more quickly at the other end. Select the size and click on **Attach**. A blank e-mail, with the file already attached, opens in your preferred e-mail program, ready for you to type in the address and a message before you send it.

Showing the World

Along with photo DVDs and screensavers, there's another even more exciting way that you can share photos, so that anyone with an Internet connection can enjoy them. Elsewhere in this book we showed you how to download Picasa 2, a free photo organizing program from the people behind Google. In the final section of this chapter we'll give you a flavor of its Web Albums feature, which allows you to create a photo album that anyone can see from anywhere in the world.

● In order to use Picasa's Web Albums feature, you will need to have a Google account. This is completely free and anyone can sign up simply by going to **www.google.com** and then clicking the **Sign in** link at the top right-hand side. This will open a page that asks you to sign in with your Google Account name and password. Since you don't yet have one, click the **Create an account now** link underneath and follow the instructions to set up your own account.

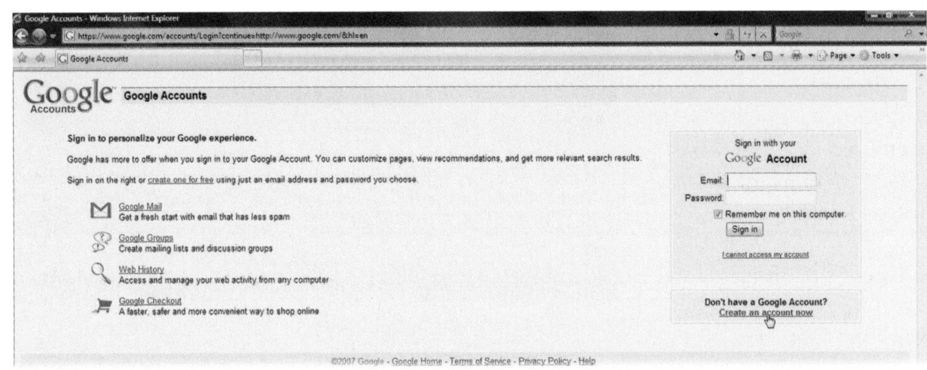

● Next, load Picasa and then navigate to a folder of photos using the list on the left of the screen so that its contents are displayed in the middle. Click the **Web Album** button at the bottom to begin.

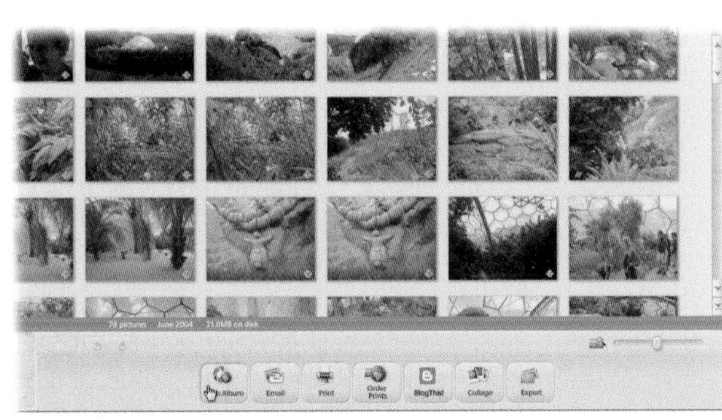

132 Downloading Programs

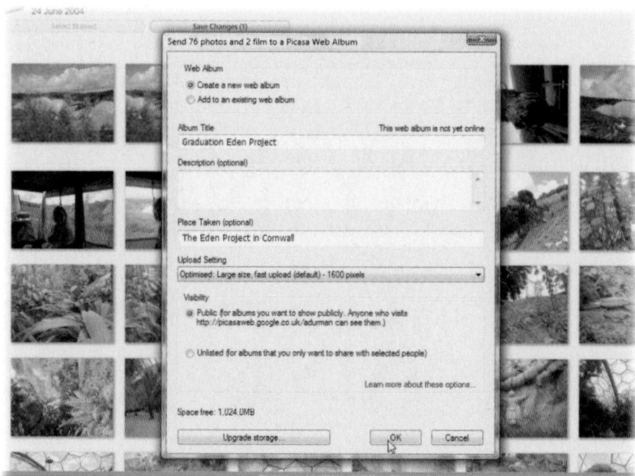

● Picasa will assume that you want to add all of the photos in the current folder to your web album, so all you have to do is fill in this simple form when it appears on the screen, giving your album a name and making sure that **Public** is selected in the **Visibility** section of the dialog. Then just click the **OK** button to upload your photos.

● Depending on how many there are, this may take a little time. Picasa keeps you informed of its progress via this dialog box.
● Once all the photos have been uploaded, you can click the **View Online** button to see them.

● Once your album is on the web, you can invite others to visit by sending them an e-mail invitation. Web Albums has a button on every page called **Share Photo or Share Album**.
● Click this and you'll be able to send friends and family a link that they can click on to go online and see your photos. They can even download the ones that they like.

PLAYING MUSIC AND DVDS

THE DAYS WHEN A PC–especially a home PC–was mainly for work are long gone, and more people are now buying computers for their entertainment value than ever before. The core of that entertainment experience is the free program that's included with Windows–Media Player version 11. With this program, you can enjoy CDs and DVD movies, you can use it to record CDs that you own (called ripping) and create a digital library on your PC's hard disk, and you can use it to make your own compilation CDs to enjoy in the car or on the move; it synchronizes digital music with many popular portable players and is even the electronic door to downloading music from web-based stores. This chapter covers all this and more.

342 Playing and Ripping CDs

350 Managing Your Music

370 Buying Music Online

378 Burning a Music CD

382 Playing DVDs

386 Windows Media Center

PLAYING AND RIPPING CDs

Media Player 11 turns your home PC into a sophisticated electronic jukebox that not only plays CDs, but can "rip" them as well, storing digital copies of your favorite songs on the hard disk.

PLAYING YOUR FIRST CD

All modern PCs are geared up to play music for you to experience in various ways. Even notebook computers include built-in speakers and a socket for headphones. Along with Media Player 11, a home PC is all you need to enjoy music to the full and, as we'll see later in this chapter, that's just the beginning.

PUTTING IN AN AUDIO CD

- Open your PC's CD-ROM or DVD drive by gently pushing the little button so that the tray slides out. Put a music CD face up onto the tray and then slide it back into the PC. The **AutoPlay** dialog box appears automatically. Then, just click on the **Play audio CD** link at the top.

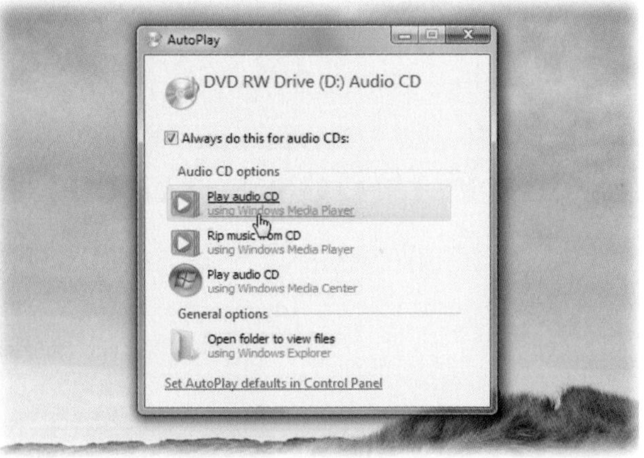

- If this is the first time you've used Media Player, it will ask to be set up.
- Click on the radio button next to **Express Settings (Recommended)** to let the program use its preferred default settings.

Choose the initial settings for the Windows Media Player. You may change these settings in the Player later.

Express Settings (Recommended)

Make Windows Media Player the default music and video player and allow it to download CD and DVD information from the Internet. If I need media usage rights, download them for me automatically. Send Microsoft anonymous usage information for the Customer Experience Improvement Program.

Online description of the Customer Experience Improvement Program

Custom Settings

Customize privacy, playback, and online store settings.

● Confirm your choice by clicking the **Finish** button.

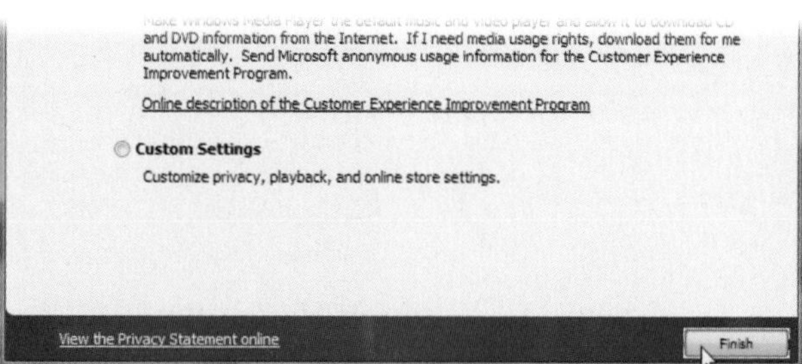

PLAYING AN AUDIO CD

● Several things will happen at once. If you're connected to the Internet, Media Player retrieves the CD name and all the track names from a database, displays them down the side, loads a colorful animation, and starts playing the CD.

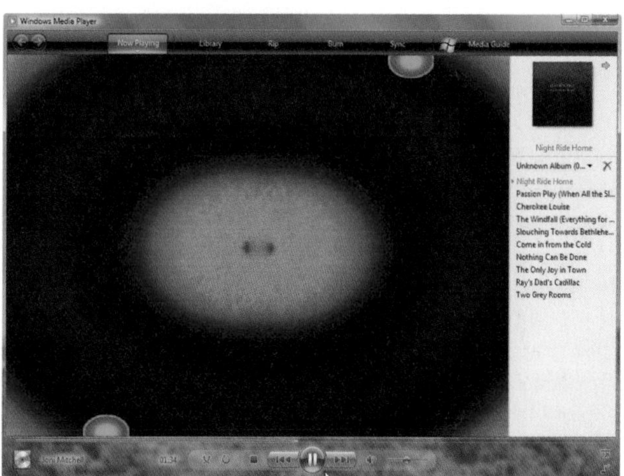

MEDIA PLAYER'S CONTROLS

❶ Shuffle
❷ Repeat
❸ Stop
❹ Previous Track
❺ Pause (becomes Play button when music is paused or stopped)
❻ Next Track
❼ Mute
❽ Volume
❾ View Full Screen
❿ Compact Mode

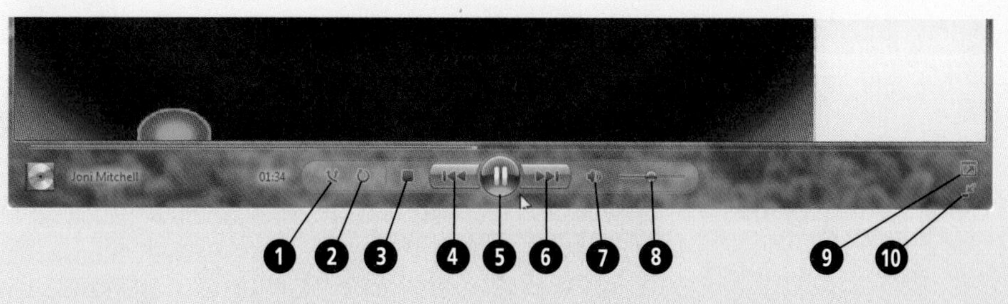

SWITCHING MEDIA PLAYER MODES

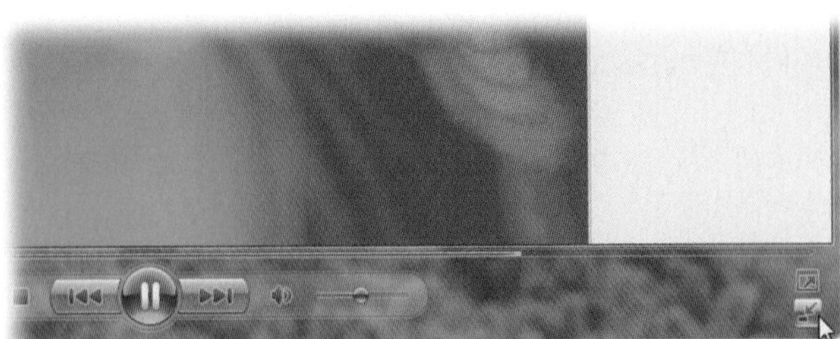

● To save screen space and give you room to run more programs, Media Player has a handy "compact" view. Turn it on by clicking on the bottom right button.

● Media Player hides one or two of its main controls, but you can still listen to and control CDs easily like this. To revert to the previous mode, click the **Returns** button.

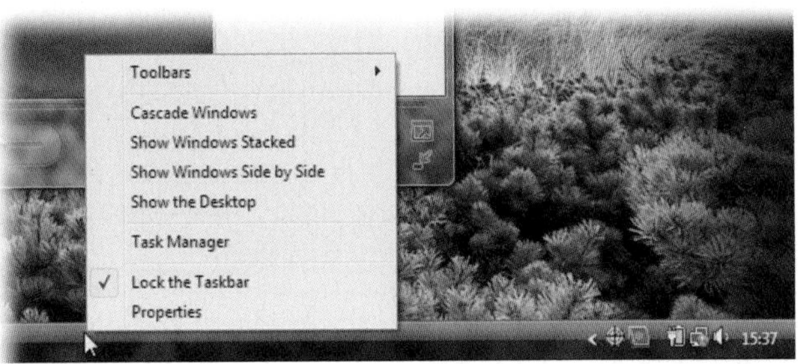

● There's an even smaller mode you can use by "docking" Media Player onto the taskbar along the bottom of the screen. Move the cursor down there and click on it with the right mouse button.

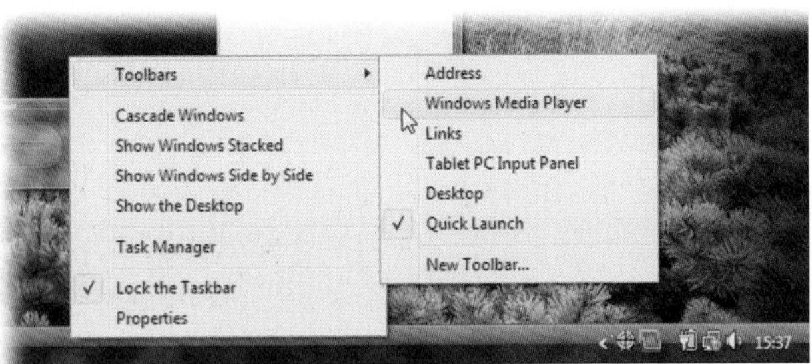

● Slide the cursor up the menu to **Toolbars** and then across to **Windows Media Player**. Click on it once with the left mouse button to select.

● Next, minimize Media Player by clicking the Minimize ("-") button at the top right corner.

• This sends the program to the taskbar along the bottom of the screen. You can still see the main Media Player controls.

• Click once on the **Show Video and Visualizations** button to the right of the Media Player controls and the visualization window will open in miniature so you can enjoy the animation as you continue to listen to the music.

• To return Media Player to its original view, click the **Restore** button below the **Show Video and Visualizations** button.

*Click the **Restore** button to return to the original view*

• The player returns to the original view again, just as we started. Click the **Stop** button to stop the CD from playing.

Ripping Your First CD

As well as playing CDs one by one, Media Player can also rip the contents of a CD onto your PC's hard disk–ripping is the term used to describe the process of making a digital copy of the music. Once tracks are stored on your PC like this, there are all sorts of things you can do with them to enhance your musical experience.

SWITCHING TO THE RIP SCREEN

● Media Player arranges its main commands as buttons along the top of the screen with the player in full screen mode. With your CD in the drive, click the **Rip** button once to start.

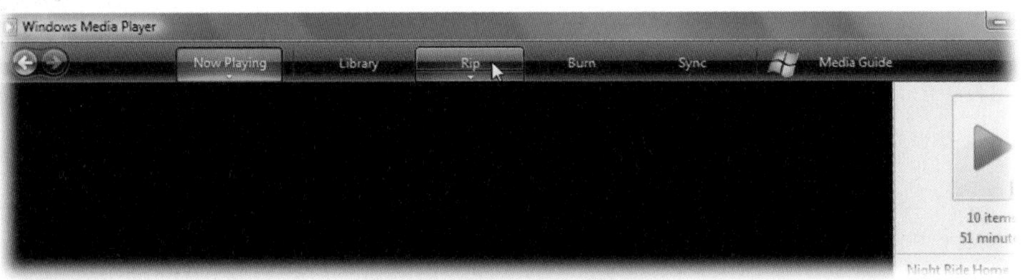

● This shows the complete track listing for the CD that we're going to copy. Note that there is a check mark beside each track, indicating that it's been selected for ripping. If there's a track you don't want to copy, simply click in the box to uncheck it.

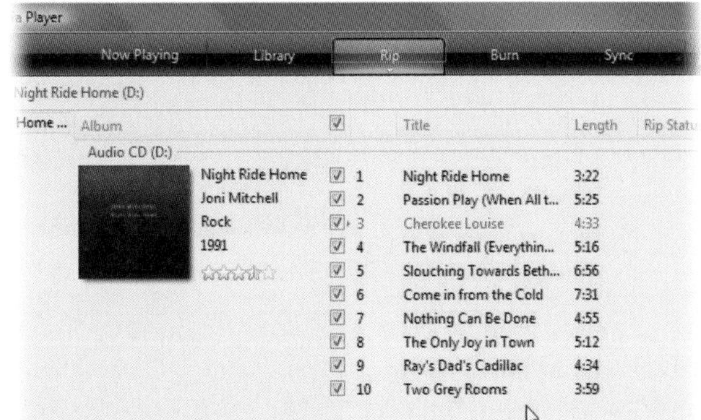

SETTING THE RIP OPTIONS

● To begin, just click on the **Start Rip** button at the bottom right of the Media Player window.

● The **Rip Options** dialog box asks whether you want to copy protect any recordings you make. Choosing not to add copy protection will allow you greater freedom in moving your music around and will ensure that it will play correctly on the broadest range of portable players.
● To continue, you must check the last box to state that you understand and agree to abide by any applicable copyright laws.

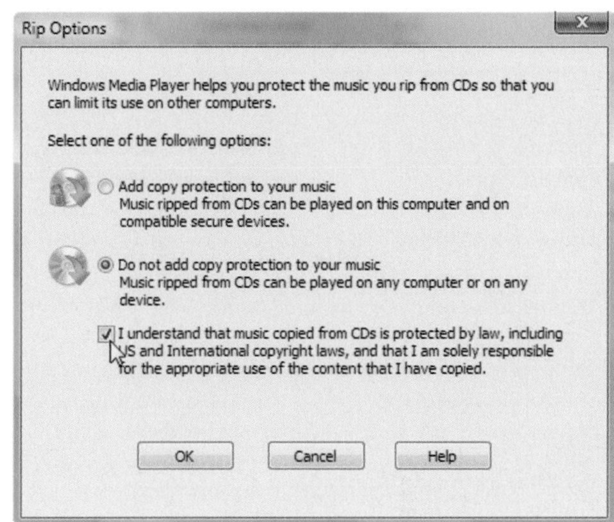

● Click **OK** to continue and then sit back as Media Player copies the CD.

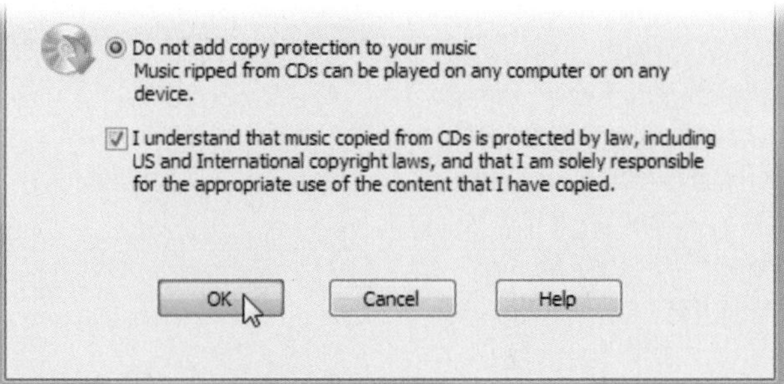

FORMAT AND BIT RATE

By default, when Media Player rips a CD it uses certain settings. Each song is saved as a Windows Media Audio file (usually abbreviated to a WMA file) at a bit rate of 128Kbps. All this means is that songs are saved in the format that Media Player prefers and with an average sound quality. Most of us never change these settings. However, if you need higher quality or would prefer to save songs as MP3 files instead of WMA files (some older digital players can't play the latter), you can. Simply click the arrow under the **Rip** button to open the menu, choose **Format** to switch between WMA and MP3, and then choose **Bit Rate** to increase or decrease the sound quality. Note that the higher the bit rate you choose, the more space a song will take up.

MISSING ALBUM ARTWORK

Sometimes when you rip a CD or even download a track from a music store, Media Player doesn't automatically find the album sleeve. If that happens, you can find it for yourself. Load Internet Explorer and go to **www.google.com**. When the page loads, click the **Images** link at the top. Type the name of the artist or album you're searching for into the box and then click **Search**. Once you've found the album cover, right click on it and choose **Copy** from the pop-up menu. Switch back to Media Player, locate the album with the missing artwork, and right click on it. Choose **Paste Album Art** from the menu, and the cover will appear in place.

RIPPING THE CD

- Here's the CD being ripped. The first four tracks have already been copied to the library, track 5 is halfway through, and the tracks below are all in line, ready to be copied. You don't have to do anything.

- When the CD has been copied, click the **Library** button at the top.

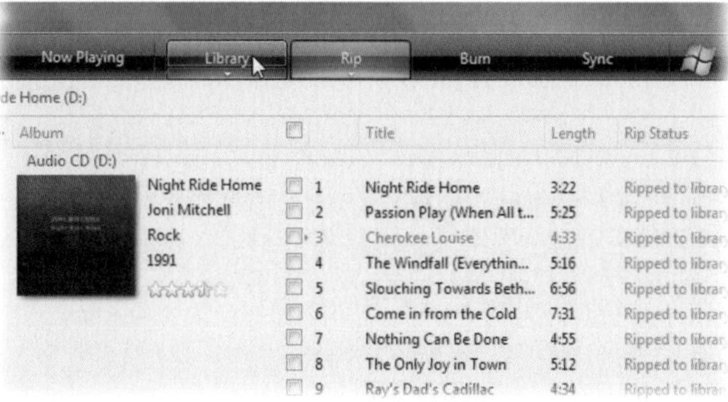

PLAYING THE RIPPED CD

● Here's the Joni Mitchell album that we just ripped, in place in Media Player's library, along with a selection of other tracks that are supplied free with Windows Vista. Double click on the first track (highlighted in blue) to start playing it.

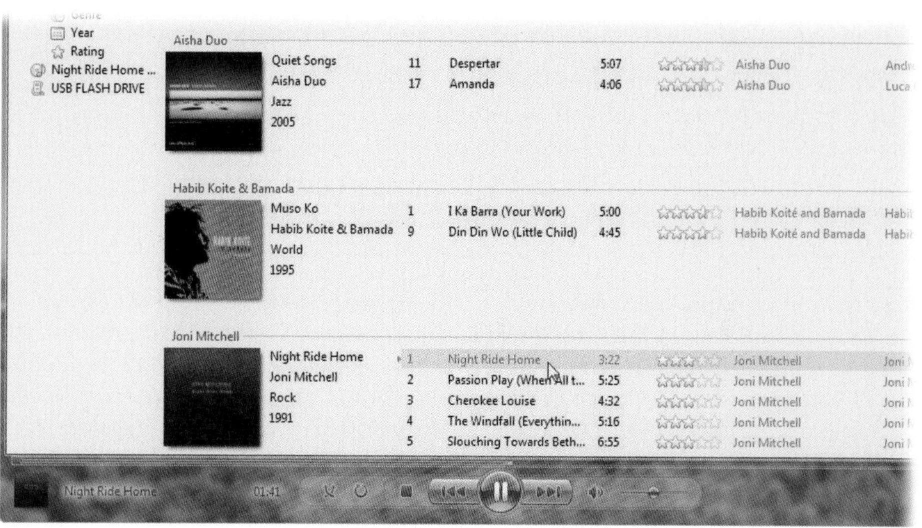

● Click the **Stop** button to stop playing the album.

STAR RATINGS

Star ratings are an important part of any good music library–it's possible for example, to create a playlist using only those songs awarded a high number of stars. To rate a song, simply move the cursor to the stars next to it–they'll be grayed out–and as you do, they will illuminate. Simply move the cursor left or right, depending on the number of stars you want to award the song, and then click once with the left mouse button.

Managing Your Music

Once your tracks are in the Media Player library you can organize them in all kinds of ways by artist, year of release, genre–you can even assign songs and albums star ratings and sort them by those.

Media Player's Views

Most traditional music collections are arranged alphabetically by artist, but Media Player can organize your music in much more interesting ways. The key to this are the "views" the program uses to arrange the music in the library. As your digital collection grows, you'll find it useful to be able to look at the contents in unusual ways in order to find what you're looking for–or be surprised by tracks you'd forgotten.

THE SONGS VIEW

Media Player's views are here, down the left-hand side under the **Library** heading. The first one, shown here, is the **Songs** view, which shows the album cover on the left and all the individual tracks from the album to the right. The reason there aren't many tracks on the first three here is that they're just samples included with Windows Vista.

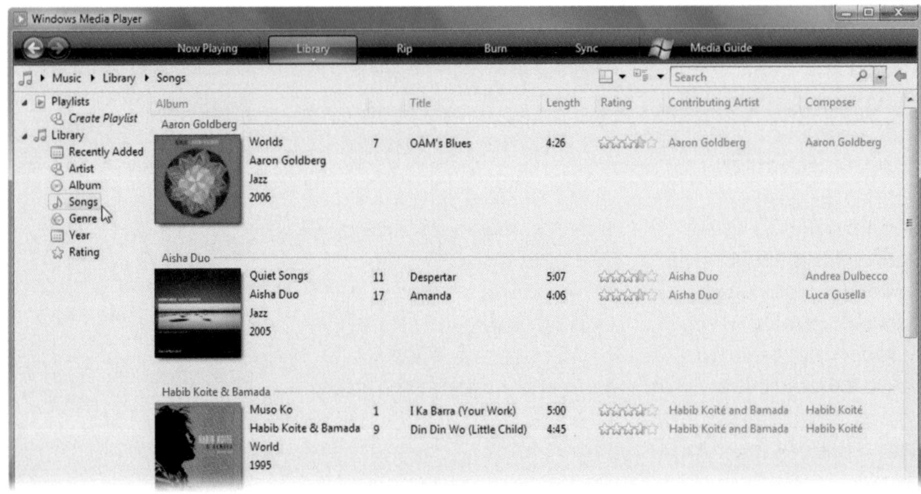

THE ARTIST VIEW

In this view, Media Player arranges the music in the library by **Artist**. Next to each album is the artist's name, the number of songs by them in the library, and their combined length.

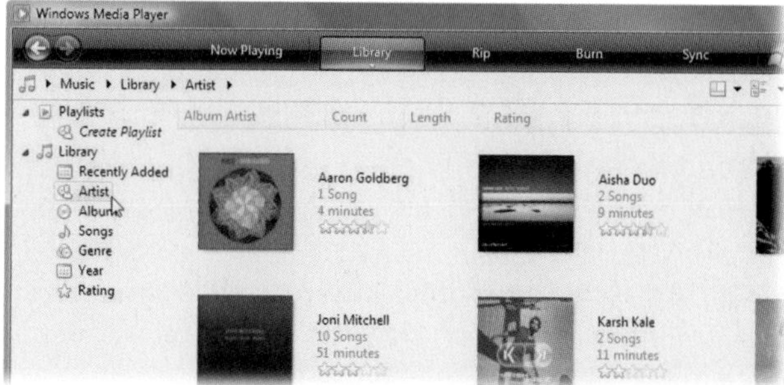

THE ALBUM VIEW

This organizes the music in the library alphabetically by album name–hence **The Best of Beethoven** comes before **Duos II**.

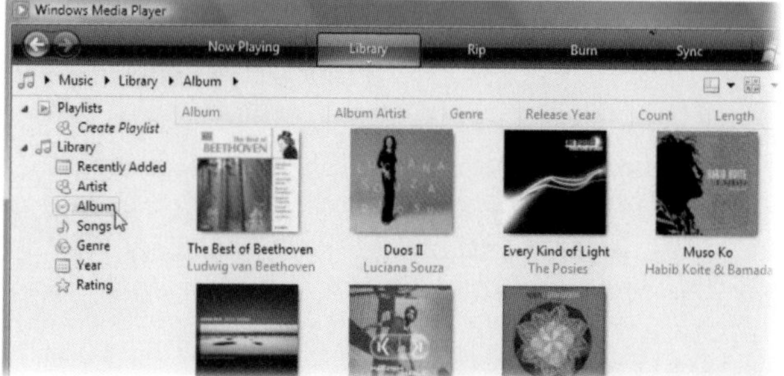

THE GENRE VIEW

Media Player can sort albums into genres such as classical, rock, world, and jazz. Where there's more than one album in the category–for example **Rock** in this screen–you can see that the albums are stacked on top of each other.

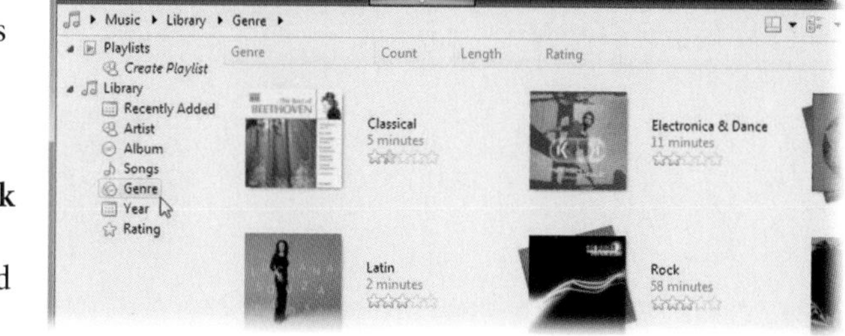

THE YEAR VIEW

Finally, this is the **Year** view, starting with the most recent year and working backward. Again, if you look at 2005, you'll see that there are three albums there, arranged in a little staggered pile.

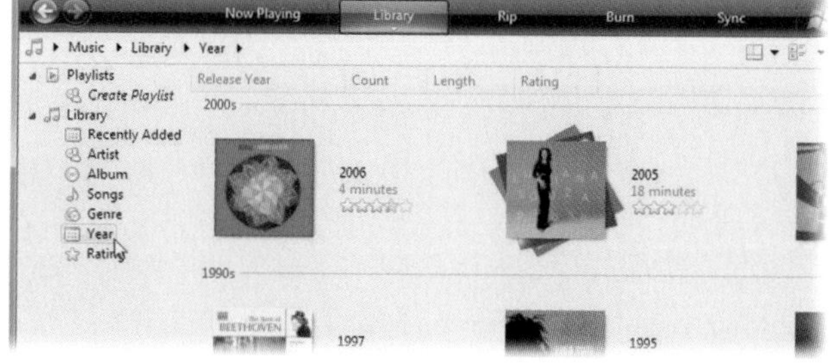

Creating a Playlist

Playlists are a simple, but brilliant idea. They allow you to cherry pick tracks from any album in your music collection, assemble them into any order you like, and then save them as a playlist that you can listen to whenever you wish. In this way you can put together a playlist for a party or for driving in the car; you can create compilations based on year of release, or of your favorite female singers. Songs can appear in many different playlists, and remain stored safely on your PC.

GIVING YOUR PLAYLIST A NAME

- Start by moving the cursor up to the **Create Playlist** command at the top left of the **Media Player** window. Click on it once with the left mouse button.

- As you do, Media Player highlights the words **New Playlist**, indicating that you can type in a new name for your compilation.

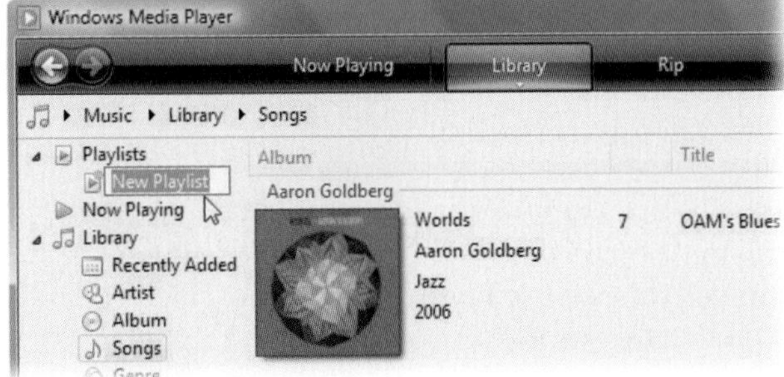

- We're going to call this **My First Compilation**. Type in the title and then press Enter↵.

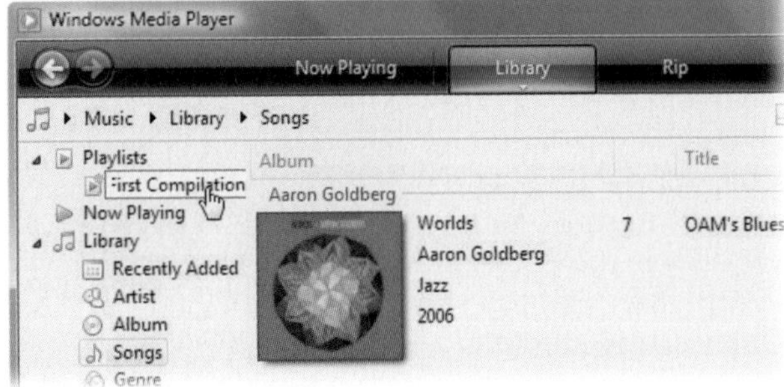

● Here's the new playlist. Note that the **Create Playlist** command has now been re-instated above **My First Compilation**. You can always create a new playlist by clicking on this again.

● At the same time as creating the new playlist name on the left of the main window, Media Player also opens a new window on the right. As the hint here suggests (**Drag items here to add them to your new playlist**), you can now drag and drop tracks from any album in the library onto the new playlist.

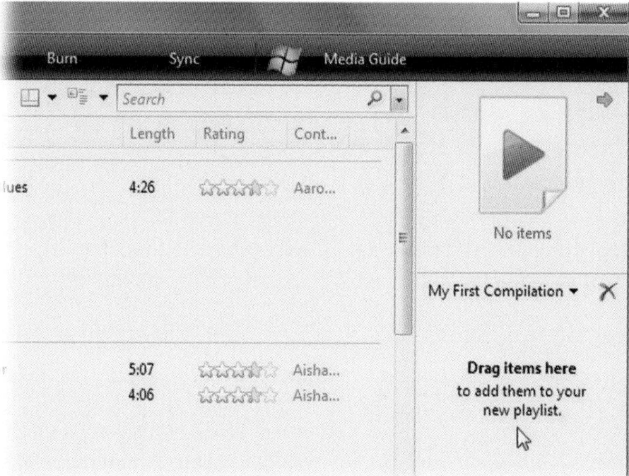

ADDING TRACKS TO THE PLAYLIST

● So, pick a track you'd like to add to the new playlist by clicking on it once with the left mouse button.

● Then, holding down the left mouse button, drag the track across to the empty playlist window on the right.

- When the track is over the playlist window, let go of the left mouse button and the track will drop into place.

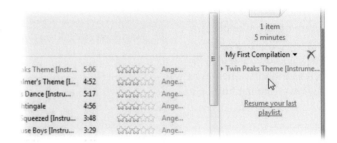

- You can continue to add tracks one by one in this way. However, if there are a few tracks from the same artist to add to the list, you can add more than one at a time. Click on the first of the consecutive tracks you want to add.

- Next, move the cursor down to the last of the tracks you want to copy from this artist and, holding down the ⇧Shift button on the keyboard, click the last track. This will highlight all the tracks between the two.

- Next, click on the highlighted tracks and, still holding down the left mouse button, drag them over into the playlist window.

● When the tracks are hovering over the playlist, let go of the left mouse button and they'll drop into place as before. Then click the **Save Playlist** button.

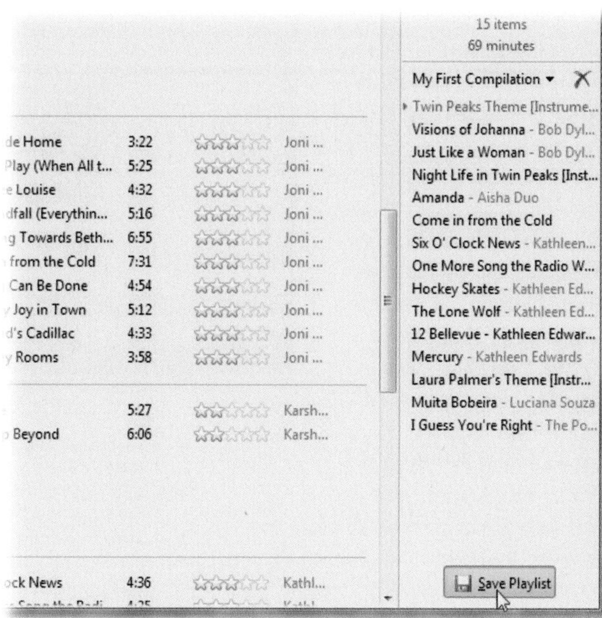

LISTENING TO THE PLAYLIST

● To listen to the playlist you've created, move the cursor up to the **My First Compilation** heading on the left.

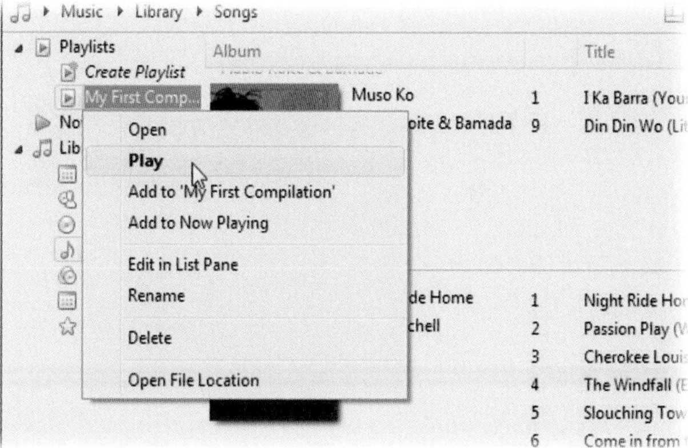

● Next, click on it once with the right mouse button and choose **Play** from the pop-up menu.

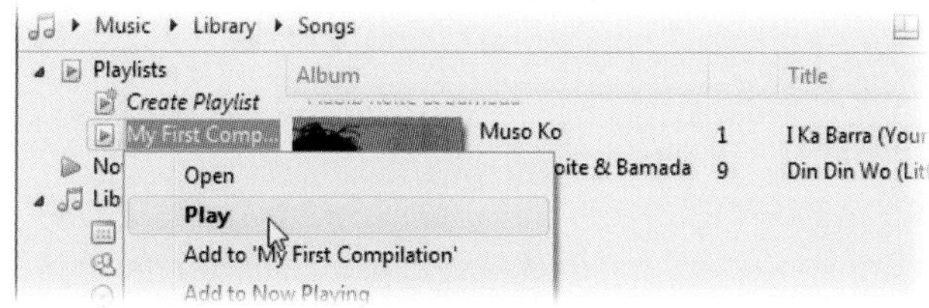

● The first track in the playlist begins to play. Here we've moved the cursor down to the bottom left of the Media Player window to show the album cover of the first track, its name, and track progress, which is indicated by the narrow blue green horizontal bar that moves from left to right as the song plays.

ADDING MORE TRACKS TO THE LIST

● If, while you're listening you decide you'd like to add another track, try this. Click on the track name that you wish to add with the right mouse button and this menu will appear.

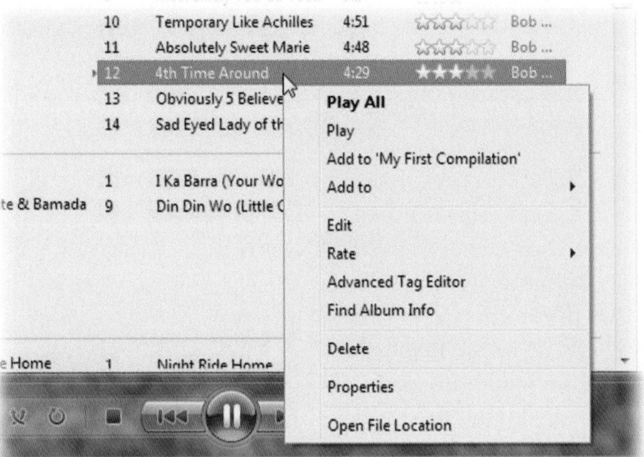

● Slide the cursor down to Add to **'My First Compilation'** and click once to select.

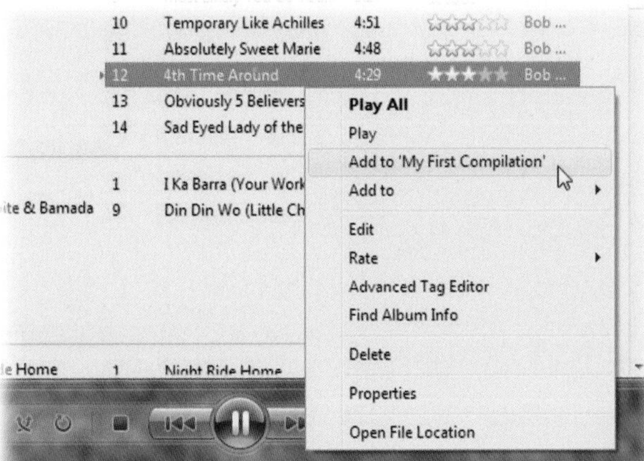

● Here's the track that we just added in place at the foot of the playlist. Some people prefer to add tracks in this manner rather than dragging and dropping.

EDITING A PLAYLIST

Once you've created a playlist, you can add or remove tracks and re-arrange the playlist in various different simply using a few straightforward commands. This helps to keep your playlists fresh and also allows you to refine them quickly and easily.

SHUFFLING THE PLAYLIST

● Let's start by changing this playlist around a little. Move the cursor up to the **My First Compilation** button and then click on the arrow to open the drop-down list.

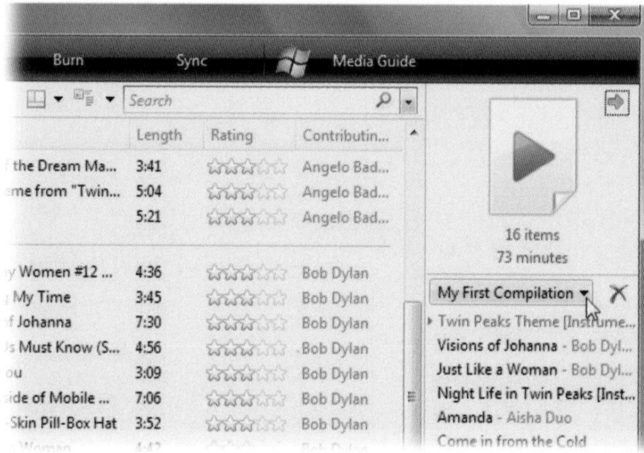

● When the menu opens, click the **Shuffle List Now** option once with the left mouse button.

● Media Player scrambles the playlist so that the same tracks appear, but in a different order.

SORTING THE PLAYLIST

● If you want to re-arrange the playlist in a rather more ordered fashion, then choose a different option from the same menu. Open the drop-down list and this time select **Sort** and choose one of the sort methods–in this example we've chosen **By Title**.

● Again, Media Player changes the playing order, this time sorting the songs into alphabetical order by their titles.

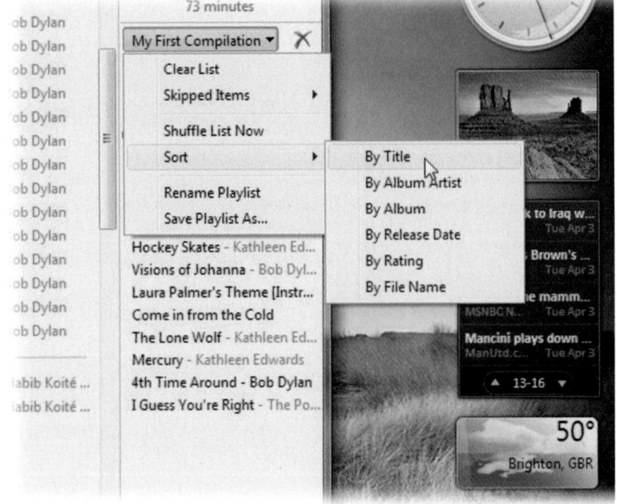

RE-ARRANGING BY DRAG AND DROP

● You can also just drag and drop songs in the list into a different order. To do this, click on a song with the left mouse button.

● Still holding down the left mouse button, drag the song into a new position– here we're moving it up a couple of songs.

● Here's the song after it has been dropped into its new position.

USING AN MP3 PLAYER

One of the pleasures of having a library of digital music that you've taken from CDs or downloaded from the web-based music stores is that you can copy it from your PC to a portable device. That way you can enjoy music when you're commuting to work or out walking or driving in the car. To get ready for this section, we've created some more playlists as described earlier in the chapter.

PLUGGING IN AN MP3 PLAYER

● Follow the instructions that came with your portable digital music player to set it up. Some come with their own software, which they may recommend you install, but usually, this isn't necessary. Just plug it into a spare USB socket on your PC and Vista will set up the required software without you having to do anything.

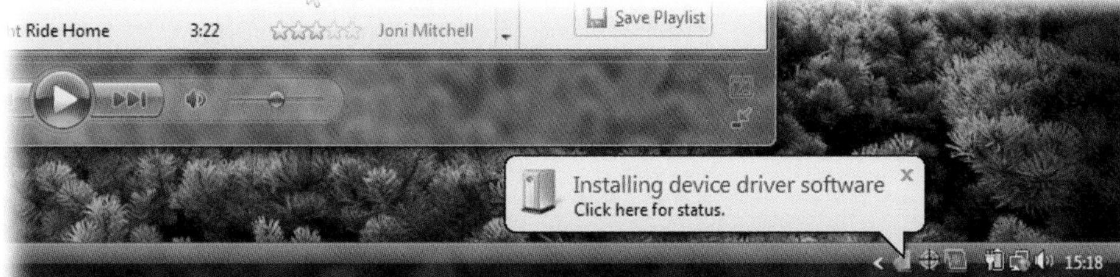

● After a moment, the **Device Setup** dialog box appears. Windows asks you to **Name your device**– this is useful if you want to use several devices with your music library–and highlights the **Audio Player** text ready for you to type over it.

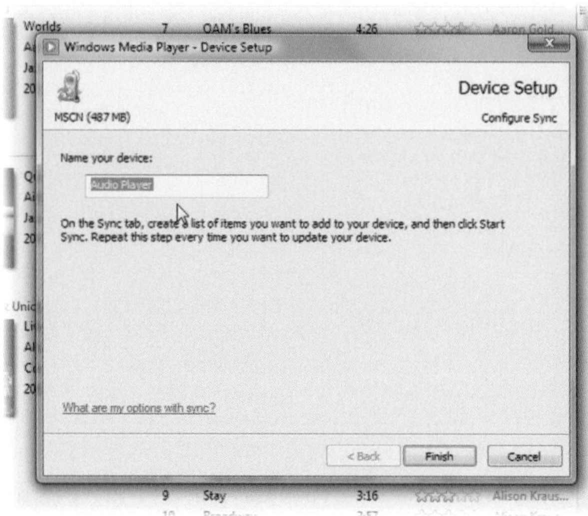

● We're going to call this **My MP3 Player**, so type this here.

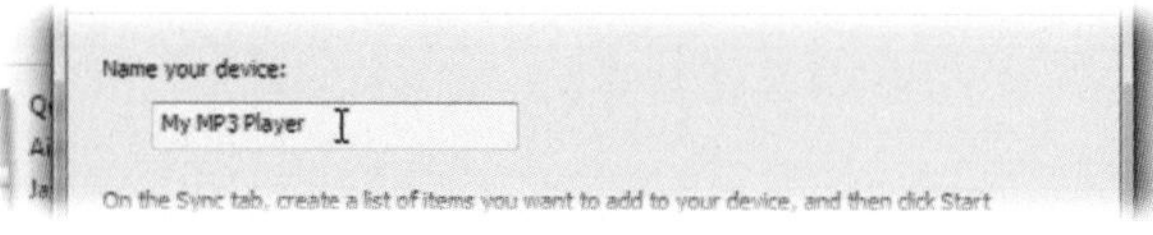

● Click the **Finish** button to conclude setting up the MP3 player. It's now ready to work with Media Player 11.

DIGITAL MUSIC FORMATS

When a program like Media Player rips a CD, it converts each track into a special format that's good for storing music, because it's able to strip out the bits of the sound spectrum that the human ear can't hear (and therefore doesn't miss), thus making each song take up less space. This is important because it means you can fit more songs onto a portable player; songs sold by music stores are recorded in the same way so they download more quickly. There are many competing formats, but the three most commonly used are Microsoft's WMA, the AAC format used by Apple, and MP3, which is used by everyone else. In practice, it is usually possible to convert a song recorded in one format so that it will play on a device that supports a different format.

SHUFFLING MUSIC TO THE PLAYER

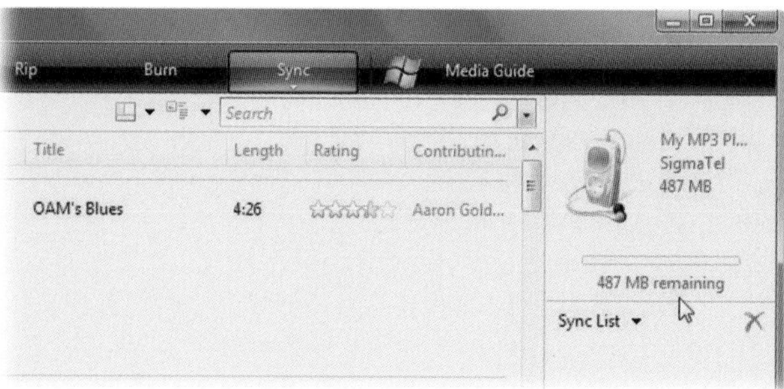

● The MP3 player now appears in the right-hand window. Media Player gives it a name, tells you its capacity (in this example it's 487MB), and indicates how much space is free for songs.

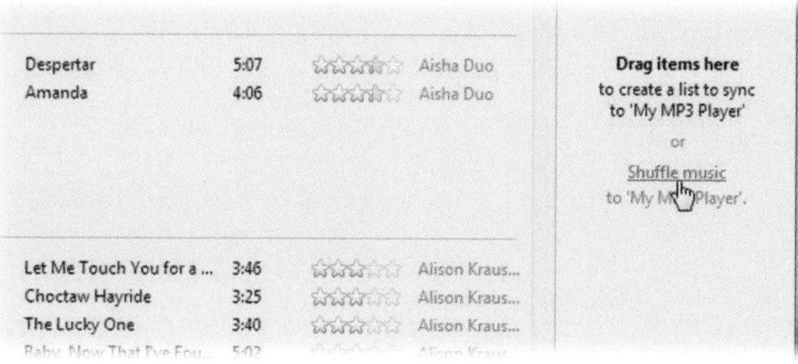

● There are lots of different ways to get music onto your player but we're going to use the quickest one first. Just move the cursor over the **Shuffle music** link in the right-hand window and then click it once with the left mouse button.

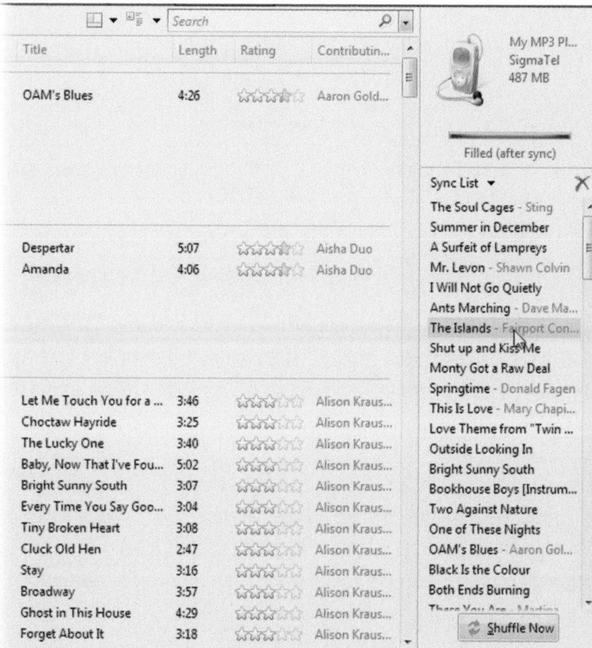

● Media Player grabs as many songs as will fit on your portable device at random and shuffles them over to the player window.

● You will notice that the "meter" above the track list is now red, fully over to one side, and marked **Filled**. Obviously, the actual number of songs will vary depending on how capacious the portable player is and the length of each individual song.

● If you thought that was quick, that's because the music hasn't actually been copied across yet! To do that, click the **Shuffle Now** button at the bottom of the right-hand column.

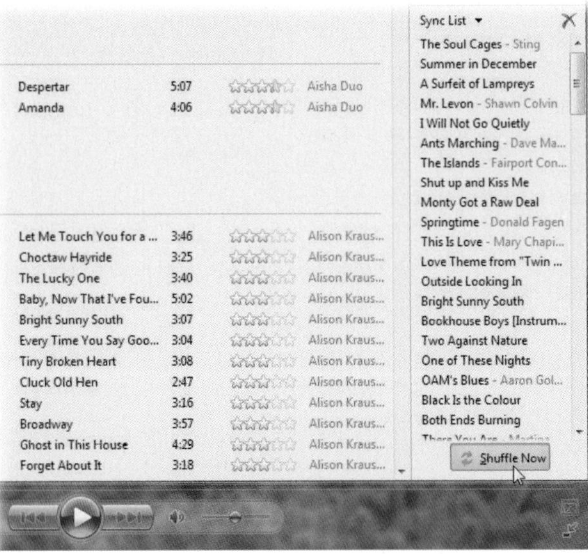

● Media Player asks if you're sure, pointing out that shuffling music onto the portable player will overwrite any music that's already stored there. Since this particularly player is empty, that's fine. Click **Yes** to continue.

APPLE'S ITUNES

Windows Media Player has a very famous competitor–iTunes, the music program developed by Apple to be both the librarian for its fantastically successful iPod series of portable digital music players, and the front end for its equally successful online music store. With the release of version 11, Media Player can approach iTunes in terms of looks and features and, as we'll see later on, it has good links with online music stores. However, if you want to use an iPod, then you should manage your music collection with iTunes because the two products (or three if you count the store) are designed to work together. If you have another brand of portable player–for example a Zune or a Creative Labs' Zen series–then Media Player is an excellent choice.

● Here you can see the tracks being copied across to the portable music player. Synchronizing from scratch like this takes some time–these 246 tracks took about 25 minutes–but since the process works unattended, you can leave it to its own devices and go and do something else.

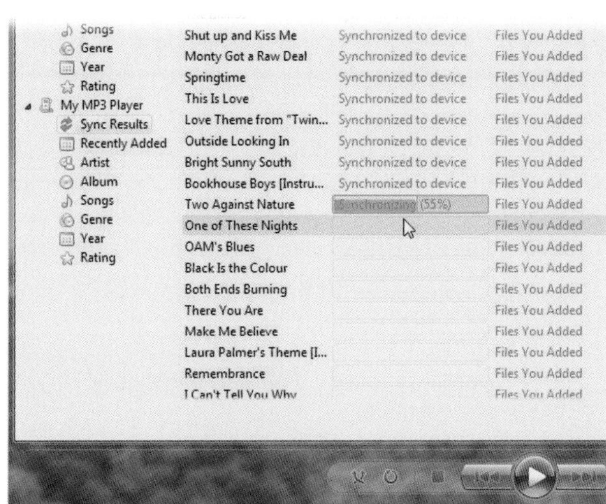

● If you have a lot of files, you can see how well it's progressing by looking at the percentage figure seen here to the right of Media Player's transport controls.

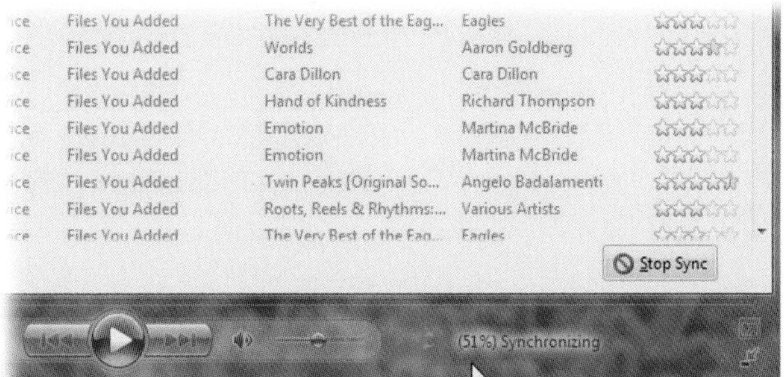

● When all the tracks have been copied, Media Player will display a message in the right-hand window saying that **You can now disconnect 'My MP3 player'**.

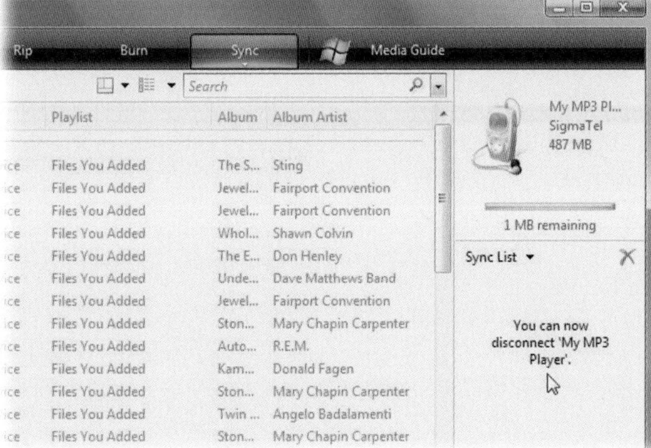

Syncing with a Portable Player

Although you can drag and drop playlists to a portable player that is plugged into your PC, there's an alternative–setting both up so that they synchronize with each other when the device is plugged in. Once a list of songs is synchronized, every time you alter that list by adding or removing songs in Media Player, those changes are reflected in what gets copied across to the portable player.

OPENING THE SYNC MENU

● With the portable player still plugged in, move the cursor up to the **Sync** button and click on it with the left mouse button to open the menu.

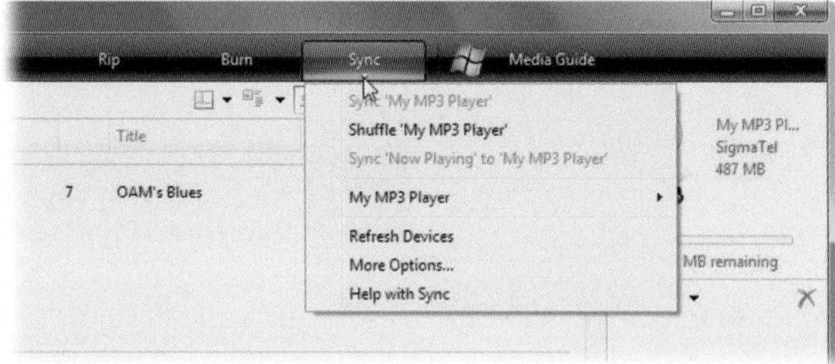

● Slide the cursor down to the **My MP3 Player** entry and a sub menu will pop out to the side.

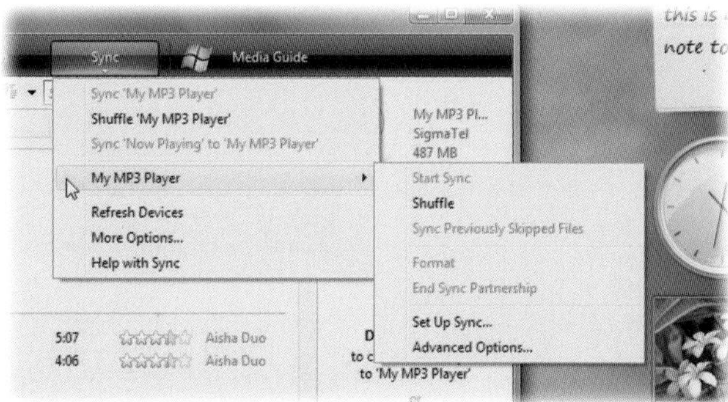

● Remember that we named the device My MP3 Player earlier on? Slide the cursor down to the **Set Up Sync** menu item and then click on it once to select that option.

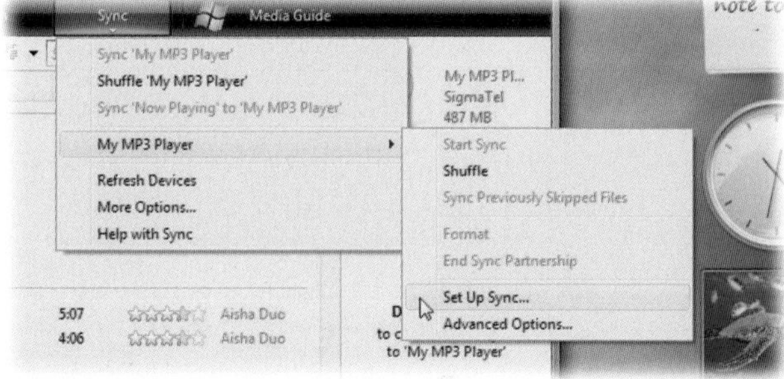

USING THE DEVICE SETUP DIALOG

● Here's the **Device Setup** dialog box, where you can configure the playlists you want to sync to your portable player. We haven't elected to synchronize the player automatically, so most of the options in the dialog are grayed out– meaning that they're not available.

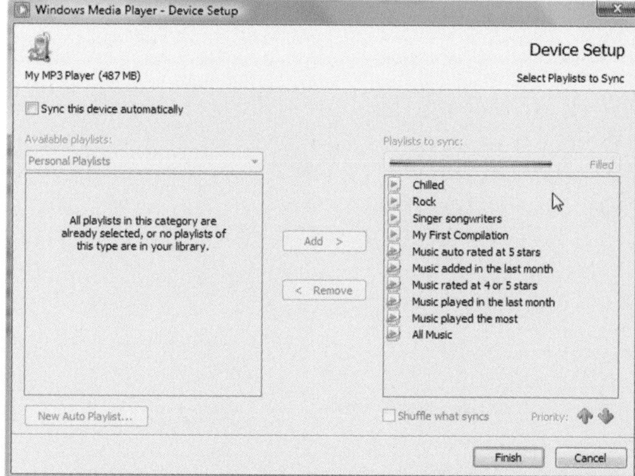

● Move the cursor over to the **Sync this device automatically** tick box.

● Click on it once to activate the feature. By default, Media Player will try to synchronize all of the playlists in the right-hand column without you asking it to. On a player with a large capacity this works fine. On a small player like this, all the tracks won't fit– hence the red bar along the top indicating the player is **Filled**.

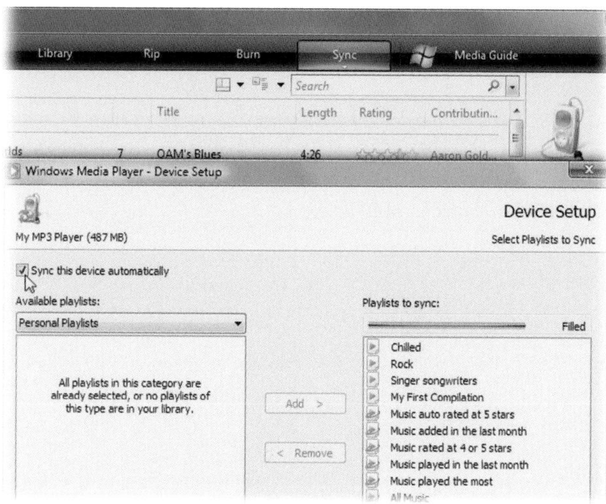

PORTABLE PLAYERS

There are a wide range of portable music players available, ranging from inexpensive models with 256MB of memory, which can only hold about 40 songs, right up to monsters with 80GB, which can store nearly 20,000 songs. Typically, portable players offer more than 10 hours of battery life, won't skip, even if you use them while exercising, and come with a range of add-ons such as speakers, cases, and connections so they can be used in the car.

EMPTYING THE SYNC PLAYLIST

● Let's remove Media Player's choices from this column and set up our own. Start by clicking once on the first playlist with the left mouse button.

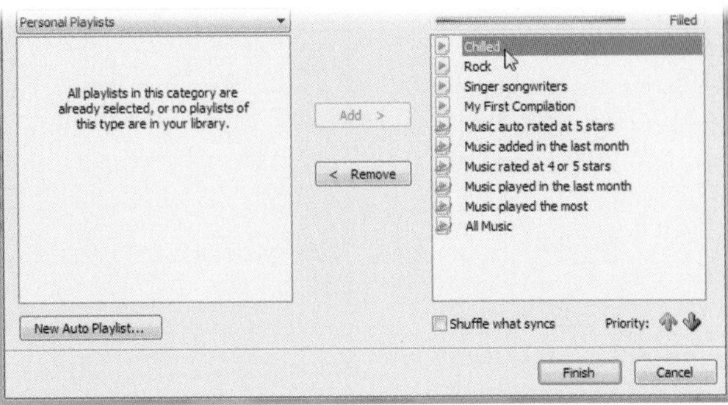

● Next, move the cursor down to the last playlist in this column. Don't click yet.

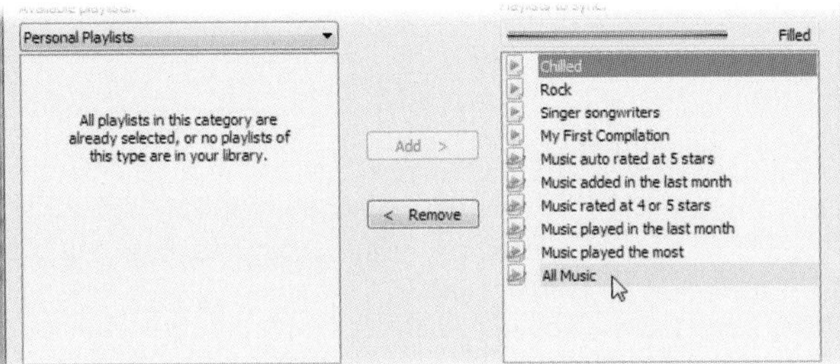

● Hold down the ⇧ Shift key on your keyboard and then click on the last item in the list with the left mouse button to highlight all the playlists.

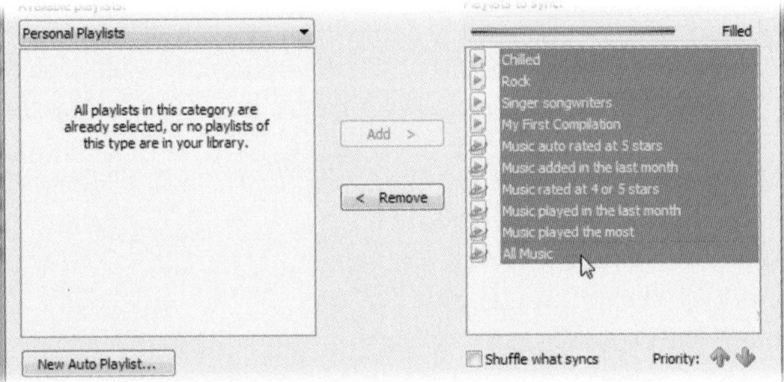

DRAG AND DROP ALBUMS

Of course, as we said in the introduction to Syncing with a Portable Player, you don't have to sync with your MP3 player if you don't want to. Instead, simply plug in your portable player, drag across the albums you want to include on it, and drop them into the right-hand window like this.

● Next, click the **Remove** button to move the playlists over to the left-hand column.

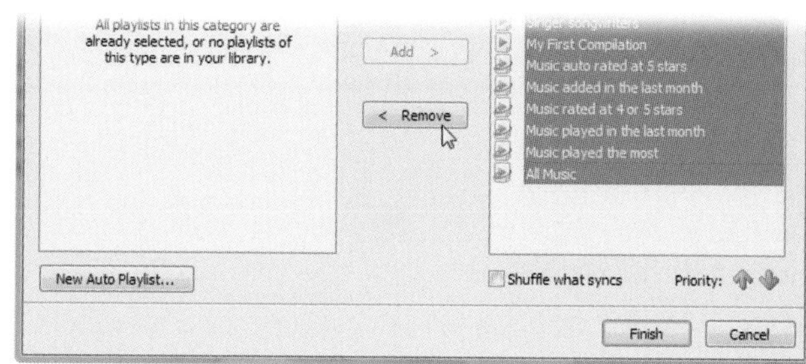

● The playlists created by Media Player vanish from the list of available choices, but the ones we created are now in the left-hand column, available for use if we want them. Note that the "meter" on the other side now reads **0% full**. That's because with the current sync setup (i.e. no playlists) the portable player will be empty before and after syncing.

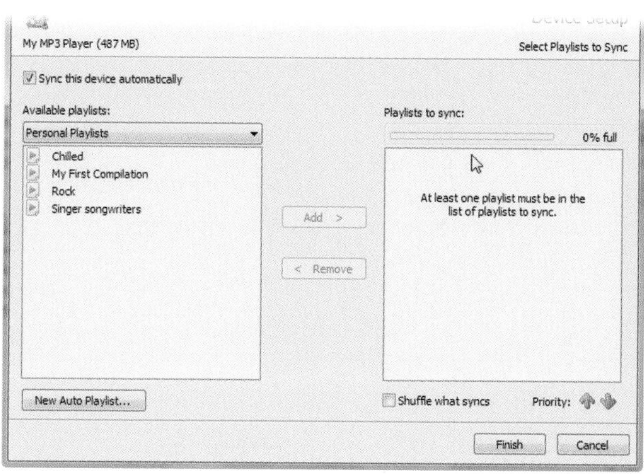

POPULATING THE SYNC PLAYLIST

● To start moving playlists back into the right-hand window–and start filling the portable player up again–click on one of the lists with the left mouse button. We're clicking on **My First Compilation**.

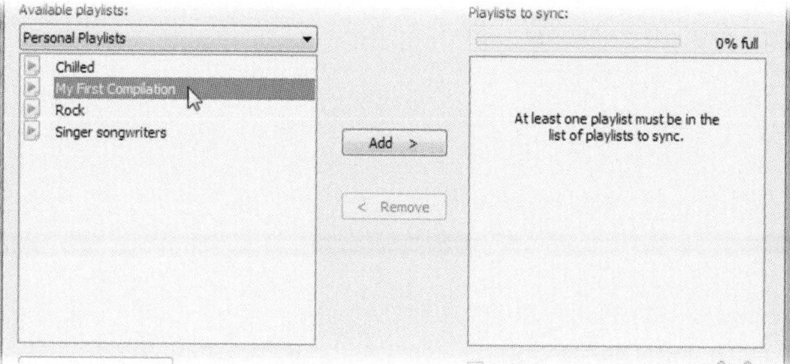

● With the playlist still highlighted, click the **Add** button in the center of the dialog box.

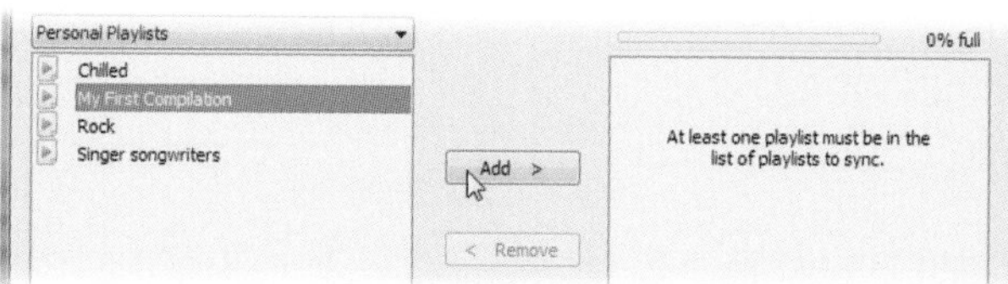

● The playlist called **My First Compilation** has moved over to the right-hand pane. Note, too, that the meter above it has moved to indicate that the player will be **14% full** after this synchronization.

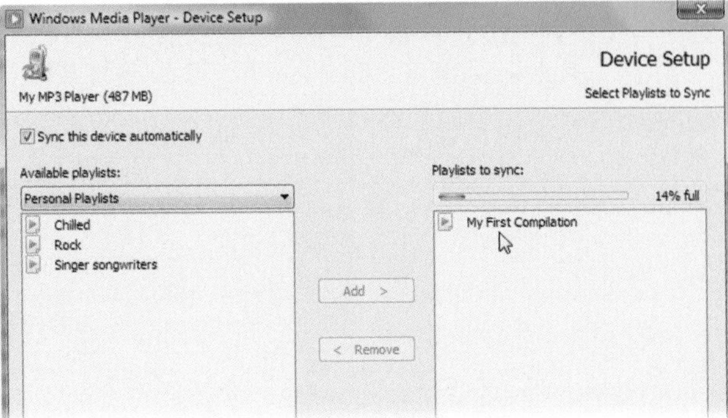

● To fill the player some more, move the cursor to the available playlists on the left and click on one to select. Then, click the **Add** button in the center and the playlist will now be added to the sync list on the right.

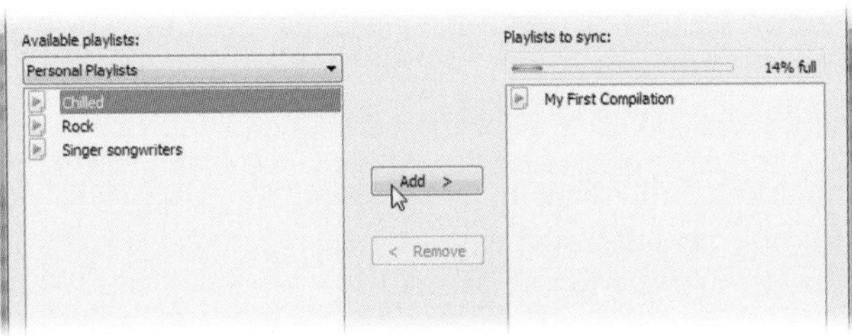

● Now there are two playlists in the pane on the right-hand side. Note again that the meter now registers that the MP3 player will be 50% full after the synchronization. You can keep adding playlists until the portable device is full.

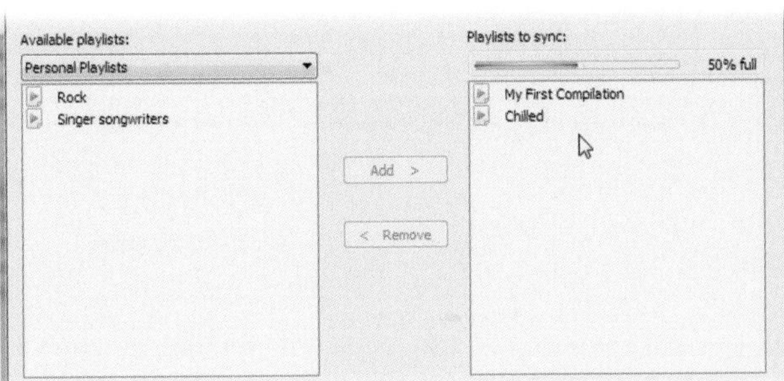

● To end the device set up, click the **Finish** button at the bottom of the dialog box with the left mouse button.

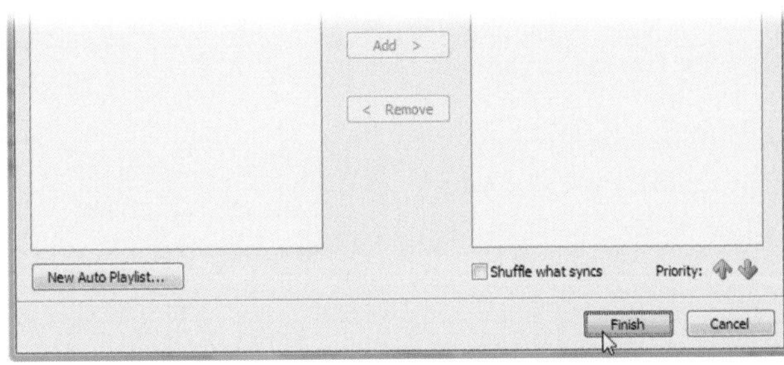

AUTOMATIC SYNCHRONIZATION

● Windows now pops up a little message from the Notification Area telling us that the device **My MP3 Player is now set up to sync.**

● Media Player now automatically synchronizes with the MP3 player and again, pops up a little box here to tell us what's going on. From now on, whenever this player is plugged in, Media Player will take a look at the latest versions of the playlists and then make sure that they are synchronized with those on the portable player, adding or removing tracks as necessary.

● The synchronization is now complete. The player is just over half full.

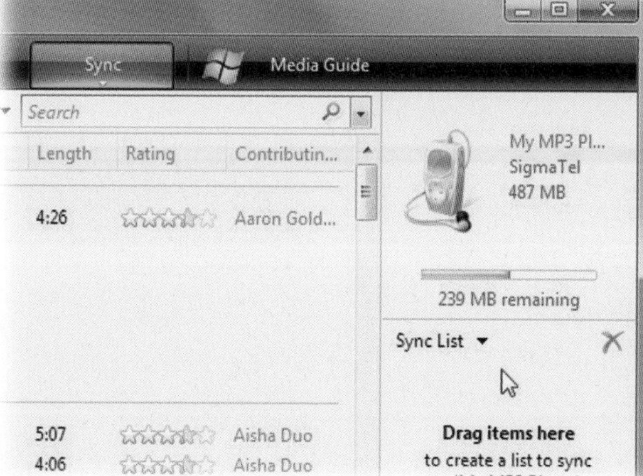

Buying Music Online

As well as digitizing your own music collection, you can also buy individual tracks and entire albums electronically from an online store.

Online Music Stores

There are many benefits to buying music online. You only have to buy the tracks you like rather than the whole album, you can shop when it suits you, and listen to songs before you decide. Also, when you buy something, all the track information and album artwork is included and downloaded to Media Player automatically.

FINDING A MUSIC STORE

● First, you have to find your store so, with Media Player loaded and an Internet connection available, click on the **Media Guide** button.

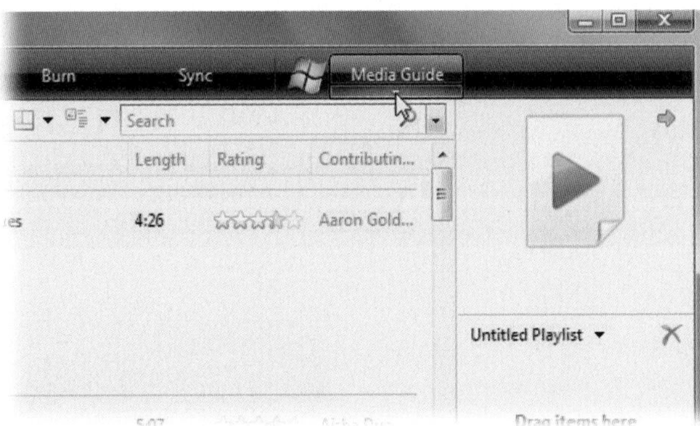

● When the menu opens, move the cursor down to **Browse all Online Stores** and then click once to select this option.

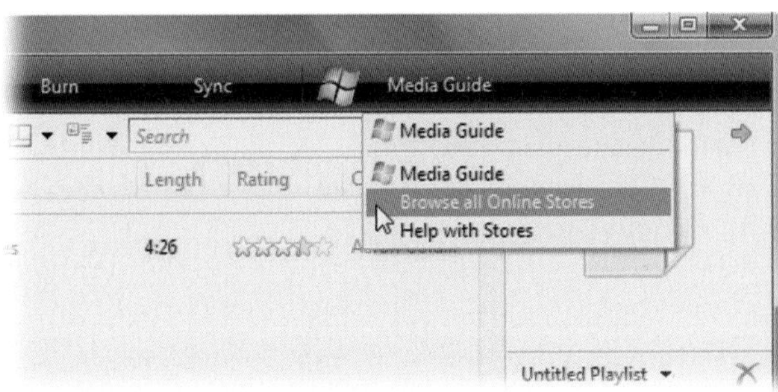

● The stores you see may be different, depending on where you live, but the principle will be the same. Choose which store you'd like to explore and click on it once with the left mouse button. Here, we're choosing eMusic.

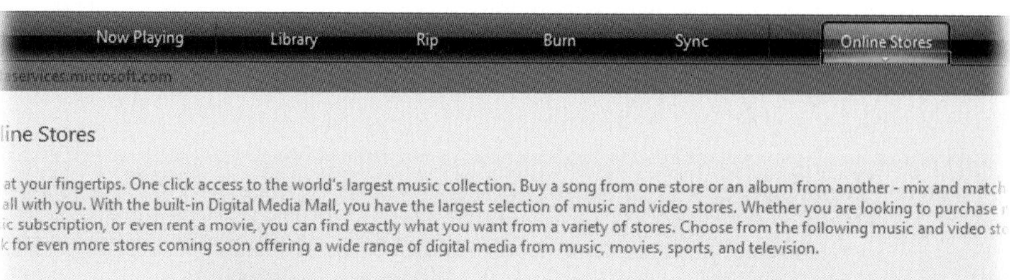

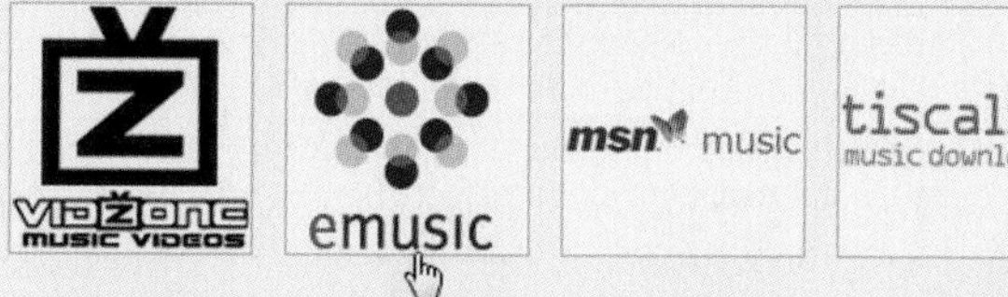

● Windows displays one of its "are-you-sure?" dialog boxes. Click **Yes** to continue.

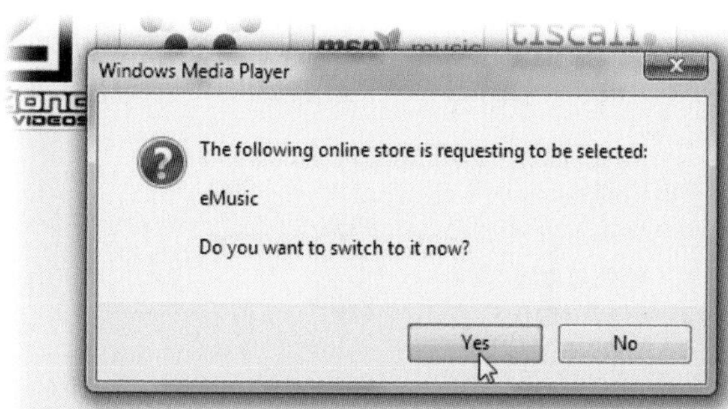

ILLEGAL DOWNLOADS

The online music stores that we mention on these pages all sell music that respects the copyright of the authors and owners and is therefore legal. Some sites–especially so-called file-sharing sites–do not. Music downloaded from an unsavory illegal source is likely to be of lower quality and may be infected with spyware; it may not even be the right track or the entire track. The price of legal music downloads is falling all the time and because you can pick and choose the songs you buy, there's really no reason to look elsewhere.

BROWSING A MUSIC STORE

● Media Player has links to a number of different music stores, and the one you choose may look different to this. However, they'll all work in more or less the same way, so we're going to spend a few pages exploring this one–eMusic.com–to show you how a typical online music store works. Here you can see the front page has various genres, some new arrivals, a search box, and links to various other parts of the eMusic website. To get started, we're going to click on the **Country/Folk** genre.

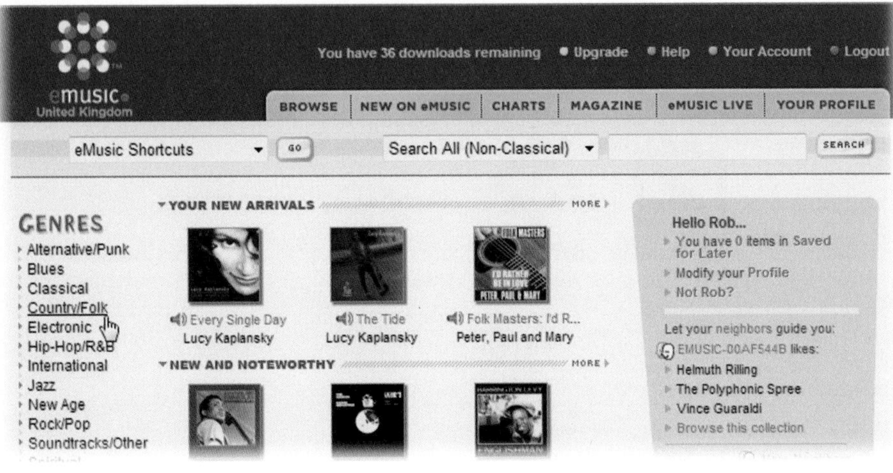

● The site breaks Country/Folk down into sub-styles on the left and offers some essential albums and favorites in the center of the screen. We're going to click on the **MORE** link here to see what else is new.

● We've scrolled down the list of new albums and found one that we like the look of–it's by Ryan Adams. We can click on the album to find out more.

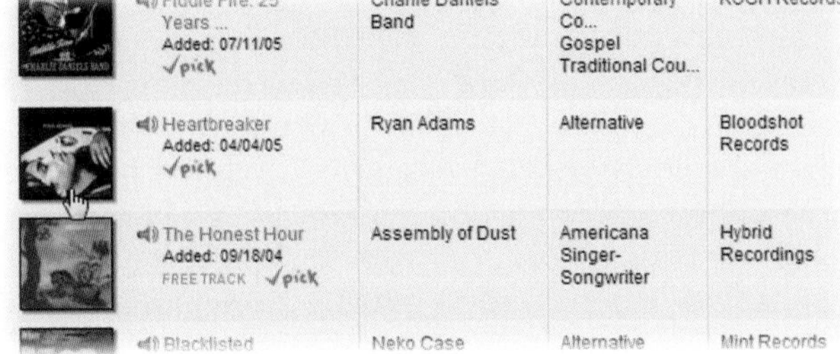

AUDITIONING A MUSIC TRACK

● This page shows the album cover, as well as a star rating and each of the tracks in a list. Music sites let you listen to snippets of songs so you can decide whether to download them or not. Clicking the little speaker icon next to any track plays a 30-second clip in Media Player.

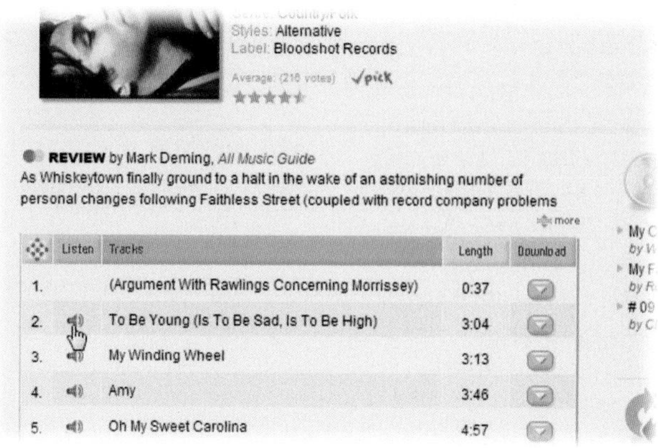

FINDING A RELATED ARTIST

● We don't particularly care for that track and having scrolled down the list and listened to one or two others, have decided not to buy the album. This is where another one of eMusic's features comes in handy–looking over at the **Related Artists** links, we can see Victoria Williams. Let's click on her and see what they've got in stock.

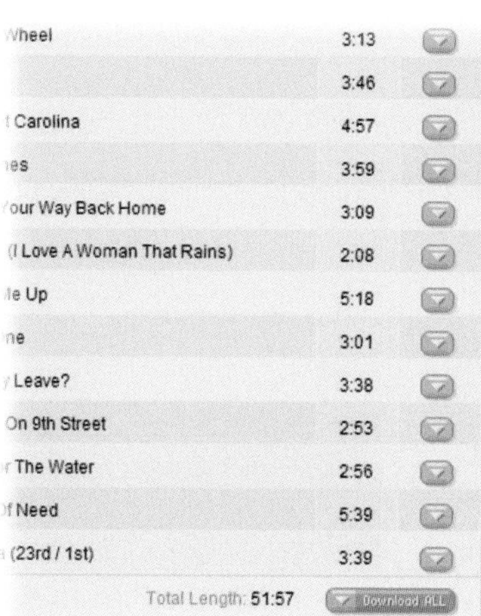

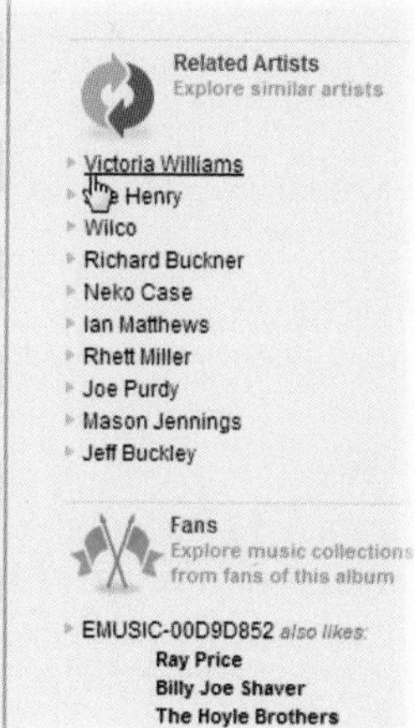

● This opens Victoria William's page on eMusic, and there are a number of her albums for sale. Here we're clicking on the first one in the list.

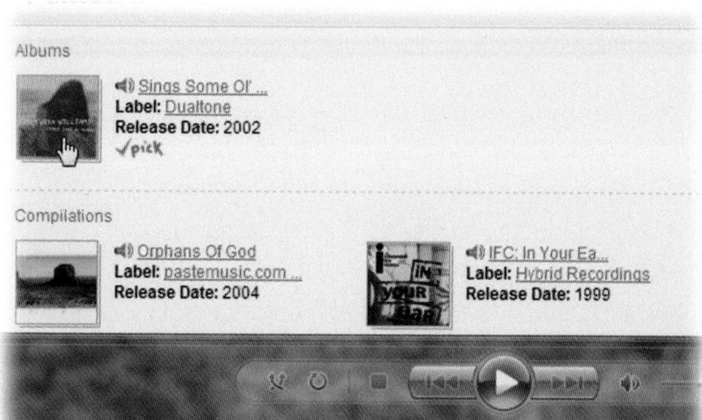

DOWNLOADING A TRACK

● As before, we can audition any of these songs and, having found one we like, we're going to buy it by clicking the blue **Download** button (see Paying for Music, below, to find out how this works).

	Listen	Tracks	Length	Download
1.		Moon River	3:18	
2.		Blue Skies	2:23	
3.		And Roses And Roses	2:30	
4.		Over The Rainbow	3:58	
5.		My Funny Valentine	2:50	
6.		Keep Sweeping Cobwebs Off The Moon	3:02	
7.		I'm Old Fashioned	3:12	

● After a moment, eMusic opens another screen and starts to download the song. On a reasonable broadband connection, this will take 20 to 30 seconds.

● When the track has finished downloading it's marked as **Completed** and we can carry on shopping by clicking the **eMusic Store** link at the top.

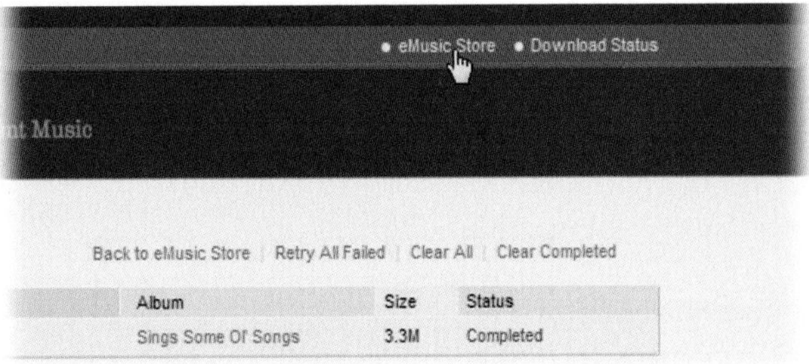

PAYING FOR MUSIC

Online music stores take money in various ways. Some sell monthly or annual subscriptions so, for a certain price, you can download 30 or so songs a month. Others take your credit card details and then debit the card whenever you buy music; most offer tokens that other people can buy as gifts. Prices can vary greatly between services, but most have some real bargains tucked away, and the choice is impressive and improving every day.

FINDING AN ARTIST

● This time, instead of browsing by categories, we're going to look for a specific artist by name. Move the cursor up to the search box and click there once with the left mouse button.

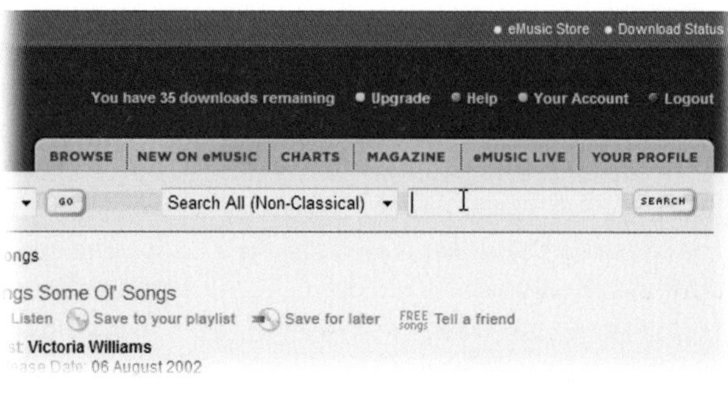

● In this example, we're going to search for the banjo player, Alison Brown. Just type her name into the empty box and then click the **Search** button.

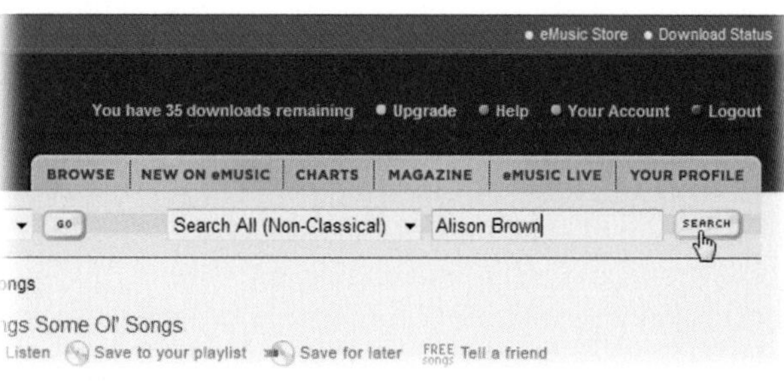

● The search only takes a few seconds and returns a link to Alison Brown at the top of the results list. Click on it with the left mouse button.

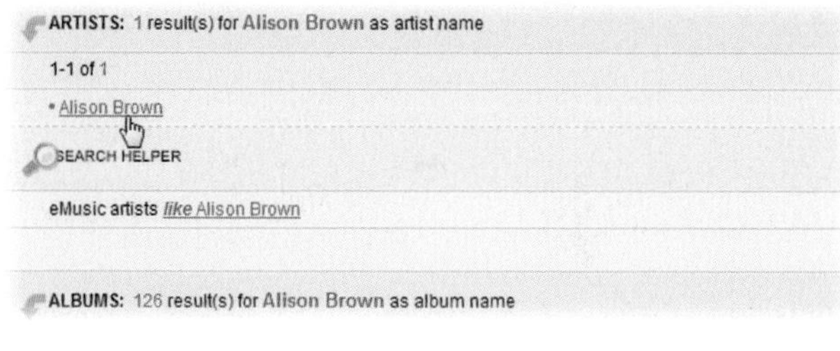

● Alison Brown's page has a number of albums, which we can open by clicking on them like this.

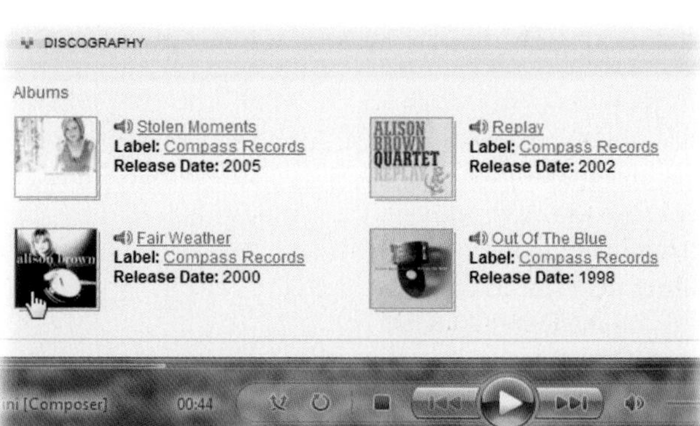

DIGITAL RIGHTS MANAGEMENT

This is a thorny subject. Digital Rights Management, or DRM, tries to balance the rights of the people who own the music we download with the rights of the consumers who purchase it. In the past, the way that DRM has been implemented has caused problems for users, sometimes specifically preventing them from playing music that they've purchased legally on the device of their choice. There are various technical and legal reasons for this, and their precise interpretation will vary according to the laws in your particular territory. Thankfully, there's been some movement recently that suggests online stores are planning to remove DRM from their downloads completely and trust to the consumers' sense of fair play. No matter what the law says, companies are not interested in taking legal action against people who download a track and then copy it onto an MP3 player for when they go jogging, or onto a CD for use in the car; they are interested in pursuing those people who flout copyright for profit, ripping off artists and selling cheap knock-offs at cut-down prices.

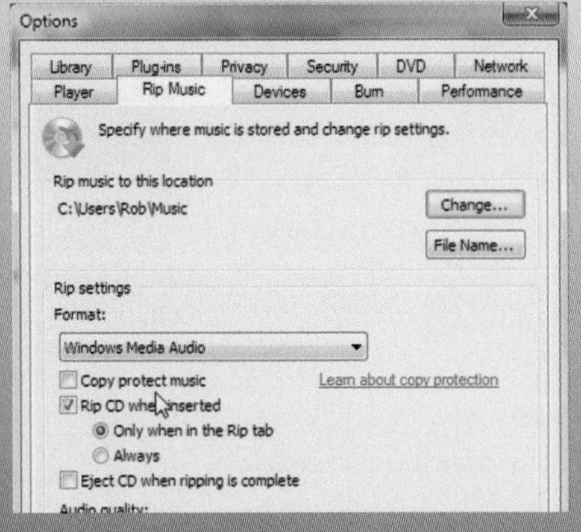

DOWNLOADING A WHOLE ALBUM

● As before, we can audition as many of the tracks as we like, and as often as we want, so that we can decide whether the album is worth buying. In this instance, we think it is, and rather than downloading each track individually, we can buy the whole album at once, by clicking the **Download All** button like this.

	Listen	Tracks	Length	Download
1.		Late On Arrival	2:32	
2.		Fair Weather	3:06	
3.		Poe's Pickin' Party	3:45	
4.		Everyday I Write The Book	3:30	
5.		The Devil Went Down To Berkeley	4:23	
6.		Hummingbird	3:58	
7.		Girl's Breakdown	3:44	
8.		Everybody's Talkin'	3:47	
9.		Deep Gap	3:54	
10.		Shake And Howdy	3:14	
11.		Leaving Cottondale	3:21	
12.		Sweet Thing	1:42	

Listen to ALL — Total Length: 40:56 — Download ALL

● Here you can see the download screen with nearly half of the album downloaded. Typically, the downloading process is automatic and you don't have to do anything.

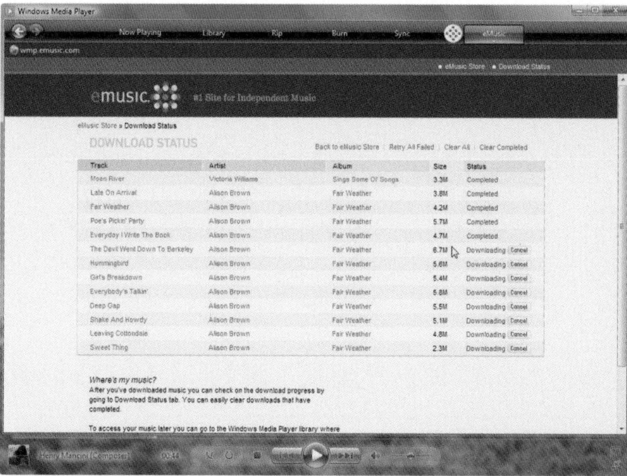

● When the album has finished downloading, you can switch back to Media Player's library and listen to the album by clicking the **Library** button at the top.

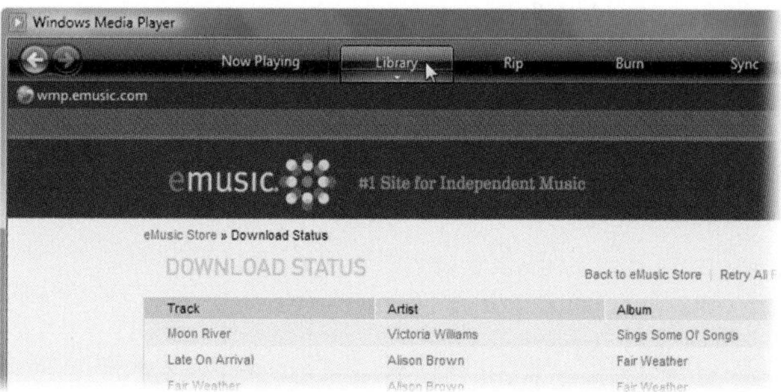

● You can see the Alison Brown album that we've just downloaded, complete with all the track information and the album cover.

BURNING A MUSIC CD

Along with ripping CDs you already own, you can use your PC to create your own compilation CDs from the music in Media Player's library.

PREPARING TO BURN A CD

It used to matter what kind of blank CDs you bought, but now the technology is so advanced that even the cheapest ones will produce good results and play on most modern hi-fis and car stereos. Remember that you should always respect the copyright of the artists who created the music and observe the relevant laws that apply in your country before copying anything onto a blank CD.

PUTTING A CD IN THE DRIVE

- Simply pop a blank CD into the CD drive of your PC and wait for a moment. Windows Vista will recognize it as a blank disc and ask what you want to do with it. Click the first choice–**Burn an audio CD**.

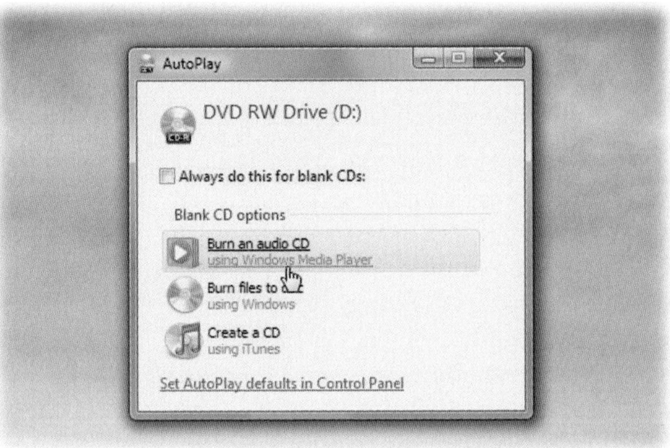

- Media Player will load. In the right-hand panel you can see the blank disc with the meter telling us that there's nearly 80 minutes recording time remaining.

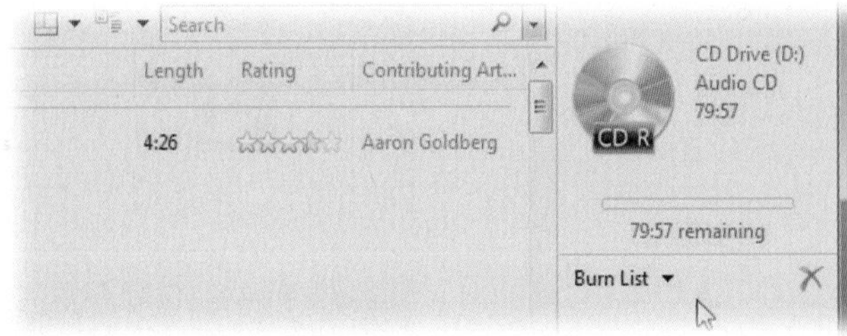

FILLING THE BLANK CD

● You can drag individual tracks or entire albums across to the right-hand panel. Alternatively, you can use one of your playlists, and that's what we're going to do in this example. Here we're clicking on the **My First Compilation** playlist.

● You can see here that we've dragged the playlist across to the panel on the right-hand side.

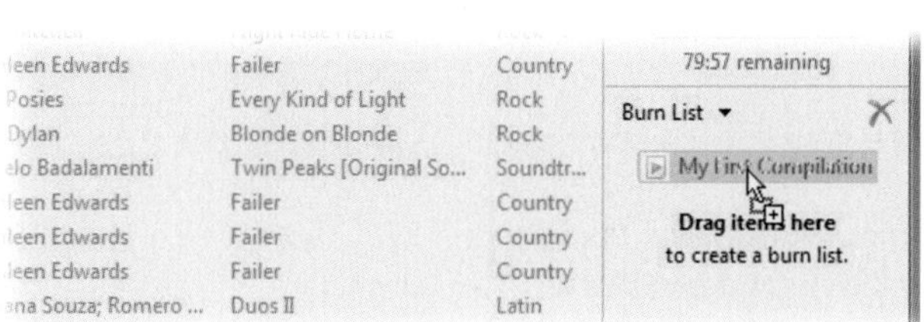

● Let go of the left mouse button and all of the tracks in the playlist drop into place in the right-hand panel ready to be burned to the blank CD in the drive.

● Note that the meter now tells us there's just over five minutes of space remaining on the CD.

● There's room for one more track on this CD, so let's move the cursor over to the **Songs** category in the left-hand list and click on it once with the left mouse button.

● When the list of songs is displayed in the main window, pick one that's short enough to fit the remaining space and click on it with the left mouse button.

● Still holding down the left mouse button, drag it across to the list on the right and position it where you'd like it to appear in the track listing–here we're dropping it in on the end.

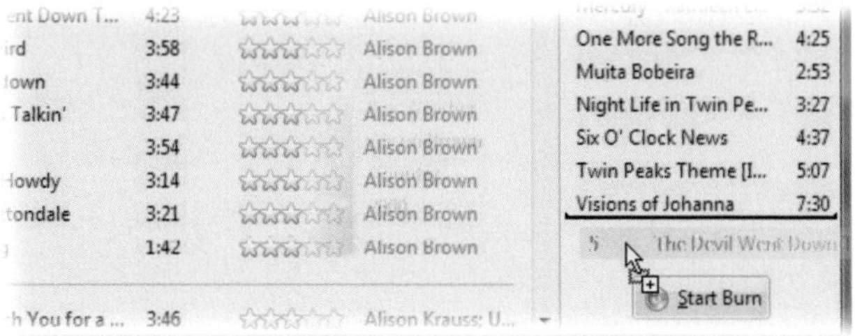

● Click the **Start Burn** button at the bottom of the track list to start creating the CD.

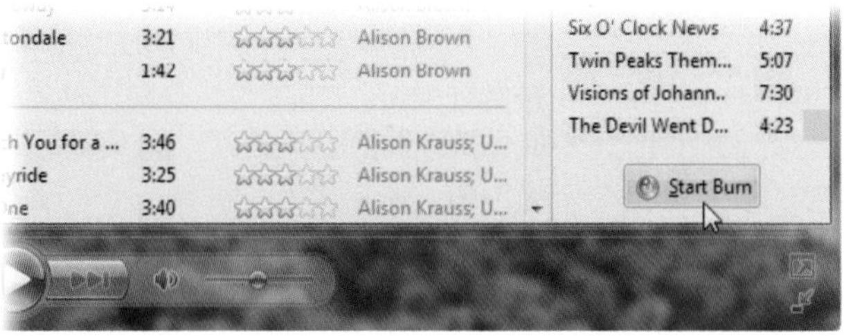

● Here we are nearly halfway through the process. Depending on the speed of your CD drive and some other technical factors, it may take up to 10 minutes to burn a CD like this.

VISUALIZATIONS

Media Player includes a wide selection of visualizations–colorful animations that play along to the music. You can choose which one you'd like to see by clicking on the arrow underneath the **Now Playing** button and then choosing **Visualizations** from the menu, followed by **Alchemy, Bars, and Waves** or **Battery** and then choosing a visualization from there.

● When the CD is finished, the disk tray will pop out and all the tracks will be marked **Complete**.

Title	Status	Length	Album
Amanda	Complete	4:06	Quiet Songs
Come in from the Cold	Complete	7:31	Night Ride Home
Hockey Skates	Complete	4:29	Failer
I Guess You're Right	Complete	3:32	Every Kind of Light
Just Like a Woman	Complete	4:43	Blonde on Blonde
Laura Palmer's Theme [I...	Complete	4:52	Twin Peaks [Original So...
The Lone Wolf	Complete	4:55	Failer
Mercury	Complete	3:32	Failer
One More Song the Radi...	Complete	4:25	Failer
Muita Bobeira	Complete	2:53	Duos II
Night Life in Twin Peaks ...	Complete	3:27	Twin Peaks [Original So...
Six O' Clock News	Complete	4:37	Failer
Twin Peaks Theme [Instr...	Complete	5:07	Twin Peaks [Original So...
Visions of Johanna	Complete	7:30	Blonde on Blonde
The Devil Went Down T...	Complete	4:23	Fair Weather

PLAYING THE FINISHED CD

● Imagine now that we've taken the CD out and put it in another computer. This is what happens. Windows recognizes that it's a music CD and displays the **AutoPlay** dialog. Click the first choice–**Play audio CD using Windows Media Player**.

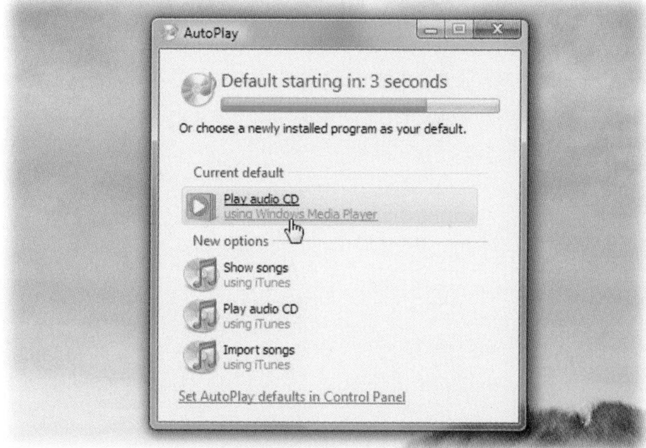

● Here's the CD playing back. Windows puts the track list in the right-hand panel and plays a striking animation that throbs and pulses in time to the music in the middle.

● All the track and artist names are in place and the CD we've created behaves just like a shop-bought CD. It can be played back on nearly all modern stereos.

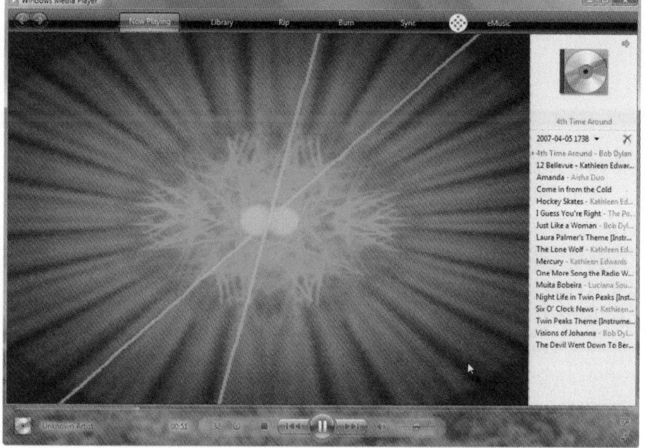

PLAYING DVDS

With their crisp, flat panel displays and wide screens, today's home PCs–and notebooks–make excellent miniature cinemas and come with everything you need to enjoy watching DVDs.

WATCHING A DVD

Trying to get a DVD to play on a home PC used to be pretty complicated, mainly because most machines didn't come with the necessary software to accomplish the task. With Windows Vista and Media Player 11, you've got everything you need to enjoy top-quality DVD movies on your home computer.

LOADING THE DVD

● The first step is similar to loading a music CD. When you put a DVD movie in the drive and close the door, Windows displays the **AutoPlay** dialog box. Choose the first option–**Play DVD movie using Windows Media Player**.

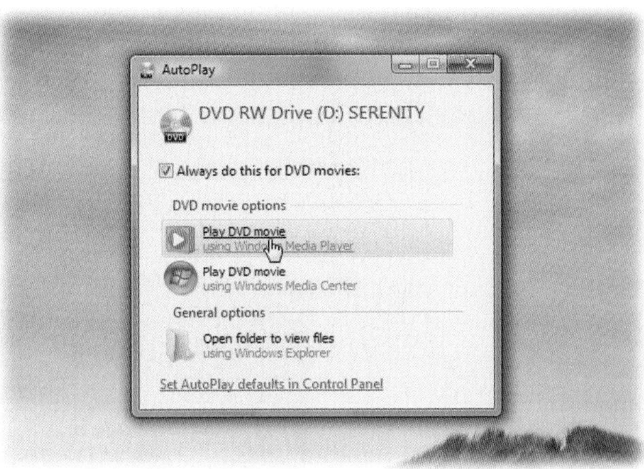

HOME-MADE DVDS

Windows Media Player will happily play back DVDs that you've created yourself or that have been made by friends. You should not have any compatibility problems–just make sure that the DVD has been "finalized" (this is the finishing off process that prepares it for playing) and it will work fine.

● After a moment, the opening credits begin to roll. Media Player assumes that you want to watch the film in as large a window size as possible, so it expands to give you give a bigger picture.

● We have loaded Joss Whedon's horse opera in outer space, *Serenity*–and the screen here is showing the opening menu of this particular DVD. As you move the mouse over the menus you can see that it turns into a pointing hand, indicating that you can click the item–in this instance, the **Scenes** screen.

● Here's a typical scene selection screen, which we can navigate using the mouse. When we've found a scene we want to watch, we can just click on it once with the left mouse button.

WATCHING THE FILM

- Here's the selected scene from the movie. You'll recognize the controls underneath from elsewhere in Media Player–they'll stop and pause the movie, mute the sound, alter the volume level, and so on.

- Although the movie's running at a good size, it's not actually full screen–you can still see the taskbar and Media Player's menus, for example. To get rid of everything except the actual film, click the **View full screen** button.

- This displays the film completely full screen, with no menus or other Windows furniture to distract you. It's the best way to watch a movie on your PC. If you need to see the controls again, just move the mouse and they'll pop up.

USING THE DVD MENU

● There's one button on the transport controls at the foot of the screen that you don't see when you're playing music–the **DVD** button. Just move the cursor to make the controls appear and then slide it over to there.

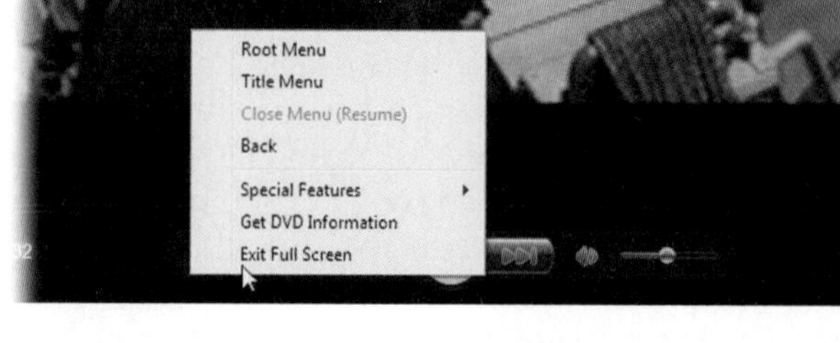

● Click once with the left mouse button on the **DVD** button to open the menu.

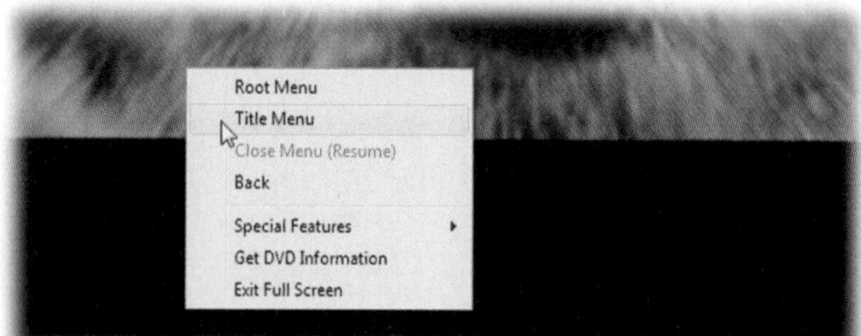

● Slide the cursor up the menu to the **Title Menu** option and click once there to select it.

● The DVD returns to the main title menu. After this splash screen, the scene selection menu will appear again, along with Bonus Materials, Language, and so on.

Windows Media Center

This software, included with Vista, turns your PC into a TV-style entertainment center, with large colorful controls for displaying photos and videos, as well as playing music and DVDs.

Launching Media Center

Media Center is really a small glimpse into the future of home entertainment, and it will really come into its own if you have a number of devices–for example, a PC, an X-Box 360, and a wireless-equipped TV–linked together in a home network. Having these will allow you to take content from your PC and display it on different devices around your home. Even without all that, Media Center is still an excellent way to enjoy the music and photos stored on your PC; and also to watch and record TV, if you have the necessary equipment. This section explains how.

SETTING UP MEDIA CENTER

● Move the cursor to the Start button and click on it to open the Start menu.

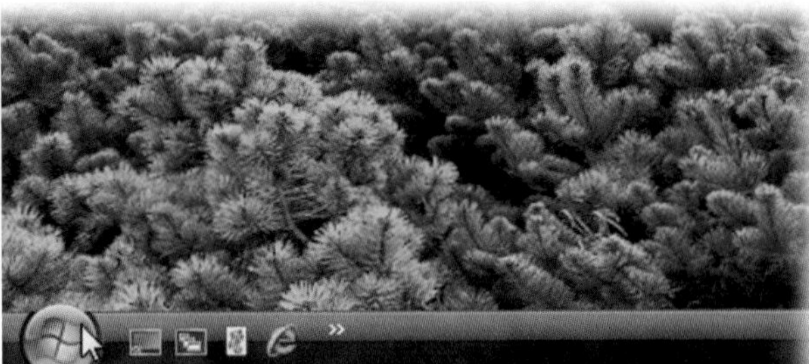

CHANGING MEDIA CENTER'S SETTINGS

It's worth exploring Media Center's settings to get the most out of it. To access the settings, load Media Center and roll the carousel around until you reach **Tasks**. Look along the line of buttons to find **Settings** and click it. Here you'll find all the controls you need to control the way Media Center looks and behaves, as well as settings for tuning in TV channels, accessing parental controls to limit the kids' access, selecting the folders where Media Center should look for photos, videos, and music, and many other features.

● When the menu opens, slide the cursor up to **All Programs** and click on that.

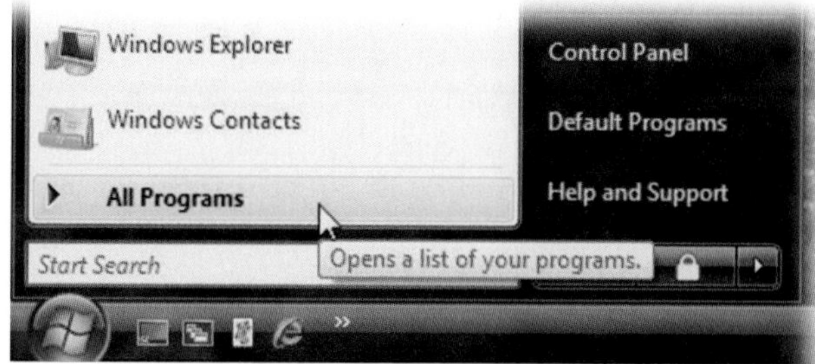

● When the All Programs menu opens, move the cursor up to the **Windows Media Center** icon and click on it once with the left mouse button to select.

● After a moment, the **Welcome** screen will load. Media Center has various settings (see Changing Media Center's Setting box opposite), but unless you've got a specific reason for doing otherwise, you needn't bother with them yet. So, leave everything as it is and click the **OK** button to continue.

THE MEDIA CENTER MENU

● The program doesn't use a Windows-style interface at all, but instead features large buttons and a central carousel that revolves through the various functions of **TV + Movies**, **Music**, **Pictures + Videos**, and so on. Let's start by selecting the **Music** menu.

● Each main menu item has a number of sub menus that stretch in a horizontal line–Music, for example, has "play all," "radio," and "search." However, we want to start with the "music library", so let's click on that now.

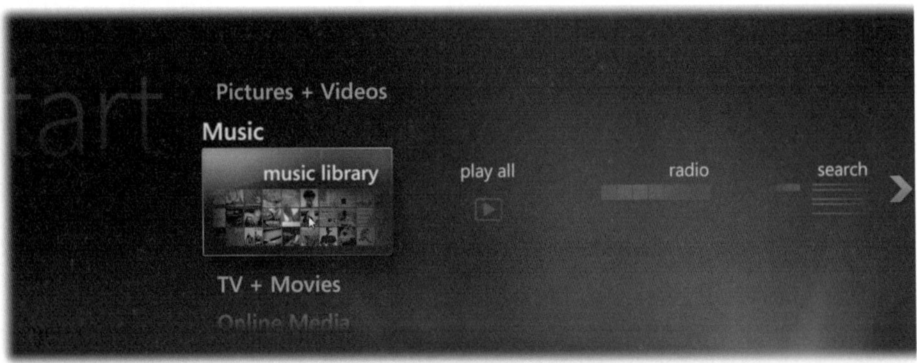

OPENING THE MUSIC LIBRARY

● This is the music library. You'll recognize some of the albums from previous pages. You can see from the pop-up box that Media Center can search other folders for music. However, as a rule, you should stick to the Music folder, so we'll click the **No** button here.

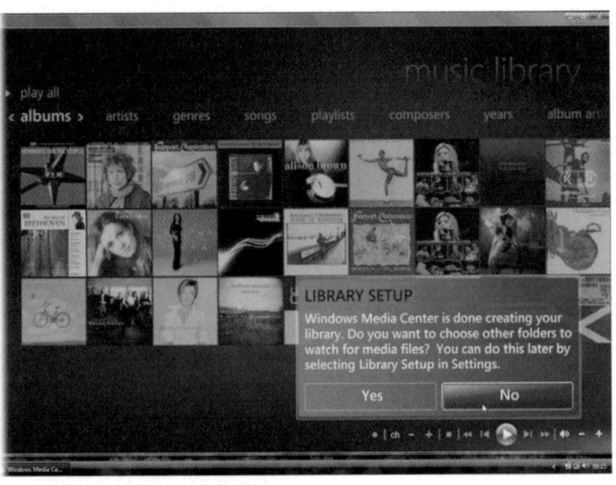

SELECTING AN ALBUM

● Select an album to play by clicking on its picture.

This album is being selected

PLAYING A TRACK

● Media Center displays the album's details and a series of controls down the left-hand side. Click the first one to play the album.

● While the music's playing, you can also watch a slide show of the pictures stored on your PC's Pictures folder. Just click **Play Slide Show** to get pictures and music together.

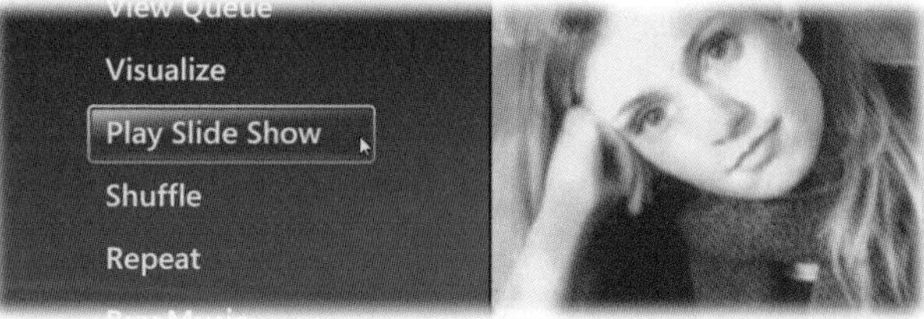

● Here's the track playing with a photo showing in the background. Media Center cycles through pictures, fading between them and zooming in and out to make the display more visually interesting.

● To quit the music library and return to the main Media Center menu, click the green Windows Vista button at the top left.

WATCHING TV

- To get to the TV menu, we need to rotate the menu carousel, so move the cursor down toward the large arrow and the menu will move round.

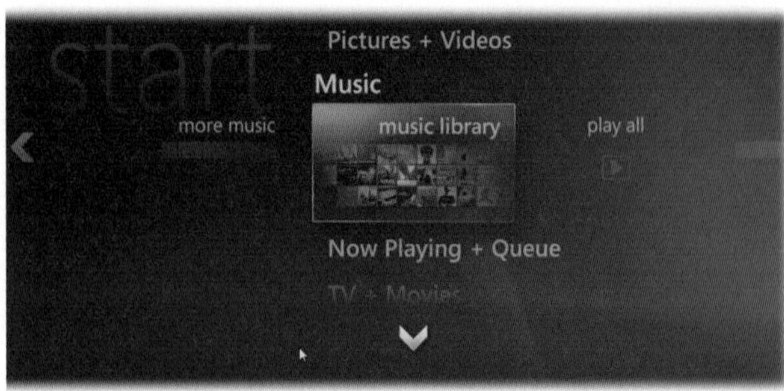

- When the **TV + Movies** menu appears, slide the cursor along to the **guide** icon on the right and click it once.

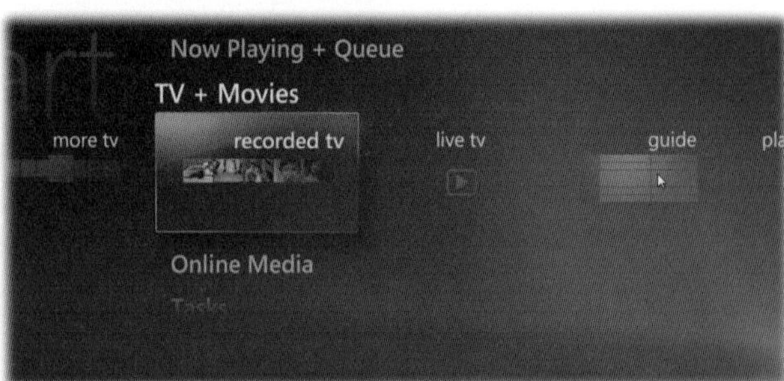

WATCHING TV ON YOUR PC

In order to watch and record TV on your PC you'll need a TV tuner, which is available either as a card that plugs inside the PC and involves taking the computer apart, or as a USB stick that just plugs into a spare USB connector. You'll also need some way to receive TV broadcasts, usually through an aerial or via a cable. Windows Media Center has all the other features you need to accomplish the task and can tune to local TV stations and download a program guide to help you work out what to watch. Exactly how this works will vary depending on where you live and what channels are available.

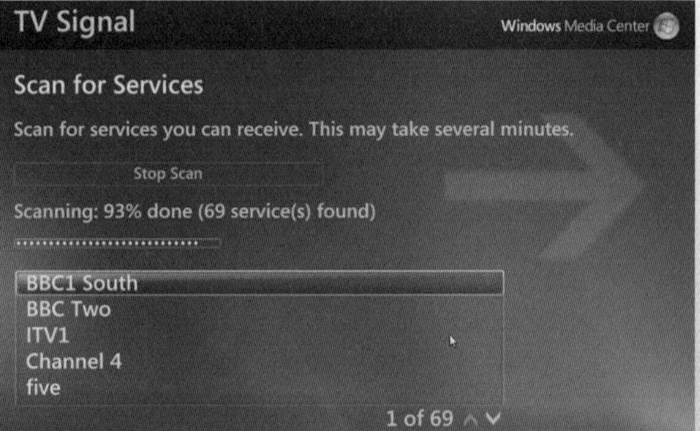

● This slides the menu along until the **guide** is highlighted in the carousel. Click once to open it.

● Your guide may look different to this one, depending on where you live and the channels you receive, but it will work in the same way.

● You can navigate up and down using the cursor, and then click on the program you want to watch with the left mouse button. Here, we are going to select *Scrubs*.

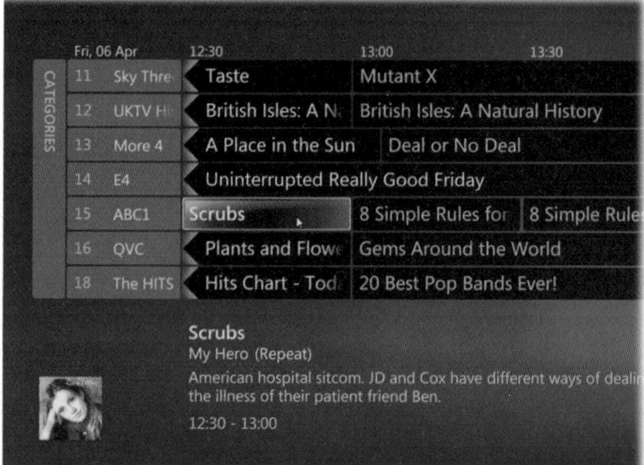

● Here's the TV show, featuring Zach Braff in the excellent comedy *Scrubs*, right here in Windows Media Center.

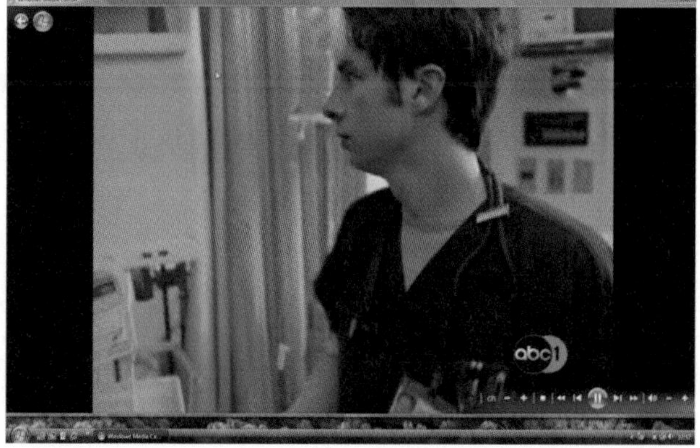

RECORDING TV

● If you're called away from your PC but don't want to miss the show you're watching, just click the red **Record** button down at the left end of the transport controls. Media Centre pops up a little message above the Notification Area to confirm that the programme is being recorded. When you've finished, just click the **Stop** button.

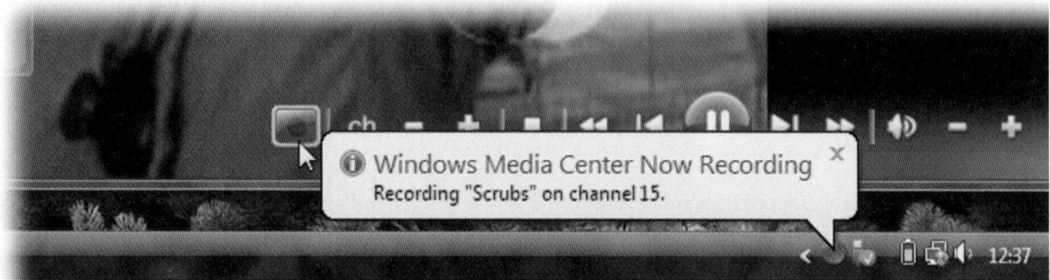

CANCELING RECORDINGS

When you click the **Record** button to record a TV show, Media Center thoughtfully sets itself up to record as many shows in the same series as you've got room for on the hard disk. You can change these and many other settings associated with recording by going to the **recorded tv** menu item on the carousel and then choosing the **series info** and then **other showings** where you can, for example, choose which episodes to record, or **series info** where you can cancel recording for the entire series.

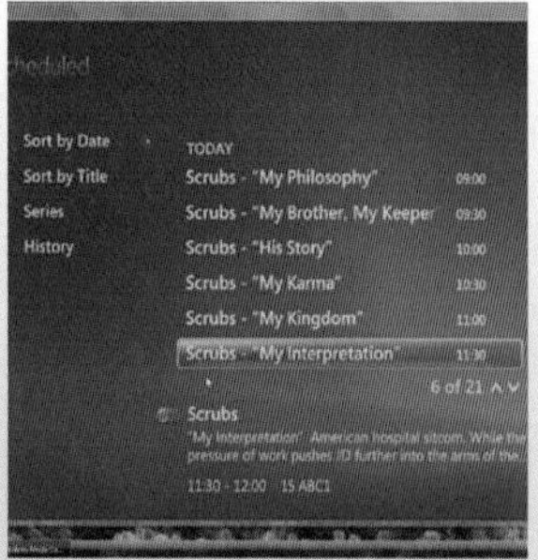

WATCHING A RECORDED PROGRAM

● When you want to watch the show you've recorded, just use the carousel to navigate to the **recorded tv** menu item and click it once with the left mouse button.

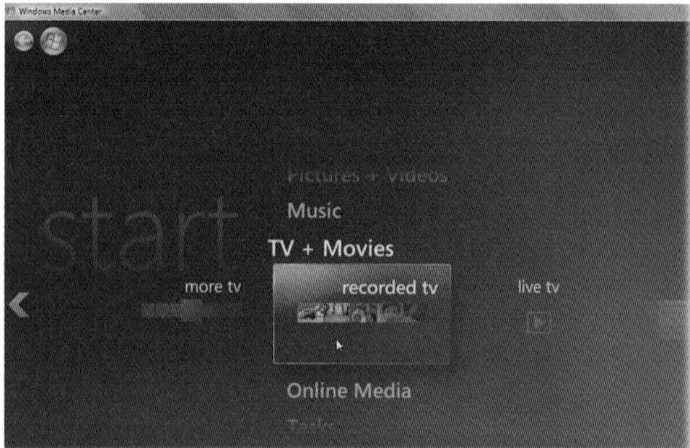

● Pick the show you want to watch by clicking on it once. Here's the short clip of *Scrubs* that we recorded previously, alongside several clips that are provided with Windows Vista.

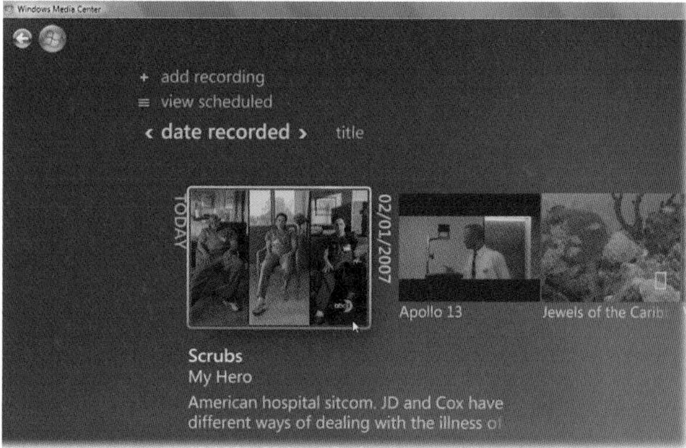

● At the **program info** screen, you'll find various bits of information about the program you've recorded. Click the **Play** button to watch it back.

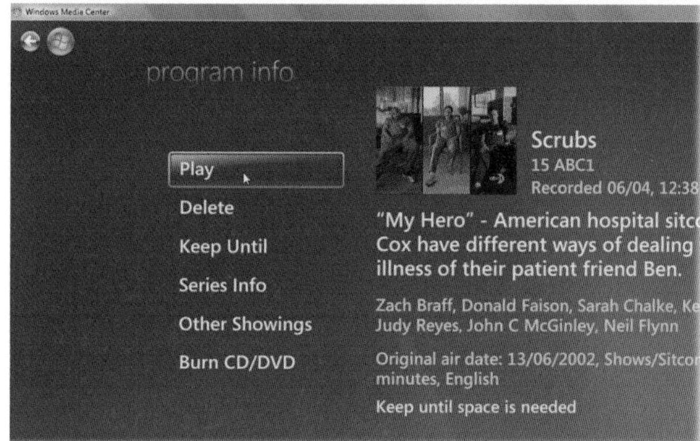

● Here's the show being played back. Media Center will continue to save the show for you to enjoy in the future until you decided to delete it.

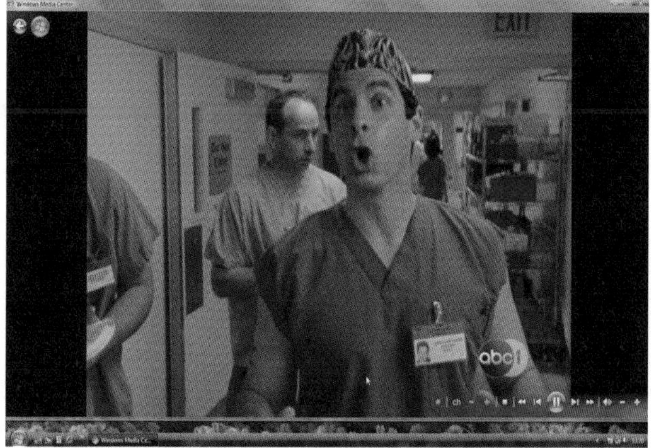

MAKING MOVIES

THE COMBINATION OF INEXPENSIVE DIGITAL VIDEO CAMERAS AND POWERFUL HOME PCs that can "talk" to them has heralded a revolution in home movie making. With the equipment now available, you can now take high definition footage, copy it to your PC with no loss of quality, edit it (just as you would a word-processed document or a photo), add titles, transitions, and even music, and then save the result onto a DVD that friends and relatives can enjoy on a standard DVD player. Courtesy of the Movie Maker program, Windows Vista provides you with everything you need to produce excellent home movies on your PC.

396 Digital Movie Making

406 Editing Your Movie

418 Adding Titles

424 Adding Music

430 Your Finished Movie

Digital Movie Making

When it comes to capturing important moments forever, there's nothing quite like home movies, and thanks to digital technology, they can now look and sound more professional than ever.

Your Home Movie Studio

These days, just about anyone can become a digital movie mogul. Digital cameras are now fairly inexpensive and are as easy to use as a point-and-shoot still camera. With the movie editing features now built into Windows Vista, you can turn even the most amateurish camera work into something worth watching.

DIGITAL EDITING

● The beauty of digital video is exactly that–it's digital. In the same way you can edit a Word document, moving text here and there, changing the fonts, the margins, and anything else you fancy and yet still produce a perfectly printed page that shows no signs of your edits, so you can do the same with a digital video clip. This is a profound improvement over analog video editing, where quality deteriorates with every change.

SAVED FOR POSTERITY

Once you've finished editing your home movie, Movie Maker lets you save it in a range of different formats so that it can be shared in various ways, each of which has its own distinctive characteristics. For example, a home movie that you want to e-mail to a friend who lives on the other side of the world needs to be small, so Movie Maker will compress both the pictures and the sound, and will reduce the number of frames it displays every second, in order to save space. The result will be small and a little jerky, but it's perfectly watchable and–more importantly–it can be sent very quickly as an e-mail attachment. On the other hand, if you're saving the results directly onto a blank DVD, there are no size constraints, so the movie will be saved with high quality, smooth-moving video and excellent stereo sound.

WHAT KIND OF PC DO I NEED?

If your computer can run Windows Vista with the Aero interface, then you can be confident it's going to be fine for editing home movies. As for software, the Movie Maker program that's included with Windows is more than enough to get you started, and you'll be pleasantly surprised at its range of effects and editing features.

NOTHING SPECIAL

- Your PC doesn't need any specialized equipment other than a socket into which you can plug a lead from your digital video camera when you want to copy a movie to your hard disk.
- Most computers have both USB and Firewire (also called 1394) connections. If you have the choice, Firewire is the faster and the more reliable of the two.

Your computer probably has both Firewire (1394) and USB ports. Firewire connections are faster.

ALTERNATIVE SOFTWARE

Should you require more sophisticated editing features, there are a number of commercial programs that are worth considering, but you really should experiment with Windows Movie Maker for a while because there's an awful lot that it can do, and it's completely free.

Meet Movie Maker

Movie Maker has all the features you need for capturing, editing, titling, and scoring your home movies. It also features a storyboard where you can plot the shape of your movie, a preview window for making fine edits, and plenty of other features that we will be exploring later on in this chapter.

FEATURES KEY

❶ Menu Bar
Standard Windows menus for opening and saving files, as well as accessing many features that are available in the Tasks menu.
❷ Movie Buttons
Use these buttons to import video clips, create an AutoMovie, and save the finished movie as a DVD, e-mail attachment, etc..
❸ Preview Window
When you play any of the clips in the storyboard or the main collection in the center of the screen, it appears here.
❹ Control Buttons
These are the transport controls for playing, pausing, rewinding, and fast forwarding video clips.
❺ Split Button
The Split button allows you to cut a video clip at the current position, thus dividing into two clips.

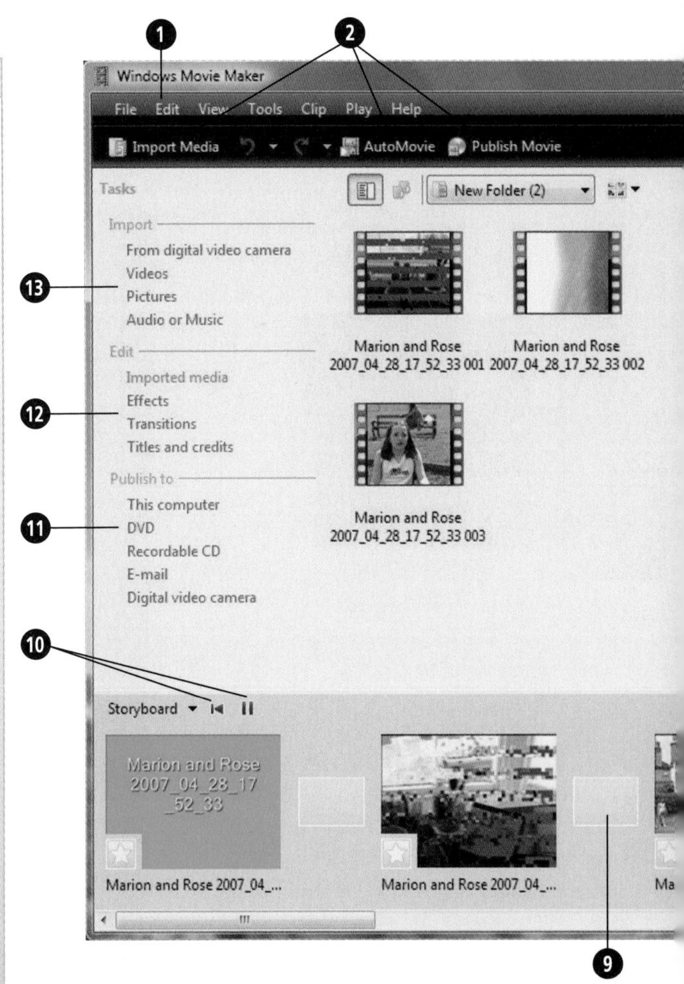

WHAT IS THE AUTOMOVIE FEATURE?

If you're short of time or have never used the program before, this is a great way to take some raw video footage and turn it into a finished movie. Windows Movie Maker makes all the decisions for you, and also offers six different styles. The Sports Highlights style, for example, uses fast cuts to create the feeling of action, while Old Movie adds a sepia tone and slower edits.

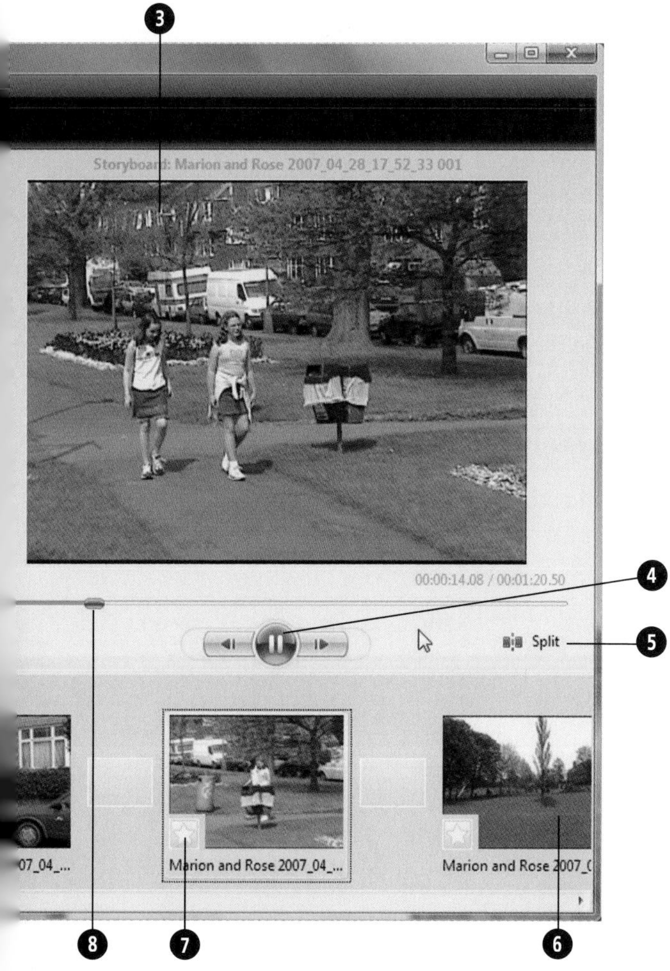

FEATURES KEY

❻ Movie Clips
Clips appear here on the storyboard. The storyboard is automatically created by Movie Maker when it imports the video.
❼ Special Effects
You can add special effects to individual clips by dragging them here. For example, you may want a scene to appear in sepia or slow motion.
❽ Progress Bar
This shows you how far you are through the current clip.
❾ Transition
You can add a transition between two clips by dragging them here. For example, you may want to add a fade.
❿ Storyboard Controls
When a clip is currently playing, the controls here will pause or rewind the video to the beginning.
⓫ Publish Options
This section of the Tasks menu handles saving your movie.
⓬ Edit Options
This section handles various editing functions such as titles and credits.
⓮ Import Options
This section handles importing video from a DV camera or other source.

3
Storyboard: Marion and Rose 2007_04_28_17_52_33 001
00:00:14.08 / 00:01:20.50
4
Split
5
07_04_...
Marion and Rose 2007_04_...
Marion and Rose 2007_(
8
7
6

IMPORTING VIDEO

Most modern home movies start life on tapes in a digital video (DV) camera. Windows Vista lets you transfer that footage onto your PC. A good modern PC will include a connector that's specifically designed to connect to a digital video camera. It's often called a Firewire connector, but is also known by its technical name–a 1394 connector; your digital video camera will also have one of these. Connect the two with an inexpensive cable and you're ready to start transferring the video from the camera to the computer.

CHOOSING AUTOPLAY SETTINGS

Follow the instructions that came with your DV camera to connect it to your PC, and then switch the camera on and put it in playback mode. After a moment, this screen appears. Choose **Import video**.

- Having recognized that you've plugged in a camera, Windows asks you to name the tape you're going to import. As is standard, it highlights a name "marker" in the top box– in this case it's "**Video Tape**."

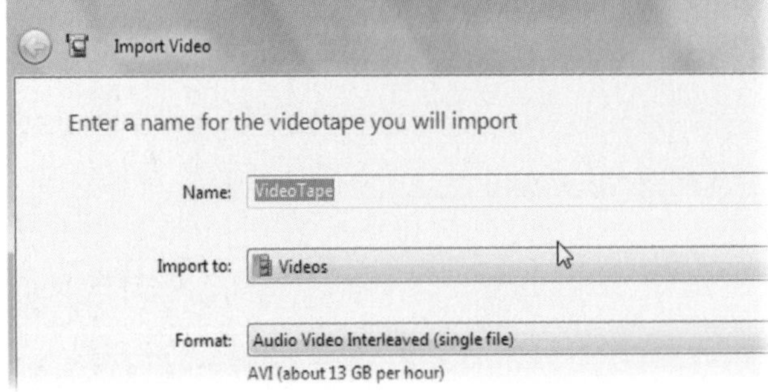

- As the marker text is highlighted, you can just start typing. This video is of a couple of kids playing in the park, so we're going to call it Marion and Rose.

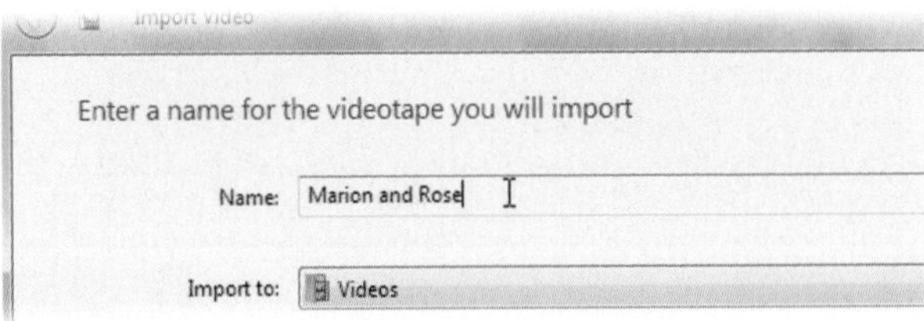

- You can change some of the video settings, but generally, the ones that Windows uses automatically are just fine, so we'll click the **Next** button to move on.

- The next dialog gives you three options. Choose the first if you only ever store one movie on each of your video tapes. Choose the second if you want Windows to automatically create a DVD of the whole tape–mistakes and wobbly camerawork included. As our tape includes different movies shot on different days, we're going to choose the third option by clicking once on the radio button as shown here.

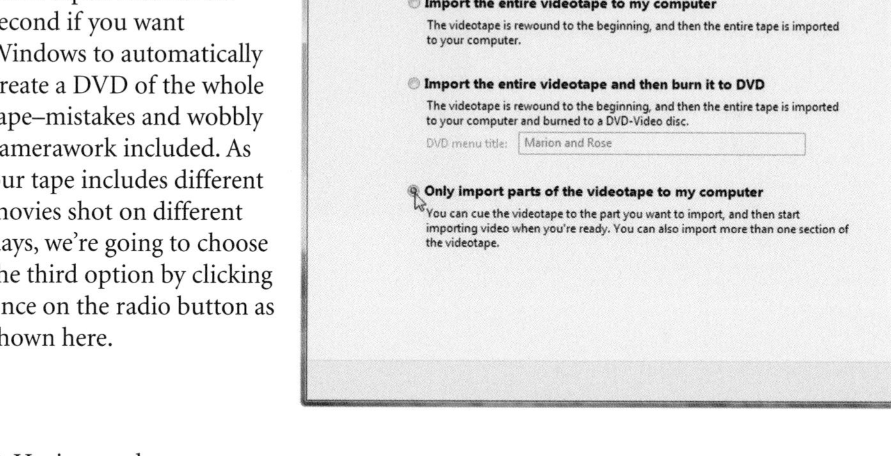

- Having made our selection, click on the **Next** button to move on.

I DON'T HAVE FIREWIRE

You can either buy a Firewire card for your PC, or try using the USB connector if that's supported. Older machines use an older, slower version of the USB communications standard, which isn't fast enough to send the video through without scrambling or dropping whole chunks of it. USB 2.0 on the other hand is fast enough if your DV camera supports it. Check the manual.

CONTROLLING VIDEO PLAYBACK

- This opens the **Import Video** screen. You can see the transport controls to the right of the cursor in this shot. We will use these to control the playback of the connected DV camera, clicking **Play** to start playing the video, **Pause** to pause, and so on. As we do so, the video will displayed in the preview window on the right of the box.

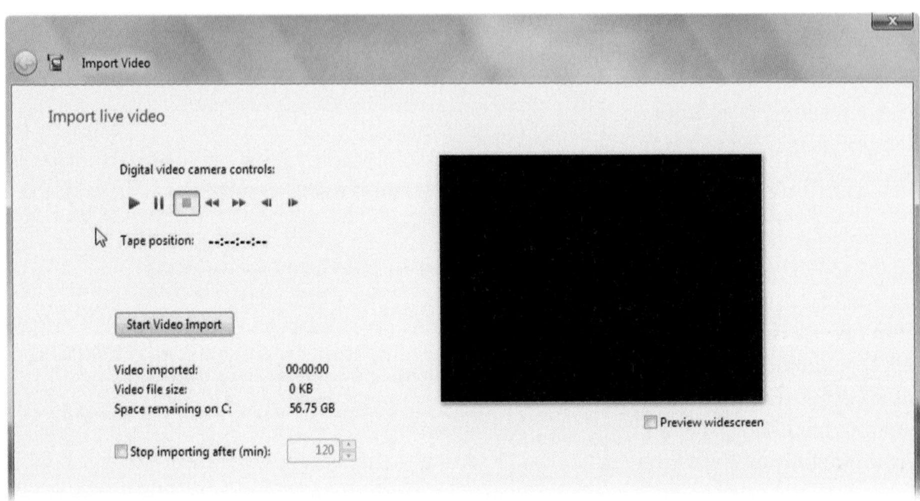

- Let's start playing the tape. Make sure the camera is switched on, move the cursor up to the **Play** button and click on it.

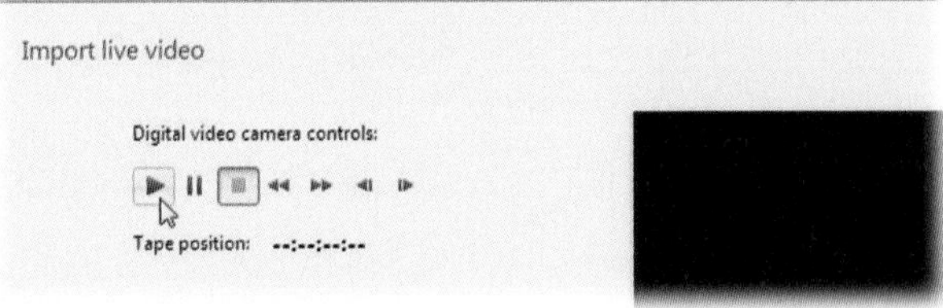

- The movie starts to play back–you'll hear the camera whirring–and we be able to watch its progress in the preview window.

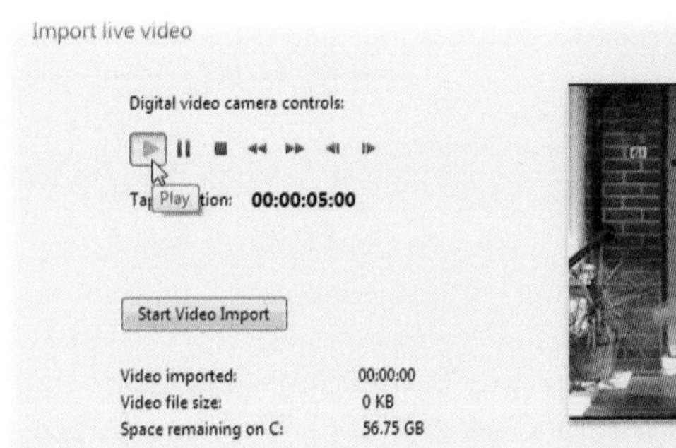

- Use the transport controls to navigate to the part of the film where you want to start copying it onto the PC, and then click the **Stop** button.

- If you have to go back to the beginning of the whole tape, just click the rewind button like this.

IMPORTING VIDEO

- When you're at the start of the clip you want to capture, click the **Play** button like this.

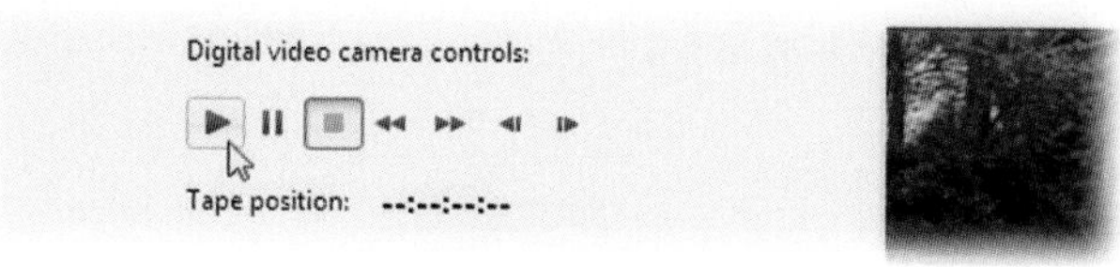

- Then, as soon as the movie begins to play back, click the large **Start Video Import** button underneath. Until you click this, you're just watching the movie play back on the screen, rather than capturing it to your PC.

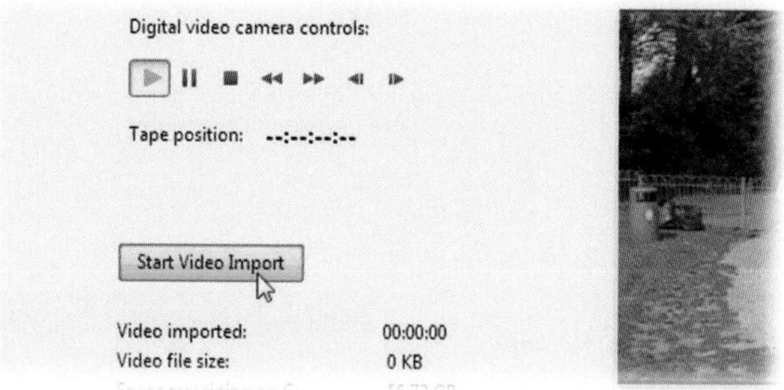

- Watch the film in the preview window until it reaches the end of the part you want to copy to your PC. When it gets there, click on the **Stop Video Import** button.

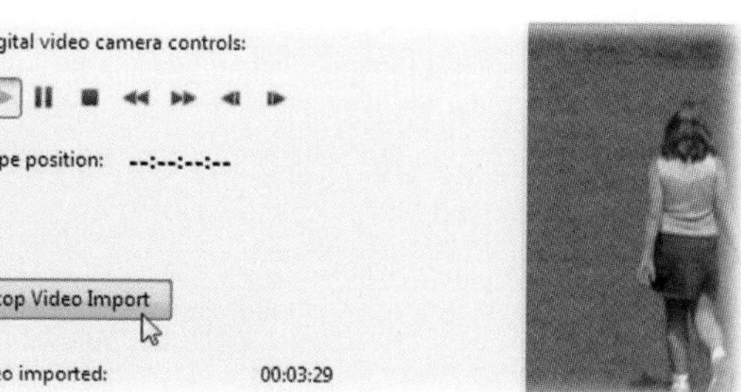

● When the movie stops playing back, click on the **Finish** button to complete the process. The movie has now been transferred to your PC.

OPENING THE VIDEO IN MOVIE MAKER

● Here is your movie! Windows closes the **Import Video** dialog and replaces it with this box–**Windows Photo Gallery**, complete with the video clip that we've just imported. The lines that you can see on the video image are the kind of things that are produced occasionally during a video capture such as this. We'll get rid of them in a few pages time. For now, click on the **Make a Movie** button to continue.

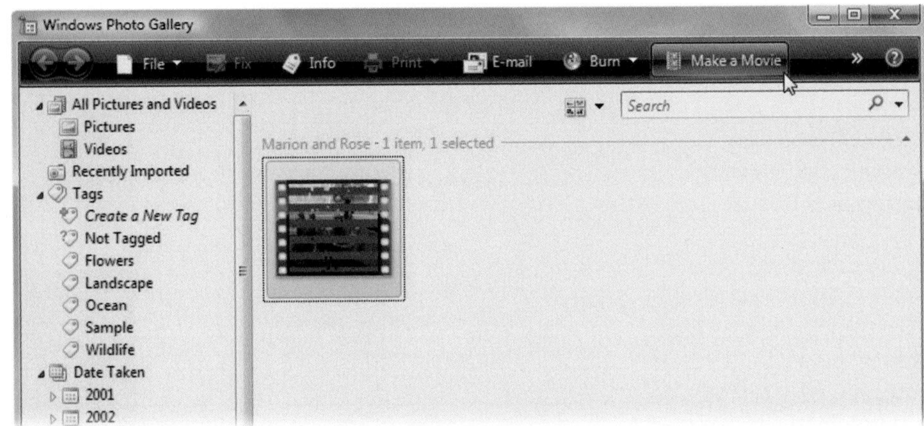

● After a moment, Windows Movie Maker loads and you will see the captured clip or clips in place at the top of the box. At the bottom of the screen, the various scenes that go to make up the clips are already in place in the storyboard.

● Before we do anything, we should save this as a project, so go to the **File** menu and click on it once with the left mouse button.
● When the menu opens, slide the cursor down and choose **Save Project** by clicking on it once.

● When the dialog box opens, you'll see that "**Untitled**" is already highlighted in the **File name** box, ready for you to type in your own title.

● Type in a name for the project–in this example, it's called **Marion and Rose**.

● Finally, click the **Save** button to finish saving the project.

WHAT IS A MOVIE MAKER PROJECT?

When you copy digital video from your camera to your computer, Windows stores it as a video file. However, when you use Movie Maker to edit that raw video, you save it as a Movie Maker project file–which is essentially a series of instructions that tells Movie Maker how to organize the video footage. This has two advantages. First, it leaves the original video untouched. Second, it means you can use the same raw video to create lots of different projects by cutting it and putting it back together again in different ways.

Editing Your Movie

Not even the most accomplished Hollywood director gets it right first time, so it's a good job that it's so easy to edit your video footage with Windows Movie Maker.

Removing Unwanted Video

When you import video the way we've done it here, Windows Movie Maker automatically takes all of the footage and then arranges it with titles, transitions, and special effects into what's called an AutoMovie. This is a great way to check out some of the key features that Movie Maker offers the budding film maker. So, let's start by having a look at the movie as created by Movie Maker.

CHECKING THE AUTOMOVIE

● To play the AutoMovie created by Movie Maker, move the mouse down to the Play button (situated above the **Storyboard**) and click on it once with the left mouse button.

● The movie will begin to play in the preview window and you can see the familiar transport-style controls for play/pause, forward, and backward.

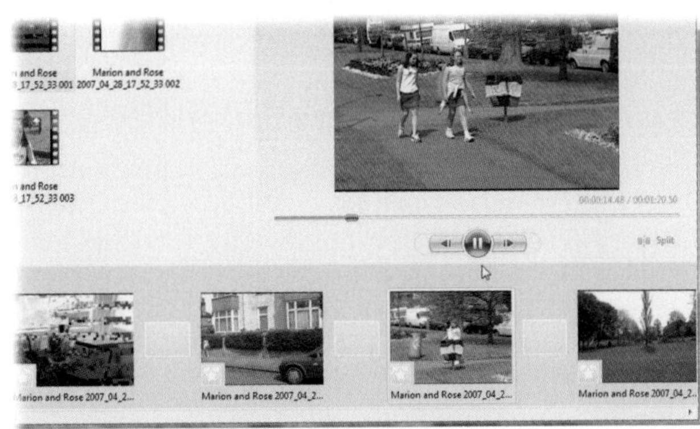

● When you've seen enough, click the Pause button to stop playback.

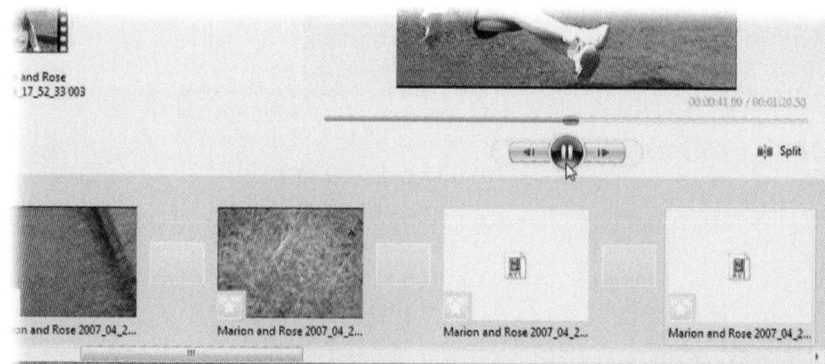

● Move the cursor back down to the transport controls above the **Storyboard** and click on the rewind button to take the movie back to the start.

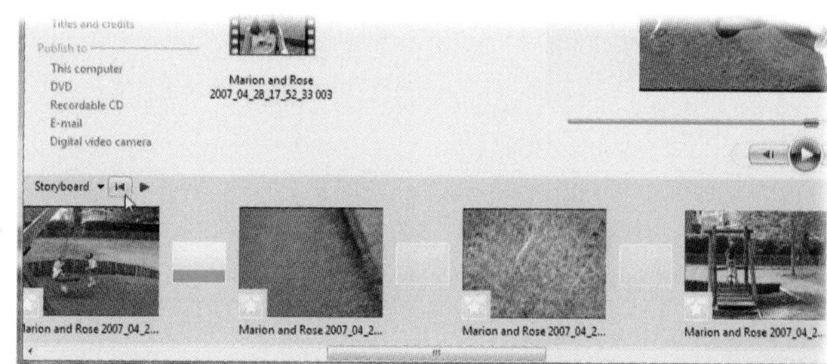

REMOVING THE AUTOMOVIE

● Movie Maker's done its best, but we think we can do better, so now that we have a taste of what a finished movie can look like, let's create our own.
● First we'll need to remove the AutoMovie.
● Start by right clicking on the first frame like this.

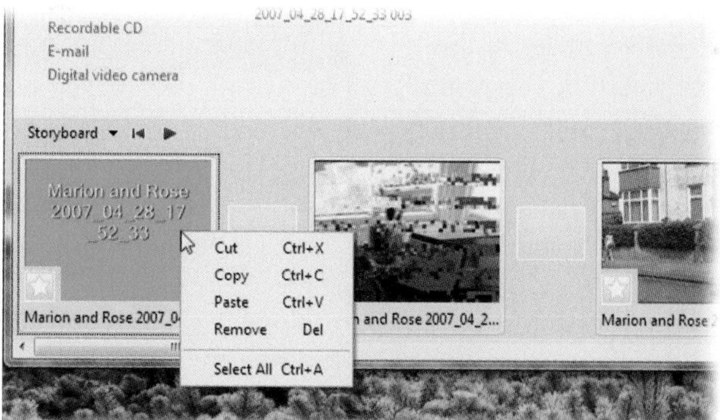

● Next, click on **Select All** from the pop-up menu– this will ensure that all the clips on the storyboard are selected.

● With all the clips selected, right mouse click again on the first frame and choose **Remove**.

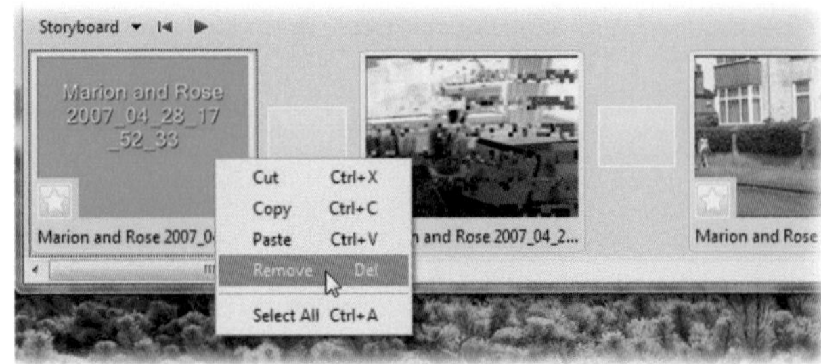

● Movie Maker removes the clips from the storyboard. However, as we'll see, it preserves all the original video, so it's easy to start again if you change your mind about your edits.

CREATING YOUR OWN MOVIE

● Start by dragging the first video clip down onto the **Storyboard**. To do this, click on it once with the left mouse button.

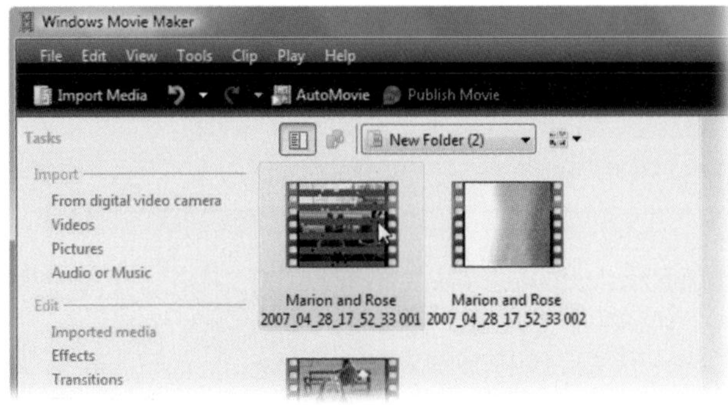

● Then, still holding the left mouse button down, drag the clip down on top of the first empty frame on the **Storyboard** like this.

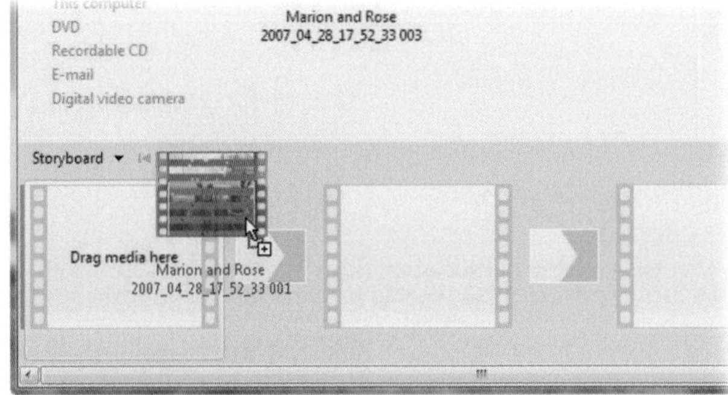

● Let go of the mouse button and the clip will snap into position. As you can see, this clip has some problems and, in any case, it isn't really the start of our film, so we'll sort that out next.

NAVIGATING MOVIE CLIPS

● With the clip still highlighted, move the cursor over to the Play button under the preview window and click it once to start playing the clip.

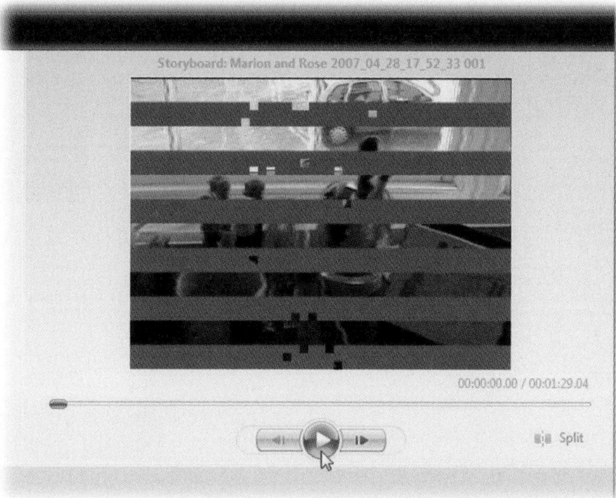

● What we're looking for here is the scene at which we want the movie to begin. When you've found it, click the Pause button.

● Unless you're very quick, you're unlikely to pause the video at the right point. That's not a problem. Just click on the rewind button like this to move back.

● Here we've gone too far back and ended up at the scene before the one we're after. We'll fix that in the next step.

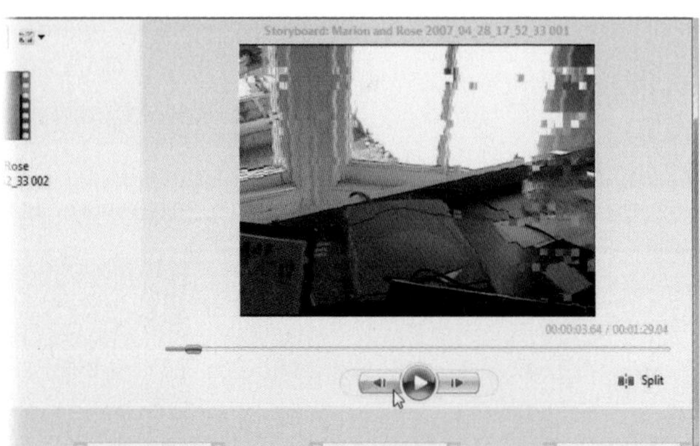

● If you go back too far, just click the Forward button once with the mouse and keep clicking until you find the scene you're looking for. Clicking once like this moves you forward a frame at a time.

● Now we are at the frame where we'd like our movie to begin–with the two girls leaving their house for a trip to the park.

SPLITTING A VIDEO CLIP

● What we're going to do is split the video at this point, so that we can get rid of the bit at the beginning that we don't want. Slide the cursor over to the **Split** button and click it once.

● Movie Maker "cuts" the video at the precise point shown in the preview window and shows the result on the Storyboard like this.

REMOVING A VIDEO CLIP

● Let's get rid of the first clip, which is now redundant, by right clicking on it with the mouse so the menu appears like this.

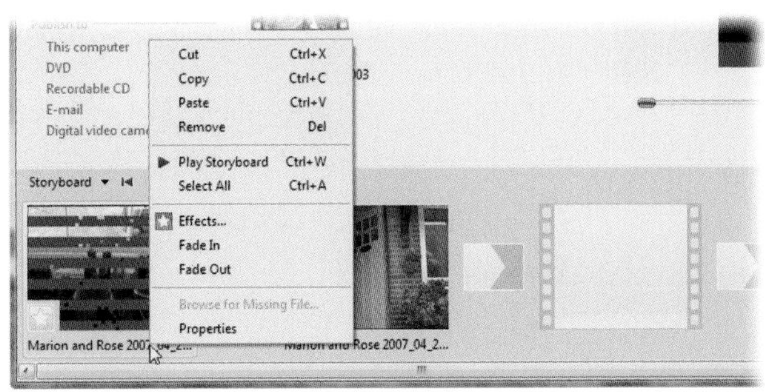

● Choose **Remove** from the menu to delete the first clip.

● The first clip is now removed, and our movie starts with the first scene of the girls leaving the house.

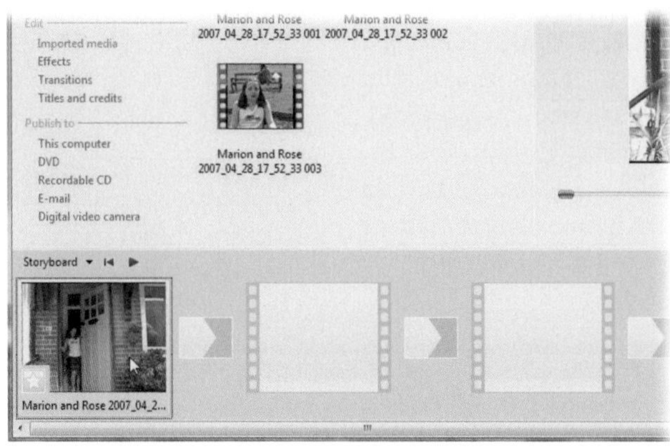

MAKING MORE CLIPS

● Let's make another cut. With the first clip in the Storyboard selected, click the Play button under the preview window.

● When you get to a point where you think you want to split the video again (either to make a cut or add a transition from the one scene to the next) click the **Pause** button like this.

● Click the Split button again to "cut" the video at the current position.

● As before, the video is now divided into two scenes on the Storyboard.

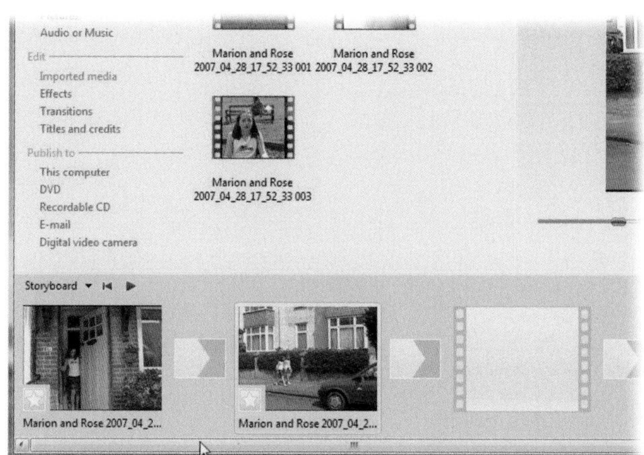

● Keep creating more clips on the Storyboard in exactly the same way until you've got enough for a short film. If you want, drag further video down from the main window to the Storyboard so you can edit that as well.

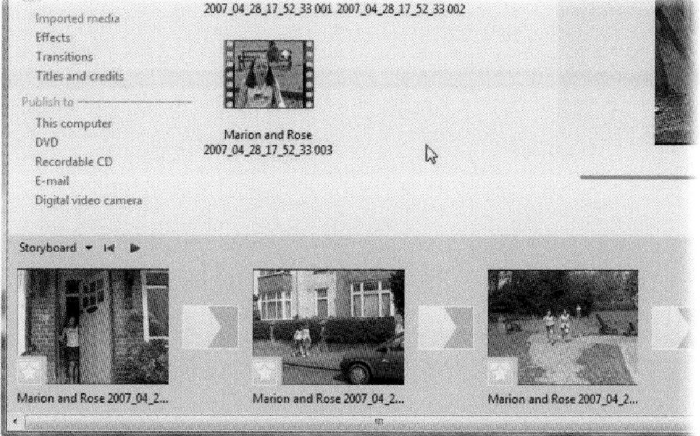

ADDING TRANSITIONS

● Movie Maker makes it easy to add interesting transitions between scenes, so that one fades into the next or opens into the next like a window blind or a chequer board. To start, click **Transitions** under the **Edit** task list on the left.

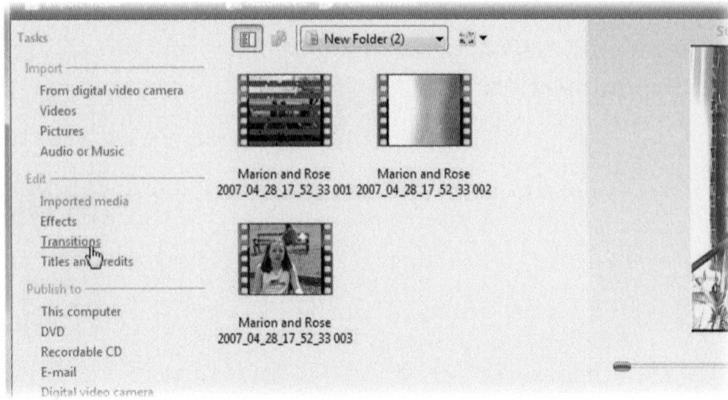

● Movie Maker has dozens of transitions with which you can experiment. For now, we're going to choose the **Bow Tie, Horizontal** transition by clicking on it with the left mouse button.

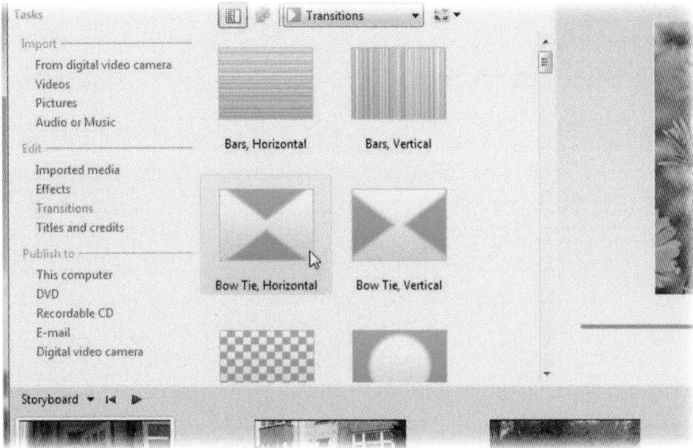

● Still holding the left mouse button down, drag the transition onto the little empty square between the first two scenes on the Storyboard like this.

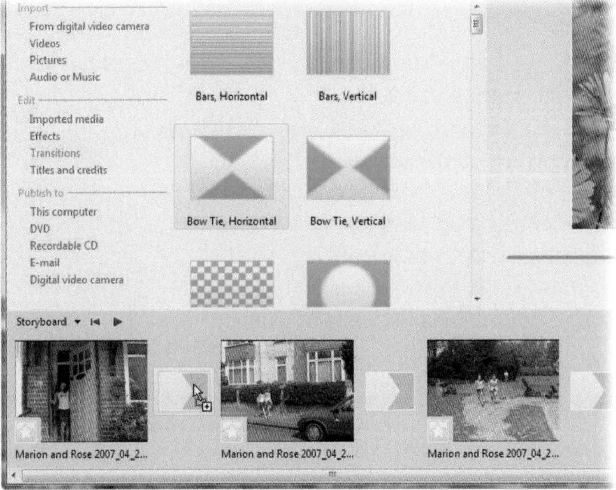

● Let go of the left mouse button and the transition appears in place. You can tell what effect you're going to get just by looking at it.

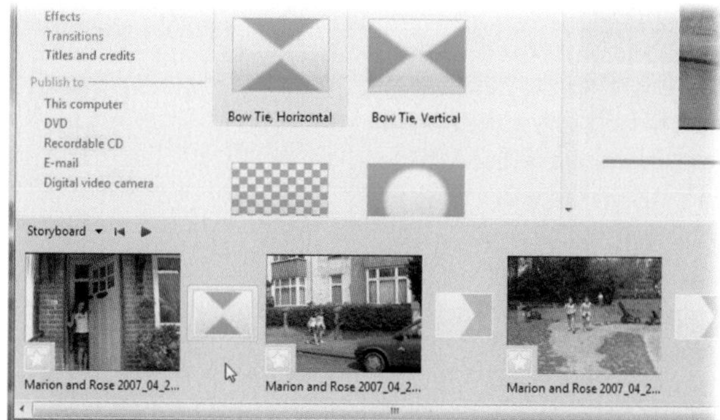

● With the transition still highlighted on the Storyboard, click on the Play button.

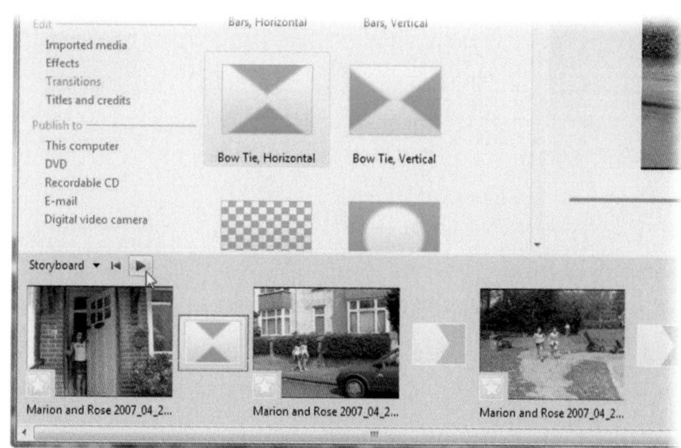

● As the movie plays, check out the preview window. Look carefully and you can see the transition being applied between these two scenes. Used sparingly, transitions can be very effective.

ADDING EFFECTS

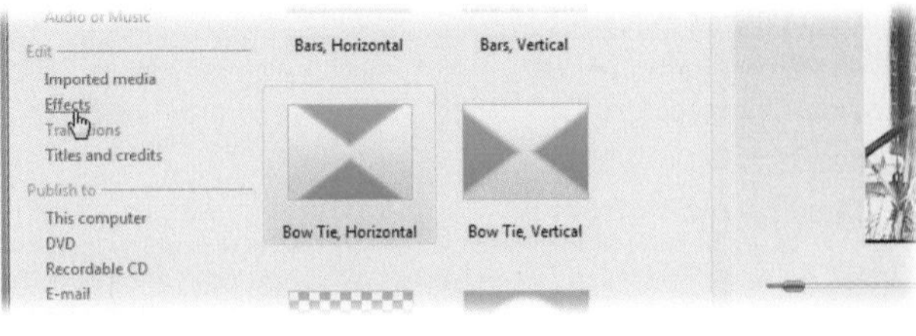

● Similarly, you can add effects to the clips themselves. Move the cursor over to **Effects** in the **Edit** task list on the left.

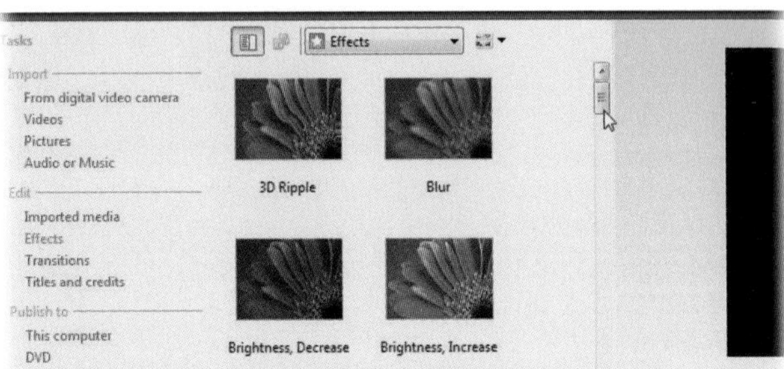

● To see more effects, grab the slider with the left mouse button and–still holding the button down–drag it down.

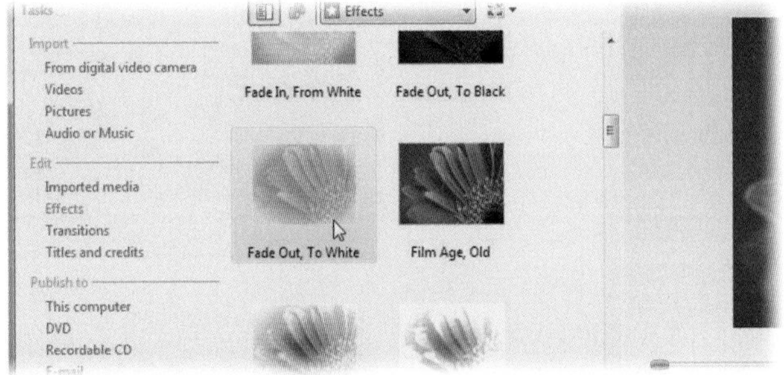

● Next, click an effect to select it. In this example, we've selected **Fade Out, To White**.

● Notice that the flower appears in the preview window. This allow us to preview the effect before adding it to our movie. Click Play to see the effect in action.

• Movie Maker demonstrates the chosen effect in the preview window like this.

• Try out a few effects in the same way until you find one you like. Then click and drag it with the mouse (just as you did the transition in the previous section), but this time drop it onto the little star/square at the bottom left of the clip in the Storyboard.

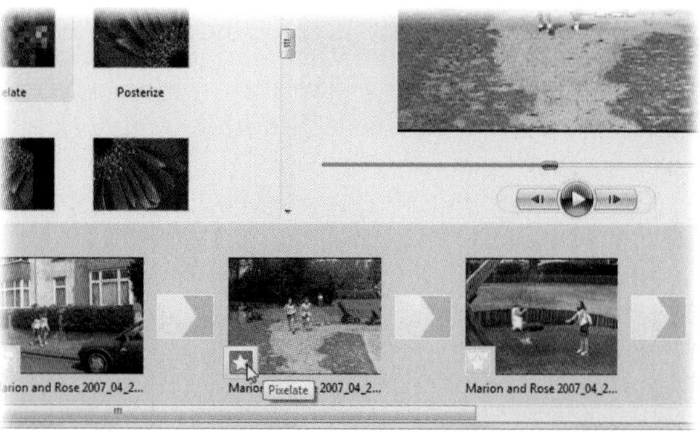

• We've chosen the pixelate effect and, with the clip still selected in the Storyboard, we can click the Play button and see the effect playing back in the preview window.

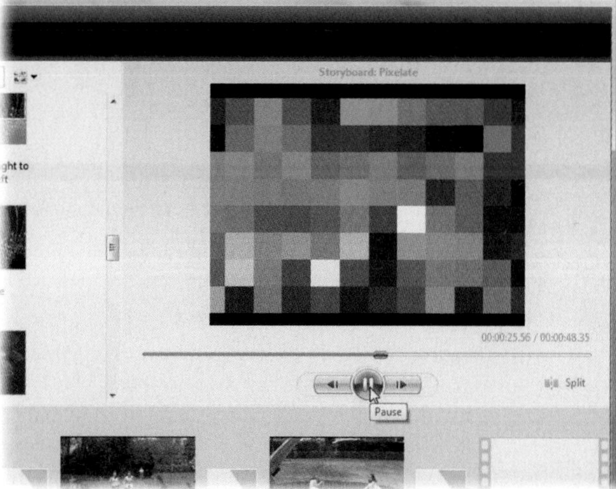

ADDING TITLES

No movie is truly complete without the opening titles and the closing credits. Movie Maker allows you to add these movie-style extras quickly and easily.

ADDING A MOVIE TITLE

One of the things that distinguishes a properly edited digital movie from the original raw footage is the extra feature or two that you can add with the help of a computer. An opening title, for example, not only tells the audience what they're about to watch, it also makes everything look that much more professional; and, although some DV cameras now have simple titling features, they really can't compare with what you can achieve with a home PC.

ADDING A MAIN TITLE

● Let's start by giving our home movie a name. Move the cursor over to the **Edit** menu on the left and click on **Titles and credits.**

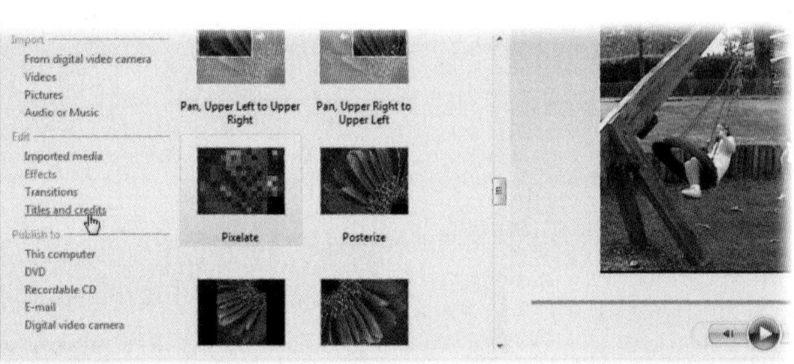

● Although you can add titles at various points in the movie, the most important ones come at the beginning and the end. To add a title for your film, click the **Title at the beginning** link.

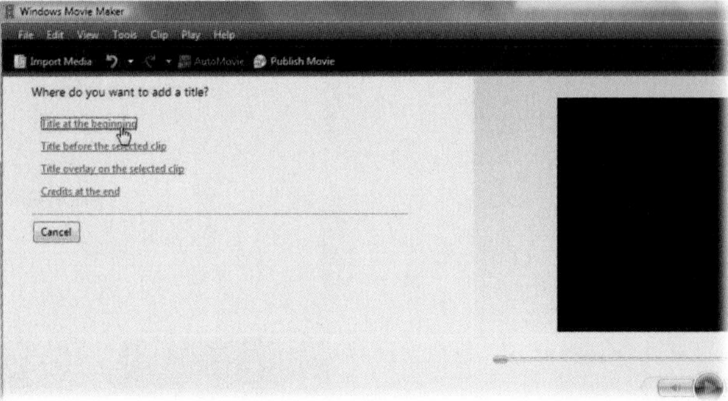

● This opens up an empty text box where you can type the name of the movie.

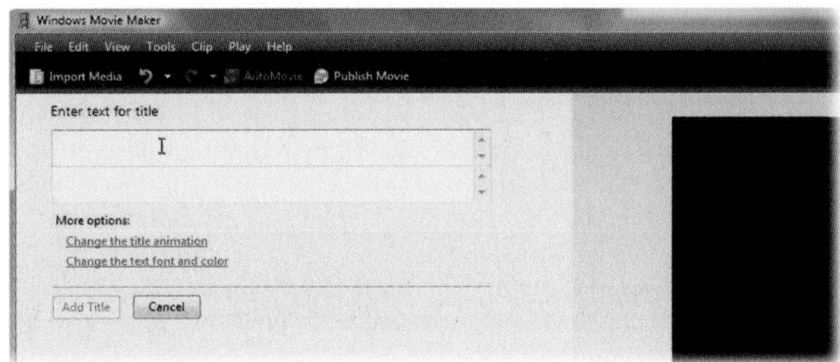

● Being big fans of the obvious, we're going to call our movie "In the park." As we type the title into the empty box on the left, Movie Maker automatically shows us what it's going to look like in the preview window. The title comes up in the default font, which we can change later if we wish.

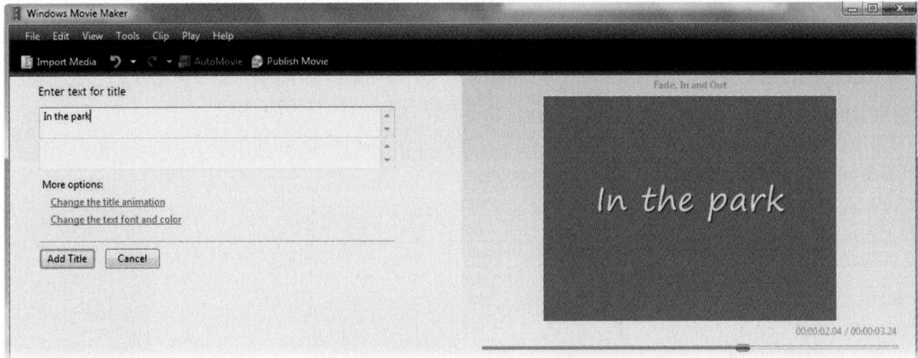

CHANGING THE TITLE ANIMATION

● By default, Movie Maker chooses to animate your title so that it scrolls up the screen, like a title in a professional movie. However, there are lots of different variations to choose from. To see them, click the **Change the title animation** link.

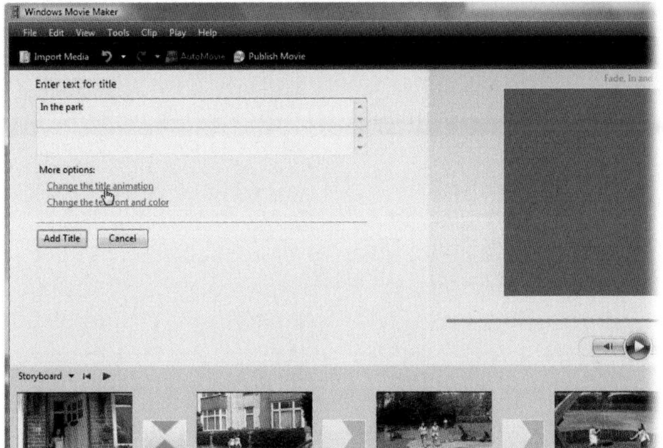

● Here you can see a whole list of different animations that Movie Maker can apply to your title. Try some of them out. Each time you click on one, it'll be shown in the preview window on the right. Here we're looking at the **Mirror** animation, in which the text flies in and out from both sides.

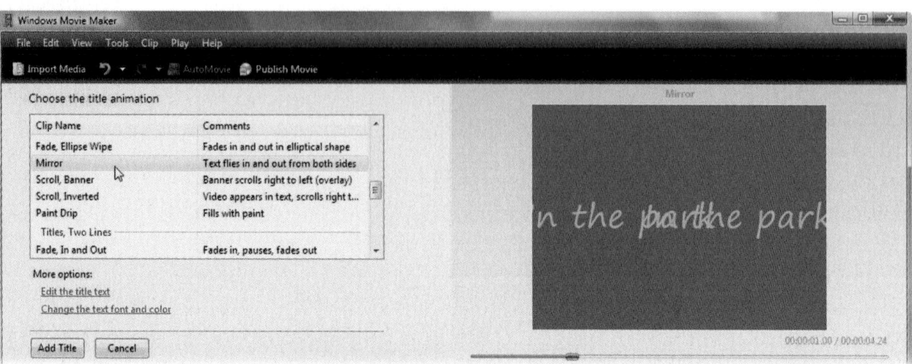

● As well as providing lots of different animation styles, Movie Maker lets you change the typestyle of your titles. Click the **Change the text font and color** to continue.

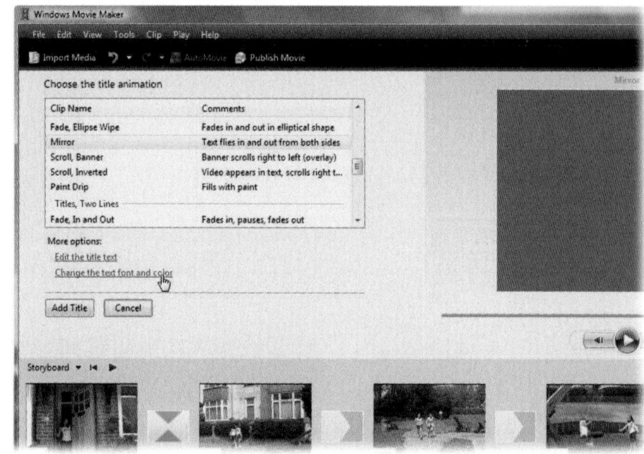

MOVIE CHAPTERS

If you'd like to divide your movie into chapters, you can give each a separate heading. Select **Titles and credits** from the **Edit** section of the **Tasks** menu and then click on the clip in the Storyboard where you'd like the chapter to fall. Click on **Title before the selected clip** to select and add the title as described elsewhere in this section. Or, you can have the title appear on top of the clip by selecting the **Title overlay on the selected clip** option.

● From here you can click the arrow to open the drop-down list and choose a different typeface, or click the color square to change the text color, or switch to bold or italics or underline by using the other commands. Experiment until you find something you like, then click the **Add Title** button.

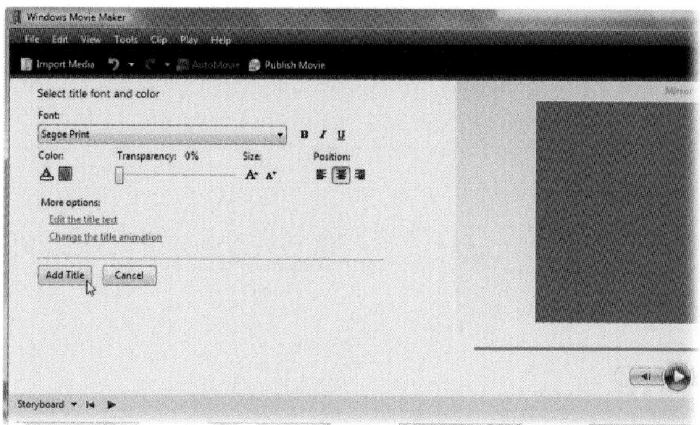

● Here you can see the title in its correct position on the Storyboard. It will now play before the actual video footage starts.

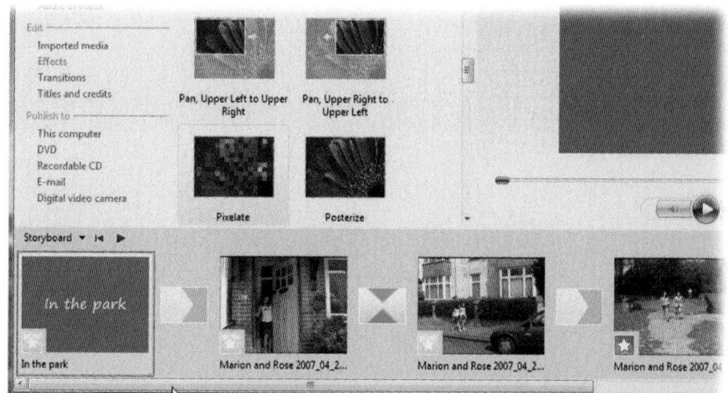

ADDING CLOSING CREDITS

● Now let's add the closing credits to our film. Move the cursor over to the **Edit** menu and click on the **Titles and credits** link.

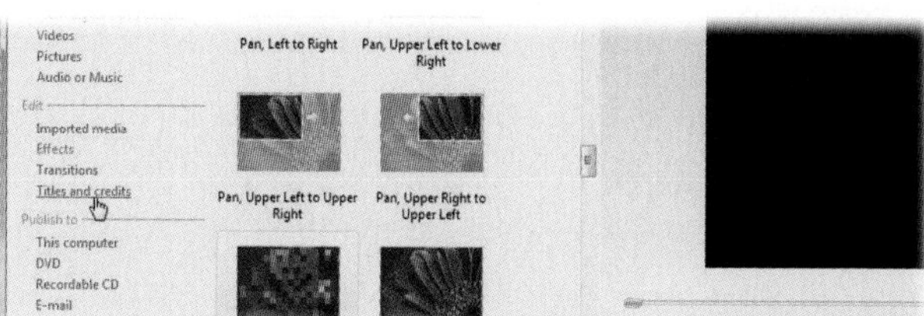

● At the next screen, find the last option–**Credits at the end**–and click on it once to select it.

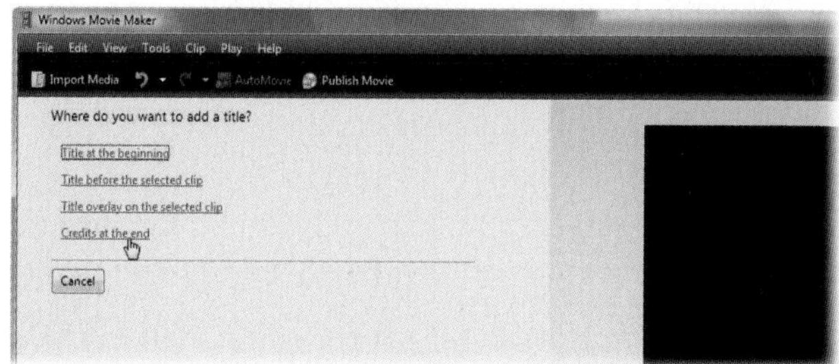

● Movie Maker displays a neat little table where we can type in the closing credits for our film.

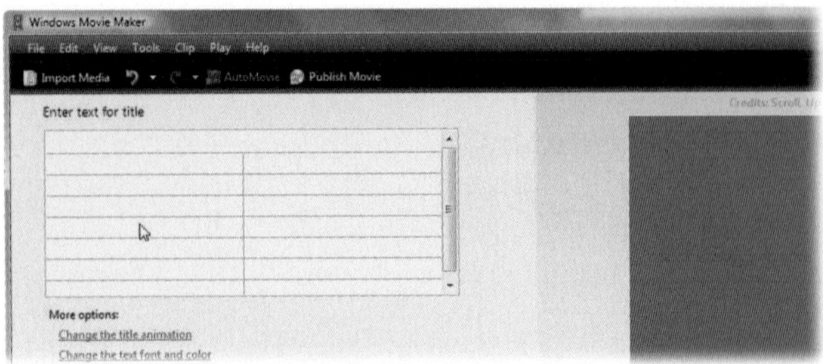

● Click in the first empty box and then type in the first of your closing credits–in this example, we're going to type in **The End.** As soon as we finish typing, Movie Maker displays the credit in the preview window.

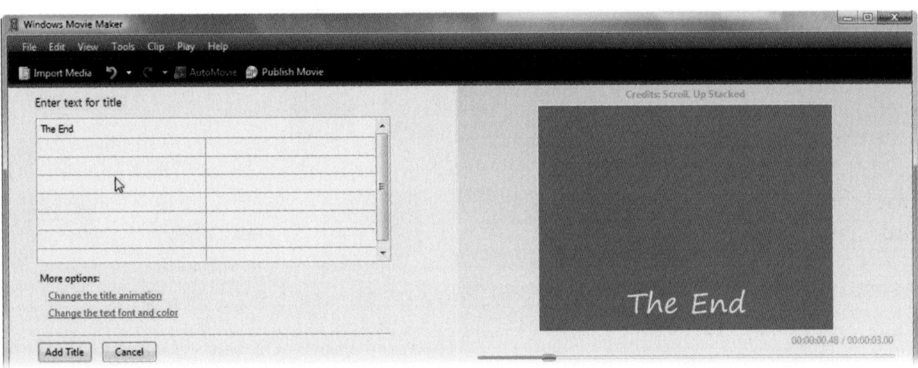

● Next, click in the box underneath and type in **Directed By** (or whatever you choose) and watch what happens in the preview window. Again, Movie Maker will display a preview of what the credit looks like.

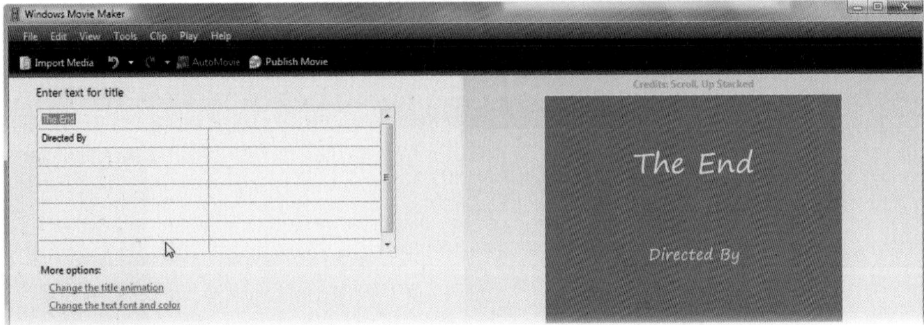

● Continue to type in your credits for your film in this way until you've credited everyone who matters. The credits will all appear in the preview window.

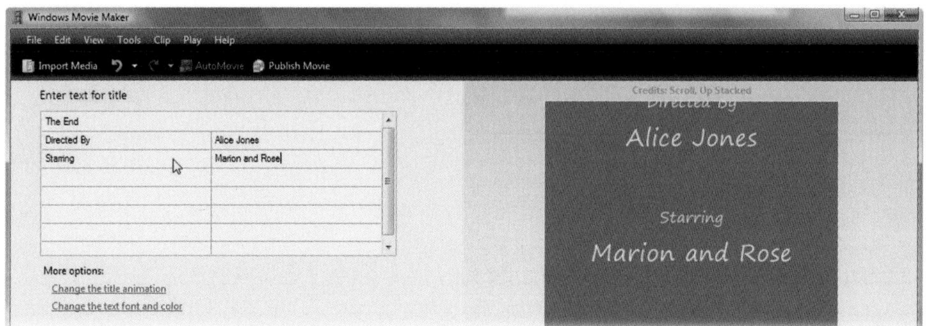

● Again, you can change the style of the animation and the text font and color as you did with the main title. When you're happy with the results, click the **Add Title** button.

● Here you can see the credits screen in place. As in a professional movie, Movie Maker automatically puts them at the end of your film.

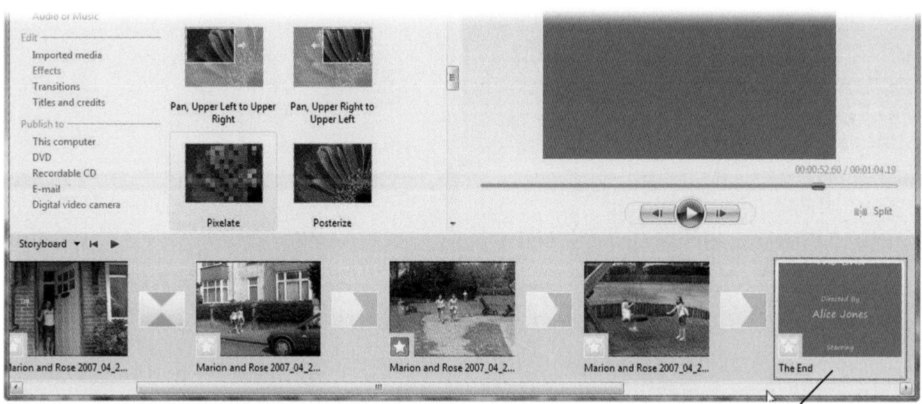

As with the opening title, Movie Maker displays our closing credits in the Storyboard, but this time in the final position

ADDING MUSIC

A good music score is one of the key components to any finished movie, adding the final touch to complete the project with panache. In this section, we will show you how to do it.

FINDING MUSIC

Although it's possible to record your own original music and add it to a movie, that's probably enough to fill another whole book, so we'll use previously recorded material in this section–a favourite CD, perhaps of instrumental, orchestral music, or something similar. In Chapter 8, we discovered how to rip CDs and store them as digital music files on your PC to play back whenever you like or copy to a portable player. You can also use these to make a soundtrack for your movie. However, just in case you haven't ripped any music yet, we'll be using some of the music that's included with Vista for free in this section.

LOCATING YOUR MUSIC

- To begin adding a soundtrack to your movie, make sure the project is still on the screen like this and move the cursor over to the **Audio or Music** link on the **Import** section of the **Tasks** list on the left.

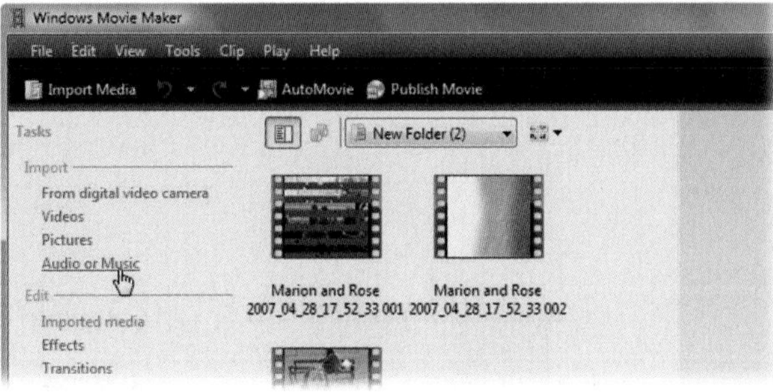

- Windows assumes you want to load something from the Music folder. In this screen, you can see we've ripped quite a few songs to our PC, but to find the one we're after we'll need to click on the navigation slider on the right of the window and, still holding down the mouse button, drag it down.

● At the bottom of the window is the folder we want–the **Sample Music** folder that's included with Windows Vista. Double click on the folder to open.

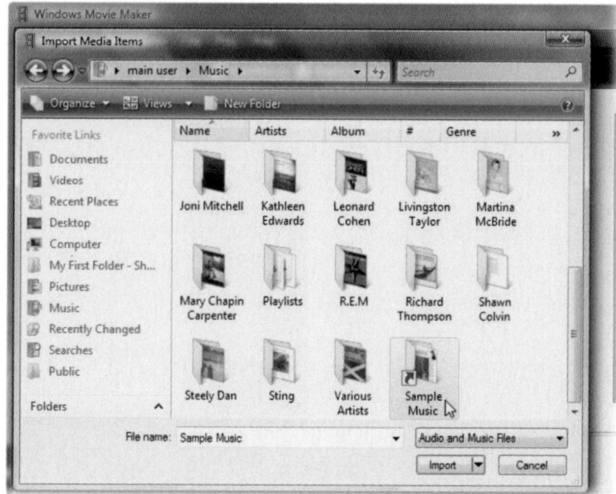

● Choose one of the songs inside the folder by clicking on it once with the left mouse button. Here we're going to choose a classical music piece.

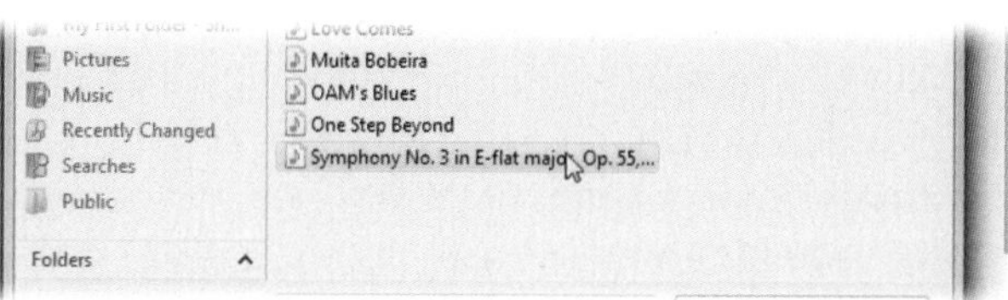

● Finally, click the **Import** button to add the song to the movie project.

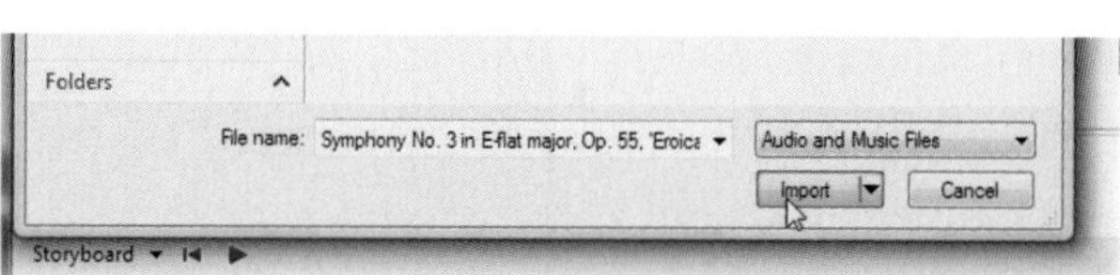

ADDING THE IMPORTED MUSIC

● You can see that the piece of music we found in the Windows Sample Music folder has been added to the project. To make it a part of our home movie, we'll need to drag it down onto the Storyboard, so click on it with the left mouse button.

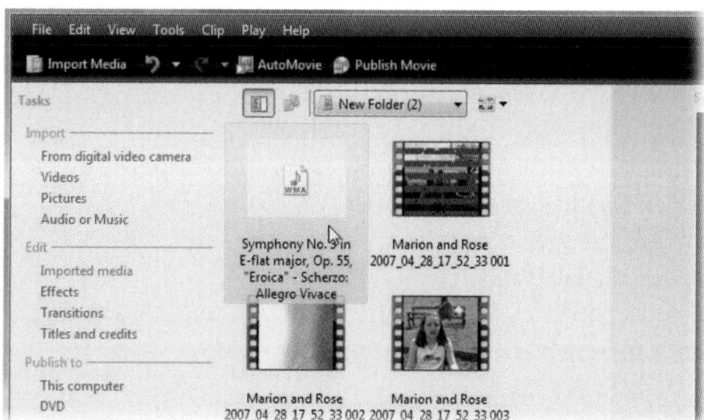

● Still holding down the left mouse button, drag the music file down onto the Storyboard. Since we want the music to start when the movie starts, we're going to position this music right at the beginning. A vertical blue line indicates the position of the music in the movie–here it's directly behind the music we're dragging and in front of the first scene.

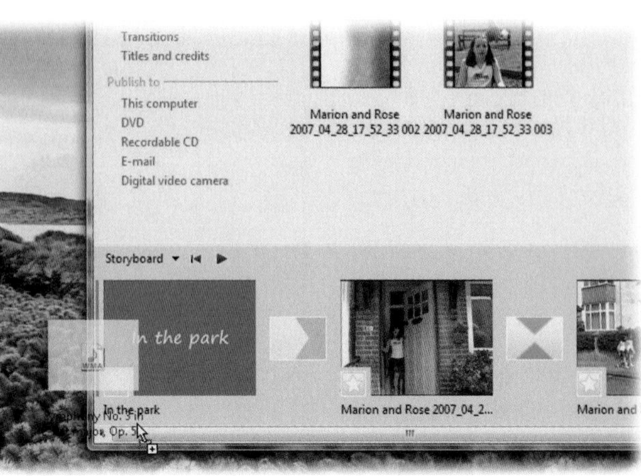

● When you let go of the mouse button to drop the music into position, two things happen. First, the Storyboard turns into a **Timeline** with much more detailed measurements; second, Windows displays a dialog box explaining what's just happened. Click the **OK** button to continue.

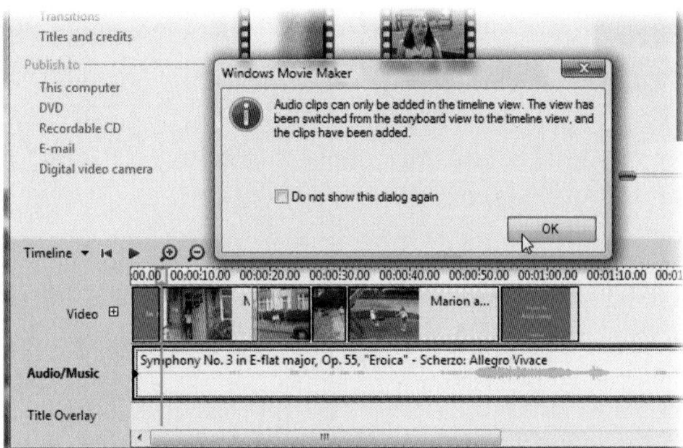

EDITING THE MUSIC

● It's unlikely that your movie and music will be the same length (here, the music is too long). We can fix that by moving the cursor over the end of the music track until it changes into a double-headed red arrow. This indicates that the track is "re-sizable" and that we can shorten it by clicking and dragging to the left.

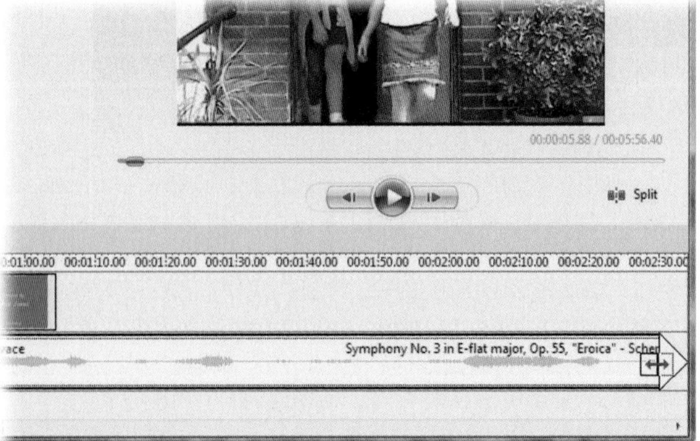

● As you start to drag the music to the left, you'll see that the entire track is highlighted in blue. Keep dragging until you reach the end of the movie.

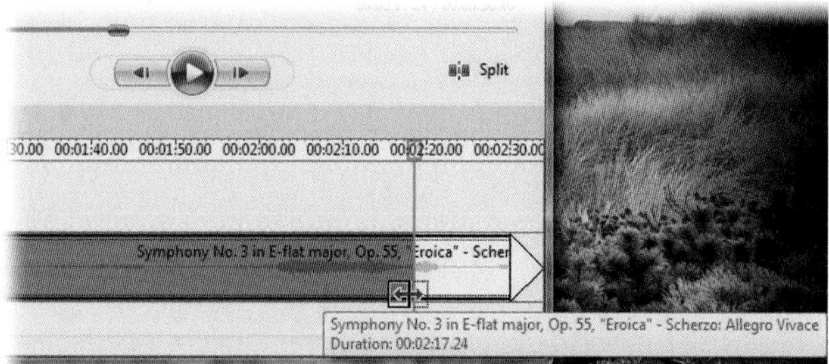

● When you've lined up the end of the music track with the end of the movie track as in this example, let go of the mouse button and it will snap into place. Your chosen piece of music will now end at the same time as your movie.

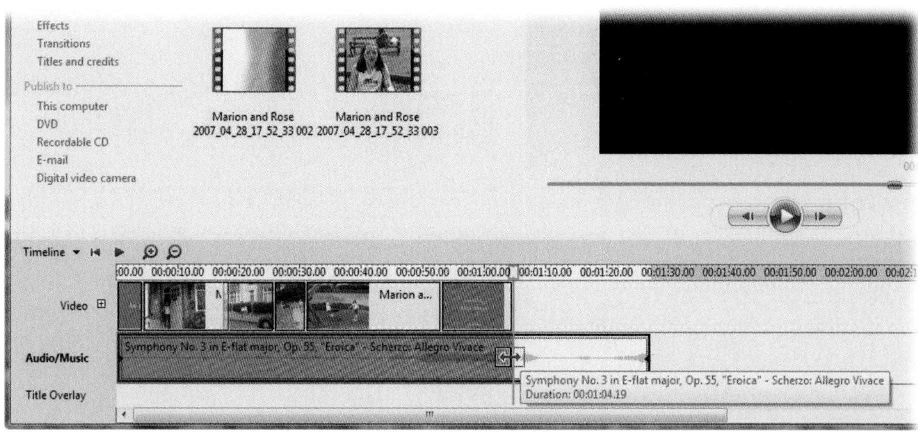

RECORDING A NARRATION

You can also record a narration to go with your movie and run it alongside– or instead of–the music track. You'll need to plug a microphone into the socket on your sound card, but after that Movie Maker takes over. With the project loaded, click the arrow next to the Storyboard button above the storyboard itself. Choose the **Narrate** timeline. If you want to speak from the beginning of the movie, just click the **Start Narration** button and speak into the microphone. When you've finished, click on **Stop Narration**. Alternatively, if you want to narrate over certain scenes but not others, click the first one in the **Timeline** and then click **Start Narration**; stop when you've finished and then move on to the next point. The narration is saved with the movie.

● Here's the music track in position. That blue line that squiggles up and down (below the title of the music) indicates the volume of the music. Where there are lots of squiggles at the end means that the music is going to be loud.

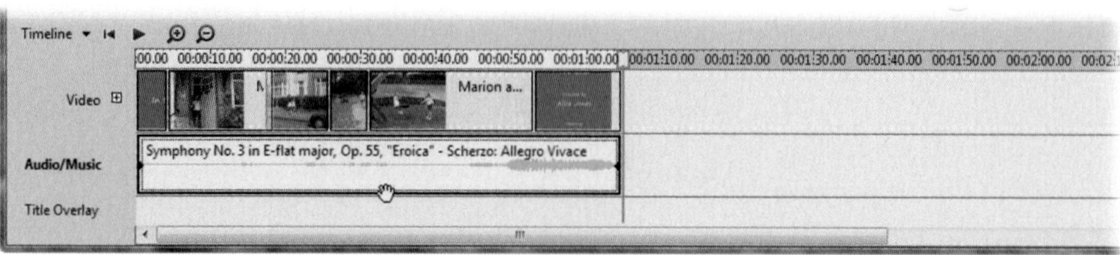

● The track looks very loud at the end and, because of the way we've shortened it, will end very abruptly. Fortunately, we can change this. Move the cursor over the music track and then click on it with the right mouse button so the menu pops up.

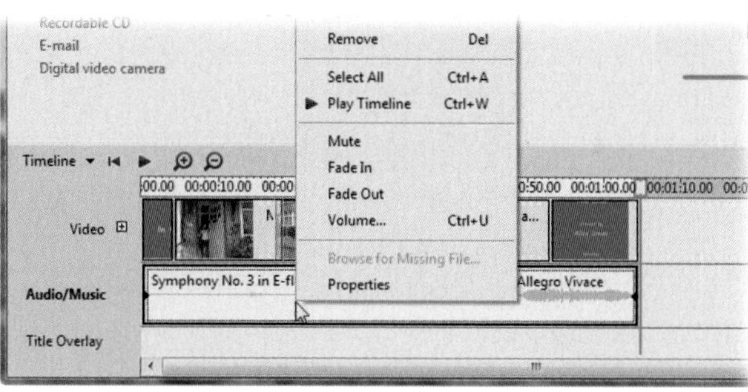

● Slide the cursor up the menu until you reach the **Fade Out** option. Click on it once to select. The music track will fade out when it nears the end.

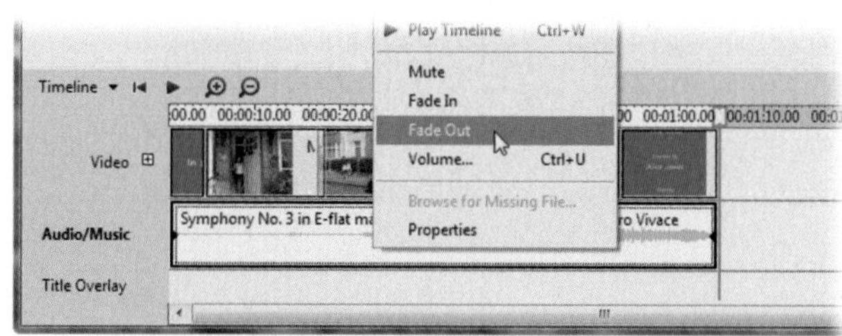

● Play the movie back as you've done before and see what it sounds like. If the music track is too intrusive, you can reduce the volume. Stop playback and then right click on the track again. Choose **Volume** from the pop-up menu.

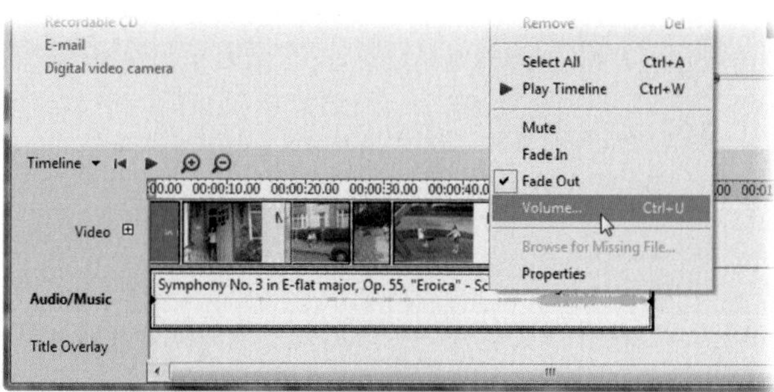

• When the **Audio Clip Volume** dialog box opens, you'll see a volume slider. In this example, it's turned up to full.

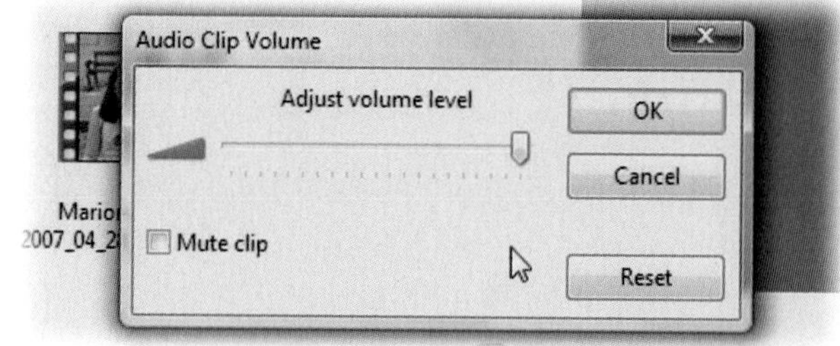

• Click on the slider with the left mouse button and then, still holding the button down, drag it slightly to the left to reduce the volume. This will help us to hear the dialog in our movie more clearly.

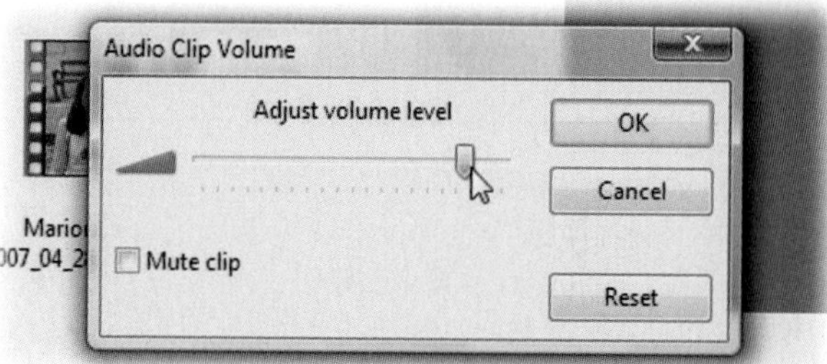

• To finish editing the music clip, click the **OK** button. This will confirm the volume change and take you back to the main Movie Maker window.

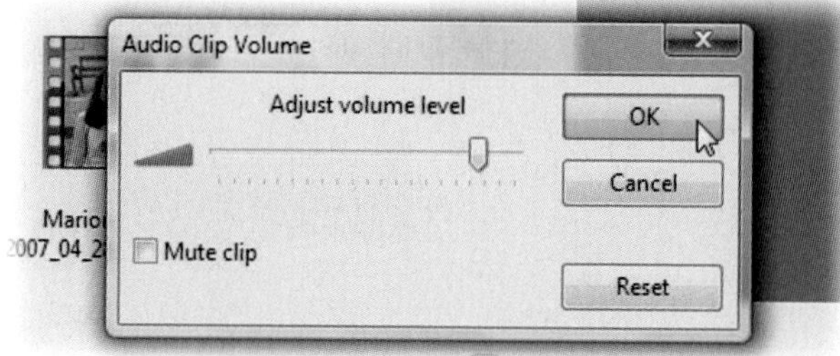

MORE THAN ONE MUSIC TRACK

Although you can't physically have multiple music tracks to accompany your movie, there's nothing to stop you from importing a range of CD tracks and then shortening them on the Timeline as we did to the classical piece in our example above. To start, choose your first piece of music and drag it down to the Timeline. Then, drag the end of the music to shorten it until it's the required length; add a fade at the end. Pick the next piece of music that you want to add to your movie and drag that down onto the same track, after the first piece. Cut that piece in the same way and fade it in and out if you think it is necessary. Carry on the music track is finished.

Your Finished Movie

Of course, having a finished movie on your own PC is very nice, but what you really want to do share it with your friends and family. That's what we'll cover in this section.

Burning Your Movie to DVD

Although Movie Maker offers a number of different ways to finish off your movie so that others can enjoy it, the most common method by far is to burn it onto a DVD that can be played on any typical home DVD player that is connected to a television set. Most modern PCs include a re-writable DVD drive that is capable of this, and blank DVD discs are inexpensive and widely available. Best of all, although Windows has supported the creation of DVDs for many versions, you used to have to buy a program from someone else to do the job properly. Fortunately, it's now included as part of Windows Vista. Here's how it works.

PREPARING TO BURN YOUR DVD

● With the project still on the screen, move the cursor over to the **Publish to** list of **Tasks** on the left and click on **DVD**.

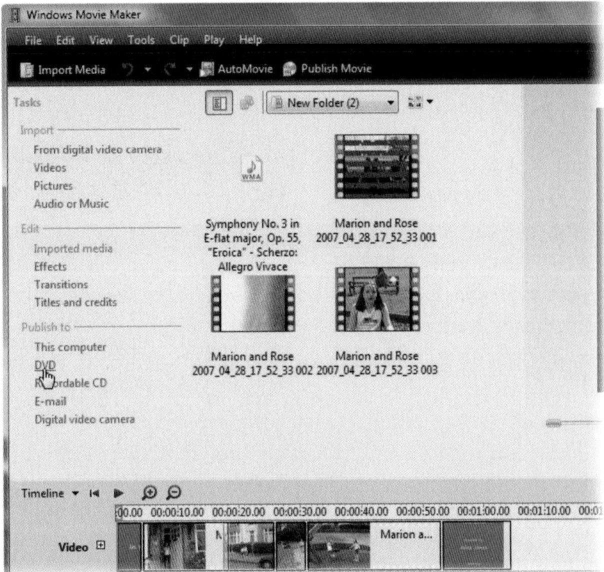

● Windows displays a dialog box that explains what happens next– basically, Movie Maker will close and Windows DVD Maker will open in its place. Click **OK** to continue.

● When the DVD Maker window appears you'll see that your film is listed there, together with its duration. In the bottom left-hand corner you will see a pie chart indicating how much of the DVD your movie is going to take up (ours is incredibly small–just long enough to show you the program's features). There's nothing more we need to do at this stage so click on **Next** to continue.

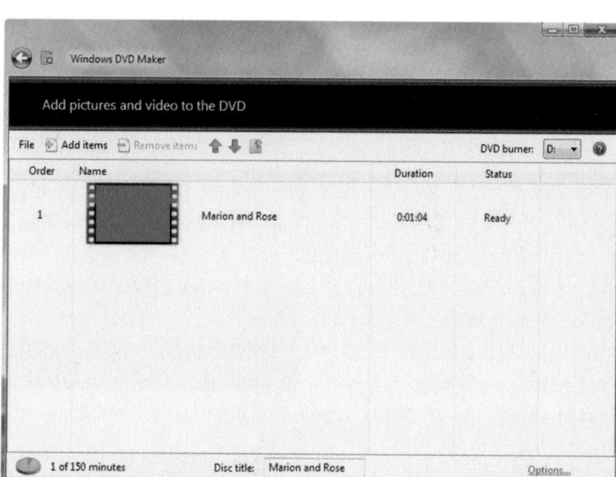

CHOOSING A STYLE

● DVD Maker includes a series of styles–visual "looks" for your DVD that make it look more professional. To see the range of available styles in the list, move the navigation slider up and down with the mouse.

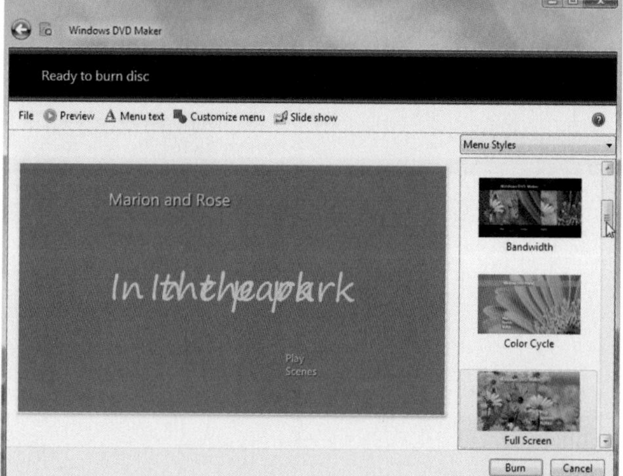

● To audition a style, just click on it with the mouse and you'll see it in the larger preview window in the middle. This is the **Photographs** style, which looks rather attractive.

● Of course you can't really tell until you see a style in action, which is why DVD Maker has a **Preview** button. Click on it now.

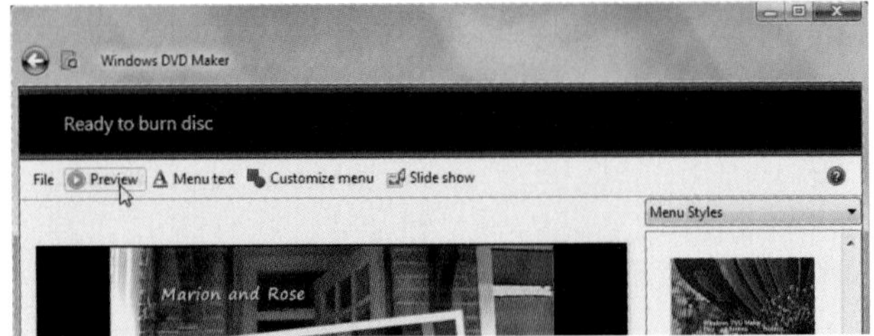

● After a moment, the movie opens in a preview window, showing DVD style controls underneath. Click the **Play** button to start the DVD.

● Watch the movie until you have a good idea of what the style is like and then click the **Menu** button to go back to the start.

● When you've finished previewing the DVD style, click on the **OK** button to return to the **Menu Styles** screen.

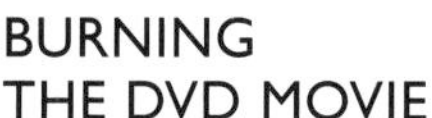

BURNING THE DVD MOVIE

● Make sure there's a new, blank DVD disc in your drive and then click on the **Burn** button.

● DVD Maker disappears and in its place you will get a small dialog box that tells you it's creating the DVD and keeping an eye on the progress.

OTHER WAYS TO SAVE MOVIES

Movie Maker offers a number of other ways to share a home movie, which you can find in the **Publish to** list of options in the **Tasks** menu. For example, you can save the movie in a format especially designed for sending by e-mail and have Windows open its mail program with the movie already attached, so all you have to do is address it and send an accompanying message. Alternatively, if you don't have a re-writable DVD, you can choose the **Recordable CD** option and use that. Finally, you can save the movie back to the tape in a connected DV camera.

● When it's finished, you'll see the message **Your disc is ready**. If you want to make another disc exactly the same, select that option. Otherwise, click the **Close** button like this.

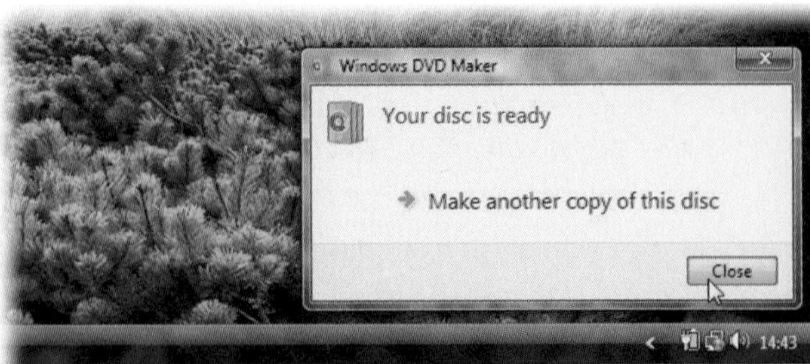

SAVING THE DVD SETTINGS

● When the DVD dialog closes, you're returned to the DVD Maker screen. If there's a chance you'll want to burn the movie again at a later date, it's worth saving it, so click on the **File** menu and choose **Save**.

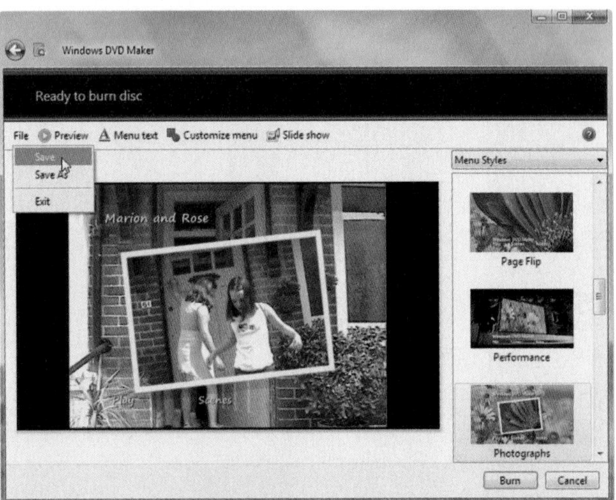

● When the dialog box opens, click in the empty box and give your DVD movie a name–ours is called Marion and Rose– and then click the **Save** button to store all of the settings used to create this particular DVD on the hard disk.

● If you've finished, close the DVD Maker by clicking on the "x" in the top right-hand corner of the window.

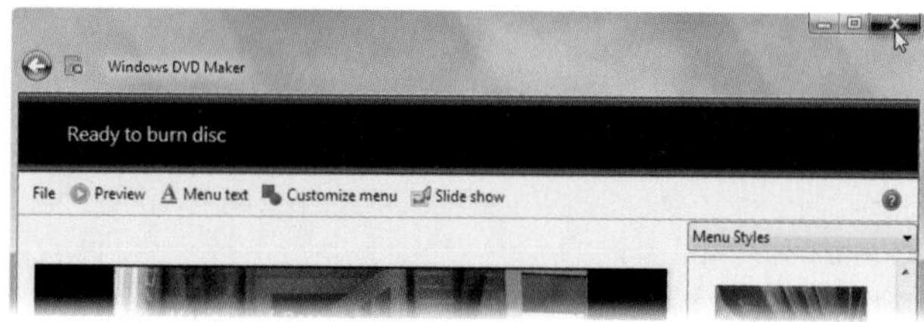

WATCHING THE DVD

● Here's the finished DVD being played in Media Player on someone else's computer, complete with the style and menu we chose in the previous steps. This will also play in a modern standalone DVD player.

MORE PUBLISHING OPTIONS

Although Movie Maker does a good job of creating DVDs and e-mail friendly movies, if you want the widest range of options when you come to publish, select **This Computer** as your source. When the **Publish Movie** dialog box appears, click **Next**. On the subsequent screen, click the radio button next to the **More settings** option. Open the drop-down list by clicking on the arrow with the left mouse button, and you'll be offered a selection including VHS, widescreen, and High Definition. Some of these options require very large amounts of space, so if space is tight, you can tell Movie Maker to set a maximum file size for the movie and it will then produce the best quality it can within that restriction.

MAINTAINING YOUR PC

DESPITE THE FACT that they're easier to use than ever before, home PCs are still complex machines and over time, as you install more programs and add more hardware, are only likely to become more complex. That means you need to know a little bit about how to maintain them. This isn't as geeky as it sounds, and Windows Vista provides lots of tools to keep your home PC in good shape. In addition to important preventative measures, Windows Vista also offers you ways to recover data, so that even if disaster does strike, it's not an all-out catastrophe for you or your PC.

438 MEET YOUR PC

448 KEEPING A TIDY HOUSE

456 SYSTEM PROTECTION

478 MANAGING PROGRAMS

486 WINDOWS SCHEDULER

496 KEEPING YOUR DATA SECURE

Meet Your PC

Although you don't need to know anything about what goes inside a home PC in order to use it, it's useful to have some basic information to hand.

Basic System Information

On the following pages, we'll look at some of the fundamental components that go to make up your PC. We're not going to ask you to open up the machine, just to get acquainted with basic information such as the processor it uses, the amount of memory installed, the size of the hard disk, and the version of Windows. If you need to get technical help at any time, these are the sorts of basic facts that will come in handy.

LOOKING AT YOUR PC'S DISKS

- Click on the **Computer** icon on the desktop.

- You will see a fairly typical PC set up. The **Local Disk** icon, marked as **C**, is our main disk where Windows, our programs, and everything else is stored. Underneath that there's a **DVD RW Drive**, which is called **D**, and next to that a third drive called **E**–this is actually a USB stick, which has taken over from the floppy disk as the easiest way to move files between PCs.

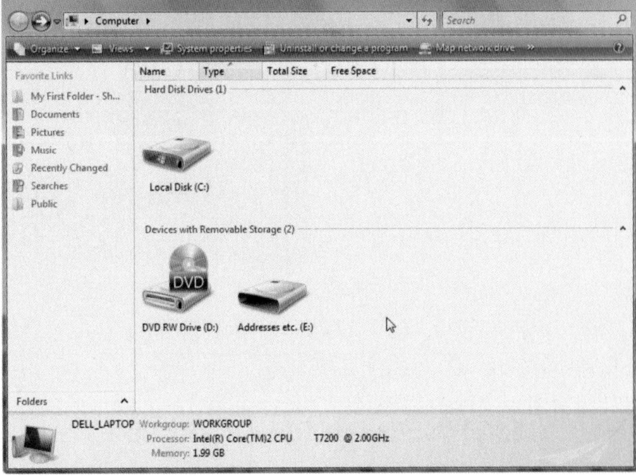

● Move the cursor over the top disk icon and let it hover there. Windows displays a little tip that tells us the size of the drive and how much space is left on it.

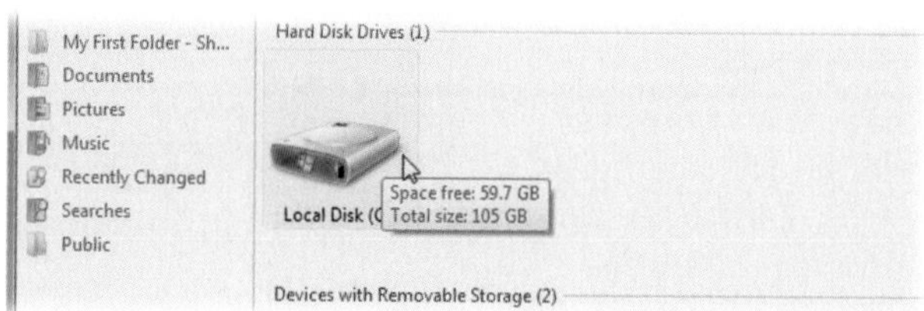

GETTING MORE INFORMATION

● To get more information, leave the cursor where it is and click once with the right mouse button. Then, when the menu appears, choose **Properties**.

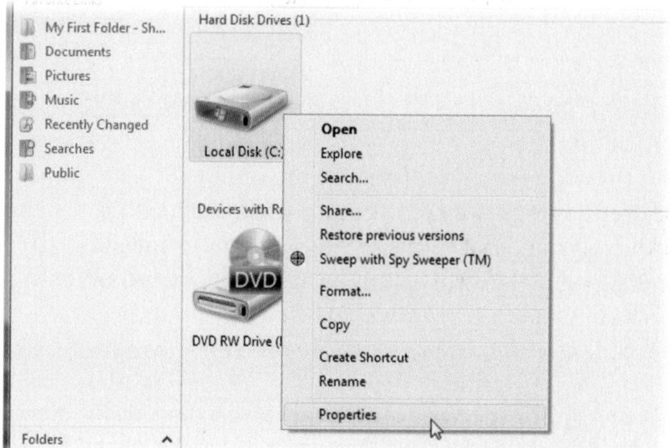

● This shows a pie chart of the disk, with the free space marked in pink. Most modern hard disks are so big that you'll need to work hard to fill them up.

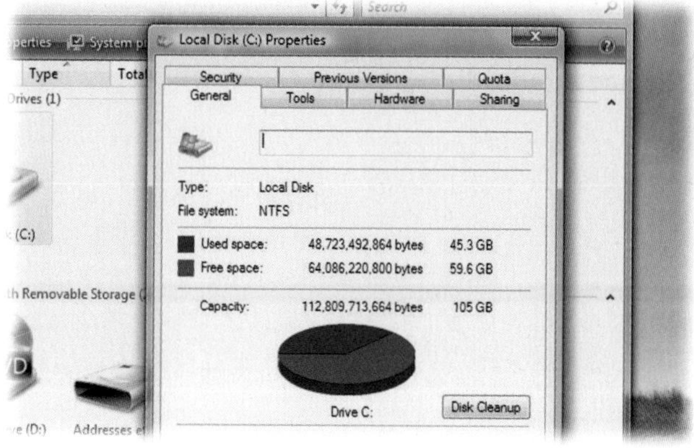

● Click the **Cancel** button to return to the **Computer** window and the disk drives.

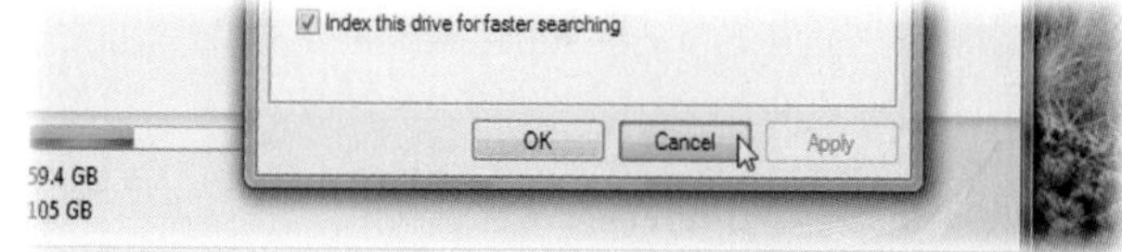

OPENING SYSTEM PROPERTIES

● Back at the Computer window, move the cursor up to the button bar that runs along the top and click on **System properties** once with the left mouse button.

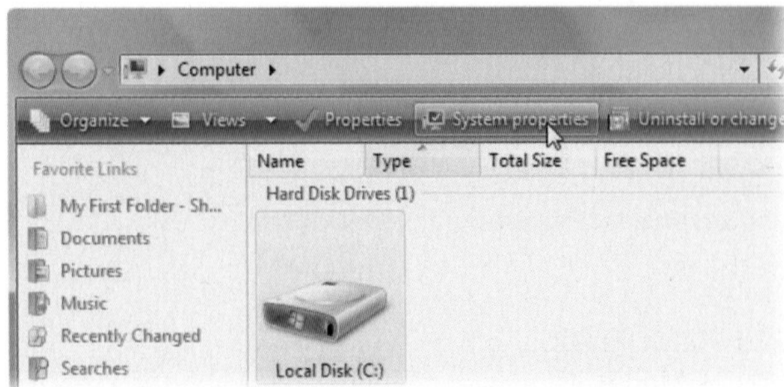

EXAMINING SYSTEM PROPERTIES

● This window tells us lots of useful things. We can see which version of Windows is running (Vista Ultimate), what processor the PC uses (an Intel Core 2), the speed it's running at (2.00GHz), as well as how much memory is installed (2038MB), and whether Windows has been activated yet. This is the kind of basic information that a technical support person will need to know–and they'll understand it, even if you don't.

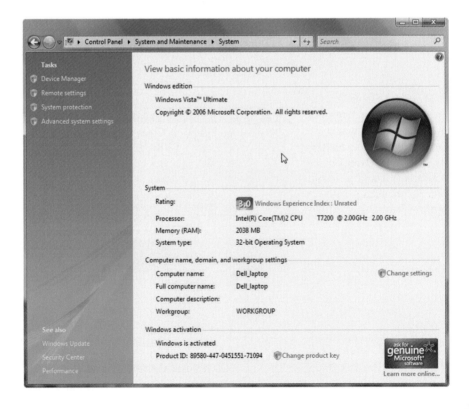

OPENING DEVICE MANAGER

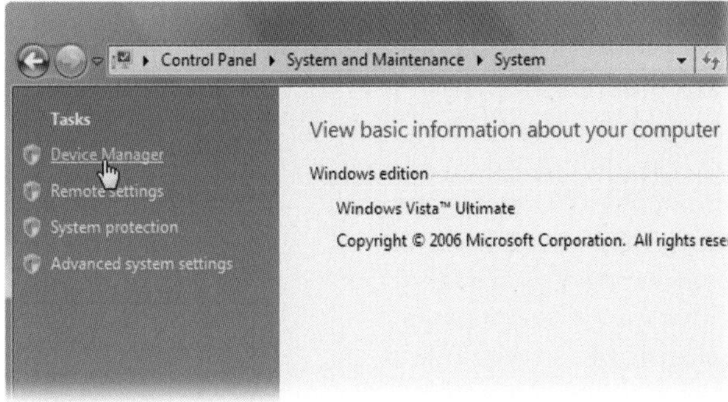

● Sometimes, a technical support person may require information about a specific device. With the **System Properties** window still open, move the cursor over to the left and click on the **Device Manager** link once.

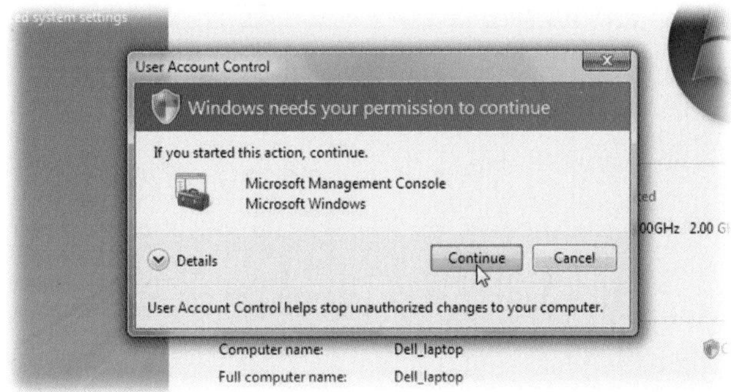

● When the **User Account Control** dialog appears, click the **Continue** button to confirm that you want to carry on.

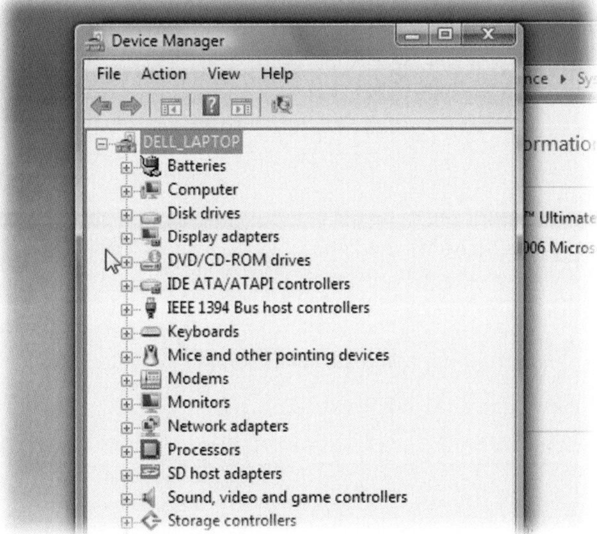

● This opens the **Device Manager** dialog box, which includes important information about the various devices inside your PC and also some that are attached to it.

GETTING MORE INFORMATION

● Note the small "+" signs next to the entries in the list. This indicates that there's either more information about this particular device available, or that there's more than one device present in this particular category. Move the cursor down to the one next to **Display adapters** and click it once.

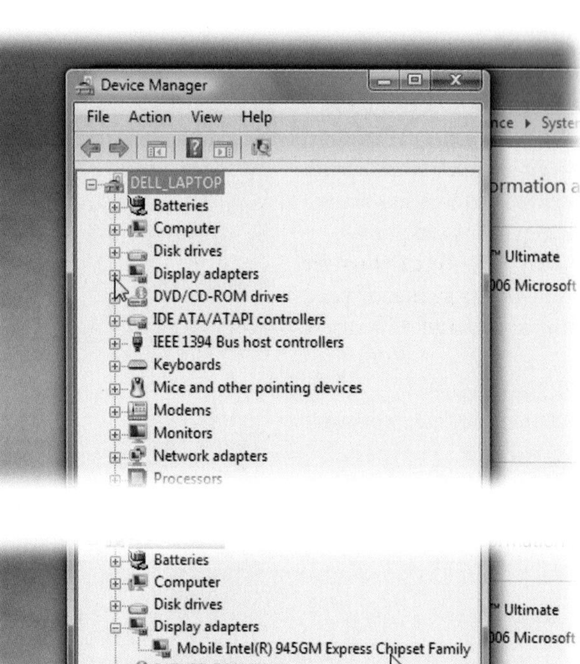

● The display adapter is the electronic device that actually sends the signals to your monitor, which produces the images you see on the screen. This reveals the name of the display adapter.

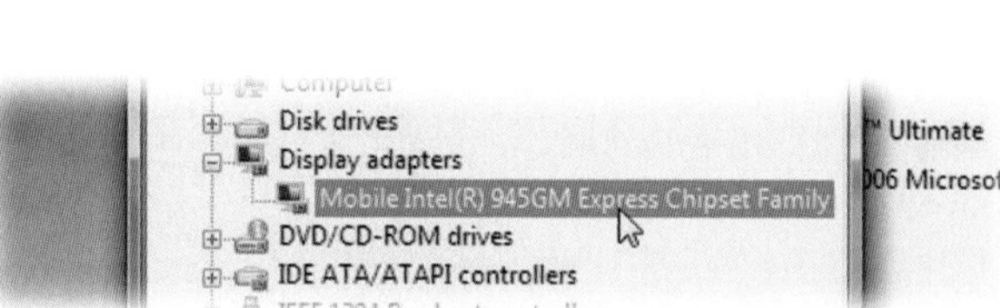

● To find out more about the adapter itself, double click on it with the left mouse button.

● This opens the dialog for this particular item and the status window tells us that the device is working properly. To get the most up-to-date information, however, click the **Driver** tab at the top.

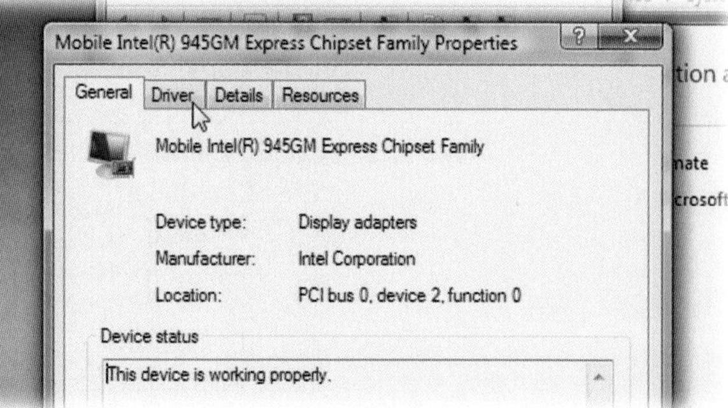

● Here you can see the version number of the driver for this device (this is the program that helps to make sure it works properly), as well as various other options such as updating or uninstalling the driver–this may help if you get into technical difficulties.

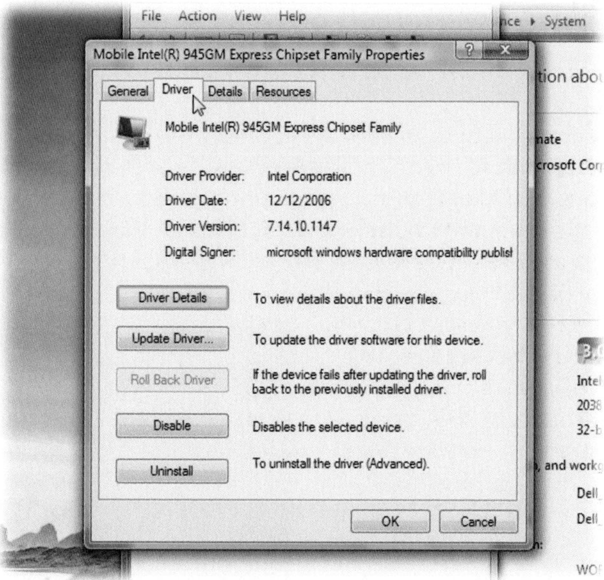

● Click the **Cancel** button to close the dialog without making any changes.

● Click the "x" to close the **Device Manager** dialog box.

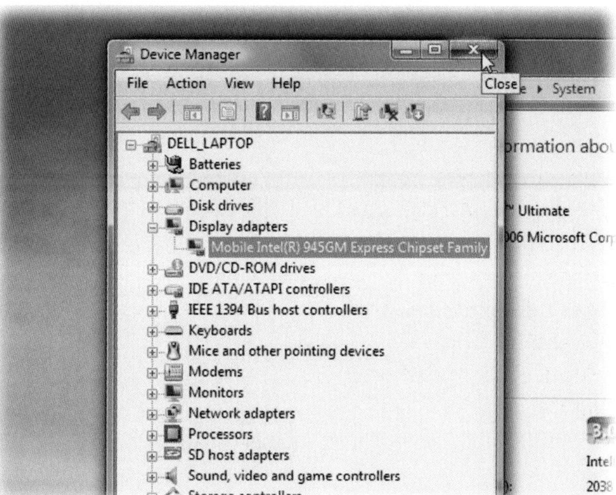

FINE TUNING YOUR PC

There are various steps that you can take to improve the overall performance of your PC. One of the most common problems with Windows Vista, for example, is that computers are sold with configurations that are only just able to run it properly, rather than being able to run it comfortably. Fortunately, it's possible to take actions yourself that can help to speed Vista up.

CHECKING WINDOWS PERFORMANCE

- The first step toward fine tuning your PC is to find out if it is necessary. Start by moving the cursor up to the **Control Panel** button and clicking on it once.

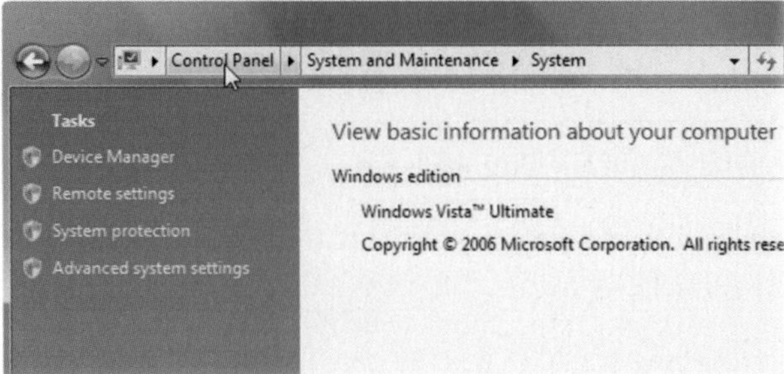

- When the **Control Panel** window opens, click the **System and Maintenance** heading at the top.

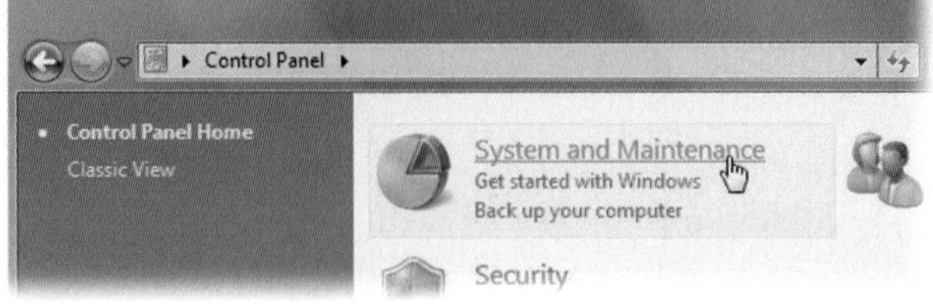

- When the System and Maintenance window appears, move the cursor down to the link that says **Check your computer's Windows Experience Index base score** and then click it once.

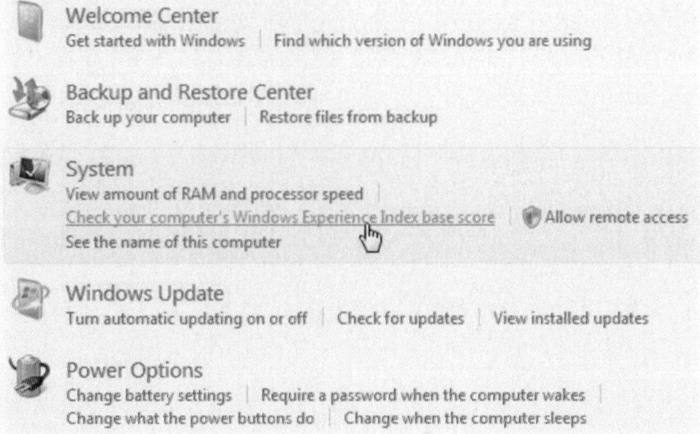

RUNNING THE EXPERIENCE INDEX

● This opens the window that measures how well your PC is able to run Windows Vista. You should run this test periodically by clicking the **Refresh Now** button as the score will change depending on whether you've made any changes to your PC.

● When the User Account Control dialog box appears, click the **Continue** button.

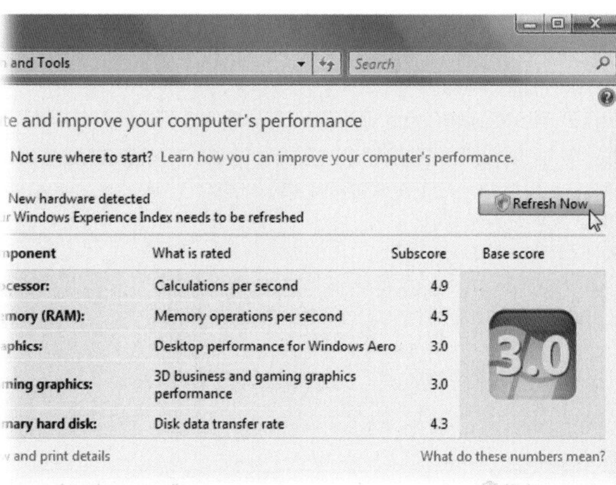

● Vista then runs the **Windows Experience Index** program. This may be a little alarming as the screen often flashes during the test–don't be concerned, it's completely normal.

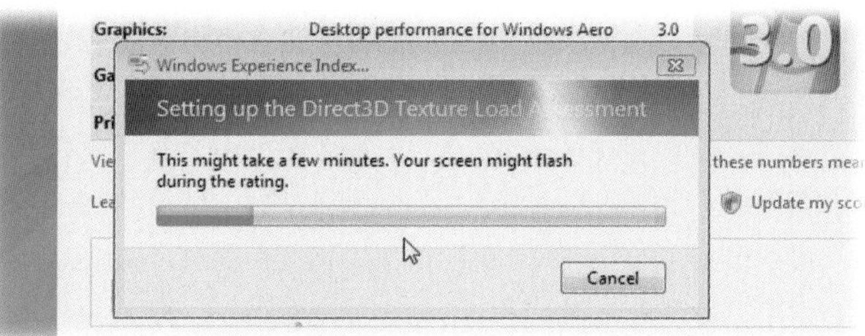

THE EXPERIENCE INDEX SCORE

● Windows will display your final overall score. Here it's 3.0, which means it's able to run most Windows tasks comfortably, including Aero, the new interface with its fancy transparency effects. However, as the visuals place most strain on your PC's hardware, it's worth looking at how to alter these, especially if your score is lower than 3.0. Slide the cursor over to the **Tasks** list and click on **Adjust visual effects** link. (Click **Continue** when the User Account Control dialog appears.)

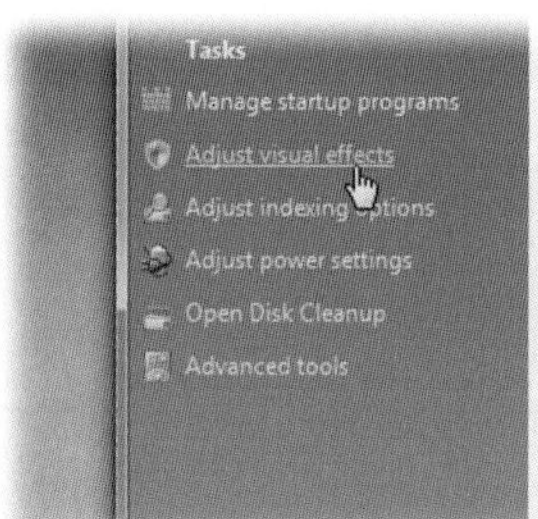

ADJUSTING VISUAL EFFECTS

● This opens the **Performance Options** dialog box. Currently it's set to **Let Windows choose what's best for my computer**. However, it's also possible to change the settings so that, for example, Windows works faster although it won't look so good.

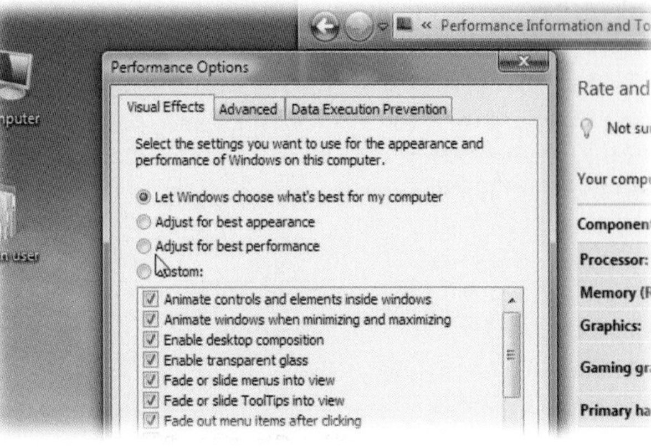

● If your PC is running slowly, this is the first thing you should try. Click the empty radio button next to the **Adjust for best performance** option.

● This will remove all of Vista's fancy visual effects but leave everything else working fine.

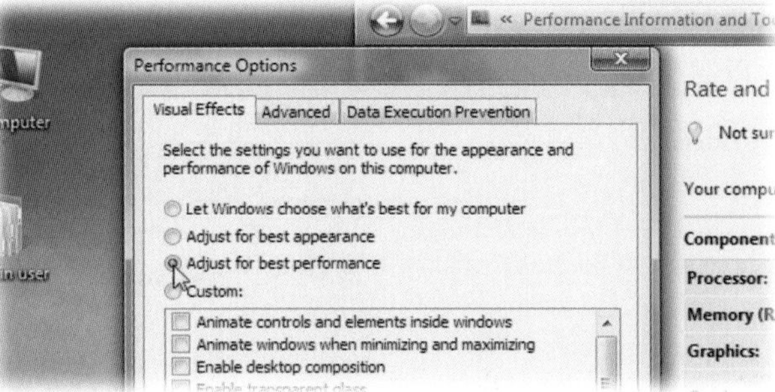

● Click the **Apply** button at the bottom of the dialog box to make your changes

● The results are dramatic. Windows reverts to the visual "look" of nine years ago, which is unattractive, but much less demanding on the PC.

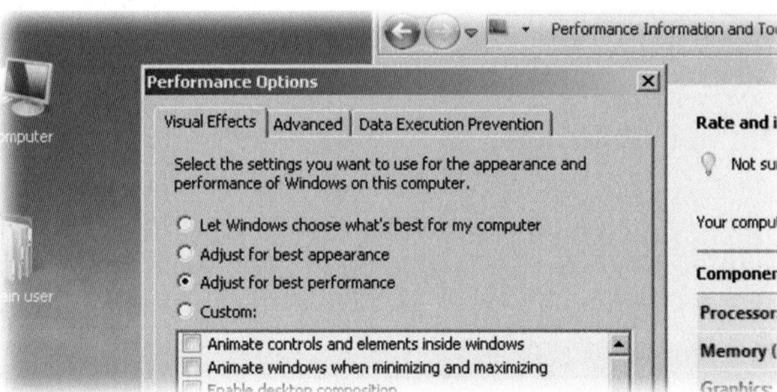

● Fortunately, this machine can cope with Vista's new look, so we can click again on the **Let Windows choose what's best for my computer** radio button.

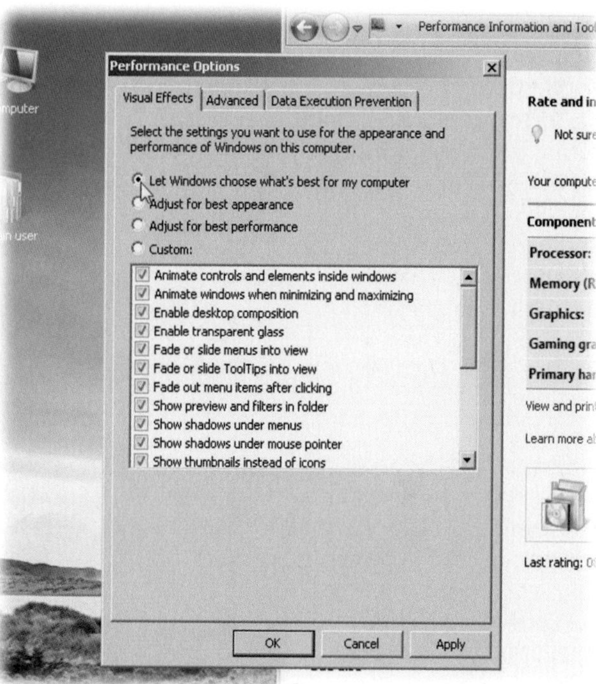

● Finally, click the **OK** button to confirm your changes and return to the smart new Vista interface.

FINE, FINE TUNING

If you like the look of the new Vista interface but are having problems because your PC is running slowly, you can turn off the single component that's likely to be causing the bottleneck, while keeping everything else. From the **Windows Experience Index** window, click on the **Adjust visual effects** links in the **Tasks** list on the left. In the dialog box, click **Continue** and then leave all the settings as they are–except one. Remove the tick next to the **Enable transparent glass** option and then click **OK**. This will improve the performance of a PC that's struggling, while retaining much of Vista's new look and feel.

Keeping a Tidy House

Computers are rather like cars, in that one of the most important things you can do to optimize their overall performance and wellbeing is the occasional bit of maintenance.

Freeing Up Hard Disk Space

Programs–and the people who use them–accumulate junk, and junk, as we all know, takes up lots of space. As you use your PC more often and for more things, your hard disk will slowly fill with data that you don't really need to keep. In this section, we'll show you how to identify the junk on your PC and how to get rid of it.

OPENING SYSTEM AND MAINTENANCE

- Move the cursor down to the Start button and click on it once.

- When the menu opens, slide the cursor across to the **Control Panel** and click once to open it.

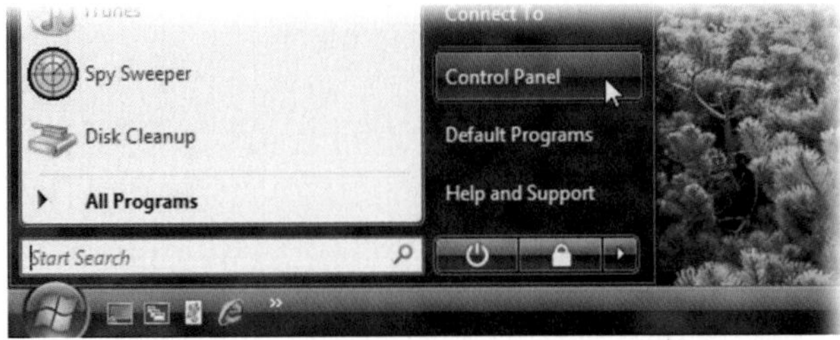

- When the **Control Panel** window appears, go to the first item, **System and Maintenance**, and click on it.

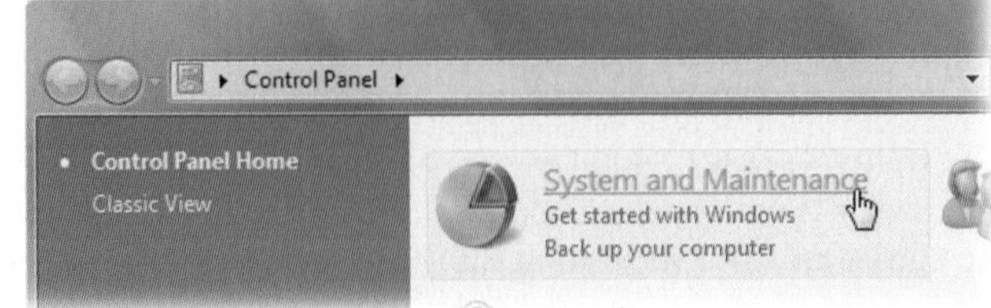

STARTING DISK CLEANUP

● Move the cursor down to the bottom of the next window until you find **Administrative Tools.** Click on the first heading underneath it–**Free up disk space**.

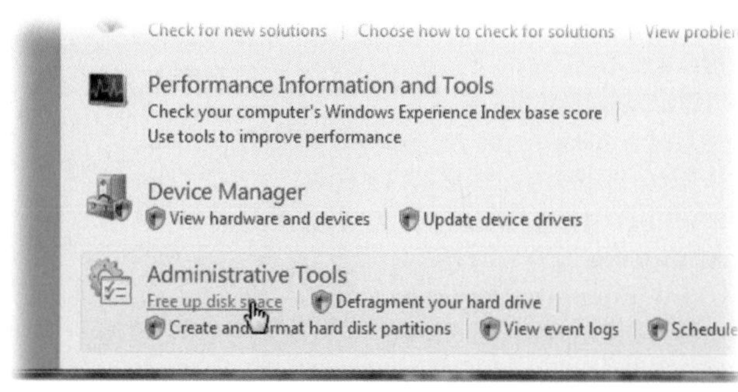

● This opens the **Disk Cleanup Options** dialog box, which asks which files you want to sort out. Select the second option–**Files from all users on this computer**–by clicking on it once.

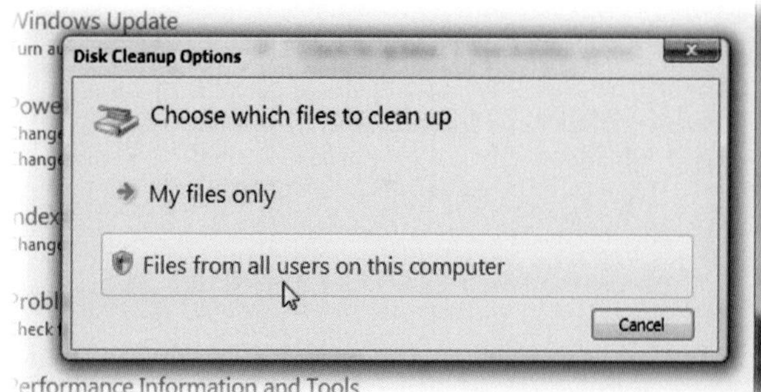

● When the **User Account** Dialog box appears, click on the **Continue** option.

● **Disk Cleanup** now does a "dry run" to estimate how much space it can save by removing those junk files that you don't really need any more. At this point, no files have been removed from your PC, so it's all perfectly safe.

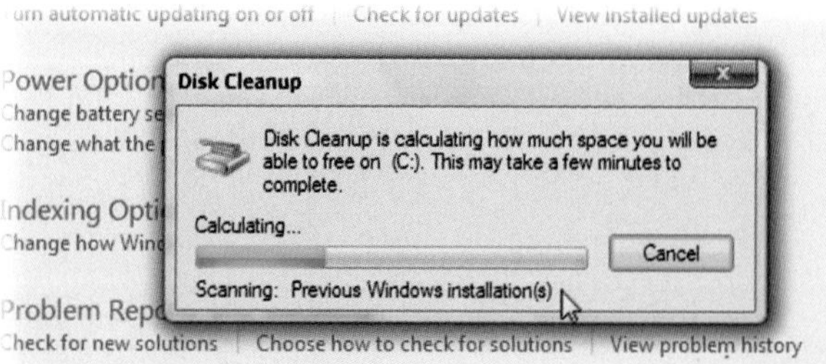

ASSESSING THE RESULTS

- Having estimated the amount of disk space you can savc, Windows displays the results in the **Disk Cleanup** dialog box. The various groups of files that can be removed are listed in the center window, together with the amount of space they will save if they are removed. Only those file groups with a tick next to them are currently included in the total.

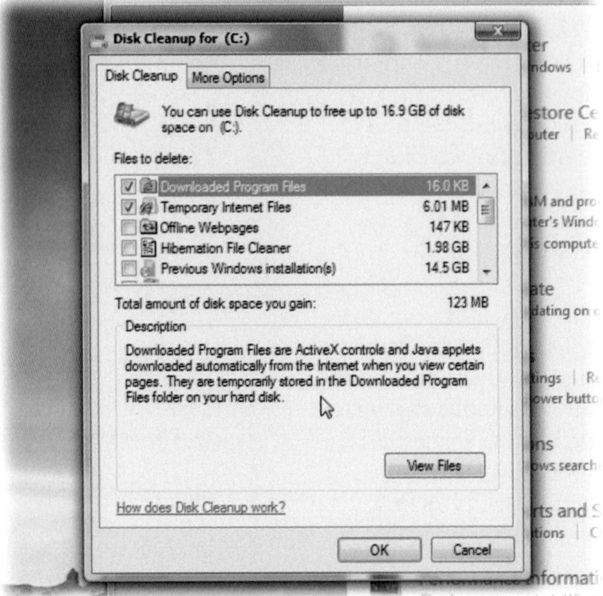

- Click on any of the groups of files in the main menu with the left mouse button and Windows will explain a bit about them in the box underneath. These **Temporary Internet Files**, for example, help webpages you've already visited load more quickly.

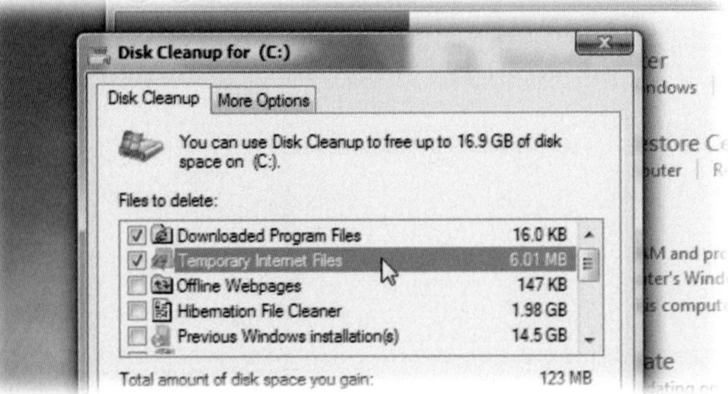

- To see the other files, click the arrow to scroll down the list of file groups.

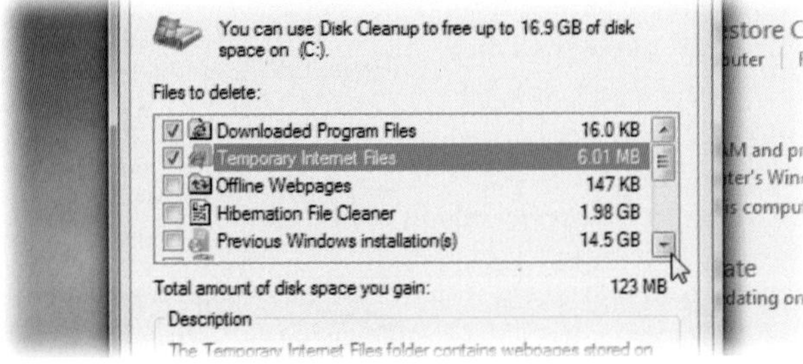

EMPTYING THE RECYCLE BIN

● Click once on the **Recycle Bin** to see what's in there. Including the Recycle Bin in a disk cleanup like this can save a lot of space.

● This looks as though it will save 341MB, which is a substantial amount of space. So, click in the empty box next to the **Recycle Bin** entry to select it–this will add it to the list of files groups that this Disk Cleanup will remove.

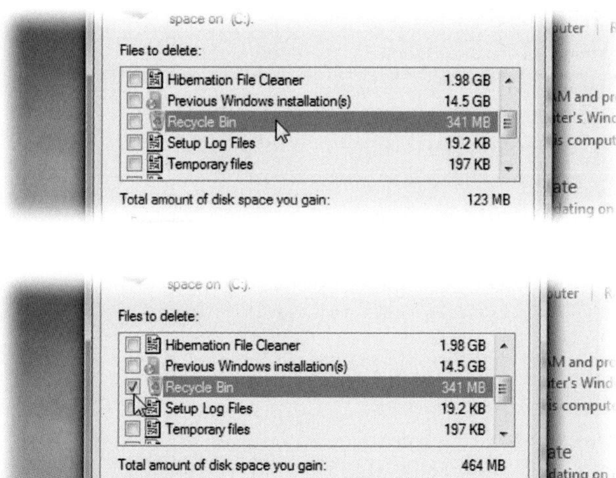

● For fun, click the **View Files** button. This will open a window into the Recycle Bin so we can see how many files are in there.

● Here you can see that there are **99 items** in the Recycle Bin. It's quite easy for this to happen when you're working with large files, such as photographs, making changes to them and dumping old versions. When you've finished, click the "x" to close the window.

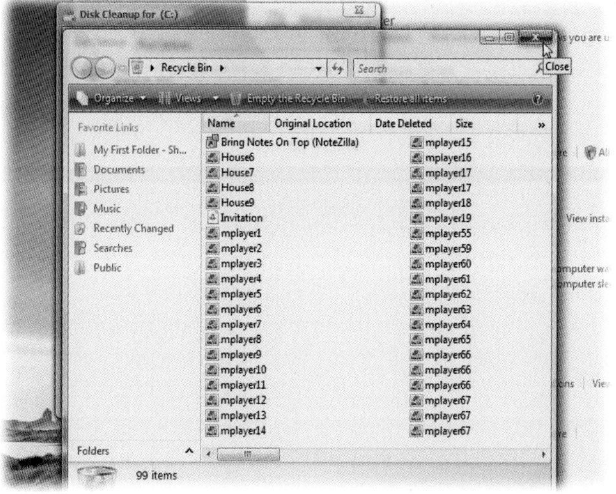

REMOVING UNWANTED FILES

- Back at the Disk Cleanup dialog box, click the **OK** button to start removing the unwanted files.

- When Windows asks if you're sure you want to permanently delete the files, click the **Delete Files** button to confirm.

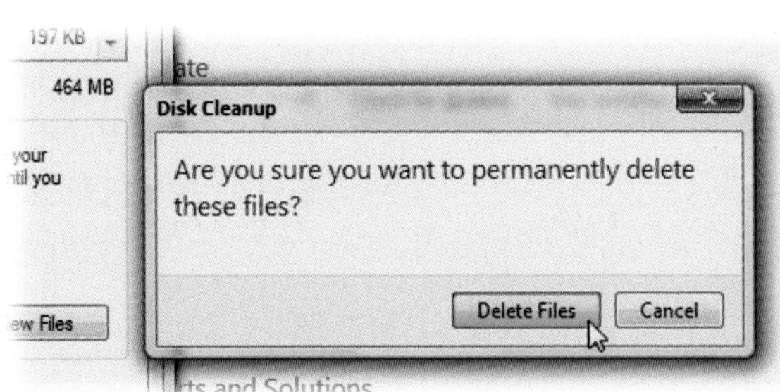

- Windows then deletes all of the marked files, creating more space on your PC's hard disk.

HOW WINDOWS USES YOUR HARD DISK

Imagine your disk is like a bookshelf filled with books that are placed in alphabetical order. When you need one of the books, Windows knows exactly where to go and finds it quickly. When you've finished with the book, however, Windows just chucks it back onto the first available space on the shelf. Over time, this means Windows has to look harder to find things, and it starts to slow down. That's why you should defragment the drive from time to time, and that's what we're going to look at next.

SPEEDING UP YOUR HARD DISK

Like any filing system, the hard disk on your PC is arranged in a particular way. Over time and with constant use, the way the data is stored can become tangled up and the best way to restore the disk's original performance is to defragment it.

This sounds geeky and complicated, but in fact it's neither. You can either defragment your disk yourself when you think it's necessary–for example, when you notice the machine running more slowly–or have Windows do it for you automatically.

THE DEFRAGMENT WINDOW

- Make sure the System and Maintenance window is still open, then find the **Administrative Tools** heading at the bottom and click on the **Defragment your hard drive** heading to begin the process.

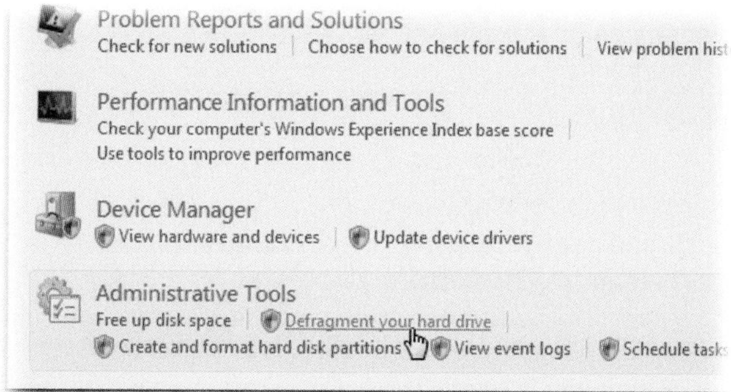

- When the User Account Control window opens, click **Continue** to proceed.

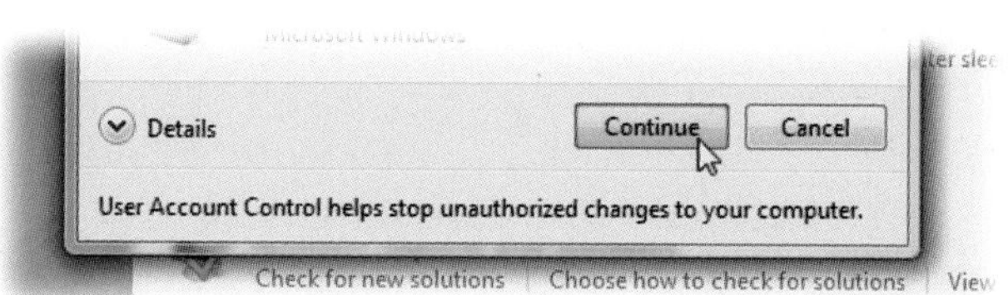

- **Disk Defragmenter** gives you two choices. You can either set up the schedule for regular defragmentation, or defragment your hard disk right here and now.

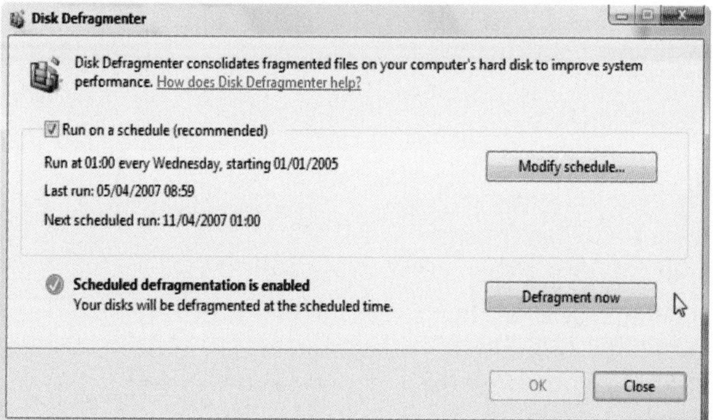

DEFRAGMENTING THE HARD DISK

● We would recommend that you choose the option to defragment now, because this way you can start with a fully defragmented hard disk before deciding on a schedule. Just do it when you can be sure that you don't need to use the PC for a while, because the defragmentation process can take some time, depending on the size of your hard drive and how fragmented it has become. (In actual fact, you can continue to use the PC while the disk is being defragmented–things just take longer.) Click the **Defragment now** button to begin the process.

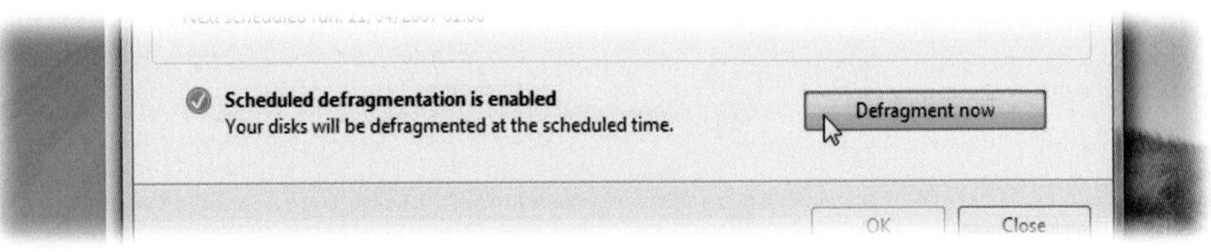

● You'll see a little spinning circle and a message saying **Defragmenting hard disks**.

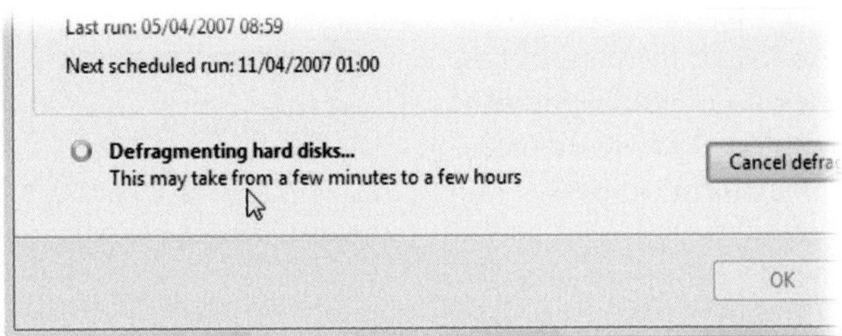

● When it's finished, you'll see a message saying that **Scheduled defragmentation is enabled**–which may seem strange since we haven't enabled it, but this is just Windows being helpful.

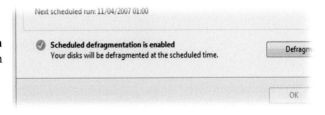

MODIFYING THE SCHEDULE

● Windows assumes you want to do defragment your drive or drives regularly using its own automatic schedule. To check that out, click the **Modify schedule** button.

- Here you can see that Windows is currently set to defragment the hard disk once a week at 1pm on a Wednesday.

- That seems excessive, particularly given that this PC is so new and hasn't had time to accumulate too much junk or get too disorganized, so we're going to change it. Click the arrow on the **How often** panel to open the drop-down list.

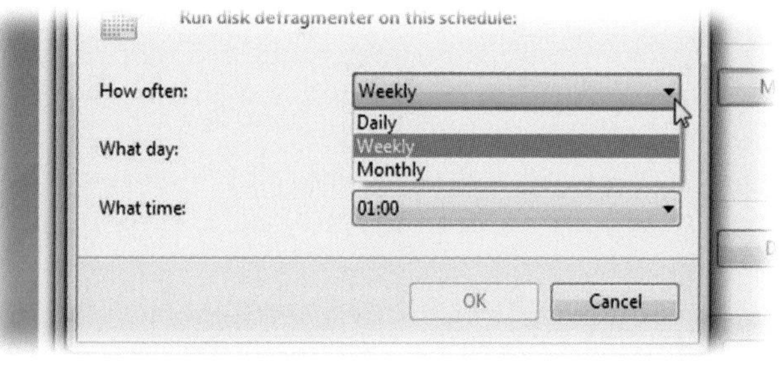

- Slide the cursor down and choose **Monthly**.

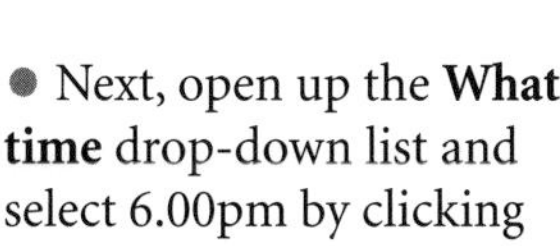

- Next, open up the **What time** drop-down list and select 6.00pm by clicking on **18:00**.

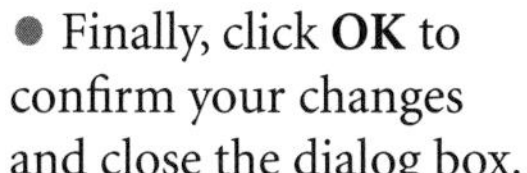

- Finally, click **OK** to confirm your changes and close the dialog box.

System Protection

If your PC stops working properly, Windows Vista can use its system protection features to go "back in time" to a point when it was last behaving itself.

Turning System Protection On

Windows Vista can create "snapshots" of your system–called restore points–and save these on the hard disk. If, at some point in the future, you discover that your PC is behaving strangely or slowing down, you can return to one of these snapshots and restore it, so that everything returns to normal. As part of this process, it will remove any programs that you have installed between now and the last snapshot, but it leave any data that you've created intact.

OPENING THE SYSTEM PROPERTIES DIALOG

- To get to the System Properties dialogue box, move the cursor over the **Computer** icon and click on it once with the right mouse button.

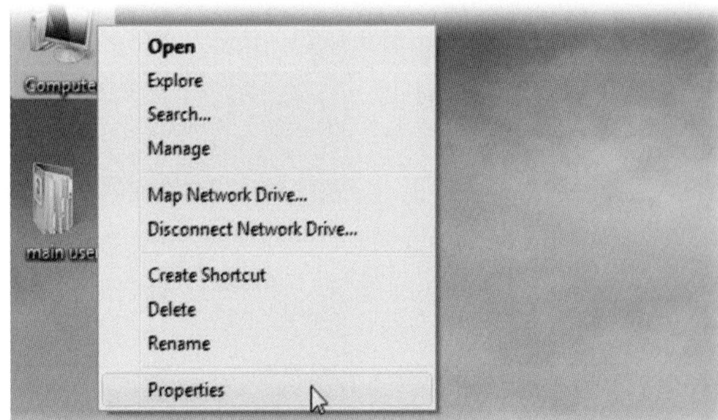

- When the pop-up menu appears, slide the cursor down to the **Properties** item and click it once.

● This takes you to the **System** window inside **System and Maintenance** in the Windows **Control Panel**. Move the cursor over to the **Tasks** list on the left and click once on the **System protection** link.

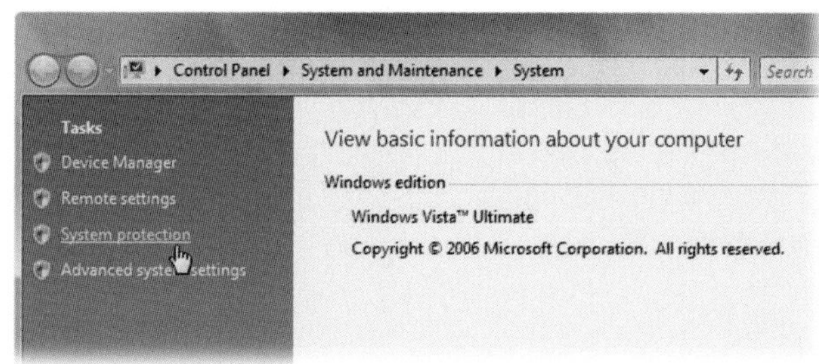

● You are about to change Windows settings, so the **User Account Control** dialog box will appear–just click the **Continue** button to move on.

STARTING SYSTEM PROTECTION

● Here's the **System Properties** dialog box, with the **System Protection** tab already highlighted at the top so we know we're in the correct section of the dialog. Note that Windows has logged our single hard disk and is displaying it in the window in the middle of the box.

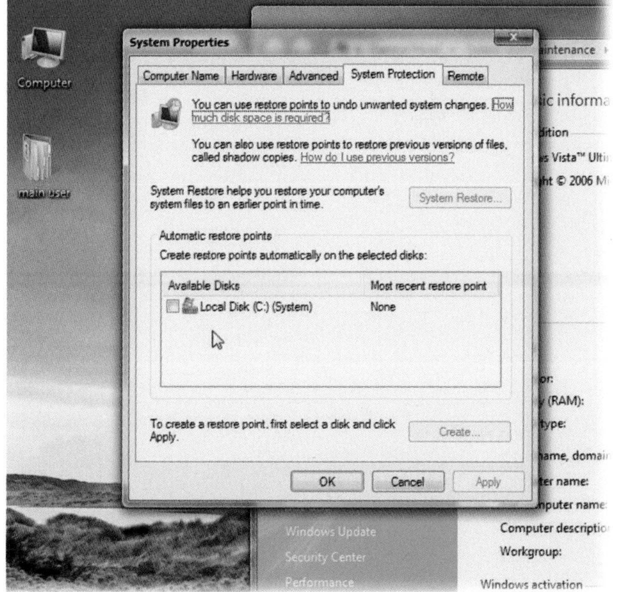

● If there's already a tick in the box next to the disk drive, then **System Protection** is already on and you can just click the **Cancel** button.

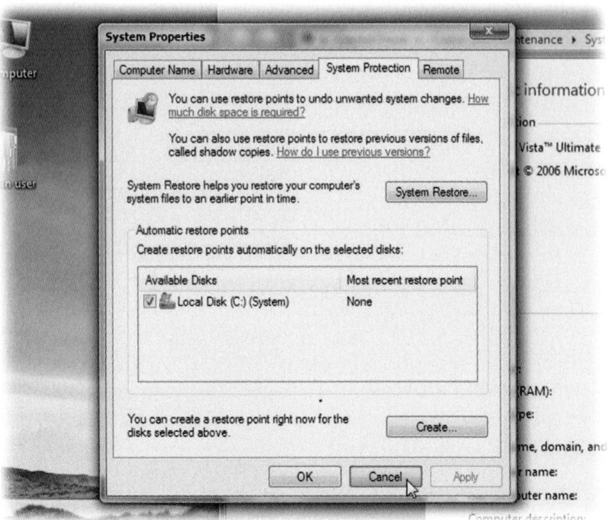

● Otherwise, to turn on System Protection, move the cursor over to the empty box next to the Local Disk icon in the middle and click there once with the left mouse button–this will tell Windows that we want to use the System Protection features.

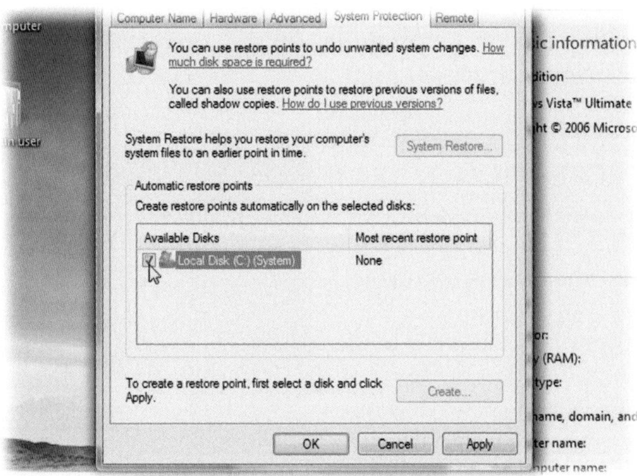

IF YOU'RE USING MORE THAN ONE DISK

Although most home PCs only have a single physical disk, this is sometimes split into partitions that appear as separate disks, each with their own name and icon. In order to take advantage of System Protection, you'll need to turn it on for each of these disks or partitions. This simply means following the steps outlined in this chapter and placing a tick next to every disk.

● To confirm your changes, click the **OK** button to close the dialog and initiate System Protection.

CREATING A RESTORE POINT

Setting up the Windows Protection System is only half the story–you can actually be much more pro-active by assessing your PC periodically yourself. How well is it running? Are all my Windows Updates installed? Is my other software up to date? Have I defragmented my hard disk recently? If things are running smoothly, don't sit back and relax, instead, create a System restore point yourself, so you've got a stable setup to return to, should things go wrong in the future.

OPENING THE SYSTEM PROPERTIES DIALOG

● With the System window still open, move the cursor over to the **System protection** link in the **Tasks** list on the left and click it once with the left mouse button.

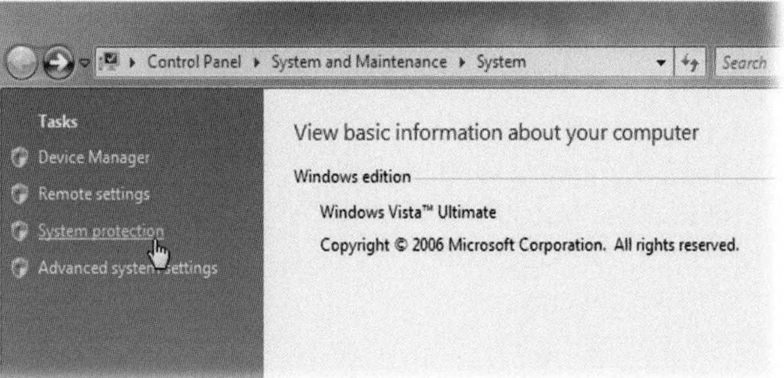

● When the **User Account Control** dialog appears, click the **Continue** button.

● The System Properties dialog box opens with the **System Protection** tab already highlighted. To create a restore point on a particular disk, select it by clicking on its name once with the left mouse button so that it's highlighted like this. Note that in the column called **Most recent restore point**, it says "**None**".

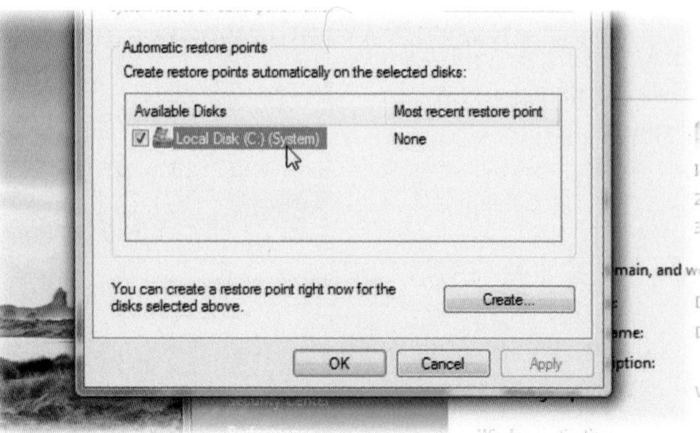

MANUALLY CREATING A RESTORE POINT

● With the correct disk name highlighted, move the cursor down to the **Create** button and click it.

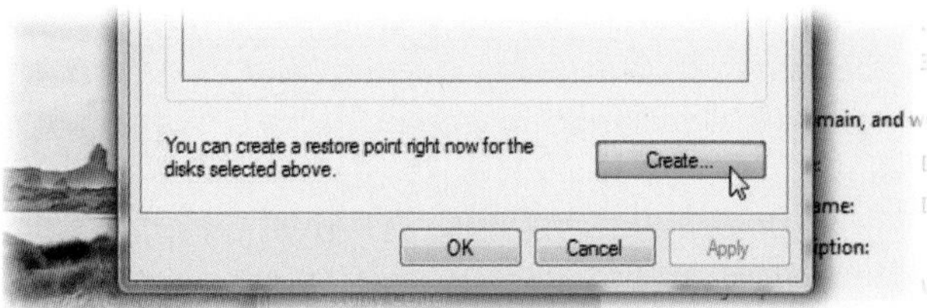

● After a second, Windows opens a dialog box with a space in it for you to type in a name for the restore point you want to create–you'll see why this is important when you come to use it in a short while.

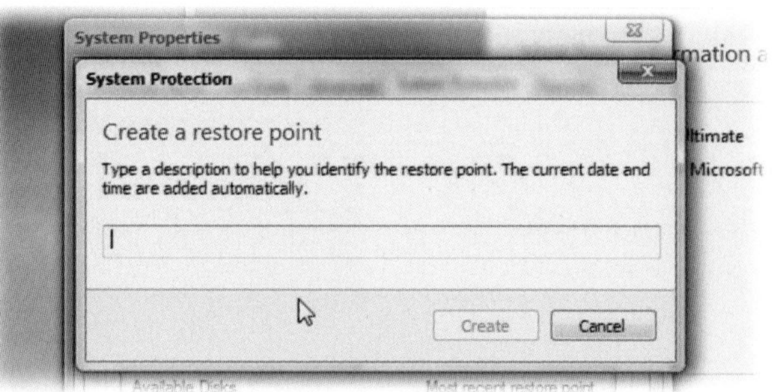

NAMING THE RESTORE POINT

● Type in a name that is meaningful and that you'll recognize later on. We're going to call this **My First Manual Restore Point**.

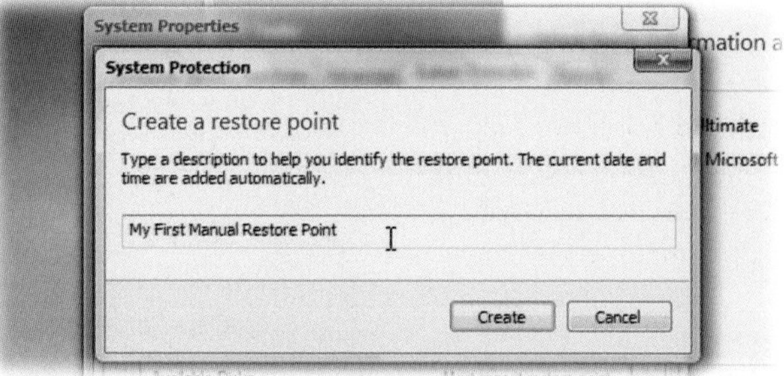

DOES SYSTEM RESTORE DAMAGE MY DATA?

One of the cleverest things about System Protection is that it keeps your data safe. For example, imagine that your computer is working fine, and you download and install a new program for creating documents from the Internet. That week, you write a dozen letters using the program, but notice that, as each day goes by, your PC is getting more and more sluggish. So, you wonder if the new program is conflicting with something else on the machine. Using System Protection, you can return to the point before you installed the new program, so that it's no longer on your system. However, Vista will protect the documents you've created so you can still use them.

- When you have typed in the name, click the **Create** button to create the restore point.

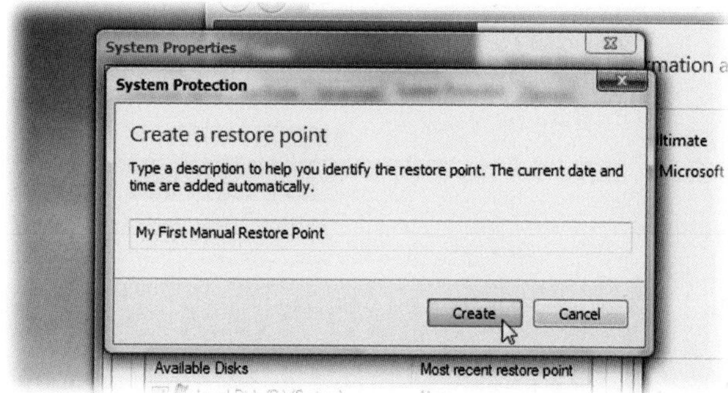

- Windows then displays one of its progress bar dialog boxes to indicate that it's working hard behind the scenes.

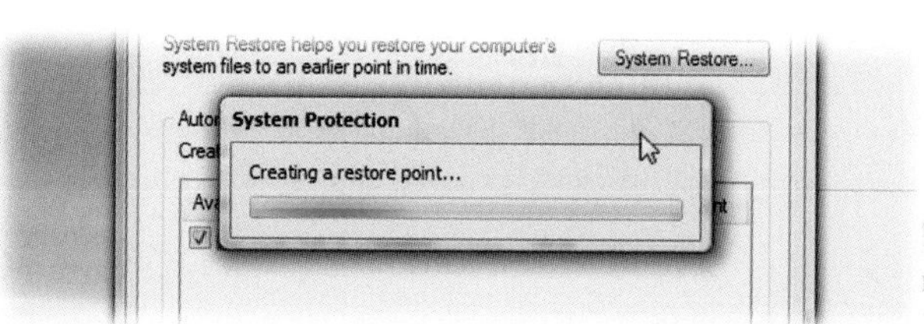

- When it's done, Windows displays another smaller **System Protection** dialog that says: **The restore point was created successfully**. Click **OK** to close the box.

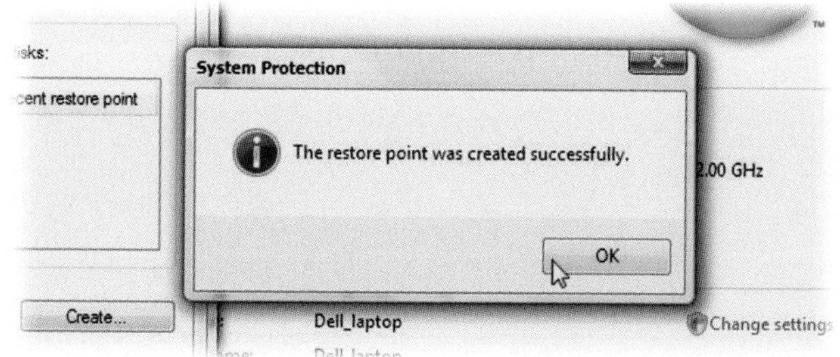

CHECKING THE RESTORE POINT

● Back at the main System Properties dialog box you can see that the **Most recent restore point** column no longer says "none"; instead, Windows displays the date of the manual restore that we've just created.

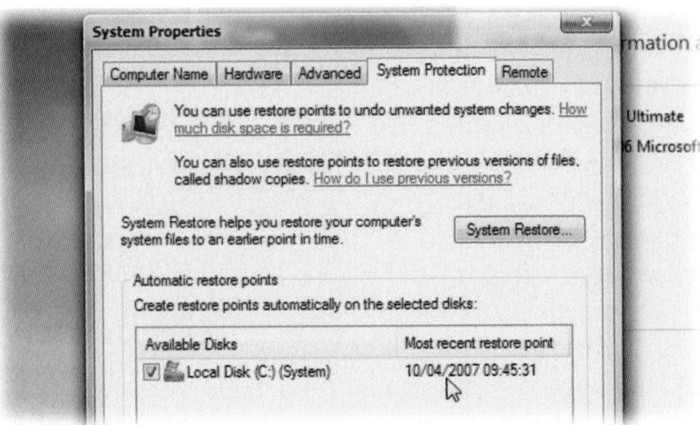

● To finish the process, click the **OK** button, which will confirm the changes and close the dialog box.

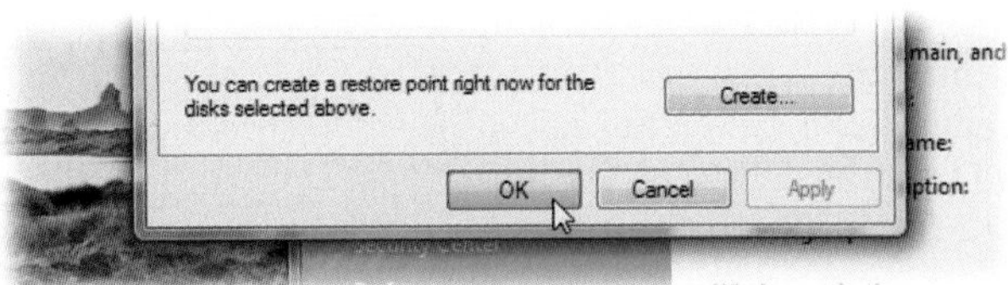

RETURNING TO A RESTORE POINT

If you've noticed that your home PC is running slowly or behaving in an odd manner, it's possible that a new program is in conflict with an existing one, or that certain important files that run in the background have become corrupted. In this case, if you've created a manual restore point as described above, you can return your PC to a state when it was last working fine. Here's how it works.

CHOOSING THE RESTORE POINT

● Before we start, let's have a look at one of the most important features of System Restore–the ability to step back in time to a point where Windows was working fine, removing programs, but leaving data intact. Click the Start button to begin.

● The Start menu opens. Our purpose here is to show how System Restore can remove programs while preserving data. So, having created a manual restore point in the previous section, we've then installed a program at random. (There's nothing wrong with this particular program, by the way–we're simply using it as an example.)

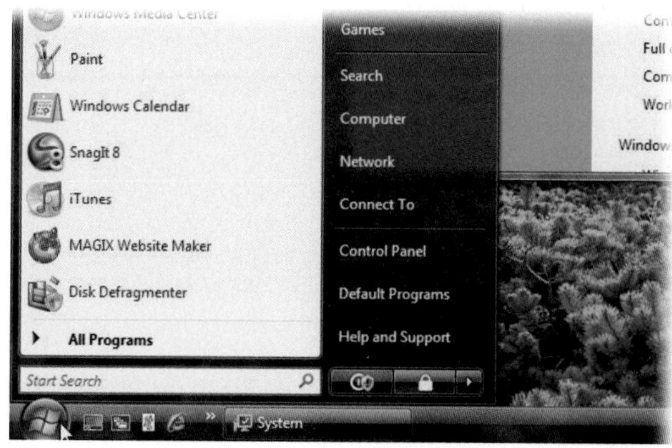

● Slide the cursor up to the **All Programs** menu item and click on it once with the left mouse button.

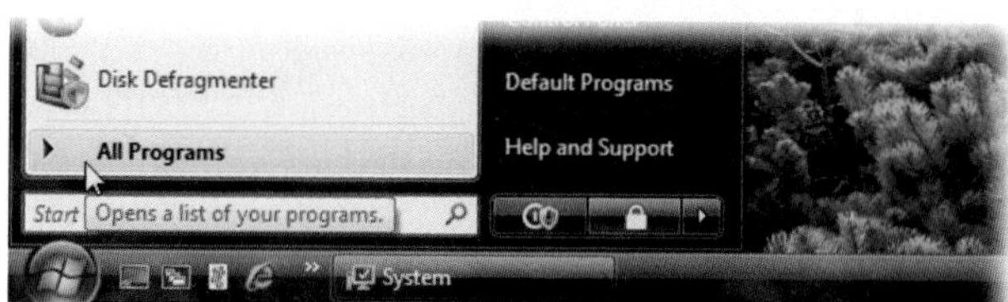

● The All Programs menu opens. Slide the cursor up to the **MAGIX** folder and click on it once.

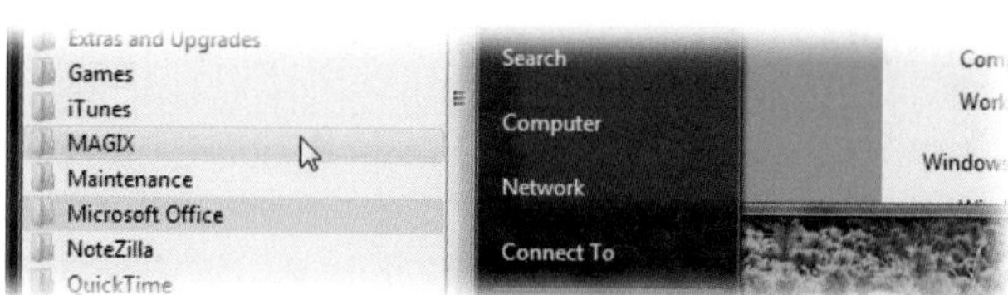

● You can see the files inside the folder. After we activate System Restore, we will return to a point before this program was installed and it will disappear.

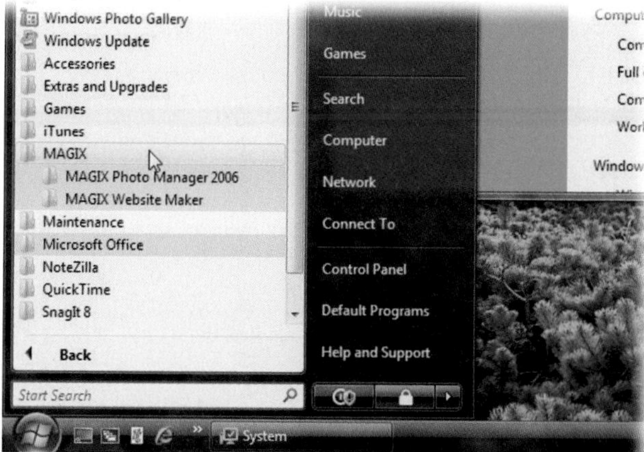

OPENING THE SYSTEM PROPERTIES WINDOW

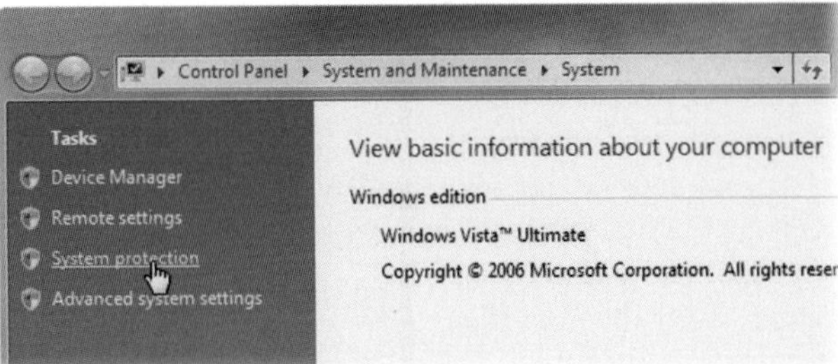

● Let's return to the System window and click the **System protection** link in the **Tasks** list on the left.

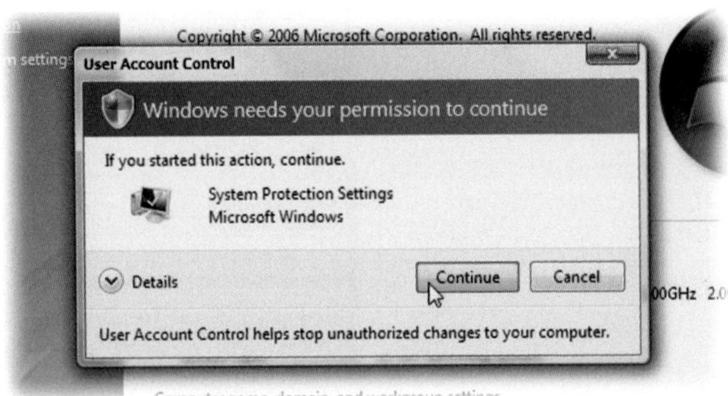

● When the **User Account Control** dialogue appears, click the **Continue** button.

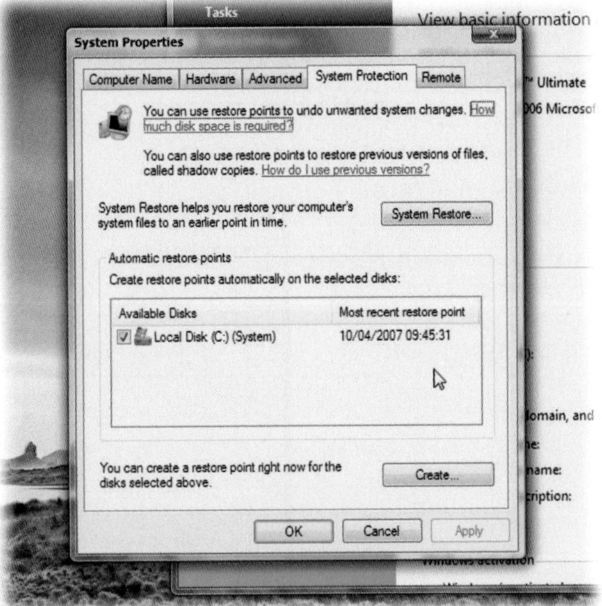

● Here's the **System Properties** dialog box. Note that the restore point we created manually in the previous section is listed in the middle window.

● We don't need to select the restore point yet, so just move the cursor up to the **System Restore** button and click it once.

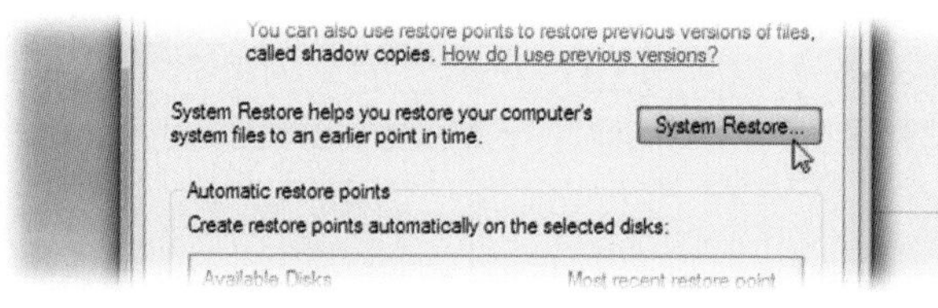

OPENING THE SYSTEM RESTORE WIZARD

● After a moment, the **System Restore** wizard appears and displays some useful explanatory text about what the process can and can't do.

● When you have had a chance to read the dialog and are ready to move on, click on the **Next** button at the bottom.

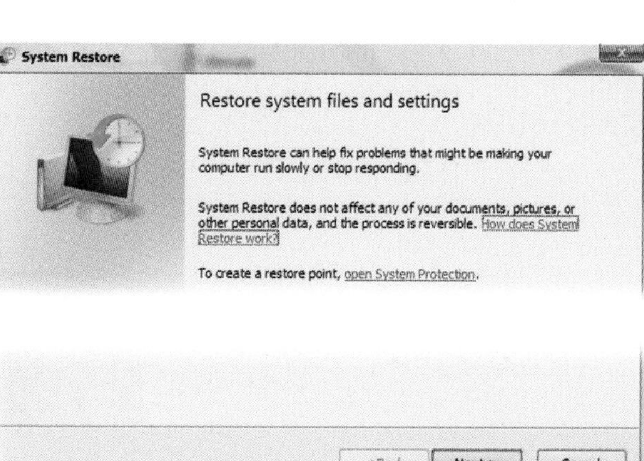

● Windows then lists the various available restore points and asks you to choose one. We've only got the one we created in the previous section, so we're going to choose that. To select your restore point, click on it once with the left mouse button.

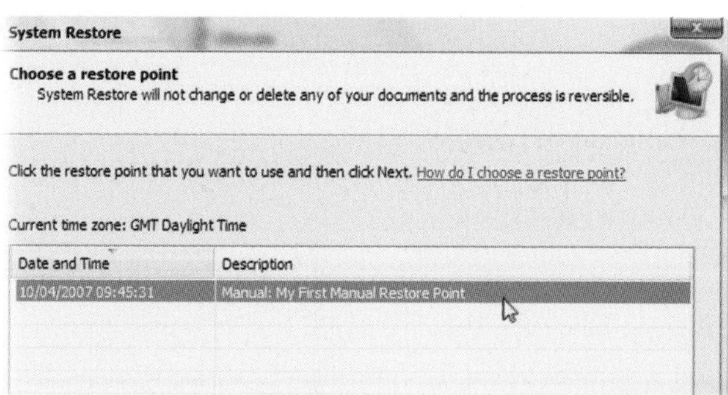

● To confirm your choice and move on, click the **Next** button at the bottom of the dialog box.

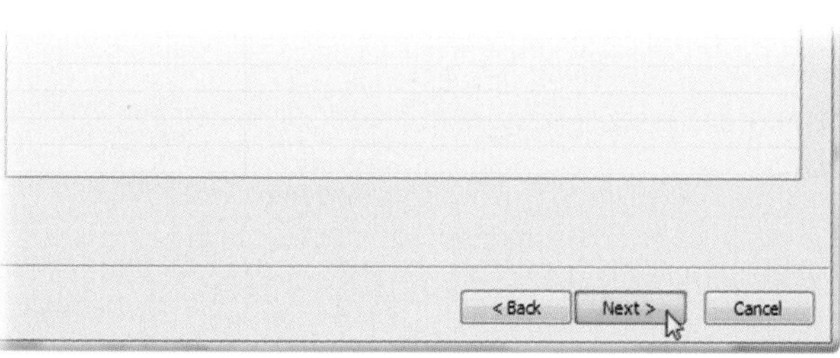

• Windows gives you an opportunity to review the restore point and make sure it's the right one.
• Remember that at any time during the process you can click the **Back** button at the bottom of the dialog box and return to a previous screen.

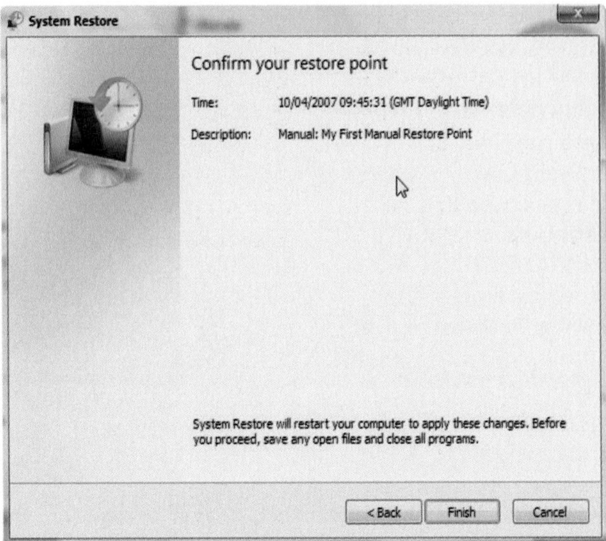

• Click the **Finish** button to confirm your choice and complete the wizard.

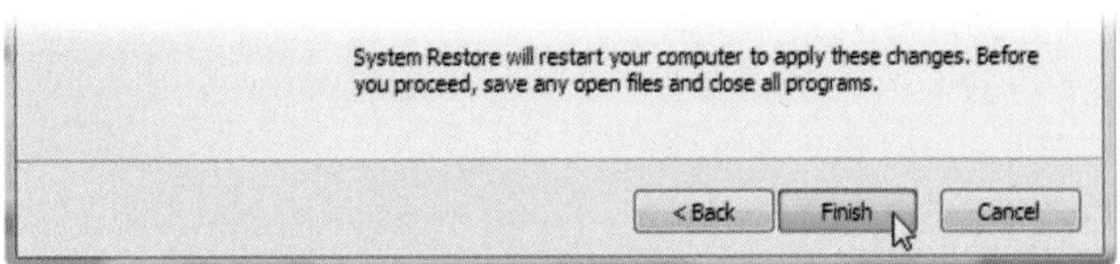

RUNNING SYSTEM RESTORE

• Windows displays a final dialog box, asking if you really want to run the program. Click the **Yes** button to continue.

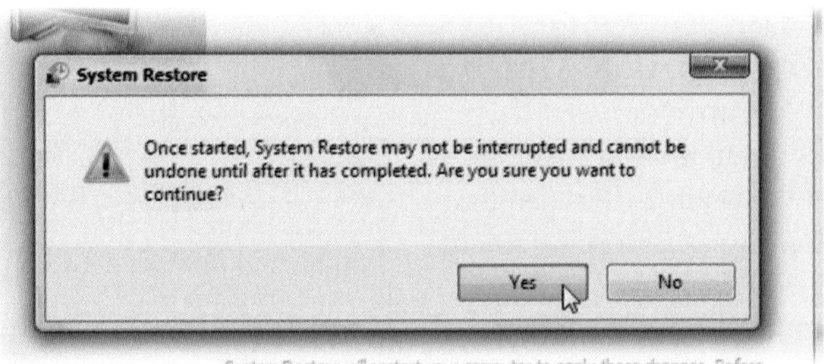

• Windows will then display the **System Restore** dialog box.

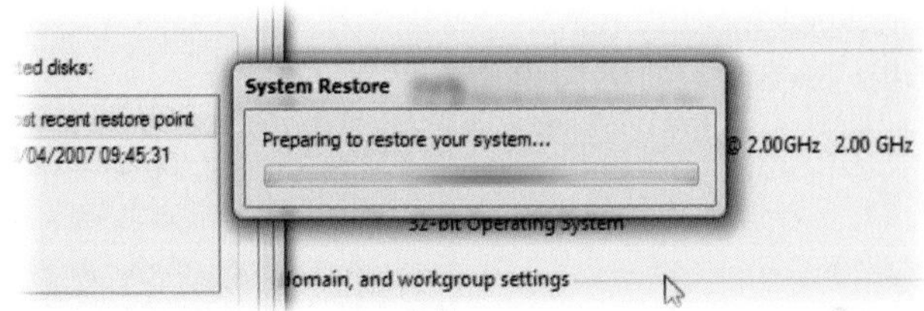

● The rest of the system restore process will take place without your help, and you shouldn't try to interrupt it in any way. Your PC will display a message on the screen that says: "**Please wait while your Windows files and settings are being restored. System Restore is initializing.**"

● Your PC will then display a message that says: "**System restore is removing temporary files.**" After that, the machine will shut down and re-start by itself. When the machine starts up again and displays the Windows desktop again, you'll see this dialog box confirming that PC has been restored as requested. Click the **Close** button.

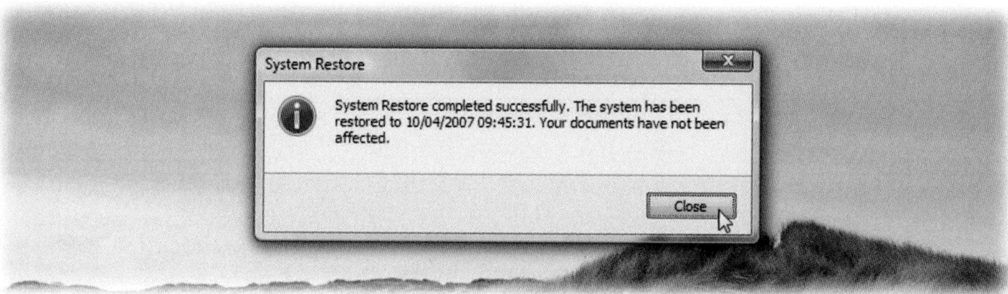

CONFIRMING THE SYSTEM RESTORE

● We now want to see the effect of Sytem Restore.

● Click on Start, go to the **All Programs** list in the Start menu, and then compare it with the Start menu we showed at the beginning of this section.

● You can see that by going back to our chosen restore point, Windows has returned the PC to the state it was in before we installed the program from MAGIX, which has disappeared from the list.

USING PREVIOUS VERSIONS

We have seen how the Windows Vista's Restore feature can be used to take your entire system back to a point in the past where it was working properly. However, sometimes, you will want to use the feature in a more subtle manner. System Restore, for example, can also be used to to roll back individual files and folders to previous versions and even restore something that's been deleted from the Recycle Bin.

FINDING A FILE TO RESTORE

● For the purposes of this section we've done a bit of preparation in order to demonstrate how to restore one of our saved files to a previous version. We created a document in Notepad and saved it. We then created a manual Restore Point . We then changed the Notepad document and saved it again. On reflection, we've now decided that we preferred the original version of the document– so how can we get it back again? Click on the Start button to begin.

● When the Start menu opens, slide the cursor up to the **Documents** menu item and click on it.

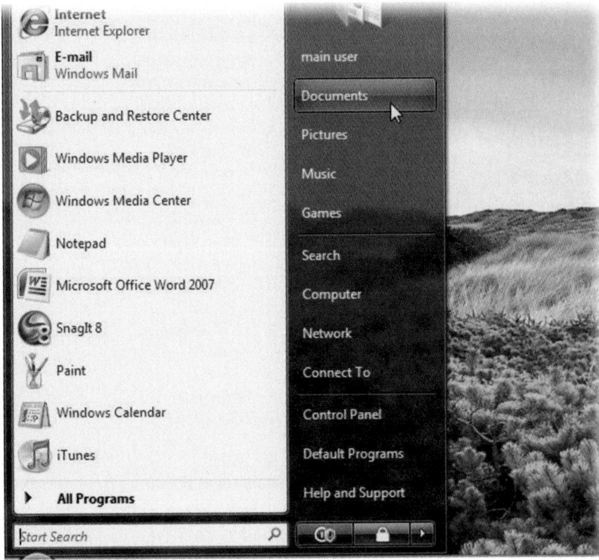

460 Manually Creating a Restore Point

● This opens the **Documents** window and we can see the Notepad document we've created, called **testnote**. Move the cursor over to the document and double click on it to open.

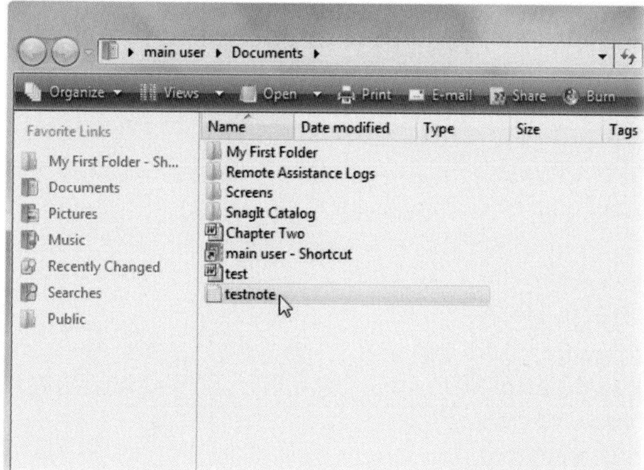

● Here's the document, displayed on top of the Documents window.

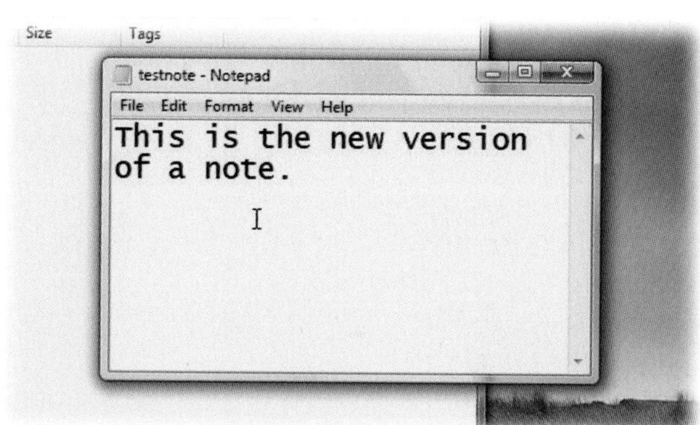

● Move the cursor back to the Documents window and this time, click on **testnote** with the right mouse button to open the menu.

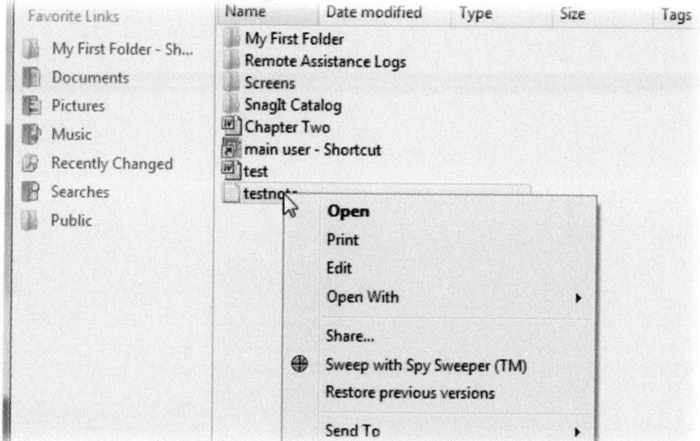

OPENING RESTORE PROPERTIES DIALOG

● Slide the cursor down to **Restore previous versions** and click on it once.

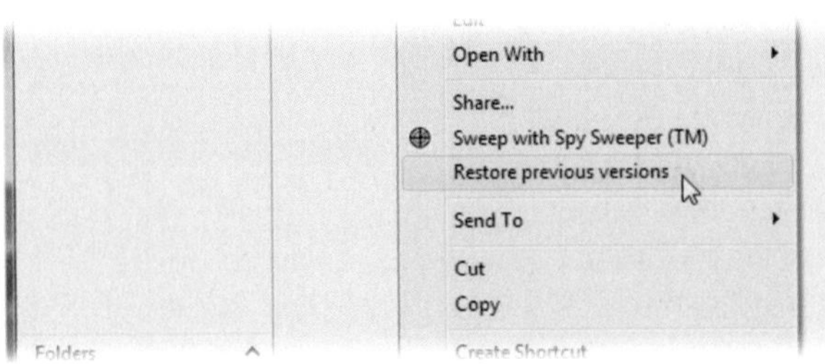

● This opens the **Properties** dialog box for this document, with the **Previous Versions** tab already selected. You can see that Windows has created a number of "shadow copies" of this particular document–one for each time Windows has created a restore point.

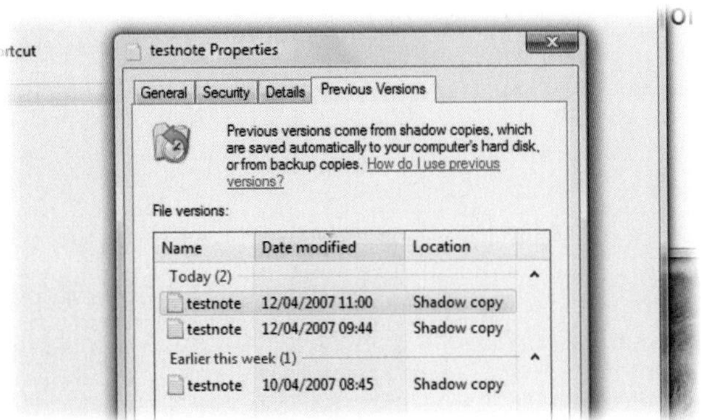

CHOOSING WHICH VERSION TO RESTORE

● Although you may be confident that you know which old version of a particular file or document you want to restore, Windows makes it easy to be certain. Start by clicking on the version to select it.

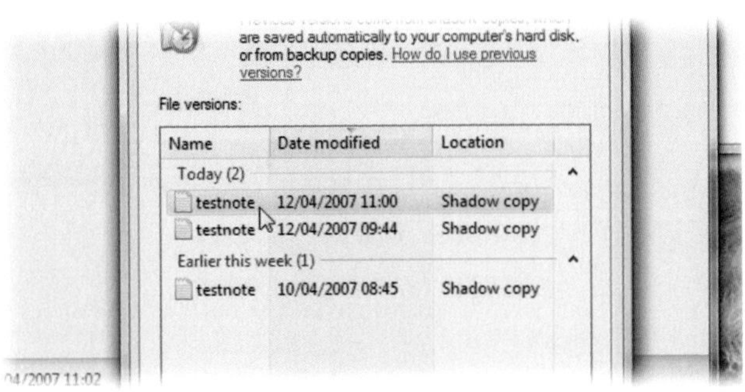

● With the version selected, click the **Open** button to check it out.

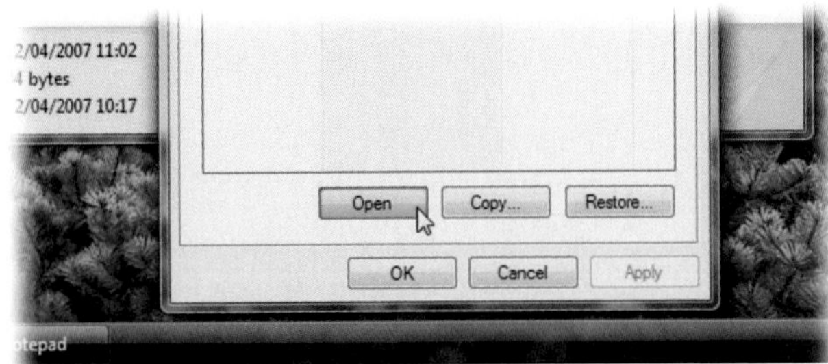

● This opens the earlier version of the document so you can make sure it's the correct one. If it isn't, simply close it and try another version. If it is, then just close it.

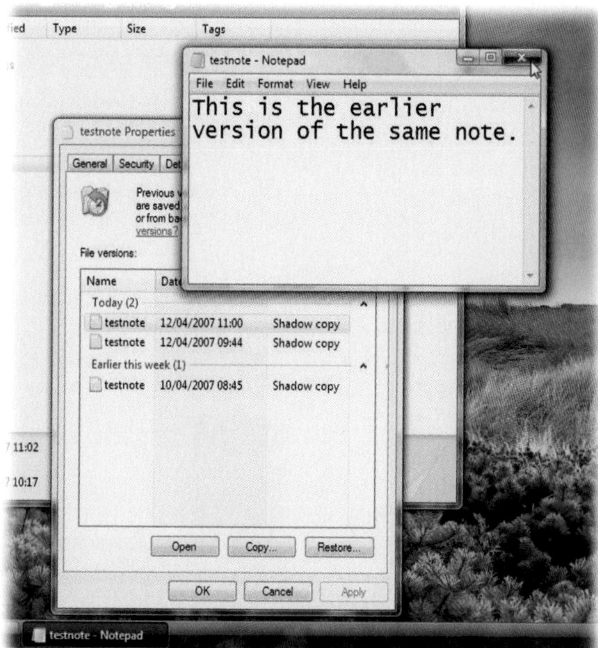

RESTORING THE DOCUMENT

● With the document still selected in the Properties dialog box, click the **Restore** button.

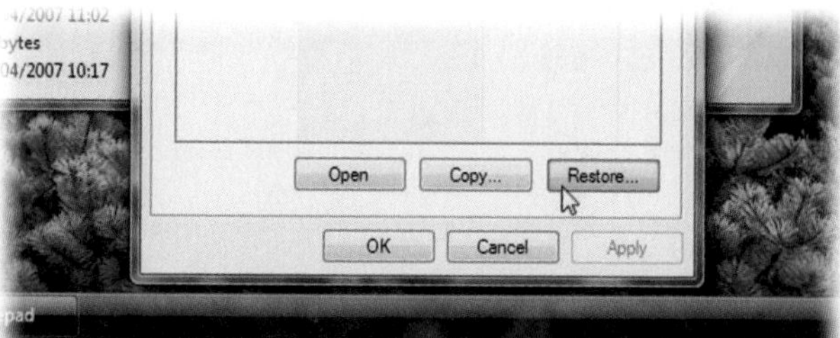

● Windows displays a dialog box asking if you're sure you want to continue. This is important, because once you've restored an old version you can't change your mind. Click **Restore** to continue or **Cancel** to think again.

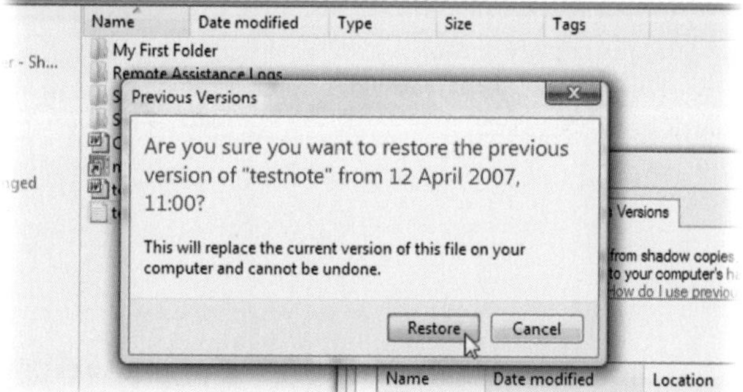

● After a few moments–depending on the size of the file or document being restored–Windows will display a confirmation dialog such as this. Click **OK** to complete the restoration process.

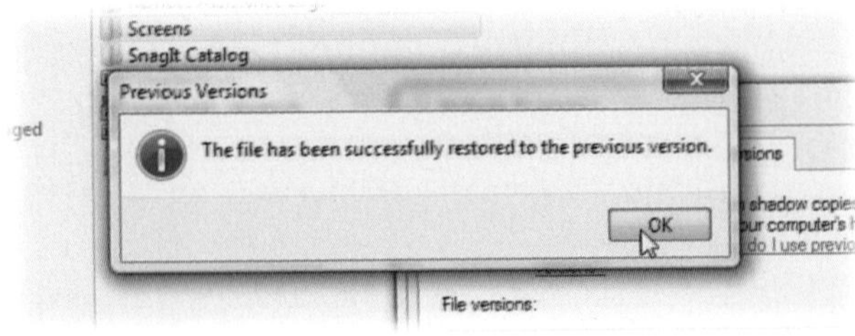

● Then click the **OK** button to close the Properties dialog box.

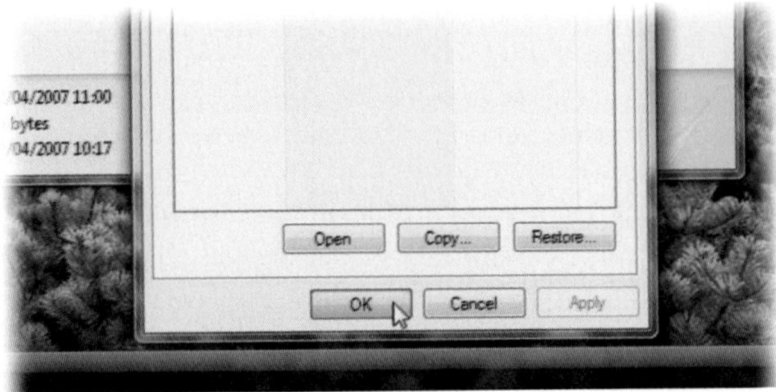

THE RESTORED DOCUMENT

● Back at the Documents window, double click on the document that has been restored.

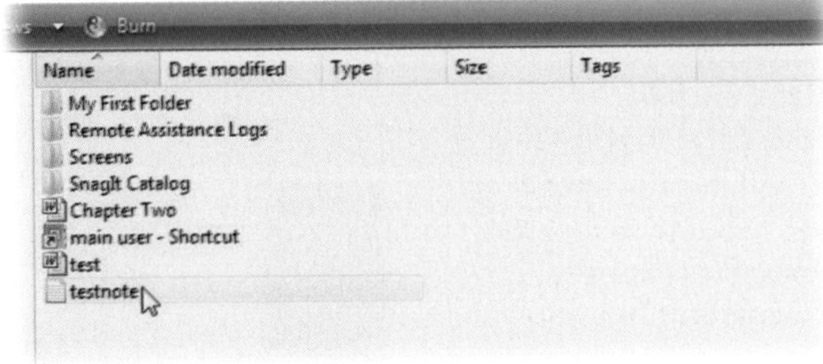

● We're looking at the version that has been successfully restored; the new version that it replaced is now gone forever.

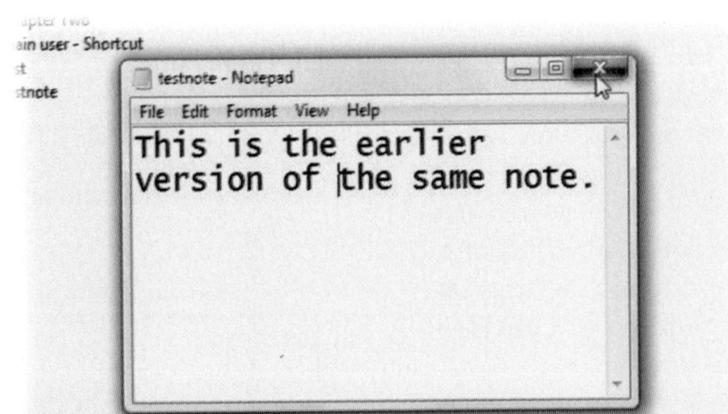

RESTORING A DELETED DOCUMENT

- In most cases, Windows can even restore a file that's been deleted.
- In this example, we've taken the testnote from the previous section, put it in the Recycle Bin and then deleted it from there as well.
- To all intents and purposes, that should have removed it from our system. As you are about to see, it hasn't.
- Start by clicking the arrow at the bottom left of the current folder window.

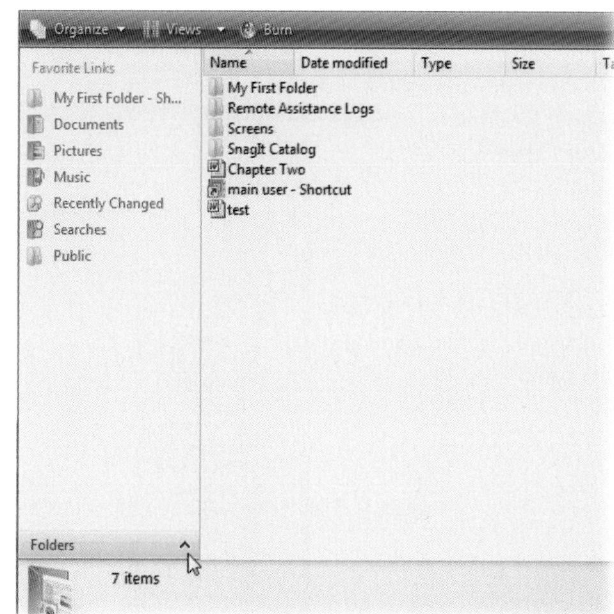

LOCATING THE FOLDER

- That opens the folder tree. Now you have to navigate to the folder where the deleted document was stored.

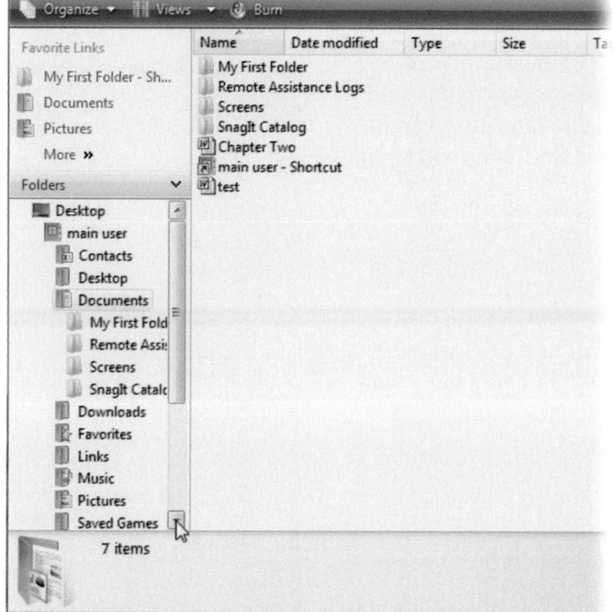

● Like most documents we have created, it was stored in the Documents folder, so we'll slide the cursor up to that folder.

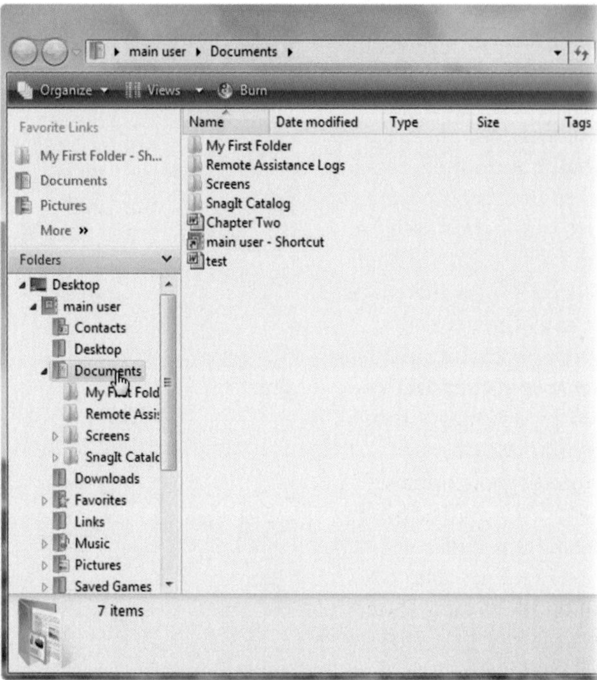

● Click once on the **Documents** folder with the right-hand mouse button and this menu will appear.

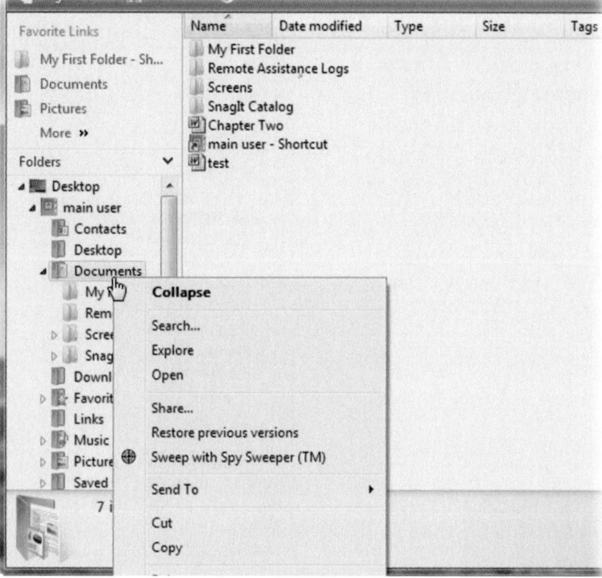

LOCATING PREVIOUS VERSIONS

- Slide the cursor down to the **Restore previous versions** menu item and click on it once.

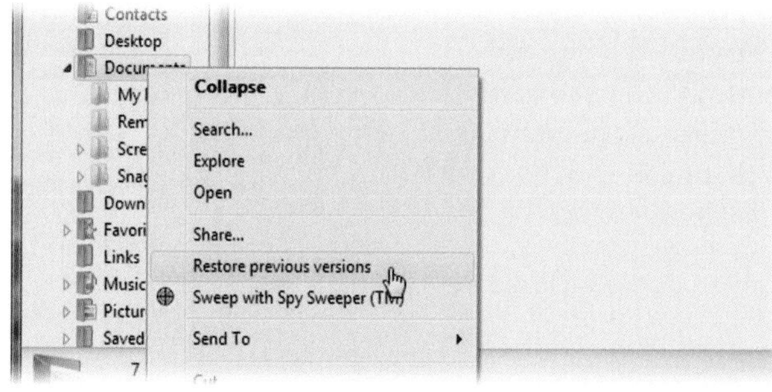

- This opens the **Documents Properties** dialog box for any items in that folder that have "shadow copies" that are created alongside a System Restore point.
- Here we're going to double click the first one, because its date is close to the time we last edited this document.

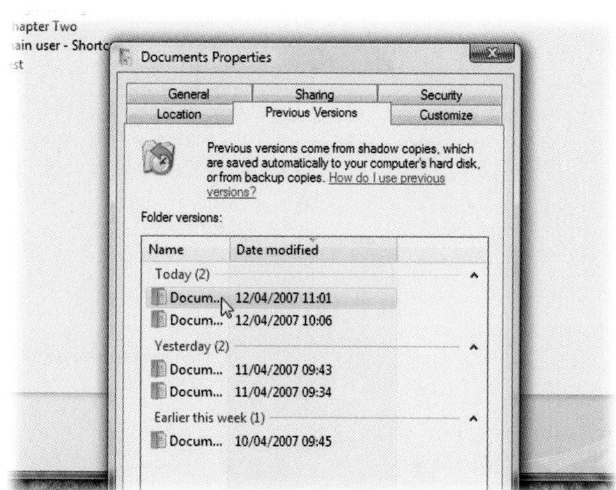

- This opens the shadow copy of the folder that contains the deleted document–**testnote**.
- You can see it at the bottom of the list.

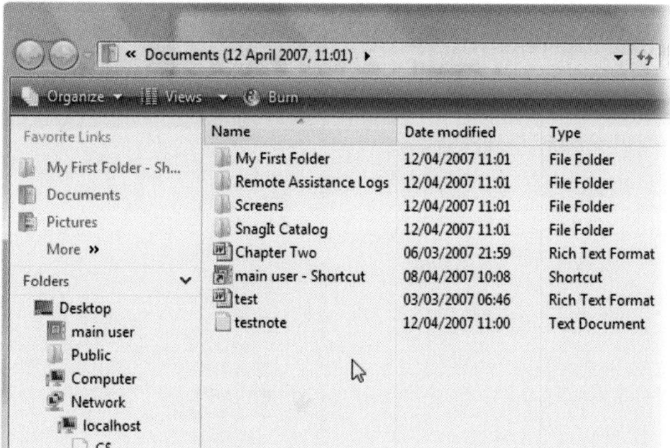

EXAMINING THE PREVIOUS VERSION

● Move the cursor over the document in question and then double click on it with the left mouse button.

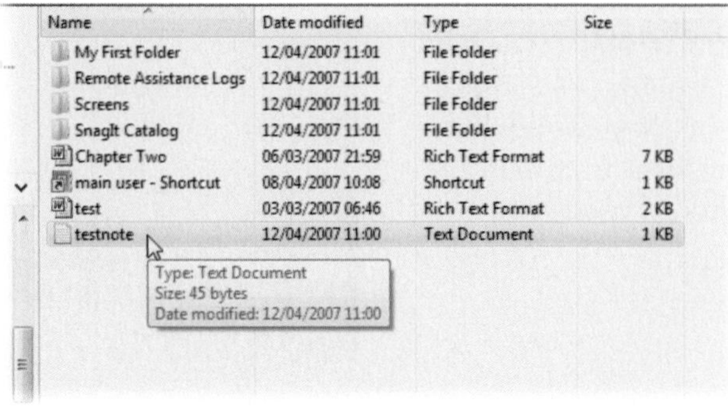

● Here's the document, despite the fact that it wasn't just dragged into the Recycle Bin–it was deleted from there as well. Close it by clicking the "x".

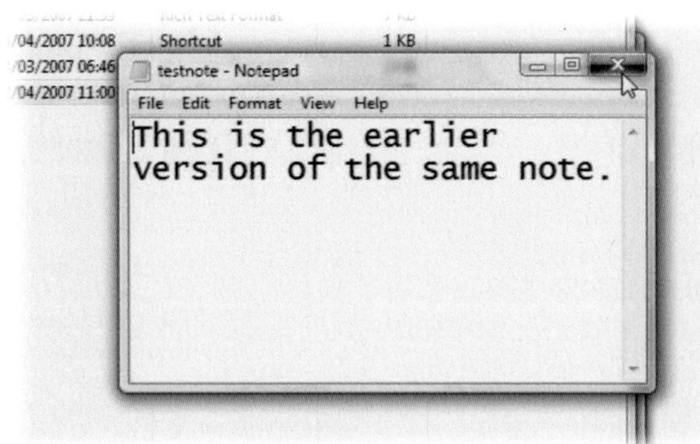

RESTORING THE DOCUMENT

● To restore the note, simply click on it with the left mouse button and then–still holding the button down–drag it out of the window and onto the desktop.

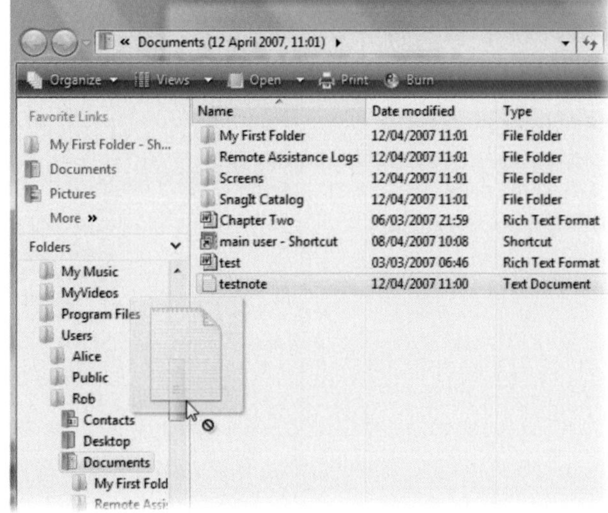

● Here we can see the note being dragged to the desktop. If you prefer, you can drag it straight to another location, for example, an open window.

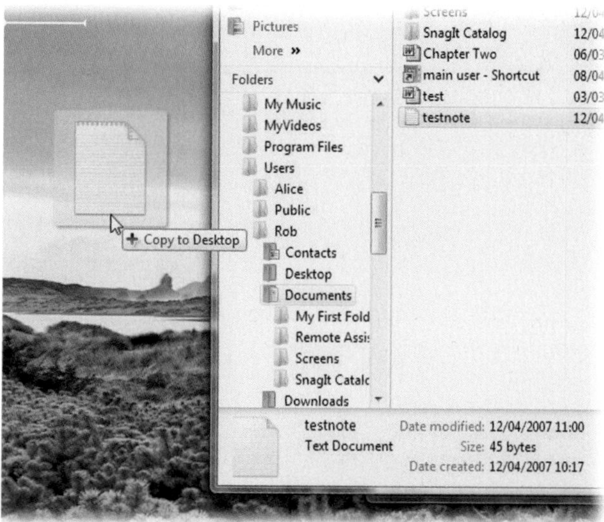

● Once the document is on the desktop, you can open the window of the folder in which it was originally stored and then drag it back into that folder like this.

● Here's the document, recovered and restored, and back in its original location, courtesy of System Restore's shadow copy feature.

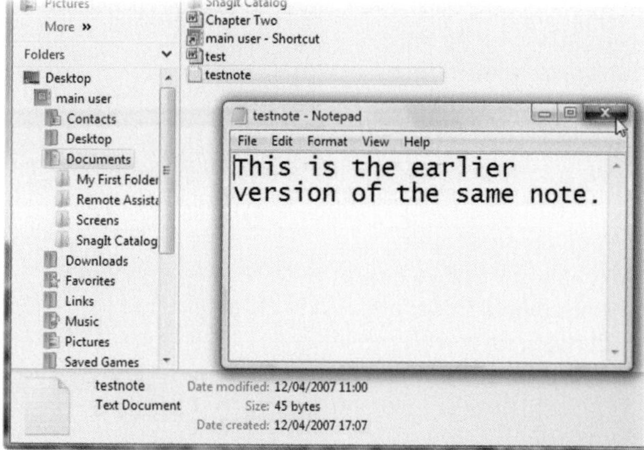

MANAGING PROGRAMS

Although Windows includes some useful programs, you'll need to install and use others to get the very best out of your PC. This section explains how to do this.

INSTALLING PROGRAMS

When you buy a program on CD or DVD, or download one from the Internet, you have to install it on your PC before you can use it. That means that each program includes a special installation file that you'll need to run. Although these will vary depending on the program, they all have many things in common and when you've done it once, installing other programs is easy.

FINDING THE PICASA DOWNLOAD

- Earlier on, when we were looking at the Internet, we downloaded a free program from Google, called Picasa, for organizing and editing photos.
- We'll start by finding that program. On the Windows desktop, move the cursor over to the **main user** folder and double click on it with the left mouse button.

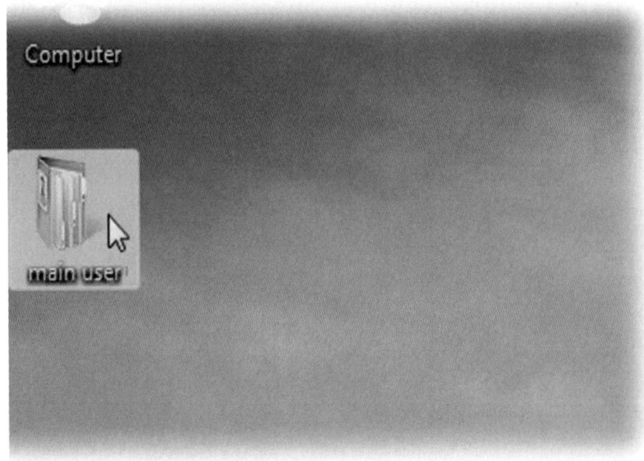

- When the main user folder window opens, locate the **Downloads** folder and double click on it with the left mouse button.

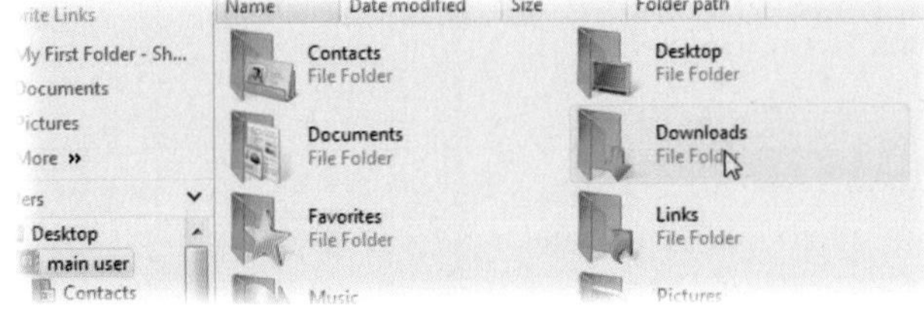

132 Downloading Programs

● Unless you've deliberately changed Windows settings, all the files you download will be stored in this folder. Here is the Picasa download, second from the bottom.

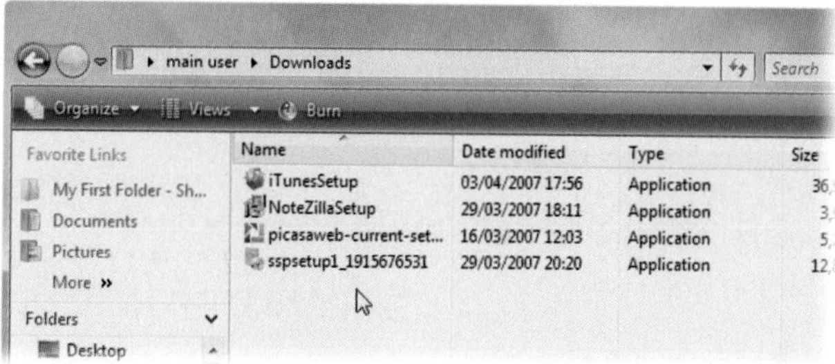

● Move the cursor over the Picasa file and double click on it. This will start the installation process– remember that a program must be installed before you can use it.

INSTALLING PICASA

● Windows displays a **Security Warning** dialog box asking if you're sure you want to run the installation program (Windows calls it a "file"). Since we know this is a bona fide download from a reputable source, click the **Run** button to continue.

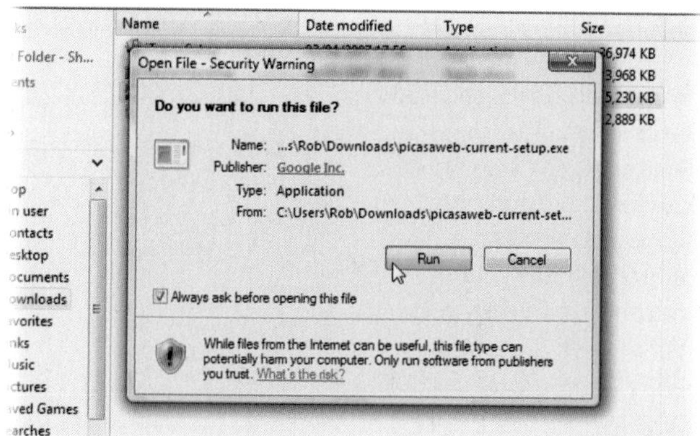

● When it comes to installing new programs, Windows doesn't take any chances, so it displays the **User Account Control** dialog box, reminding you that this particular program needs your permission to continue. Click **Continue** to start the installation.

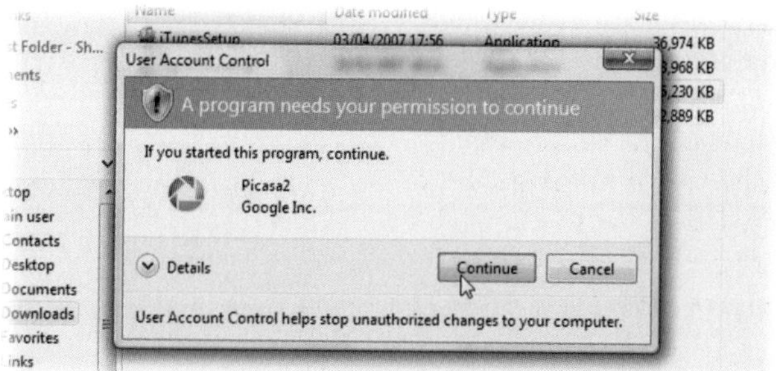

● All programs come with a license agreement, which sets out what you can and can't do with the product, along with your rights and responsibilities. Read through it, and when you've finished, click the **I Agree** button to continue with the installation.

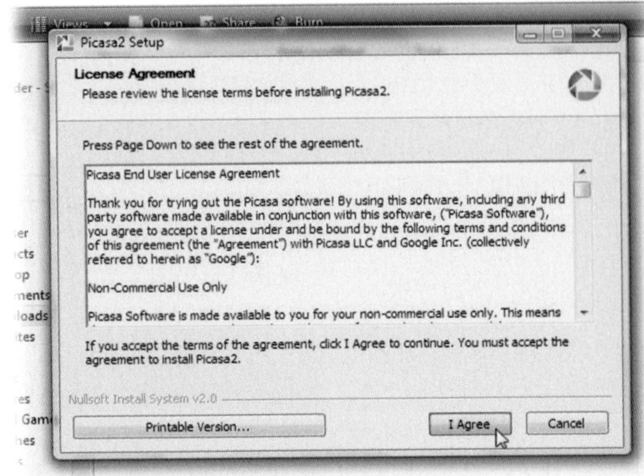

● Unless you have a specific reason for doing otherwise, don't change any of the settings in this dialog box.
● Basically, the installation program knows what it's doing and will copy all of its files into the correct places on your PC.
● Just click the **Install** button to start the process.

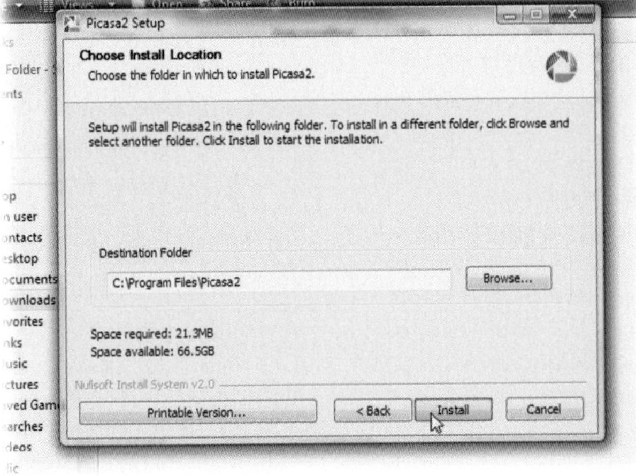

● Picasa then installs itself on your PC. You can follow the program's progress in this dialog box. You don't have to do anything.

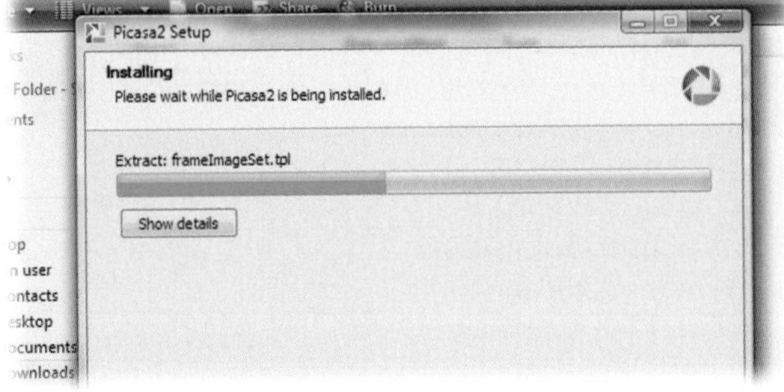

CHECKING ANY CHANGES

- At the end of the setup process, many programs will display a screen similar to this, asking permission to add a shortcut to the Windows desktop or in the Quick Launch bar.
- Some will even cheekily try to change some of the setting in their favor.
- Here, for example, the setup program is offering to set Google as the default search engine in Internet Explorer. We're happy to confirm that, but other programs may try and make changes you're less comfortable with, so read dialog boxes such as this one with care.
- Click the **Finish** button to complete the installation and run the program.

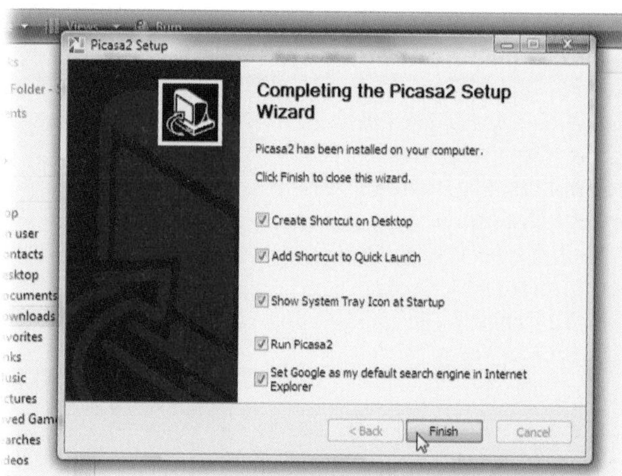

INSTALLING A PROGRAM FROM A CD

There is almost no difference between installing a program that you have downloaded from the Internet and installing one that you have bought on a CD from a shop. Simply pop the CD in the drive and Windows should start the installation process immediately. After that, just follow the onscreen instructions.

RUNNING THE PROGRAM

- Before it loads properly, Picasa–which is, after all, a program designed to organize and edit photos–offers to scan the whole of your computer (including additional hard drives) for images. If you have photos stored in many different areas of your computer, then keep this choice.

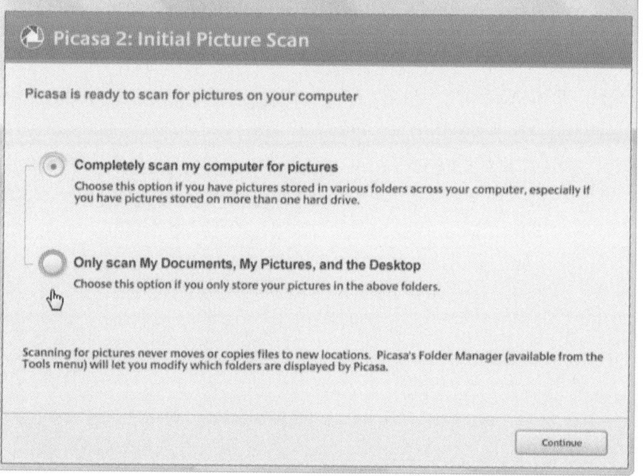

● Typically, however, you will store photos in the Pictures folder, so you should choose the second option, **Only scan My Documents, My Pictures, and the Deskop**.
● Click once on the radio button next to the second option to select it, and then click the **Continue** button.

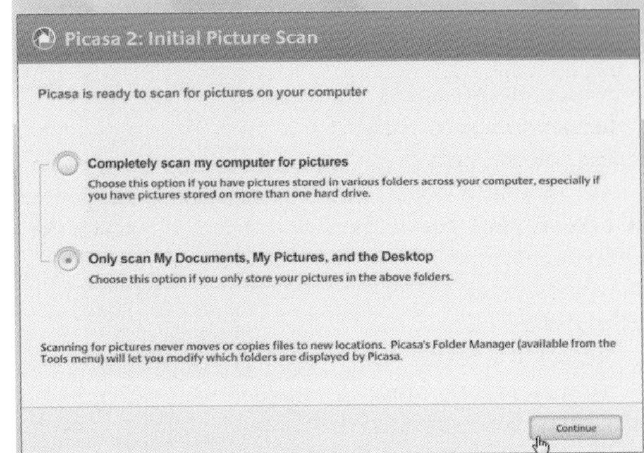

● Here we see Picasa, installed on the PC, having scanned the Pictures folder and added everything in there to its library.
● Although Windows' own Photo Gallery is very good, Picasa has lots of additional features that make it well worth downloading.

● To close the program, just click the little "x" in the top right hand corner.

Uninstalling a Program

When a program is installed on your PC it doesn't all go into a single folder–it installs bits of itself in various locations, usually in order to get access to the different components of Windows that it needs to work properly. That means you can't remove a program in the same way as you can remove a file–by dragging it to the Recycle Bin. Instead, you need to uninstall it. This section explains how that works.

FINDING THE UNINSTALL PROGRAM

- Most software comes with its own uninstall program, which is usually located in the same place as the program itself. So, to being uninstalling Picasa, we need to locate it on the Start menu. Begin by clicking on the Start button once.

- When the menu opens, click the **All Programs** menu item to open it.

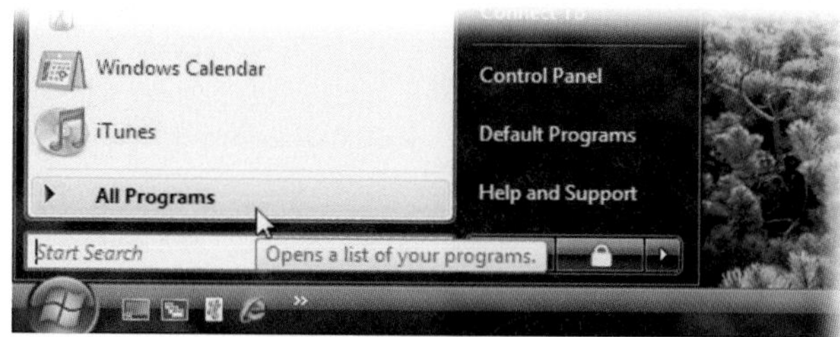

- Slide the cursor up the menu until you find he Picasa folder and then click it once with the left mouse button to open it.

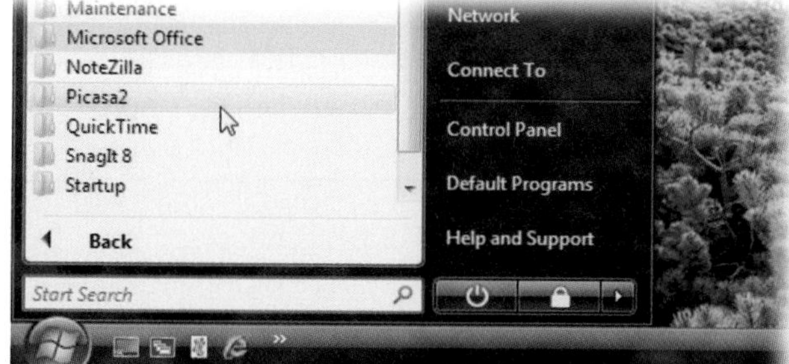

● The Picasa folder opens, revealing the program itself (Picasa2) and the **Uninstall** program. Select that by clicking on it once.
● If the program you want to remove doesn't include an uninstall program, see the box below.

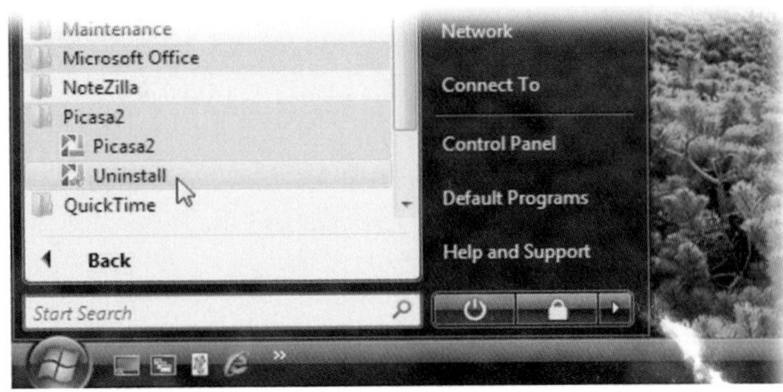

RUNNING THE UNINSTALL PROGRAM

● As we're about to make a basic change to the PC, Windows will display the **User Account Control** dialog box, explaining that **An unidentified program wants access to your computer**. Since this is fine, and we trust the uninstall program, we're going to click the **Allow** button.

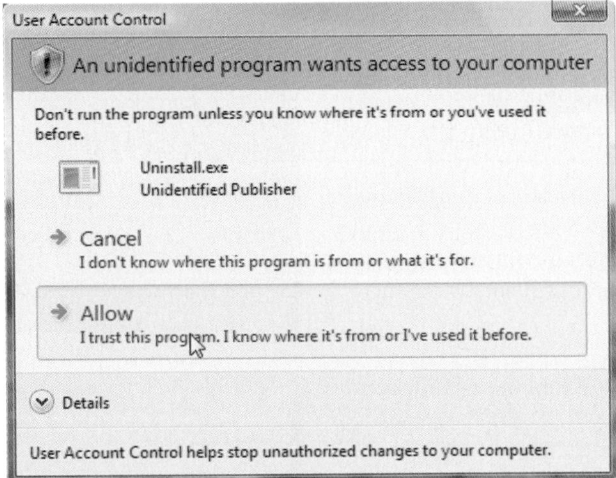

● The rest of the process is all but automatic. Just click the **Uninstall** button to allow it to continue.

WHEN YOU CAN'T FIND AN UNINSTALL PROGRAM

If your software doesn't include an uninstall program, you can use Windows to remove it. Click the Start button and then the entry for the **Control Panel**. When that opens, find **Programs** and click the link underneath– **Uninstall a program**. Windows displays a list of the programs installed on your PC. Click on the one you want to remove with the left mouse button, then on the **Uninstall** button that appears, and follow the instructions.

● Some programs ask if you would also like to remove any files that they may have created. In this example, Picasa wants to know whether to remove the database it created for our photographs. Since we don't want that database any more either, we'll click the **Yes** option. There will be some occasions when you will want to keep files created by one program so that you can use them at a later time with another program, in which case you should click **No.**

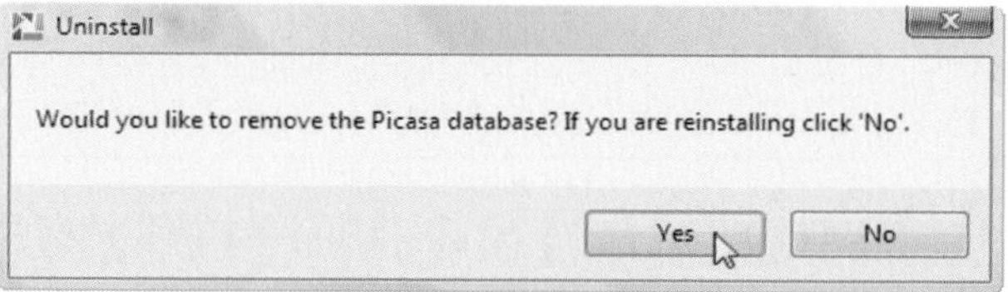

PARTICIPATING IN FEEDBACK

● The authors of some programs are keen to know why you would choose to uninstall their product.
● In this case, Picasa has loaded Internet Explorer and then linked to a website that invites you to post feedback about the program.
● If you don't want to, simply click the "x" to close the browser window.

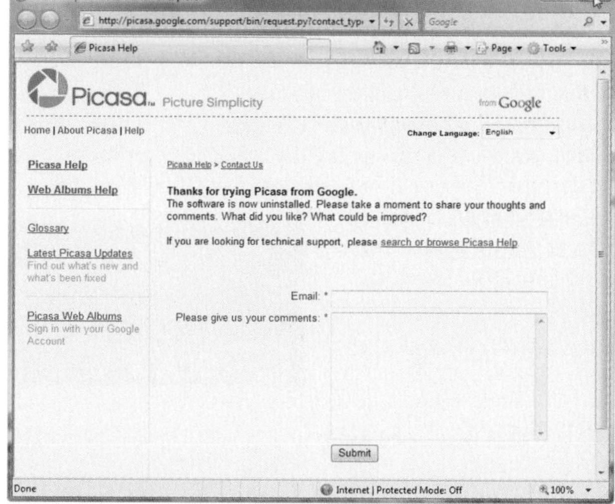

● Finally, Picasa displays a dialog box explaining that it has finished the uninstallation process. Click the **Finish** button to completely remove the product from your PC.

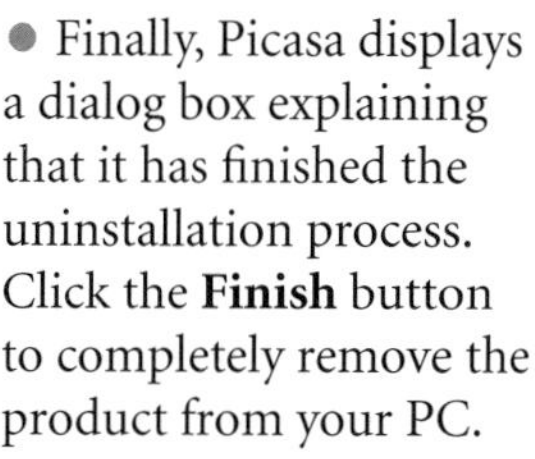

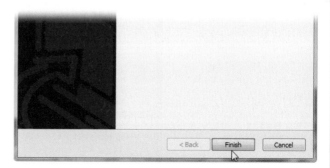

Windows Scheduler

One of the problems with housekeeping is that no-one really wants to do it. With Windows Scheduler, those tedious but necessary tasks can be run regularly and automatically.

Introducing Windows Scheduler

Windows Vista never sleeps–or rather it never sleeps so long as the PC is switched on. That means you can set your PC up to run important housekeeping tasks automatically, whether you're at your machine or not. This is where the Scheduler comes into its own. It's a program that is included with Windows and it can be set up to do various jobs at the times you specify. In this section, we'll show you how to set up a schedule that runs the Disk Cleanup program every month.

1 Opening the Scheduler

- To open the Scheduler and start creating a new, automated task, click the Start button.

- After a moment or two, the Start menu opens. find the **Control Panel** entry–it's in the dark side on the right-hand side of the menu.
- Next, slide the cursor over to the **Control Panel** entry and click on it once with the left mouse button to open.

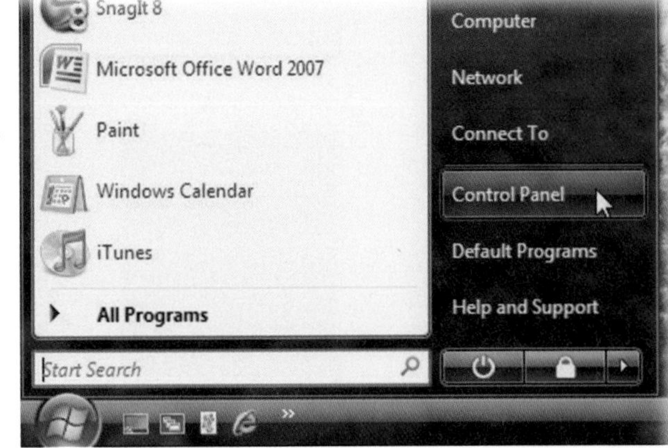

● The Scheduler is part of Windows' System and Maintenance functions. That's the first heading in the **Control Panel** list, so click it once to open it.

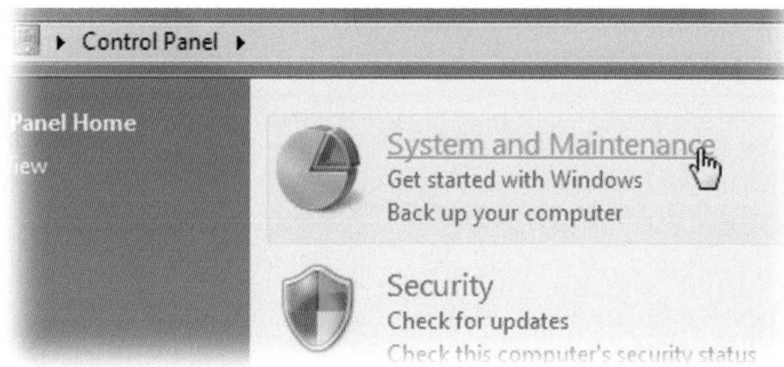

● When the new window opens, move right the way down to the bottom right and find the **Schedule tasks** link. Click on it once.

● When Windows displays the **User Account Control** dialog box, click on the **Continue** button.

● This opens the **Task Scheduler** window–the central place in Windows for creating and carrying out all the automatic tasks you need to run those tedious housekeeping jobs that you might otherwise ignore.

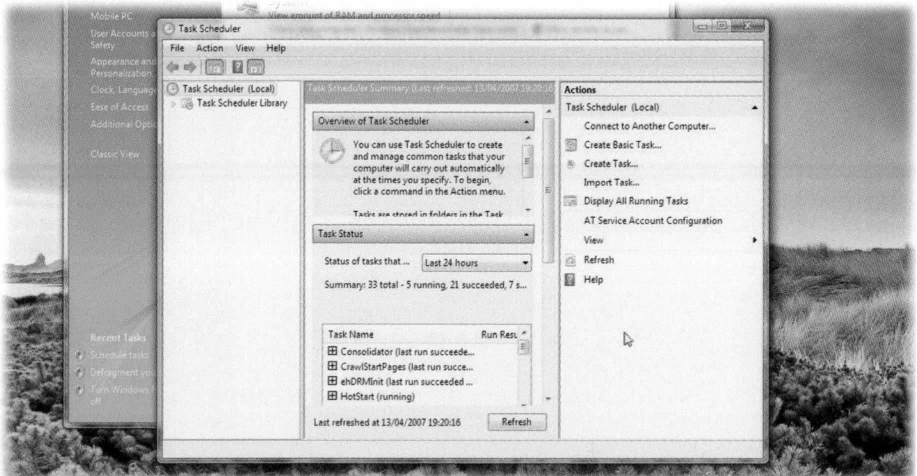

2 CREATING A NEW BASIC TASK

● The Scheduler is a complex and capable tool, which is able to set up sophisticated routines that accomplish very specific goals. Fortunately, it also has a "wizard" mode that will take us through the creation of a task step by step. To begin, move the cursor over to the **Create Basic Task** heading in the right-hand column and click on it once with the left mouse button.

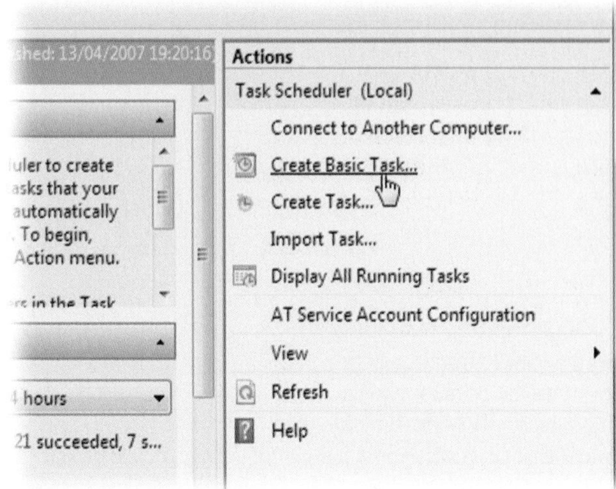

3 RUNNING THE TASK WIZARD

● This opens the **Create Basic Task Wizard**, which will help you through the set-up process by asking a series of simple questions– a little like filling in a questionnaire.

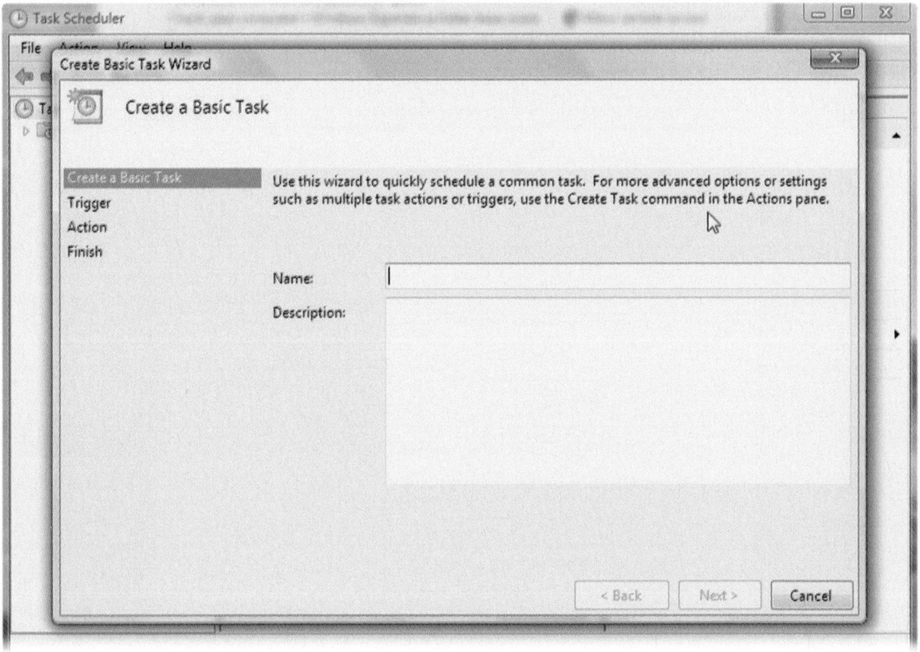

4 NAMING THE TASK

- Start by giving the task a name that you'll remember and that makes sense. In this example, we'll be calling it "**Getting rid of junk**." Type the name into the empty **Name** box.

- If you like, you can also type in an optional description. These kind of details may seem unnecessary, but if you end up setting up lots of scheduled tasks, you'll appreciate being able to tell which one is which.

- Once you've typed in the name and description of the task, click the **Next** button to move on to the next part of the wizard.

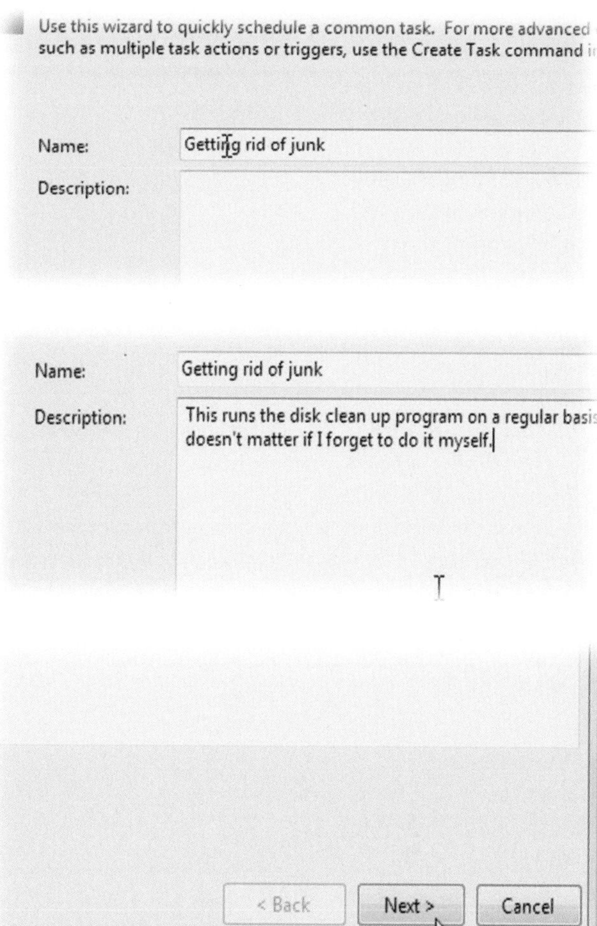

5 SCHEDULING THE TASK

- Having given the task a name, the next stage is to tell Windows when it needs to run. This is where we can do that.

When do you want the task to start?

- Daily
- Weekly
- Monthly
- One time
- When the computer starts
- When I log on
- When a specific event is logged

● Since this is going to run Disk Cleanup, and we're using a new PC that hasn't accumulated too much junk, we're going to run this task once a month. Select **Monthly** by clicking the radio button next to it.

● To move on, click the **Next** button at the bottom of the dialog box.

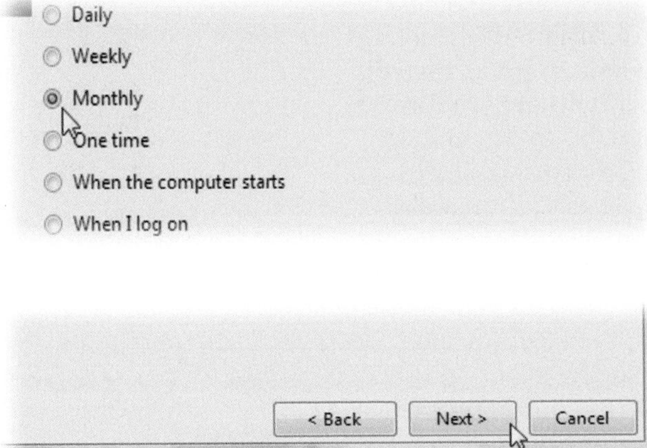

● In the next dialog box we can choose the specific time at which we would like the task to run, as well as specifying other important details, such as the day of the month on which it takes place and so on. This dialog box takes care of all that.

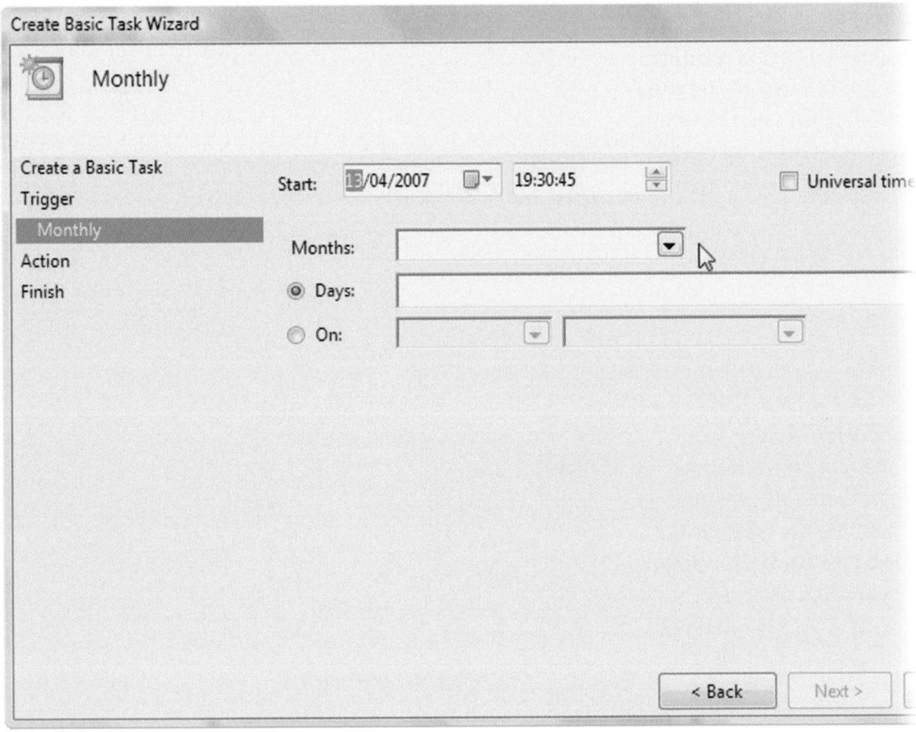

• We'd like to create the schedule from this moment in time, which means we can leave the **Start** date and time as they are. So, to continue, we're going to open the drop-down list next to the **Months** heading by clicking the arrow there with the left mouse button.

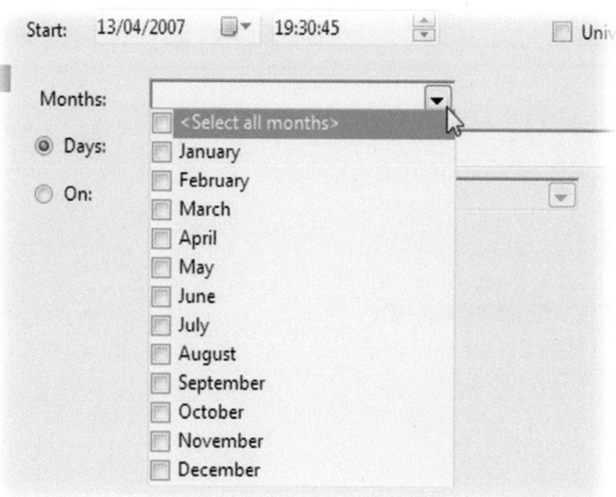

• As we want the task to run once a month, we're going choose the **Select all months** option by putting a tick in the box at the top of the list.

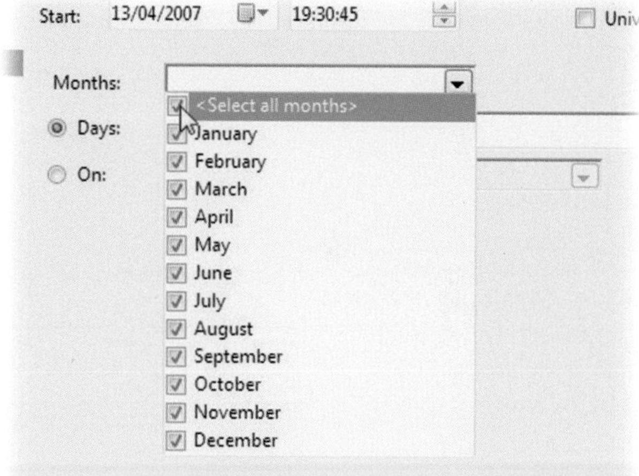

• Next, we need to choose which day the task should run on, so move the cursor over to the arrow next to the **Days** heading and click on it once to open it.

• When you click the arrow, a drop-down list of available dates appears– from the 1st to the 31st, as well as an option for the last day of the month.

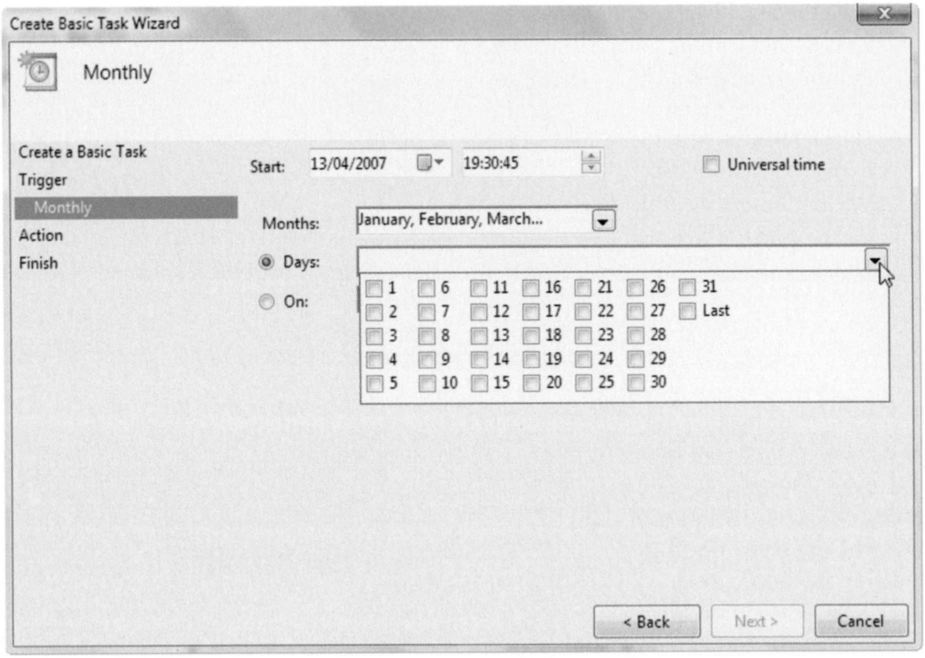

• We're going to run this task on the last day of every calendar month, so we'll click in the box labeled **Last**, like this.

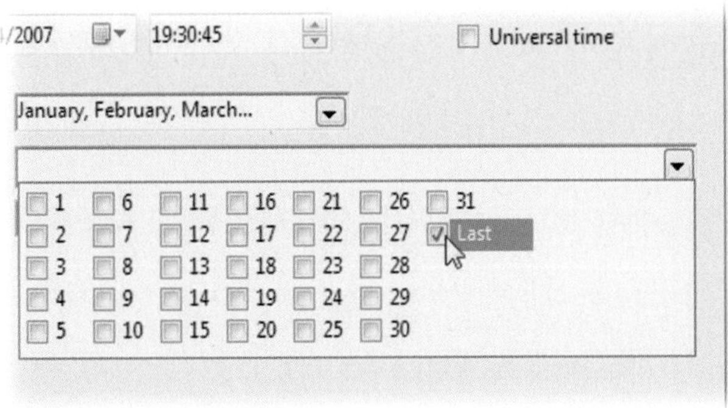

• When you've finished with these settings, click the **Next** button to move on.

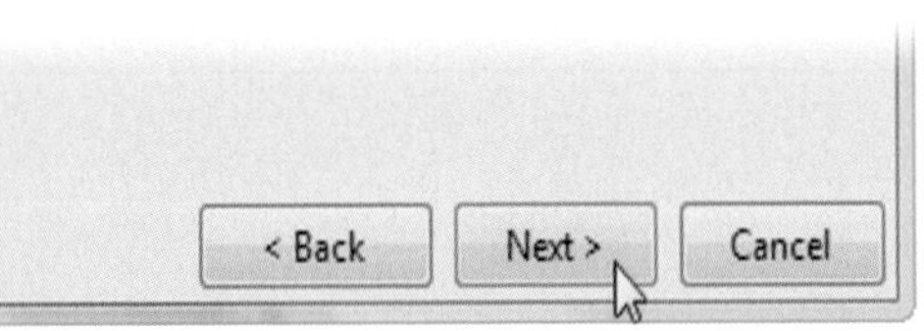

6 SELECTING THE TASK TYPE

● You can run different kinds of tasks using the Task Scheduler, and the available types are listed in this dialog box. Since we want to run a program–Disk Cleanup–we're going to leave the settings as they are (**Start a program** is selected) and just click the **Next** button.

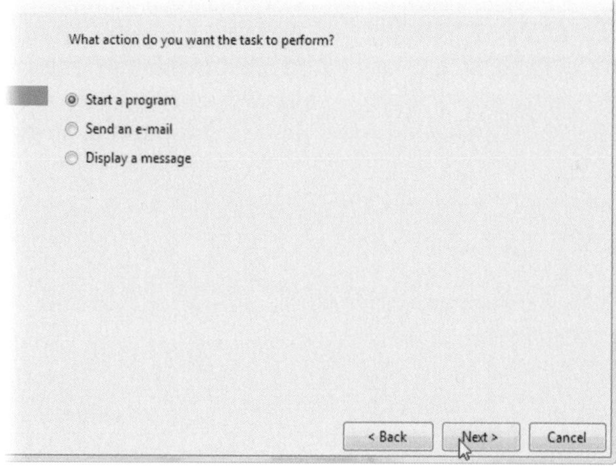

● You can now tell Windows which program you want to run. We're going to run the Disk Cleanup program, so we'll type its name into the empty box–**cleanmgr**–like this. How did we know the name of the program? By investigating the properties of Disk Cleanup .

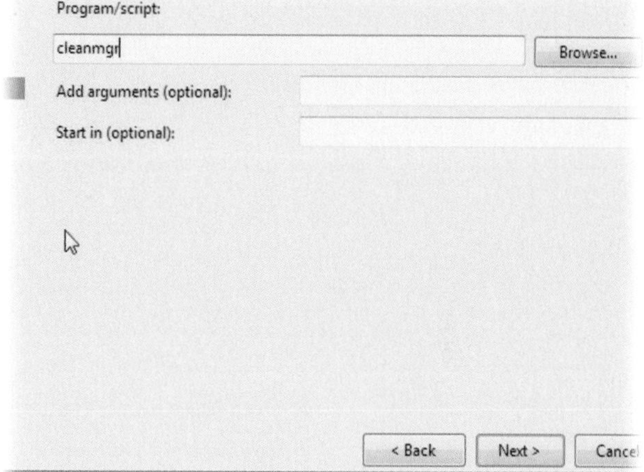

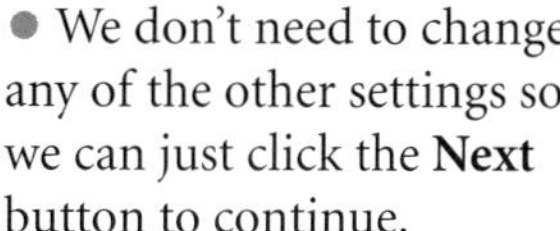

● We don't need to change any of the other settings so we can just click the **Next** button to continue.

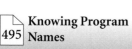

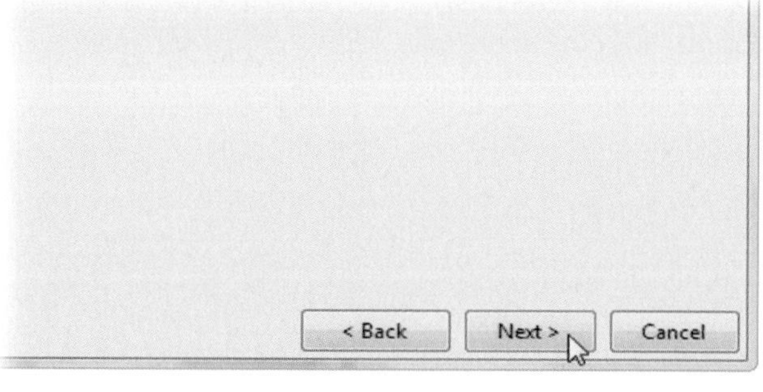

495 **Knowing Program Names**

7 REVIEWING YOUR TASK SETTINGS

• The final dialog in the wizard gives you the opportunity to review your settings and make sure you're happy with all your choices. Remember, you can always click the **Back** button at the bottom to go back to any of the screens in the wizard and change the settings there. For now, though, click the **Finish** button to close the box.

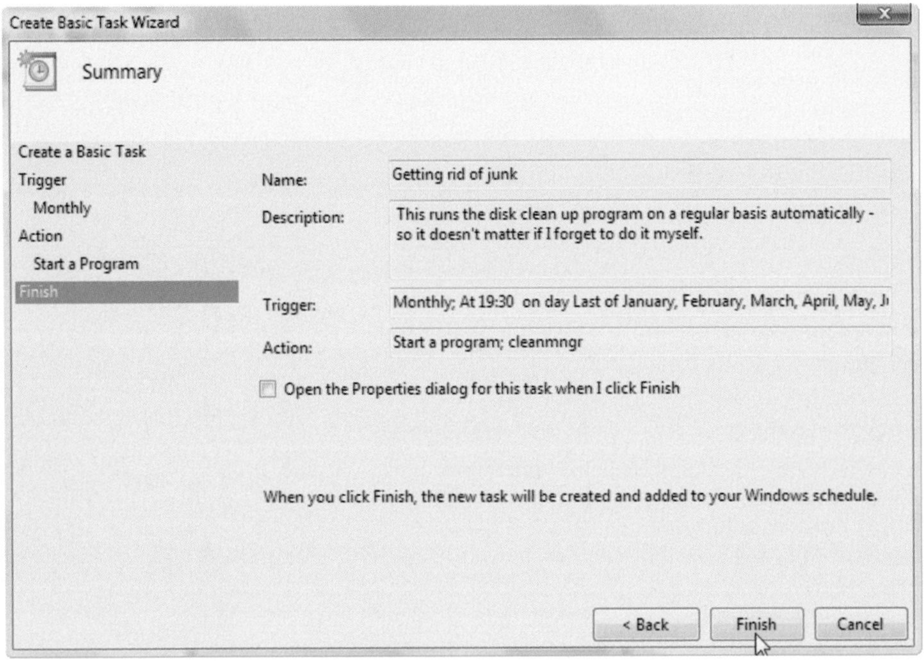

Create Basic Task Wizard
Summary
Create a Basic Task
Trigger
Monthly
Action
Start a Program
Finish
Name:
Getting rid of junk
Description:
This runs the disk clean up program on a regular basis automatically - so it doesn't matter if I forget to do it myself.
Trigger:
Monthly; At 19:30 on day Last of January, February, March, April, May, J
Action:
Start a program; cleanmngr
Open the Properties dialog for this task when I click Finish
When you click Finish, the new task will be created and added to your Windows schedule.
< Back
Finish
Cancel

• This returns you to the **Task Scheduler** window. To check that your new task has been included correctly, click the **Task Scheduler Library** heading in the left-hand column like this.

Task Scheduler
File Action View Help
Task Scheduler (Local)
Task Scheduler Library
Overview of Task Scheduler
Task Status

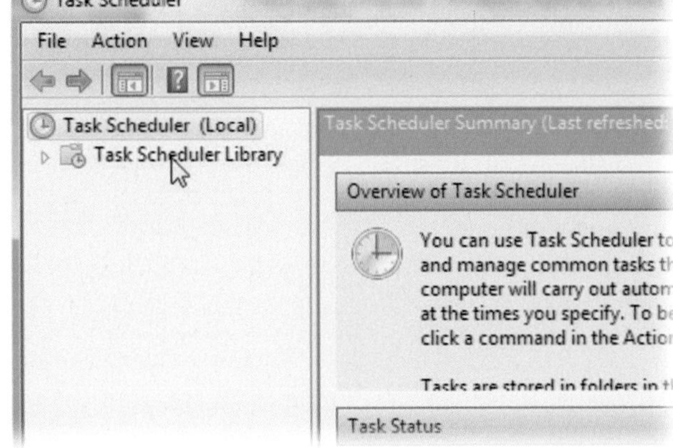

● There, in the center of the window, is the task that we've just created–**Getting rid of junk**. We can see from the **Triggers** list that it is now scheduled to run automatically at 19.30 hours (7.30pm) on the last day of every month.

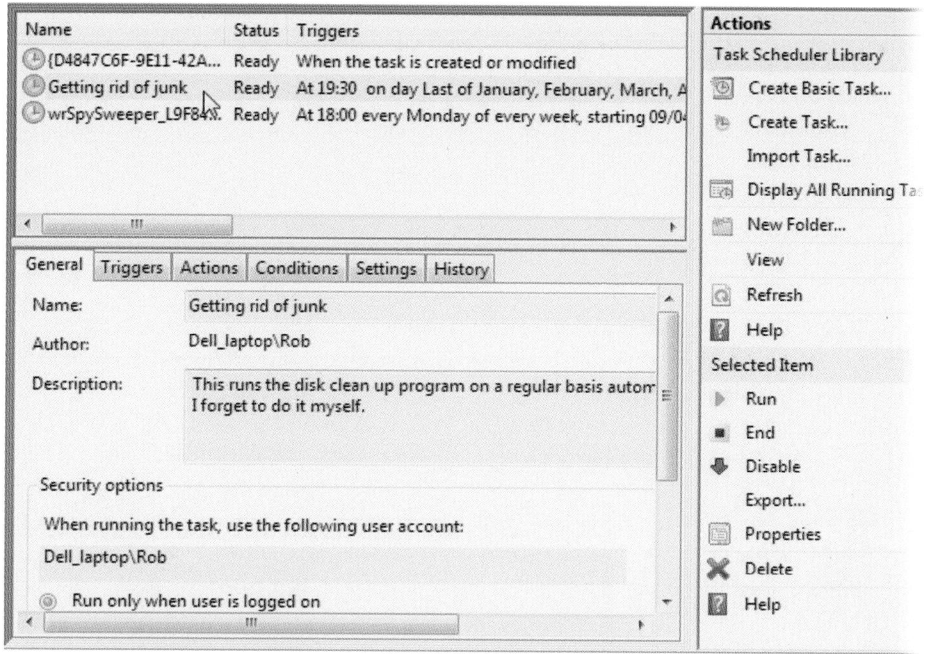

KNOWING PROGRAM NAMES

Windows programs sometimes have two names. For example, the Disk Cleanup program is actually called "cleanmgr.exe" and it's this second name that you need to type into the empty box when you're scheduling a disk cleanup to run. To demonstrate, click the Start button and then start typing the name **Disk Cleanup** into the Search box. You will see the Disk Cleanup icon appear on the menu. Slide the cursor up to it and then click on it with the right mouse button. Choose **Properties** from the pop-up menu and when the dialog box appears, make sure the **Shortcut** tab at the top is selected. Look in the **Target** section of the dialog and in the Target panel you will see the location and the Windows name of Disk Cleanup. It's in the **system32** folder and is called **cleanmgr.exe**. You don't have to bother with the **.exe** part of the name because that is just the suffix that tells Windows that it's an executable program, so just type in **cleanmgr**.

Keeping Your Data Secure

Of all the routine jobs required to keep a home PC running smoothly, making regular backups of your data is by far the most important.

Backing Up

Although you can simply drag and drop files onto an external hard disk or burn them to a CD, Windows Vista includes a backup program that's able to do all this, and more, in an ordered fashion–thus ensuring that you don't overlook anything. It can also be set to run regularly–say every week–so that you don't have to remember to do it yourself. In this section, we'll look at Vista's file backup features.

1 OPENING THE CONTROL PANEL

- To start backing up, you'll need to navigate to the Windows Control Panel. Begin by clicking the Start button.
- When the menu opens, have a look at the entries down the right-hand side and you'll find the **Control Panel**. This is where Windows keeps most of its controls and settings.
- Click the **Control Panel** entry once with the left mouse button to open it.

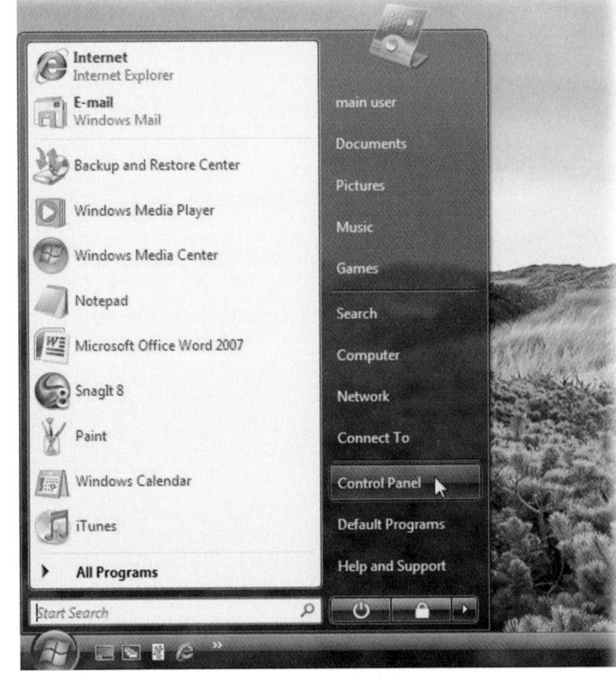

2 OPENING THE BACKUP PROGRAM

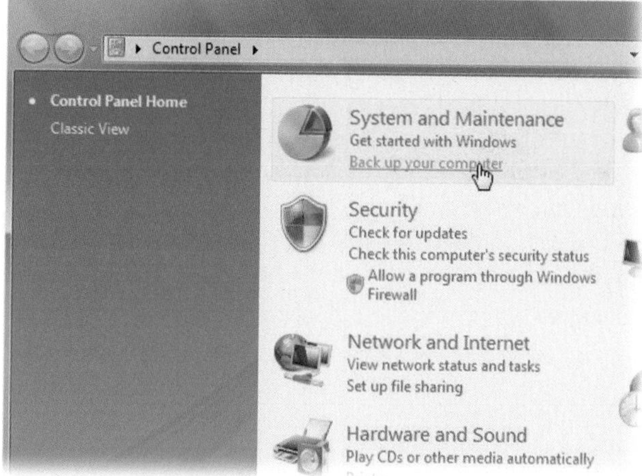

- When the **Control Panel** window opens, find the section heading called **System and Maintenance** at the top and then left click the second link underneath it–it's called **Back up your computer**.

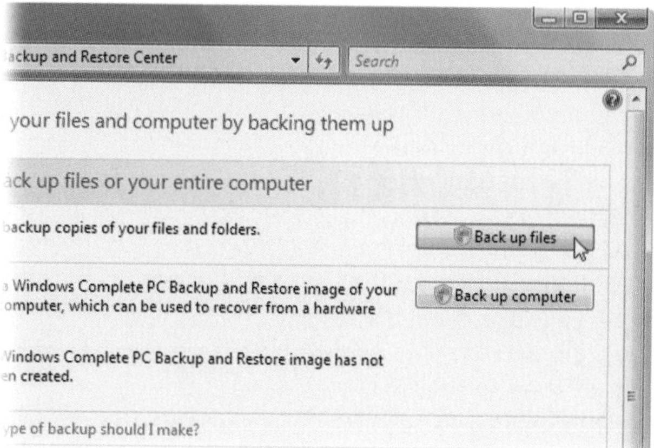

- This opens the **Backup and Restore Center**. The most common use for this Windows' feature is to backup files, so we'll start by clicking the **Back up files** button.

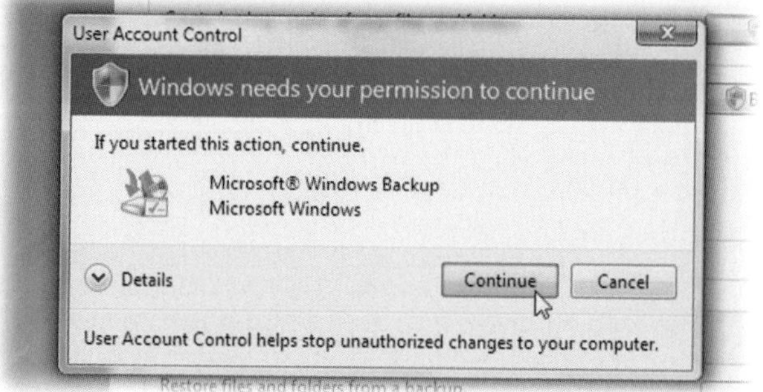

- As usual, Windows displays the **User Account Control** dialog box and asks for your permission to carry on–just click the **Continue** button.

3 RUNNING THE BACKUP WIZARD

● Windows checks your hardware and then suggests which device you can backup onto. The PC we're using has a re-writable DVD drive, so Windows suggests we use that.

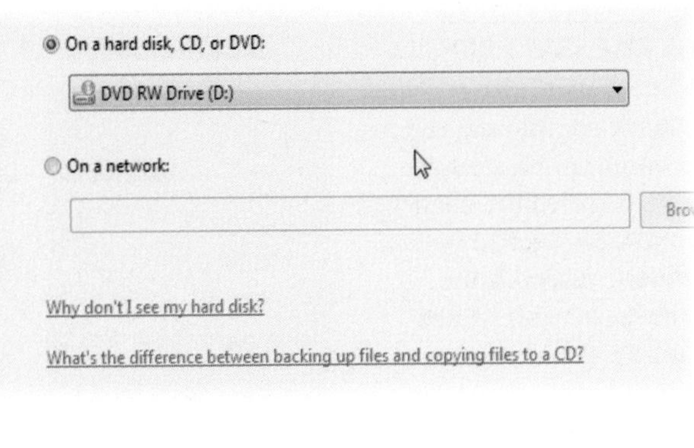

● To continue using the **Back Up Files** wizard, click the **Next** button.

● Windows automatically suggests the files it thinks you should backup. These include everything in the list on the left of the dialog that has a tick next to it.

● Move the mouse over each of the file types in turn to see an explanation in the **Category details** section of the dialog. Here's the description for **Documents**.

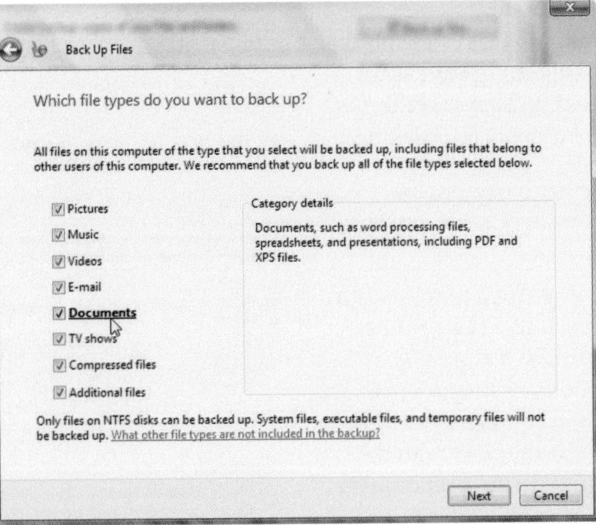

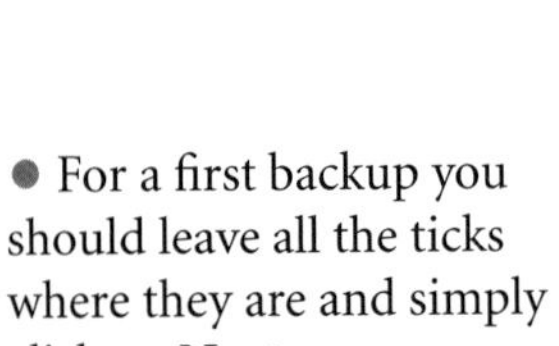

● For a first backup you should leave all the ticks where they are and simply click on **Next**.

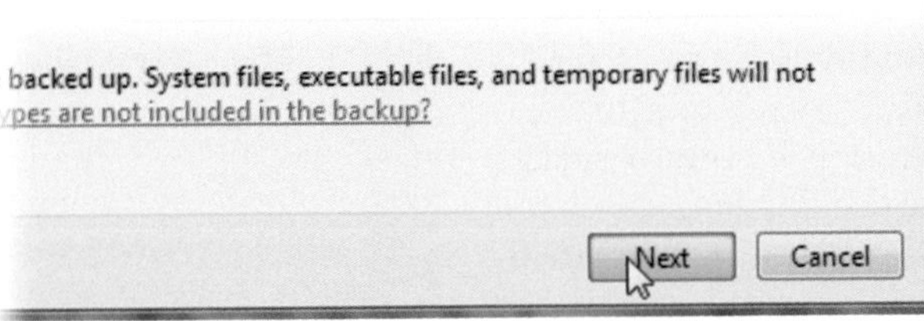

4 SCHEDULING THE BACKUP

- Windows suggests a schedule for making regular backups–once a week on a Sunday at 7.00pm. Let's say you'd rather back up on a different day, click the arrow next to the **What day**? option like this.

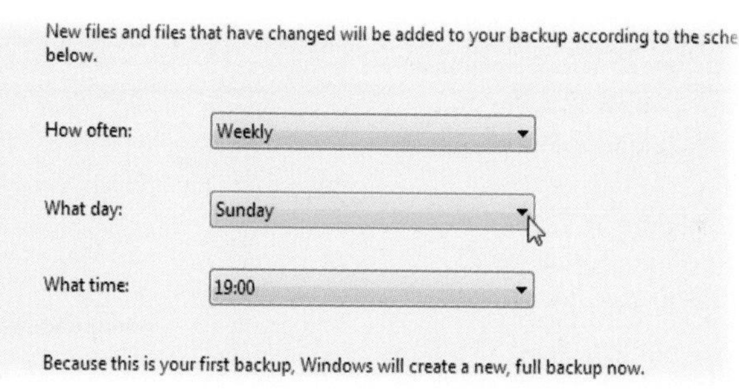

- When the drop-down list opens, pick the day you'd like the backup to run–in this example we're going to choose **Monday**.

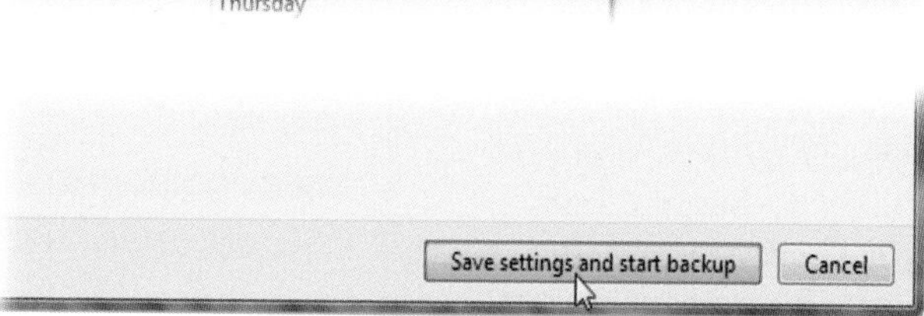

- That's the only change we want to make, so click the **Save settings and start backup** button at the bottom of the dialog box.

5 SETTING UP A BLANK DVD

- Next, you'll see a dialog box asking you to insert a blank DVD into your re-writable DVD drive. Windows suggests you label the disc like this with the name of the PC and the date and time. Click **OK** when you're ready.

- If you've just taken the disc out of the box, then Windows will need to format it for use, so you'll see this dialog. Just click the **Format** button to continue.

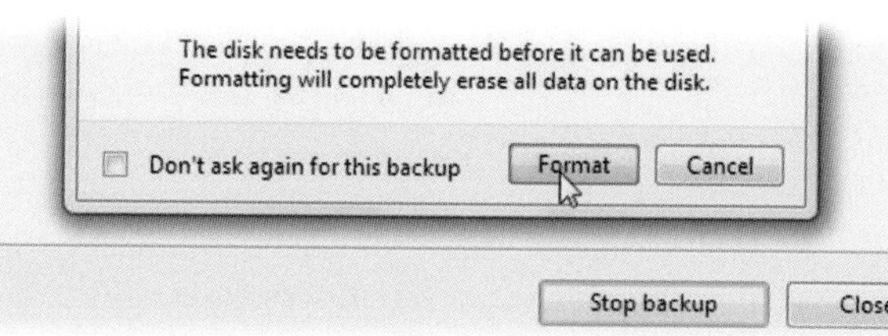

● Windows then formats the disc. It usually takes less than a minute and you don't have to do anything.

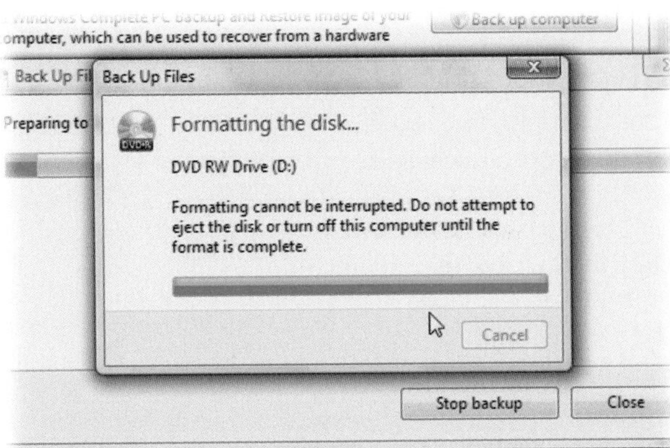

6 RUNNING THE BACKUP

● Windows then starts backing up your files. How long this takes depends on a number of factors–the speed of your re-writable drive (or external hard disk if you're using one of those), the number of files being backed up, and how large they are. You can follow the backup's progress in this dialog box.

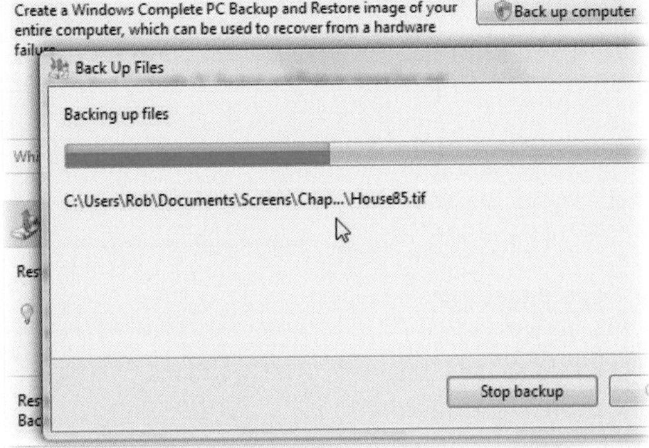

● Here's the finished backup. Windows tells us that we've successfully backed up all the selected files and folders and tells us when the next backup is scheduled. The next step is to make sure you put your backup disc (or discs) somewhere safe in case you ever need them.

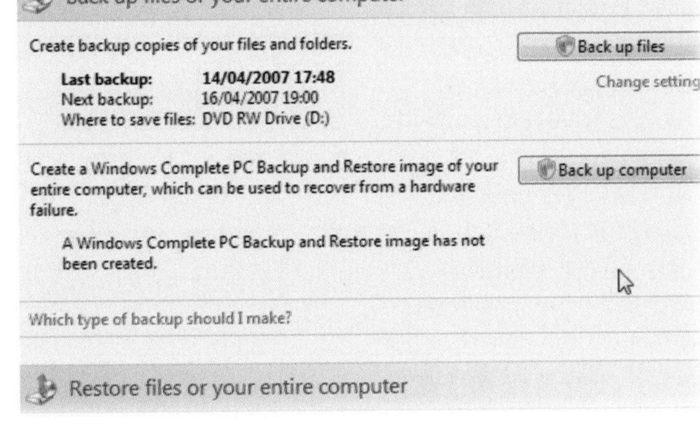

Restoring from a Backup

The whole point to backing up is so that you've got copies of your important files and data in case disaster strikes. Everyone who's used a computer knows how easy it is, for example, to delete a file or folder accidentally. If you have a recent backup, then you can simply load it and then restore the file or folder from there.

1 STARTING A RESTORE

• For this example we've deliberately dropped a folder–the Letters folder–into the Recycle Bin and then emptied it. This means the folder is now deleted from our hard disk. Now we're going to restore it from the backup that we've just created. Navigate to the **Backup and Restore Center** and click the **Restore files** button like this.

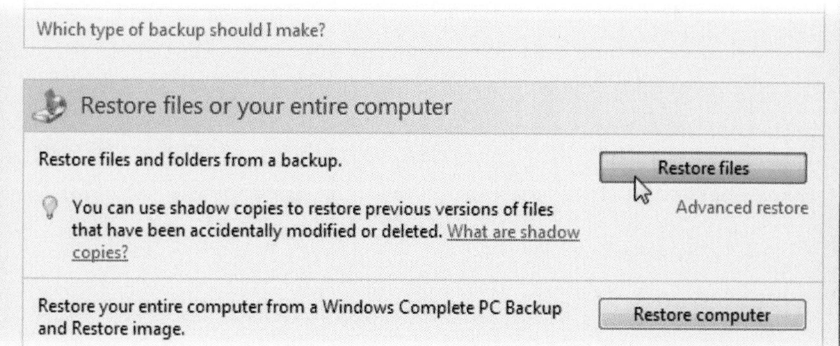

2 SELECTING THE SOURCE

• Windows then displays a dialog box asking you what you want to restore. It assumes that you're keeping regular backups and want to restore files from the latest one. That's the case here, so we can leave the settings as they are. You will, however, have to put the backup DVD into the drive, ready for action.

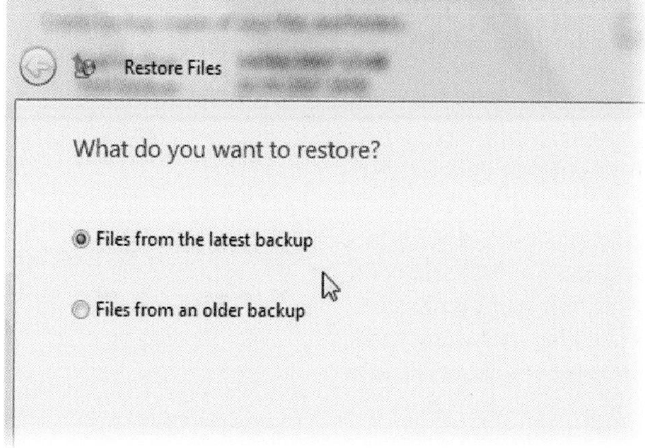

● Click the **Next** button at the bottom of the dialog box to move on.

3 SELECTING WHAT TO RESTORE

● At the next step in the process, the dialog box asks us to select the files or folders that we want to restore by adding them to the list in the middle of the screen. We haven't as yet selected any files or folders to restore, so currently the list is empty.

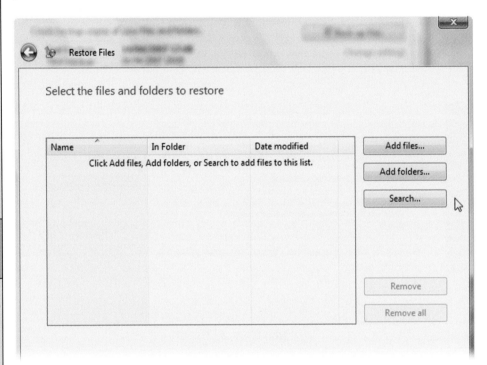

● Remember that we said earlier that we deliberately deleted a folder–the Letters folder–from our hard disk? That's the one we want to restore, so we'll start the process by clicking the **Add folders** button on the right.

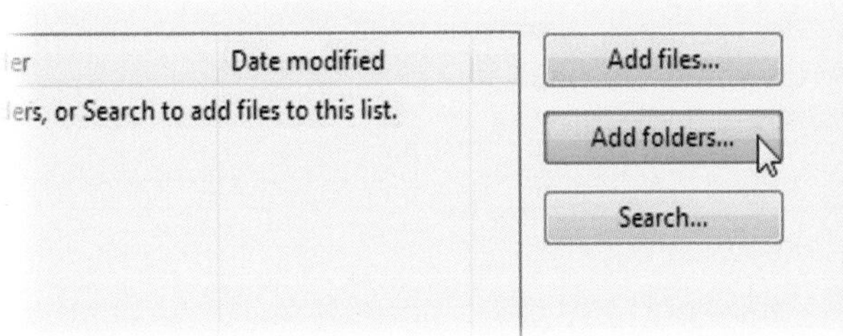

● Windows displays a list of the files and folders that formed the last backup you did. Just click on the folder (or file) that you want to restore with the left mouse button. You can select more than one file or folder like this.

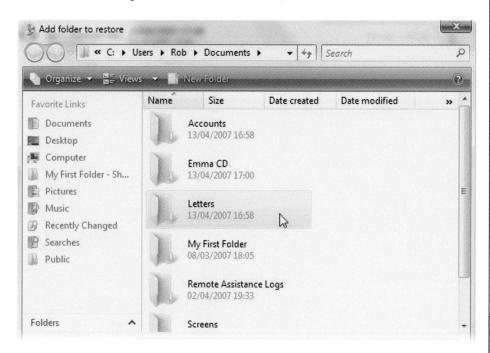

● Once you've selected the files and folders that you want to restore, click on the **Add** button.

● Windows now displays the files or folders that you want to restore in the center of the dialog box–here, it's the **Letters** folder.

● Click the **Next** button to move on.

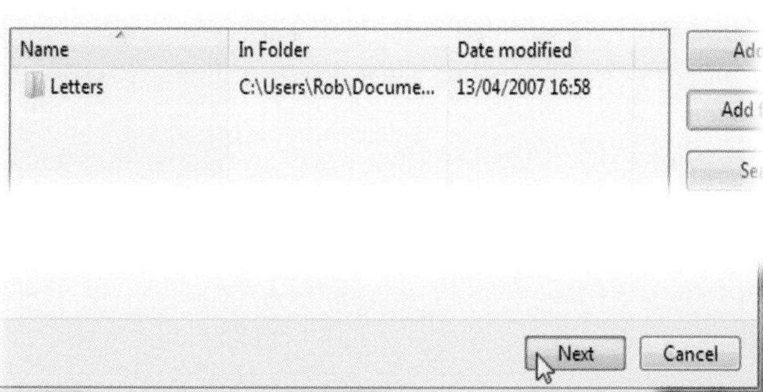

4 SELECTING THE DESTINATION

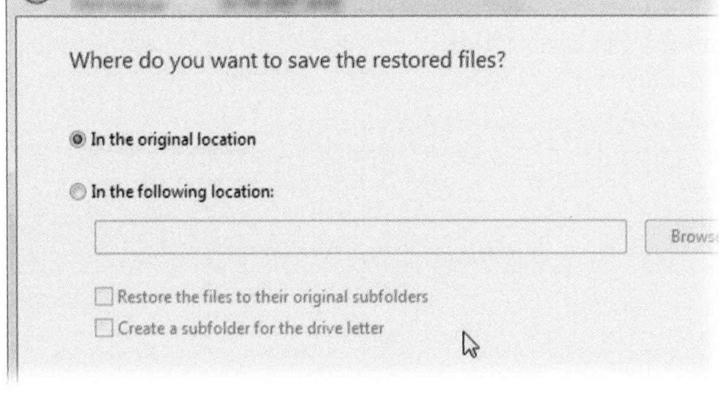

- The next step is to tell Windows where you want to put the restored files or folders. In most cases, you'll want them back in their original location, and by default this is already selected for you.

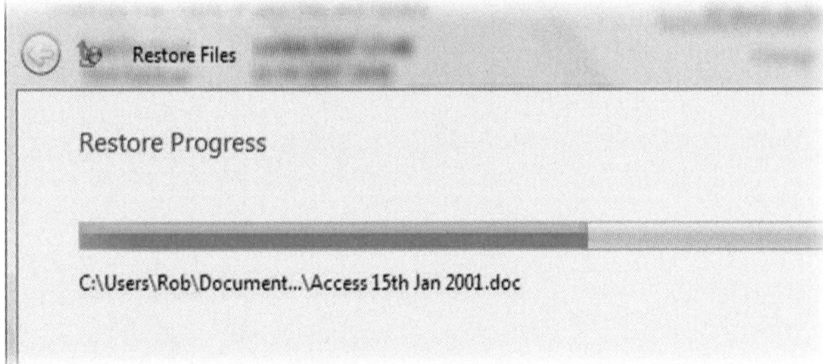

- Once you've told Windows where you want the restored files and folders to go, click the **Start restore** button to continue.

5 RESTORING THE DELETED FILES

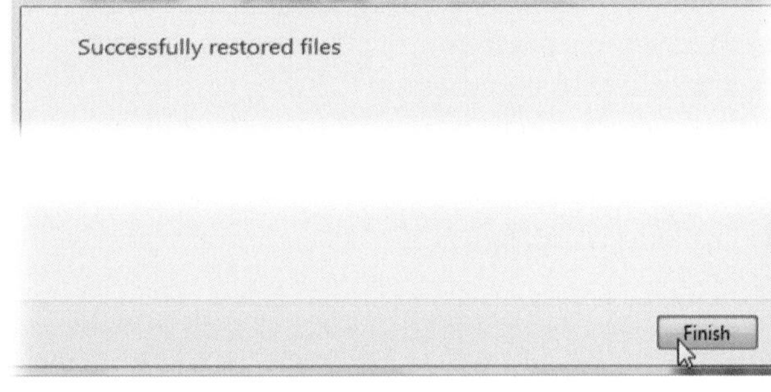

- Here you can see Windows restoring the Letters folder from our backup. It's being copied back to its original location on the hard disk.

- When the process is complete, you'll see this dialog box telling you that Windows has **Successfully restored files**.

- Just click the **Finish** button to close the box.

● Here we have navigated back to the Documents folder to show that the Letters folder has been successfully restored back into its original position.

● Keeping regular backups is one of the most essential housekeeping tasks you can do on your computer. Don't neglect it, or you may live to regret it!

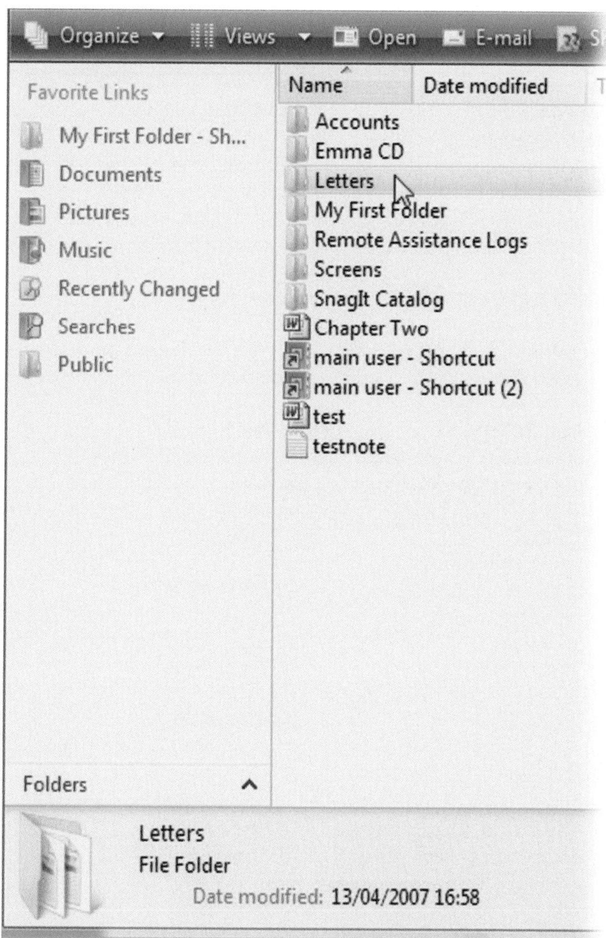

BEFORE YOU BACKUP

First, decide what you're going to backup–typically you should backup the files you've created, rather than the programs you've installed, since you've still got the CDs for those and can re-install them if necessary. Second, decide what medium you're going to use for your backup. DVDs are a good choice because many PCs include a re-writable DVD drive as standard and they can store up to 4.7GB. Alternatively, consider an external hard disk; these are inexpensive and can typically store 200GB of information. Whichever method you choose, you need to have DVDs or the external disk ready and waiting.

Glossary

ActiveX
Small programs or "controls" used by websites that do tasks such as gather or help you view information, or display animations of various kinds.

AERO INTERFACE
Stands for Authentic, Energetic, Reflective, and Open and is the new visual "look" for Windows.

APPLICATION
Another term for a piece of software, usually a program.

ARCHIVE
A file, which is usually compressed, containing back-up copies of your work.

ATTACHMENT
A file that is "attached" to an email message.

BACK UP
To create copies of your work on an external device, such as a DVD or external hard drive, in case you lose documents or your computer develops a fault.

BLOG
Short for web log, this is a kind of diary stored on a webpage.

BROADBAND
A way of connecting to the Internet, that is many times faster than using a traditional modem and that is always "on," so you can browse websites and send and receive e-mail without having to connect every time.

CD-ROM
Compact Disk–Read Only Memory. A disk containing data such as games and programs. Data can only be read from the disk, not written to it.

COMPRESSION
The act of reducing the size of a file by using software to "compact" it into an archive.

CRASH
The term applied when a computer suddenly stops working during a routine operation.

DEFRAGMENTING
The process of reassembling and arranging badly distributed files on a hard drive.

DOCUMENT
A file containing user data, such as text written in Word.

DOWNLOAD
The process of file-transfer from a remote computer to your own computer.

DV
Stands for digital video, the format used by almost all home movie cameras.

DVD
Stands variously for Digital Video Disc or Digital Versatile Disc and has replaced CD-ROM as the preferred medium for storing backups as well as home movies

E-MAIL (ELECTRONIC MAIL)
A system for sending messages between computers that are linked over a network.

FILE
A discrete collection of data stored on your computer.

FILE NAME EXTENSION
Three letters added to the end of a file name that indicate what type of file the document is, e.g. .txt (a text file).

FILE PROPERTIES
Information about a file, such as its size and creation date, and attributes that determine what actions can be carried out on the file and how it behaves.

FOLDER
A folder stores files and other folders to keep files organized.

FONT
The typeface in which text appears onscreen and when it is printed out.

FORMULA
In Excel, an expression entered into a cell that calculates the value of that cell from a combination of constants, arithmetic operators, and (often) the values of other cells.

FREEWARE
Software that can be freely used and distributed, but over which the author retains copyright.

FUNCTION
In Excel, a defined operation or set of operations that can be performed on one or more selected cell values, cell addresses, or other data.

GIF (GRAPHICS INTERCHANGE FORMAT)
A widely used file format for web-based images.

HARD DRIVE/HARD DISK
The physical device on your computer where programs and files are stored.

HARDWARE
Hardware is the part of a computer that you can physically see or touch.

HTML (HYPERTEXT MARK-UP LANGUAGE)
The formatting language used to create webpages. HTML specifies how a page should look onscreen.

HYPERLINK
A "hot" part of a webpage (e.g., text, image, table, etc.) that links to another part of the same document or another document on the Internet.

ICON
A graphic symbol, attached to a file, that indicates its type or the program it was created in.

IMAGE EDITING
The process of altering an image on the computer, either to improve its quality or to apply a special effect.

INSERTION POINT
A blinking upright line on the screen. As you type, text appears at the insertion point.

INSTALLING
The process of "loading" an item of software onto a hard drive. *See also* Uninstalling.

INTERNET SERVICE PROVIDER (ISP)
A business that provides a gateway to the Internet.

JPG
A graphic file format used on many websites for storing photos thanks to the way in which it preserves quality while reducing file size.

MODEM
A device used to connect a computer to the Internet via a telephone line.

NETWORK
A collection of computers that are linked together.

ONLINE
Connected to the Internet.

PATH
The address of a file on a computer system.

PERIPHERAL
Any hardware device that is connected to your computer.

PIXELS
The individual grayscale or color dots that make up an image on a computer screen.

PLUG-IN
A program that adds features to a web browser so that it can handle files containing, for example, multimedia elements.

PORT
The socket on the back or front of a computer, or other piece of hardware, into which you plug the cables in order to connect peripherals.

PROGRAM
A software package that allows you to perform a specific task on your computer (also known as an application).

PROTOCOL
A shared set of rules that any two computers must follow when they communicate with each other.

RADIO BUTTON
Small onscreen button within an application that visibly turns on and off when clicked with a mouse.

RECYCLE BIN
The location on your desktop where deleted files are stored. Files remain here until the Recycle Bin is emptied.

RESOLUTION
The density of the pixels that make up an image on a computer screen or the dots that make up an image, measured in pixels or dpi (dots per inch).

RESTORE
To return data from the Recycle Bin to its original location.

RGB
Red, Green, and Blue. An image displayed on a computer screen is created from a combination of these three colors.

RIBBON
Easily accessible toolbar format, common to Microsoft Office 2007 programs.

RULER
Indicator at the top and left of the screen, with marks in inches or centimeters like a real ruler. Rulers also show the indents and margins of the text.

SCROLL
To scroll is to move up or down a document or screen.

SCROLL BARS
Bars at the foot and on the right of the screen that can be used to move around the document.

SELECT
Highlighting files or folders to enable you to perform certain activities on them.

SERVER
Any computer that allows users to connect to it and share its information and resources.

SHAREWARE
Software that is made freely available for use on a try-before-you-buy basis.

SHORTCUT
A link to a document, folder, or program located elsewhere on your computer that, when you double click on it, takes you directly to the original.

SIDEBAR
A component of Windows Vista designed to display Gadgets– small programs such as a clock or a newsfeed, calendar, or currency converter.

SOFTWARE
A computer needs software to function. Software ranges from simple utilities to immense computer games.

STATUS BAR
The small panel at the foot of an open window that displays information about the items located there.

TASKBAR
The panel at the bottom of the desktop screen that contains the Start button, along with quick-access buttons to open programs and windows.

TIFF
Tagged Image File Format. A file format that retains a high level of information in an image, therefore suited to images that contain a lot of detail.

TROJAN
A malicious program hidden inside another, harmless or even useful, program.

UNINSTALLING
The process of removing an item of software from the hard drive by deleting all its files.

USB FLASH DRIVE
A storage device with no moving parts, about the size of a stick of gum, that can store many megabytes of information

USB PORT
Universal Serial Bus. A type of port that allows for very simple installation of hardware devices to your computer.

VIRUS
A program or piece of computer code deliberately created and distributed to destroy or disorganize data on other computer systems.

WEB BROWSER
A program used for viewing and accessing information on the Web.

WEBSITE
A collection of webpages that are linked together, and possibly to other websites, by hyperlinks.

WINDOW
A panel displaying the contents of a folder or disk drive.

WIZARDS
Interactive sequences that lead you, step by step, through processes on your computer.

WORLD WIDE WEB (WWW, W3, THE WEB)
The collection of websites on the Internet.

WORM
A malicious, self-replicating computer program

INDEX

A

Accessories, 34–35
accounts, 234–235
antivirus program
  choosing, 216–218
  quarantining files, 226–227
  scanning, 220, 224
  scheduling scans, 227–229
  setting up, 224–226
  updates, 219

B

back up
  opening program, 496–497
  restoring, 501–505
  scheduling, 499–500
  wizard, 498

C

Calendar
  appointments, 43–48
  basics, 42
  monthly view, 52–53
  new, 50–52
  tasks, 49
CDs
  album artwork, 348
  audio, 342–349
  burning, 378–381
  formats, 347
  ripping, 346
computer
  Experience Index, 445
  performance, 444
  speed, 447
  visual effects, 446
Control Panel, 60–61

D

Desktop
  choosing, 54
  color scheme, 56–57
  icons, 59
Device Manager, 441–443
digital music formats, 360
DVDs
  loading, 382–383
  menu, 385
  watching, 384

E

e-mail
  account, new, 172–174
  address, 181
  attachments, 178–180
  backgrounds, 196
  creating, 176
  deleting, 188–189
  draft, 182
  features, 171, 175, 177
  formatting, 177
  junk. *See* junk mail
  managing, 188
  message, new, 176
  opening, 170
  printing, 188
  reading, 185–186
  receiving, 184–185
  responding, 186–187
  sending, 183
  signatures, 194–195
  stationery, 197
  storing, 189–190
Excel
  calculations, 292
  cells, 285–286
  charts, 296
  column headings, 288
  column widths, 288–289
  corrections, 288
  features, 280–281
  fonts, 294
  formulas, 291–294
  launching, 279
  numbers, 289–290
  saving, 283
  text, 287
  themes, 295
  workbook, 282, 284
  worksheet, 278, 280, 282

F

Family Tree Maker
  adding data, 299–302
  description, 298
  online search, 303–305
  places, 302
  publishing options, 308–309
  viewing, 306–308
favorites, 98–99
files
  deleting, 83, 85–86
  moving, 89–95
  naming, 81
  new, 79
  previewing, 73–76
  removing, 452
  retrieving, 82
  See also WordPad, files
Firewall
  configuring, 212–213
  exceptions, 213–215
  outbound connections, 215
  turning off, 222
Flash player
  downloading, 140–143
  managing, 143
  using, 144
folders
  features, 64–65
  layout menu, 73
  moving, 87–89
  moving between, 68–71
  naming, 78
  new, 77–78
  viewing, 66, 73

G

genealogy software. *See* Family Tree Maker

H

Hard Disk,
  clean up, 449–450
  defragmenting, 453–455

I
images
burning to disc, 334–335
captions, adding, 328
dating, 327
deleting, 321
emailing, 337
improving, 330–333
rating, 327
red eye, correcting, 333
tags, 322–326
See also Photo Gallery
internet
browsers, 115
connecting to, 108
hyperlinks, 111
plug-ins,145
web addresses (URLs), 112
web browser, 111
webpages, 109–110
Internet Explorer
button bar, 117
favorites, 124–127
home page, 119
launching, 114–115
navigation, 118–120
tabs, 121–124
window, 116–117
internet searching
downloading programs, 132–136
Google search, 130–131
Live search, 128–129
internet security
phishing filter, 138–139. *See also* phishing
pop-ups, 136–137
See also antivirus program
See also malware, protection
See also Security
internet sites, top 10
www.amazon.com, 154–155
www.ebay.com, 152-153
www.flickr.com, 160–161
www.google.com, 48–149
www.local.live.com, 158–159
www.myspace.com, 164–165
www.netvibes.com, 156–157
www.videojug.com, 166–167
internet sites, top 10 (cont.)
www.wikipedia.org, 162–163
www.youtube.com, 150–151
iTunes, 362

J
junk mail
avoiding, 190–191
settings, 192

L
limiting Internet access, 238–241
Local Disk, 438–439

M
Mail, Windows. *See* e-mail
maintenance, 436-447
malware
description, 201
protection, 216–218
See also antivirus program
Media Center
launching, 386
menu, 387–388
music library, 388–389
recording TV, 392–393
settings, 386–387
watching TV, 390–391
Media Player
controls, 343
playlist, 352–359
views, 350–351
movies
digital editing, 396
saving, 396
See also Movie Maker
Movie Maker
AutoMovie, 406–408
burning a DVD, 430–435
closing credits, 421–423
creating a movie in, 408–410
editing video clips, 411–413
effects, 416–417
features, 398–399
Firewire, 401
importing video to, 400–404
narration, 427
Movie Maker (cont.)
opening a video in, 404–405
project file, 405
publishing options, 433, 435
soundtrack, 424–429
title, 418–421
transitions, 414–415
MP3 player
downloading music to, 361–363
plugging in, 359–360
syncing with, 364–369
types of, 365
music, managing. *See* Media Player
music, online. *See* online music stores

N
Notepad, 79
Notification Area, 27

O
online music stores
browsing, 370–373, 375
downloading, 374, 376–377
paying, 374
online photo album, 338–339

P
parental controls, 236–241
password protection, 230–233
phishing, 200
Photo Gallery
burning to disc, 334–335
features, 312–313
filtering images, 328–329
import settings, 317
importing images, 314–317
reverting to original, 332
searching, 328–329
screen saver. *See* screen saver
viewing images, 318–319
zooming, 320
See also images
photos. *See* Photo Gallery; images
Picasa, 132, 338
plug-ins. *See* internet, plug-ins

portable player. *See* MP3 player
programs
  installing from CD, 481
  installing from internet, 478–481
  running, 481–482
  uninstalling, 483–485

Q
Quick Launch toolbar, 26

R
Recycle Bin, emptying, 451
Restore Point
  checking, 462
  creating, 460–461
  returning to, 462–464
  wizard, 465–466
restoring
  deleted documents, 473–477
  previous document versions, 470–472
ripping. *See* CDs, ripping

S
screen saver, 336–337
shortcuts, creating, 96–97
searching
  by file type, 105
  from Start menu, 100–102
  within a folder, 102–105
Security,
  Center, 204–205
  Defender, 220–222
Sidebar, 28–33
spam, 202
speed. *See* computer, speed
spyware, 203
Start menu, 20–25
System
  properties, 439–440, 456–457
  protection, 457–458
  restore point. *See* Restore Point
  See also Device Manager

T
time limit. *See* parental controls
trojan, 201

U
updates
  help, 211
  history, 208
  manual installation, 206–208
  notifications, 208
  settings, 209–210
Universal Serial Bus. *See* USB
URLs. *See* internet, web addresses
USB (Universal Serial Bus), 438

V
virus, 201
visual effects, 416–417

W
Web (World Wide Web). *See* internet
Windows Mail. *See* e-mail
Windows Vista
  features, 10–13
Windows Vista (cont.)
  Help, 36–41
  Media Center. *See* Media Center
  Media Player. *See* Media Player
  Photo Gallery. *See* Photo Gallery
  Scheduler, 486–495
  Security Center. *See* Security, Center
  updates, 206–211
  versions, 13
Word 2007
  clipboard, 266–268
  Editing group, 273
  features, 262–263
  fonts, 268–272
  launching, 260–261
  Office button, 264
  Paragraph group, 272–273
  Quick Access Toolbar, 265
  Styles, 274–277
  Themes tab, 277
WordPad
  bulleted list, 257
  corrections, 251, 255
  features, 245
  files, 258–259
  fonts, 252–254
  format bar, 258
  layout, 255–257
  opening, 244
  text, 246–250
worm, 201

ACKNOWLEDGMENTS

Dorling Kindersley would like to thank the following:

Dawn Cambrin, Gibsons, BC, Canada, for the index.

The Generations Network for permission to reproduce screens from within Family Tree Maker™; Canon Inc.; Hewlett-Packard Company; Iomega Corporation for permission to reproduce photos of the Iomega Zip USB Drive. Copyright© 2003 Iomega Corporation. All Rights Reserved; Microsoft Corporation for permission to reproduce screens from within Microsoft® Windows® Vista Ultimate™ Edition, Microsoft® Notepad, Microsoft® WordPad, Microsoft® Windows® Mail, Microsoft® Internet Explorer, Microsoft® Windows® Media Player, Microsoft® Windows® Movie Maker, Microsoft® Windows® Photo Gallery, Microsoft® Office Word 2007, Microsoft® Office Excel 2007; SanDisk for permission to reproduce photos of the SanDisk® USB Flash Drive; Techsmith Corporation for supplying SnagIt Screen Capture and Image Editing software.

amazon.com; cnn.com; ebay.com; flickr.com; google.com; local.live.com; msn.com; myspace.com; nasa.gov; netvibes.com; videojug.com; wikipedia.com; youtube.com